This is a study of British foreign policy in a crucial period of international political development. It provides a comprehensive account of the subject, and acts as a guide to the nature of the British state in the period and to international relations.

In 1783 Britain had lost America and was unstable domestically. By 1793 she had regained her position as the leading global maritime, colonial and commercial power. During the intervening years Britain went several times to the brink of war, in 1787 with France over control of the Dutch and their empire, in 1790 with Spain over the British claim to settle on the Pacific coast of modern Canada, and in 1791 with Russia over the fate of the Turkish Empire. In 1793 Britain and revolutionary France went beyond the brink, a struggle which was to be crucial for both countries. Each of these crises is examined in an effort to throw light on the British state in an 'age of revolutions'.

British foreign policy in an age
of revolutions, 1783–1793

British foreign policy
in an age of revolutions,
1783–1793

Jeremy Black

Reader in History, University of Durham

CAMBRIDGE
UNIVERSITY PRESS

Published by the Press Syndicate of the University of Cambridge
The Pitt Building, Trumpington Street, Cambridge, CB2 1RP
40 West 20th Street, New York, NY 10011-4211, USA
10 Stamford Road, Oakleigh, Melbourne 3166, Australia

© Cambridge University Press 1994

First published 1994

Printed in Great Britain at the University Press, Cambridge

A catalogue record for this book is available from the British Library

Library of Congress cataloguing in publication data

Black, Jeremy.
British foreign policy in an age of revolutions, 1783–1793 / Jeremy
Black.
    p.   cm.
ISBN 0 521 45001 2
1. Great Britain – Foreign relations – 1760–1820.   2. Revolutions
– History – 18th century.   I. Title.
DA505.B66   1994
327.41′009′033 – dc20   93-13513   CIP

ISBN 0 521 45001 2 hardback

For Sarah again

... in this age of Revolutions it is not easy to be over-vigilant

Lord Auckland, Ambassador at The Hague,
to the Duke of Leeds, Foreign Secretary, March 1790

A new system is now opening to the view of the world; the European courts are plotting to counteract it. Alliances, contrary to all former systems, are agitating, and a common interest of courts is forming... This combination draws a line that runs throughout Europe and presents a cause so entirely new, as to exclude all calculations from former circumstances.

Public Advertiser, 10 March 1792

Contents

Maps

Acknowledgements

I first began work on this subject in 1977, and archival work the following year, with the Keith papers for 1787. Since then I have accumulated many debts of gratitude. In sixteen years work on this period, I have been helped by a large number of people. This help has included the loan or gift of material, published or unpublished, from many parts of the world: Geoffrey Rice's photocopying of material he was able to borrow for me from Dunedin Public Library being the most far-flung. My work in archives and libraries has been facilitated by the help of numerous archivists and librarians, not least through the willingness to let me consult uncatalogued material or to work in archives when they were officially closed. While not always sharing the conclusions of other scholars, I have always profited from reading their work and from discussing the period with them. My interest in the period was awakened by Tim Blanning, who has written on it in a perceptive and exciting fashion. I am most grateful for his assistance and inspiration in a number of respects, and it is more than appropriate that he should figure prominently in the acknowledgements. Matthew Anderson, Roy Bridge, Ian Christie, John Derry, Grayson Ditchfield, Alan Frost, Munro Price and Brendan Simms read earlier drafts of part of this work and made many useful comments. I am most grateful for the advice of two anonymous readers. I would like to thank Leopold Auer, Christopher Bayly, Peter Carey, Hugh Dunthorne, Robert Harris, Colin Jones, George Lukowski, David Saunders and Dennis Showalter for answering enquiries, and Edna Lemay, John Lynn, Peter Marshall, Charles Middleton, Nicolaas van Sas and Gerhard Wolf for providing offprints. Michael Duffy was characteristically generous in drawing my attention to the Stafford-Thurlow correspondence. The generosity of the British Academy, the Staff Travel and Research Fund of Durham University and the Wolfson Foundation made much of the research possible and I am also grateful to a host of friends for putting me up or rather putting up with me on my research trips. Work in American archives was assisted by fellowships from the Beinecke and Huntington libraries. I would like to thank the Earl of Elgin for his hospitality at Broomhall and Sir Hector Monro for his at Williamwood. The Earl of Malmesbury, the Earl of Shelburne, Lady Lucas and Richard Head kindly gave permission to consult and quote from the papers of the first Earl of Malmesbury, the first Marquess of Lansdowne, the second Lord Grantham and James Bland Burges respectively. I am most grateful to Wendy Duery for all her help.

I initially planned to do my thesis on this subject, but had to abandon my early work because another scholar, who never completed, had a 'prior claim' to part of the field. I continued to work on the subject, however, publishing three articles on it in 1984 and 1987. If I have been somewhat distracted by other topics, I nevertheless hope that my other research and writing has contributed to this larger study. My *British Foreign Policy in the Age of Walpole* (1985) and *A System of Ambition? British Foreign Policy 1660–1793* (1991) can be seen as preludes to this book, dealing as they do with the 'structural' aspects of foreign policy in the Hanoverian period. Regrettably, it has proved necessary to omit the bibliography of this work for reasons of space.

The dedication is one that I could offer for all my books but it is especially appropriate for this one, which has been the longest in its genesis. If thankfully I am a more content person than I was in the mid-1970s, it is thanks to Sarah.

Newcastle
January 1993

Abbreviations

Add.	Additional Manuscripts
AE	Paris, Quai d'Orsay, Ministère des Affaires Étrangères
AN AM	Paris, Archives Nationales, Archives de la Marine
Ang.	Angleterre
AP	*Archives parlementaires de 1787 à 1860 : Recueil complet des débats législatifs et politiques des chambres françaises* (127 vols., Paris, 1879–1913)
Aspinall, *George III*	A. Aspinall (ed.), *The Later Correspondence of George III* I (Cambridge, 1962)
AST	Turin, Archivio di Stato
Aut.	Autriche
Beinecke	New Haven, Beinecke Library
BL	London, British Library, Department of Manuscripts
Bod.	Oxford, Bodleian Library, Department of Western Manuscripts
Bowood	Bowood, Earl of Shelburne, papers of 2nd Earl of Shelburne (1st Marquess of Lansdowne)
Broomhall	Broomhall, Fife, Earl of Elgin, Elgin papers
Cobbett	W. Cobbett (ed.), *Cobbett's Parliamentary History of England ... 1066 to ... 1803* (36 vols., London, 1806–20)
Court and Cabinets	Richard, 2nd Duke of Buckingham (ed.), *Memoirs of the Court and Cabinets of George the Third* (4 vols., London, 1853–5)
CP	Correspondance Politique
CRO	Country Record Office
CUL	Cambridge, University Library, Department of Manuscripts
Eg.	Egerton Manuscripts

EK	Englische Korrespondenz
Esp.	Espagne
FO	Foreign Office
HHStA	Vienna, Haus-, Hof-, und Staatsarchiv, Staatskanzlei
HL	San Marino, California, Huntington Library
HMC *Dropmore*	Historical Manuscripts Commission, *The Manuscripts of J. B. Fortescue, Esq., Preserved at Dropmore* (10 vols., London, 1892–1927)
Ing.	Inghilterra
Ipswich	Ipswich, Suffolk Record Office
KAO	Maidstone, Kent Archives Office, Sackville papers (U 269)
LM	Lettere Ministri
Malmesbury	Winchester, Hampshire Record Office, Malmesbury papers
Marburg	Marburg, Staatsarchiv
MD	Mémoires et Documents
Munich	Munich, Bayerisches Hauptstaatsarchiv, Gesandtschaften
NLS	Edinburgh, National Library of Scotland, Department of Manuscripts
Polit. Corresp.	*Politische Correspondenz Friedrichs des Grossen* (46 vols., Berlin, 1879–1939)
PRO	London, Public Record Office
RA	Windsor, Royal Archives
Recueil	*Recueil des Instructions aux Ambassadeurs et Ministres de France depuis les Traités de Westphalie jusqu'à la Révolution Française*
SP	State Papers
STG	Stowe papers
Williamwood	Williamwood, Sir Hector Monro, Ewart papers

Unless otherwise stated, place of publication for publications in the notes is London.

Introduction

The game of projects and discussions between nations is like many other games liable to be affected both by the chance and combination of the cards and by the manner of playing them; but it varies in an essential respect, the game is never lost.

Lord Auckland, Ambassador at The Hague, to Joseph Ewart, Envoy Extraordinary in Berlin, June 1791[1]

The 1780s and early 1790s were an age of revolutions and were seen as such by contemporaries. It is the revolutions within states of this period that have attracted the greatest subsequent and scholarly attention, and one, the French Revolution, was indeed spectacular in its course and seminal in its consequences. Though between 1782 and 1795 revolutions in Geneva, the United Provinces (modern Netherlands), Austrian Netherlands (essentially modern Belgium and Luxemburg), the Prince-Bishopric of Liège (part of Belgium centring on Liège and the Meuse valley), and Poland were all suppressed, they helped to increase the general sense of government and society under challenge and, more specifically, to exacerbate British concern about the international situation. Elsewhere in Europe, especially in the Habsburg dominions of Hungary and Galicia, serious challenges were mounted to the authority and power of central government. The concurrence of so many challenges led contemporaries, bewildered, frightened or exhilarated, to search for common, often conspiratorial, causes, a task that scholars have taken up, though their search has been for more long-term factors, often 'structural' in their nature. The notion of a general crisis, variously economic, social, political or intellectual, has been presented in a number of guises, including that of an Atlantic Revolution. This process is not free from difficulty. It entails the amalgamation of some very disparate problems and developments and a tendency to exaggerate signs of conflict and to see them all as aspects of a common crisis. Much of Europe was not affected by insurrections in the last decades of the century, while loyalist movements were not limited to those in authority. The extent of loyalist

[1] Auckland to Ewart, 21 June 1791, Matlock, Derbyshire CRO 239 M/O 759.

1

and counter-revolutionary sentiment suggests that the impact of radical ideas and revolutionary pressures, social, economic and political, was less universal, automatic and popular than the notion of a general crisis would imply. Furthermore, many tensions and disturbances in the period can be seen best as aspects of traditional eighteenth-century society, rather than as evidence of an Age of Revolution.[2]

It has also been argued recently by Christopher Bayly that the years 1780–1820 witnessed a 'world crisis', that 'the European "Age of Revolutions" was only one part of a general crisis affecting the Asian and Islamic world and the colonies of European settlement ... when the long-term political conflicts unleashed by the decline of the great hegemonies of the Ottomans, Iran, the Mughals and the monarchies of the Far East and southeast Asia came to a head'.[3] This exciting thesis suffers, however, from some of the problems facing that of a European or Atlantic revolution. Furthermore, different chronologies of crisis can be given for some of the Asian states with, for example, earlier peaks for Iran, Burma and Siam. Nevertheless, Bayly's thesis is important not only because it introduces a welcome note of comparative analysis, but also because it provides an analytical context within which the global consequences of the actions of the European powers of 1783–93 can be considered. Their relationships with the Asiatic empires discussed by Bayly were indeed important in this period, though less so than during the following fifteen years, but the most striking area of European expansion, the Pacific, was very different in its character to Asia, and the most important impact of a European power on the trans-oceanic world,

[2] J. Godechot, *La Grand Nation: L'Expansion révolutionnaire dans le monde 1789–1799* (2 vols., Paris, 1956); R. R. Palmer, *The Age of the Democratic Revolution* (2 vols., Princeton, 1959–64); J. Pelenski (ed.), *The American and European Revolutions, 1776–1848: SocioPolitical and Ideological Aspects* (Iowa City, 1980); H. A. Barton, 'Scandinavia and the Atlantic Revolution, 1760–1815', *Proceedings of the Twelfth Consortium on Revolutionary Europe, 1750–1850* (1983), 145–58; F. Venturi, *Settecento riformatore. IV. La caduta dell' Antico Regime (1776–1789)* (2 vols., Turin, 1984). For a 'new political culture' and 'the invention of modern politics' that was not restricted to France, N. C. F. van Sas, 'The Patriot Revolution: New Perspectives', in M. C. Jacob and W. W. Mijnhardt (eds.), *The Dutch Republic in the Eighteenth Century. Decline, Enlightenment, and Revolution* (Ithaca, 1992), p. 118. For recent work on Spanish America, P. K. Liss, *Atlantic Empires: The Network of Trade and Revolution, 1713–1826* (Baltimore, 1983); S. O'Phelan Godoy, *Rebellions and Revolts in Eighteenth Century Peru and Upper Peru* (Cologne, 1985) and J. R. Fisher, A. J. Kuethe and A. McFarlane (eds.), *Reform and Insurrection in Bourbon New Granada and Peru* (Baton Rouge, 1990), pp. 197–326. For criticism of the thesis as applied to Britain, I. R. Christie, *Stress and Stability in Late Eighteenth-Century Britain* (Oxford, 1984), pp. 3–26, and Europe, T. C. W. Blanning, *The French Revolution in Germany: Occupation and Resistance in the Rhineland, 1792–1802* (Oxford, 1983); J. Black, *Eighteenth Century Europe 1700–1789* (1990), pp. 415–23.

[3] C. A. Bayly, *Imperial Meridian. The British Empire and the World 1780–1830* (Harlow, 1989), pp. 164–92, esp. 164–5.

the establishment of a British colony in Australia in 1788, was somewhat different from the consequences of declining Asian hegemonies discussed by Bayly.

A different facet of the concurrence of so many domestic challenges to authority in European states is provided by the question of their relationship to contemporary developments in the intensely competitive international relations of the period. This aspect of the period has been generally avoided in recent scholarship, which has tended to treat the international dimensions of the French Revolution largely as a question of relations with foreign radicals, rather than as one of the foreign policies of states. The most conspicuous recent exception is offered by the sparkling and incisive work of T. C. W. Blanning, and it is significant that this is well grounded in the solid writings of the scholars of the great age of diplomatic history in the late nineteenth and early twentieth century.[4] Blanning's *Origins of the French Revolutionary Wars* is very valuable, but it is all too short, and suggestive rather than comprehensive. His insights will be returned to as they are very important for an understanding of international developments in the period. Blanning's 'George III, Hanover and the *Fürstenbund*' is also the best article on an important crisis for British foreign policy; but he has not had the opportunity to produce a wider-ranging study of this policy.[5]

The notion of international relations playing a central role in the crises within individual states in this period appears less remarkable if the literature surrounding the 'general crisis' of the mid-seventeenth century is considered, or if those of the 1560s, 1590s and 1700s are considered. Such a thesis has been advanced more generally by Theda Skocpol in her comparative study of the French, Russian and Chinese revolutions.[6] The financial and political pressures arising from military developments and war finance are an incessant theme in the literature on the early-modern

---

[4] T. C. W. Blanning, *The Origins of the French Revolutionary Wars* (1986), 'The French Revolution and Europe' in C. Lucas (ed.), *Rewriting the French Revolution* (Oxford, 1991), pp. 183–206, esp. 183–96.

[5] T. C. W. Blanning, '"That Horrid Electorate" or "Ma Patrie Germanique"? George III, Hanover, and the *Fürstenbund* of 1785', *Historical Journal*, 20 (1977), 311–44.

[6] The extensive literature can be approached through T. Aston (ed.), *Crisis in Europe 1560–1660* (1965); R. Forster and J. Greene (eds.), *Preconditions of Revolution in Early Modern Europe* (Baltimore, 1970); G. Parker and L. M. Smith (eds.), *The General Crisis of the Seventeenth Century* (1978); P. Zagorin, *Rebels and Rulers 1500–1660* (2 vols., Cambridge, 1982); P. Clark (ed.), *The European Crisis of the 1590s* (1985); O. Subtelny, *Domination of Eastern Europe. Native Nobilities and Foreign Absolutism 1500–1715* (Kingston, Ontario, 1986); L. and M. Frey, *Societies in Upheaval. Insurrections in France, Hungary, and Spain in the Early Eighteenth Century* (Westport, Conn., 1987); T. Skocpol, *States and Social Revolutions* (Cambridge, 1979), though see criticism in J. A. Goldstone, *Revolution and Rebellion in the Early Modern World* (Berkeley, 1991), pp. 19–21.

period, as are the interrelationships between external strength and domestic stability, and between peace and stability.

The 1780s and early 1790s were a period of volatility in European international relations, of diplomatic revolutions, planned or realised, imminent or actual.[7] These arose largely from changes in the configurations of alliances, the most important being the Austro-Russian understanding of 1781, and, in the early 1790s, the interrelated collapse of the Austro-French connection, Austro-Prussian reconciliation and recreation of the Austro-Prussian-Russian understanding that had already been responsible for the First Partition of Poland in 1772. Such shifts could be related closely, however, to changes within individual states and, in part, states sought to achieve their international goals by sponsoring disorder in the territories of their rivals. Although this process is classically associated with the radicals who rose to influence and power in revolutionary France, it was neither restricted to them nor new. The French politicians who sponsored revolution in Ireland or the Low Countries in the 1790s were in part adopting practices that Louis XIV had followed in Hungary.[8] The French radicals were eager to encourage activity by those who were not natural leaders of society, to replace the intervention on behalf of particularist forces that had frequently characterised the *ancien régime* situation, by a more obvious social component, but this ambition would not have surprised, for example, rulers seeking to encourage co-religionists in the sixteenth century.

Excluding the French radicals, it is possible to point to other instances of intervention in domestic politics and the encouragement of discontent in 1783–93. The British encouraged frontier separatists in America, especially in Vermont, and, to a lesser extent, Kentucky. Gustavus III of Sweden sought to encourage discontent in Norway, Livonia and Estonia in order to facilitate his plans to acquire the first from the King of Denmark and to weaken Catherine II of Russia in her Baltic provinces. Catherine, in turn, followed the same policy in Sweden and Finland. British and French intervention in the crisis in the United Provinces in 1785–7 was followed by Russian and Austrian encouragement of insurrection in the Turkish Empire, and by Prussian incitement of discontent in Habsburg territories,[9] incitement that played a role in

---

[7] The most recent introduction is J. Black, *The Rise of the European Powers 1679–1793* (1990), pp. 129–48. M. S. Anderson, 'European Diplomatic Relations 1763–90' in *New Cambridge Modern History*, 8 (1968), pp. 252–78 is valuable.

[8] M. Elliott, *Partners in Revolution. The United Irishmen and France* (New Haven, 1982); B. Köpeczi, *La France et la Hongrie au début du XVIIIe siècle* (Budapest, 1971).

[9] C. Williamson, *Vermont in Quandry: 1763–1825* (Montpelier, Vermont, 1949), pp. 151–64; H. A. Barton, *Scandinavia in the Revolutionary Era 1760–1815* (Minneapolis,

Prussian plans in the late 1780s and 1790–1 for a major reordering of the territorial system of Europe, a planned revolution to which insurrection, war and diplomacy were all to contribute. In some respects this was very different from the last occasion when an extensive redrawing of the European territorial system had been attempted, 1741. Then, France, Bavaria, Spain, Saxony, Prussia and Sweden had sought largely by direct military means to challenge the hegemony in central and eastern Europe that Austria and Russia had created in 1683–1721. Encouraging insurrection played a larger role in Prussian plans fifty years later, though the appeal to popular support was far from unknown in the 1740s, as was demonstrated when Bavaria invaded Bohemia in 1741, and Russia Finland in 1742.

A comparison between the early 1790s and the early 1740s is far from idle. Too often the question of how far the French Revolution altered the conduct and content of international relations is based on a chronologically limited survey of the *ancien régime* situation. This is unhelpful and reflects the erroneous assumption that *ancien régime* international relations were relatively fixed, so that a comparison of the period 1763–89 with subsequent years suffices. Instead, both for British foreign policy and for Continental international relations, it is necessary to adopt a longer time-span in order to make sound evaluations. An example of the problem that neglecting such a time-span creates is provided by one of Blanning's many suggestive remarks, 'The collapse of French power that was the French Revolution allowed Russia to achieve hegemony of Eastern Europe; yet that same hegemony ensured the Revolution's survival.' In fact, Russian power was in some respects more obvious, and certainly newer and more unexpected, in 1716–17, when Peter the Great's troops wintered in Mecklenburg and controlled Poland, or 1735, when, having subjugated Poland in the War of the Polish Succession (and crushed a French attempt to relieve Danzig (Gdansk) in 1734), Russian troops moved into the Empire (roughly modern Germany), helping to encourage France to end the war. Between 1733 and 1743, until the start of 1742 a period of marked French resurgence, Russia successively defeated the Poles, the Turks and the Swedes. Austrian difficulties in this period made Russian strength even more apparent. In short, there was no necessary relationship between French weakness and Russian strength, let alone between the Revolution and

1986), pp. 154–5; A. Cobban, *Ambassadors and Secret Agents. The Diplomacy of the First Earl of Malmesbury at the Hague* (1954); P. Bernard, 'Austria's Last Turkish War: Some Further Thoughts', *Austrian History Yearbook*, 19–20 (1983–4), 21–9; F. C. Wittichen, *Preussen und die Revolutionen in Belgien und Lüttich* (Göttingen, 1905); R. Gragger, *Preussen, Weimar und die ungarische Königskrone* (Berlin/Leipzig, 1923).

Russian hegemony. In claiming that Russia's emergence as a European great power covered the period from the 1760s to the 1790s, Hamish Scott similarly underrates Russia's strength earlier in the century.[10]

Another instance of the need to adopt a long time-span is provided by an apparently imminent revolution of the 1780s, the destruction of Turkish power in Europe. In 1783 Vergennes, the capable French Foreign Minister and a former Ambassador in Constantinople, wrote of 'la révolution dont l'Empire Ottoman semble être menacée'.[11] The 'Eastern Question' has been seen as arising in this period,[12] but serious plans for the conquest of the Turkish Empire had first been advanced nearly a century earlier as, following the Turkish defeat at Vienna in 1683, Austrian forces conquered Hungary and pressed south into Serbia and towards the Balkans. The interrelationship of Swedish, Polish and Turkish developments, which was such a major theme in the conflicts and confrontations of 1787–92, had been a major theme in the 1710s, 1730s and during the last Russo-Turkish conflict of 1768–74.

Thus, the question of the revolutionary nature of the international developments of 1783–93 has to be addressed against a time-span bounded by the major changes of the 1680s. This is equally true of British foreign policy, for it was the 'Glorious Revolution' of 1688–9, and its consequences, the resulting dynastic arrangement that led in 1714 to the succession of the Hanoverian dynasty under the Act of Settlement of 1701, and the Anglo-French wars of 1689–97 (Nine Years) and 1702–13 (Spanish Succession), that led to much closer British concern with and intervention in the affairs of the Continent.[13] A study of British foreign policy in the 1780s and early 1790s offers an opportunity for re-examining the international relations of the period and, in particular, the vexed question of the impact of the French Revolution. France was the foreign country and state that successive governments of Britain, as well as its population, were most concerned with. Alexander Straton, Secretary of Legation in Vienna, wrote in August 1791 to Lord Grenville, the new Foreign Secretary, of 'his persuasion that everything which has a reference to France, cannot but be more or less connected with the politics of Great Britain'.[14]

Alongside the strong sense that the two countries were inevitable

---

[10] Blanning, 'The French Revolution and Europe', p. 188; H. M. Scott, 'Russia as a European Great Power', in R. Bartlett and J. M. Hartley (eds.), *Russia in the Age of the Enlightenment* (1990), pp. 8–11.

[11] P. Vaucher (ed.), *Recueil des Instructions données aux Ambassadeurs et Ministres de France depuis les Traités de Westphalie jusqu'à la Révolution Française. Angleterre III* (Paris, 1965), p. 522.   [12] M. S. Anderson, *The Eastern Question, 1774–1923* (1966).

[13] J. Black, *A System of Ambition? British Foreign Policy 1660–1793* (Harlow, 1991).

[14] Straton to Grenville, 3 Aug. 1791, PRO FO 7/24 fol. 256.

enemies – an attitude that linked the Foreign Secretary, from December 1783 until 1791 Francis, Marquis of Carmarthen (from 1789, 5th Duke of Leeds), to the most splenetic of xenophobic patriots – it was claimed by some that such inevitabilities did not exist in international relations and that contingent circumstances, improved by diplomatic skill, could lead to better relations. This was argued most forcefully in defence of the Anglo-French Commercial Treaty of 1786. The treaty is commonly named after its British negotiator, William Eden (later Lord Auckland), and, never one to neglect his role, he wrote in April 1786 to William Pitt the Younger, First Lord of the Treasury and the head of George III's government from December 1783, 'It is even highly possible that this treaty may form a new epoch in history.' Defending the treaty in the Commons the following February, Pitt argued that 'to suppose that any nation could be unalterably the enemy of another, was weak and childish. It had neither its foundation in the experience of nations nor in the history of man.' A critic, Sir Grey Cooper, formerly a Lord of the Treasury, said of the treaty that it

> was an experiment of the greatest magnitude and extent, and that it was an innovation which made a wide and comprehensive alteration in a system, which had long prevailed in this country, and which had taken so deep a root, that the sudden disturbance and change of it might shake and impair the foundation of the pillars which supported the strength and power of the kingdom.[15]

The unpredictability of international developments was abundantly demonstrated in 1787, for that autumn Britain staged a major naval mobilisation in order to prevent France from acting against the British-encouraged Prussian invasion of the United Provinces. There was to be no diplomatic revolution, in the shape of the Anglo-French diplomatic co-operation that Vergennes sought, but, instead, the collapse of French power in 1787 was to usher in the French Revolution as far as international relations were concerned. It was also crucial for British foreign policy, as French weakness enabled Britain to take a more assertive role in Europe in 1787–91, and in a trans-oceanic confrontation with Spain, the Nootka Sound Crisis, in 1790. This stage of the French Revolution persisted until 1791–2. In 1791 the future of the French constitution and the nature of France's place in international relations became a prominent topic of diplomatic discussion and negotiation. The following year, after war had broken out between France and Austria, dramatic French successes made it apparent that France could not be ignored and, instead, that the territorial future of western Europe was again an issue, as it had not been since 1748.

---

[15] Eden to Pitt, 13 Apr. 1786, PRO 30/8/110 fol. 19; Cobbett 21, 149.

The study of British foreign policy also provides an opportunity for assessing the nature of the British state in this period. A consideration of the most influential pressures and ideas in the formulation and execution of foreign policy raises questions about the functioning of the political community. The extent to which political practice accorded with constitutional theory is of importance, as is the influence of public debate, the openness of government to external ideas and the nature of public opinion. Foreign policy is a crucial sphere for the discussion of these and other questions, because it was important and believed to be so. This was a sphere in which monarch, ministers and politicians had both considerable interest and views of their own, and, in so far as this led to clashes over policy, it provides an opportunity for assessing the nature of power and influence within the political community and the sophistication of public debate.

The most recent monograph devoted to eighteenth-century British foreign policy, an important work by Hamish Scott, argues that the scope and focus of such a study, at least for the period 1763–83, should not dwell on domestic factors such as the press and Parliament, because foreign policy was not at the centre of political debate. It is, however, possible that Scott's scholarly work with his heavy diplomatic emphasis rather underrates the role of political debate in these years. Though its direct consequences in terms of policy decisions are difficult to demonstrate, this debate and the constitutional, political and financial roles of Parliament had perhaps a wider importance. Scott has expanded his argument to claim that Britain's eighteenth-century diplomacy as a whole 'was conducted by a tiny political elite whose eyes were usually upon Europe rather than upon the domestic consequences of their actions ... the "diplomatic maze" ... and not the domestic context, was always the principal influence upon Hanoverian foreign policy'.[16] This thesis is not supported by any detailed discussion of the situation prior to 1763 or after 1783, and Scott's conclusions for 1763–83 are more surprising given the apparent importance of parliamentary and public pressures in the following decade, 1783–93, most obviously in the Ochakov affair of 1791. As Augustus, 3rd Duke of Grafton, an ex-Secretary of State and First Lord of the Treasury familiar with the nature of eighteenth-century politics, noted of the last, 'Mr. Pitt, unwilling to meet the disapprobation of the nation, who were throughout clamorous against a rupture with Russia, was persuaded to abandon the measure entirely.' George III observed, 'how impossible it would be at

[16] H. M. Scott, *British Foreign Policy in the Age of the American Revolution* (Oxford, 1990), pp. 7–8, and 'The Second "Hundred Years War", 1689–1815', *Historical Journal*, 35 (1992) 449.

present to incline this country to take a cordial part in any measures that might involve it in a war'. Clearly influenced by the recent crisis, Lord Grenville, the new Foreign Secretary, referred to the impact of 'the commercial stumbling block...' on the negotiations for the Anglo-Spanish alliance that he was 'very favourable' to: 'There was no possibility of resisting what was urged on the subject of our commercial grievances, and of the prodigious clamour that we should have raised against us here, if we had appeared, by concluding the alliance separately, or even with only the general article, to acquiesce in all the infractions of the former treaties.' The following year, Grenville wrote of 'the meeting of Parliament, on which all depends'.[17] These pressures require notice, for no study of eighteenth-century British foreign policy can be restricted to a work on diplomacy, nor limited by a concentration on the diplomatic sources.

It is not easy to offer a coherent account of foreign policy that relates domestic circumstances to diplomatic developments, in part because of lacunae and ambiguities in the sources, and also because there was no neat pattern of influences and policies. Instead, there were varied pressures, the impact of which was generally episodic, and in understanding them it is necessary first to consider those cited by the ministers and diplomats of the period. It is also important to appreciate that the formulation and conduct of foreign policy were sometimes within the domestic political arena, but often not. To approach it solely from the diplomatic angle would be misleading, but so, equally, would be any undue stress on domestic parameters, if they are seen as determinants of particular policies, and on the political context and politicisation of policy. Important differences of opinion over policy reflected clashing ministerial views on diplomatic strategy, most obviously over policy towards France in 1786–7 and Russia in 1791,[18] as much as those of rival political parties. Public and political debate over foreign policy varied in its extent and intensity. Britain was not a political system operating in accordance with rigid guidelines. There was much in the constitution and in the political culture of the period that was inconstant or ambiguous, and the formulation, execution and discussion of foreign policy reflected this. The content of the public discussion particularly requires attention for it tends to be underrated, if not ignored, by

[17] W. R. Anson (ed.), *Autobiography and Political Correspondence of Augustus Henry Third Duke of Grafton* (1898), pp. 399–400; George III to Grenville, 19 Apr., Grenville to Lord St Helens, envoy in Madrid, 26 Aug. 1791, Grenville to Auckland, 4 Dec. 1792, BL Add. 58856 fol. 34, 59022 fol. 27, 58921 fol. 10; Pitt to Ewart, 24 May 1791, PRO 30/8/102 fols. 127–33.

[18] M. S. Anderson, *The Discovery of Russia, 1553–1815* (1958), pp. 143–85; A. Cunningham, 'The Oczakow Debate', *Middle Eastern Studies*, 1 (1964), 209–37.

diplomatic historians, while their domestic counterparts, though ready to assess the influence of public agitations, are less happy with judging the intelligence of analyses and predictions.

This study is devoted to the period from 19 December 1783 when Pitt became First Lord of the Treasury, and George III thus created and enjoyed anew a ministry in which he had confidence, until 1 February 1793, when the French Convention voted to declare war on Britain. These were years of great importance for Britain and the other European states, but also years of consequence in the world including as they did the first British settlements in Australia and on the Pacific coast of Canada. The struggle for control over the United Provinces was part of that between Britain and France for hegemony in the Indian Ocean. Despite Vergennes' interest in Anglo-French co-operation as part of a new European and oceanic order, the years from 1783 until 1790, when the Nootka Sound crisis demonstrated France's weakness even more than that of her Spanish ally, can be seen as a continuation of the Anglo-Bourbon struggle, which had been resumed when France came to the assistance of the revolting American colonists in 1778. At the same time, the fate of the Turkish and Austrian Empires, the future of Poland and the position of Austria within the Empire and of Russia within eastern Europe were all uncertain and contested. These were crucial years for the European great powers, an age of confrontation and struggle as much as of revolutions.

1   The aftermath of war

> If a lasting and honourable peace could be secured by the public measures of any minister, it undoubtedly would be the wish of every man of virtue, to see those measures enforced; but such is the nature of man, that *rivalship* between states will always produce *war*; superiority (especially in *commerce*) will never be borne by any power for one moment, after it feels itself strong enough to enter into a new contest.
>
> *Felix Farley's Bristol Journal*, 24 March 1787

As the guns fell silent shortly after 10 on the morning of 17 October 1781 an empire seemed to be drawing to its close. No longer able to reply to the cannon of the American–French besieging force, Charles, 2nd Earl Cornwallis, the commander of the British army that had set off from the Carolinas to conquer Virginia, felt obliged to seek terms for the surrender of his army. On 5 September the British navy had failed to defeat the superior French fleet that blocked the relief or withdrawal of Cornwallis' force at Yorktown. It was not only the North American colonies that now seemed lost. The entire British military system appeared in ruins. Naval power had served as the basis for the conduct of war and the conquest of empire earlier in the century. Its failure in 1781 suggested that British power would soon be defeated throughout the world, and isolated British posts would be obliged to surrender to larger Bourbon forces, as Pensacola, the last base in West Florida, had already done in 1781 and as Minorca was to do the following year. The *Leeds Intelligencer*, one of the most perceptive papers of the period, warned in its issue of 18 December 1781 that France and the Americans threatened to ruin Britain as a naval power.

Yorktown led directly to the fall of the British government and the abandonment of claims to the Thirteen Colonies. News of the defeat led to a collapse in confidence in Britain about the continuation of the war. On 27 February 1782 the government lost a motion in the House of Commons relating to the further prosecution of the war in America. On 20 March Frederick, Lord North, First Lord of the Treasury and head of a ministry that had brought governmental stability since 1770, announced his resignation. Despite talking of abdication, George III turned to a political grouping that he distrusted, the Rockinghamites, who were pledged to independence for America. Although the new ministry was reconstituted around William, 2nd Earl of Shelburne after the death of the Marquis of Rockingham in July 1782, and was in turn replaced by the Fox–North government in April 1783, the peace momentum was maintained. Preliminaries of an Anglo-American peace were signed in Paris in November 1782. American independence was acknowledged and, although the British kept Canada, they yielded the 'Old North West', the area between the Great Lakes and the Ohio river.

The signature of Anglo-Bourbon peace preliminaries followed on 20 January 1783, the definitive peace treaty with the Bourbons (France and Spain) and America being signed at Versailles on 3 September 1783. The terms were less severe for Britain than had been considered and feared. Though on 3 December 1782 the British cabinet had agreed to the Spanish demand to cede Gibraltar in return for gains in the West Indies, French pressure on Spain led to the dropping of this demand which had exposed the British ministry to considerable criticism. Nevertheless, Spain gained Minorca and West and East Florida. In May 1782 Thomas Grenville had reported from Paris to the then Foreign Secretary, Charles James Fox, that France sought, among her other demands, 'very extensive surrenders of commerce and territory in the East Indies'. She did not obtain these, but Britain ceded Tobago and Senegal, agreed to the fortification of Dunkirk and consented to improved terms for the French in the crucial Newfoundland fisheries.[1]

That the terms were not worse reflected British successes in the war against the Bourbons after Yorktown, especially Admiral Rodney's victory at the Saints on 12 April 1782, which prevented an attack on Jamaica, and the successful defence of Gibraltar. Vergennes was aware that in financial and naval terms the war appeared to be going Britain's way. Her naval strength was increasing rapidly, while financially the Bourbons were succumbing to the strain of war. Though without any ally to distract the Bourbons, the British were winning the naval race. In addition, Vergennes was concerned about Russian designs on the Turkish Empire and wanted France to be in a position to oppose them.[2]

---

[1] S. Conn, *Gibraltar in British Diplomacy in the Eighteenth Century* (New Haven, 1942), pp. 220, 228–31; Grenville to Fox, 14 May 1782, PRO FO 27/2 fol. 72; V. T. Harlow, *The Founding of the Second British Empire 1763–1793* (2 vols., 1952–64), I, 223–447; R. B. Morris, *The Peacemakers: The Great Powers and American Independence* (New York, 1965); R. Hoffman and P. J. Albert (eds.), *Peace and Peacemakers: The Treaty of 1783* (Charlottesville, Virginia, 1986); Scott, *Foreign Policy*, pp. 321–38.

[2] D. A. Baugh, 'Why did Britain lose command of the sea during the war for America?' in J. Black and P. L. Woodfine (eds.), *The British Navy and the Use of Naval Power in the*

Britain had thus retained most of her empire, both in the war and in the subsequent peace. The failure of the Bourbon invasion attempt on England of 1779 had ensured that control over the British Isles themselves was not contested by the Bourbons. And yet, to contemporaries, both in Britain and abroad, it was defeat and failure that were most obvious. The Anglo-American English-speaking world had been shattered, Britain had lost her most populous colonies and it was generally believed that her trade with them would inevitably collapse. The rapid changes in government in 1782–3, which culminated in December 1783 when George III inspired the replacement of the Fox–North ministry by an untried team around the young William Pitt who lacked a majority in the House of Commons, created an impression of weakness and instability. Thomas, 2nd Lord Grantham, the Foreign Secretary of the Shelburne ministry, expressed the hope 'that our civil revolutions may not destroy all confidence from abroad in our councils'.[3]

Frequent changes in ministry had a number of consequences. They lessened foreign confidence in British strength, ministerial change being seen as evidence of governmental weakness. British envoys complained frequently that foreign rulers and ministers did not understand British politics.[4] Changes also led to a lack of confidence in the stability of ministries with which negotiations might be or were being conducted. The veteran diplomat, Sir James Harris MP, in London just after the formation of the Pitt ministry, assured Sir Robert Murray Keith, Envoy Extraordinary in Vienna, that the governmental change would not affect foreign policy,

the same system will be pursued and however fluctuating we may be at home we shall be systematic as far as relates to the continent, for I am now convinced by experience of what I have so often taken upon me to say from presumption that it is neither candid or wise in foreign courts to suppose that our sentiments relative to them alter with any change of administration. To recover our weight on the continent by judicious alliances is the general wish of every man the least acquainted with the interests of this country, and this object will be pursued with the same assiduity whether Mr. Fox or Lord Carmarthen is the channel through which the King's sentiments are to pass – of this I am certain.[5]

Harris was a man of firmly held convictions and like many such tended to overlook the ambiguities of reality. Although he was correct to argue that

Eighteenth Century (Leicester, 1988), pp. 158–63; J. R. Dull, *A Diplomatic History of the American Revolution* (New Haven, 1985), p. 133.
[3] Grantham to Sir Robert Murray Keith, Envoy Extraordinary in Vienna, 22 Feb. 1783, BL Add. 35528 fol. 22.
[4] Keith, 'Heads of a Conversation with the Emperor [Joseph II]', 19 Aug. 1782, BL Add. 35526 fol. 119.   [5] Harris to Keith, 22 Dec. 1783, BL Add. 35530 fols. 276–7.

both the Fox–North and the Pitt ministries wished to 'recover our weight on the continent by judicious alliances', he was wrong to argue that policies and priorities did not change with ministries and ministers. Fox was more hopeful of creating an Anglo-Prusso-Russian system than Grantham or David, Viscount Stormont, Secretary of State for the Northern Department from October 1779 to March 1782, who had looked to an Austrian alliance. Shelburne wanted to use the negotiation of peace with France as the opportunity for and basis of an Anglo-French alliance designed to bring stability to Europe.[6] This was scarcely the goal of Fox or Carmarthen, both of whom saw peace as but a stage on a continuing path of Anglo-French enmity.

In these circumstances, ministerial changes made Britain an unreliable partner. As Alleyne Fitzherbert, Envoy Extraordinary in St Petersburg, observed in February 1784:

> It would indeed be unreasonable to expect that when these total changes take place in our government, foreign courts should veer about with the same celerity that we do, and be ready to enter into a cordial and confidential communication with a set of ministers with whose principles and notions they have little acquaintance, and as little reason to rely upon their political stability.[7]

Britain was scarcely alone in having changed ministers, policy and partners in recent decades, but the nature of the British political system made it easier to dwell on her apparent tendency to do so. British statesmen of the age of the American Revolution have recently been accused of a lack of flexibility in their thinking about foreign policy, of minds that 'ran along familiar grooves',[8] but such predictability was not apparent to foreign commentators in the early 1780s. Change also affected the conduct of British foreign policy. William Fraser, the Under Secretary at the Foreign Office, was evidence of continuity of a type. He had entered the office of the Secretary of State of the Southern Department in 1751, first became an Under Secretary in 1765 and was not to retire until 1789. In December 1783, however, he wrote, 'the business of this office can be little attended to at present ... the instability of things'. The Senior Clerk, George Aust, wrote to Robert Liston, Secretary of Embassy at Madrid, on 16 December:

---

[6] H. Doniol, 'La première négociation de la paix de 1783 entre la France et la Grande-Bretagne', *Revue d'histoire diplomatique*, 6 (1892), 56–89.

[7] Fitzherbert to Keith, 10 Feb., Fitzherbert to Carmarthen, 2 Feb., Duke of Dorset, envoy in Paris, to Carmarthen, 22 Feb. 1784, BL Add. 35531 fol. 79, Eg. 3500 fol. 1, 3499 fol. 11; Viscount Torrington, Minister Plenipotentiary in Brussels, to Harris, 9 Jan. 1784, Winchester CRO Malmesbury vol. 169; Count Kageneck, Austrian Envoy Extraordinary in London, to Count Kaunitz, Austrian Chancellor, 19 Oct. 1784, HHStA EK 123.   [8] Scott, *Foreign Policy*, p. 342.

You must not wonder at not hearing officially from us at present – Read the turn the India business took last night in the House of Lords and when I tell you the *interference* alluded to gains universal credit, you will naturally believe that we are *totally unhinged.* I am not able at present to give you a single ray of light upon the probable consequences.[9]

Diplomats were also affected. There was no professional service separate from the world of politics. Patronage was crucial in appointments, and in the senior ranks this was often political in nature. Some diplomats, such as Harris, were MPs, while all the English peers sat in the House of Lords, and some of the diplomat-peers were really politicians. When Pitt replaced Fox–North it was necessary to appoint new envoys to Paris and Madrid because their followers were either dismissed or sought to undermine the new minister by a collective resignation. This led to the departure of the existing envoys, George, 4th Duke of Manchester and John, Viscount Mountstuart, as well as of the Under Secretary at the Foreign Office, St Andrew St John, an MP friend of Fox's, and Anthony Storer, the Secretary to the Embassy at Paris, and an MP. The previous May, Elizabeth, Duchess of Manchester had warned her husband, then in Paris, 'I think it may be *prudent* not to engage any house till the stability of this ministry is a little more certain.' Governmental instability did not only, however, affect the 'political' diplomats. In October 1783 Keith, a former, though not active, MP, wrote to his cousin Frances Murray, a sounding board for his frequent complaints about the trials of diplomatic life, 'I presume the parties in Parliament are whetting their knives to assassinate each other at the opening [of the session] without any regard to the welfare of old England. You are a set of hardened sinners, and nothing will reclaim you.' The absence of 'steady govern-ment' in Britain left Keith neglected and unable to plan his life.[10]

That summer John, 2nd Earl of Buckinghamshire, a former diplomat, took time off from admiring the scantily clad bathing beauties at Weymouth, to reflect on,

this unhappy disgraced country surrounded by every species of embarrassment, and without even a distant prospect of establishing an Administration so firm and so respectable as to restore to England any proportion of her defeated dignity. The state is now circumstanced as a human body in the last stage of a decline.

---

[9] Fraser to Keith, 16 Dec. 1783, BL Add. 35530 fol. 252; Aust to Liston, 16 Dec. 1783, NLS 5539 fol. 27.

[10] Harris to his wife, 22 July 1782, Merton College, Oxford, F.3.3; Mountstuart to Liston, 26 Dec. 1783, NLS 5539 fol. 65; Duchess to Duke of Manchester, 7 May 1783, Huntingdon CRO dd M21 B; Keith to Murray, 10 Oct., 18 Dec., 1783, HL HM. 18940 pp. 266, 270–1; Viscount Dalrymple, Minister Plenipotentiary in Warsaw, to Liston, 21 Jan. 1784, NLS 5540 fol. 25.

Like George III, who had been driven to consider abdication, the political crisis led Buckinghamshire to question his assumptions,

Whig as I am and sufficiently vain of my descent from Maynard and Hampden, it sometimes occurs to me that something might be obtained by strengthening the hands of the Crown, but then school recollection suggests to me the Fable of the Horse.[11]

The British political system appeared to have failed. Defeat abroad, the crisis of the imperial system, was matched by instability at home. The eventual resolution, in the shape of a ministry enjoying active royal support and victory in the general elections of 1784 and 1790, was scarcely prefigured in the chaos and enmity of 1782–3. Indeed, in February and March 1783 Pitt had rejected royal invitations to form a government.[12]

A sense that Britain was weak and weakening was not new. Her triumphs in the Seven Years War (1756–63) had been followed by the ministerial and domestic instability of the 1760s, especially the prominent Wilkite troubles, which had encouraged foreign commentators to discern weakness.[13] As with the Excise Crisis in 1733, the significance of public disturbances was exaggerated. The ministerial changes of 1782–3 were the culmination of nearly two decades of continual harping on British debility, especially the apparent malaise of her political system. The emphasis placed by foreign commentators varied, in accordance with their own perception of Britain and the chronology of crisis there. The Wilkite troubles of the 1760s were succeeded by the imperial crisis of the 1770s and then, in 1780–4, first by troubles in Ireland and England, including the spectacular Gordon Riots of 1780, and secondly by a collapse of the North ministry and a protracted political crisis. Rulers such as Catherine II (the Great) of Russia, Frederick II (the Great) of Prussia and Joseph II of Austria, argued in the early 1780s that Britain was weak, that this was due to inherent characteristics of her political system which would probably lead to the dissolution of her empire, and that in the meantime this weakness made her an undesirable ally. Selected for the Madrid embassy, John, Viscount Mountstuart was warned that he would meet with 'contemptuous treatment' from the ministers of France and Spain, 'They feel the superiority gained in the contest over Great Britain, and it is a measure adopted to make it public to the whole world.'[14] Asked at the beginning of that decade what major

---

[11] Buckinghamshire to Sir Charles Hotham, 12 July 1783, Hull UL DDHo/4/22.
[12] Pitt to George III, 25 Mar. 1783, PRO 30/8/101 fol. 1.
[13] M. Roberts, *Splendid Isolation 1763–1780* (Reading, 1970), pp. 4–7.
[14] Mountstuart to Liston, 24 Dec. 1782, BL Add. 36804 fol. 27.

state was most likely to have a revolution by its close, an impartial European commentator would almost certainly have replied Britain, not France or Austria. Crisis at the centre would make Britain less able to protect her empire and Ireland, Canada and, in particular, her position in India seemed vulnerable.[15] Thus any alliance with Britain would entail co-operation with a power that was not only not interested in seeing territorial changes in Europe, but would also be preoccupied with defending her own colonial and maritime position. In 1739 Portugal and the United Provinces had been unwilling to help their ally Britain in the War of Jenkins' Ear with Spain; in 1755 Austria and the United Provinces had been similarly uninterested in helping Britain in her developing North American conflict with France, though not because British power was regarded as finished. In the 1780s it seemed likely that any new Anglo-French conflict would again see Britain on the defensive. Though the causes were not identical, Britain appeared to be following Spain, Turkey, the United Provinces and Poland into the category of vulnerable, weak powers. Such a classification need not be permanent, as the revival of Spanish strength under Bourbon rule, first Philip V (1700–46) and later Charles III (1759–88), or of Austrian power under Maria Theresa and Joseph II indicated, but the situation did not seem propitious for Britain. Recently defeated, she was isolated, her government was unstable and her empire vulnerable.

Recent and, as it turned out, short-term problems were not alone responsible, however, for Britain's diplomatic weakness and international situation. There were also long-term reasons why Britain was an unattractive ally and why her foreign policy tended to caution. In part, caution was a product of Britain's military weakness. Britain possessed 'sinews of power' sufficient to win Canada from France (1758–60), to intimidate Spain over the Falklands (1770) and to retain Jamaica and Gibraltar (1782), but not those that could influence the fate of Poland, persuade Catherine II to disgorge Ochakov or prevent the French, whether in 1746–7 under Saxe, or in 1792 under revolutionary colours, from seizing the Scheldt and threatening the Dutch. Caution, however, was also a consequence of Britain's international position and the central theme of her foreign policy. Britain essentially acted in Europe as a 'satisfied' power. This was especially so after the interventionist, if not aggressive, activity associated with George I's attempts to gain territory with Hanover, was replaced from 1731–3 by a sense of vulnerability and caution that reflected both the collapse of the Anglo-French and Anglo-

---

[15] Lord Camden to Shelburne, 2 Sept. 1780, Thomas Orde MP, Secretary to the Lord Lieutenant of Ireland, to Shelburne, 30 Aug. 1784, Bowood 38, 27; Andrew Drummond to Keith, 13 Sept. 1784, BL Add. 35535 fol. 125; Bayly, *Imperial Meridian*, p. 98.

Austrian alliances in 1731 and 1733 respectively, the failure to improve relations with Prussia in 1730, and the fall of Townshend in 1730 and the greater influence of Walpole.[16] Britain was an unsatisfactory ally for many powers because she opposed European war and would not support aggression. British ministries refused to participate in the War of the Polish Succession (1733–5), were reluctant to become involved in the War of the Austrian Succession and resisted involvement in the rivalries of the central and eastern European powers during the Baltic crisis of 1748–9 and in 1756. In 1787 David Parry, the Governor of Barbados, wrote to the Marquess of Lansdowne, formerly Earl of Shelburne:

I am quite of your Lordship's opinion with respect to the Continent, the less we have to do with it the better, no Partition can do us much harm; it may affect France, and the lesser states of Germany by adding dominion, and strength to the two Imperial powers; but as long as England has the command at sea (which when she has not, she will cease to exist as a great power, and, as she was wont to do, keep the political scales of Europe, and the world in equilibre) she will have little to fear from either of those states; for to meet them on land would in us be madness, and at sea they cannot hurt us.[17]

Such an attitude made Britain an unsatisfactory ally for an aggressive power, as Philip V of Spain had appreciated when he abandoned his British alliance in 1733, and yet the major continental powers other than France sought territorial gains. This was true of Austria under Joseph II, Russia under Catherine II and Prussia under Frederick William II, although less so in the second half of the reign of Frederick II. It was therefore impossible for Britain to ally with any of them and retain a quiescent European position and a peace policy for any length of time. Britain thus demonstrated the problems of a reactive power allying with any active one, a difficulty that also characterised the Franco-Austrian alliance.[18] Ewart asked Pitt in 1791 'if the events of the last four years do not clearly prove that there was no alternative for this country, between taking a leading part in the affairs of Europe, and submitting to be led by other powers'.[19] He advocated the former, but his policy was to collapse in ruins that year in the Ochakov crisis, and the British ministry was then to adopt a non-interventionist and passive policy. As a reactive power, the foreign policy of Britain, whether she was part of an alliance system or not, remained one of expedients. She was never in control of the situation and arguably never would be while she preferred to be inactive in great power politics. During the reign of Louis XVI, the French

---

[16] J. Black, *British Foreign Policy in the Age of Walpole* (Edinburgh, 1985).
[17] Parry to Lansdowne, 14 June 1787, Bowood 60.
[18] J. Hardman, *Louis XVI* (New Haven, 1993), p. 95.
[19] Ewart to Pitt, 14 Feb. 1791, PRO 30/8/133 fol. 294.

government was not inactive but was similarly opposed to European war, and, specifically, to the ambitions of the predatory rulers. As a result, however, of the British fear of France, arising both from her actions in the American War and from concern about her objectives in Asia, British ministers failed to appreciate that Britain and France were the only powers who wished to maintain peace and the present distribution of territories in Europe. In addition, ministerial consideration of policy took place against the background of a powerful francophobia, not that that determined diplomatic strategy.[20] This francophobia was reflected in the public discussion of foreign policy. It was especially marked in print: in the press, in pamphlets and in caricatures.[21] Thus, the Anglo-French commercial treaty of 1786, the Eden Treaty, led to a blast of hostile comment. France was presented as Britain's natural enemy, 'although an enemy of that stamp may be converted into an artificial ally, yet the ultimate result of such an union must be the ruin of one or other of the contracting nations'.[22] It was also claimed that France's political interests were never more opposed to those of Britain than then.[23] As a consequence, public discussion of British diplomatic options concentrated on the question of which continental power was most able and willing to oppose France.[24] Furthermore, concern with France helped to set the geography of British diplomatic and, still more, public concern. Writing of the early nineteenth century, Paul Schroeder has queried whether 'any lasting European settlement' could have developed from, or rested on, a view that limited 'Britain's interests in Europe to a narrow strip of territory stretching from Holland to Portugal'.[25] Such an attitude was of scant interest to Austria, Prussia and Russia.

Part of the interest of British foreign policy in 1783–93 is provided by the attempt of the Pitt ministry in 1788–91 to widen these horizons and to adopt a more active approach to international problems. The chosen means was an alliance system, the Triple Alliance of 1788 of Britain,

---

[20] J. Black, *Natural and Necessary Enemies. Anglo-French Relations in the Eighteenth Century* (1986).

[21] For example, *The Commercial Treaty; or, John Bull changing Beef and Pudding for Frogs and Soup Maigre!* (1786), British Museum Catalogue 6995, illustrated in M. Duffy, *The Englishman and the Foreigner* (Cambridge, 1986), p. 265.

[22] Anon., *Sentiments on the interests of Great Britain with thoughts on the politics of France and on the accession of the Elector of Hanover to the German League* (1787), pp. 36–7.

[23] Anon., *The Principles of British Policy, contrasted with a French Alliance* (1787), p. 2.

[24] *Sentiments*, p. 46; Sir John Dalrymple, *Queries concerning the Conduct which England should follow in Foreign Politics in the Present State of Europe, written in October 1788* (1789), pp. 35–6, 38–9.

[25] P. W. Schroeder, 'Old Wine in Old Bottles: Recent Contributions to British Foreign Policy and European International Politics, 1789–1848', *Journal of British Studies*, 36 (1987), 9.

Prussia and the United Provinces,[26] the desired goal a stable European system bound together by a guarantee for mutual protection. The last prefigured both what the British sought in late 1792 to restrain Revolutionary France and, again, Pitt's objectives in 1805.[27] The failure of the Triple Alliance is one of the major themes of this book, a failure that throws much light both on the international relations of the period and on the potential role of Britain in European power politics. The failure to restrain Revolutionary France is another theme, although its domestic context was different to that of the Ochakov Crisis: British policy and public debate achieved a greater consistency of purpose when France became aggressive again and did so with revolutionary zeal, pretensions and unpredictability. A description of policy in terms of failure runs the risks of anachronism, arrogance and a spurious omniscience. All are inappropriate. Instead, it is the difficulties of the challenges facing British ministers and diplomats that must be appreciated. The British alone were not, of course, faced with serious problems. Such an anglocentric perspective would be inappropriate. Changes in power relationships and the particular views of individual rulers ensured that the European system was far from stable. The costs of military strength, confrontation and war were a significant drain on the resources of all major states. A sense of unpredictability combined with an awareness of opportunities to produce opportunism and anxiety. Europe was at peace when the Pitt ministry came to power; but it was a peace that neither experience nor an awareness of current and likely future tensions suggested would be harmonious or lasting.

[26] This was based not on an alliance of the three powers, but on bilateral alliances between them.

[27] Pitt, 'Official Communication made to the Russian Ambassador at London... explanatory of the views which His Majesty and the Emperor of Russia formed for the deliverance and security of Europe', 19 Jan. 1805, PRO FO 65/60, C. K. Webster (ed.), *British Diplomacy 1813–1815. Select Documents Dealing with the Reconstruction of Europe* (1921), pp. 389–93.

2   Years of isolation, 1783–1786

The very contradictory reports daily propagated in respect to the views and intentions of the principal powers of Europe are almost beyond the limits of newspaper speculation, and I do not believe a period ever existed in which so much was surmised and so little really known. However by following a clear and distinct line, at least by keeping it in view and only deviating from the direct course of it, in cases of absolute necessity, I flatter myself England may still profit of the unsettled state of other powers. Some of the principal ones of these should be convinced the friendship of England is not to be despised. Should they reject it, it may to their astonishment take a very different direction indeed, and then it may be too late for them to renew ancient professions of friendship and good wishes.

Marquis of Carmarthen, Foreign Secretary, 1784[1]

Political crisis

Political survival, not foreign policy, was the first priority of the new Pitt government. Whereas the Rockingham, Shelburne and Fox–North ministries had had to bring a world war to a close and to obtain the best terms possible with a weak hand, the new government's international problems were less urgent. Because of Dutch reluctance to accept the disadvantageous terms that their poor performance in the war led Britain and France to consider reasonable, Anglo-Dutch peace preliminaries were not signed until September 1783, and the definitive treaty until 20 May 1784. Nevertheless, these negotiations were not at the forefront of governmental attention. Instead, the new ministry was involved in a desperate struggle to establish itself. Recent work on its early months has emphasised its political weakness.[2] It was not inevitable that Pitt would

---

[1] Carmarthen to Keith, 18 June 1784, PRO FO 7/8.
[2] P. Kelly, 'The Pitt–Temple Administration: 19–22 December 1783', *Historical Journal*, 17 (1974), 157–61; P. Kelly, 'British Politics, 1783–4: the Emergence and Triumph of the Younger Pitt's Administration', *Bulletin of the Institute of Historical Research*, 54 (1981), 62–78; H. Furber (ed.), *The Correspondence of Edmund Burke* V (Cambridge, 1965), p. 119; W. C. Lowe, 'George III, Peerage Creations and Politics, 1760–1784', *Historical Journal*, 35 (1992), 608.

21

secure a majority in the Commons simply because George III had appointed him to office. George's actions, which were regarded by some as unconstitutional, were countered by a collective resignation of office-holders, similar to the step that had forced George II to abandon his attempt to create a ministry under Lord Carteret in February 1746 or the resignation of Rockingham's supporters in protest at the appointment of Shelburne in July 1782; though at least one of those who has been listed as having resigned, Edmund Burke, was in fact sacked in December 1783. The unsuccessful attempt of the new ministers to reach an agreement with Fox on 21 December 1783 and the resignation on 22 December of Earl Temple, both Home and Foreign Secretary, in order to lessen the danger of impeachment for his role in the fall of the previous government, were evidence of weakness. On the morning of 23 December George saw himself as 'on the edge of a precipice'.[3] Though a Cabinet had been formed by that evening, the government was still weak after the Christmas recess. Having lost two Commons divisions on 12 January 1784, Pitt thought of resigning. Distressed to find the Commons 'much more willing to enter into any intemperate resolutions of desperate men than I could have imagined', George III characteristically reiterated his hostility to 'this faction', his readiness to struggle against them until the end of his life and his willingness to abdicate if they gained office. On 23 January Pitt's bill for the government of British India, a crucial and contentious piece of legislation, was also defeated. Four days later the ministry was referred to as 'this no government'.[4]

The conduct of foreign policy in the new ministry was in the hands of Francis, Marquis of Carmarthen, who was appointed Foreign Secretary on 23 December 1783. He explained his willingness to accept the post as due to 'motives of the most disinterested duty'. The Secretaryship had first been offered to Thomas, 2nd Lord Grantham, an ex-diplomat who had been Foreign Secretary in the Shelburne administration, but he was reluctant to take office. Grantham was clearly seen as the best choice, and was indeed pressed to accept the Foreign Office by Temple, Sydney and Pitt.[5] Envoys were selected, John, 3rd Duke of Dorset, very much George III's choice, but without any diplomatic experience, reaching Paris on the evening of 13 January 1784, having been driven by the wind to Boulogne, rather than his intended landfall of Calais. Dorset sent

---

[3] George III to Pitt, 23 Dec. 1783, PRO 30/8/103 fol. 14.
[4] George III to Pitt, 13 Jan. 1784, PRO 30/8/103 fol. 30; Lord George Germain to 3rd Duke of Dorset, 27 Jan. 1784, KAO C192.
[5] Leeds Political Memoranda, BL Add. 27918 fols. 106–8; Carmarthen to Shelburne, 31 Dec. 1783, Bowood, 39; I. R. Christie, 'Lord Grantham and William Pitt: 12 December 1783 ... ', Historical Journal, 34 (1991), 144–5.

Carmarthen his proxy vote in the Lords to give 'to anybody the King approves'; as a diplomat-peer this was his first obligation.[6] Instructions were drawn up, dispatches answered and assurances of continuity of policy proffered.[7] And yet, despite George III's determination, it was still unclear whether Pitt's tenure on office would be much longer than Temple's. An attempt by independent MPs to create a broad-based government of national union, a frequently expressed aspiration during the century, gave Pitt breathing space in early February, and his position was further improved by a swelling tide of favourable public opinion, betokened by a large number of addresses from counties and boroughs, with over 50,000 signatures in total, in favour of George III and the free exercise of the royal prerogative in choosing ministers. They also reflected hostility to what was seen as the opportunism of the Fox–North coalition. George's confidence in public support was reflected on 13 February 1784 when he wrote of

the present strange phenomenon, a majority not exceeding 30 in the House of Commons thinking that justifies the stopping the necessary supplies when the House of Lords by a majority of near two to one and at least that of the People at large approve of my conduct and see as I do that not less is meant than to render the Crown and the Lords perfect cyphers; but it will be seen that I will never submit.[8]

On the positive side, if the formation of the Pitt government had not ended the crisis created by the poor relations between George III and the Fox–North ministry, it had changed its nature, made it more public and united monarch and government. The more public nature of the transformed crisis led to an upsurge in popular interest and this focused on support for George and thus his new ministers. That so many of the latter were little known was very advantageous: they lacked the experience of office that could lead to political charges of opportunism and inconsistency. Edward Gibbon referred to the country as being 'governed by a set of most respectable boys, who were at school half a

[6] Adhémar, French Ambassador, to Vergennes, 23 Dec. 1783, AE CP Ang. 546 fol. 254; Dorset to Carmarthen, 11, 23, 24 Jan. 1784, BL Eg. 3499 fols. 3–7.
[7] Carmarthen to Fitzherbert, 23, 29 Dec. 1783, Carmarthen to Anthony Storer, Minister Plenipotentiary in Paris, 6 Jan. 1784, PRO FO 65/11, 27/11 fol. 16.
[8] George III to Pitt, 17, 25, 30 Jan., 3, 4 Feb. 1784, PRO 30/8/103 fols. 35, 41, 44, 48; Thomas, 1st Earl of Clarendon, to Harris, 15, 23 Dec. 1783, Winchester, Malmesbury, 147; J. Cannon, The Fox–North Coalition. Crisis of the Constitution (Cambridge, 1969), pp. 178–80, 185–96; R. W. Davis, Political Change and Continuity 1760–1885. A Buckinghamshire Study (Newton Abbot, 1972), pp. 33–4; E. S. Wortley (ed.), A Prime Minister and His Son. From the Correspondence of the 3rd Earl of Bute and of … Charles Stuart (1925), p. 203; George to Richard Grenville, 13 Feb. 1784, BL Add. 70957. This correspondence is one of several not included in the Aspinall collection of George's letters.

dozen years ago', Lord Sheffield to 'the young gentlemen who have taken the empire into their hands'.[9] Pitt was further aided by the active support of many peers, not least their influence with dependants in the Commons; and by the uncertainty of his opponents as to whether they should use Parliament's power to refuse supplies in order to force a change of government. By 5 March 1784 Fox's majority in the Commons was down to one, and Pitt felt able to face a general election: Parliament was dissolved on 25 March and the elections, many of which were contested on national political grounds,[10] were very favourable for the ministry. The hostile William Eden referred to a 'frenzy of the people'. William Fraser suggested, 'The tide is so favourable here for the present ministry, that I think they may undertake anything that is for the advantage of this country ... The elections I may now say are three parts over and beyond expectation favourable.'[11] Secure in the backing of the king and of both houses of Parliament, and with clear popular backing, the new government now appeared stable. Even so, ministries that won general elections could fall soon after: Newcastle's overwhelming success in the elections of 1754 and North's success in 1780, did not prevent their fall from office in 1756 and 1782. Many seats were not contested on national political grounds. And yet, ministries that had won an election were likely to be longer-lasting than those that had not had an opportunity to do so. Such ministries were, however, vulnerable to failure in war. That had played a major role in the fall of Newcastle in 1756 and North in 1782. An absence or loss of royal favour could also be fatal to ministries, as Godolphin had discovered in 1710, Newcastle in 1762, Grenville in 1765, Rockingham in 1766 and Fox–North in 1783.

Both these factors were to play an important background role in British foreign policy in the early years of the Pitt ministry. The government wanted peace for political, financial, economic and military reasons, all of which took precedence over diplomatic considerations; while the ministers were well aware that, although George III was hardly likely to

---

[9] J. R. Norton (ed.), *The Letters of Edward Gibbon* (3 vols., 1956), III, 44; Bishop of Bath and Wells (ed.), *The Journal and Correspondence of William, Lord Auckland* (4 vols., 1861–2), I, 72; Germain to Dorset, 14 July 1784, KAO C192.

[10] M. W. McCahill, *Order and Equipoise. The Peerage and the House of Lords, 1783–1806* (1978), pp. 31–6; Cannon, *Fox–North*, p. 225; F. O'Gorman, *Voters, Patrons and Parties. The Unreformed Electorate of Hanoverian England, 1734–1832* (Oxford, 1989), pp. 295–6. For other factors at work in the elections, T. R. Knox, '"Peace for Ages to Come": The Newcastle Elections of 1780 and 1784', *Durham University Journal*, 84 (1992), 13–15; P. D. G. Thomas, 'The Rise of Plas Newydd: Sir Nicholas Bayly and County Elections in Anglesey, 1734–84', *Welsh History Review*, 16 (1992), 174–6.

[11] Eden to Lord Sheffield, 10 Apr. 1784, BL Add. 45728; Fraser to Keith, 23 Apr. 1784, BL Add. 35531 fol. 240; George III note, 4 Apr. 1784, New York, Public Library, Montague collection vol. 4.

turn to the Fox–North opposition, his support had been crucial to the foundation and establishment of the ministry and his views had to be considered. There were divisions in the government, Lord Chancellor Thurlow, an experienced minister, not wishing to defer to Pitt, who also had uneasy relations with Charles, 3rd Duke of Richmond, Master General of the Ordnance, and with Charles Jenkinson, very much a King's man, who was from 1786 Lord Hawkesbury and President of the Board of Trade. There were persistent rumours of rifts within the ministry and likely changes of office, as well as of the strengthening of the government by the recruitment of new ministers, such as Shelburne, that might lead to a change of policy. Thus, the *Daily Universal Register* of 1 January 1785 reported that Grantham would replace Carmarthen, the *Newcastle Courant* of 19 July 1788 that Hawkesbury would become Home Secretary. Such rumours attracted considerable interest among foreign envoys, keen to probe possible causes of changes in British policy, and needing to fill their dispatches. Thomas Orde MP, Secretary to the Lord Lieutenant of Ireland, argued that Pitt was thwarted over Irish trade in 1785 by the narrow views of Cabinet colleagues.[12]

The ministry also faced major defeats in the Commons. George, Lord Herbert, observed in March 1785, 'Ireland, India and Reform are terrible stumbling blocks, but not content with them, Government seems ...to be grasping for others.' That month it was defeated over the Westminster scrutiny, a division that ensured that Fox, the leading opposition MP, was returned for such a prominent seat. That August the ministry withdrew its proposals for a new commercial and financial relationship between England and Ireland in the face of serious opposition from the Irish House of Commons. The proposals had earlier been substantially modified in the face of British mercantile and parliamentary hostility. In February 1786 the British House of Commons rejected a plan, sponsored by Richmond and supported by Pitt, for fortifying Plymouth and Portsmouth, naval bases that were crucial to the use of a Western Squadron to blockade Brest and guard the Western Approaches.[13]

---

[12] Barthélemy, French envoy, to Vergennes, 11, 18 July, 22 Aug., 5 Sept., 5, 26 Dec. 1786, AE CP Ang. 557 fols. 31–2, 45, 197–8, 262, 558 fols. 232, 321; Pollon, Sardinian envoy, to Victor Amadeus III, 19 Dec. 1786, 23, 30 Jan. 1787, AST LM Ing. 88; Germain to Dorset, 8 Dec. 1784, 11 May 1785, KAO C192; Orde to Lansdowne, 31 July 1785, Bowood, 27.

[13] Herbert to Harris, 1 Mar., Grantham to Harris, 4 Dec. 1785, Winchester, Malmesbury 157, 155; Orde to Lansdowne, 24 Jan., Francis Baring MP to Lansdowne, 20 May 1786, Bowood, 27, 9; P. Kelly, 'British Parliamentary Politics, 1784–1786', *Historical Journal*, 17 (1974); D. R. Schweitzer, 'The Failure of William Pitt's Irish Trade Propositions 1785', *Parliamentary History*, 3 (1984), 129–45; I. R. Christie, 'The Anatomy of the

These defeats were noted abroad and commented on by foreign envoys. John Trevor, Envoy Extraordinary in Turin, remarked in April 1785, 'can I mention England without making some gloomy reflections upon the continuation of that unfortunate spirit of party which still mars all our affairs'. In July 1786 François de Barthélemy, the French Minister Plenipotentiary in London, reported that the session had gone badly for Pitt, who had been unwise to support Richmond's fortification project.[14] Writing to Liston in Madrid, Aust, however, argued that the defeat was without consequence, as the issue had not been 'a ministerial question', i.e. a matter of government policy.[15]

The defeats are of importance for British foreign policy, though it is unclear that they were sufficiently spectacular to do more than underline the sense that Britain was unstable and thus to cast doubts on reports that under the new government she was becoming more united and stronger. In January 1784 Samuel Greig, a Scottish admiral in Russian service, warned Harris:

Its now high time that party rage should subside, and people begin to think soberly of the situation of the country; and ministers (whoever they are) be allowed some breathing time, for to apply to public business. For really those intestine broils and dissensions and continual changes of ministers tend greatly to lessen the weight and influence of the nation abroad ... I know that we abroad look upon those things in a much more serious light, than those at home.

In May Prince Wenzel Anton Kaunitz, the Austrian Chancellor, wrote to the Austrian envoy Kageneck suggesting that chronic instability was preventing the new ministry from following the Foxite policy of continental alliances. That August Joseph II spoke to the Marquis de Noailles, French ambassador in Vienna, at a ball that was being held for Frederick, Duke of York, the visiting second son of George III. In response to Joseph's comments on the extent to which Britain was affected by *toutes sortes de divisions*, Noailles, who had been Ambassador in London in 1776–8, replied that this would discourage Britain from fighting another war, and that the need to win parliamentary support limited the ministry's ability to mobilise national resources swiftly. The same month the Danish envoy in London reported that Britain and her government needed peace. The following February, Harris feared that

Opposition in the Parliament of 1784', *Parliamentary History*, 9 (1990), 50–77; M. Duffy, 'The Establishment of the Western Squadron as the Linchpin of British Naval Strategy', in Duffy (ed.), *Parameters of British Naval Power 1650–1850* (Exeter, 1992), pp. 60–81. On the situation at Portsmouth, P. A. Magrath, *Fort Cumberland 1747–1850 : Key to an Island's Defence* (Portsmouth, 1992), pp. 12–13.

[14] Trevor to Keith, 3 Apr. 1785, BL Add. 35534 fol. 56; Barthélemy to Vergennes, 11 July 1786, AE CP Ang. 557 fol. 30.

[15] Aust to Liston, 16 Mar. 1786, NLS 5544 fol. 95.

parliamentary business would prevent ministers from devoting the necessary attention to Dutch affairs.[16]

Signs of domestic weakness and ministerial failure were clearly important, though they were not the only reasons why Britain was an unattractive ally. The parliamentary defeats are of interest for two other reasons. First, recent studies have suggested that Pitt did not handle the issues well. He has been criticised for inexperience, inattention to detail, a failure to understand parliamentary management, and a refusal to accept good advice, and some of the criticism has been in very harsh terms with phrases such as 'a faith that bordered on being blind'.[17] This is significant because the literature on British foreign policy in this period generally takes a very favourable line towards Pitt's objectives, ability and activity, despite reservations over the Ochakov affair. It can, however, be suggested that the situation was less clear-cut, that Pitt's reputation requires re-evaluation, and that a sense *within* governmental circles that his achievements, views and abilities could be questioned accounted both for the criticism that he encountered and for the tensions over foreign policy within the ministry, at certain periods, most obviously in 1786–7 and early 1791.

The parliamentary defeats are also important, as they cast light on the nature of parliamentary politics in this period. The defeats occurred not because of the strength of the opposition, but because on specific issues the ministry lost the support of the influential and numerous independent MPs. The *Daily Universal Register*, a newly launched London newspaper that was to become the *Times*, declared on 15 January 1785:

Mr. Pitt has more to dread from the opposition of the independent country gentlemen, than the most formidable avowed opposition in the House of Commons. It is the independent part of the country who feel the taxes, and these are known to be the first who create party and set their faces against them.

In February 1786 Pitt's sister Harriet explained the defeat of the Fortification Bill

The Opposition brought up all their forces, but they are not very considerable; and the question was lost by the disinclination of the country gentlemen particularly of all the western gentlemen.

Harris was informed that 'the Cornwall gentlemen had the weight ... the friends of ministry are at pains to treat this particular question about

[16] Greig to Harris, 16/27 Jan. 1784, Winchester, Malmesbury 155; Kaunitz to Kageneck, 19 May 1784, HHStA EK 129; Noailles to Vergennes, 4 Aug. 1784, AE CP Aut. 348 fols. 3–4; Dreyer to Count Andreas Bernstorff, Danish first minister, 27 Aug. 1784, PRO FO 95/8 fol. 593; Harris to Keith, 8 Feb. 1785, BL Add. 35533 fol. 213.
[17] Kelly, 'British Parliamentary Politics', HJ, 739, 743; Schweitzer, 'Irish Trade Propositions 1785', 134, 140–4.

these fortifications as one separate from the general system of association on which a party is supposed to act'. The Duke of York, who supported the Bill as a means to free the fleet for wartime offensive operations, argued that its defeat had 'by no means shaken Mr. Pitt in his seat'. In the Dorset county meeting held in early 1789 to discuss sending a congratulatory address to Pitt for his conduct in the Regency Crisis, Charles Sturt, MP for Dorset and an opponent of such an address, felt it pertinent to attack Pitt over the Fortification Bill.[18] The role of independent MPs reflected the limited nature of the party configuration in Parliament. Independents generally gave their support to the crown and the ministers who enjoyed the confidence of the monarch, which was why George III's withdrawal of his backing from the Fox–North government had been so crucial in the Lords. They were, however, willing to withdraw support over particular issues, and this represented an important, but unpredictable, constraint on government policy. Lord Walsingham expressed his concern to Pitt in July 1786 about 'a loose House of Commons, whose firm and systematic support is not to be depended upon in the way which it must be had to carry on a war effectually'. Three years earlier Fox, then in office, had written of a near defeat in the Commons, that 'considering the great unpopularity of the question, what passed seems to me rather a proof of strength than of weakness'.[19] Such a convenient assessment was not without weight on a number of occasions, but it was not surprising that foreign commentators failed to subscribe to it.

The political history of the period 1783–93 demonstrated that in some crises, such as that posed by the apparent rise of French-inspired domestic radicalism in 1792, the independents would back the crown, but in 1782 they had withdrawn their support from North and in early 1784 many preferred to pursue the chimera of independent politicians, a broad-based, apparently national government. In the field of foreign policy the Pitt ministry could not count on Parliament. This was to be demonstrated over Ochakov, but the lesson did not have to wait until 1791. It was, for example, by no means impossible that the Eden Treaty of 1786 would go the way of the Irish commercial propositions, and be

---

[18] Harriet Pitt to her mother, the Countess of Chatham, 28 Feb. 1786, Manchester, John Rylands Library, Eng. Mss. 1272 no. 54; Anne Lindsay to Harris, 1 Mar. 1786, Winchester CRO Malmesbury vol. 159; York to Richard Grenville, 24 May 1786, BL Add. 70958; *Salisbury and Winchester Journal*, 2 Feb. 1789.

[19] Walsingham to Pitt, 16 July 1786, CUL Add. 6958; Fox to Sir John Stepney, envoy in Berlin, 20 May 1783, BL Add. 47562 fol. 115; I. R. Christie, 'Party in Politics in the Age of Lord North's Administration', *Parliamentary History*, 6 (1987), 47–8, 62, and 'The Changing Nature of Parliamentary Politics 1742–1789', in J. Black (ed.), *British Politics and Society from Walpole to Pitt 1742–89* (1990), p. 122.

heavily amended or even defeated, and this explains both the ministry's care in sounding out manufacturing and mercantile opinion and support before and during the negotiations, and the diplomatic tactics adopted in the negotiations with the French. In 1785 George III and Pitt expressed their satisfaction with the session.[20] Parliament was, however, an ever-present factor, though it did not of course sit for as long as its modern successor. Fraser observed in March 1785, 'I hope we are now freer from party than we have been for some time, though the business of Parliament will ever keep it up to a certain degree.'[21]

Parliamentary considerations and, more obscurely, ministerial divisions were to be of importance in the mid-1780s. Ministers were divided over some parliamentary business, such as parliamentary reform in 1785 and the Fortifications Bill in 1786.[22] But after the Pitt government had survived the early months of 1784 and triumphed in the general election, it was freer from immediate domestic pressures and abler therefore to consider the international situation, the specific challenges facing Britain and the diplomatic options available. Foreign powers were, however, to take longer to become convinced of the stability, let alone strength of the British state, and their hesitation was an aspect of the international context of British foreign policy in the mid-1780s.

The international situation: the Americas and the Eastern question

In many respects the most interesting and important challenges facing Britain in 1784 were non-European. In the western hemisphere there was the question of how Britain was to respond to the newly independent thirteen states, and especially to the outstanding issues arising from the implementation of the recent peace treaty. In addition, it was unclear whether the Americans would remain united with the French, and, if so, what impact this would have on Britain's position, or whether Shelburne's hope of an entente between Britain and her former colonies could bear fruit. Relations with America were of obvious importance, for aside from the possible domestic reaction within Britain if the implementation of the peace was too unfavourable or humiliating, there was the question of the security of Canada and of Britain's Caribbean possessions. In a report from Paris of 1786, William Eden struck a prophetic note about

[20] Aspinall, *George III* no. 206; Philip, 5th Earl Stanhope (ed.), *Miscellanies* (1863), p. 6.
[21] Fraser to Keith, 22 Mar. 1785, BL Add. 35534 fol. 15.
[22] Richmond to Pitt, 15 Jan. 1786, PRO 30/8/170 fol. 64; Germain to Dorset, 14 Jan. 1784, KAO C192.

the possibility that the New World would challenge the interests and power of Europe,

there are strong appearances here of a disposition to believe that Great Britain and France ought to unite in some solid plan of permanent peace: and many of the most considerable and efficient people talk with little reserve of the dangers to be apprehended from the revolted colonies, if they should be encouraged to gain commercial strength and consistency of government.

This was not seen as a serious prospect in London, and had few echoes, although in 1787 the new French Foreign Minister Montmorin, expressed his hope that the Americans would not be able to establish a new constitution and his fear that, if they did, they would be able to develop a strength that they would probably be eager to abuse. In Britain, American–French co-operation was feared, there was no interest in an Anglo-French alignment directed against the Americans, and better relations with the last were sought. Dorset thought it 'worth our while to sooth the Americans as no pains are spared by the French to render us still odious in their eyes'. Post-war bitterness and suspicion on both sides, however, proved a major hindrance to the improvement of Anglo-American relations, and the rapid and profitable recovery of commercial links was not matched in the political sphere. In order to limit French influence, the British government insisted that negotiations must take place in London, not Paris. John Adams, the first American diplomat accredited to the British Court, was presented to George III on 1 June 1785, but the draft treaties he submitted to Carmarthen in July 1785 and April 1786 were unacceptable as they challenged the British imperial trading system as outlined in the Navigation Acts. British anger about the American refusal to pay debts, a point that Pitt stressed in December 1785, and to compensate Loyalists led to a refusal to evacuate frontier posts near the Canadian frontier. Relations did not improve until 1791 when George Hammond was appointed as the first British Minister Plenipotentiary to the United States. He arrived in Philadelphia in October 1791, but the suspicions, indeed hostility towards British policy, of Thomas Jefferson, the American Secretary of State, hindered the progress of negotiations. Canada was now an issue in Anglo-American rather than Anglo-French relations. The French paid little heed to their 1783 agreement not to fortify St Pierre and Miquelon in the St Lawrence estuary to the extent of causing *jalousie*, but their awareness of the limited potential of the islands ensured that they did not give rise to serious dispute.[23]

[23] Eden to Carmarthen, 6 June 1786, Carmarthen to Dorset, 12 Nov. 1784, PRO FO 27/19 fol. 116, 27/13 fol. 175; Montmorin, *American Historical Review* 8 (1903), 713; Dorset to Earl Gower, Lord President of the Council, 29 July 1784, PRO 30/29/1/15

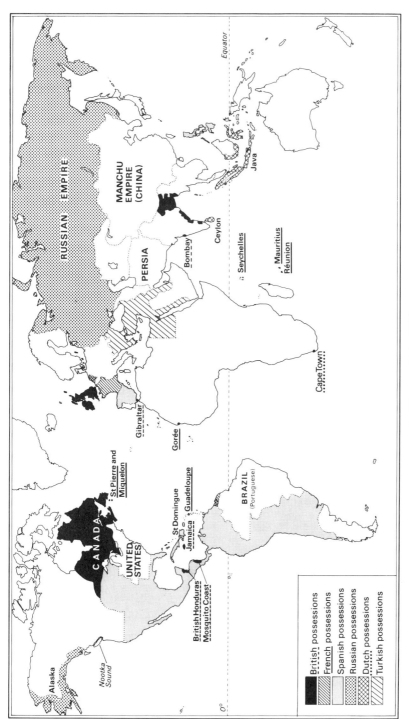

1. The world in 1783

The situation in Spanish America was not of great concern for Britain in 1783–4, but it was pregnant with future possibilities. Signs of discontent in the Spanish colonies were plentiful, most obviously the recent serious Túpac Amaru rebellion, and during the recent war there had been suggestions that Britain should seek to exploit them, an idea that was first discussed widely in the late 1730s. In 1780 North had planned an expedition from Madras to the Pacific coast of South America in order to encourage rebellion there.[24] After the war was over, Spanish America still seemed unstable, Robert Liston, Minister Plenipotentiary in Madrid, reporting in November 1783, 'I am assured the insurrections in Spanish America still continue, and people of sense appear to consider a revolution as certainly brewing.'[25] Once war was over, however, Spanish America largely ceased to be a subject of interest to the British government. No support was provided to the East Florida Loyalists under John Cruden who wished to thwart the cession of East Florida to Spain. Disputes over the British position in Honduras, where logwood-cutting settlements at Belize and, especially, on the Mosquito Coast were a long-standing source of disagreement, were not settled by the peace treaty,[26] though a Convention of 14 July 1786 largely resolved the matter. The British government reiterated that it would evacuate and demolish all fortifications on the Mosquito Coast, while Spain made concessions over Belize. Carmarthen regretted having to 'perform the unfortunate engagement we entered into some time ago' and argued that in any future conflict the British should re-establish themselves on the Shore and not thereafter give it up. Though criticised by the British settlers and in the London press, the Convention was implemented, and in the subsequent

no. 47; Pitt to Carmarthen, 16 Dec. 1785, BL Eg. 3498 fol. 155; Hammond to Grenville, 1 Nov. 1791, BL Add. 58939 fols. 6–7; G. S. Graham, *Sea Power and British North America 1783–1820. A Study in British Colonial Policy* (Cambridge, Mass., 1941), pp. 79–83; C. R. Ritcheson, *Aftermath of Revolution: British Policy towards the United States 1782–1795* (Dallas, 1969); J. L. Wright, *Britain and the American Frontier, 1783–1815* (Athens, Georgia, 1975), pp. 1–85; R. C. Stuart, *United States Expansionism and British North America, 1775–1871* (Chapel Hill, 1988), pp. 28–41; P. P. Hill, *French Perceptions of the Early American Republic 1783–1793* (Philadelphia, 1988). On the definition of an American national culture, different from and often in opposition to that of the former mother culture, R. A. Burchell (ed.), *The End of Anglo-America* (Manchester, 1991).

[24] L. E. Fisher, *The Last Inca Revolt 1780–1783* (Norman, Oklahoma, 1966); Sir Charles Middleton, Comptroller of the Navy, memorandum, 3 Oct. 1782, Bowood, box 57; Straton to Keith, 31 Dec. 1782, BL Add. 35527 fol. 163.

[25] Liston to Keith, 22 Nov. 1783, BL Add. 35530 fol. 198.

[26] Wright, *American Frontier*, p. 27; J. McLeish, 'British Activities in Yutacan and on the Mosquito Shore in the Eighteenth Century' (unpublished MA, London, 1926); C. A. Anderson, 'Anglo-Spanish Negotiations involving Central America in 1783', in E. R. Huck and E. H. Moseley (eds.), *Militarists, Merchants and Missionaries: United States Expansion in Middle America* (Tuscaloosa, 1970), pp. 23–37.

British evacuation of the Coast in 1787, 2,214 settlers, mostly slaves, moved from the Black River settlements to Belize. The Spanish flag was raised at Black River on 29 August 1787.[27]

The future of the Spanish colonies was not though a matter of British governmental concern until the Nootka Sound crisis of 1790 brought the prospect of war close, and thus made British conquests, or action on behalf of Latin American opponents of Spain, possible, both as a means of waging war in order to secure a better peace and as a way to extend British power.[28] In the 1780s, however, such an agenda, imperialist certainly in the sense of centring on the clash of empires, was not that of the Pitt ministry. It sought good relations with Spain, and, in peacetime, expansionist imperial goals, in so far as they existed, were essentially pursued at the expense of native peoples and non-European empires. This excluded Spanish America, until the crisis in 1790 seemed to offer a new chance to fulfil the schemes unattempted during the War of American Independence. As hostilities did not break out, 1790 was a false dawn of empire, in so far as Spanish America was concerned, though the basis of Britain's position in British Columbia was assured. It was not to be until the Revolutionary and Napoleonic wars that Britain was to have an opportunity to make gains at the expense of other European colonial empires, indeed to see them fatally weakened.[29]

If Spanish America was not an issue, everything implied by the term India was a pressing concern for the Pitt ministry. The future of the East India Company was not simply a contentious issue in domestic politics, the occasion of the fall of the Fox–North ministry. The company was also

[27] Sir Alder Burdon (ed.), *Archives of British Honduras* (3 vols., 1931–5), I, 154–7; Carmarthen to Pitt, 24, 27 Dec. 1786, BL Eg. 3498 fols. 167–9; Bourgoing, French *chargé d'affaires* in Madrid, to Vergennes, 17 Jan. 1785, AE CP Esp. 616 fols. 47–9; Carmarthen to Fitzherbert, 12 Nov. 1786, BL Eg. 3500 fol. 17; Carmarthen to Liston, 9 Apr. 1787, NLS 5546 fol. 109; HMC, *Dropmore*, I, 572–7; Leeds, Foreign Secretary, to Anthony Merry, Consul in Madrid, 25 Dec. 1789, PRO FO 72/15 fols. 375–85; R. A. Humphreys, *The Diplomatic History of British Honduras 1638–1901* (Oxford, 1961), pp. 5–6; W. Sorsby, 'Spanish Colonization of the Mosquito Coast 1787–1800', *Revista de Historica de América*, 73–4 (1972), 145–53; F. G. Dawson, 'William Pitt's Settlement at Black River on the Mosquito Shore: A Challenge to Spain in Central America, 1732–87', *Hispanic American Historical Review*, 63 (1983), 702–4; B. Potthast, *Die Mosquitoküste im Spannungsfeld britischer und spanischer Politik 1502–1821* (Cologne, 1988), pp. 295–302; R. A. Naylor, *Penny Ante Imperialism: The Mosquito Shore and the Bay of Honduras, 1600–1914. A Case Study in British Informal Empire* (1989), pp. 64–7.
[28] W. S. Robertson, 'Francisco de Miranda and the Revolutionizing of Spanish America', *Annual Report of the American Historical Association for 1907* I (1908); F. J. Turner, 'English Policy towards America in 1790–1791', *American Historical Review*, 7 (1902), 711–12; L. B. Kinnaird, 'Creassey's Plan for seizing Panama', *Hispanic American Historical Review*, 13 (1933), 46–78.
[29] J. Lynch, 'British Policy and Spanish America 1783–1808', *Journal of Latin American Studies*, 1 (1969), 1–30.

crucial to British public finances and foreign trade, and was seen as such. In December 1782 Sir John Macpherson wrote to Shelburne, 'India has sent in specie and in goods and in drafts upon foreign nations to England since the year 1757 upwards of 50 millions sterling upon balance of account with Britain.'[30] India was also the pivot of British activities throughout Asia.[31] The fate of India implied the British position in the China trade,[32] her attempts to challenge the Dutch in the East Indies, particularly Sumatra, or to accommodate differences with them in an acceptable fashion,[33] the possibility of Pacific expansion, and the future of the maritime route to India, which included such interests as the East India Company island of St Helena, and the plan to develop a base on the southwest coast of Africa which led to the *Nautilus* survey of the coast north of St Helena Bay from February to May 1786. The last was found unsatisfactory as an area for colonisation, even for convicts. In order to open up the 'Middle Passage' to India, the Court of Directors of the East India Company in July 1785 ordered that a base be established at Diego Garcia in the Chagos Archipelago. It was seen as a source of refreshments for ships en route to India, but the *Admiral Hughes* which reached the island in June 1786 found plenty of rats but no grain or local building supplies. That November, the British evacuated their settlement, although that month Lieutenant Archibald Blair hoisted the flag on what he called, after the Governor of Bombay, Governor Boddam's Islands, now the Salomon Islands.[34] The loss of America made the British position in India even more important, not least because this was the best base from which to give effect to rising interest in the Pacific and

---

[30] Macpherson to Shelburne, 6 Dec. 1782, Bowood 56; Lord Bulkeley to Keith, 27 Oct. 1785, BL Add. 35535 fol. 220; L. S. Sutherland, *The East India Company in Eighteenth-Century Politics* (Oxford, 1952); H. V. Bowen, *Revenue and Reform. The Indian Problem in British Politics 1757–1773* (Cambridge, 1991).

[31] H. Furber, *John Company at Work, A Study of European Expansion in India in the later Eighteenth Century* (Cambridge Mass., 1948).

[32] E. H. Pritchard, *The Crucial Years of Early Anglo-Chinese Relations 1750–1800* (Pullman, Washington, 1936), pp. 236–311; J. L. Cranmer-Byng, 'Lord Macartney's Embassy to Peking in 1793, from Official Chinese Documents', *Journal of Oriental Studies*, 4 (1957–8), 117–87, and *An Embassy to China … the Journal kept by Lord Macartney* (1962); P. Roebuck (ed.), *Macartney of Lisanoure 1737–1806* (Belfast, 1983), pp. 216–43.

[33] P. N. Tarling, *Anglo-Dutch Rivalry in the Malay World, 1780–1824* (St Lucia, Queensland, 1962), pp. 1–50; J. Bastin, *The British in West Sumatra, 1685–1825* (Kuala Lumpur, 1965), is disappointing for this period; J. Kathirithamby-Wells, *The British West Sumatran Presidency 1760–1785: Problems of Early Colonial Enterprise* (Kuala Lumpur, 1977).

[34] H. Fry, 'Early British Interest in the Chagos Archipelago and the Maldive Islands', *Mariners' Mirror*, 53 (1967), 344–9; A. Frost, *Convicts and Empire: A Naval Question, 1776–1811* (Melbourne, 1980), pp. 37–44; D. Mackay, *In the wake of Cook. Exploration, Science and Empire, 1780–1801* (Wellington, 1985), pp.30–6.

Australasia. *A Voyage to the Pacific Ocean*, based on Cook's last voyage, was published to great excitement in 1784. The India Act of that year created a new structure for governmental control over the East India Company, and it was one in which Pitt was active. In January 1787 Henry Dundas noted that Pitt signed all the Board of Control for India's 'correspondence with the India House', unlike another fellow-member, the Home Secretary, Viscount Sydney who claimed to be too busy.[35]

The Commutation Act of August 1784 cut the duties on tea from an average of 119 per cent to a uniform 25 per cent. This hit smuggling, priced the East India Company's competitors out of the British and much of the continental market, helped the finances of the company and eventually boosted government revenues. Tea imports from China grew greatly, to more than 13 million pounds in 1788 and to $17\frac{1}{4}$ million of the $19\frac{1}{2}$ million sold at Canton in 1791, and this in turn stimulated exports from India to China. A new structure of trans-oceanic links, in the creation of which Pitt had played a major role, was created rapidly. In 1785–6 local initiative by a merchant, Francis Light, led to the occupation of the island of Penang as a base on the route to China, a move designed, in part, to check French ambitions to the east of the Bay of Bengal. The island was renamed Prince of Wales Island when the British flag was hoisted on 11 August 1786. Cornwallis saw it as a possible naval base. It was also hoped that India and South-East Asia would provide goods that could be exported to China, and thus reduce the need to finance tea imports by sending silver to China. Plans in 1787 to negotiate 'a commercial establishment' in China were motivated both by a desire to sell British and Indian manufactures and by national rivalry: 'there is every reason to believe the French are at this moment very anxious to acquire such a situation'.[36] By 1793 India was contributing £500,000 per annum to the British Exchequer. The Asian trading system being developed by the British was seen as crucial to the finances of the British state. These had given rise to acute concern in the early 1780s, as the national debt rose to unprecedented heights, and Pitt, who was very

[35] Dundas to Cornwallis, 29 Jan. 1787, PRO 30/11/111 fols. 66–7; Holden Furber, *Henry Dundas* (1931), pp. 29–62; C. H. Philips, 'The New East India Board and the Court of Directors, 1784', *English Historical Review*, 55 (1940), 438–46, *The East India Company 1784–1834* (2nd edn, Manchester, 1961); H. Moi and L. H. Mui, *The Management of Monopoly: A Study of the English East India Company's Conduct of its Tea Trade, 1784–1833* (Vancouver, 1984).

[36] Harlow, *Second British Empire* II, 350–7; R. Bonney, *Kedah 1771–1821. The Search for Security and Independence* (Oxford, 1971), vi, pp. 52–101; D. K. Bassett, *British Trade and Policy in Indonesia and Malaysia in the Late Eighteenth Century* (Hull, 1971), pp. 73–80; P. Nightingale, *Trade and Empire in Western India 1784–1806* (Cambridge, 1970), pp. 51–5; Cornwallis to Sir Archibald Campbell, 9 Dec. 1787, Dundas to Cornwallis, 21 July 1787, PRO 30/11/159 fol. 88, 30/11/112 fol. 37.

much a First Lord of the Treasury made Prime Minister, made the improvement of the national finances his prime objective.

In some respects India was a central theme in British foreign policy in 1784-7, but the security of Britain's position in Asia was pursued in the shipyards of Britain and the muddied factional politics of the United Provinces rather than along the shores of the Indian Ocean itself. As a result of her successes in mid-century conflicts with France and certain Indian rulers, Britain was the dominant European power in India, though the French and Dutch each had a presence in the sub-continent, in the shape of trading stations (otherwise known as factories), as indeed had the Portuguese and the Danes. The British feared the competition of these bases, for example French-ruled Mahé. In addition both France and the United Provinces had important establishments in the region. France ruled Réunion, Mauritius and the Seychelles, island bases from which Britain's position in India could be challenged. The Dutch dominated the East Indies, especially Java, and Ceylon, and they controlled Cape Town on the sea route from Europe. In 1785 the Dutch overran Rhio (Riau, Riouw), an island off the southern tip of Malaya that controlled the eastern approach to the Strait of Malacca, and thus preempted the attempt to develop it as an entrepôt for British trade. British bases in the Bay of Bengal were vulnerable to ships based in Ceylon.[37]

In the War of American Independence the French had mounted a powerful challenge to the British position in India, and revealed its vulnerability. Admiral Suffren's naval threat was made more serious by the attack on the British position on land mounted by Haidar Ali, the bellicose ruler of Mysore (1761-82). In 1780 he invaded the Carnatic destroying a vastly outnumbered force under Colonel William Baillie near Polilore on 10 September, and in 1781 threatened Madras. The French landed 3,000 troops to assist him and they jointly captured Cuddalore, winning a port for Haidar Ali, and thus increasing the chance of successful co-operation between the two powers.[38]

The immediate threat to the British position in southern India, and to the profitability of the East India Company, was ended by the peace with

[37] S. P. Sen, *The French in India, 1763-1816* (Calcutta, 1958, 2nd edn New Delhi, 1971); Nightingale, *Trade and Empire*, p. 66; Tarling, *Anglo-Dutch Rivalry*, pp. 12-13; B. W. and L. Y. Andaya, *A History of Malaysia* (1982), p. 105.

[38] G. B. Malleson, *Final French Struggles in India and on the Indian Seas 1778-1816* (1878), pp. 1-78; E. Barbé, *Le Nabab René Madec. Histoire diplomatique des projets de la France sur le Bengale et le Penjab, 1772-1808* (Paris, 1894); H. W. Richmond, *The Navy in India 1763-83* (1931); P. Pluchon, *Histoire de la Colonisation Française. I. Le Premier Empire Colonial* (Paris, 1991), pp. 718-39; S. Das, 'British Reactions to the French Bugbear in India, 1763-83', *European History Quarterly*, 22 (1992), 50-7.

France. Nevertheless, the situation was still worrying for a number of reasons. Haidar Ali's son and successor Tipu Sultan (1782–99) was bellicose, anti-British and keen to secure French assistance, while French officers served with the Maratha chieftain Sindhia.[39] Even if no challenge was mounted, the 'protection cost' of Britain's Indian empire had risen significantly as long as the possibility of a French–Mysore alliance persisted. If the French did wish to harm Britain, the existence of powerful native rulers who could be helped provided them with an opportunity for doing so without risking a breach in relations, offering them a possibility of repeating the strategy followed towards the Americans in 1776–7. France's position in the Indian Ocean was still intact, and was made far stronger by the close relations with the Dutch which survived the war.[40] Though Vergennes told Dorset in July 1784 that the Dutch settlements were 'much too far to the eastward' to be of any real advantage to France, the Dutch defeat of the Bugis siege of Malacca on 18 June 1784 caused concern in British circles; for J. P. van Braam's naval squadron was strong enough to close the Malacca Strait to Britain in the event of war, and thus to wreck the crucial Canton–India axis on which the fortunes of the East India Company increasingly depended. The Dutch victory was followed by Braam's capture of Kuala Selangor and Rhio (1785), the local bases of power in the Strait's region, and in 1787 the Dutch had fresh successes in western Borneo. That year, the British recorded two Dutch 54-gunners in the East Indies, as well as two 36-gunners, two 24s and two sloops.[41]

The vulnerability of the Dutch in Indian waters and the importance of the French there had been demonstrated during the recent conflict. The Dutch-ruled mainland port of Negapatam fell to the British in November 1781; their Ceylonese port of Trincomalee, the only all-weather harbour in the Bay of Bengal, falling the following January. The Dutch bases on the western coast of Sumatra fell in 1781 to attack from the East India Company's base of Benkulen. And yet Suffren had dissuaded the British from attacking Cape Town, by reinforcing it in 1781 before the British

[39] W. Miles (ed.), *Kirmani's History of Hyder Ali and Tipoo Sultaun* (1844); B. E. Kennedy, 'Anglo-French Rivalry in India and in the Eastern Seas, 1763–93: A study of Anglo-French Tensions and of their impact on the consolidation of British power in the region' (unpublished Ph.D., Australian National University, 1969), pp. 222–39, 242; D. Forrest, *Tiger of Mysore: The Life and Death of Tipu Sultan* (1970); B. Lenman, 'The Transition to European Military Ascendancy in India, 1600–1800', in J. A. Lynn (ed.), *Tools of War. Instruments, Ideas, and Institutions of Warfare, 1445–1871* (Urbana, 1990), p. 120.
[40] Dorset to Liston, 20 Mar. 1786, NLS 5544 fol. 98; Grenville to Dundas, 26 Aug. 1787, BL Add. 58914 fol. 20.
[41] Dorset to Carmarthen, 8 July 1784, PRO FO 27/12 fol. 138; Bassett, *Trade and Policy*, pp. 69, 71, 73, 86; Naval intelligence, 24 July 1787, PRO 30/11/112 fol. 180.

expeditionary force, initially intended for first South America and then the Spanish colonies of Mindano and the Celebes, could arrive, and had managed to force the British garrison in Trincomalee to capitulate in August 1782. When war ended, he was planning a final attack on Madras. Peace robbed him of his chance, just as it prevented what might have been a decisive battle between the French–Mysore army in Cuddalore and the British forces outside the town.[42]

The British had preserved their position in India in the peace negotiations, Shelburne making it clear that 'it was not to be expected that the king could cede two continents', but they had failed to gain Trincomalee, despite considerable efforts centred on the belief expressed by Richmond that 'the preservation of our possessions in the East Indies will in future greatly depend' on it.[43] In 1783–4 India acted as the focus of the sense of British vulnerability bred out of recent defeat and of distrust of France.[44] Peace was not made with Mysore until 1784. That January the British garrison at Mangalore surrendered after a ten-month siege, and though the Treaty of Mangalore of 11 March 1784 was based on the notion of the *status quo ante bellum* (the mutual return of territories seized during the conflict), it was seriously criticised by the Governor General, Warren Hastings, because it failed to protect the position of Britain's principal ally in southern India, the Nawab of the Carnatic. The local British commander, Colonel William Fullarton, complained in July 1784 that Tipu had failed to fulfil the peace terms and that British eagerness for peace only led him to be less accommodating, and he concluded ominously 'that Tippo Sultan or the English must fall for his conduct is such as cannot be compatible with our safety'. By October 1784 Tipu had seriously undermined the British position in the Carnatic. The following year he took measures that hit the British spice trade on the Malabar coast. In 1786 the Bombay presidency yielded to the Rajah of Cherika who, with Tipu's support, had demanded the return of the territory of Randaterra. In 1787 Governor Boddam feared that Tipu would deprive Britain of the pepper trade by overrunning Travancore.[45] Suspicion of Franco-Indian links and plans to drive the British out of

---

[42] L. C. F. Turner, 'The Cape of Good Hope and Anglo-French Rivalry, 1778–1796', *Historical Studies. Australia and New Zealand*, 12 (1966), 166–85.

[43] Shelburne to Grantham, 15 Sept. 1782, Richmond to Grantham, 23 Jan. 1783, Bedford CRO L30/14/306/36, 30/14/221/5; Middleton to Shelburne, 27 Aug., Major General Sir John Burgoyne of Sutton to?, 1 Nov. 1782, Bowood, box 57, 37.

[44] Liston to Fitzherbert, 1 Feb. 1783, Matlock CRO 239 M/O 515.

[45] Fullarton to Dorset, 28 July, Fullarton to Carmarthen, 29 July 1784, KAO C188/23, BL Eg. 3504 fol. 15; T. G. Fraser, 'India 1780–86', in P. Roebuck (ed.), *Macartney of Lisanoure 1737–1806* (Belfast, 1983), pp. 201–2; Nightingale, *Trade and Empire*, pp. 13, 37–9, 44; unsigned letter from Madras, 14 Oct. 1784, Aspinall, *George III* no. 137.

India remained strong until the Dutch crisis of 1787 and the subsequent collapse of French power.[46]

Peace provided the British with an opportunity to strengthen their position in India and the Indian Ocean, though George III was sceptical, writing in September 1784, that 'whilst the army in India remains in such unfit hands as those of a company of merchants I cannot expect any good can be done'. The army was indeed in a bad state. In November 1784 Dundas wrote:

It must readily occur to everybody, that an exceeding good establishment of artillery, a considerable establishment of cavalry, and a large European force must at all times be kept in India, particularly on the Coast ... our force now and hereafter must be regulated by the intelligence we have of the force that our European rivals have at Mauritius, Pondicherry, Ceylon and other places. Taking it for granted that India is the quarter to be first attacked, we must never lose sight of having such a force there as to baffle all surprise.

This led to the appointment of Cornwallis as Governor General and Commander in Chief in India in 1786, to the plan for a reorganisation of the East India Company army, involving the dispatch of 5,000 troops from Britain, and, eventually, to its reinforcement in 1788 by four British regiments. The army in India continued, however, to suffer from serious weaknesses.[47]

The naval situation was also worrying and there was concern about naval bases, especially the vulnerability of the British roadsteads in the Bay of Bengal. In December 1784 Richard, Viscount Howe, 1st Lord of the Admiralty, warned Pitt of the danger that France would establish a naval base at Acheen (Atjeh, Achin) on the north-western tip of Sumatra, where the British had a commercial base. Discussing where Britain could found a naval base, Howe wrote, 'The Nicobar Islands are highly spoken of ... and seem much the most eligible station for ships of war, were commercial purposes less in contemplation for fixing at Acheen.' Howe continued that there was, however, an Austrian (in fact Danish) settlement already there, and he added of the Bay of Bengal,

---

[46] [G. Ellis], *History of the Late Revolution in the Dutch Republic* (1789), pp. 96–7, 122–30. Ellis was employed by Harris at The Hague, and sought his advice on the book, Ellis to Malmesbury, 'Monday Morning', Winchester, Malmesbury 151. For differing assessments of the book, Joseph Yorke, Lord Dover, to Keith, 15 June 1789, BL Add. 35541 fol. 251; S. J. Pratt, *Gleanings through Wales, Holland and Westphalia* (3 vols., 1795), III, 8.

[47] George III to Pitt, 23 Sept. 1784, unsigned letter, Aspinall, *George III* nos. 128, 137; Dundas to Sydney, Nov. 1784, PRO 30/11/112 fol. 60; Cornwallis to Sir Archibald Campbell, 23 Dec. 1786, 9 Dec. 1787, PRO 30/11/159 fols. 20, 88; F. and M. Wickwire, *Cornwallis. The Imperial Years* (Chapel Hill, 1980), pp. 101–13; E. Ingram, *In Defence of British India. Great Britain in the Middle East, 1775–1842* (1984), pp. 56–7.

in either case, it would require a long time before magazines could be formed for keeping a squadron on that side India, all the year. The settlement would be exposed in the meantime, or in the absence of the squadron, to the attacks of an enemy, before notice could be conveyed for obtaining reasonable assistance from the other British settlements where the squadron might be stationed.

No secure base, however, was established in the mid-1780s. The local sultan closed the British entrepôt at Acheen in 1786 and the British did not reestablish themselves there until 1810. Proposals in 1784 for a base on the Andaman Islands, Rhio or St Matthew's Island (off the Kara Isthmus) were not realised, and Britain only gained the Nicobars in 1869. In 1787, however, a lack of reliable information about 'the most proper stations for the shelter, refitting, refreshment, or protection of squadrons and ships of war, as well as convoys or East India ship ... in case of a future war ... as well as ... for offensive or defensive operations', led the Board of Control to decide to investigate whether Diego Garcia could be fortified as a base for naval stores and for transmitting information. After that a base on the west coast of Sumatra was to be considered, and then Acheen, Penang, Junk Ceylon (Jung Saylang in the Mergui Archipelago), the Nicobars, the Bengal Coast, the Andamans, the Indian coastline, and, if necessary, the eastern coast of Malaya. The wild, in British eyes, Andaman Islands were acquired in 1789, Port Cornwallis being established. Cornwallis felt that the base would be very important in any future naval conflict with France. His brother, Commodore William Cornwallis MP, who had been appointed commander-in-chief of naval forces in the East Indies, and had been responsible for establishing the base in the Andamans, was also interested in Nancowry in the Nicobars. Earl Cornwallis suggested that Britain negotiate with Denmark to acquire the Nicobars, not least in order to prevent the Danes from ever ceding them to France. The idea was not pursued.[48]

While the war with Mysore continued, concern about French attentions had been acute. In August 1783 Lord North was worried by signs that the Bourbons would resume hostilities.[49] George, Viscount Torrington, Minister Plenipotentiary in Brussels, and an excitable weathervane who recorded the changing shifts of attitudes within the diplomatic corps, wrote in February 1784, 'What a deplorable situation we are in; we shall lose the East Indies, for Holland and France are united

[48] Howe to Pitt, 25 Dec. 1784, PRO 30/8/146 fols. 172–3, Ipswich CRO HA 119 T108/33; Dundas to Cornwallis, 20 July 1787 and enclosed anonymous and undated memorandum, PRO 30/11/112 fols. 1–7; Cornwallis to Pitt, 9 Aug. 1789, Cornwallis to Dundas, 1 Apr., 31 Dec. 1790, 4 Mar. 1792, Cornwallis to Court of Directors, 26 Aug. 1792, PRO 30/11/175 fol. 14, 30/11/151 fols. 21, 75, 108, 30/11/155 fol. 301; Bassett, *Trade and Policy*, pp. 41–3, 52–3, 66; Tarling, *Anglo-Dutch Rivalry*, pp. 12, 39.

[49] North to Fox, 27 Aug. 1783, BL Add. 47561 fol. 7.

to ruin our trade and in order to drive us out of the East Indies.' The same month he claimed,

The great object of the French Ministry is to ruin us in the East-Indies, which they hope to accomplish by the means of the Dutch traducing Great Britain. The French, by the late Treaty of Versailles, cannot assist the Indian Princes in their wars, but as our treaty with Holland is not ratified, the French cabinet means to support them through the channel of those allies.

Kageneck reported that France and the Dutch were united to harm the British position in India. Carmarthen argued that the French idea of a mutual naval reduction in Indian waters could not be accepted unless Dutch intentions were ascertained.[50]

Torrington's letters are a useful reminder that although possible post-war scenarios had been sketched out throughout the recent negotiations, the diplomacy of 1782–4 should also be seen in the context of continuing conflict, and that the transition to a world of new options and problems was by no means clear-cut. This was especially true of the colonial and maritime sphere, William Grenville MP, joint Paymaster General and a member both of the Board of Trade and of the Board of Control for India, writing in September 1784 to his elder brother, Earl Temple, about 'the safety of the British government in India now believed (and I fear with too much reason) to be shaken to its center'. France seemed most of a threat in India, and Carmarthen, fully convinced of the danger, wrote in February 1784 about

those plans which they have so much at heart I mean the injuring in every way in their power the British interests in India, both commercial and political, and which they will regard as more practical now than at any former period on account of their new connection with Holland. I have heard that a treaty actually subsists between France and the United Provinces the great if not the sole purport of which is to endeavour to drive the English from the East Indies.[51]

Dorset was instructed to seek from Vergennes an explicit declaration of the number of ships the French intended to keep in the Indian Ocean, to press for a mutual reduction and, separately, to report on French naval moves in the region. British warships in Indian waters seemed out-

[50] Torrington to Keith, 4, 28 Feb. 1784, BL Add. 35531 fols. 62, 129; Kageneck to Kaunitz, 20 Feb. 1784, HHStA EK 123; Carmarthen to Daniel Hailes, Secretary of Embassy at Paris, 1 June, Carmarthen to Dorset, 23 Dec. 1784, PRO FO 27/12 fol. 88, 27/13 fol. 243; Horace Walpole to Horace Mann, 15 Apr. 1784, W. S. Lewis et al. (eds.), *The Yale Edition of Horace Walpole's Correspondence* (New Haven, 1937–83), IX, 491; William Coxe to Harris, 26 May, 31 Aug. 1784, Winchester, Malmesbury 148.

[51] Grenville to Temple, 30 Sept. 1784, HL STG. Box 39(1); Storer to Carmarthen, 11 Jan. Carmarthen to Dorset, 13 Feb. 1784, PRO FO 27/11 fols. 38, 111–12; Carmarthen to George III, 10 Apr., and reply, 11 Apr. 1784, Aspinall, *George III* no. 65.

numbered by the French squadron at Mauritius, although Howe
reassured Carmarthen that French warships being sent to the East Indies
were old and probably for trade or transporting troops, not combat.[52]
Dorset reported the apparently accurate rumour that the French were to
send six regiments to India in Dutch ships,[53] while Carmarthen was
worried about 'intelligence' that Dutch warships in the Mediterranean
were to be sent to the East Indies.[54] In May 1784 another rumour, that
Suffren was to return to India, led Carmarthen to express concern and
seek information.[55] He continued concerned thereafter,[56] despite French
assurances, Dorset's efforts to assuage his fears, and Vergennes' attempt
to reach an agreement on naval forces in the Indian Ocean.[57]

Carmarthen was wrong about the Franco-Dutch treaty and, to a
certain extent, about French policy. Though there were disputes in
1785–6 over the implementation of the Treaty of Versailles in India,[58]
Vergennes was not greatly interested in India, was certainly keen, as he
assured Dorset,[59] on better Anglo-French relations and was well aware
that these might be thwarted by British concern that the French sought
more than trade in India. And yet, as after the War of the Austrian
Succession when Vergennes was on his first diplomatic mission, a general
desire to improve Anglo-French relations was accompanied by opposition to British interests in both Europe and elsewhere.[60] These aims
were not necessarily incompatible: alliances between equal partners were
characterised by the pursuit of interests both through and in spite of the
alliances.[61] In the case of France, a policy advocated by the foreign

[52] Carmarthen to Dorset, 16 Feb., and enclosure, 26 Mar. 1784, PRO FO 27/11 fols.
134–6, 262; Howe to Carmarthen, 11 Apr. 1784, BL Eg. 3498 fol. 178.
[53] Dorset to Carmarthen, 26 Feb. 1784, PRO FO 27/11 fol. 198.
[54] Carmarthen to Dorset, 5 Mar. 1784, PRO FO 27/11 fol. 226–7; Pitt to Carmarthen, 10
Apr. 1784, BL Eg. 3498 fol. 30.
[55] Carmarthen to Hailes, 28 May 1784, PRO FO 27/12 fol. 79.
[56] Carmarthen to Dorset, 2, 9, 27 July, 10, 20 Aug., 6 Nov., 25 Dec., Dorset to
Carmarthen, 22 July 1784, PRO FO 27/12 fols. 133, 149, 183, 238, 271, 27/13 fols. 162,
242–3, 27/12 fol. 176.
[57] Dorset to Carmarthen, 8 July, 30 Dec. 1784, PRO FO 27/12 fols. 137–8, 27/13 fol. 256,
BL Eg. 3499 fol. 31; Dorset to Gower, 29 July 1784, PRO 30/29/1/15 no. 47; Pitt to
Carmarthen, 30 Oct. 1784, Howe to Carmarthen, 15, 17 Apr., Howe memorandum, 17
Apr. 1785, BL Eg. 3498 fols. 64, 186, 188–9.
[58] G. C. Bolton and B. E. Kennedy, 'William Eden and the Treaty of Mauritius
1786–1787', *Historical Journal*, 16 (1973), 686–7; Vergennes to Adhémar, Ambassador
in London, 4 Apr. 1784, AE CP 548 fol. 185.
[59] Pluchon, *Colonisation Française*, pp. 737–42; Dorset to Carmarthen, 22 Feb. 1784, PRO
FO 27/11 fol. 187.
[60] O. T. Murphy, *Charles Gravier, Comte de Vergennes. French Diplomacy in the Age of
Revolutions 1791–1787* (Albany, 1982), pp. 16–50; J. Black, *Natural and Necessary
Enemies. Anglo-French Relations in the Eighteenth Century* (1986), pp. 51–9.
[61] J. Black, 'Britain's Foreign Alliances in the Eighteenth Century', *Albion*, 20 (1988),
573–602.

ministry had to cope with the different interpretations of French interests advanced not so much by diplomats, though some of them had experience of seeking to thwart their chief minister, not least in response to suggestions or orders from courtiers, other ministers, or indeed Louis XV, as by the separate ministry of the marine which controlled the colonies. The minister, Marshal Castries, was anti-British and favoured a war of *revanche* in India and the development of French influence along the route to India, especially in Egypt. In 1785 he referred to Britain as France's principal and natural enemy. Castries argued that a war in India would pay for itself. He had wanted war to continue in 1783, and had argued that France was then in a very good position in India. Castries sought to maintain the French navy on a wartime footing in preparation for the resumption of hostilities. Jean-Balthazar, Comte d'Adhémar, the Ambassador in London, also sought an aggressive policy. Vergennes rejected the idea, and was less than enthusiastic about closer relations with the Dutch; but nevertheless, the French government was unwilling to accept simply a commercial role in India, which was all, and then only within limits, that the British wished to leave it.[62]

There was in fact a distinctive forward direction in French policy outside Europe in the mid-1780s, that much concerned the British. The period witnessed a steep climb in the volume of French trade, one in which major efforts were made to increase commerce with Asia via Mauritius in order to diversify trade beyond an excessive reliance on the substantial re-export of goods from the French West Indies. Adam Smith had favourably compared the production of sugar there with the situation in the British islands and France's sugar exports boomed after the return of peace. The French negotiated commercial treaties with Portugal (1783), Russia (1787) and Spain (1788). The French navy charted the coast of Asia from Suez to Korea in the 1780s and France established a settlement on Diego Garcia in 1784. As, however, it could not be cultivated successfully, Diego Garcia was evacuated by the French in August 1786. In 1784–9 France sent ten naval expeditions into the Indian and Pacific oceans, that of La Pérouse in 1785–8 being seen as a sign that the French might establish a convict base on New Zealand. Carmarthen was informed of this intention in 1785. In fact, La Pérouse, having reached the Pacific, first followed the American coast south from Alaska to Monterey, before crossing to Macao, en route being the first European to discover what he named Necker Island in the Hawaiian group. It was only after exploring part of the north-western Pacific, an

[62] Castries, mémoire, 2 Jan. 1785, AE CP Aut, 349 fol. 8; Duc de Castries, *Le Maréchal de Castries*, 1727–1800 (Paris, 1956), p. 131; Hardman, *Louis XVI*, pp. 73, 79; Vaucher (ed.), *Recueil*, pp. 531–2; Kennedy, 'Anglo-French Rivalry', pp. 323, 330–2.

area of growing European interest, that La Pérouse sailed to Australasia. On 24 January 1788 La Pérouse reached Botany Bay, six days after the British had arrived in order to found a penal colony there. La Pérouse had played a major role the previous summer in the exploration of the north-western Pacific, following the coast of Korea, Sakhalin, Hokkaido and Kamchatka. Although scientific aims played a part in his expedition, political and economic considerations stemming from competition with Britain were also very important.[63]

There were more immediate French threats to the British position in the Indian Ocean. Though the French had abandoned their commercial establishment at Rangoon in 1784, in 1787 the dynamic Bo-daw-hpaya, King of Burma, was able to negotiate with the French at their Bengal base of Chandernagore in his search for western arms. This was a threatening development because in 1784–5 Burma had conquered Arakan, destroyed it as an independent political entity, and thus created a tense situation in relations with the neighbouring domain of the East India Company in Bengal. There was concern both about Franco-Burmese links and about a possible Franco-Burmese-Annamese invasion of Siam, and Light compared Bo-daw-hpaya to Haider Ali, though, in fact, France played no role in the Burmese attack on Siam in 1786. The French had also been asked to intervene in the civil war in Cochin China (the area around the Mekong area). The arrival in France of the son of N'guyen Anh, one of the claimants, in early 1787 aroused British concern, as did the earlier appeal to the Governor of Pondicherry in 1785 by Pigneau de Béhaine, Bishop of Adran and Vicar Apostolic of Cochin China, plenipotentiary for N'guyen Anh. By the Treaty of Versailles of 28 November 1787 with N'guyen Anh, France acquired a claim to bases in Cochin China. Lieutenant-Colonel Charles Cathcart MP, who had served in India and negotiated with the French in Mauritius in 1786, told Pitt the following year that although the French had no immediate offensive plans, 'their systematick views both military and commercial, were pursued with

[63] P. Butel, 'France, the Antilles, and Europe in the seventeenth and eighteenth centuries: renewals of foreign trade', in J. D. Tracy (ed.), *The Rise of Merchant Empires* (Cambridge, 1990), pp. 164, 172; F. Crouzet, 'Angleterre et France au XVIIIᵉ siècle: essai d'analyse comparée de deux croissances économiques', *Annales*, 21 (1966), 261–3; A. Smith, *An Inquiry into the Nature and Causes of the Wealth of Nations*, edn R. H. Campbell and A. S. Skinner (Oxford, 1979), p. 586; Murphy, *Vergennes*, pp. 450–6; Kennedy, 'Anglo-French Rivalry', pp. 279–82; Dalrymple, then in Paris, to Carmarthen, 8 June 1785, BL Eg. 3501 fol. 39; S. Chapin, 'Scientific Profit from the Profit Motive: the Case of the LaPerouse Expedition', *Actes du XIIᵉ Congrès International d'Histoire des Sciences* XI (Paris, 1971), 45–9, and 'The Men from across La Manche: French Voyages, 1660–1790', in D. Howse (ed.), *Background to Discovery. Pacific Exploration from Dampier to Cook* (Berkeley, 1990), p. 113; C. Gaziello, *L'Expédition de Lapérouse 1785–1788* (Paris, 1984).

unremitting attention', and to that end they were seeking another base in the Indian Ocean. In fact, the Treaty of Versailles was not implemented. France lacked the resources to send assistance. In place of royal forces, N'guyen Anh received only a small number of Frenchmen, hired thanks to the help of French merchants. With these, however, he was able to train his forces and to reconquer much of modern Vietnam.[64]

Rumour played an especially important role in arousing British fears, because it was very difficult to check on French moves in Asia. They appeared more alarming because some of them seemed new, though France had in fact developed relations with Siam in the 1680s and played a role in the mid-eighteenth-century civil conflicts in Burma. Aside from the development of the French position on their Indian Ocean islands, what aroused most concern was evidence of French activity on other routes to India, especially via Egypt and the Red Sea, and via the Persian Gulf and Oman. The western Mediterranean was not an area of concern. Diplomatic relations with the Barbary states and Morocco were left to naval officers, such as Commodore Sir Roger Curtis, who was ordered in 1783 to renew the Anglo-Moroccan treaty of friendship, and Captain John Blankett. The eastern Mediterranean was, however, becoming of much greater concern. The French government definitely received a number of memoranda proposing an alliance with the Dutch and the Venetians and the development of the Suez route to the Indian Ocean. In March 1784 Carmarthen ordered Dorset to check reports that the Turks had ceded Candia (Crete) and Scio (Chios) to France and that the French had sent two regiments to the former.[65] The following month Daniel Hailes, Secretary of Embassy at Paris, reported that it was probable

that the plan of the French Cabinet is to establish a communication with India by the way of Alexandria, Suez, and the Red Sea; and that the good offices of mediation between Russia and the Porte have been paid by the latter with the

---

[64] W. J. Koenig, *The Burmese Polity, 1752–1819* (Ann Arbor, 1990), pp. 22–5; Bassett, *Trade and Policy*, pp. 74–5; Kennedy, 'Anglo-French Rivalry', p. 290; Cathcart to Pitt, 29 Sept. 1787, BL Add. 58906 fols. 31–2. On the Cathcart negotiations, Kennedy, 'Anglo-French Rivalry', pp. 167–82; on Cochin China, Bassett, *Trade and Policy*, pp. 74–5; text of Treaty of Versailles, A. Faure, *Les Français en Cochinchine au XVIIIe siècle. Mgr. Pigneau de Behaine* (Paris, 1891), pp. 123–7; G. Taboulet, *La Geste française en Indochine* (2 vols., Paris, 1955–6), I, 161–279; Pluchon, *Colonisation française* pp. 760–4; Harlow, *Second British Empire* II, 351 does not distinguish fact from rumour.

[65] Carmarthen to Dorset, 26 Mar. 1784, PRO FO 27/11 fols. 262–3; Captain John Blankett RN to Shelburne, 9 Feb. 1784, Bowood 11; Kennedy, 'Anglo-French Rivalry', p. 332. The increasing strategic importance of Egypt emerges from F. Charles-Roux, 'La politique française en Egypte à la fin du XVIIIe siècle', *Revue Historique*, 92 (1906), *Les Origines de l'expédition d'Egypte* (Paris, 1910), *L'Angleterre, l'Isthme de Suez et l'Egypte au XVIIIe siècle* (Paris, 1922), *Le Projet français de conquête de l'Égypte sous le règne de Louis XVI* (Cairo, 1929).

island of Candia, which is conveniently situated in the same line of communication from the Mediterranean.[66]

In short, the eastern Mediterranean was but a stage on the route to India. Suspicion of French intentions led British commentators to perceive her individual steps, real or rumoured, as but aspects of a general malevolent design. Dorset argued in July 1784 'that the Archipelago is intended for a line of communication with the East Indies'. The previous month the newly appointed French Ambassador in Constantinople had indeed been instructed to seek means to improve French relations with Iran, both for commercial reasons and in order to facilitate French trade with India.[67] The following year Carmarthen ordered Ainslie to investigate French projects for developing trade to India via Egypt, while Captain John Blankett, commander of a British warship in the Mediterranean, reported that the French were employing a surveyor and engineers in the Isthmus of Suez to estimate the cost of building roads across it, in order to open up a new commercial link between India and Europe.[68] In January 1787 Ainslie sent a warning about bold French plans spanning from the Near East to India:

I am told the principal motive which engaged France to send a minister to Isfahan [Iran] is to cooperate in the views of Russia, for extending her dominions to the Persian provinces bordering upon the Caspian Sea; In return for which France is to enjoy the exclusive privilege of exporting cloth, by way of the Black Sea for the consumption of the northern provinces of Persia, and to carry on a trade between India and Europe by land carriage, from the Persian Gulf, through that empire, to the Caspian Sea, and from thence in Russian ships to the Black Sea (in case that communication is open) or through Russia by land carriage, with a modest duty; all which it seems may be performed at reasonable expense with rich articles, such as silks.[69]

By the 1780s France had achieved a dominant position in the foreign trade of the Levant and eastern Mediterranean. For both political and commercial reasons, she was the most influential foreign power in the Turkish Empire. In the mid-1780s, experts helped to direct the construction of Turkish warships and of fortifications at the major Black Sea base of Ochakov. The French government also sought to extend this influence. Sartine, Minister of the Marine 1774–80, had sought to

---

[66] Hailes to Carmarthen, 28 Apr. 1784, PRO FO 27/11 fol. 337; Keith to Dorset, 17 Mar. 1784, KAO C191.
[67] Dorset to Carmarthen, 22 July 1784, PRO FO 27/12 fol. 177; P. Duparc (ed.), *Recueil ... Turquie* (Paris, 1969), p. 473.
[68] Carmarthen to Ainslie, 16 Aug., Fraser to C. W. Boughton Rouse MP, Secretary to the Board of Control for India, 22 Aug. 1785, Ainslie to Carmarthen, 9 Aug. 1786, PRO 30/8/137 fols. 27–8, FO 78/7 fol. 221; Blankett to Lansdowne, 26 Aug. 1785, Bowood 11.   [69] Ainslie to Carmarthen, 11 Jan. 1787, PRO FO 78/8 fol. 7.

2. The route to India

develop what has recently been termed *l'axe Méditerranée–mer des Indes*. In 1785 the French negotiated an agreement with the beys who wielded most influence in Egypt, opening the Red Sea route to India to overland trade, over the Isthmus of Suez. Marseilles merchants sought to exploit the route. The French were less successful in negotiating alliances with Iran and with the Iman of Oman, but the making of French–native alliances throughout the Middle East, complementing and supporting that with Mysore, seemed a prospect. The Iman seemed interested in the idea of joint action against Bombay. The French East India Company was refounded in 1785. Two years later a French memorandum suggested that if France joined her ally Austria, and Russia, against Turkey she could hope to acquire Crete and Egypt from the latter. The occupation of Cyprus and Rhodes was also suggested, and the need to prevent Britain occupying Egypt was emphasised. British agents in Baghdad, Basra and Shiraz warned in 1784–7 of signs of French activity in Iran and the Gulf, including the arrival of French ships at Muscat and Basra, and anticipated French designs on Bandar Rig and Kharg.[70]

Although it was not at the forefront of government attention, some Englishmen themselves were interested in Egypt. In 1784 Colonel James Capper of the East India Company army published his *Observations on the Passage to India through Egypt*, an argument in favour of the importance of the Egyptian route. It was reprinted in 1785. George Baldwin had been interested in trade via Egypt since the late 1760s. In 1784 he published his *The Communication with India by the Isthmus of Suez, vindicated from the Prejudices which have prevailed against it*. Baldwin pressed the East India Company on the threat to British interests in India posed by the growth of French influence in Egypt. In 1786 he was appointed both British Consul-General in Alexandria and Agent of the East India Company, his mission to ensure that the French gained no advantage over the British. Baldwin wanted to develop trade to India via the Red Sea, but the Turkish government was opposed to the idea, and the successes in 1786–7 of the Turkish forces sent to reimpose control over Egypt thwarted Baldwin's scheme. In 1791 Richard Willis,

[70] P. W. Bamford, *Forests and French Sea Power 1660–1789* (Toronto, 1956), p. 204; Pluchon, *Colonisation française*, pp. 710–18, 750–2; J. Charles-Roux, *L'Isthme et le Canal de Suez* (2 vols., Paris, 1901), I, pp. 110–11, 421–2; F. Charles-Roux, *Le Projet français de commerce avec l'Inde par Suez sous le règne de Louis XIV* (Paris, 1925), pp. 45, 67; A. Auzoux, 'La France et Muscate', *Revue d'histoire diplomatique*, 23 (1909), 529–36; Ingram, *British India*, p. 28; F. L. Nussbaum, 'The Formation of the New East India Company of Calonne', *American Historical Review*, 38 (1933), 475–97; J. Conan, *La Dernière Compagnie française des Indes, 1785–1875* (Paris, 1942); Anon., – July 1787, AE MD Russie 16 fols. 279–83; Charles-Roux, *L'Angleterre, L'Isthme*, p. 276; Furber, *Dundas*, p. 65; *Cambridge History of Iran*, VII (Cambridge, 1991), p. 368.

an English merchant who had settled in the Crimea, wrote to Pitt from the Dardanelles to suggest that Britain help arrange a Russo-Turkish settlement. He added that that would be an appropriate occasion to press the Turks 'upon that neglected business, my friend Mr. Baldwin's plan of the Suez Navigation. An arrangement with the Turks might probably be made in that part of the world, which would be a security to our Possessions in India.'[71]

In some respects much of British foreign policy in the period 1783–91 was a matter of two eastern questions. The first centred on the Indian Ocean, more particularly India, and related to the French challenge. There was a 'swing to the east' in the concerns of foreign policy, which was a reflection of fears for the security of Britain's existing eastern position. This prefigured British concern at the end of the 1790s and in the nineteenth century about the threat to India posed by French and Russian ambitions in the Near and Middle East. Carmarthen referred in July 1784 to issues 'which so deeply concern not only the present interests but, perhaps, the future existence of Great Britain as an independent; at any rate as a respectable power'.[72] The successful resolution, for the British, of the Dutch crisis in 1787 pushed the issue from the forefront of governmental attention, although it continued to be a source of concern in the late 1780s. The next matter, however, over which French naval power was a threat, related not to Asia, but to the Nootka Sound crisis with Spain in 1790. Although arising from growing competition in the Pacific, had war broken out, it would have been waged largely in European and Caribbean waters.

The second eastern question related to Russia and culminated in the Ochakov crisis of 1791. In some respects, it was very different from the first. There was no immediate colonial or maritime threat to British interests. And yet, the concern about the fate of the Turkish Empire that was expressed in 1790–1 directly related to a major theme in the mid-1780s, for the condition of that empire and growing French interests in the Near and Middle East seemed to threaten the British position in India and, more generally, existing European territorial arrangements, often somewhat misleadingly described as the balance of power. At the same time as Britain was vying with the Franco-Dutch alliance for

---

[71] George Baldwin, *Political Recollections Relative to Egypt* (1801), p. 79; Charles-Roux, *L'Angleterre, L'Isthme*, pp. 201–49, 299; H. L. Hoskins, *British Routes to India* (1928), pp. 6–41; A. C. Wood, *A History of the Levant Company* (1935), pp. 165–74; Ingram, *British India*, pp. 21–35; H. Furber, 'The Overland Route to India in the Seventeenth and Eighteenth Centuries', *Journal of Indian History*, 29 (1951), 123–33; Willis to Pitt, 31 Jan. 1791, CUL Add. 6958 no. 910: on Willis, Christie (ed.), *The Correspondence of Jeremy Bentham* III, 439, 446–7.

[72] Ingram, *British India*, p. 9; Carmarthen to Dorset, 9 July 1784, PRO FO 27/12 fol. 149.

dominance over the maritime route to India, Russia and France, though from different directions and only episodically and very loosely in co-operation, were apparently becoming more influential over the overland route. In 1781 Catherine established a base in the Gulf of Asterabad (Gorgan) on the south-eastern shore of the Caspian Sea because of its location on the trade route to Bukhara and India. In 1783–4 France had vigorously maintained her earlier policy of opposing Russian gains at the expense of the Turks. There was Russian interest in the idea of a partition of the Turkish Empire by Austria, Russia and Iran, and Vergennes sought to thwart Russian influence in Iran, sending an embassy to Isfahan in 1784 that angered Catherine II. There were signs, however, of a shift in French policy towards interest in joining Austria and Russia in making gains at the expense of the Turks and thus creating a new territorial order, although the shift did not really develop until after the death of Vergennes in 1787. Nevertheless, French interest in Egypt, the Russian annexation and development of the Crimea and their growing presence in the Caucasus, and the Franco-Russian trade treaty of January 1787 could all seem to be different aspects of a common threat, prefiguring closer Franco-Russian relations in 1800–1 and Napoleon's plans of 1808 for joint action in Asia.[73]

Ainslie warned in 1784 that France was seeking to gain 'the same advantages in point of trade including the navigation of the Black Sea, ceded by the Porte to those of Russia'. He claimed that this would provide sources of copper and timber for the French navy, a crucial issue, and 'open a mercantile communication with the Emperor's dominions', in short creating an economic nexus to bind together France, Austria and Russia, one that would strengthen the French naval threat to Britain and be immune to British naval pressure. Later that year Dorset noted the report that France was to send two frigates to the Black Sea.[74] Indeed, in May 1783, Choiseul-Gouffier, who had travelled extensively in the Levant in the late 1770s and was soon to be the French Ambassador at

[73] D. M. Lang, *The Last Years of the Georgian Monarchy 1658–1832* (New York, 1957), pp. 180, 207–8; *Cambridge History of Iran*, VII, 326; J. L. van Regemorter, 'Commerce et politique: préparation et négociation du traité franco-russe de 1787', *Cahiers du monde russe et soviétique*, 4 (1963), 230–58; F. Fox, 'Negotiating with the Russians: Ambassador Ségur's Mission to St Petersburg, 1784–1787', *French Historical Studies*, 7 (1971), 47–72; J. Savant, 'Louis XVI et l'alliance Russe', *La Nouvelle Revue des deux mondes* (1975), 306–24; H. Ragsdale, *Détente in the Napoleonic Era: Bonaparte and the Russians* (Lawrence, 1980); O. Feldbaek, 'The Foreign Policy of Tsar Paul I, 1800–1801: An Interpretation', *Jahrbücher für Geschichte Osteuropas*, 30 (1982), 16–36; J. W. Strong, 'Russia's Plans for an Invasion of India in 1801', *Canadian Slavonic Papers*, 7 (1965), 114–26.

[74] Ainslie to Dorset, forwarded to Carmarthen, 24 Jan., Dorset to Carmarthen, 7 Oct. 1784, PRO FO 27/11 fols. 232–3, 27/13 fol. 77.

Constantinople, had submitted a memorandum proposing that France expand her influence in the Levant by increasing her trade there. He argued that it would be possible both to preserve the Turkish Empire and to develop trade with Russia via the Black Sea. In August 1784 Louis XVI wrote to the Sultan seeking admission to the Black Sea for ships flying the French flag; Choiseul-Gouffier had been given instructions to the same end on 2 June. The Turks refused, but Marseilles ships flying the flag of Russia were acceptable. In 1785 a French trading company was established at Kherson, at the mouth of the Dnieper. The French government provided a credit of 100,000 livres for the purchase of naval stores and a French master mastman organised inspections of timber in Poland and the Ukraine. The route offered the prospect of France gaining a new source of supply for timber and other naval stores from Poland and neighbouring states, and one that was not subject in wartime to British naval control of the North Sea. Trade on the route, though profitable, was still very small-scale. Prospects for expansion were shattered by the outbreak of Russo-Turkish hostilities in 1787. Ships were seized, cargoes confiscated and in the end the commercial facilities at Kherson had to be closed and the trade suspended.[75] However, as Poland freed herself from Russian influence and speculation about possible scenarios for the end of the conflict and for the post-war world developed in 1789–91, the British government also was to become interested in trade with the Black Sea.

Russian pressure on trans-Pontine Europe was for Britain a distant threat: a line could be traced from the fate of the Crimea in 1783 or of Ochakov in 1791 to that of the entire Turkish Empire, but it was less urgent a problem than that apparently posed by French power and rumoured French intentions. 'We cannot keep too strict an eye upon every motion of the French in the East Indies' wrote John Trevor from Turin in April 1786, a true representative of the francophobe style of most British diplomats, the majority of whom had served as envoys during the American war.[76] Ministers were continually pressed on the threat, and, of all the British colonial interests, it was India, with the East India Company, the Board of Control and the parliamentarians with interests there, that was most conspicuous. Of the 558 MPs in the 1784–90 House of Commons there were 45 Directors of the East India Company and 'nabobs', men who had been in India, a figure that

---

[75] Charles-Roux, 'La Monarchie Française d'Ancien Régime et la Question de La Mer Noire', *Revue de la Méditerranée*, 27 (1948), pp. 533, 537; Duparc (ed.), *Recueil…Turquie* pp. 472–3; Bamford, *Forests and French Sea Power*, pp. 194–205; Regemorter, 'Commerce et politique', p. 243.
[76] Trevor to Carmarthen, 8 Apr. 1786, PRO FO 67/5.

excluded major proprietors of stock and politicians, such as Henry Dundas, who were very concerned about India. The comparable figure of 'West Indians' was 8.[77] The *Leeds Intelligencer* of 6 July 1784 claimed that the East India Company 'are known to have above sixty members in the House *in their immediate interest,* and *at the absolute command* of the Ministerial Junto'. Typical of the letters received by ministers was that which Lord Walsingham sent Pitt in July 1786. Both men were members of the newly established Board of Control, a powerful group which also consisted of Viscount Sydney, the Home Secretary, William Grenville, Lord Mulgrave, and Dundas, Treasurer of the Navy and the government's political manager for Scotland. Walsingham wrote

look at the naval force in India at this moment of the French and of the Dutch compared with our own ... The Governor General says 2 French frigates could stop all supplies and all communication with Madras, and, he adds, the worst of consequences will follow unless you have a naval force on a rupture equal to your enemies.[78]

Concern about India was not equally expressed in all the Foreign Office diplomatic series, being most marked in correspondence with Paris, but in April 1784 Carmarthen explained to Keith at Vienna his views on the interrelationship of Britain's European and extra-European policies in the aftermath of the crisis caused by the Russian annexation of the Crimea in 1783,

This storm having blown over for the present, leaves France at liberty to pursue her plans of resentment and ambition in the East Indies. To obviate their designs in that quarter no method can be devised more likely to succeed than by finding employment for that restless spirit on the Continent of Europe.

Though only stated on occasions, this thesis was clearly attractive to British ministers, the influential Duke of Richmond writing of France in December 1785, 'Instead of drawing her off from the continent to the ocean, we want some power to draw her attention from the ocean to the continent.' The strategic notion of conquering Canada in Germany, popularised by Pitt the Elder, was thus seen as offering a possible guide to peace-time diplomacy, not least because it was widely believed that the absence of such a diversion for French efforts had handicapped Britain in the War of American Independence, and war with her appeared close again.[79]

[77] L. Namier and J. Brooke (eds.), *The House of Commons 1754–1790* (3 vols., 1964), I, 149–57; R. Thorne (ed.), *The House of Commons 1790–1820* (5 vols., 1986) I, 325.
[78] Walsingham to Pitt, 16 July 1786, CUL Add. 6958.
[79] Carmarthen to Keith, 23 Apr. 1784, Richmond to Carmarthen, 30 Dec. 1785, PRO FO 7/8, 30/8/322 fol. 24.

3. India

New ministry

Till I see this country in a situation more respectable as to army, navy and finances I cannot think anything that may draw us into troubled waters either safe or rational. George III, July 1784[80]

When the Pitt government came to power, Britain was isolated, without allies in a world that was directly threatening for British interests and in which the ambitions of the two most powerful European monarchs, Catherine II of Russia (1762–96) and Joseph II of Austria (1780–90), seemed to be the precursors of major changes that might well also harm Britain. The new government had to consider how best to meet these challenges. Whereas most eighteenth-century British ministries included senior members with considerable experience in the conduct of foreign policy, either as ministers (Secretaries of State for the Northern or Southern Departments prior to the creation of the Foreign Office in 1782), or as diplomats,[81] this was not the case with the Pitt government. True, two of the most notable Secretaries of State, the Duke of Newcastle (1724–54) and William Pitt the Elder (1756–61), had had no diplomatic experience, and indeed neither of them was renowned for his sensitivity to foreign views; but over the last two decades there had been a Secretary of State with such experience for much of the time: the Earl of Sandwich (1763–5, 1770–1), Earl of Rochford (1768–75), Viscount Stormont (1779–82), while Lord Grantham, the Foreign Secretary in the Shelburne ministry (1782–3), had been Ambassador in Madrid. Indeed, when the Pitt ministry was formed Grantham and Stormont were both active in politics and both were to be mentioned as possible Foreign Secretaries, but neither was chosen, Grantham because he refused and Stormont because he stayed loyal to North. Another former Secretary, Viscount Weymouth (1768–70, 1775–9), was also mentioned, as were Earl Gower and Viscount Sydney.[82]

The choice as Foreign Secretary, first, briefly, of Temple and then of Francis, Marquis of Carmarthen (1751–99), from March 1789 5th Duke of Leeds, reflected and hardly relieved the weakness of the ministry, for neither had any aptitude or experience for this key office. Carmarthen had accepted the Paris embassy from Shelburne shortly before he fell, though he had never gone. He was not the most committed of politicians, was not to be the most active of ministers and himself doubted the

[80] George III to Carmarthen, 6 July 1784, BL Add. 27914 fol. 3.
[81] M. A. Thomson, *The Secretaries of State 1681–1782* (1932); D. B. Horn, 'The Diplomatic Experience of Secretaries of State, 1660–1852', *History*, 41 (1956), 88–99.
[82] Aust to Liston, 19 Dec. 1783, NLS 5539 fol. 34.

wisdom of his appointment. A former MP (1774–5), Carmarthen was not a prominent member of any political connection, though he had a view of his own importance. He was not to be a success as leader of the Lords in 1790. The experienced former minister, Lord George Germain would have supported the government but for this appointment. He wrote to his nephew Dorset, 'What assistance the Ministry can derive from his experience or abilities I cannot guess ... a composition of self conceit, ingratitude, malignity and illiberality.' Eden snapped, 'if we may judge from the Embassies to Spain and France, and from the Secretarys' Offices, they are in desperate streights even for old men and boys to accept situations'. Dorset felt that Carmarthen failed to keep him informed and hoped that he would be dismissed. Carmarthen's active role against the East India bill may have been crucial to his appointment. He had canvassed against it among the Lords. Carmarthen has possibly been underrated. His vigorous anti-French attitudes were to be vindicated in the crisis of 1787, while his approaches to Austria and Russia, though unsuccessful, were in line with the earlier efforts of ministers usually regarded as more able.[83]

Pitt had as little experience of foreign affairs as Carmarthen and in his first months in office he understandably devoted little attention to them, although that summer he was clearly reading dispatches. Though the Austrian Envoy Extraordinary Friedrich, Count Kageneck, attributed the fall of the Fox–North ministry to the intrigues of the francophile Shelburne and the French ambassador, and presented the new government as pro-French,[84] this reflected the understandable tendency of diplomats to see diplomatic developments in the light of their own preoccupations. In contrast to the situation during the early decades of the century or indeed towards the close of the Seven Years War, when the Prussians sought to undermine the Bute ministry, foreign intervention and envoys played very little role either in the crisis of 1782–4 or in the subsequent course of the Pitt ministry until 1791. Whereas in 1710 the Austrian and Dutch envoys had pressed their ally Queen Anne not to part with the Godolphin ministry, no such action occurred in the early 1780s. Rather than being pro-French, as Kageneck suspected, Pitt appears to have shared the views of most of his ministerial colleagues. In May 1784 Carmarthen recorded, after a discussion with Pitt,

---

[83] Germain to Dorset, 27 Dec. 1783, KAO C192; Dorset to Stafford, 9 Mar. 1786, 15 Mar. 1787, PRO 30/29/1/15 nos. 52, 57; Eden to Sheffield, 4 Jan. 1784, BL Add. 45728 fol. 12; J. Black, 'The Marquis of Carmarthen and Relations with France 1784–1787', *Francia*, 12 (1984), 283–303. For a more critical view, McCahill, *Order and Equipoise*, pp. 129, 131.

[84] Pitt to Carmarthen, 24 June 1784, BL Eg. 3498 fol. 41; Kageneck to Kaunitz, 3 Feb., 14 May 1784, HHStA EK 123.

I was very happy to find our ideas were similar on the great object of separating if possible the House of Austria from France, as likewise a degree of desire to form some system on the continent in order to counterbalance the House of Bourbon, though at the same time the strongest conviction of the necessity of avoiding, if possible, the entering into any engagement likely to embroil us in a new war.[85]

The most experienced member of the government in the field of foreign policy was George III. This was very different to the situation under his three predecessors, and, instead, a return, in some respects, to that under William III. Throughout their reigns, Anne, George I and George II had been served by ministers who had long experience in the field, a situation that owed much to the continuity of Old Corps Whiggery during the reigns of Georges I and II. In contrast, the reign of George III was one of governmental discontinuity.[86] Whereas, however, in 1762 George III, who had come to the throne in 1760, had broken with his experienced ministers but had himself lacked expertise in the field of foreign policy, that was not true in 1783. George, born in 1738 was both older than Carmarthen and Pitt and more experienced than either of them, although he had never visited the Continent. George III's interest and views was to be a central theme in British foreign policy throughout this period, made, if anything, more conspicuous during the Regency Crisis of 1788–9 when the collapse of his health made the importance of the monarch's views starkly apparent.

Aside from George III, Pitt and Carmarthen, most of the other members of the government generally devoted little attention to foreign affairs. Sydney, Home Secretary and government leader in the Lords (1783–9), was a lightweight, Viscount Howe, First Lord of the Admiralty (1783–8), was chiefly concerned with Admiralty matters. Earl Gower (who in 1786 was created Marquis of Stafford), Lord President of the Council 1783–4 and Lord Privy Seal 1784–94 and an ally of Thurlow, did not exhaust himself in the service of government, while Gower's successor as Lord President, the able but elderly Lord Camden lacked the determination of Thurlow, the Lord Chancellor and very much the king's man in the Cabinet, or of the more mercurial Duke of Richmond, Master General of the Ordnance, both of whom did have views of interest and importance. Letters by Camden, Richmond and Thurlow on foreign policy reveal them to have been thoughtful and well-informed politicians. Excusing his failure to come to London from his country seat during the

---

[85] Leeds memoranda, May 1784, BL Add. 27918 fol. 122.
[86] I. R. Christie, 'George III and the Historians – Thirty Years on', *History*, 71 (1986), 205–21; Scott, *Foreign Policy*, pp. 15–18; Black, *System of Ambition?* pp. 38–42.

Dutch crisis, Stafford informed Pitt that he was 'perfectly satisfied' that his advice would be of 'little use'. The Cabinet was not united by party or connection, while it was divided on such policies as parliamentary reform and measures against the slave trade. Cabinet ministers were consulted on matters of diplomatic importance and saw dispatches, although in December 1785 Thurlow complained 'it is not easy to make much of a single link of correspondence'.[87] The Cabinet was to play an important role at moments of crisis in 1787 and 1791, but its lack of unity and a certain lack of corporate and in some cases individual interest, lessened its actual role and increased the room for manoeuvre of George III, Pitt and Carmarthen. Carmarthen wrote of the 1784 Cabinet, 'I found I could not prevail upon them to give that attention to foreign affairs that I thought necessary, and consequently afterwards gave them little trouble on the subject', and on 24 May 1784 he recorded that Richmond, 'could not help lamenting to me a want of confidential communication in the Cabinet, and of the dilatory proceedings in the Cabinet'. Two years later, Richmond, an industrious complainer, wrote, 'I cannot help regretting that we cannot allow more time for settling at our meetings, and when we are all present, the precise words on which so much depends in such important dispatches; or at least that we could see them before they are sent away.'[88]

European problems and options

For the past century the ending of European wars had frequently been precipitated, accompanied or followed by major diplomatic realignments. Britain had broken with her allies towards the end of the War of the Spanish Succession, negotiated the Peace of Utrecht in co-operation with her former enemy France, and then followed the peace by first close links with France (1713–14) and later an alliance (1716–31). At the end of the War of the Polish Succession (1733–5), France had abandoned her

---

[87] Thurlow to Carmarthen, 8 Dec. 1785, Pitt to Carmarthen, 24 June, 11 Dec. 1784, BL Eg. 3498 fols. 247, 41, 90; Dorset to Gower, 3 Feb. 1785, PRO 30/29/1/15 no. 48; Richmond to Carmarthen, 24 May 1785, BL Eg. 3498 fol. 221; George III to Carmarthen, 12 Nov. 1785, BL Add. 27914 fol. 11; Carmarthen to Pitt, 26 Dec., Carmarthen to Richmond, 27 Dec. 1785, Richmond to Pitt, 5, 30 July, 4 Sept. 1787, PRO 30/8/151 fols. 32–3, 30/8/170 fols. 81–8; Stafford to Pitt, 17 Sept. 1787, HL Hastings Mss. 26018; I. R. Christie, 'The Cabinet in the Reign of George III, to 1790' in his *Myth and Reality in Late Eighteenth-Century British Politics* (1970) pp. 55–108; McCahill, *Order and Equipoise*, pp. 130–5, 137; A. Aspinall, *The Cabinet Council 1783–1835* (The Raleigh Lecture, 1952) concentrates on the early nineteenth century.
[88] Leeds Political Memoranda, BL Add. 27918 fols. 121–2; Richmond to Carmarthen, 26 Mar. 1786, BL Eg. 3498 fol. 233.

Sardinian and Spanish allies and negotiated a settlement with her former enemy Austria. Austria, Sardinia and Spain negotiated a comprehensive settlement of their Italian differences after the War of the Austrian Succession, while the death of Elizabeth of Russia in 1762 led to a Russo-Prussian reconciliation that wrecked the Russo-Austrian alliance and the coalition fighting Prussia. There was a major contrast between the theory of international relations, of a system in which states rationally pursued natural interests and were affected by a discernible balance of power, and a reality that was less regular, predictable, measurable and systemic, and more affected by the play of contingency and the role of individual rulers and ministers.[89] If a systemic perspective is adopted, then British policy can appear foolish and futile, the product of outdated thinking, and this charge can be brought against the Pitt ministry, as well as against its predecessors.[90] However, the frequently kaleidoscopic nature of eighteenth-century international relations cannot be readily judged from such a perspective. The negotiation of an Austro-Russian understanding in 1781 underlined the unpredictability of alignments; and the disagreements between Britain's enemies both during the War of American Independence and in the subsequent peace negotiations demonstrated the fragility of alliances. Spain had come close to abandoning France during the war, while the Franco-American alliance did not survive it.[91] It was not, therefore, necessarily foolish to hope that existing continental alliances might dissolve and that Britain might benefit. The coming of peace suggested both that Britain might appear as a more attractive ally and that existing links that excluded her could be broken.

Britain could search for allies among either former enemies or powers that had played no role in the recent conflict. Both policies were to be followed, though more hope and energy were devoted to the latter. This represented an obvious continuity with the policies of previous ministries. During the war Britain had devoted considerable effort to improving relations with both Austria and Russia. In December 1780 Stormont, then Secretary of State for the Northern Department, ordered Keith to take advantage of the accession of Joseph II as sole ruler of Austria, by proposing an alliance of Britain, Austria and Russia. The following month Stormont wrote of his support for an Austro-Russian defensive alliance, 'Such an alliance would be the cornerstone of that system, which every friend to this country, and the general interests of Europe, must wish to see restored.'[92] Now at war with the United Provinces, the British government had no compunction in seeking to win

[89] Black, *The Rise of the European Powers.*   [90] Scott, *Foreign Policy,* pp. 342–3.
[91] Hill, *French Perceptions.*
[92] Stormont to Keith, 12 Dec. 1780, 9, 12 Jan. 1781, PRO SP. 80/223, FO 7/1.

Austrian support by encouraging Joseph II's aggressive views, in this case his wish to reverse the prohibition under the Peace of Westphalia (1648) of trade on the river Scheldt.[93] This had succeeded in the objective of its Dutch sponsors in ruining the trade of Antwerp, the principal port on the Scheldt, and thus of lessening commercial competition from the then Spanish, later Austrian, Netherlands. Stormont declared of the opening of the Scheldt, which was to bulk large in the British case when going to war against Revolutionary France in 1793,

This is a very general wish in this country; At Berlin it might savour of that partiality to the House of Austria, of which we there stand accused, a partiality I shall never disown, as it is approved by my reason, and consistent with every wish I can form for the prosperity of Great Britain ... Our present position with the United Provinces fully authorizes our concurrence in any project for opening the Scheldt; which at another time could not have done consistently with the faith of treaties.[94]

Stormont hoped that Austria could and would dispel hostile French and Prussian influences in Russia, and indeed Frederick II, an ally of France, feared an Anglo-Austro-Russian alliance. Austria, however, did not seek better relations with Russia in order to help Britain; Keith did not raise the idea of an alliance because he was convinced that Austria would not desert France for Britain; and Kaunitz did not pursue, for the time being, the idea of opening the Scheldt.[95]

In early 1782 Stormont returned to the theme of using Austria to influence Russia, and sought, as numerous earlier ministers had done, to persuade Vienna to see Europe in terms of a struggle against French influence. His tone, however, was pessimistic,

I am afraid no real assistance can be expected from the Court of Vienna, who are wedded to the system they have embraced, and will not suffer themselves to see how much their own interests are concerned in the great contest in which we are engaged, and how much every great power in Europe, France alone excepted, would be affected by Great Britain losing the weight she has hitherto had in the general scale. Without taking an active part himself, the Emperor could render us most essential service by insinuating to the Empress of Russia, the propriety of her standing forth upon this occasion ... I am well aware that nothing of this kind can be suggested by you to Prince Kaunitz, but if the Emperor and his ministers can once be brought to see the actual situation of the country and that of Europe in a proper light, such a measure may be the result of reflections arising in their own mind.[96]

[93] S. T. Bindoff, *The Scheldt Question to 1839* (1945), pp. 138–9.
[94] Stormont to Keith, 20 Jan., 4 Feb. 1781, PRO FO 7/1.
[95] Keith to Stormont, 7, 28 Feb. 1781, PRO FO 7/1; A. Beer (ed.), *Joseph II, Leopold II und Kaunitz. Ihr Briefwechsel* (Vienna, 1873), pp. 81–2.
[96] Stormont to Keith, 15 Jan. 1782, PRO FO 7/4.

4. Europe in 1783

Stormont's pessimism led him to welcome better Austro-Russian relations while appreciating that they would be of no immediate benefit to Britain. He was hopeful that the developing crisis in relations between Russia and Turkey, a traditional ally of France, would strain Austro-French relations, an essential precondition, in Stormont's eyes, to any reassessment by Joseph II of his position towards Britain. Grantham also hoped that Austrian support for Russia's Balkan schemes would lead to the end of the Austro-French connection, while his successor Fox, shared these hopes and the view that the state of Austro-French relations was the key to British policy towards Austria, 'everything to be said and done that can contribute to break the connection between France and Austria; when that connection shall be broken every assistance to be given short of actual war; till that connection shall be broken nothing'.[97] In this respect, the Pitt government followed the policy of its predecessors. The hope that an understanding with Austria could be negotiated played a major role in 1784–5, Carmarthen writing to Keith in August 1784,

No difficulty ought ever to deter us from the steady and determined pursuit of the great and important object this country should ever keep in view. I mean detaching the Emperor from France; this cannot be too often repeated, or too closely attended to, and no one circumstance, however trivial in itself, ought to be neglected.[98]

The need to balance French power by a continental alliance was a theme that linked the foreign policy of the Pitt ministry with that of its predecessor. Fox had hoped to use the crisis in Russo-Turkish relations caused by the Russian annexation of the Crimea in 1783 to negotiate an alliance with Russia. This had been seen both as a prerequisite of an Anglo-Prussian alliance,[99] and as crucial to Fox's basic plan. In September 1783 he had written to the Duke of Manchester, Ambassador in Paris and a political ally, of the need to form

a League to balance the Family Compact, and in this article of a continental Alliance as a balance to the House of Bourbon, consists the whole of my foreign politics; and I am very happy to find that *every one* of the present ministers agree with me in this respect. Some have their partialities to the Emperor as I own I have to the King of Prussia, but between these two, the circumstance of the time will decide too forcibly to admit of the operation of either of these biasses.[100]

[97] Stormont to Keith, 25 Jan., 12 Feb. 1782, Grantham to Keith, 27 Sept. 1782, Fox to Keith, 29 July, 8 Sept. 1783, PRO FO 7/4–7; J. Black, 'British Policy towards Austria, 1780–93', *Mitteilungen des Österreichischen Staatsarchivs*, 42 (1992), 197–8.
[98] Carmarthen to Keith, 16 Aug. 1784, PRO FO 7/9.
[99] Stepney to Fox, 3, 14 June 1783, BL Add. 47562 fols., 121, 128–9.
[100] Fox to Manchester, 12 Sept. 1783, BL Add. 47563 fol. 129 .

The emphasis on circumstances was justified, both in light of the experience of recent attempts to secure allies, and because the choice of ally was apparently less important than the need for an alliance designed against France. Joseph II would make a valuable ally because of his possessions, his army and his Russian alliance. Paul Kennedy has argued that 'the Habsburg Empire had already become a *marginal* first-class power', an ambiguous phrase, but that was not how Austria struck contemporaries. A stress on the rise of Prussia and Russia has led to an underrating of Austrian power and resilience in the eighteenth century. In the late 1710s and 1720s the Austria of Charles VI seemed the strongest power in Europe and, though the wars of 1733–48 placed a severe strain on Austrian power, she emerged with the bulk of her territories, and with hopes of a partition of Austria decisively thwarted. In turn, Austrian hopes of regaining Silesia from Prussia in the Seven Years War and of crushing Frederick II had been disappointed, but her stronger finances, administration and army underlay her recovery from the defeats and chaos of the late 1730s and early 1740s.[101]

Austria is a convenient but misleading term for the variety of Joseph II's territories. These included principalities comprising most of modern Austria, the Kingdom of Bohemia, Moravia and Austrian (part of Upper) Silesia, the lands gained in the First Partition of Poland, Transylvania (modern north-western Romania), the Duchies of Milan and Mantua in northern Italy and a number of possessions in southern Germany. Joseph was also ruler of the Austrian Netherlands and of Hungary, a kingdom that included modern Slovakia and Croatia, although in both his authority was less than in Austria. The Austrian army had grown considerably in size. The establishment had risen from 157,000 in 1740 to 174,000 in 1775 and 307,000 in 1783, and the rise in the number of effectives was even more impressive. In contrast, the size of the French army in 1786 was 156,000, that of the Prussian, 194,000 men.[102]

Austrian power was supplemented from a number of sources. Joseph's brother and heir Leopold was Grand Duke of Tuscany, a state which in Leghorn (Livorno) included the leading Mediterranean port for British trade. Another brother, Max Franz, became coadjutor to the Archbishop-Elector of Cologne and Prince-Bishop of Münster in 1780 and succeeded to both sees in 1784. This increased Habsburg power in north-western Germany and the Rhineland, an area which, after several

[101] P. Kennedy, *The Rise and Fall of the Great Powers* (1988), pp. 118–19; P. G. M. Dickson, *Finance and Government under Maria Theresia 1740–1780* (2 vols., Oxford, 1987).

[102] Dickson, *Finance and Government*, I, 354–7. Frederick II was less impressed, *Polit. Corresp.* 46, 120.

decades of peace and quiet, was becoming more important in diplomatic terms. Münster brought Habsburg power to the frontiers of the Electorate of Hanover and to the eastern frontier of the United Provinces, though, in fact, Max Franz was to offer his brother little support.[103]

As Holy Roman Emperor, Joseph II was heir to a mass of legal powers and pretensions, which, in combination with Austrian strength, gave him the ability to intervene in disputes throughout Germany.[104] His assertive, often aggressive, instincts were not, however, restricted to the Empire. Throughout his territories, Joseph sought to increase his power and authority, and this materially affected other states. Thus, in 1781, Joseph expelled the Dutch garrisons from the Barrier, the fortifications near the French frontier of the Austrian Netherlands that were designed to lessen the possibility or success of a French attack. These garrisons appeared as an affront to Joseph's authority, as well as unnecessary in light of the alignment with France that had lasted since 1756. Though Britain had been instrumental in the negotiations leading to the establishment of the Barrier system during and after the War of the Spanish Succession, she was not consulted. Had the Barrier still been in place in 1787, the crises in the Low Countries that year might well have taken a different course. More obviously, Dutch garrisons in the Barrier in 1792 would, had they been attacked by France, probably have led to the earlier outbreak of Franco-Dutch and Anglo-French hostilities.

Compared by Frederick II in August 1781 to a chemist who kept the affairs of Europe in fermentation, Joseph II took a number of steps that increased his reputation for unpredictability and disrespect for international agreements. Unsympathetic to compromise and the views of others, and unwilling to honour accepted conventions and privileges, either domestically or internationally, Joseph prefigured to a certain extent the attitudes of Revolutionary France. He was, however, less willing than the revolutionaries were to be to push issues to a crisis, as he demonstrated in his confrontations with the Dutch over the Scheldt in 1784 and with Prussia over the Bavarian Exchange Scheme in 1785. Compromise or co-existence was easier for Joseph, because he did not publicly advance unacceptable universal principles as a basis for his diplomacy, as the Revolutionary French were to do; because other

---

[103] M. Braubach, *Maria Theresias jüngster Sohn Max Franz* (Vienna/Munich, 1961); G. Livet (ed.), *Recueil ... Cologne* (Paris, 1963), pp. l–li, 349, 358–62; A. Schulte, *Ein englischer Gesandter am Rhein. George Cressener als Bevollmächtiger Gesandter an den Höfen der geistlichen Kurfürsten und beim Niederrheinisch-Westfälischen Kreis 1763–1781* (Bonn, 1971), pp. 200–15.

[104] K. O. von Aretin, *Heiliges Römisches Reich 1776–1806 : Reichsverfassung und Staatssouveränität* (2 vols., Wiesbaden, 1967), I, 7–109; J. G. Gagliardo, *Reich and Nation. The Holy Roman Empire as Idea and Reality, 1763–1806* (Bloomington, 1980), 16–46.

powers were willing to act to reduce tension, the French defusing the Scheldt crisis of 1784; and because, in the last resort, Joseph was less aggressive in action than aspiration, certainly less bold than Catherine II.

The Austro-Russian understanding joined the two most powerful of the three states that had carried out the First Partition of Poland in 1772. The union then of Austria, Prussia and Russia had led to fears that those powers would dominate Europe and carry out further partitions, fears voiced by, among others, the Earl of Suffolk, Secretary of State for the Northern Department, and the Duke de Broglie, director of the *secret du roi*, the secret French diplomatic network created by Louis XV. Contemporaries, like later commentators, argued that the First Partition inaugurated a new era in international relations, one characterised by a use of force to gain territory without consideration of even tenuous legal claims, or, in a more modern light, by the use of 'reason' as a justification for territorial expansion.[105] In fact, not only had treaties been cynically breached on many occasions in the past, but the actual or planned despoliation of neighbours, alone or in combination, was far from novel. The First Partition created such a shock in part because Europe had been territorially stable since 1748, but also thanks to the combination and seeming apparent invulnerability of the three partitioning powers. The loss of a *sense* of balance (more important than any nebulous reality of one), destroyed any element of predictability and it was apparently no longer the case that schemes would be opposed by states that could hope to block them.

The best comment on these fears, but one that was most apparent in hindsight was the absence of significant territorial changes in the two decades after the First Partition, where they had been most feared, in Germany and northern Italy. This reflected the distrust between the partitioning powers that had led them to the attempt to balance gains by the First Partition. Distrust ensured that these powers did not create co-operative arrangements or plan their policies jointly. Partly as a result, differing views over the first major dispute, the Bavarian Succession, led to war.[106] Neither Maximilian Joseph of Bavaria (1745–77) nor his successor, Karl Theodor of the Palatinate, had any direct heirs, and Joseph II saw this as an opportunity to gain part of Bavaria. After Maximilian Joseph's death, Joseph II reached an agreement with Karl Theodor by which he gained much of Lower Bavaria. Such a gain,

---

[105] Frederick II to his niece Wilhelmina, 13 Aug. 1781, *Polit. Corresp.*, 46, 107; E. Boutaric, *Correspondance sècrete inédite de Louis XV sur la politique étrangère* (2 vols., Paris, 1886), II, 497–8; D. Kaiser, *Politics and War. European Conflict from Philip II to Hitler* (Cambridge Mass., 1990), pp. 204–6.
[106] Black, *European Powers*, pp. 123–30.

without any compensating advantages for other powers, would have dramatically increased Austrian power in the Empire and breached the principle on which the First Partition had been negotiated. In particular, it was a threat to the second German power, Prussia, which feared yet another Austrian attempt to reverse Frederick II's conquest of the bulk of Silesia in 1741.

These competing interests led to the War of Bavarian Succession (1778–9) in which Austria was able to thwart Frederick militarily, but suffered from a lack of diplomatic support. Her French ally and most of the German states were opposed to substantial Austrian gains, while Catherine gave important diplomatic support to Frederick. By the Peace of Teschen, concluded under Franco-Russian mediation in May 1779 and with both powers becoming guarantors of the treaty, Austria gained the Innviertel, a small but strategic area of south-eastern Bavaria, that was far less than the gains stipulated in the agreement with Karl Theodor. Prussia obtained the reversion to the Hohenzollern principalities of Ansbach and Bayreuth, bringing the prospect of Prussian power extending south of the River Main. The failure of either power to achieve victory in the war, and the Russian role in the peace, led to an important increase in Russian prestige, particularly in the Empire, an increase that was advertised in Britain, the writer John Richard observing, 'the Russians may now be considered as the arbiters of Germany, since it is evident that their conjunction with either power must overwhelm the other'.[107]

This war and a revival of concern about the Balkans led to a diplomatic realignment. Joseph's determination to destroy the Prusso-Russian alliance took precedence over his earlier worries about Russian expansion against the Turks, which had led to an Austro-Turkish defensive concert in 1771.[108] The death in November 1780 of his mother, Maria Theresa, who was hostile to Catherine, helped, but more important was Catherine's shift towards ambitious anti-Turkish schemes, including the Greek Project, the plan for the expulsion of the Turks from the Balkans and the creation of an empire ruled by her grandson born in 1779 who was symbolically christened Constantine. These schemes were associated with an influential former lover Potemkin, who was closely involved in the development of Russia's gains from the Turks in the war of 1768–74. He was the central figure in a political grouping that centred on military

---

[107] J. Richard, *A Tour from London to Petersburg* (1780), p. 159; K. O. Aretin, 'Russia as a Guarantor Power of the Imperial Constitution under Catherine II', *Journal of Modern History*, 58 (1986) suppl., 141–7. The best guide to Austrian diplomacy in this period is D. Beales, *Joseph II. 1. In the Shadow of Maria Theresa 1741–1780* (Cambridge, 1987), pp. 386–438.

[108] K. Roider, *Austria's Eastern Question 1700–1790* (Princeton, 1982), pp. 109–29.

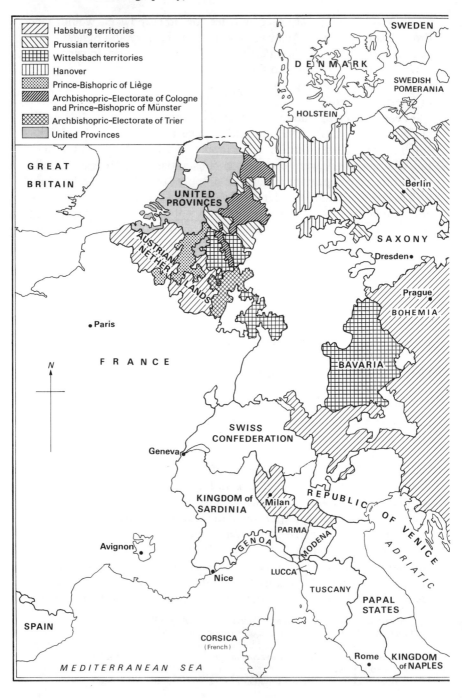

Habsburg territories
Prussian territories
Wittelsbach territories
Hanover
Prince-Bishopric of Liège
Archbishopric–Electorate of Cologne and Prince–Bishopric of Münster
Archbishopric–Electorate of Trier
United Provinces

SWEDEN

DENMARK

SWEDISH POMERANIA

HOLSTEIN

GREAT BRITAIN

Berlin

UNITED PROVINCES

SAXONY

Dresden

AUSTRIAN NETHERLANDS

Prague

BOHEMIA

Paris

BAVARIA

FRANCE

N

SWISS CONFEDERATION

Geneva

KINGDOM of SARDINIA

Milan

REPUBLIC OF VENICE

PARMA

ADRIATIC

GENOA

MODENA

Avignon

LUCCA

Nice

TUSCANY

PAPAL STATES

SPAIN

CORSICA (French)

Rome

KINGDOM of NAPLES

MEDITERRANEAN SEA

5. Central Europe in 1783

command and an interest in Russia's borderlands. Catherine's personal commitment to the Greek Project has been doubted, but it seems likely that her government sought territory to act as an equivalent to the colonial gains of the western European powers.[109] Intervention in the Crimea in 1776, in support of a client khan, Sahin Giray, and the Convention of Aynali Kavak (1779) increased Russian control of the Crimea. Catherine sought Austrian support for her plans, and, though her claims to an imperial title which Joseph found unacceptable prevented the negotiation of a formal treaty, the two rulers exchanged letters in May and June 1781 that in practice constituted a secret treaty of defensive alliance. This alliance was to be of considerable benefit to Catherine both in facilitating her peaceful annexation of the Crimea and in freeing her from having to fight the Turks alone, after they declared war on Russia in 1787. Instability in the Crimea, where Sahin Giray proved a weak and unreliable client ruler, led to Russian military intervention in the autumn of 1782 and annexation on 19 April 1783.[110]

The European response to this and the possibility that it would provide opportunities for British diplomacy was the first question facing the Pitt ministry, one inherited from the Fox–North government. It was at once a matter of negotiation that required immediate action and an issue that posed a central question about the direction of British foreign policy, for Vergennes sought British co-operation in thwarting Russian gains at the expense of the Turks, which he held to be the most obvious sign of the threat to the European system and status quo posed by the partitioning powers. To the French, Russia appeared especially threatening, both because her policies challenged traditional French protégés, Sweden, Poland and Turkey, and because she pressed her claims most vigorously. In March 1777 Vergennes had already written of the need for Anglo-French co-operation against measures to weaken Turkey, and it has been argued that Vergennes hoped that, once defeated in America, Britain would support France in eastern Europe. The possibility of such co-operation in order to thwart the aggressive designs of the partitioning powers was held out by Shelburne in discussions with Gérard de

[109] E. Hösch, 'Das sogenannte "griechische Projekt" Katharinas II', *Jahrbücher für Geschichte Osteuropas*, 12 (1964), pp. 168–206; J. P. LeDonne, *Ruling Russia. Politics and Administration in the Age of Absolutism, 1762–1796* (Princeton, 1984), pp. 56–65, 302–3; M. Atkin, *Russia and Iran, 1780–1828* (Minneapolis, 1980), pp. 23–5.

[110] A. von Arneth (ed.), *Joseph II und Katharina von Russland: Ihr Briefwechsel* (Vienna, 1869), pp. 72–81; A. Trachevsky, 'Das russisch-österreichische Bündnis im Jahr 1781', *Historische Zeitschrift*, 30 (1875); I. de Madariaga, 'The Secret Austro-Russian Treaty of 1781', *Slavonic and East European Review*, 38 (1959–60), 114–45; M. S. Anderson, 'The Great Powers and the Russian Annexation of the Crimea, 1783–4', *Slavonic and East European Review*, 37 (1958–9), 17–41; A. W. Fisher, *The Russian Annexation of the Crimea, 1772–1783* (Cambridge, 1970), pp. 75–138.

Rayneval, a *premier commis* in the French foreign ministry, in late 1782, and they were accompanied by the idea of a commercial treaty, a repetition of the plans advanced in 1713 at the end of the War of the Spanish Succession.[111]

Such ideas were held not only in London and Paris, but also in Madrid and in Turin, whence Trevor wrote in December 1783,

this court is very uneasy at the ambitious projects of the Emperor and still more alarmed that he should aggrandize himself by negotiation, than by … war. Hints are frequently given to me, by the minister of the necessity of a system among the western powers of Europe, to form a barrier against the dangerous ambition of the two Imperial courts that the House of Bourbon and we should forget all our old jealousies and prejudices, and recollect that, in this affair, we have one common cause.[112]

Both during the course of the peace negotiations and subsequently, as the Crimean crisis neared the point when full-scale war between Russia and Turkey and the danger of the realisation of wider Russian ambitions seemed imminent, the French pressed the British for support.[113] Despite Joseph II's suggestion that France could gain Egypt from a partition of the Turkish Empire – a scheme that envisaged no role for Britain and that was not in British interests – Vergennes felt that it was in France's interests that the balance of power should not be overthrown by Austrian and Russian gains and that the empire should survive. He realised that any war was bound to result in a further weakening of the Turks, as indeed had happened in 1768–74.[114] Vergennes' solution was to prevent such wars and to try by diplomacy either to maintain the *status quo* or to limit Russia's and Austria's advance.

It is understandable that French approaches were unwelcome to the British government, though the growing French concern about pleas for help from Constantinople and their hope of enlisting British support appear to have softened their attitude on the peace terms. There was little doubt that the Turks were vulnerable. Sir James Porter, a former Ambassador in Constantinople, had already suggested that Russian possessions in the Crimea would 'hold any navy in Europe … they may

---

[111] AE CP Ang. 522 fols. 117–22, 134, 162–3, 401; Dull, *Diplomatic History*, p. 59; Doniol, 'Première négociation', 70, 81.

[112] Trevor to Keith, 10 Dec. 1783, BL Add. 35530 fol. 244; Liston to Grantham, 15 Jan. 1783, PRO FO 62/3, p. 14.

[113] Vergennes to Rayneval, 1 Feb. 1783, AE CP Ang. 540 fol. 318; Manchester to Fox, 18 June 1783, PRO FO 27/6.

[114] Vergennes to Bertin, Controlleur General, 11 July 1783, Paris, Archives Nationales, nouvelles acquisitions françaises 6498 fol. 298; Vergennes to Adhémar, 25 Apr. 1783, Vaucher (ed.), *Recueil*, p. 522; P. Duparc (ed.), *Recueil … Venise* (Paris, 1958), pp. 282–3, *Recueil … Turquie*, p. 475; R. Salomon, *La politique orientale de Vergennes* (Paris, 1934).

soon have one superior to the Turks in which case with a fresh north-east wind they may be masters of Constantinople in 48 hours'. In January 1784 Greig reminded Harris that he had often said to him when they were both in St Petersburg that there was no alternative between Russia 'keeping the Crimea, and the Turks leaving Europe, sooner or later'.[115] On the other hand, following the French lead would jeopardise British chances of improving relations with Austria and Russia, and would do so in favour of a policy whose costs would be heavy and consequences unpredictable. Grantham wrote of the Balkans in February 1783,

The Court of France is anxious that we should concur in some plan of neutrality. I have in general admitted the eligibility of such a system but at the same time have carefully avoided committing His Majesty in any measures which should preclude him from taking such part as may suit his interests and those of his kingdoms.[116]

The French tried to present Britain as co-operating with them, Harris reporting from St Petersburg that

the French ministry have taken great pains, both directly through their minister here, and indirectly through the court of Vienna, to insinuate to the Empress that we have promised them to oppose any project she may have in contemplation, which may tend to produce a new war in Europe; and that our conduct towards Russia will be widely different from what it was during the last Turkish war,

(1768–74) when Britain had favoured Russia, though without becoming a combatant. Harris denied this; and in response to 'very pressing solicitations' from the French, Fox replied in a 'very cold manner'.[117] The dilemma facing Britain was indicated in a conversation between George III and North in September 1783. The king

spoke of the Russian Manifesto with much ill humour and resentment, and intimated some degree of apprehension of being drawn into taking a part with the Empress, but upon Lord North's submitting to him the impolicy of joining France, in opposition to Russia, he very readily concurred in it, and said that certainly would be going a great deal too far.[118]

Any alliance with France would be intended by the latter as active and the British government did not seek this, whether the activity in question was pro-active or re-active. The Anglo-Prussian alignment that was to confront Russia in 1788–91, and that had been prefigured by George

[115] Bedford CRO L30/14/314; Greig to Harris, 16/27 Jan. 1784, Winchester, Malmesbury 155; Blankett to Lansdowne, 26 Aug. 1785, Bowood, 11.
[116] Grantham to Keith, 22 Feb. 1783, PRO FO 7/6.
[117] Harris to Fitzherbert, 10/21 Mar. 1783, Matlock CRO 239 M/O. 522; Fox to Keith, 29 July, Fox to Manchester, 4 Aug. 1783, PRO FO 7/7, 27/6 fol. 391.
[118] Portland to Fox, 7 Sept. 1783, BL Add. 47561 fol. 61.

III's negotiation of the *Fürstenbund* in 1785, was not practical in 1783–4; nor was such confrontation desirable. The Pitt ministry inherited this situation.

For the time being, in fact, Vergennes was reasonably successful even without British help: his tactic was one of pressing the Turks to make concessions and avoid at all costs a war that could only lead to further Russian advances. His efforts to mediate or influence a solution to the Crimean crisis prevented Austria from making any gains, while Russia's were kept to a minimum and the Greek Plan remained only an aspiration. Vergennes did so by persuading the Turks to appease Russia and buy her off by acknowledging the Russian gain of the Khanate of the Crimea, which included not only the Crimean peninsula but also the Kuban region to the east of the Sea of Azov and the land to the north of the Crimea between the Sea of Azov and the Dnieper. This policy assumed a measure of French influence at Constantinople, that would limit the role of the war party there; and Vergennes was also helped by Austrian diplomatic pressure on the Turks. In 1784 Vergennes was successful. Three years later, however, French efforts to prevent war between Russia and Turkey failed. British hesitation about supporting France in 1783–4 should be seen in part against the background of a possible Balkan war. Such a conflict would be desirable if it shattered the Franco-Austrian alliance, but not if it found Britain allied to France. The French Ambassador urged the new British government to support France in pressing Russia to moderate her demands, and in guaranteeing any Russo-Turkish settlement, and thus protecting the interests of the weaker power, Turkey.[119] The British response was cautious, and George III praised Carmarthen's unenthusiastic response to the French move. Simolin, the Russian envoy, was informed of the French approach, and the British were clear that they would not be willing to guarantee any settlement unless Russia wanted it. In the event no such guarantee was to be required. By the second Convention of Aynali Kavak, the Turks accepted Russian terms on 8 January 1784. Without much cause, Keith wrote of the Convention as a measure 'to which His Majesty's friendly intervention contributed most essentially ... the public tranquillity of Europe is thereby reestablished'.[120]

The problem facing the Pitt ministry at its outset and its response were to set the pattern for much of British foreign policy in the following years. The aims of this policy were clear. Despite French desires for improved

---

[119] Vergennes to Adhémar, 4 Jan. 1784, AE CP Ang. 547 fols. 38–41; Adhémar to Carmarthen, 8 Jan. 1784, PRO FO 27/11 fol. 31; *Recueil ... Turquie*, pp. 476, 486.

[120] George III to Carmarthen, 28 Dec. 1783, BL Add. 27914 fol. 1; Fisher, *Annexation*, p. 138; Keith to Richard Grenville, 28 Jan. 1784, BL Add. 70958.

relations, Carmarthen sought a strong alliance system that could counteract, or, in the language of the period, balance Bourbon strength; in short he was preparing for another Anglo-Bourbon struggle and seeking, as with Pitt's extensive and expensive naval rebuilding plan,[121] to remedy the deficiencies of Britain's position in the last conflict. Such a system could include all powers that wished to enter it, and in 1784 the British government were willing to probe widely. In September 1784, for example, Carmarthen wanted Count Andreas Peter Bernstorff, the Danish Foreign Minister, sounded on 'such a system as he may think necessary, to preserve the tranquillity of the north in the first instance, and in its general tendency to prevent any future ill effects from the restless and ambitious views of the House of Bourbon'. Later that month Carmarthen was hopeful that the Scheldt crisis would cause the break up of the Franco-Austrian alliance and lead to 'the revival of the old system', the Anglo-Austrian alliance that had played such a major role in British policy between 1689 and 1755. The following month he pressed Simolin on the need for an alliance between Britain, Denmark and Russia.[122] Such widely spread approaches might suggest confusion and a lack of consistency, but British policy was motivated by a central theme of hostility to France and an attempt to exploit any difficulties that she faced. Having envoys at foreign courts, the government lost nothing in instructing the diplomats to investigate the possibilities of better relations and, to that end, it was understandable that the stress should be on common interests, however anachronistic and mistaken this might appear in hindsight.

Such an opportunistic approach was necessary if alliances were sought in a continent where existing alignments left no satisfactory place for Britain, for it was by no means clear what changes would occur, and recent history suggested that major and sudden realignments were possible. In addition, the language used, of common interests and a balanced system, which can be seen as evidence of outmoded ideas that bore no relation to shifts in the international system, can also be presented in a different light. British politicians revealed an understandable desire to assume that the arrangements they made were natural, an inevitable consequence of the nature of international relations; but, rather than being trapped in their rhetoric, British ministries were flexible, yet keen to describe their goals and achievements as consistent. This was understandable psychologically; it represented

[121] P. L. C. Webb, 'The Rebuilding and Repair of the Fleet 1783–1793', *Bulletin of the Institute of Historical Research*, 50 (1977), 194–209.
[122] Carmarthen to Hugh Elliot, Envoy Extraordinary in Copenhagen, 7 Sept., 22 Oct., Carmarthen to Keith, 21 Sept. 1784, PRO FO 22/6 fols. 269, 297, 7/9.

the need to organize, and thus better understand and make meaningful, the otherwise apparently inchoate nature of international developments, and was also important in the domestic political debate about foreign policy. In 1783–93 hostility to France was a consistent note in British policy. The different alliances that were sought to further that end were given unity by that goal, while continuity with the situation in the decades prior to the formation of the Pitt ministry was provided by the central problem, not of whose alliance should be sought, but rather of what commitments could and should be made to further the creation of an alliance. Indeed, the flexibility of diplomatic speculation in this period was indicated by Fitzherbert's suggestion that a negotiation with Spain to exchange Gibraltar would be the best way to seek to weaken France. He felt that the Family Compact could not be battered 'down by main force', that the other European powers were neither able nor willing to serve Britain's purposes and that it was necessary to distinguish between an alliance for 'the purpose of the present hour' and 'a solid and lasting counterpoise' to the Family Compact. The last was a good point, and the objective of such a counterpoise was, Fitzherbert suggested, unrealistic. His conclusion was that Britain should negotiate with Spain, but approaches that were made to Spain in the mid-1780s were unsuccessful.[123]

Carmarthen's alliance-goal in 1784–5 was clear: the most powerful alliance system on the Continent. He had, however, to cope with the reluctance of, in particular, George III and Pitt to commit Britain to the consequences of such a system. Carmarthen tackled this concern in writing to Pitt on 9 June 1784,

Were it possible for England to be permitted to remain perfectly quiet and undisturbed, so as to be able by a prudent line of conduct in her domestic government to recruit her strength almost exhausted by the late long and expensive war no one could hesitate a moment to adopt that system of tranquility ... I cannot however by any means flatter myself with the hopes of our being permitted to pursue so salutary a plan.

A 'system in Europe' was therefore necessary, as Carmarthen argued that September, in order both to 'secure to this country a prospect of remaining unmolested by France' and, more generally, to keep Bourbon ambitions in check. Pitt, in contrast, was worried about getting 'involved in the quarrels' of continental powers and about 'how to employ anything more than very vague unmeaning professions, without pledging ourselves, to more than could be prudent'. This tension was to

---

[123] Fitzherbert to Liston, 30 Dec. 1783, NLS 5539 fols. 80–2; S. Conn, *Gibraltar in British Diplomacy in the Eighteenth Century* (New Haven, 1942), pp. 237–55.

characterise British foreign policy throughout the period. In 1784, Carmarthen thought 'the recovery of our former connection with Austria ... the most desirable object'. To the monarchs and ministers of Europe, Austria appeared a powerful and aggressive state whose alliance was worth seeking, or that had to be guarded against. The Russian alliance made Austria an even more desirable ally and ensured that there were a number of powers which could be approached in order to negotiate an alliance: Austria, Russia and Russia's ally Denmark. The only alternatives as alliance partners were France and Prussia but it was felt that France could not be trusted. Carmarthen was willing to think of Prussia if Austria and Russia were unresponsive, but Frederick II was unwilling to jeopardise his relations with France, contemptuous about George III and British stability, unwilling to move towards Britain beyond talk of common interests in Dutch politics, feared Russia and was seen as untrustworthy. Prussia lacked the demographic, military, political and economic strength of the Austro-Russian alliance.[124]

In 1784 Denmark, Austria and Russia were sounded by Britain. In 1783 letters discussing the plans of Gustavus III of Sweden for an attack on Denmark and the occupation of her possession of Norway were intercepted in Hanover, one of the most successful centres for postal interception and decipherment in Europe, and, as such, a major asset for the British. In late December 1783 Carmarthen ordered Fitzherbert and Elliot to pass on the information to the Russian and Danish governments, though neither was impressed. The peaceful settlement of the Crimean crisis which Gustavus had hoped would lead to a Russo-Turkish war, and Russian pressure in June 1784, in the form of a declaration that any attack on Denmark–Norway would be resisted, both dissuaded Gustavus from acting; and Catherine did not feel it necessary to seek British support. On the other hand, Elliot helped to encourage the bloodless Danish coup of 14 April by which the government of Ove Høegh Guldberg was replaced by one dominated by Bernstorff as Crown Prince Frederick asserted his authority on coming to age; Christian VII was insane. The new government was more pro-British and replaced Christof Dreyer, the anglophobe Envoy Extraordinary in London, in response to British pressure.[125]

[124] Carmarthen to Pitt, 9, 23 June, 28 Sept., Pitt to Carmarthen, 24 June 1784, BL Eg. 3498 fols. 36–8, 56, 40; Keith to Carmarthen, 30 Apr. 1785, BL Eg. 3501 fol. 82.
[125] S. Oakley, 'Gustavus III's Plans for War with Denmark in 1783–84', in R. Hatton and Anderson (eds.), *Studies in Diplomatic History* (1970), pp. 280–5; Kageneck to Kaunitz, 8 June, 24 Sept. 1784, HHStA EK 123; Coxe to Harris, 31 Aug. 1784, Winchester, Malmesbury, 148. Barton, *Scandinavia*, pp. 129–31 is the best short introduction to the coup, though Elliot's role is not mentioned. On Dreyer, Stormont to Morton Eden, Envoy Extraordinary in Copenhagen, 22 Jan. 1782, Elliot to

An opportunity for improving relations with both Denmark and Russia was soon seemingly offered by Gustavus and his French ally. In July rumours of a treaty by which France ceded the small West Indian island of St Barthélemy to Gustavus, who was then visiting France, in return for being granted a depot for naval stores at Gothenburg circulated. On 19 July, a secret treaty between Louis XVI and Gustavus III was signed at Versailles. The French were granted a commercial position at Gothenburg and promised help if Sweden was attacked by Denmark or Russia, as well as annual subsidies; the cession of the tiny island of St Barthélemy had been agreed in March. Simolin was ordered to establish what the British response would be, and Carmarthen, who saw a threat to British maritime interests, pressed for concerted action by Britain, Denmark and Russia to demand an explanation from France and Sweden. Dorset was initially sceptical about the supposed exchange, though he subsequently felt tricked by the French; but Pitt, although he did not want Britain committed 'too far', was hopeful 'that the business of Gothenburg may perhaps be improved into a groundwork of some farther connexion with Russia and Denmark... some more comprehensive and permanent junction' with Catherine II. Carmarthen made it clear that such a system would be designed against France, that assertive British diplomacy was designed to serve a defensive purpose,

in order to establish that system in Europe, which can alone secure to this country a prospect of remaining unmolested by France, and of providing at the same time for effectual assistance in case that restless power should think proper to proceed to extremities in her attempt to throw Ireland into actual rebellion... I have already told the Russian minister that I flatter myself this measure concocted by Sweden at the instigation of France would promote the formation of the system which had so long been in contemplation, which if brought to perfection would operate so forcibly on the general system of Europe as not only to secure the tranquility of the north, but to keep within bounds any other dangerous projects of the House of Bourbon. I own I think a very small exertion of our former spirit would now be of infinite service, Russia must go through with us, and a small portion of danger to that power from the designs of Sweden (as the instrument of France) sugared over with a large quantity of well turned flattery to the Empress herself might I think produce the most beneficial consequences... I should think the measure of *at least* a Triple Alliance, though at first having only this particular object in view may produce a good effect, I mean the preventing a war with France for some time longer, and providing against one at a future period, at all events preventing her exertions being directed solely at Great Britain.[126]

Carmarthen, 24 Apr., Carmarthen to Elliot, 27 Apr. 1784, PRO FO 22/3 fol. 38, 22/6 fols. 206–8.
[126] Dorset to Carmarthen, 1, 8, 29 July, Carmarthen to Dorset, 9 July 1784, PRO FO 27/2 fols. 132, 139, 219, 148–9; Carmarthen to George III and reply, 6 July 1784, Aspinall, *George III* no. 95; Carmarthen to Pitt, 23 June, 28 Sept., Pitt to Carmarthen, 24 June,

The approach was unsuccessful, as Catherine II was unwilling to join in pressing Sweden for an explanation. Vergennes' argument that the importance of the agreement had been exaggerated was to be vindicated.[127] Catherine had already shown herself uninterested in better relations with Britain, and this discouraged the Danes. The Russian response to British approaches for an alliance in 1784 and early 1785 was evasive. Fitzherbert argued that Russia had seemed responsive while war in the Balkans threatened, but that the settlement of the Crimean crisis at the beginning of 1784 had led to a cooling in relations. The Russian government had preferred the Fox–North ministry. A more cautious Carmarthen returned in April 1785 to the idea of an approach to Denmark, though now it was not to be linked to one to Russia, but the continuation of Dano-Russian links combined with the *Fürstenbund* undercut the notion.[128]

Joseph II had also been unresponsive to British approaches, through Kageneck, Keith, and, acting initially on his own initiative, George, 3rd Earl Cowper, who lived in Florence and had met Joseph in the spring of 1784. On 7 March Cowper had written enthusiastically to Carmarthen describing a lengthy recent audience with Joseph at Pisa,

in which, besides the great distinction he showed me, [he] spoke very highly of our nation, and by what I could observe [is] very partial to us: if your Lordship should think an alliance with his Imperial Majesty could be advantageous to us, permit me to bring it about: I really believe that between myself and the Imperial Resident here, who is a great friend of mine it might be brought about, and I flatter myself that nobody could succeed in the affair better than myself; as his Imperial Majesty has on all occasions treated me with distinction.

Carmarthen's reply was encouraging,

an alliance with the Emperor would no doubt be a most desirable object, but the utmost care will be necessary to ascertain whether H. I. M. is sincerely disposed to enter into a closer connection with this country, and of course dissolve the unnatural alliance which subsists between Austria and France.

10 Sept. 1784, BL Eg. 3498, fols. 38, 40–1, 54–7; Kageneck to Kaunitz, 20 July 1784, HHStA EK 123; C. Nordmann, *Grandeur et liberté de la Suède, 1660–1792* (Paris, 1971), pp. 373–4.
[127] Fitzherbert to Keith, 10 Oct. 1784, BL Add. 35532 fols. 295–6; Vergennes to Noailles, 1 Oct. 1784, AE CP Aut. suppl. 23 fol. 29.
[128] Fitzherbert to Dorset, incomplete letter received 3 May 1784, KAO C188/1; Fitzherbert to Keith, 10 Feb. 1784, BL Add. 35531 fol. 79; Carmarthen to Keith, 2 July 1784, PRO FO 7/9; Carmarthen to Pitt, 9 June 1784, BL Eg. 3498 fol. 36; George III to Carmarthen, 6 July 1784, BL Add. 27914 fol. 3; J. W. Marcum, 'Semen R. Vorontsov: Minister to the Court of St James's for Catherine II, 1785–1796' (unpublished Ph.D., Chapel Hill, 1970), p. 57; W. Stribrny (ed.), Johann Eustach Graf von Goertz, *Mémoire sur la Russie* (Wiesbaden, 1969), p. 31; Carmarthen to Elliot, 11 Apr., Elliot to Pitt, 14 Aug. 1785, NLS 12999 fols. 54–5, 74–5.

Cowper was asked to send information on the subject, but was informed that any regular negotiation 'would of course be carried on at Vienna'. Joseph II's response to Cowper's approach was negative and the Earl's advice that the affair should not be dropped was mere whistling in the wind. The Emperor's reply was interesting both because of its range of reference – back to British conduct during the War of the Austrian Succession when Austria had been successfully pressed to cede territory to both Prussia and Sardinia – and because of his reference to the 'true fundamental political laws' that should direct international relations, an assessment that failed to pay sufficient attention to their volatility. Joseph, however, was not writing a text on the subject, simply a crisp and cutting reply whose closing remark, that it was easier to break than to repair alliances, failed to consider Austria's responsibility for the breach in friendly relations.[129]

The British ministry was disheartened by Austrian replies. In June 1785 a demoralised Keith, who criticised Kaunitz and blamed Austrian partiality to France, sought leave for a year.[130] The absence of a positive response, however, freed the government from the necessity of having to decide what they were willing to offer a prospective ally. This was a point on which George III and Pitt stressed caution more than Carmarthen, though the last had instructed Elliot in Copenhagen in June 1784 to obtain better relations 'by every means in your power short of engaging this court in difficulties which your own good sense will immediately point out to you', a very ambiguous formulation.[131]

The Scheldt crisis

The notion of waiting on developments while stressing good wishes, led Carmarthen to look to all points of the diplomatic compass. He was hopeful, for example, of tension between Austria and Spain, both allies of France, over the succession to Naples, and wrote in October 1784 to Sir William Hamilton, Envoy Extraordinary in Naples, about Austria and Spain 'the latter of which I have good reason to believe regards with an unfriendly eye every accession of influence which the former either actually has, or is likely to acquire at Naples, and which may perhaps in its consequences become interesting to the general system of Europe'.[132]

[129] Cowper to Carmarthen, 7 Mar., 5 June, Carmarthen to Cowper, 8 Apr., copie de la réponse reçue de Vienne, no date, Hertford CRO D/EP F 318, 310/90, BL Add. 28060 fols. 107–29; B. Moloney, *Florence and England: Essays on Cultural Relations in the Second Half of the Eighteenth Century* (Florence, 1969), pp. 108–9.

[130] Keith to Carmarthen, 30 Apr., 18 June 1785, BL Eg. 3501 fols. 82, 88.

[131] Pitt to Carmarthen, 24 June 1784, BL Eg. 3498; Carmarthen to Elliot, 25 June 1784, PRO FO 22/6 fol. 143.

[132] Carmarthen to Hamilton, 12 Oct. 1784, PRO FO 70/3 pp. 610–12.

This opportunistic policy appeared more likely to succeed in the second half of 1784, as a serious rift developed in the French alliance system between Austria and the United Provinces, with whom France was seeking to turn wartime alliance against Britain into a more permanent relationship. The British ministry feared, with reason, that any Franco-Dutch alliance could only be designed against British interests. The issue was the Scheldt.

At a conference held in Brussels to try to settle frontier differences, the Austrians on 4 May 1784 presented an ultimatum demanding from the Dutch not only territory, including the major fortress of Maastricht, and indemnities for supposed injustices, but also the withdrawal of the Dutch guardship on the Scheldt. The Dutch rejected the demands in May 1784, the Patriot government fearing accusations of surrendering national interests. Both parties turned to Louis XVI for help, while Frederick II urged the Dutch to stand firm. Both sides began military preparations, while the Austrians prepared to force the passage of the river with a warship.[133]

The extent to which the Dutch and Austrians sought French support was a ready measure of Britain's diplomatic insignificance, but Carmarthen was sounded in May about the opening of the Scheldt, though significantly the Austrian envoy concentrated on the likely commercial advantages for Britain, reflecting the widely held perception that British policy was dominated by mercantile considerations,

Count Kageneck has assured me it will be of the greatest advantage to this country as it will greatly expedite the transport of many considerable articles of British commerce with which a great part of Flanders and Germany are supplied, and for which a much greater demand will be made, should this scheme be carried into execution.

The British government was indeed advised that the opening of the Scheldt would probably help British trade. Carmarthen sought information from Hailes concerning the nature of Austro-French relations and the extent to which France supported the Austrian stance over the Scheldt. Hailes was also ordered to sound the Austrian envoy in Paris, Florimond, Comte de Mercy-Argenteau, in order to discover Austrian views, and

at the same time you may continue to suggest to that Minister, of what essential service England might be to His Imperial Majesty's commercial plan, if once a confidential intercourse could be established upon the subject, though at the same time France must be a stranger to that as well as to every other subject of

---

[133]   F. Magnette, *Joseph II et la liberté de l'Escaut* (Paris, 1897); Dorset to Keith, 27 July, Keith to Dorset, 18 Aug 1784, KAO C191.

mutual advantage which may be discussed between the Courts of London and Vienna.

Mercy explained the Austrian claims to Hailes, and said that no commercial treaties were envisaged. His response was friendly but offered no opening for negotiations. Hailes also reported his view that Austrian plans were not concerted with France.[134]

Initially, it did not seem likely to the British that the dispute would lead to war, and therefore it appeared to offer a painless way to improve relations with Joseph II, Kageneck being given assurances accordingly. In August, however, the crisis worsened. On the 23rd the Austrian plenipotentiary presented a fresh ultimatum, this time demanding the opening of the Scheldt, claiming that the river should be regarded as open and stating that if the Dutch committed any act on it against Joseph's flag, i.e. any ship flying the Emperor's flag, he would regard it as a declaration of war.[135]

While British tourists noted the assembling of large forces,[136] the Dutch decided to defy Joseph, so that when two Austrian ships tried to force the Scheldt in the second week of October they were seized, the first on 8 October. Joseph withdrew his envoy from The Hague and announced that an army of 60,000 men would obtain satisfaction for the outrage against his flag, which Kaunitz likened to a declaration of war.[137] French diplomatic pressure on both powers to be conciliatory was unsuccessful,[138] and with war seeming 'inevitable',[139] France prepared to come to the assistance of the United Provinces. In early November Calonne, the finance minister, told Frederick II's brother Prince Henry that France would have 60,000 troops ready within a fortnight. Dorset kept London informed of French military preparations.[140]

The crisis appeared to vindicate British attitudes and to provide a marvellous opportunity to obtain the long-sought alliance with Austria, though it also offered a hint of the forthcoming controversy over the *Fürstenbund*, for on 18 January 1785 the *Daily Universal Register* raised the conduct of George III's brother-in-law, Duke Adolf,

---

[134] Carmarthen to Keith, 11 May, Carmarthen to Hailes, 1 June, Hailes to Carmarthen, 7 June 1784, PRO FO 7/8, 27/12 fols. 88–9, 103–4; memorandum by Mr Hollier, 9 June 1784, BL Eg. 3504 fol. 12; Kageneck to Kaunitz, 2 Apr. 1784, HHStA EK 123.

[135] Hailes to Carmarthen, 6 Sept. 1784, PRO FO 27/13 fol. 23.

[136] Aylesbury, Buckinghamshire CRO D/DR/8/12/3.

[137] Kaunitz to Kageneck, 23 Oct. 1784, Ipswich CRO HA 119 T108/33.

[138] French note for Austrian government, 20 Nov., Vergennes to Noailles, 1, 28 Oct., 20 Nov. 1784, AE CP Aut. 348 fol. 225, suppl. 23 fols. 28, 31–2, 34–6.

[139] Harris to sister Gertrude, 2 Nov. 1784, Merton College Oxford, Malmesbury papers F.3.3 (a); Dorset to Fitzherbert, 21 Dec. 1784, KAO C188/1.

[140] J. Flammermont, *Les Correspondances des agents diplomatiques étrangers en France avant La Révolution* (Paris, 1896) p. 115; Dorset to Liston, 13 Dec. 1784, KAO C184.

The conduct of the Prince of Mecklenburg-Strelitz, in consenting to be subsidised by the Dutch, or rather courting them to take his battalion into their pay, has confounded our politicians. They were of opinion that England would observe a strict neutrality in case of a rupture between Holland and the Emperor; but as they conceive that the Prince would not take this step without the advice of the British Cabinet, they are afraid that England will unfortunately engage herself in the quarrel.

Such sensitivity about possible royal connections was without resonance in the Scheldt crisis, for George III did not take a distinct role.[141] In April 1784 Carmarthen had seen developments in the Low Countries as both threatening and a possible occasion for reconciliation with Austria. He had written then of the projected Franco-Dutch treaty,

The Barrier Towns dismantled and the French nation masters of the councils as well as of the marine of Holland surely call upon the Court of Vienna to avow its sentiments upon the subject.[142]

The Scheldt crisis apparently focused the issue to an extent that the treaty did not. Franco-Prussian support for the Dutch offered the prospect of the dissolution of the Austro-French alliance, and this was not just British wishful thinking, for Vergennes was of the same opinion.[143] Indeed the crisis was to have a serious long-term impact on Franco-Austrian relations, producing a situation in which Joseph II wanted Vergennes replaced. Britain had the opportunity of seeing French influence in the Low Countries challenged by a German army, prefiguring the British-encouraged Prussian invasion of the United Provinces in 1787. There was also the hope that the crisis could harm Franco-Dutch relations. As in 1787, however, it was unclear what Britain should do beyond encouraging the German power to act. This was precisely what Carmarthen sought to do by making it clear that Britain supported the opening of the Scheldt and by responding coolly to a French approach for diplomatic support for the Dutch, a policy that was approved by Pitt. With a, for him, characteristic allusion, Harris, then the most experienced member of the British diplomatic corps, wrote to his sister, 'I advise and my advice is listened to, the playing the back game and by keeping back we certainly shall win the rubber.' Dorset struck a similar note, writing from Paris to Nathaniel Wraxall, a Pittite MP with whom he conducted an unbuttoned correspondence,

---

[141] Hailes to Carmarthen, 25 Nov. 1784, BL Eg. 3499 fol. 64.
[142] Carmarthen to Keith, 23 Apr. 1784, PRO FO 7/8.
[143] Vergennes to Noailles, 20 Nov. 1784, AE CP Aut. suppl. 23 fol. 35; Mercy to Kaunitz, 27 Nov. 1784, Alfred von Arneth and J. Flammermont (eds.), *Correspondance secrète du Comte Mercy-Argenteau avec l'Empereur Joseph et le Prince de Kaunitz* (2 vols., Paris, 1889–91) I, 341; George III to Carmarthen, 5 Dec. 1784, Aspinall, *George III* no. 154.

I can send you no *positive* news from hence as to peace or war, the latter is to be hoped will be the case and if we can keep out of the scrape which I am confident our ministers can easily do we shall have fine cards to play. The Emperor is a fine obstinate fellow. By all accounts he will persevere. His honour seems to be so deeply engaged that I don't see any chance of his being bought off. Vergennes is confoundedly embarrassed and devilishly vexed at our *affected* neutrality. We owe him a good grudge for the American war.[144]

The last was a frequently made comment in British correspondence of the period. It was clear throughout Europe that Britain took the Austrian side in the dispute, and Hailes encouraged his Austrian counterpart Thugut accordingly. Vergennes complained that Carmarthen was uncommunicative when approached by Barthélemy.[145] It was equally unclear what the British were prepared to do, bar seek to exploit Austro-French differences. Germain noted 'our court is too wise to be drawn into another war for the sake of either party'.[146] At a time of military preparations on the Continent, this understandable caution did not make Britain an attractive ally in the event of any confrontation or war. The notion that, in the shape of George III's negotiations for the *Fürstenbund*, 'a time-bomb had been ticking away under British plans for an Austrian alliance for many months and was about to explode',[147] has to be supplemented by the realisation that a more serious bar than Hanoverian interests, as advanced by George III, challenged any such alliance. As in 1714–31, the British ministry did not wish to appreciate the consequences of Austrian dynamism. Joseph II was unwilling to confine himself to past roles, whether within his dominions, including the Austrian Netherlands, in the Empire or in the world of European diplomacy. In 1783 Shelburne acclaimed Joseph as a monarch who would 'secure the happiness of his own subjects and command the admiration of the whole world',[148] but the Emperor sought to do neither on terms laid down by others. His wilfulness could be criticised by those who sought, at least in

---

[144] Carmarthen to Pitt, 8 Nov., Pitt to Carmarthen, 9 Nov., Hailes to Carmarthen, 28 Oct., 25 Nov. 1784, BL Eg. 3498, fols. 72, 74, 3499 fols. 45, 64; Carmarthen to Keith, 8 Nov., Carmarthen to Dorset, 3 Dec. 1784, PRO FO 7/9, 27/13 fol. 222; Harris to Gertrude, 12 Nov. 1784, Merton F. 3.3 (a); Dorset to Wraxall, 10 Dec. 1784, Beinecke, Osborn Files, Dorset; Kageneck to Kaunitz, 29 Nov. 1784, HHStA EK 123; Magnette, *L'Escaut*, pp. 203–7.

[145] Hailes to Carmarthen, 18 Nov. 1784, BL Eg. 3499 fol. 62; Vaucher (ed.), *Recueil*, p. 529; Harris to Keith, 14 Dec. 1784, Winchester, Malmesbury vol. 204 p. 3; Noailles to Vergennes, 22 Jan. 1785, AE CP Aut. 349 fols. 73–4; Trevor to Carmarthen, 29 Jan. 1785, PRO FO 67/4 p. 636.

[146] Carmarthen to Dorset, 6 Nov., 3 Dec., Dorset to Carmarthen, 9 Dec. 1784, PRO FO 27/13 fols. 161, 222, 226; Dorset to Keith, 6 Dec., Dorset to Fitzherbert, 21 Dec. 1784, Germain to Dorset, 11 May 1785, KAO C191, 188/1, 192; Dorset to Gower, 3 Feb. 1785, PRO 30/29/1/15 no. 48.   [147] Blanning, '*Fürstenbund* of 1785', 320.

[148] Shelburne to Keith, 10 Nov. 1783, BL Add. 35530 fol. 167.

Europe, to work on the basis of stability, but Joseph responded to the mixture of opportunity, opportunism and anxiety that characterised the volatile international system of the period and helped to make it more volatile.

It was understandable that Britain, a power that did not seek European territorial gains, should not respond in a similar fashion, but that helped to make her a less attractive ally. If in 1784, as in 1781, she was willing to consider changes over the Scheldt, that was only a minor alteration, and, more seriously, there was little sign that Britain would act to achieve even such a minor change, let alone anything more. In August 1785 Pitt informed Charles, 4th Duke of Rutland, with whom he had close links, that Britain needed five years peace, and would be best served by not getting involved in continental affairs. It has been argued that British policy in this period was not that of support for the status quo and that the British government was ready to make 'commitments to adventurous allies'. Zartz, however, does not produce evidence to support his thesis. Britain was not, as during her subsequent war with France, in a desperate situation that obliged her to accept the undesirable views of allies, and in 1784–6 George III and Pitt were convinced of the need to do nothing for the sake of gaining allies that would compromise the peacetime recovery of governmental strength and economic power that they sought.[149] Carmarthen might be willing to encourage Austria in late 1784, but he could offer no prospect of assistance in any confrontation. This problem over means was more important than the clear anti-French goal of British policy, and was to emerge on a number of occasions over the following decade. It helped to explain why, irrespective of George III's Hanoverian policy, there was little that the British ministry could do to develop an alliance system in 1785. The controversy over the *Fürstenbund* disguised this fundamental weakness.

The Bavarian Exchange Scheme and the *Fürstenbund*

In this age of perpetual vicissitude there is no answering for futurity. Keith, March 1785.[150]

The Scheldt crisis was to be complicated and superseded by the revival of the Bavarian exchange scheme, although the extent to which

---

[149] *Correspondence between the Right Honble. William Pitt and Charles Duke of Rutland ... 1781–1787* (1890), pp. 111–12; F. Zartz, 'The "Pole-Carew Memorandum" in the Context of British Policy towards Russia in the 1780s', *Study Group on Eighteenth-Century Russian Newsletter*, 10 (1982), 15, 17; C. J. Fedorak, 'In Search of a Necessary Ally: Addington, Hawkesbury, and Russia, 1801–1804', *International History Review*, 13 (1991), 245; George III to Pitt, 24 Jan. 1786, Aspinall, *George III* no. 274.

[150] Keith to Frances Murray, 30 Mar. 1785, HL HM. 18940 p. 313.

perspectives on the international relations of the period can vary is suggested by the limited attention devoted to that scheme in one important recent study.[151] The idea that the Bavarian branch of the Wittelsbach family should exchange Bavaria for territories elsewhere had played a major role in negotiations over the Spanish Succession, to which they had a claim, in 1698–1712. The Spanish Netherlands, of which Elector Max Emmanuel of Bavaria had become Lieutenant Governor and Captain General in 1691, Naples, Sicily, Lombardy and the island of Sardinia had all been seriously considered as Bavarian gains, sometimes in return for the Habsburg acquisition of Bavaria.[152] The issue was revived in 1764, when Kaunitz discussed the possibility of Austria gaining Bavaria by means of an exchange, and, more seriously in 1776–7 when Karl Theodor of the Palatinate negotiated with Austria in order to further an exchange of Bavaria and the Austrian Netherlands. Kaunitz and, though less consistently, Joseph II felt that the respective revenues of the dominions made such an exchange disadvantageous for Austria, and it was anyway subordinated to the more immediate crisis that led to the War of the Bavarian Succession.[153]

Though Count Rumyantsev, Russian envoy to the Empire, raised the project when he first met Joseph II in May 1782, seeking unsuccessfully to press Joseph to win the indebted Duke of Zweibrücken, heir to Bavaria, with money,[154] it was not until 1784 that it was pushed actively again. Rumyantsev was sent to Zweibrücken that autumn to win the Duke over to the exchange scheme, while in November Joseph sought the support of Zweibrücken's principal ally, Louis XVI, because he wanted Louis to press the Duke and Karl Theodor. Joseph informed Louis, whom he also sought to influence through his sister Marie Antoinette, that he would accept a French plan for a settlement of the Scheldt dispute if the Bavarian exchange scheme went through. After an initially promising response in the French Council of State on 1 December 1784, the final decision taken on 2 January 1785 was negative. All the ministers bar Vergennes opposed the scheme, arguing that a rise in Austrian power would lead to a relative fall in that of France.[155] Indeed, their arguments were a reminder of the fragility of the Austro-French connection, and thus, to a certain extent, a vindication of British hopes that it would collapse. It has been argued that Vergennes, who did

[151] Murphy, *Vergennes*.
[152] D. A. Gaeddert, 'The Franco-Bavarian Alliance during the War of the Spanish Succession' (unpublished Ph.D., Ohio State, 1969).
[153] Beales, *Joseph II*, I, 389–92, 397, 413.
[154] Aretin, 'Russia as a Guarantor Power', 148.
[155] Memoranda of 2 Jan. 1785, AE CP Aut. 349 fols. 6, 11, 21, 24.

not enjoy the support of Joseph II, was playing a double game,[156] though he informed Noailles, who was very opposed to the scheme, that he thought the objections were balanced by the advantages.[157] On 6 January Louis XVI wrote to inform Joseph II that the exchange could not take place without Prussian consent, thus wrecking it unless, as seemed most unlikely, Joseph made concessions to Frederick II in order to obtain it. This echoed French policy in the early 1750s towards the Imperial Election Scheme in which Vergennes and Frederick had been active in thwarting British support for Austrian pretensions, in this case on behalf of the young Joseph. The Duke of Zweibrücken appealed for Prussian help on 3 January 1785, and, in response to Louis XVI's letter of the 6th, Joseph II wrote on the 19th that he would abandon the scheme.[158] Prussian consent was not simply a spoiling device, because France did not wish to become involved in another continental war, a second war of the Bavarian Succession; though it was unlikely that Frederick, who had suffered badly in the Seven Years War, would choose to challenge France, Austria and Russia again.

The British were not formally notified of the scheme by Austria, though Kaunitz subsequently claimed that Britain would have been consulted had the first obstacle of Zweibrücken approval been sur-mounted.[159] The British response developed slowly. On 25 January 1785 Harris wrote to Carmarthen to suggest that all would depend on whether a new ruler of the Austrian Netherlands would be pro-British or pro-French, but by 1 February he had changed his tone. Reports that Joseph had reserved Luxemburg and Namur for France suggested that France would dominate the new state and gain 'the key of Germany'. Harris referred directly to 'acquisitions which were the great objects of the ambition of Louis the Fourteenth'.[160] Whereas in January 1784 it had seemed to Torrington, in another echo of an earlier age, that Austria should take more care to defend Luxemburg against a surprise French attack, than it had been doing, now the Austrians seemed to be inspiring a wholesale revolution in the Low Countries. Kageneck gave 'some reason to suspect France may have been consulted at least, if not concerned in the transaction', but, to Carmarthen's anger, the Austrians

---

[156] P. P. Bernard, *Joseph II and Bavaria: two eighteenth century attempts at German unification* (The Hague, 1965), p. 203; Blanning, '*Fürstenbund* of 1785', p. 324 fn. 65; Hardman, *Louis XVI*, pp. 98–9.

[157] Vergennes to Noailles, 4 Jan., Noailles to Vergennes, 17 Jan. 1785, AE CP Aut. 349 fols. 33, 52–7.

[158] Vergennes to Noailles, 4, 6 Jan. 1785, AE CP Aut. 349 fols. 33, 35; Bernard, *Joseph*, p. 158.

[159] Kaunitz to Count Reviczky, Kageneck's replacement, 3 Apr. 1786, HHStA, EK 129.

[160] 3rd Earl of Malmesbury (ed.), *Diaries and Correspondence of James Harris, First Earl of Malmesbury* (4 vols., 1844), II, 96, 100.

made no attempt to clarify the matter. The Bavarian government denied that an exchange would take place. Carmarthen feared that the exchange would lead to France gaining the Austrian Netherlands with the Elector of Bavaria receiving Alsace and Lorraine.[161]

The Austrian failure to keep the British ministry informed led to disproportionate importance being attached to the reports from Joseph Ewart, who, in the absence on leave of Sir John Stepney, the envoy, was representing Britain at Berlin. These reports reflected the Prussian conviction that France was supporting the exchange scheme, and this led the British government to decide to approach Prussia in May. Convinced of 'the concert of measures between the courts of Vienna and Versailles and their plan of extending their views and interests by every possible means', Carmarthen instructed Ewart on the need for 'a great and more comprehensive system' which would 'contribute in the most essential degree to the maintaining the interests of both on the most secure and dignified footing against any encroachments liable to affect them'. Carmarthen pressed for joint Anglo-Prussian efforts to free the United Provinces from French influence, but also emphasised the need not to commit Britain until there were good grounds to believe Frederick favourable. He wrote to Richmond of his hope that the approach would lay 'the ground work of some real and permanent system of defence against the dangerous views of the respective rivals of England and Prussia now so apparently and so closely connected'. As, however, it was planned to support Prussian efforts at St Petersburg to weaken Austro-Russian links, it is clear that this initiative was aimed against Austria and France, but not Russia.[162]

The Prussian reply offered no support over the United Provinces, but far from abandoning 'their half-hearted flirtation with Prussia', as has been suggested, a pleased British ministry decided to respond to Frederick's willingness for a confidential communication by sending back Stepney. At the same time, the government responded positively to a suggestion by Simolin's successor, Count Vorontsov, that Catherine II should be asked to improve Anglo-Austrian relations. It was decided to 'apply for the intercession of the Empress at Vienna', while also warning that failure would lead Britain to turn to 'other quarters', i.e. Prussia. On

[161] Torrington to Keith, 21 Jan. 1784, BL Add. 35531 fol. 35; Carmarthen to Keith, 4 Feb., 7 Mar., 8 Apr., 15 July, Keith to Carmarthen, 19 Feb., Fraser to Joseph Ewart, in charge of British affairs in Berlin, 15 Feb. 1785, PRO FO 7/10–11, 64/7; Vieregg, Bavarian Foreign Minister, to Fossey, chargé in London, 27 Feb. 1785, Munich, London 261; Carmarthen to Richmond, 20 May 1785, BL Eg. 3498 fol. 219.
[162] Fraser to Ewart, 13 May, Carmarthen to Ewart, 14 May 1785, PRO FO 64/7; Pitt to Carmarthen, 15 May, Carmarthen to Richmond, 20 May, Richmond to Carmarthen, 24 May 1785, BL Eg. 3498 fols. 116–17, 219, 221.

5 July Carmarthen, Pitt, Harris, then on leave in London, and Vorontsov agreed over dinner at Carmarthen's that both Britain and Russia wanted an alliance but that Austria was a stumbling block.[163]

Vorontsov had also made it clear that there was another related stumbling block, Hanover. News of the Bavarian exchange scheme had brought new urgency to proposals that had been circulating in the early 1780s for a *Fürstenbund* (league of German rulers) designed to support imperial institutions against, in particular, the assertive imperial policies of Joseph II. It was a measure of the suspicion aroused by Joseph that the rulers, who had traditionally supported the Emperor or been wary of opposing him, and had thus tended to isolate Frederick II within the Empire, were willing publicly to form a league against him. Many of the ecclesiastical princes were also unhappy about Joseph's attitude to the church and his moves against foreign ecclesiastical influences in Austria, and suspected him of being willing to support secularization. The *Fürstenbund* that was created in 1785 was more powerful than the last major league unrelated to external sponsorship, the Wittelsbach *Hausunion* (Family alliance) of the 1720s, and it represented a revival of the alliance of 1719–26 between George I of Britain–Hanover and Frederick William I of Prussia that had opposed the apparent determination of Charles VI to increase imperial authority in the Empire.

Relations between Austria and Hanover had deteriorated in the 1770s and this was reported in the British press, one newspaper declaring in 1774 that the Austrian envoy expressed himself to this effect: 'If the King of Great Britain avowed the language lately held by his Electoral minister, he must expect the Emperor to oppose him in every step he took in the Empire.' The Electoral government opposed what it saw as Joseph II's dictatorial attitude in the Empire, while Joseph was angered by Hanoverian independence. In 1774 the Austrian envoy in London threatened to suspend all good relations with Hanover, while in Vienna they were regarded as broken. The Hanoverian minister attached to George III in London, Johann Friedrich Carl von Alvensleben, declared that Joseph was the chief, but not the master of the Empire. Antagonism between Joseph and Elector George led the latter towards Frederick II, and it is not surprising that during the War of the Bavarian Succession the Elector adopted a pro-Prussian position, to the anger of British diplomats, such as Keith, who feared that this policy was needlessly irritating to Joseph. This policy was reversed in 1780, and both Britain

---

[163] Blanning, '*Fürstenbund* of 1785', p. 331; Carmarthen to Ewart, 17 June 1785, PRO FO 64/7; Carmarthen to George III and reply, both 16 June 1785, Aspinall, *George III* no. 219 and fn. 3; Pitt to Carmarthen, 25–8 June 1785, BL Eg. 3498 fol. 118; Marcum, 'Vorontsov'.

and Hanover refused to help Frederick II block Max Franz's election to the coadjutorships of Cologne and Münster, but by 1781 concern about Joseph's policies in the Empire had pushed Hanover back towards Prussia. In March 1784 Kaunitz referred to close co-operation between Hanover and Prussia, but he was also hopeful that disillusionment would make it possible to woo Hanover via Alvensleben.[164] Many of the themes of Anglo-Austrian relations in 1784–5 had, therefore, already been clearly enunciated in the previous decade: the British government's hope that incompatible French and Austrian interests would drive the two powers apart and lead Joseph II to turn to Britain, combined with Hanoverian hostility to imperial pretensions and a consequent closeness to Prussia that bred Austrian distrust of Hanover *and* Britain.

The policies of both Britain and Hanover were to be affected both by the views and policies of the other, and by those attributed to them. It could be suggested that there was already a dangerous failure of communication between kingdom and electorate in the late 1770s, one for which George III was responsible, and that was to have serious results in 1785. There was also, however, a genuine problem in combining Hanoverian policy, and, in particular, the need to respond to specific issues and initiatives by other German states, with the British aspiration for better relations with Austria. It was too easy for British diplomats and ministers who sought the latter and believed that it was in Austria's interest, to blame their failure on Hanover.

In 1784 Hanover and Prussia, the two leading German Protestant powers, began to move closer together, though George III and his Hanoverian ministers were suspicious about Prussian intentions. News of the Bavarian Exchange scheme led to a renewal of the Prussian advance on George III, through Spiridion, Count Lusi, Prussian Minister Plenipotentiary in London, the Hanoverian ministry, and Frederick, Duke of York, then in Hanover, who was approached by Frederick through the Duke of Brunswick, the same route that Frederick

---

[164] M. Naumann, *Österreich, England und Das Reich* (Berlin, 1936); M. Hughes, *Law and Politics in Eighteenth Century Germany. The Imperial Aulic Council in the Reign of Charles VI* (Woodbridge, 1988); *Westminster Journal* 3, 17 Sept., 1 Oct. 1774; Haslang, Wittelsbach envoy in London, to Beckers, Palatine Foreign Minister, 14 June, 19 Aug. 1774, Beckers to Haslang, 10 Dec. 1774, Ritter, envoy in Vienna, to Beckers, 27 Apr., 3, 24, 31 Aug., 7 Sept., 5, 26 Oct. 1774, Munich, London 252, Wien 702; Beales, *Joseph II* I, 276, 304, 396; Elliot to Keith, 11 Aug. 1778, Joseph Yorke, envoy at The Hague, to Keith, 9 Oct. 1778, Keith to Stormont, 4 Dec. 1779, BL Add. 35514 fol. 242, 35515 fol. 154, 35517 fol. 311; Kaunitz to Kageneck, 9 Mar., 13 Nov. 1784, HHStA EK 129. There are introductions to Hanoverian policy in S. Conrady, 'Die Wirksamkeit König Georgs III für die hannoverschen kurlande', *Niedersächsisches Jahrbuch für Landesgeschichte*, 39 (1969), 150–91; V. Press, 'Kurhannover im System des alten Reiches 1692–1803' in A. Birke and K. Kluxen (eds.), *England und Hannover* (Munich, 1986), pp. 53–79.

had used forty years earlier when opening negotiations for an alliance with George II. York, George III's favourite son and, as Prince-Bishop of Osnabrück, resident in Germany since 1781, was tangible proof of George's growing personal commitment to Hanover. He added to his letter conveying Frederick's memorandum a statement that would alarm George more directly than the Bavarian exchange, namely that Max Franz was seeking the coadjutorships of Paderborn and Hildesheim.[165] Held by previous pluralist Archbishop-Electors of Cologne, these had not been too serious a threat for Hanover, as Cologne was not a major military power, but Habsburg control would be a different matter. The frontier of Hildesheim was within a few miles of the city of Hanover and the prince-bishopric helped to separate it from the southern portion of the Electorate. Whereas in 1761 a newly acceded George, who gloried 'in the name of Britain', had abandoned his grandfather George II's attempt to acquire Hildesheim, in May 1784 Alvensleben told Lusi that George III would try to block any Habsburg attempt to add the sees to Max Franz's portfolio.[166] In 1785 Frederick was to help block Max Franz's election to the coadjutorship of Hildesheim.

The Electorate of Hanover was militarily vulnerable. Its army was small and it lacked major fortifications or readily defensible frontiers. In 1762 the Hanoverian minister Baron Behr had suggested to the Wittelsbach Envoy Extraordinary, Joseph, Count Haslang, that a German league, of at least the leading Electors, should be formed, so that the participants were not always at risk of being invaded on the slightest pretext.[167] Nothing had been done, and the peaceful nature of the Empire in 1763–77 had helped to keep Hanoverian concerns away from the forefront of George III's attention; though there had been anxiety in 1772–3 that if Britain sought, as the French Foreign Minister D'Aiguillon and, to a lesser extent, George wanted, to oppose the partitioning powers, Prussia would invade Hanover. Defiance of either Austria or Prussia without the active assistance of the other was not credible.

George III responded rapidly to Prussian approaches in early 1785,[168]

---

[165] York to George III, 28 Feb. 1785, Aspinall, *George III* no. 178.

[166] J. Black, 'The Crown, Hanover and the Shift in British Foreign Policy in the 1760s', in Black (ed.), *Knights Errant and True Englishmen. British Foreign Policy 1660–1800* (Edinburgh, 1989), pp. 121, 125; Blanning, '*Fürstenbund* of 1785', 323. On Britain, not Briton, see J. Brooke, *King George III* (1972), pp. 390–1. Brooke was not sure why the change came about, but as the colloquial pronunciation was Britun, so in terms of sound there would have been no distinction between the two literate spellings.

[167] Haslang to the Palatine and Bavarian Foreign Ministers, Counts Wachtendonck and Preysing, 7 Sept. 1762, Munich, London 239.

[168] Draft in George III's hand, RA 6071. The dates at the top were written by former archivists. Misfiled in accordance with one of these, 18 Aug. 1785. In fact an answer to Frederick II's memorandum of 19 February 1785 sent to York and forwarded by him

more so than his Hanoverian ministers, who had to be pushed on by George and the Duke of York. This contrast was hardly new; indeed the tendency in British public debate and, though to a lesser extent, among British ministers, to treat Hanover as a unit motivated by clear Hanoverian concerns was generally inaccurate. Throughout the century, there were major differences of opinion within Hanoverian governmental circles, especially over relations towards Austria and Prussia, and over the extent to which Hanover should take an assertive, indeed forceful, line in international relations. In general, George I and George II supported a more forceful line than their ministers in Hanover, and in 1785 George III adopted the same approach. As a result, negotiations were pressed on, so that at Berlin on 23 July 1785 representatives of Prussia, Hanover and Saxony signed a treaty.[169] They agreed to the preservation of the imperial system as currently constituted, to co-operation at the Diet and to opposition to the Bavarian exchange and any similar future projects. The resulting *Fürstenbund* or League of Princes grew rapidly in the following months. An interesting contrast therefore appears between George III's bold stance as Elector and his cautious response as King, in 1784 and subsequently, to ministerial suggestions about alliances and commitments. A degree of speculation about George's views is necessary in light of the patchy nature of the surviving evidence, but he appears to have responded as Elector in 1785 to an immediate challenge that was more threatening than any that had yet faced Britain on the Continent.

The *Fürstenbund* was negotiated in the face of bitter Russian and Austrian protests. Both Joseph II and Catherine II claimed that the Bavarian Exchange had been dropped already, which was substantially true,[170] and argued that the *Fürstenbund* would be an unfriendly step. Catherine saw it as designed to stop her from supporting Joseph within the Empire and was so angry that she talked of war with him against Prussia.[171] Prior to the signature of the treaty, the British government argued that it was a justifiable step, Carmarthen telling Kageneck on 26 May, 'that I made no doubt His Majesty, in His Electoral Capacity, would ever prove himself a zealous assertor of the liberties and rights of

to George III on 28 February, Aspinall, *George III* no. 178. This is the document mentioned by Blanning '*Fürstenbund* of 1785', fn 71, though he suggests it was written by York.

[169] U. Dann, *Hannover und England 1740–1760. Diplomatie und Selbsterhaltung* (Hildesheim, 1986). The best short guide to the negotiations leading to the *Fürstenbund* is provided by Blanning's excellent article, pp. 321–6.

[170] Hallberg, Bavarian envoy in Vienna, to Seinsheim, Bavarian minister, 15 June 1785, Munich, Wien 724, but see Noailles to Vergennes, 22 June 1785, AE CP Aut. 349 fol. 380.   [171] Aretin, 'Russia as a Guarantor Power', p. 151.

the Empire; and that, if there was a design of infringing them, I thought no measures of a defensive nature, in favour of them, could give offence anywhere'.[172] Later British ministerial criticisms of the *Fürstenbund* have to be viewed in the light of their earlier comments, though instructions can scarcely be seen as private letters. On 7 June 1785 Carmarthen, who had expressed his irritation over Austrian policy two months earlier, informed Keith that 'the courts of Vienna and Versailles appear as intimately connected as ever'. He added that the Bavarian Exchange 'as far as the Netherlands are concerned, cannot be an object of indifference to England'. Keith was told that he could let Kaunitz know unofficially that better relations with Prussia were a natural response to Austrian coolness towards Britain. Fraser sent Keith a private letter clearly directed against Joseph on the same day,

these strange disjointed times. Where there is no system, but that of striving to ... overreach. Surely things must mend, and we shall again see a right understanding in those who ought to form a balance for the preservation of mankind, and not for the destruction of those they are born to protect and render happy, merely for the purpose of gratifying their own ambition.

Ten days later, Carmarthen informed Ewart that

the friendly manner in which His Prussian Majesty appears to have received the proposals made from hence of a more friendly communication between the two courts, upon the subject of their mutual interests had given the king great satisfaction ... The very idea of the German League appears already to have made a considerable degree of impression upon several of the principal courts of Europe and I trust it may, in the event, be productive of the most beneficial consequences to this country in particular, as well as to the more immediate concerns of the Empire.[173]

Thus, prior to the Austrian and Russian complaints, the British ministry were prepared to defend what they knew of the *Fürstenbund*, though the limited nature of their knowledge was to be an important issue. It was Russian, rather than Austrian, complaints that aroused disquiet, as did the sense that, far from forcing Austria to adopt a more acceptable position, George III's policy had restricted British options. Complaints were made in London, St Petersburg and Vienna.[174] Vorontsov pressed

[172] Minute of conversation with Kageneck, 26 May 1785, PRO FO 7/10; Kageneck to Kaunitz, 31 May 1785, HHStA EK 124.
[173] Carmarthen to Keith, 12 Apr., 7 June 1785, BL Eg. 3501 fol. 80, PRO FO 7/10; Fraser to Keith, 7 June 1785, BL Add. 35534 fol. 208; Carmarthen to Ewart, 17 June 1785, PRO FO 64/7. On Austro-French closeness, Fitzherbert to Carmarthen, 4 June 1785, BL Eg. 3500 fol. 7.
[174] Fitzherbert to Keith, 2 Aug., Harris to Keith, 9 Aug. 1785, BL Add. 35535 fols. 31, 51–2; Carmarthen to Keith, 16 Sept. 1785, PRO FO 7/11; Fitzherbert to Carmarthen, 14 Oct. 1785, BL Eg. 3500 fol. 12; Eden to Sheffield, 29 Nov. 1785, BL Add. 45728 fol.

Carmarthen, Pitt, Thurlow and Sydney to prevent the ratification of the treaty; Fitzherbert was told that it would harm Anglo-Russian relations. The Danish envoy also proved unwilling to accept Carmarthen's distinction between British and Hanoverian policy. George III replied robustly to Vorontsov's pressure on his British ministers, arguing that the *Fürstenbund*, a defensive league, could give no umbrage if no one had views contrary to the Imperial constitution. Vorontsov was told on 18 August that George sought good Anglo-Russian relations and that the *Fürstenbund* involved George solely as Elector and was only a defensive association. Pitt suggested, if possible, supporting Russian views over Danzig.[175]

Carmarthen was to be very bitter at George and Hanover's expense, blaming the *Fürstenbund* for the failure of his hopes of better relations with Austria and Russia. He criticised the failure to keep him informed and the danger of Britain becoming 'involved in a German quarrel', for example over Danzig, 'with no other ally but the King of Prussia and his connections, or... obliged to unite with the House of Bourbon'. Carmarthen also expressed his distrust of Frederick II. It is clear, however, that more than the *Fürstenbund* lay between Britain and an anti-French alliance system. Harris was correct to focus attention on Joseph II and Catherine II rather than George III.[176] Conscious of Anglo-French antipathy, Joseph and Kaunitz regarded the prospect of a British alliance with disfavour. The French refusal to support the Bavarian Exchange Scheme, and indeed their sympathy for the *Fürstenbund*, did not wreck the Austro-French connection, although it was already devoid of much positive content. Nevertheless, Britain appeared an unattractive ally. Kageneck had reported in February 1785 that domestic problems would prevent Britain from taking an active part in a continental war. Kaunitz was to argue in February 1787 that only practical help, not protestations of good intentions, could restore an Anglo-Austrian alliance.[177]

66; Carmarthen to Pitt, 26 Dec. 1785, PRO 30/8/151 fol. 32; J. W. Marcum, 'Vorontsov and Pitt: The Russian Assessment of a British Statesman, 1785–1792', *Rocky Mountain Social Science Journal*, 10 (1973), 50 and 'Vorontsov', pp. 61–7.

[175] Carmarthen to Vorontsov, 5, 7 Aug., Vorontsov to Carmarthen, 6 Aug., Thurlow to Carmarthen and reply, both 5 Aug., Sydney to Carmarthen and reply, both 6 Aug., Pitt to Carmarthen, 8 Aug. 1785, BL Eg. 3504 fols. 83–7, 3498 fols. 243–5, 209–12, 122; George III to Pitt, 7, 10 Aug. 1785, PRO 30/8/103 fols. 172, 178; Memorandum by George III, 18 Aug. 1785, RA 6070; Pitt to Carmarthen, 15 Sept. 1785, BL Eg. 3498 fol. 130.

[176] Carmarthen to Thurlow, 5 Aug., Carmarthen to Sydney, 6 Aug. 1785, BL Eg. 3498 fols. 245–6, 211–12; Harris to Keith, 9 Aug. 1785, *Malmesbury*, II, 204.

[177] Joseph II to Mercy, 29 Sept. 1785, *Mercy*, I, 455; Kaunitz to Joseph, 28 Sept. 1785, Beer (ed.), *Joseph, Leopold, Kaunitz*, p. 224; Vergennes to Noailles, 27 May 1785, AE

Despite Carmarthen's hopes for an Austro-Dutch conflict, and the military moves that left routes taken by British tourists, such as that from Verviers to Aachen, crowded,[178] Joseph did not in the autumn of 1785 press his still rumbling dispute with the United Provinces over Maastricht to the point of conflict, and thus did not precipitate a crisis in Austro-French relations. In St Petersburg, Russian complaints, which had more force because, in the absence of a Hanoverian envoy, Fitzherbert had to represent the Electorate,[179] were countered by a British proposal for an Anglo-Austro-Russian alliance. The Russian Vice-Chancellor, Count Osterman, was told that it was only diplomatic isolation that had led George towards Prussia.[180] Joseph II, however, was opposed to this proposal. In August, Fitzherbert attributed British difficulties at St Petersburg to Austria, not the *Fürstenbund*, which, he wrote, Catherine saw correctly as a defensive measure. At the end of the year, however, Fitzherbert reported,

The business wore at first a pretty favourable appearance, but it was speedily nipped in the bud by the conclusion of the Germanic League, in consequence of which this court declared that by entering into this measure His Majesty had ipso facto destroyed all possibility of a connection between himself and the Emperor. The reasoning of the Russian Ministers upon this subject is in brief as follows – admitting the government of Great Britain and of the Electorate of Hanover to be entirely distinct and disparate from each other as to all internal affairs, yet the system of the two countries in regard to foreign, and more especially to German politics must necessarily be one and the same, and therefore though the Germanic League has been subscribed to by Hanover only, the principles of it are to be considered as having been adopted equally by both. Now (add they) we have the strongest reason to be persuaded that whatever may be the ostensible purport of this confederacy, it is in fact levelled directly against the Emperor as head of the House of Austria, and calculated to lessen his weight in the scale of Germany, and to augment in the same proportion that of his rival and enemy the King of Prussia. Consequently then it would be the heights of imprudence in the former of these monarchs was he at this time to listen to the proposals made by Great Britain for the formation of a system of alliance; neither can any such proposals … be listened to by this court, connected as it is with that of Vienna.[181]

The *Fürstenbund* led Elliot, then in London, to desist from presenting Pitt with a memorandum on foreign policy, for, as he explained to the minister,

CP Aut. suppl. 23 fols. 85–6; Kageneck to Kaunitz, 1 Feb. 1785, Kaunitz to Reviczky, 15 Feb. 1787, HHStA EK 124, 126.

[178] Diary of William Bennet, 13 July 1785, Bod. MS. Eng. Misc. f. 54 fol. 31.

[179] Ewart to Fraser, 2 Aug. 1785, PRO FO 64/8.

[180] Aretin, 'Russia as a Guarantor Power', p. 150. Aretin confuses Fitzherbert and Carmarthen.

[181] Fitzherbert to Keith, 2 Aug., 8 Dec. 1785, BL Add. 35535 fols. 31, 33, 292.

The die is cast; and I consider every return to the Imperial Courts as impossible, except the King of England shall be prevailed upon to break the treaty so lately signed by the Elector of Hanover. Were such a measure practicable without throwing the interior government of this country into confusion I doubt whether even it would have its full effect abroad. The personal inclinations of the King are now too strongly marked not to create distrust in foreigners of the stability of a contrary system.[182]

The search for a continental ally, 1785–1786

Hanoverian participation in the *Fürstenbund* was criticised by British ministers and diplomats, and by knowledgeable politicians in opposition or not in office, such as Fox, Stormont and Shelburne; and it also led to an upsurge in press criticism of specific aspects of the Hanoverian connection, such as the education of royal princes at Göttingen, the patronage of German plays, music and army officers and the 'Germanic' habit of excluding the public from royal gardens. Such criticism was a warning of the possible sensitivity of unpopular royal moves in the field of international relations. More seriously, moves against British trade by both Catherine II and Joseph II were blamed on the *Fürstenbund* and there was call for 'redress ... the people have no remedy but in themselves'.[183]

The formation of the *Fürstenbund* helped to encourage the British approach to Frederick II, which had already been taking shape prior to the negotiation of the League. In early May 1785 Harris had pressed the Cabinet to make such an approach, and later that month his dispatch to Berlin was planned.[184] In fact, it was Stepney who set off for Berlin at the start of July, but, ill, depressed, worried about his finances and sceptical about the chances of gaining Frederick II's diplomatic support, he abandoned his mission at Harwich.[185] John, Viscount Dalrymple, later 6th Earl of Stair, replaced him. Dalrymple, an officer who had served in the War of American Independence, was a good choice, who had had diplomatic experience, as Minister Plenipotentiary in Warsaw. His new embassy was complemented by a special mission by Earl Cornwallis.

[182] Elliot to Pitt, 14 Aug. 1785, NLS 12999 fols. 74–5.
[183] Carmarthen to Pitt, 28 Oct. 1785, 4 Jan., Richmond to Pitt, 15 Jan. 1786, PRO 30/8/151 fols. 29–30, 35, 30/8/170 fols. 70–1; Trevor to Keith, 22 Oct. 1785, BL Add. 35535 fol. 210; Fox to Richard Fitzpatrick, Nov. 1785, BL Add. 47580 fols. 126–7; Thomas Orde to Duke of Rutland, 19 Oct. 1785, HMC *Rutland III* (1894) p. 250; *Daily Universal Register*, 5 Jan., 4, 15, 22, 26 July, 14 Aug., 1 Sept. 1786, trade: 2, 3 (quote) Jan. 1786.
[184] Harris, 'Heads given in to the Cabinet', 12 May 1785, Winchester, Malmesbury vol. 204; Carmarthen to Richmond, 20 May 1785, BL Eg. 3498 fol. 219.
[185] Stepney to Carmarthen [4 July], Carmarthen to Stepney, 5 July 1785, BL Eg. 3501 fols. 19–21.

Cornwallis, who went to Prussia to attend the military manoeuvres, was instructed to act in a confidential manner, without any ostensible mission, in order to probe the possibility of improved relations. Carmarthen's instructions revealed the central role that France played in British concerns and the difference that was drawn between cultivating friendly conduct and committing the government, a distinction that was crucial to British diplomacy in this period, as more generally since 1763, and one that needs to be kept in mind when the intentions and effectiveness of this diplomacy are considered:

The earnest desire of the King of Prussia to open a more direct and confidential intercourse with England, I am apt to believe, originates rather in a desire of sounding the intentions of this court, than from any real intention of a fair and candid communication either of future views or even of present opinions: it behoves us, however, at all events to cultivate this apparently friendly conduct on the part of that Prince, and, by not committing ourselves, to meet him precisely upon his ground... before any serious connexion could be entered into with Prussia, it would be absolutely necessary to know how far that power might be depended upon in respect to France, and whether the former intercourse between them was either diminished or maintained; and the only circumstance which could probably totally break that intercourse would be the King of Prussia discovering some new plan of aggrandizement, projected by the Emperor in concert with, and to be supported by, the Court of Versailles. Should such an event take place, this country must then give up all hopes of an alliance with the Emperor; at the same time Prussia could no longer reckon upon the assistance of France; and in that case it might be prudent for England and Prussia to form a more close and intimate connexion.

Though claiming to be impressed by Pitt's fiscal policy and the state of British public finances compared to those of France, Frederick said there was no point in an Anglo-Prussian alliance, because France, Spain, Austria and Russia would be too powerful for them, but that if Russia could be won over the situation would be very different. Frederick also warned that France was trying to foment disaffection in Ireland; indeed the previous December Kaunitz had been interested in reports of turbulence in Ireland.[186] Thus, for Frederick, growing British domestic strength did not entail a stronger international position, because continental alignments were hostile. The attraction of Britain as a possible ally would depend not upon Pittite stability and financial reforms, though these were clearly of importance to British policy, but upon shifts in these alignments. The Duke of York thought that in the current situation all that could be expected was that Frederick would

---

[186] C. Ross (ed.), *Correspondence of Charles, First Marquis Cornwallis* (3 vols., 1859), I, 196–203; The Cornwallis papers in the Public Record Office do not add to this account; Kaunitz to Kageneck, 27 Dec. 1784, HHStA EK 129.

hold out the prospect of better relations. Thus the *Fürstenbund* had made only limited difference to Anglo-Prussian relations. As at the beginning of 1785, Frederick was cautious, unwilling to become too involved in the affairs of the Low Countries and to alienate France, and worried about Russian intentions. A fortnight before Frederick met Cornwallis the French envoy was assured that there was no Anglo-Prussian alliance. Harris argued that Frederick would do nothing, because he wanted to stay on good terms with France. Indeed, in the spring of 1786, Vergennes sought to improve relations with Frederick.[187] Frederick's caution, though unwelcome to some British commentators, such as Carmarthen and Harris, was applauded by George III, who thought that Britain should emulate it.[188] George also appreciated Cornwallis' efforts, and in 1786 he was appointed Governor General and Commander in Chief in India and awarded the Garter. Carmarthen remained suspicious about Franco-Prussian links and in early 1786 he told Kageneck that Frederick was primarily concerned to avoid upsetting France. Vorontsov urged Pitt against closer Anglo-Prussian relations. The Austrian and Russian conviction that George had acted a deceitful part, was matched by British suspicions about Frederick.[189] It is easy to appreciate why the *Fürstenbund* was criticised so bitterly.

Anglo-Prussian relations and the general impact of the *Fürstenbund* have to be seen in the context of a disagreement between those who wanted to push Britain into achieving her foreign policy goals of opposition to France through active commitments, of which Harris was an advocate, and others, of whom George III was most prominent, who were more cautious, for whom the avoidance of (excessive) commitments was itself a goal.[190] At the same time, there was a difference between those, such as Carmarthen, for whom European international relations and Britain's role centred on opposition to France, and others, of whom again George was most prominent, who had wider interests. This tension was not new. It had played a major role in British foreign policy in 1741–57 and, as then, alliances or commitments could be seen in more

---

[187] York to George III, 18 Nov. 1785, Aspinall, *George III* no. 258; Harris to Ewart, 27 Sept. 1785, Winchester, Malmesbury 204 p. 69; S. Schama, *Patriots and Liberators: Revolution in the Netherlands 1780–1813* (1977), p. 123.

[188] Carmarthen to Dalrymple, 13 Dec. 1785, PRO FO 64/9; Harris to Keith, 27 Dec., Dalrymple to Keith, 31 Dec. 1785, BL Add. 35535 fols. 326, 334–5; George III to Carmarthen, 4 Oct. 1785, BL Add. 27914 fol. 9, misdated in Aspinall, *George III* no. 250; George III to Pitt, 24 Jan. 1786, Aspinall, *George III* no. 274.

[189] Kageneck to Kaunitz, 20 Jan., 21 Mar. 1786, HHStA EK 125; Pitt to Carmarthen, 27 Dec. 1785, BL Eg. 3498 fol. 159; Dalrymple to Liston, 24 Jan. 1786, NLS 5544 fols. 47–8.

[190] George III to Pitt, 24 Jan. 1786, Aspinall, *George III* no. 274; George III to Carmarthen, 26 Aug. 1786, BL Add. 27914 fol. 17.

than one light, and designed to serve more than one purpose.[191] Though a major difference between George III's conduct as King and Elector has been discerned,[192] this was not new, and there was also a basic consistency between the two, as well as continuity with policy earlier in the century: Austria must be persuaded to act the role she should, both in the Empire and more generally, and pressing her to that end did not make George III a bad German Elector or British King.

In early 1786 Keith was instructed to approach Joseph again, though his orders were not seen by George III until after they were sent. Justifying the *Fürstenbund* as a defensive measure, Carmarthen added,

The court of Vienna ought to be convinced that the aggrandisement of Austria, taken as a general position cannot be looked upon as injurious to England, the means however by which this aggrandisement is to be procured, may it is true in some particular instances prove greatly so. I mean supposing that in order to purchase the consent or even the connivance of France, this latter power should be permitted to increase ... could this apprehension be removed, there could be no doubt of the advantage that must accrue to this country from seeing a power established on the continent, sufficiently formidable not only to control (if need be) the ambitious views of France, but of such a nature as to require her to keep up a constant, numerous and of course expensive army and thereby necessarily divert her attention, as well as resources, from the increase at least, if not the support of her marine. Such are the fixed and unalterable sentiments of this government.

Kageneck was given similar assurances by Carmarthen, though the minister was aware, from an intercepted dispatch, that the envoy was in touch with opposition leaders.[193] Yet Joseph was not interested in turning against France, which was what Carmarthen sought, and the Austrians were suspicious of Anglo-Prussian relations.[194] As the possibility of a Balkan conflict increased in the summer of 1786, Carmarthen returned to the old hope that French ties with the Ottoman empire would anger Austria. This led him to hesitate about seeking any improvement in relations with Prussia.[195] The year 1786 passed without any negotiation of an alliance with Prussia, any major international disturbance that might lead to a realignment of the powers and without any improvement

[191] Dann, *Hannover und England*; Black, 'The British Attempt to Preserve the Peace in Europe 1748–1755', in H. Duchhardt (ed.), *Zwischenstaatliche Friedenswahrung in Mittelalter und Früher Neuzeit* (Cologne, 1991), pp. 227–43.

[192] Blanning, '*Fürstenbund* of 1785', p. 340.

[193] Carmarthen to Keith, 17 Jan. 1786, PRO FO 7/12; Kageneck to Kaunitz, 28 Feb., 28 Mar. 1786, HHStA EK 125; Carmarthen to Pitt, 28 Oct. 1785, PRO 30/8/151 fols. 29–30.

[194] Carmarthen to Keith, 4 Apr. 1786, PRO FO 7/12; Harris to Keith, 7 Apr., 26 May 1786, BL Add. 35536 fols. 207, 309–11.

[195] Carmarthen to Keith, 18 July 1786, PRO FO 7/12; Carmarthen to Harris, 24 July, Harris to Ewart, 8 Aug. 1786, *Malmesbury*, II, 211–12, 218.

in Anglo-Austrian relations. In January 1787 Carmarthen's renewed expression of a wish for good relations was accompanied by an outburst of irritation directed against Joseph.[196]

Isolation and irritation; these were the consequences of over three years of diplomatic effort. It was all too easy to blame the *Fürstenbund* for this failure, crucially for exasperating Joseph II.[197] And yet that was arguably as misleading as George III's attempt in October 1787 to ascribe the successful resolution of the Dutch crisis through Prussian intervention to his participation in the League.[198] Exasperation and irritation were important, but they did not prevent realignments, as the diplomacy of the 1780s and of previous decades demonstrated. Richmond was not wrong to suggest that the negotiation of the *Fürstenbund* did not preclude better Anglo-Austrian relations. A critic of the League, he was to write to Pitt in July 1787,

If some idea could be conveyed to the Emperor that the effects of the German League would probably be much weakened and in time done away by an alliance between him and England, I should think it would have a very good effect ... it would be saying no more than the truth for without the assistance of England Hanover would make but a poor figure in a continental war, and I do not believe that His Majesty's German purse could possibly support his army in the field above one campaign. But if England was on the other side it is next to impossible he could act at all.[199]

Richmond underrated the importance of George III in British foreign policy. The early summer of 1785 had scarcely been a period for ministers to confront the King. They were divided over parliamentary reform and about to be thwarted over trade with Ireland. Both Pitt and Carmarthen realised that the country needed to restore its strength before confronting France in Europe too actively. Had the long lasting Austro-Dutch crisis led to war then Britain would not have been able or willing to play much of a military role in the crisis, and would certainly not have been prepared or able to defend the Austrian Netherlands against attack by France, the United Provinces, or Prussia from the Prussian bases on the lower Rhine.

The British failure to improve relations with Spain and weaken the Franco-Spanish alliance offers an instructive parallel. There was no equivalent to the *Fürstenbund*, and yet the Spanish government was not greatly interested in better relations, despite definite strains in the alliance with France. As with France and Austria, Britain had little to

---

[196] Carmarthen to Keith, 16 Jan. 1787, PRO FO 7/13 fols. 11–14.
[197] Carmarthen to Harris, 24 July 1786, *Malmesbury*, II, 212.
[198] George III to Carmarthen, 12 Oct. 1787, Aspinall, *George III* no. 406 fn. 1.
[199] Richmond to Pitt, 30 July 1787, PRO 30/8/170 fols. 85–6.

offer, and that was despite the fact that, as George III appreciated, Charles III (1759–88), unlike Joseph II, but like George III, was against European territorial changes.[200] There was little point in Spain seeking better relations with Britain, while Austria and France were allied, and this also deterred the more anglophile Victor Amadeus III of Sardinia. Had George III refused to participate in the *Fürstenbund*, as the Kings of Denmark and Sweden, as, respectively, Dukes of Holstein and Pomerania were to do, then this would simply have alienated Frederick II, and made him less likely to break with France, without in any way ensuring that Catherine and, still more, Joseph would be interested in better relations in order to thwart French interests in Europe.

The Franco-Dutch defensive treaty signed at Fontainebleau on 10 November 1785[201] ensured that Britain became more, rather than less, isolated in western Europe in this period. Along with the successful French mediation of Austro-Dutch differences, this was a significant blow for those in Britain who had pressed for a more active policy, and had hoped that France would not be able to settle the Scheldt question.[202] Harris' attempts to prevent the signature of the treaty and the Dutch ratification of it were both unsuccessful.[203] It was scarcely surprising that Joseph preferred the France of his despised brother-in-law Louis XVI to the Britain of the despised George III, nor that Frederick was unwilling to provoke France, and indeed that in 1786 the Pitt ministry responded to French pressure to negotiate a trade treaty. Keith noted in December 1785 that Joseph was primarily concerned to maintain his Russian alliance and he added, 'England seems to be almost entirely out of the question, in the present juncture, and matters, in general, must take a new and more favourable turn, before she can again resume her place and weight amongst the nations of Europe.'[204]

---

[200] George III to Carmarthen, 30 Jan. 1786, BL Add. 27914 fol. 15; Liston to Carmarthen, 5 Jan. 1786, CUL Add. 6958 no. 38; Liston to Dorset, 25 Oct. 1784, 30 Mar. 1785, 19 Apr. 1786, KAO C184.   [201] Murphy, *Vergennes*, pp. 467–8.

[202] Carmarthen to Pitt, 13 Nov. 1785, PRO 30/8/151 fol. 31.

[203] Carmarthen to Richmond, 13 Nov., and reply, 16 Nov. 1785, BL Eg. 3498 fols. 223, 227; Cobban, *Ambassadors and Secret Agents*, pp. 63–9.

[204] Keith to Hailes, 12 Dec. 1785, KAO C191.

3　Trade, France and the Dutch, 1786–1787

M. de Ségur it is reported affects to say that in respect to the general system of Europe his court can answer for that of London, and the other ministers of France in different courts are I am told authorised to hold the same language.

Carmarthen, January 1786

everything bears the appearance of tranquillity, but I believe the cabinet at Versailles is working hard in every cabinet in Europe... the spirit of intrigue which Vergennes is endowed with is more dangerous ... to the balance of power than all the mighty armies of Louis XIV.

Dorset, February 1786[1]

There were signs in 1786 of the international crisis that was to engulf Europe the following year, but it was far from clear what was to happen. A developing confrontation in the Caucasus, combined with the growth of a war party in Constantinople and a tendency in the Russian government to underrate the Turks, was helping to push the two powers towards war.[2] Domestic tension was rising in the Low Countries, both in the Austrian Netherlands where Joseph II's 'reform' policies were not appreciated by the population and the existing elites,[3] and in the United Provinces.[4] Municipal autonomy, federal republicanism and hostility to the House of Orange were powerful political and constitutional traditions in the United Provinces, and municipal coups, urban disorder and the creation of unofficial citizen militias were customary means of procedure

---

[1] Carmarthen to Keith, 17 Jan. 1786, PRO FO 7/12; Dorset to Wraxall, 9 Feb. 1786, Beinecke, Osborn Files, Dorset.

[2] Dalrymple to Carmarthen, 12 May 1785, BL Eg. 3501 fol. 34; D. M. Lang, *The Last Years of the Georgian Monarchy 1658–1832* (New York, 1957), pp. 185, 205–10; A. Bennigsen, 'Un mouvement populaire au Caucase au XVIIIe siècle: la "Guerre Sainte" au Sheikh Mansur', *Cahiers du monde russe et soviétique*, 5 (1964), 159–97; Fisher, *Annexation*, p. 154.

[3] W. W. Davis, *Joseph II: An Imperial Reformer for the Austrian Netherlands* (The Hague, 1974).

[4] S. Schama, *Patriots and Liberators: Revolution in the Netherlands 1780–1813* (1977), pp. 64–135; W. Te Brake, *Regents and Rebels. The Revolutionary World of an Eighteenth Century Dutch City* (Oxford, 1989); N. C. F. van Sas, 'The Patriot Revolution' in Jacob and Mijnhardt (eds.), *The Dutch Republic in the Eighteenth Century*, pp. 91–119.

in periods of instability. Traditional republican sentiment and opposition to William V of Orange, Stadtholder (governor) of all the provinces of this federal state from 1751 to 1795, especially in light of his ambiguous stance during the Fourth Anglo-Dutch War (1780–4), combined to produce the Patriot movement of the 1780s. As with the popular pro-Orangist agitation of the late 1740s, its main support came from the lesser bourgeoisie and not from the wealthy urban oligarchs, the Regent caste or class. The Regents in the towns of the wealthiest and most populous province, Holland, were interested in limiting the power of the Prince of Orange, but were unhappy about the direction of the movement. Bourgeois Free Corps were formed to lend force to the overthrowing of Orangist municipal and provincial governments. William's constitutional rights in numerous municipalities and provinces were abolished, and, as agitation increased, the prince had to leave The Hague, the federal capital, in September 1785. The British government followed the traditional policy of supporting the Orangist cause and Anglo-Dutch relations were thus affected by the growing weakness of William V's position. Harris wrote to Carmarthen that month,

I am very much afraid that the game is entirely lost here and that we must lay on our oars, till a fresh gale springs up ... there is however some kind of foundation laid for taking it up again at another opportunity and I have acquired a good deal of experience of the characters and connections of the people here ... events must arise in Europe and this country be involved in the general convulsion – it is also more than probable that sooner or later the evil will cure itself by a popular insurrection.[5]

The sense that something would turn up was scarcely the basis for a diplomatic strategy, and indeed the Orangist position continued to deteriorate. The following spring the Patriots discussed dismissing William as Stadtholder. Far from seeking to create a unitary state, the Patriots sought to follow the American example of republican federalism with an extension of political rights, though the idea of a representative assembly of the whole 'Netherlands People' was discussed at a meeting of the national federation of Free Corps in Utrecht in 1786. Like the American revolutionaries, the Dutch Patriots faced substantial internal opposition and received French political and financial support. Unlike the American case, however, the opposition was stronger, the Patriots being especially weak in the provinces bordering Germany where, unlike the Loyalists, the Orangists were not dependent on foreign military assistance; while, again unlike the American revolutionaries, the Patriot movement had not sufficient time in which to establish itself.

[5] Harris to Carmarthen, 17 Sept. 1785, PRO 30/8/155 fol. 47A.

In the autumn of 1787, the confrontations in the Balkans and the Low Countries were to lead to conflict in which the major powers were involved directly or indirectly. The war in the Balkans was to last until 1792 and, as with the previous Russo-Turkish war of 1768–74, to lead to major changes in Poland and to threaten a fundamental alteration of the situation in eastern Europe. The crisis in the Low Countries was to precipitate French isolation and reveal the collapse of her power. Though some of the alignments in at least the initial stages of the crisis were expected, for example the hostility of Russia and Turkey and the opposition of Austria and Prussia, there was much about the course, configuration and interrelationships of the international crisis of 1787 that was surprising or unpredictable. In part for this reason, it is necessary to be cautious in assuming that the British triumph in 1787 can be ascribed to a well-conceived and skilfully executed foreign policy. The destruction of French influence in the United Provinces through the forcible reimposition of Orangist power in the provinces of Holland and Utrecht was seen as a triumph; although arguably the step itself, especially the Prussian invasion that achieved it, and, more particularly the subsequent diplomatic vacuum in much of Europe, that enabled it to be seen as such a triumph, owed much to chance factors over which Britain had little influence, namely the crisis in the Balkans and French weakness.

Anglo-French relations and the Eden Treaty

British policy in the Dutch crisis was motivated by hostility to France, and yet the negotiation of the Eden Treaty in 1786 had led to expectations of better relations. This commercial treaty with France helped to return foreign policy to the field of partisan political debate, from which it had been absent in 1784–5. In the debates over the Address of Thanks in January 1786, the opposition had sought to make capital out of the *Fürstenbund*, blaming it as a step that would provoke Joseph II, but Pitt had countered this by insisting on the constitutional proprieties, namely that Britain was not committed by Hanoverian policies. Reginald Pole Carew, a former MP, thought that Pitt answered Fox 'as well as the delicacy of the subject and the ticklish ground he stood on would admit'.[6] Fox made it clear in the Commons that the importance of the issue arose from its impact on Anglo-French relations. Freed from the fear of Austrian attack, France, he claimed, would be a more formidable naval opponent for Britain.[7] Fox also stated that France was 'the natural enemy

[6] Cobbett, 25, 1014; Pole Carew to Harris, 30 Jan. 1786, Winchester, Malmesbury 146.
[7] Cobbett, 25, 1006–7.

of Great Britain', and, in speaking of Anglo-Russian relations, gave a clear warning of the likely response to any trade treaty with France,

> He well knew the fashionable mode of calling treaties commercial, and treaties political, distinct and separate sorts of treaties; but he was not to be blinded by any such new-fangled and ill-founded distinctions; treaties of commerce entered into between two countries always had influenced their politics in a very great degree.[8]

Trade negotiations were politically a problematic aspect of foreign policy, but those with France were most so. France was a formidable economic power, Britain's principal political and commercial rival, she was able to negotiate from a position of strength, and it was likely that any agreement would affect sectional interests in Britain and worry those concerned about the future of the national economy. More seriously, such terms, and the more general point of any negotiations with France, would provide a clear focus for the customary opposition criticism of any government's foreign policy, namely that it failed to defend national interests, that the country was not safe in ministerial hands. The parliamentary defeat in 1713 of the last Anglo-French commercial treaty was a serious warning, but so also were the difficulties in the British Parliament in 1785 over Irish trade, while the delicacy of trade as an issue was highlighted in the debates over the Address in January 1786 when the opposition mentioned recent Austrian and French regulations that affected British imports. The savage scene of dogs, with the faces of politicians, fighting over the Eden Treaty, depicted in Gillray's cari-cature, *Commercial Treaty with France attacked in the Commons* (1786), underlined the sensitivity of the issue. In November 1784, Pitt had referred to 'the clamour of our manufacturers' in the face of new Austrian regulations.[9]

It would not have been surprising had the British government chosen not to respond to French pressure for a trade treaty. That would certainly have been in line with the clear antagonism to France voiced so prominently both within and outside the ministry. Opposition spokes-men, such as the nominal leader, William, 3rd Duke of Portland, Fox, and Stormont, could stress the necessity of rivalry from the luxury of

---

[8] Cobbett, 25, 1020, 1007.
[9] D. A. E. Harkness, 'The Opposition to the 8th and 9th Articles of the Commercial Treaty of Utrecht', *Scottish Historical Review*, 21 (1923–4), 219–21; E. C. Bogle, 'A Stand for Tradition: the Rejection of the Anglo-French Commercial Treaty of Utrecht' (unpublished Ph.D. thesis, University of Maryland, 1972); D. C. Coleman, 'Politics and Economics in the Age of Anne: The Case of the Anglo-French Trade Treaty of 1713', in D. C. Coleman and A. H. John (eds.), *Trade, Government and Economy in Pre-Industrial England* (1976) pp. 187–211; Pitt to Carmarthen, 2 Nov. 1784, BL Eg. 3498 fol. 66.

opposition, but such views were also held by George III, Carmarthen, Richmond, Howe and many diplomats, including Harris, Dorset, Hailes, Fitzherbert and Ewart. Carmarthen received continual reports of French hostility. Some were masterpieces of prejudice, Hailes writing in September 1785 that 'in general ... every Frenchman of any condition that goes to England is more or less a spy and brings back all the intelligence he can to ingratiate himself with the minister'.[10]

Many accusations were more specific. Aside from continual anxiety about India, there were reports of French intrigues in Canada and Ireland. The expansion of the French navy agitated many members of the British government, including George III, Howe and Dorset. In 1784 Carmarthen mentioned the size of the Danish navy as one reason for seeking an alliance with Denmark.[11] The development of a major harbour at Cherbourg aroused particular concern. It was seen correctly as aimed specifically at Britain. Allegedly designed to hold over seventy ships of the line, it was argued that France hoped to use Cherbourg to attain strategic mastery over the Channel. If an invasion attempt should be mounted, Cherbourg would offer a better and closer base than Brest which had been used in 1779. Hailes suggested in September 1784 that developments at Cherbourg were related to the attempt to develop a base at Gothenburg. He warned that the harbour would be able to contain 100 ships of the line, and that a tower 60 foot high could be built nearby that would command the entire Channel, not least British naval movements from Portsmouth.[12] In January 1786 Richmond outlined the dangers of invasion to Pitt and linked them to British isolation,

By the combinations that are formed against us we must expect numerous enemies, probably some losses abroad, and it will be after having been successful against our foreign possessions and whilst our naval and military force is strained to the utmost abroad or is exhausted there that they will attempt anything here or possibly before we can get on our legs at the very first breaking out of hostilities.

[10] Hailes to Carmarthen, 1 Sept. 1785, BL Eg. 3499; Carmarthen to Dorset, 27 July, 12 Nov. 1784, PRO FO 27/12 fols. 183–4, 27/13 fols. 174–5; Harris to Keith, 24 Jan., 26 May, Ewart to Keith, 24 May, Harris to Pitt, 22 Dec. 1786, BL Add. 35536 fols. 32, 310, 298, 28068 fol. 194; Harris to Elliot, 17 Jan. 1786, NLS 12999 fols. 116–17; Dorset to Wraxall, 9 Feb. 1786, Beinecke, Osborn Files, Dorset; Noailles to Vergennes, 17 Aug. 1785, AE CP Aut. 350 fol. 102. For Portland, A. S. Turberville, *A History of Welbeck Abbey and its Owners* (2 vols., 1939), I, 208.
[11] Sydney to Carmarthen, 4 Apr. 1785, BL Eg. 3498 fols. 199–200; Dorset to Gower, 23 June 1785, PRO 30/29/1/15 no. 49; Hailes to Carmarthen, 28 Oct., 4 Nov., Carmarthen to Dorset, 19 Oct. 1784, Carmarthen to Pitt, 23 June 1784, BL Eg. 3499 fols. 45, 52, 101, 3498 fol. 38.
[12] Hailes to Carmarthen, 2, 9 Sept. 1784, PRO 27/13 fols. 7, 26; Simolin, memorandum, 12 Aug. 1784, BL Eg. 3504 fol. 17; Castries, *Castries*, pp. 149–52.

Louis XVI's visit to Cherbourg in 1786 helped to focus British public concern. Eden predicted accurately that 'John Bull will rub his eyes.'[13]

Hostility to France extended to suspicion of commercial negotiations with her, as Carmarthen made clear. And yet, the ministry not only proceeded with the negotiations, but brought them to a successful conclusion, unlike other British commercial initiatives of the period,[14] and then defended them successfully in Parliament. This caused considerable political controversy and was seen as indicative of an attempt to obtain better diplomatic relations. Philip Francis, an opposition MP, argued that 'the polemic laurels of the father', the Elder Pitt, were yielding 'to pacific myrtles which shadow the forehead of the son' and warned that 'there may be a strict union between the two crowns though never between the two nations'. His colleague Henry Flood stated that 'the idea of rendering peace durable by entering into a Commercial Treaty with France was, as experience proved, a false suggestion'.[15]

The commercial negotiations therefore represented a significant political risk. If they failed, the ministry would be criticised domestically for attempting them. If they succeeded, there would also be criticism, but, in addition, there might be diplomatic consequences. The *Fürstenbund* demonstrated that it was not within the government's control to determine the foreign perception of British intentions. A trade treaty with France might well create the impression that Britain sought better relations with her and would not, therefore, play an active role in thwarting French schemes. That was certainly the impression created among British diplomats, who feared that Pitt was abandoning national interests in order to concentrate on commercial objectives and financial considerations. Ewart wrote in February 1787 of 'the backwardness shown by our Court', Harris referred to 'a system of pounds, shillings and pences', and, two months earlier, Carmarthen, who felt 'we are dwindled down to tradesmen', stated 'we must not suffer Holland to be sacrificed either to lawn or cambric', a reference to issues in commercial negotiations.[16]

A lack of ministerial cohesion was not new. Ministers served the king as individuals, not as representatives of a political party, and the Pitt

---

[13] Richmond to Pitt, 15 Jan., Eden to Pitt, 8 June 1786, PRO 30/8/170 fol. 67, 30/8/110 fol. 50; Barthélemy to Vergennes, 18 July 1786, AE CP Ang. 557 fol. 45.

[14] Carmarthen to Eden, 25 Apr. 1786, The Bishop of Bath and Wells (ed.). *The Journal and Correspondence of William, Lord Auckland* (4 vols. 1861–2), I, 112–13; J. Ehrman, *The British Government and Commercial Negotiations with Europe 1783–1793* (Cambridge, 1962).   [15] Cobbett, 26, 422, 432.

[16] Ewart to Keith, 1 Feb., Harris to Keith, 9 Feb. 1787, BL Add. 35538; Carmarthen to Fitzherbert, 12 Nov., Carmarthen to Harris, 14, 21 Nov. 1786, BL Eg. 3500 fols. 16–17.

ministry had come to office in response to a specific crisis and in order to defend the royal position, rather than in fulfilment of political pressure designed to further a particular agenda. The ministry had divided the previous year over parliamentary reform, on which Pitt was opposed by George III and a host of prominent figures, such as Dorset and Grenville. Dorset provided an authentic voice of conservatism,

as to the reform I wish to God he may be beaten by a thumping majority. It is too foolish a thing to hear of. If the *rotten boroughs* are destroyed England will soon become a rotten country and it will [be] time to seek for protection and shelter elsewhere. It seems a paradox, but it is true that the fewer means we have left us of corruption, the quicker we shall become rotten and have at last no government at all.

In February 1786 the government divided again over Richmond's fortification bill which was supported by George III and Pitt, and opposed, to a varying extent, by Howe, Thurlow and Dundas.[17] There was little continuity between such disputes. Ministers responded to particular issues on their merits, but for Pitt the Eden Treaty was more worrying than parliamentary reform, because there was no prospect of any opposition support, unlike over the earlier issue. Pitt has been criticised for taking political risks over the Irish trade legislation, and he was well aware that parliamentary defeats could harm the government. In March 1785 he wrote to Gower over parliamentary reform,

it is indeed material that what is proposed should as far as possible be supported or at least not opposed by the weight of government, for I do sincerely fear that if it should be thrown out, and that by a majority of our friends; it may have an effect on the public opinion, fatal, I will not say personally to myself, but to the cause in which we are all embarked.[18]

This had not been the case in 1785: the opposition was in no position to exploit the issue. The Eden Treaty was, however, more dangerous. Developments abroad might well throw doubt on the possibility or desirability of improving relations in any respect and the extent to which Pitt could rely on George III or his colleagues was unclear. Though the *Fürstenbund* issue related specifically to Hanover, George's unwillingness to consult Pitt over it suggested a less than total confidence in the field of foreign policy.

The Eden Treaty can be seen as another instance of Pitt's idealism and optimism leading him into a potentially dangerous political situation.

[17] G. M. Ditchfield, 'The House of Lords and Parliamentary Reform in the Seventeen-Eighties', *Bulletin of the Institute of Historical Research*, 54 (1981), 211–12; Richmond to Pitt, 15 Jan. 1786, PRO 30/8/170 fol. 65; Dorset to Wraxall, 17 Mar. 1785, Beinecke, Osborn Files, Dorset.   [18] Pitt to Gower, 19 Mar. 1785, PRO 30/29/384.

The need for the treaty arose from the peace treaties of 1783–4 which provided for the selection of commissioners to reach new commercial arrangements, based on reciprocity and mutual convenience, between Britain on the one hand, and France, Spain and The Netherlands on the other, and, in the case of the first two, stated that these should be completed by 1 January 1786. These clauses reflected French pressure, though Shelburne was interested in better commercial relations as a means to further reconciliation between the two powers. French officials made it clear that they wanted a major change in commercial relations. Rayneval told Hailes in May 1784 'that the wish of the French Ministry was to establish their trade with England on the broadest basis possible and to open all their ports'.[19] Ministerial instability, more pressing problems and a lack of enthusiasm led to a lack of movement by Britain, but, under French pressure, the British first nominated and then eventually sent George Craufurd to Paris in 1784.

The dispatch of such an inconspicuous figure as Craufurd, who received his instructions on 2 September 1784, indicated lack of interest on the British part, and this aroused French anger.[20] Rayneval, the

[19] Draft to Fitzherbert, 9 Jan. 1783, Hailes to Carmarthen, 20 May 1785, PRO FO 27/5 fol. 125, 27/12 fol. 34. The best treatment of the negotiations is M. M. Donaghay, 'The Anglo-French Negotiations of 1786–1787' (unpublished Ph.D., University of Virginia, 1970). Professor Donaghay has published a number of articles including, 'Calonne and the Anglo-French Commercial Treaty of 1786', *Journal of Modern History*, 50 (1978) suppl., 1157–84, 'The Maréchal de Castries and the Anglo-French Commercial Negotiations of 1786–1787', *Historical Journal*, 22 (1979), 295–312, 'The Ghosts of Ruined Ships: The Commercial Treaty of 1786 and the Lessons of the Past', *Proceedings of the Consortium on Revolutionary Europe* (Athens, Georgia, 1981), 111–18, 'Textiles and the Anglo-French Commercial Treaty of 1786', *Textile History*, 13 (1982), 215–22, 'A propos du traité commercial franco-anglais de 1786', *Revue d'histoire diplomatique*, 101 (1987), 371–4, 'The Exchange of Products of the Soil and Industrial Goods in the Anglo-French Commercial Treaty of 1786', *Journal of European Economic History*, 19 (1990), 377–401, 'The Vicious Circle: The Anglo-French Commercial Treaty of 1786 and the Dutch Crisis of 1787', *Consortium on Revolutionary Europe. Proceedings 1989*, 447–56. Aside from important discussions in Ehrman, *Commercial Negotiations*, and Murphy, *Vergennes*, other relevant works include O. Browning, 'The Treaty of Commerce between England and France, 1786', *Transactions of the Royal Historical Society*, new ser., 2 (1885), 349–64; C. Bloch, 'Le Traité de commerce de 1786 entre la France et l'Angleterre', *Études sur l'histoire economique de la France 1760–1789* (Paris, 1900), pp. 239–69; F. Dumas, *Étude sur le traité de commerce de 1786 entre la France et l'Angleterre* (Toulouse, 1904); J. Holland Rose, 'The Franco-British Commercial Treaty 1786', *English Historical Review*, 23 (1908), 709–24; W. Bowden, 'The English Manufacturers and the Commercial Treaty with France', *American Historical Review*, 25 (1919), 18–35, W. Cahen, 'Une Nouvelle Interpretation de traité franco-anglaise de 1786–1787', *Revue Historique*, 185 (1939), 271–85; W. O. Henderson, 'The Anglo-French Commercial Treaty of 1786', *Economic History Review*, 2nd ser., 10 (1957–8), 104–12; J. Kelly, 'The Anglo-French Commercial Treaty of 1786: The Irish Dimension', *Eighteenth-Century Ireland*, 4 (1989), 93–112.

[20] Instructions for Craufurd, 2 Sept., Dorset to Carmarthen, 1 July 1784, PRO FO 27/13 fols. 2–5, 27/12 fol. 131.

French commissioner, suggested in September that reciprocity serve as the basis of negotiations, but the British did not respond.[21] Having lowered duties on some British goods as an encouragement to get talks going, the French took the opposite tack the following year. Raised duties and outright prohibitions had a considerable impact in Britain, helping to push the government towards serious negotiations, and thus apparently demonstrating that British policy could be influenced through trade. In February 1785, for example, the French raised the duty on imported carriages, then fashionable in France. This affected British tourists, Thomas Brand, a 'bearleader' or travelling tutor, writing a year later, 'We were obliged to deposit 1200 livres at the customhouse at Calais for the importation of an English carriage, a tax which the French court have thought proper to lay on to prevent the sale of them and perhaps to hasten the intended treaty of *commerce*.' Prohibitions and heavy duties certainly affected the exports of both countries. Frances Crewe, the wife of an MP, wrote from Paris in early 1786,

There is … no kind of comparison between the most common sort of china in France and the best our country ever produced; and one pays a fourth part only here for what is at least four times as beautiful. The great objection however against buying French china is the duty laid upon it in England, and which actually comes to as much as the purchase.[22]

In the Lords debate on the Address of Thanks on 24 January 1786, an opposition speaker, Earl Fitzwilliam referred to Britain as being 'in an hostility of commerce' with Austria and France.[23] Three months earlier, Pitt had argued that it was necessary to show that Britain was in earnest, and on 9 December 1785 Carmarthen instructed Craufurd to extend the date by which a settlement had to be made from 1 January to 1 June 1786, and informed him that he would be replaced by an envoy with greater status and powers.[24] This was an aspect of Pitt's general determination to step up the pace of commercial negotiations throughout Europe, but the political and diplomatic importance of Anglo-French relations lent special urgency to the prospect of a trade treaty with France. The new envoy chosen for the negotiations was William Eden, a controversial choice, which was risky given the politically contentious nature of the object of his negotiations. Whereas the choice of Harris, who was close to Fox, as Envoy Extraordinary at The Hague possibly helped to defuse the

[21] Craufurd to Carmarthen, 25 Nov. 1784, PRO FO 27/13 fol. 200.
[22] Dorset to Liston, 20 Mar. 1786, NLS 5544 fol. 98; Brand to Robert Wharton, 10 Feb. 1786, Durham UL Wharton MSS; Crewe, BL Add. 37926 fol. 34; Donaghay, 'Anglo-French Negotiations', p. 57.   [23] Cobbett, 25, 989.
[24] Pitt to Carmarthen, 13 Oct. 1785, BL Eg. 3498 fol. 136; Carmarthen to Craufurd, 9 Dec. 1785, PRO FO 27/17.

issue of Britain's Dutch policy, Stormont only attacking Carmarthen briefly in the Lords over this issue in January 1786,[25] the appointment of Eden helped to focus attention on negotiations in Paris. Harris' appointment at The Hague had been acceptable to Fox, but Eden was regarded as a turncoat. There was no doubt of his talent for commercial negotiations, as Fox acknowledged in the Commons. Eden (1744–1814), had been an Under Secretary of State (1772–8), an MP since 1774, a member of the Board of Trade (1776–82) and a member of the select committee on East Indian affairs since 1784. He had been an active spokesman for the opposition in the sessions of 1784 and 1785, especially over Irish trade. His move to the ministry was seen as desertion, though he argued in 1783 that politics had nothing to do with diplomatic appointments, a surprising view for an MP who in 1786 must have been aware of the contentious nature of his mission. Eden would have preferred the Speakership of the Commons. Like some other younger sons in politics, he had an insecure position and was very much a man on the make and was distrusted accordingly.[26]

Eden was disliked by Carmarthen, who knew 'nothing right or honourable about him', thought him suited for 'narrow and illiberal intrigue' and in August 1784 proposed sending him as envoy to America, in order to get him out of the way, and by Harris and Dorset; and his defection and appointment gave rise to much criticism. Carmarthen claimed that George III disliked Eden. The *Daily Universal Register* of 27 September 1786 was to carry a mock advertisement, a characteristic eighteenth-century feature, in this case for a new book, 'Perpetual Deviation, the only political consistency, by the Right Hon. W. Ed-n'. He was still referred to in the press in 1788 as 'Billy the Apostate'.[27] Nevertheless, Eden devoted himself with his characteristic energy to gathering information from mercantile and manufacturing circles in

[25] Cobbett, 25, 993.
[26] Eden to brother Morton Eden, 30 Dec. 1783, *Auckland*, I, 70–1; Eden to Pitt, 12 Oct. 1785, PRO 30/8/110 fol. 1; Eden to Sheffield, 6 Dec. 1785, BL Add. 45728 fol. 70; I. R. Christie, 'The Anatomy of Opposition in the Parliament of 1784', *Parliamentary History*, 9 (1990), pp. 70–1; J. Black, *Pitt the Elder* (Cambridge, 1992), pp. 12–16. Eden's attitude was shared by the 2nd Earl of Hardwicke, Hardwicke to Rockingham, 21 June 1782, Sheffield City Archive, Wentworth Woodhouse Mss R1–2124. On Harris' appointment, *Malmesbury*, II, 69–72; HMC *Rutland* III, 102.
[27] Carmarthen to Pitt, 18 Aug. 1784, Eden to Sheffield, 11 Dec., Fraser to Keith, 23 Dec. 1785, journal of Frances Crewe, – Jan., Lord Bulkeley to Keith, 31 Jan. 1786, BL Eg. 3498, fol. 42, Add. 45728 fol. 72, Add. 35535 fol. 319, 37926 fol. 51, 35536 fol. 44; Harris to Frederick Robinson, 23 Dec. 1785, Bedford L30/15/26/16; Dorset to Wraxall, 5 Jan. 1786, Beinecke, Osborn Files, Dorset; O. Browning (ed.), *Political Memoranda of…* Leeds (1884), p. 140; John Hatsell to John Hey, 15 Dec. 1785, Exeter, Devon CRO 63/2/11/2/7; Barthélemy to Vergennes, 1 Jan. 1786, AE CP Ang. 555 fol. 6; *Felix Farley's Bristol Journal*, 1 Nov. 1788.

Britain in formal hearings, before setting out for Paris. With instructions drawn up on 10 March 1786, Eden left London on 21 March and reached Paris ten days later. Though ready to voice doubts about French political intentions,[28] Eden was enthusiastic about the prospect for a trade treaty and, pressing Pitt to move fast, critical of British hesitation and protectionist sentiment. He wrote to the minister on 13 April 1786,

> this French negotiation takes the turn that we wished and even beyond our speculations ... France shows a disposition to encourage our trade if we remove the senseless and peevish distinctions which fill so many lines in our Book of Rates ... we shall derive extensive and solid advantages from the alteration which the French ministers will immediately make in the restrictions which affect our trade ... this Treaty may form a new epoch in history ... temporary considerations are trifling when compared first with the importance of avoiding the farther embarrassments which were prepared, and would actually have been put in execution against our trade, if I had not arrived: but more especially when compared with the advantage of instituting a system of right understanding between the two Empires.

Four days later Eden transmitted the French Project for a treaty to London.[29] A statement of principle, it envisaged negotiations in detail after the ratification of an agreement, but the Pitt ministry wanted all details to be part of any agreement, and Carmarthen responded to Eden by seeking detailed information on specific duties and commercial regulations.[30] This problem could not be solved by talk, such as Eden's, of Britain and France uniting 'in some solemn plan of permanent peace'. A more conciliatory British line towards France was noted by commentators. Kageneck argued that it was designed to preserve the British position in India and to allow George III a free hand in the Empire (Germany), though there is no evidence to support this suggestion.[31] Eden was unhappy at what he saw as a hesitant British response, and feared that this was making the French ministers more cautious, and his own position more difficult.[32] In response to the French Project, the British ministry drew up a declaration, drafted by Pitt, which accepted, in its first article, the principle of most favoured nation treatment between the two countries. While waiting for the French response, Eden remained convinced that the French ministry were keen to negotiate the

---

[28] Instructions for Eden, 10 Mar. 1786, PRO FO 27/19 fols. 1–5; Eden to Carmarthen, 13 Apr. 1786, *Auckland*, I, 99.
[29] Eden to Pitt, 13 Apr. 1786, PRO 30/8/110 fol. 16; Eden to Carmarthen, 17 Apr. 1786, PRO FO 27/19 fols. 13–18.
[30] Carmarthen to Eden, 20 Apr., 11 May 1786, PRO FO 27/19 fols. 25–39, 46.
[31] Eden to Carmarthen, 25 Apr. 1786, PRO FO 27/19; Kageneck to Kaunitz, 9 May 1786, HHStA EK 125.
[32] Eden to Carmarthen, 25 Apr. 1786, PRO FO 27/19 fol. 41; Eden to Pitt, 6, 25, May, 1, 6, 8 June 1786, PRO 30/8/110 fols. 26, 38, 43–5, 49–50.

treaty 'upon any plan not grossly unreasonable'. He was made more optimistic by the imminent end of the parliamentary session,

whilst the Parliament was sitting it was very possible that any body of men whose interests were not included to their satisfaction in the treaty might have raised among themselves some expression ... but this would not be the case during the prorogation; we should have the advantage of information from any body of men, who might think their interests capable of being forwarded.[33]

Nevertheless there was no prorogation until 11 July, and, till then, parliamentary business and other ministerial commitments delayed a British reply to the French Contre-Déclaration of 16 June, which had accepted most of the points in the British Declaration.[34] Eden feared that delay would lead to the loss of opportunity not least because of the development of opposition in certain French ministerial circles. At the same time, he hoped that it would be possible to reduce colonial differences with France by negotiating a separate treaty. Though Eden was enthusiastic about the prospect of better relations with a French ministry that was wooing him personally very successfully,[35] he was still conscious of serious points in dispute, especially over the United Provinces and the Dutch colonies. Indeed, on 8 August, Eden wrote to Pitt, with whom he maintained a confidential correspondence during the negotiations,

the great danger to the peace between the two countries is certainly in our Asiatic possessions: but such a plan settled respecting the commerce for the same term as our other Commercial Treaty would put that danger to a distance. – At the same time it is very material to watch what this Court is doing as to the Dutch settlements in the East Indies: her influence over Dutch politics is grown quite decisive, and will root itself deeply if no struggle takes place soon in the Dutch provinces.[36]

The signature of the main treaty was delayed while negotiations took place over specific tariffs, a policy criticised by Eden.[37] Such attention to detail, however, was clearly necessary in light of the vociferous nature of British mercantile and industrial opinion and the need to defuse press and political criticism.[38] Though Parliament was not sitting, newspaper

---

[33] Draft by Pitt, PRO 30/8/333, Eden to Pitt, 15, 17 June 1786, PRO 30/8/110.
[34] Carmarthen to Eden, 23 June 1786, PRO FO 27/19 fol. 132.
[35] Eden to Pitt, 17 June, Eden to Carmarthen, 6 June 1786, PRO 30/8/110 fol. 56, FO 27/19 fol. 116; Eden to Liston, 18 Sept. 1786, NLS 5545 fol. 68.
[36] Eden to Pitt, 8 Aug. 1786, PRO 30/8/110 fol. 70.
[37] Eden to Pitt, 17, 22, 28, 29 June 1786, PRO 30/8/110 fols. 56–61.
[38] W. Bowden, *Industrial Society in England Towards the End of the Eighteenth Century* (New York, 1925), pp. 181–91; J. M. Norris, 'Samuel Garbett and the Early Development of Industrial Lobbying in Great Britain', *Economic History Review*, 2nd ser. 10 (1958); E. Robinson, 'Matthew Boulton and the Art of Parliamentary Lobbying',

attacks offered a pointed reminder of the sensitive nature of trade negotiations with France. The *Daily Universal Register* of 22 August 1786 declared that,

The demands of each country militate so much against the staple manufactures of both, which are rivals to each other, that the policy of either must be injured by a surrender of the advantages they at present enjoy. Most countries have articles of which we stand in need, and without injury exchange them for ours they have not; but England and France have the same manufactures, are vying with each other for competition. How then can we take off duties from foreign commodities to undersell our own, or vice versa.

It was necessary to demonstrate that British industry would not suffer, and, with Pitt receiving expert opinion from Hawkesbury, the head of the Board of Trade, the British took a firm line in the negotiations over duties and prohibitions.[39] Eden's support for Rayneval's argument that there should be an understanding that neither power would insist on the rigid enforcement of unforeseen advantages that created 'a sudden and mischievous revolution in commerce', was sensibly rejected in favour of precision, clarity and detail.[40] The British determination, despite French complaints,[41] to continue the exclusion of French silk imports was successful in the final treaty,[42] as was pressure for favourable terms for some of the principal British exports, and the demands made on behalf of Ireland. The French, however, apparently gained one important goal, the reduction of duties on French wines to a rate no greater than that on Portuguese wines, which had enjoyed a marked preference since the Methuen Treaty of 1703. The terms were so good for Britain that Eden feared the treaty would not be sustainable for the French. The terms indeed were to be blamed for problems affecting French industry in the late 1780s. British textile exports were to be especially competitive. The treaty, signed at Versailles, on 26 September 1786, covered the full range of Anglo-French commercial relations in Europe and was to be approved by Parliament the following year. The crucial Commons division, at 2 am on 13 February 1787, was 252 to 118, a 'pretty decent' majority.[43] The

Historical Journal, 7 (1964), 209–29; J. Brewer, *The Sinews of Power. War, Money and the English State, 1688–1763* (1989), pp. 231–49. The topic is not addressed in N. McKendrick, J. Brewer and J. H. Plumb, *The Birth of a Consumer Society. The Commercialization of Eighteenth-Century England* (1982).

[39] Eden to Pitt, 23 Aug. 1786, PRO 30/8/110 fol. 73.
[40] Eden to Carmarthen, 27 Aug., Carmarthen to Eden, 4, 12, Sept. 1786, PRO FO 27/20 fols. 4–5, 21–7, 64, 68–9.   [41] Eden to Pitt, 23 Aug. 1786, PRO 30/8/110 fol. 74.
[42] Donaghay, 'Textiles', 210–16.
[43] Eden to Carmarthen, 18 Oct. 1786, *Auckland*, I, 167; Sydney to Cornwallis, 6 Jan., Dundas to Cornwallis, 29 Jan, 21 Mar., 1787, PRO 30/11/138 fol. 10, 30/11/111 fols. 67, 81; W. Morton Pitt MP to Harris, 13 Feb. 1787, Winchester, Malmesbury 163; Aust to Liston, 15, 27 Feb, 9 Mar. 1787, NLS 5546 fols. 41, 49, 61.

impact of the treaty on British diplomacy was, however, to be slight, a victim of international developments.

Developing crisis: late 1786

The steps that were to lead to the major crisis of 1787, a crisis that involved both western and eastern Europe, but whose effects were felt more widely, both in the Near East and in the Indian Ocean, were taken both that year and in 1786. In the Low Countries, the Empire and the Balkans, the international situation appeared increasingly unstable. Relations between William V of Orange and the Patriots appeared to be moving towards a crisis in the United Provinces. On 27 July 1786 the Estates General removed the command of the Hague garrison from William V, a step that Vergennes disapproved of. In September William was suspended as Captain-General of Holland. The potential seriousness of these developments for Britain had been underlined in March 1786 when Harris reported that the French government had warned the Patriots that a war between Britain and France in India would break out soon, and that they would require Dutch support, a measure the Patriots were willing to offer. Harris saw no hope for William unless through 'a revolution effectuated by force', and he looked to Prussia for action.[44] The French envoy, Vérac, was becoming steadily more involved in Patriot plans, in spite of warnings from Vergennes that he should be careful not to over-commit France in Dutch internal affairs.

The death of Frederick II on the morning of 17 August 1786, news of which reached London at 10 pm on 25 August, was seen as likely to lead to changes in central Europe, although George III was hopeful that it would not lead to war. The Duke of York had written from Hanover six months earlier, 'everybody expects war as soon as the King of Prussia dies'. Carmarthen thought that the situation was propitious for an Austrian attack on Silesia. Vergennes had pointed out the previous year that Prussia lacked allies and had less than half the power of Austria.[45] Even if Joseph II did not launch the long contemplated, expected and feared war to regain Silesia, it was likely that his nephew and heir, Frederick William II, would face a difficult task in resisting Austro-Russian initiatives in the Empire. The *Fürstenbund* had apparently

[44] Harris to Carmarthen, 7, 10 Mar., 12 Sept., 3 Oct. 1786, *Malmesbury*, II, 189–90, 231–2, BL Eg. 3500 fol. 20.

[45] Aust to Liston, 25 Aug. 1786, NLS 5545 fol. 28; George III to Carmarthen, 26 Aug., York to Richard Grenville, 7 Feb. 1786, BL Add. 27914 fol. 17, 70958; Carmarthen to Keith, 16 May 1786, PRO FO 7/12; Vergennes to Noailles, 27 May 1785, AE CP Aut. suppl. 23 fol. 84.

thwarted Joseph in 1785, but Frederick II had been quite correct to point out to Cornwallis in September 1785 that the alliance system to which Joseph could look was stronger than any Anglo-Prussian alliance would prove. Militarily, there was little to the *Fürstenbund* besides Prussia. The alliance of Hesse-Cassel and Brunswick was worth having, but Hanover, Saxony, Mainz, Anhalt, Ansbach, Baden, the two Mecklenburg duchies, Gotha, Osnabrück and Weimar were militarily weak and vulnerable. Given Prussia's failure to defeat Austria in the War of the Bavarian Succession, it was likely that she would fare far worse in a crisis that also forced her to face Russia. The expulsion of the Saxon Duke of Courland in 1763 in order to make way for a Russian, and the First Partition of Poland had put Russia in a better position to intervene further west. Politically, the refusal of Denmark and Sweden to join the *Fürstenbund* helped to weaken it, as did Austrian influence in Bavaria and the Rhineland. The historic pattern of divisions among the non-Habsburg, indeed the Protestant, rulers of the Empire at a time of confrontation with the Emperor was maintained in this crisis. Bavaria, Hesse-Darmstadt, Oldenburg, Württemburg and Würzburg all remained outside the League. Such differences were scarcely new. Hesse-Cassel and Hesse-Darmstadt had generally been on different sides over German issues since the Thirty Years War.

While central Europe seemed unstable, the prospect of war in the Balkans grew closer. Russian military expansion in Pontic Europe was well advertised, and Catherine II made no secret of her determination to make Russia a major power on the Black Sea. In 1787 Catherine was to meet Joseph II at the new naval base at Kherson. Trouble developed, however, in the Caucasus, a region where Turkey, Russia and Iran had competed for control or influence for over fifty years, and where there were religious and ethnic rivalries, an absence of clearly defined boundaries and a lack of control over rival local protégés. Russia had moved into an area that Iran and Turkey had been disputing since the sixteenth century. On 24 July 1783, by the Treaty of Georgievsk, Erekle (Irakli) II, ruler of Kart'li-Kakhet'i, the principal Georgian state, who had actively sought Russian intervention, placed himself under Russian protection, and in November 1783 Russian troops entered Tibilisi. Erekle swore allegiance to Catherine, while in 1784 a military road through the Dariel Pass, linking Russia and eastern Georgia, was completed. These moves alarmed the Turkish frontier pashas, especially Sulayman of Akhaltsikhe and in 1785 he and Omar Khan of Avaria raided Georgia, leading to Russian complaints. In 1785 Russia and Turkey were drawn in to support competing protégés in Transcaucasia, where the Russians had upset the balance of power. In the North

Caucasus, a rising under Sheikh Mansur Ushurma, a Chechen Naqsh-bandi sheikh, who launched a holy war against the Russians in 1785, posed serious problems for the latter. In 1785 a Russian force was encircled and destroyed on the banks of the river Sunja, and it has been claimed that this was the worst-ever defeat inflicted on Catherine's armies. By 1786 Russo-Turkish relations were deteriorating rapidly. Russian actions were in breach of the Treaty of Kutchuk–Kainardji (1774), which had established that all Georgians were under the protection of the Sultan, though the Russians argued that the treaty was an error and that they had only intended to recognise Turkish suzerainty over part of Georgia. In addition, the treaty had been ambiguous about the status of the Black Sea coast of the Caucasus region, which included both Circassian and Georgian lands. In May 1786 Bulgakow, the Russian envoy at Constantinople, presented an aggressive memorial demanding compliance with Russian views in Georgia.[46]

French claims in late 1786 to have settled Russo-Turkish disputes proved inaccurate, although the Turks had ordered Sulayman to cease attacking Georgia. In January 1787 Choiseul-Gouffier, the French Ambassador at Constantinople, reported a new aggressive Russian stance on Georgia, and the following month he and Ainslie noted warlike steps by both powers. In a conference on 20 January 1787 Bulgakow had renewed the Russian demand for a consul at Varna, a step that the Turks feared would lead to an extension of pro-Russian agitation in the Balkans, and demanded that the Turks prevent the Kuban Tartars and the people of the Caucasus from committing hostilities against Russia and her allies, demands that the Turks were determined to reject. A week later Turkish troops were sent to reinforce the crucial Black Sea fortress of Ochakov, and on 1 February the Reis Effendi, the Turkish minister responsible for the negotiations, was dismissed and a less pacific replacement appointed.[47] In addition to the issues already mentioned, there were a

[46] Ainslie to Carmarthen, 25 Jan., 11 Mar., 10 June, 24 July, 9 Aug., 10 Nov., Russian memoranda, 18 May, 3 July 1786, PRO FO 78/7 fols. 15, 79, 179, 210, 222, 308, 219-19; Ségur, French envoy at St Petersburg, to Vergennes, 1, 9 Sept. 1786, AE CP Russie 119 fols. 3–9, 21; Lang, *Georgian Monarchy*, pp. 182–5, 205–6; Atkin, *Russia and Iran*, pp. 29–30, 37; *Cambridge History of Iran*, VII, 327–8; Fisher, *Annexation*, p. 154; Bennigsen, 'Un mouvement populaire', 159–97; M. B. Broxup, 'Russia and the North Caucasus', and P. B. Henze, 'Circassian Resistance to Russia', in Broxup (ed.), *The North Caucasus Barrier. The Russian Advance towards the Muslim World* (1992), pp. 3, 73–6.

[47] Noailles to Vergennes, 13, 18 Nov. 1786, AE CP Aut. 351 fols. 405, 411; Lang, *Georgian Monarchy*, p. 207; Ainslie to Carmarthen, 9 Dec. 1786, PRO FO 78/7 fol. 352; Choiseul-Gouffier to Vergennes, 25 Jan., 10, 23 Feb., memorandum read at Conseil d'Etat, 28 Feb. 1787, AE CP Turquie 175 fols. 40–1, 57–8, 84, 90; Ainslie to Carmarthen, 11, 15 Jan., 10, 23 Feb. 1787, PRO FO 78/8 fols. 5, 15–16, 21–7, 30, 36;

host of others, including Russian anger about the expulsion of a sympathetic Hospodar of Moldavia by the Turks and disputes over the return of deserters. It had already been widely predicted the previous year that problems in the Balkans would prevent Russia's ally Austria from making aggressive moves in Germany.[48] Vergennes undermined his policy of persuading the Turks to avoid war by the trade treaty with Russia, the news of which was greeted in Constantinople with anger and dismay. The internal coherence of his diplomatic strategy, the desire to keep the Turks calm while at the same time to improve relations with Russia (and perhaps also restrain her), was destroyed by the interaction of its own contradictions, and by events in eastern Europe. In a similar fashion, France's policy in the Dutch crisis was to collapse.

The stages by which the crisis in the Balkans and the Low Countries developed and interacted have a misleading air of inevitability in hindsight, combining to create an international crisis that spanned Europe. Such a crisis was not unprecedented: that of 1733 encompassed different struggles in eastern and western Europe that interacted to produce hostilities in Poland, Italy and the Rhineland. The crisis of 1787 was confined to Europe though its effects were felt in Asia. Britain and France did not press their differences to the point of hostilities, and there was therefore nothing comparable to the trans-oceanic span of the crisis of 1754–6 that had led to the Seven Years War. Nevertheless, the crisis of 1787 was a major one because of the number and strength of the participants and the importance of the consequences. As well as revealing French weakness and leading to the outbreak of a major conflict in eastern Europe, the first to involve Austria since the Austro-Turkish war of 1737–9, the crisis dramatically altered European diplomacy, and therefore fulfilled British ministerial hopes over recent years.

And yet the unpredictability of international developments was amply demonstrated in 1786–7. Austria did not attack Prussia after the death of Frederick II; indeed Joseph II saw it as an opportunity for better relations, though he was dissuaded from making an approach by Kaunitz.[49] In addition, the Turks attacked the Russians, instead of, as was generally expected, waiting passively for Catherine II. The Austrian

A. I. Bagis, *Britain and the Struggle for the Integrity of the Ottoman Empire. Sir Robert Ainslie's Embassy to Istanbul 1776–1794* (Istanbul, 1984), pp. 32–3; O. T. Murphy, 'Louis XVI and the Pattern and Costs of a Policy Dilemma: Russia and the Eastern Question, 1787–1788', *The Consortium on Revolutionary Europe, 1986. Proceedings*, 267–8. On the role of Russian consuls, G. F. Jewsbury, *The Russian Annexation of Bessarabia: 1774–1828. A Study of Imperial Expansion* (Boulder, 1976), p. 19.

[48] Pollon, reporting British ministerial opinion, to Victor Amadeus III, 23 May 1786, AST LM Ing. 88; *Daily Universal Register*, 10 Aug., 1 Sept. 1786.

[49] Roider, *Austria's Eastern Question*, pp. 170–1.

Netherlands rebelled, the French were unable to act convincingly in the crisis, the Prussians militarily intervened in the United Provinces and the British found themselves co-operating with Prussia not Austria. Given these unexpected developments, it is inappropriate to criticise the British ministry for failing to anticipate events. It is also clear that their room for manoeuvre was still very limited, as it had been in 1784–5. In 1786 the most promising development paradoxically seemed to be better relations with France. Vergennes had certainly sought such an end, and that was the major reason behind his interest in a commercial treaty.[50] In many respects he was a thoughtful and perceptive Foreign Minister and he has enjoyed a much more favourable scholarly reputation than his predecessors, though he has been criticised for indifference to German questions, and his American biographer has seen Vergennes' skill as compromised by his failure to appreciate the domestic costs of his diplomacy, so that unwillingly he helped to precipitate the Revolution, while, from the perspective of French colonial history, he has been condemned recently for mediocrity, lack of vision and failing to support the imperial schemes of Sartine and Castries.[51]

Vergennes' attempt to improve Anglo-French relations was scarcely unprecedented. Dubois, Morville and Puysieulx had all pursued the same goal. However, whereas Dubois, Morville and the other ministers responsible for the negotiation and maintenance of the Anglo-French alliance of 1716–31, had done so within a diplomatic context in which Spain, Russia and, though to a lesser extent, Austria, but definitely not France, had seemed rising and aggressive powers, unwilling to be restrained by the views of others, and, in various ways, threats to the views of George I and his ministers, Puysieulx had failed in the different context of the late 1740s. By then, France had recovered from her weakness at the end of the War of Spanish Succession, Britain was no longer anxious about Russian strength and was, instead, keen to use Austria and Russia to balance the strength of France and her ally Prussia. At the same time, British colonial and maritime rivalry with France had become more acute and more politically contentious.

Vergennes' failure has to be seen as a repetition of that of Puysieulx, and indeed of D'Aiguillon in 1772–3, rather than as an inability to repeat Dubois' success. Better Anglo-French relations were unlikely while the

[50] Eden to Pitt, 22 Oct. 1786, PRO 30/8/110 fols. 89–90; Vergennes to Barthélemy, 26 Nov. 1786, AE CP Ang. 558 fol. 191.
[51] 'Un Nouveau Vergennes?', Colloquium at Sorbonne, 1987, proceedings printed in *Revue d'historique diplomatique*, 101 (1987), nos. 3–4; A. Tratchevsky, 'La diplomatie de Vergennes ou la France et l'Allemagne sous Louis XVI', *Revue historique*, 15 (1981), 43; Murphy, *Vergennes*, pp. 473–6; Pluchon, *Colonisation française*, pp. 686–8, 715, 737–7, 761.

two powers remained colonial rivals and until Britain became more concerned about the ambitions of another continental power.[52] This was not to be the case until 1791. In late 1786 Eden complained about a poor response to his reports of French good intentions and of Vergennes' wish for further negotiations. Yet, the same day he also wrote to Pitt about the strong possibility of a Franco-Dutch negotiation to give France possession of the Dutch ports in the East Indies.[53]

At the beginning of 1786 George III had made clear to Pitt the advantages of peace and the danger that alliances would lead to war, a thesis he returned to that March. In one sense this argument was a defence of the *Fürstenbund* from accusations that it had jeopardised Britain's chances of negotiating an alliance with Austria or Russia, and, indeed, George was writing in response to Stormont's parliamentary attack on the League of Princes. In another sense, George was responding to the alarmism about French intentions by arguing that growing domestic British strength would be the best counter, while he was also remaining true to a continual theme of his reign: that in negotiations with foreign powers the British government should not be too ready to be the suppliant. This was part of George III's 'Tory' education, his response to the expensive and contentious interventionism of his grandfather George II and the Duke of Newcastle.[54]

And yet such a policy seemed more hazardous in early 1786 as French influence grew in the United Provinces, especially in the affairs of the Dutch East India Company. Unimpressed by Orangist chances under the pusillanimous William V, Harris warned that France was seeking 'to form a mass of maritime power' against Britain. There was talk of Spain acceding to the Franco-Dutch treaty. Prussia preferred to try to influence Dutch affairs by co-operating with France rather than Britain. Dorset was convinced that no Anglo-French commercial treaty would last.[55] Thus the voices within the diplomatic corps warning that France could not be trusted were not stilled at all during the negotiations for the trade treaty. This distrust led Harris to press for a more interventionist British policy, a move that his personal involvement in Dutch affairs made him more eager for. Closer relations with France anyway entailed diplomatic,

[52] Black, *Natural and Necessary Enemies.*
[53] Eden to Pitt, 9 Nov. 1786, PRO 30/8/110 fols. 91–3.
[54] George III to Pitt, 24 Jan., 30 Mar. 1786, Aspinall, *George III* no. 274; Philip, 5th Earl of Stanhope, *Life of … Pitt* (3rd edn, 3 vols., 1879), I, 480; J. Black, 'The Crown, Hanover and the Shift in British Foreign Policy in the 1760s', in Black (ed.), *Knights Errant*, pp. 113–34.
[55] Harris to Keith, 28 Feb., 26 May, Ewart to Keith, 24 May 1786, BL Add. 35536 fols. 106–07, 309, 298; Harris to Ewart, 25 Jan. 1785, Winchester, Malmesbury 204 p. 18; Dorset to Wraxall, 9 Feb. 1786, Beinecke, Osborn Files, Dorset.

as well as political, risks. Carmarthen was concerned that reports about them might both jeopardise chances of improving relations with Joseph II and Catherine II and disconcert the Orangists, and that the French might deliberately spread reports to these ends.[56]

It was, however, far from clear how best Britain could pursue such an interventionist policy. Support for Orangist interests in the United Provinces could not serve as the basis for any major diplomatic realignment, or so it appeared. In 1747 the British had supported an Orangist coup in the province of Zeeland, but that had been an aspect of a wider struggle, and in 1747 Britain was part of a powerful alliance system.[57] Seeking the defeat of the Dutch Patriots in 1786 without foreign assistance seemed foolish. That year Harris, who attributed French success in Holland to their use of bribery, was given about £9,000 from secret funds to support the Orangists;[58] but no further commitments were made and Harris complained about a lack of support.[59] As foreign intervention in the United Provinces was not anticipated, talk of Prussian co-operation having hitherto only led to disappointments,[60] it seemed clear that Britain would have to seek a different basis for interventionism, an instance of the extent to which the configuration of the crisis of 1787, specifically in this case Prussian intervention in the United Provinces, was unexpected, though the Duke of Brunswick, who was to command the force discussed the practicality of an invasion the previous autumn. Dalrymple, who complained that he was not being kept informed of British policy, was convinced that Prussia was being discouraged from negotiating with Britain by means of advice through an unspecified 'indirect channel', possibly an allusion to the Hanoverian ministry. Carmarthen was fully conscious of the problems posed by the unpredictability of other powers.[61]

The government was hopeful in 1786 that Anglo-Russian commercial negotiations might lead to closer political relations, that the developing crisis in the Balkans would destroy the Franco-Austrian connection[62]

---

[56] Harris to Keith, 26 May 1786, BL Add. 35536 fol. 310; Carmarthen to Fitzherbert, 30 Dec., Carmarthen to Harris, 21 Nov. 1785, BL Eg. 3500 fols. 13–14, 30–1.
[57] P. Geyl, *Willem IV en Engeland tot 1748* (The Hague, 1924); H. L. A. Dunthorne, 'Prince and Republic: The House of Orange in Dutch and Anglo-Dutch Politics during the first half of the Eighteenth Century', in J. Black and K. Schweizer (eds.), *Essays in European History in Honour of Ragnhild Hatton* (Lennoxville, 1985), pp. 19–34.
[58] Harris to Carmarthen, 1 Aug. 1786, *Malmesbury*, II, 217; Cobban, *Ambassadors and Secret Agents*, p. 523.
[59] Harris to Carmarthen, 11 Oct. 1786, BL Eg. 3500 fol. 22.
[60] Harris to Carmarthen, 11 Oct. 1786, BL Eg. 3500 fols. 22–3.
[61] Dalrymple to Harris, 2 Sept. 1786, *Malmesbury*, II, 225; Carmarthen to Keith, 3 Apr. 1787, PRO FO 7/13 fol. 105.
[62] Carmarthen to Keith, 18 July 1786, PRO FO 7/12.

and that Frederick William II would be easier to deal with than his uncle. Carmarthen continued to prefer an Austrian alliance, only wanting one with Prussia if Denmark and Russia could be included.[63] The latter idea could be traced back through Fox to Chatham in 1766, and to earlier responses to poor Anglo-Austrian relations in the winter of 1755–6 and in the late 1730s. Prussia alone was weak militarily and of less diplomatic weight than Austria or Russia. There was no real basis however for hopes about an Anglo-Austrian alliance at this juncture. Had Carmarthen been able to see the instructions Kaunitz drew up on 3 April 1786 for the new Envoy Extraordinary in London, Count Karl Reviczky, he would have found his doubts about that minister's views confirmed to an extent that might have shaken his confidence in the prospect of an alliance. Kaunitz, who thought that France and her Dutch allies might drive Britain from India, was convinced that Britain was an unacceptable ally, her policy unreliable and contradictory, flawed by the contrasting views of George III as King and Elector. George and Hanover were presented as very anti-Austrian, and therefore, it was argued, the British government was unwilling to restore Austrian hegemony in the Empire.[64]

There had been hints in early 1786 of an Austrian desire to improve relations with Frederick II, but these had led to nothing to the disappointment of some British observers. Dalrymple wrote from Berlin in May 1786, 'could a reconciliation be brought about between them, a system might be formed that would reduce the overgrown influence of our neighbours to its proper bounds'.[65] In light of British concern over the intentions of the partitioning powers when they had all been united, such a notion might appear surprising, but it reflected heightened anxiety over French views, and a somewhat naive sense that such reconciliation would be good for Britain, a view that recurred in 1790 and early in 1791. Whereas in 1772–3 France had appeared to present no danger to the territorial situation in western Europe, as indeed had been the case since 1748, in the mid-1780s this threat appeared to be revived in the shape of a puppet government in the United Provinces, while the challenge from French colonial and commercial competition also seemed more serious. In 1786 the influence of Kaunitz and the legacy of distrust and German rivalry was too strong for an Austro-Prussian reconciliation, but George III was convinced that the death of Frederick II would not lead to conflict and he used the occasion to remind Carmarthen of the danger that war posed to Britain.[66] The accession of Frederick William II was

[63] Carmarthen to Harris, 24 July, Harris to Ewart, 8 Aug. 1786, *Malmesbury*, II, 211–12, 218.   [64] Kaunitz to Reviczky, 3 Apr. 1786, HHStA EK 129.
[65] Dalrymple to Keith, 24 May 1786, BL Add. 35536 fol. 294.
[66] George III to Carmarthen, 26 Aug. 1786, BL Add. 27914 fol. 17.

indeed to lead to conflict, though in an unexpected fashion, not with Austria, but rather with the Dutch Patriots. The Londoners who gambled that war would be declared between Prussia and Austria by 1 September 1788 were to lose their money.[67] Frederick William's sister, Wilhelmina, was married to William V of Orange, and she was to be the cause of Prussian action, but prior to the summer of 1787 this seemed unlikely. Though the *Daily Universal Register* of 22 September 1786 suggested that 'a continental war... may spring from the troubles of Holland', the possibility of Frederick William II confronting France was most improbable. Joseph might leap at such an opportunity to revenge the loss of Silesia, and would probably be supported by Catherine II. Frederick William, though indecisive and subject to contradictory ministerial pressures, was capable of bold steps, but he had no wish to repeat the experience of the Seven Years War, which had been marked by the devastation of Prussia at the hands of Austria and Russia, as much as by the 'miracle' of its survival. Louis XVI argued on 11 September 1786 that, although Britain was delighted to sow dissension in the United Provinces, she would not provide William V with effective assistance, and that only Frederick William II could do so.

Nevertheless, Carmarthen hoped that Prussian diplomatic pressure in the United Provinces would help William V and harm Franco-Prussian relations. The collapse of the influence of Frederick William's francophile uncle Prince Henry was welcome, as was the dispatch in September 1786 to The Hague of a Prussian special envoy, Count Johann von Görtz.[68] Yet, the British response was still cautious, a sensible policy given the strength of francophile elements in Berlin, the extent to which Frederick William was an unknown quantity, the marked British preference for Austria[69] and the more general reluctance to over-commit Britain. Carmarthen sent Dalrymple fresh instructions on 22 September,

Holland... it is not possible for the King to commit himself until it is clearly evident what part France, as well as Prussia may be inclined to take, every degree of encouragement, short of engaging ourselves too far, ought to be held out to those who may be disposed to oppose the views of France and, of course, the ruling faction in Holland, at the same time we ought not to hold out false hopes of assistance and support to any one. The most desirable object for England might be to see France and Prussia so far engaged and Holland suffering

[67] *Gazette De La Haye*, 22 Sept. 1786, London report.
[68] Hardman, *Louis XVI*, p. 100; York to Keith, 22 Sept. 1786, G. Smyth (ed.), *Memoirs and correspondence of Sir Robert Murray Keith* (2 vols., 1849), II, 190; Cobban, *Ambassadors and Secret Agents*, pp. 93–6.
[69] Carmarthen to Keith, 16 Jan. 1787, PRO FO 7/13 fols. 13–14; *Sentiments on the Interests of Great Britain* (1787), p. 46.

in the general conflict, as to render the King's mediation as necessary as it would undoubtedly be both favourable and advantageous … Prussia should be encouraged to prevent Holland being sacrificed either directly or indirectly to France, without England being at least for the present committed.[70]

This was a reflection both of long-established British caution about actual commitments, as opposed to protestations of good wishes, and of the assessment of Prussia as the least desirable ally among the partitioning powers.[71] Carmarthen was not keen on the idea of an alliance with Prussia, unless Russia and Denmark were also parties. Without such allies, Prussia would be an insufficient basis for a strong alliance system.[72] He found Lusi's language more friendly than in the past, though the envoy was also cautious not to commit Prussia, and the Foreign Secretary reiterated his instruction to Dalrymple to encourage Frederick William to take an anti-French line in the Dutch crisis while at the same time not committing Britain so far 'as to hazard the continuance of our tranquility'.[73] The British response suggests that critics who blamed the *Fürstenbund* for the failure to win the alliance of Austria and Russia were misinformed: there was a fundamental ambivalence about the very notion of any alliance involving commitments, and indeed in October 1786 Pitt referred, though in a different context, to another reason for reluctance about new initiatives, the prospect of direct domestic pressure. He wrote to Carmarthen, 'I have also some doubts as to any mode of treating the delicate subject of Gibraltar and I would submit to you, whether upon the whole it is not better to omit any mention of it for the present.'[74] Given the great attention and effort being devoted by the ministry at this time to commercial negotiations with France, Portugal, Russia and Spain, it is not surprising that foreign envoys, such as Barthélemy, were convinced that British policy was determined by trade, nor that Carmarthen feared the same.[75]

Dalrymple himself was sceptical about the possibility of improved relations with Prussia. He reported that although Frederick William II and his most influential adviser, Count Ewald von Hertzberg, were friendly towards Britain, they would never want to break with France as long as Austria and Russia were united and Prussia therefore vulnerable.

[70] Carmarthen to Dalrymple, 22 Sept., Carmarthen to Harris, 26 Sept. 1786, PRO FO 64/10, 37/12; Harris to Carmarthen, 3 Oct. 1786, BL Eg. 3500 fol. 20.
[71] Carmarthen to Harris, 20 Oct. 1786, BL Eg. 3500 fol. 34.
[72] Carmarthen to Dalrymple, 16 Nov. 1786, BL Eg. 3501 fol. 43.
[73] Carmarthen to Dalrymple, 6 Oct. 1786, PRO FO 64/10; Carmarthen to Harris, 20 Oct. 1786, BL Eg. 3500 fol. 24; Pollone to Victor Amadeus III, 17 Oct. 1786, AST LM Ing. 88.   [74] Pitt to Carmarthen, 24 Oct. 1786, BL Add. 27915 fol. 15.
[75] Carmarthen to Harris, 21 Nov. 1786, BL Eg. 3500; Barthélemy to Vergennes, 5 Dec. 1786, AE CP Ang. 558 fol. 231.

Dalrymple saw no more than the prospect of temporary co-operation with Prussia. Harris was depressed by the Prussian failure to sustain earlier hopes.[76] Carmarthen sought to shift the emphasis of British policy by focusing Pitt's attention on the Dutch crisis and by suggesting a more active role there to George III. He suggested to Harris that he write directly to Pitt,[77] and, in response to Harris' warnings of the seriousness of the situation, Pitt made clear to Carmarthen, to whom he showed Harris' letter, that he was inhibited from acting only because of concern about how best to do so, not because he doubted the need to resist French influence. After receiving Pitt's letter, Harris wrote again to Pitt:

I was very happy to find by your letter of the 5th inst that your ideas relative to this country are perfectly conformable to the principles on which I am acting – I feel the extreme imprudence of committing ourselves in a most forcible manner, and I consider, the endeavour to keep together a party which may be put into activity, whenever circumstances admit, as the only line of conduct we can pursue here either with safety or success … from every thing I can collect, France is endeavouring to lull us to sleep in Europe, in order the more effectually to attack there whenever she feels herself prepared.

As a result of this initiative, Pitt made it clear to Harris that he wished to be fully informed of developments.[78] Irrespective of diplomatic issues, such a move was prudent because the Eden Treaty was most likely to be attacked in the forthcoming parliamentary session on the grounds that French policy was hostile.

In that session Pitt was to declare that 'to suppose that any nation could be unalterably the enemy of another, was weak and childish',[79] a statement that, however hedged with qualifications, revealed the political danger of the Eden Treaty. Not only did such a statement conflict with the prejudices and experience of most of the British political nation, but it also clashed with important aspects of British foreign policy, notably concern with the developing Dutch crisis. Indeed on 22 December 1786 Harris had written to Pitt to tell him that France could never be trusted.[80]

Pitt's discussion of the Dutch crisis with Carmarthen is especially interesting in light of the instruction that Carmarthen sent Sir Robert Ainslie at Constantinople on 19 December 1786. The instruction might appear to arise from a new determination that Pitt's intervention had

[76] Dalrymple to Carmarthen, 20 Oct. 1786, PRO FO 64/10; Harris to Carmarthen, 11 Oct. 1786, BL Eg. 3500 fol. 23; Eden to Carmarthen, 10 Oct. 1786, PRO FO 27/20 fol. 255.

[77] Browning (ed.), *Memoranda of … Leeds*, pp. 117–18; Carmarthen to Harris, 21 Nov., Harris to Carmarthen, 28 Nov. 1786, BL Eg. 3500 fol. 30, 28061; Harris to Pitt, 28 Nov., Carmarthen to Harris, 5 Dec. 1786, *Malmesbury*, II, 251–5.

[78] Harris to Pitt, 8 Dec. 1786, PRO 30/8/155 fols. 53–4; Pitt to Harris, 26 Dec. 1786, *Malmesbury*, II, 263.   [79] Cobbett, 26, 392.

[80] Harris to Pitt, 22 Dec. 1786, BL Add. 28068 fol. 194.

given to British policy, but it casts serious doubt upon either the wisdom or the integrity of the ministry's parliamentary defence of the Eden Treaty, in which Pitt told the Commons on 12 February 1787 that 'her [France's] assurances and frankness during the present negotiation, were such as, in his opinion, might be confided in'.[81] Ainslie, who Carmarthen recommended for the Order of the Bath in January 1787 on the basis of his ability, zeal and success, was instructed of 'the necessity as well as propriety upon every occasion, of endeavouring to combat the views of France as far as possible with caution and discretion in order to serve and promote the interests of England, unless you receive very positive and direct instructions to the contrary from home', a somewhat ambiguous order. French interests were to be combated by exploiting Russo-Turkish disputes, 'this difference ought certainly to be blown into a flame if possible ... ' The prospect of France supporting her Turkish ally was seen as the key, 'in the event of a rupture between Russia and the Porte it is easily to be judged whether the situation in which Russia, Austria, and France must necessarily be placed, might not be productive of the most important, and perhaps permanent advantage to Great Britain'. Carmarthen relied on Ainslie's knowledge of the situation in Constantinople, where he had been since 1776, to decide 'how far the resolution of the present Divan can be encouraged so far as at least to hamper France if not actually break with Russia without at the same time committing England till things are ripe for our taking what we ought to do, on every possible occasion, a decided and effective part'. Ainslie was assured that it was 'by no means the wish of England to create, or even encourage, a breach of public tranquillity, except where some restless and ambitious power renders it necessary for our own defence [and that] a diversion of the attention of France on the side of Turkey would now be of the most important service to England'. The letter reached Ainslie on 3 February 1787. Promising to obey the orders, he noted that his views coincided with Carmarthen's.[82] Carmarthen's instruction fell into the pattern of British attempts to exploit possible difficulties facing the Franco-Austro-Russian power bloc, but it proposed a more active role for Britain than during the Balkan crisis of 1783–4. Carmarthen hoped that the Balkan crisis would not only divide France from Russia, but also lead to poor relations between Catherine and Joseph.[83] The instructions are of importance, not only because of the allegations that Ainslie was in part responsible for the Turkish declaration of war in 1787, and thus for

[81] Cobbett, 26, 393.
[82] Carmarthen to Pitt, 14 Jan. 1787, BL Eg. 3498 fol. 171; Carmarthen to Ainslie, 19 Dec. 1786, Ainslie to Carmarthen, 10 Feb. 1787, PRO FO 78/7 fols. 361–4, 78/8 fol. 20.
[83] Carmarthen to Keith, 16 Jan. 1787, PRO FO 7/13 fol. 13.

the beginning of the great European crisis,[84] but also because it suggests that British policy had become hopelessly confused, with major disagreements over the extent to which France could be trusted. It has been customary to attribute the successful (for Britain) resolution of the Dutch crisis in large part to Pitt's skill,[85] but this can be re-examined. In the winter of 1786–7 Pitt can be seen as beginning to appreciate that he had committed himself to a policy of reconciliation with France that was diplomatically questionable and politically dangerous. In the summer of 1787 he was to yield to the advocacy of strong anti-French policies by Harris and Carmarthen, and he had begun to move towards them the previous winter. The beginning of his correspondence with Harris was more probably part cause of this move, rather than effect. It is significant that for most of 1786 Pitt had corresponded with the more francophile Eden, but not with Harris. The forceful Harris was believed to have considerable influence with Carmarthen, who both knew far less about foreign policy than the envoy and who shared his views about France, Eden and trade treaties.[86] In late 1786 an ill Carmarthen survived a rather obscure attempt to replace him. The persistence of reports to this end in 1784–7 suggest that his position in the ministry was at least believed to be insecure, although it is unclear whether this arose from his policies or his lack of apparent, certainly of obvious and ostentatious, dedication to the details of his post. In October 1784 when Pitt suggested that Carmarthen move to the Foreign Office in order to free the post for Grafton, Carmarthen replied that he was ready to be replaced and would not seek another post. The presence of Fox at a dinner Carmarthen held in mid-January 1787 gave rise to comment.[87]

Carmarthen was to remain at his post, helping to direct British policy in an anti-French direction. It is not clear that policy would have been different had he been replaced by Grantham, Germain or Stormont, as was rumoured at various times, though, another suggestion, Hawkes-

---

[84] Lang, *Georgian Monarchy*, p. 210; Bagis, *Ainslie*, pp. 38–46; J. Black, 'Sir Robert Ainslie: His Majesty's Agent-provocateur? British Foreign Policy and the International Crisis of 1787', *European History Quarterly*, 14 (1984), 253–83.

[85] J. Ehrman, *The Younger Pitt* (2 vols. to date, 1969, 1983), pp. 536–8.

[86] Barthélemy to Vergennes, 26 Sept. 1786, AE CP Ang. 557 fol. 319; Carmarthen to Harris, 20 Oct. 1786, BL Eg. 3500 fol. 24.

[87] Pitt to Carmarthen, and reply, both 15 Oct. 1784, BL Eg. 3498 fols. 59, 62–3; Pollone to Victor Amadeus III, 19 Dec. 1786, 23 Jan. 1787, AST LM Ing. 88; Barthélemy to Vergennes, 26 Dec. 1786, AE CP Ang. 558 fol. 321; Carmarthen to Pitt, 8 Jan. 1787, PRO 30/8/151 fol. 38; Horatio Walpole memorandum, 18 Jan. 1787, Lewis (ed.), *Walpole – Countess of Upper Ossory Corresp.* II, 554 fn. 6; *Newcastle Chronicle* 20 Jan. 1787; Marquis of Lothian to Rutland, 22 Jan. 1787, HMC *Rutland* III, 367; Lady Chatham to Edward Eliot, 25 Jan. 1787, Belfast, Public Record Office of Northern Ireland, papers of Edward Gibson F2/2; Bulkeley to Keith, 13 Mar. 1787, BL Add. 35538 fol. 63.

bury, would have represented a major shift, as he was a protégé of George III, and George remained opposed to what he saw as unwise and potentially expensive commitments, while Shelburne, now Marquess of Lansdowne, would have been more keen on co-operation with France. The extent to which Ainslie was responsible for the Turkish declaration of war was contentious and is obscure. It would have required a wide interpretation of his instructions for Ainslie to have pressed the Turks to fight, as it is difficult to see how he could have done so without compromising the British government, though it would have been perfectly in accord with them for him to assure the Turks that there would be no British aid for the Russian navy, as there had been in the previous Russo-Turkish conflict. In February 1787 Ainslie assured the Grand Vizir that Russia would probably act alone. Vergennes' successor, Montmorin, claimed that Ainslie refused a Turkish request to put in writing what he had said in order to press the Turks to fight,[88] but it is difficult to perceive what he could have offered that would have persuaded the Turks to attack. Given Ainslie's known friendship with many Turkish dignitaries and the convenience of the conflict for British policy, it is easy to appreciate the accusations that were pressed. The available evidence indicates that the Turks were not decisively influenced by Ainslie, though it does not free him from the suspicion of having encouraged them to fight. Ministerial changes in Constantinople were doubtless more important. On 24 January 1786 Koca Yusuf Paşa, a Georgian convert and the Governor of the Morea, became Grand Vizir. He was a supporter of immediate war with Russia, which he saw as a major threat to the Turkish Empire. His influence was increased by the departure of the more cautious Grand Admiral Gazi Hasan Paşa to Egypt in order to restore Turkish authority over the Mamelukes who had taken effective control over that important part of the empire. Gazi Hasan left in June 1786 and did not return until November 1787. The Sultan, Abdulhamit I (1774–89), does not appear to have taken a forceful role, and was threatened by Koca Yusuf Paşa with deposition unless he agreed to war to regain the Crimea.[89]

Distance was to help ensure that the British government played a less direct role in the Balkan crisis than in its Dutch counterpart, but it is necessary to bear in mind that, as the Dutch crisis developed, the British

[88] Ainslie to Carmarthen, 10 Feb. 1787, PRO FO 78/8 fol. 25; Montmorin to Ségur, 5 Feb. 1788, AE CP Russie 123 fol. 187.
[89] D. Gerhard, *England und der Aufstieg Russlands* (Munich, 1933), pp. 197–9; S. J. Shaw, *Between Old and New. The Ottoman Empire under Sultan Selim III 1789–1807* (Cambridge, Mass., 1971), pp. 25–6, and *History of the Ottoman Empire and Modern Turkey I* (Cambridge, 1976), p. 258; Bagis, *Ainslie*, pp. 26, 40–1; Fisher, *Annexation*, p. 155; A. Cunningham, 'The Oczakov Debate', *Middle Eastern Studies* 1 (1964), 213–14.

ministry were aware that it might interact with the outbreak of war in the Balkans, and it is possible that they had acted to encourage the latter. That was certainly the intent of Carmarthen's instruction of 19 December 1786. This is significant because it underlines the danger of judging Britain's Dutch policy in isolation.

An additional complication arises from the Russian interpretation of British policy, for this centred on George III and offers the possibility that the Balkan and Dutch policies should be carefully separated. The Russian government believed that Ainslie had obeyed orders, but orders from George III, not Pitt. Catherine II, several members of the College of Foreign Affairs, such as Bezborodko and Markov, and the envoys in London and Frankfurt, Vorontsov and Rumyantsev, all believed that British policy was controlled by George for the benefit of Hanover and Prussia. This belief arose largely from the *Fürstenbund*. George III had not only negotiated the treaty, but had also taken an active role in seeking the support of German princes, such as the rulers of Baden, Hesse-Cassel, Mainz, Mecklenburg and Würzburg. Fox and Stormont told Kageneck that George not only was very attached to Hanover, but also kept his British ministers in the dark about German affairs. His ability to do so contributed to the growing conviction in St Petersburg and Vienna that George operated in a deceitful fashion. In July 1786 Kaunitz asked how the British ministry could believe an Austrian alliance possible, given George III's views. He suggested that Reviczky make a personal approach to Pitt and Carmarthen in order to explain the situation from the Austrian viewpoint.[90] Catherine II wrote of George as a weak puppet of his German connections. This view led her to regard the British government as a foreign element, out of sympathy with the British nation and its 'natural interests'. Vorontsov's reports helped to confirm Catherine in her views. He argued that the influence of Berlin, by way of Hanover, was directing the actions of George III, and that the king could override Pitt. Vorontsov reported that George was greatly influenced by the Hanoverian minister Alvensleben, who had important Prussian links, by Baron Seckendorf, a German agent working in London on behalf of Prussia, and by the Duke of York, who also had Prussian links. He also complained that Harris was working on behalf of Prussia, and was leading Carmarthen around 'by the nose' thereby directing the ministry towards Berlin. Vorontsov reported that Harris and Carmarthen were in league with George III and misleading Pitt, who was kept ignorant. These reports had an effect. In April 1789 the British envoy in St

---

[90] Kageneck to Kaunitz, 18, 25 Oct. 1785, Kaunitz to Reviczky, 27 July 1786, HHStA EK 124, 129; Aretin, *Reich*, I, 178, 9.

Petersburg, Charles Whitworth, reported that Vorontsov's reports were abusive and scurrilous, and harmed relations, and that in Russia he heard 'daily of the most extravagant and exaggerated stories of a personal dislike to the Empress; of a determination to force her to accept of peace, on the most humiliating terms'.[91]

The Austrian envoy Kageneck reported in June 1786 that only Pitt still seemed to favour Austria and Russia, and that George III and Carmarthen were very cold to both him and Vorontsov. That was certainly a failure to understand the attitude of Carmarthen, who remained pro-Austrian. If the *Fürstenbund* was seen not simply as a Hanoverian move, but as an attempt by George III to commit Britain to a Prussian alliance, then it was understandable that subsequent Anglo-Prussian co-operation should be seen as originating with the League and arising from George III's views and actions. In April 1787 Reviczky reported that George was close to Prussia, and that all talk of a British alliance with Austria and Russia had ceased. The following month Reviczky presented Britain as the dupe of Prussia, helping her to stir up the Turks.[92]

The Russian argument is given added importance in light of Blanning's contention that George III had taken control of British foreign policy in 1785, and that it was in 1787 that 'Pitt and his colleagues regained freedom of action',[93] a phrase that avoids the problem of differences within the ministry and makes it unclear how far this process of regaining involved conflict. By combining both arguments, a *secret du roi*, a royal foreign policy, can be readily discerned and it can be argued that, having achieved the *Fürstenbund*, the policy continued in 1787, maybe not in the Dutch crisis, in which the Cabinet rather than George was responsible for policy, but with the King instigating war in the Balkans. The notion of a bi-focal foreign policy, only one part of which was closely directed by the King, is not implausible. It had existed in the latter stages of the War of the Austrian Succession, in which George II, operating through the Hanoverian government and the British Ambassador in St Petersburg, John, 3rd Earl of Hyndford, had followed an anti-Prussian policy, that contradicted the anti-French emphasis of the British ministry. Hano-verian concerns in central and eastern Europe were stronger than those of British ministries, and it was more in the interest of the Electorate to

[91] Marcum, 'Vorontsov and Pitt', 50–1; Marcum, 'Vorontsov', pp. 69–81; I. de Madariaga, *Russia in the Age of Catherine the Great* (1981), p. 395; Whitworth to Carmarthen, 10 Apr. 1789, PRO FO 65/17 fols. 89–91. For the claim that anti-Russian moves in 1788 were entirely due to George III, Luzerne to Montmorin, 3 June 1788, AE CP Ang. 565 fol. 235.

[92] Kageneck to Kaunitz, 9 June 1786, Reviczky to Kaunitz, 13 Apr., 22 May 1787, HHStA EK 126.   [93] Blanning, '*Fürstenbund* of 1785', pp. 337–44.

follow policies against Austria, Prussia or Russia, whereas, for Britain, France took clear precedence. The Dutch crisis had little distinctive importance for George III. He could share his ministers' desire to thwart France, and like them, hope that it would be achieved in part through Prussian assistance, but he certainly did not force the pace of British action. Indeed Carmarthen was made very uneasy in January 1787 by George III's reluctance both to approve his plan for an active stance in the Dutch crisis and to support Harris' demand for money to this end. At a crucial moment in the Dutch crisis that summer the Duke of York saw Frederick William II on behalf of George III, but it was to discuss the coadjutorship of Mainz, not Dutch affairs.[94]

On the other hand, the notion of a royal foreign policy, of British diplomacy directed, at least in part, by George III to the objectives suggested, and in the manner described, by Russian commentators is questionable. The *Fürstenbund* had shown that George III was more ready than his British ministers to give effect to policies that offended Joseph II and Catherine II, and he was believed to have little personal esteem for either.[95] It was also, however, clear that British ministers did not alter their attitudes to conform to George III's moves. The Russian notion that Ainslie's activities were another instance of George's personal policy has, however, to be seen in the context of the long-standing British attempt to seek to exploit tensions in the opposing power bloc. Furthermore, whereas the *Fürstenbund* arose from Hanoverian policy in a sphere that was within the competence of the Electorate, however inconvenient it might be for the British government, there was no Hanoverian dimension to the Turkish policy. Nevertheless, it is important to stress that the *Fürstenbund* did not cease in 1785. The issues that had given rise to it remained pressing. Concern about Joseph's plans in the Empire continued and there were frequent reports of plans to revive the Bavarian Exchange Scheme, for example in January 1787. Joseph claimed that the Exchange was finished after the Duke of Zweibrücken had rejected it, but there was widespread suspicion about his intentions.[96] Hanoverian–Prussian co-operation in the Empire remained important, for example in the winter of 1786–7 over the contested election to the coadjutorship of Mainz, and this helped to keep Catherine II and Joseph II aware of that diplomatic axis. Accessions to the *Fürstenbund* continued, the Duke of Mecklenburg-Schwerin joining

[94] Carmarthen to Pitt, 8 Jan., Carmarthen to Harris, 8 Jan., George III to Pitt, 8 Jan. 1787, PRO 30/8/151 fol. 38, *Malmesbury*, II, 267–8, CUL Add. 6958 no. 262; York to George III, 1, 8 June 1787, Aspinall, *George III*, no. 370; Carmarthen to Fitzherbert, 12 Nov. 1786, BL Eg. 3500 fol. 17.
[95] Barthélemy to Montmorin, 14 Aug. 1787, AE CP Ang. 561 fol. 55.
[96] Joseph II to Mercy, 18 Mar. 1787, Arneth, II, 83.

on 16 January 1787. Proposals for imperial reform through the League circulated in late 1786 and 1787 and received a sympathetic response from Frederick William II.[97]

The suspicions of contemporary diplomats about Ainslie need to be placed in the context of the widespread habit of ascribing the actions of certain powers, especially Turkey, throughout the century, Sweden, during the Age of Liberty, and Russia, between the reigns of Peter I and Catherine II, to the influence, often pecuniary, of foreign diplomats. The Russo-Turkish war of 1768–74, for example, had been blamed on the French. In January 1785 the British ministry had insisted that the French were stirring up the Turks. It was easy to jump to such conclusions and to make such claims. Scholarly investigations have usually failed to substantiate these accusations. The cautious attitude adopted in 1738 by Grantham's father, Thomas Robinson, Minister Plenipotentiary in Vienna, was more appropriate,

neither those who are unacquainted with the vicissitudes of the Turkish councils, nor those who are unacquainted with the brigues of the Seraglio and of the priests and of the men of the law, which are more difficult to be penetrated than like factions and intrigues in European courts and governments, can well pretend to judge what may be the resolutions of that assembly.

When, on 2 January 1787, Ainslie sent presents to the total value of 1,000 piastres to leading ministers and favourites, he added 'I know from experience [they] will turn to very good account, when I shall have occasion for their services', but he did not suggest that he would therefore be able to dictate policy.[98] It was all too tempting, however, to argue that unexpected or unwelcome decisions arose from the manipulations of rivals. Ainslie claimed that his Austrian and Russian counterparts had totally failed to appreciate that the Turks would not give way to threats. The erroneous report that Joseph II had not gone to war

[97] F. C. Wittichen, *Preussen und England in der europäischen Politik 1785–1788* (Heidelberg, 1902), p. 117; Gagliardo, *Reich and Nation*, p. 74.
[98] Robinson to Lord Harrington, Secretary of State, 8 Nov. 1738, PRO SP. 80/132 fol. 36; Earl Harcourt, envoy in Paris, to Viscount Weymouth, Secretary of State, 20 Feb. 1769, PRO SP. 78/277 fol. 129; Kageneck to Kaunitz, 11 Jan. 1785, HHStA EK 124; R. M. Hatton, 'Gratifications and Foreign Policy: Anglo-French Rivalry in Sweden during the Nine Years War', in Hatton and J. S. Bromley (eds.), *William III and Louis XIV. Essays 1680–1720 by and for Mark A. Thomson* (Liverpool, 1968), pp. 68–94; M. F. Metcalf, *Russia, England, and Swedish Party Politics, 1762–1766: the interplay between great power diplomacy and domestic politics during Sweden's Age of Liberty* (Stockholm, 1977); R. M. Hatton, 'Presents and Pensions: a methodological search and the case study of Count Nils Bielke's prosecution for treason in connection with gratifications from France', in P. Mack and M. C. Jacob (eds.), *Politics and Culture in Early Modern Europe: Essays in Honour of H. G. Koenigsberger* (Cambridge, 1987), pp. 101–17; Ainslie to Carmarthen, 11 Jan. 1787, PRO FO 78/8 fol. 7.

during the Scheldt dispute because he feared Turkish attack could only have encouraged a sense that the two spheres were interrelated, and that this would lead to attempts to influence developments in western Europe by manipulating those in the Balkans. The Russians were most surprised by the Turkish declaration of war and Vorontsov did not believe the news.[99] It was customary to stress the impending dissolution of the Turkish Empire and most commentators, who had expected a Russian attack, found it impossible to believe that the Turks would risk a war unless they had been encouraged by promises of support.[100]

The Dutch crisis

Rather than searching for a master plan in British policy, one directed by George III, that scored two major successes in 1787, it is more appropriate to notice the hesitant way in which British policy developed in the Dutch crisis. This hesitation owed much to differences over the extent to which Britain should commit herself, but there was also considerable uncertainty over the likely response of other powers; indeed it was this unpredictability that was the most obvious feature of the crisis.

The Dutch situation became more complex in the winter of 1786–7 as the growing radicalism of the Patriots and their worsening rift with the Orangists led to deteriorating relations between the Regents, the oligarchical patriciate of Holland, and the Patriots. Whereas France in 1789 had a single centre of authority, Paris, the federal nature of the United Provinces led to differing relationships between authority and power throughout the state and ensured that rising tension led to civil war between the forces of various authorities. This offered fertile ground for external intervention, and both Harris and his French counterpart, Vérac, thought it necessary to do so, a process that was blamed for the failure to settle differences.[101] In light of 'the progress of French influence in almost every cabinet in Europe', Harris greeted the new year by pressing Carmarthen on the need to build up the Orangist party in the United Provinces, and, while stressing to the more cautious Pitt that he did not want to commit Britain too far, the minister took up the challenge,

eager as I am for preventing France acquiring the absolute command of Holland: I have always thought that we might succeed by means of private negotiation and intrigue. The experiment of trying to combat her with her own weapons would

[99] Ainslie to Carmarthen, 10 Oct. 1787, PRO FO 78/8 fol. 218; *Daily Universal Register*, 10 Aug. 1786; Fraser to Eden, 8 Sept. 1787, BL Add. 34426 fol. 141.
[100] Ségur to Montmorin, 28 Aug., 5 Sept. 1787, AE CP Russie 121 fols. 285–6, 122 fol. 7.
[101] Bütemeister, report from The Hague, 26 Dec. 1786, Marburg, 4 f. Niederlande 769.

have some merit, and convinced as I am that she has reckoned all along upon England's not interfering I think the present moment must not be suffered to pass by without our endeavouring to make the most we can of the provinces who are opposed to Holland and of the present firmness of the Prince and Princess of Orange.

Carmarthen also focussed attention on what was to be a major theme not only of the crisis of 1787, but even more of international relations over the next few years, the first French Revolution, the impact of French domestic difficulties on her international status. The financial crisis of the French monarchy led to increasing governmental interest in reform and constitutional change; indeed, as elsewhere in Europe, the political impetus for innovations came in the mid-1780s largely from the government. An Assembly of Notables comprised of leading figures nominated by Louis XVI assembled in February 1787, but refused to accept the proposals from first Calonne, who was compromised by suspicions of corruption, and then Brienne, that the taxation system be reorganised and that both a universal land tax and provincial assemblies elected by landowners be introduced. Instead the Notables sought government economies and assemblies that were virtually autonomous, not mere organs for consultation and collaboration. At the outset of 1787 it was far from clear that the Assembly of Notables would not produce a degree of reform and renewal, indeed that was the expectation of Vergennes' successor, Montmorin, but Carmarthen argued that 'L'Assemblé des Notables is I think some security for the pacific dispositions of France, or rather for her inability of indulging any of a contrary nature at present.'[102] Ewart, who felt that the British had been too hesitant in becoming involved in Dutch affairs, shared similar hopes.[103] Eden, however, offered the contrary view, that Calonne might well achieve reform. He also suggested that this might be done through an extreme solution, a national bankruptcy. By pointing out that the resources of the country were always great, Eden argued that no reliance could be placed upon temporary French difficulties. Richmond had

---

[102] Harris to Pitt, 2 Jan., Carmarthen to Pitt, 8 Jan., Harris to Carmarthen, 3, 8, 9 Jan. 1787, PRO 30/8/155 fol. 57, 30/8/151 fols. 38–9, CUL Add. 6958 no. 261, *Malmesbury*, II, 266–70; Montmorin to ?, 20 Feb. 1787, 'Melanges', *Revue d'histoire diplomatique*, 105 (1991), 178; J. Egret, *The French Prerevolution, 1787–1788* (Chicago, 1977), pp. 1–35; V. R. Gruder, 'Class and Politics in the Pre-Revolution: The Assembly of Notables of 1787', in E. Hinrichs et al., *Vom Ancien Régime zur Französischen Revolution* (Göttingen, 1978); V. R. Gruder, 'Paths to Political Consciousness: The Assembly of Notables of 1787 and the "Pre-Revolution" in France', *French Historical Studies*, 13 (1984), 323–55; V. R. Gruder, 'A Mutation in Elite Political Culture: The French Notables and the Defence of Property and Participation', *Journal of Modern History*, 56 (1984), 598–634; Hardman, *Louis XVI*, pp. 103–27.   [103] Ewart to Keith, 1 Feb. 1787, BL Add. 35538 fols. 6–8.

claimed the previous year that financial problems would not prevent hostile French steps. Grenville was warned that French attempts to improve government finances might be preparations for war.[104]

Britain still lacked a continental ally, but the Dutch crisis was pushing relations with France to a more acute level. The crisis of 1787 helped to emphasise Anglo-French rivalry and to encourage an interpretation of the previous years in that light, as a pre-history of the crisis, but the position was in fact less clear. It is clear that the tension of 1787 is not a reliable guide to French intentions in 1784–6. Vergennes did not seek war with Britain, and, to that extent, Carmarthen's fears of French policy were unjustified. It is equally true, though, that the French view of the status quo was one that left little room for British action. Victor Amadeus III of Sardinia told the British envoy 'Peace is certainly a great blessing ... but I do not like a peace of which France seems to have the arbitration, and a mischievous one too.' Carmarthen replied in December 1785 to Richmond's idea of Britain joining the Franco-Dutch alliance by pointing out not only that Britain would therefore have to assist France in the event of a Franco-Austrian conflict, but also that she would 'be called upon to interpose our good offices whenever France chose to represent herself as even *menacée d'une attaque*, an expression so vague as to admit of almost infinite doubt and discussion'. The Spanish minister Floridablanca complained in July 1787 that the French government's interpretation of the alliance between the two states was one of French domination and Spanish subordination.[105] Excluded from influence in European affairs, Britain appeared to have to accept what seemed to be an active and aggressive French policy of gaining control of European trade, or so the Franco-Dutch and Franco-Russian treaties suggested. Yet the extent to which the French diplomatic dominance of western Europe affected vital British interests is questionable. The Scheldt and Bavarian Exchange issues arguably did not, although had they led to greater French influence in the Low Countries, the situation might have appeared more threatening. The French position certainly challenged British perceptions of their respective roles in European affairs.

The growing bitterness of Dutch internal struggles and, more crucially, the increase in diplomatic attention devoted to them, altered this situation; not least in Britain by focussing attention on Harris. He

[104] Eden to Pitt, 3 Feb. 1787, CUL Add. 6958 no. 274; Richmond to Pitt, 15 Jan. 1786, PRO 30/8/170 fols. 65–6; John Gray to Grenville, 21 May 1787, BL Add. 59354 fol. 34.
[105] Trevor to Carmarthen, 3 Jan. 1787, PRO FO 67/5; Carmarthen to Richmond, 27 Dec. 1785, BL Eg. 3498 fol. 229; J.-R. Aymes, 'Spain and the French Revolution', *Mediterranean Historical Review*, 6 (1991), 64.

sent a private letter to Carmarthen in October 1786 explaining why he believed a combination of French hegemony and British isolationism was dangerous,

I much fear the indifference with which we suffer this republic to pass under the French yoke, far from ensuring the duration of peace, will tend to shorten its term – France will naturally attribute this condescension on our side to an inability to resist her, and this idea will necessarily prompt her to quarrel with us – There is no doubt of our growing richer in a much quicker proportion than France, but if France does not augment her national wealth, France is augmenting her political influence in Europe and of course her political strength with such success and rapidity, as to make it a very serious and formidable apprehension – my standing principle, is that France will go to war with England, whenever she is ready, and that till she is ready nothing short of a direct insult will induce her to draw the sword.

Harris' arguments accorded with and lent direction to Carmarthen's views.[106] The Dutch crisis, with its naval and colonial repercussions, engrossed British ministerial and public attention to an extent that previous issues had failed to do. It was easy to relate the crisis to the British conviction of a French threat to the British naval and colonial position. The previous March, Harris had warned that the Patriots were seeking French guidance

on the degree of force ... which they require the Dutch to keep in the East Indies ... by a late regulation the East India direction here is now entirely in the hands of the Patriots and that they have it in their power to make its wealth and influence absolutely subservient to ... the Court of Versailles.

Dorset was, in turn, convinced that the French wished the Dutch to be as strong as possible in the Indian Ocean, and that they were making plans in the event of war.[107]

As attention focussed increasingly on the United Provinces, and as the situation there deteriorated markedly, acceptable Anglo-French relations became progressively more difficult. Neither government acted purposefully to restrain their envoys' ardent endorsement of clashing Dutch factions.[108] As so often with great power intervention in the complicated affairs of a smaller state, the policies of the great powers were influenced substantially by their local protégés. The British were acutely sensitive to signs of French intervention in Dutch politics, and French policy, handicapped by internal tensions and by the natural difficulty of a change after the death of Vergennes on 13 February 1787, was sufficiently

---

[106] Harris to Carmarthen, 11 Oct., Carmarthen to Fitzherbert, 12 Nov. 1786, BL Eg. 3500 fols. 22, 16–17.
[107] Harris to Dorset, 7 Mar., Dorset to Harris, 20 Mar., Dorset to Liston, 20 Mar. 1786, KAO C188/3, 184.   [108] Eden to Liston, 19 Aug. 1787, NLS 5547 fol. 180.

interventionist to increase British fears. Had his successor Montmorin been more in control of French policy, then it is possible, as Eden suggested, that it would have been perceived as less aggressive. On the other hand, it was seen as aggressive when Vergennes was alive even though he sought an amicable settlement of the Dutch crisis.

The almost obsessive concentration on the struggle between British and French protégés in the United Provinces to the detriment of other aspects of Anglo-French relations was largely due to Harris' success in May 1787 in forcing the issue to the forefront of ministerial attention. Hawkesbury complained in early August 1787 that ministers were 'wholly engrossed with what is passing in Holland, and in other parts with reference to this particular point'. In warning Barthélemy in 1788 not to make British policy appear too profound, reflective and complicated, Montmorin attributed British intervention in the Dutch crisis to Harris.[109] In the summer of 1787 British ministerial attitudes toward France hardened *and* there was a greater willingness to support the Orangists, a reversal of the policy of late 1786 of relying on Frederick William II. The implications of French policy in the United Provinces were extremely serious for Britain. The War of American Independence had revealed the crucial importance of sea power and colonial strength. Responding to instructions about commercial issues, Harris wrote in February 1787, 'I wish instead of the production of the Moluccas you would instruct me to ask for the Moluccas themselves. If *we* do not get them the *French* will, as it is impossible, in its present state of disorder that the Republic should preserve its distant settlements.'[110] Carmarthen and his supporters were justified in viewing the French position with grave suspicion, even though their interpretation of French policy was based on a misunderstanding of the extent of Vergennes' interest in weakening Britain. Vergennes' views, however, were not shared by influential ministerial colleagues, in particular Castries, the minister for the Marine, and Calonne who emphasised that Britain was a natural enemy. Dorset, although confident that Vergennes and Calonne sought good relations, was concerned about the situation after the death of the first and the fall of the second. In 1790 Sir John Macpherson recorded discussing with Castries, then an *émigré* in Lausanne, his 'plans in 1786 [sic] for the subversion of our Empire in India. These were found, and frustrated, by the Duke of Brunswick when he took Amsterdam.' The Duke of York, who in August 1787 wanted war with France over the

---

[109] Montmorin to Vérac, 23 June 1787, Montmorin to Barthélemy, 23 Sept. 1788, AE CP Hollande 573 fol. 215, Ang. 566 fol. 309; Hawkesbury to Walsingham, 6 Aug. 1787, BL Add. 38310 fol. 3.
[110] Harris to Carmarthen, 6 Feb. 1787, BL Eg. 3500 fol. 38.

Dutch, argued that 'the addition of the ships which she [the United Provinces] is able to fit out, will give them the complete empire of the sea'.[111] Carmarthen and Harris were correct not only in regarding the Dutch situation as serious, but also in feeling that it might be possible to confront France successfully over the issue, and without excessive cost to Britain.

Initially the prospect of success in the United Provinces had seemed unlikely. Most crucially, Frederick William II had not persisted with his support for the Orangists because of disillusionment with William V, and a wish not to alienate France in the face of rumoured Austro-Russian plans to revive the Bavarian Exchange and even possibly attack Prussia, which were skilfully exploited by France. Frederick William argued that Dutch affairs were of more concern to Britain than Prussia.[112] Harris became totally disillusioned about the prospects of Prussian action, and, instead, remained committed to his plan for a British-supported revolution in Holland, a repetition in short of the coup of 1747, while he hoped to see Austria and possibly Russia join Britain in achieving this. Harris promised that within a week of Joseph II allying with Britain he would 'overset the whole influence of France' in the United Provinces.[113] The caution that George III and Pitt displayed in the Dutch crisis is understandable in light of the improbability of this scenario. Nevertheless, it was government policy to seek such an alliance, Camarthen starkly contrasting it with what he saw as the two other scenarios,

such a connection must be deemed desirable by every person who has at all times their mind to the consideration of foreign politics, unless either mad enough to suppose this country perfectly secure in her own internal resources, against all possible contingencies, or foolish enough to give, I do not say implicit, but even any considerable degree of credit to the pacific or friendly assurances of France.[114]

The spring of 1787 brought no improvement in relations with Austria and Russia, but the failure of the Assembly of Notables in France to bring the hoped for renewal was increasingly obvious. Calonne was dismissed on 8 April, being replaced eventually as first minister by Brienne, who Louis XVI hoped would have more success. Hawkesbury

[111] Memoranda, 2 Jan. 1785, AE CP Aut. 349 fols. 8, 21; Dorset to Stafford, 12 Apr., Thurlow to Stafford, 17 Oct. 1787, PRO 30/29/1/15 nos. 58, 68; A. Aspinall (ed.), *Correspondence of George Prince of Wales 1770–1812* II (1964), p. 99; York to Richard Grenville, 30 Aug. 1787, BL Add. 70958; Donaghay, 'Vicious Circle', pp. 448–9.
[112] Frederick William to Wilhelmina, 31 Oct. 1786, Wittichen, *Preussen und England*, p. 64; Dalrymple to Keith, 1 Feb., Ewart to Keith, 1 Feb. 1787, BL Add. 35538 fols. 1–4.
[113] Harris to Carmarthen, 11 Oct. 1786, Ewart to Keith, 1 Feb., Harris to Keith, 9 Feb., 20 Mar., 4 May 1787, BL Eg. 3500 fols. 22–3, Add. 35538 fols. 7, 19–20, 77, 138.
[114] Carmarthen to Keith, 3 Apr. 1787, PRO FO 7/13 fol. 103.

was not alone among British ministers in wondering how these changes would affect French finances, and he noted smugly that 'the revolutions that have lately happened in the government of France afford a very flattering contrast to the stability and prosperity of our administration'.[115] British finances were also contrasted favourably with those of France,[116] although Montmorin noted opposition claims that British finances were poor, as many previous French foreign ministers had done. This encouraged the French to hope that Britain would be obliged to maintain a pacific foreign policy, which they saw as the conclusion to which Pitt had come.[117] On the other hand, the British were struck by the rising opposition to monarchical pretensions in France, Eden writing of the Assembly 'nothing ever was more contrary to the principles of a monarchical government'. Commercial recovery after the American war and an inflow of foreign funds brought a measure of buoyancy to the British financial system, providing a helpful context for Pitt's measures of fiscal reorganization. Whereas the bullion balance at the Bank of England had been only £590,000 in August 1783, by August 1785 it stood at £1,540,000 and by August 1791 £8,056,000. The 3 per cents rose from under 60 in 1784 to over 70 in late 1785. The extent to which stronger government finances helped encourage Britain to take a firmer role in Dutch affairs is unclear. Given their attitude towards commercial matters, financial considerations were probably of limited weight with Carmarthen and Harris. W. Morton Pitt MP, wrote to the latter of his, Harris', hating 'everything which regards trade'. Carmarthen and Harris would presumably have been affected, however, had the difficult financial circumstances of 1783 persisted. Foreign subsidies and other expenditure would certainly have been difficult. Pitt was probably far more concerned. At the Cabinet meeting on 23 May 1787, he referred to Britain's 'growing affluence and prosperity', and, if Pitt did so in order to doubt whether it was worth disturbing, he did not argue that intervention in the Dutch crisis, in the shape of substantial expenditure, would impose an unacceptable financial burden.[118]

[115] Hawkesbury to Eden, 30 Apr., Hawkesbury to Cornwallis, 23 July 1787, BL Add. 38309 fol. 151, 38310 fol. 1; York to Richard Grenville, 30 Aug. 1787, BL Add. 70958.
[116] William Fawkener, Clerk to the Privy Council, to Elliot, 30 Apr. 1787, NLS 12999 fol. 170; Fraser to Keith, 11 May 1787, BL Add. 35538 fols. 149–50; Elliot, reporting Danish views, to Carmarthen, 15 May 1787, PRO FO 22/9 fol. 46; Pitt to Cornwallis, 2 Aug. 1787, PRO 30/8/102 fol. 84.
[117] Montmorin to Adhémar, 20 May, Barthélemy to Montmorin, 29 May 1787, AE CP Ang. 563 fols. 8–9.
[118] Eden to Lord Sheffield, 24 May, Dalrymple to Keith, 24 May 1787, BL Add. 61980 fol. 40, 35538 fol. 182; Dorset to Wraxall, 24 May 1787, Beinecke, Osborn Files, Dorset; J. Clapham, The Bank of England (2 vols., 1945), I, 256–7; W. Morton Pitt to Harris, 8 Jan. 1786, Winchester, Malmesbury 163; Cabinet, 23 May 1787, Malmesbury II, 305.

Meanwhile, the situation in the Balkans became more tense as both Russia and Turkey prepared for war. As with the Austrians and France in 1792, the Russians over-estimated the weakness of their opponent and mistakenly thought that they would be readily intimidated. Instead, as Ainslie reported, the Turkish Empire was unusually quiet, which encouraged its government to feel that it could act, as did the sense that Russia would never be satisfied with concessions. At Kherson, Joseph II found Catherine 'dying' to fight with the Turks, and so eager that she was willing to fight alone. He urged her to keep the peace.[119] Alongside continued signs of tension,[120] there were still indications that war would be avoided. Fitzherbert, who accompanied Catherine to Kherson, thought that the unprepared nature of the military system in southern Russia would oblige her to keep the peace, while Montmorin was hopeful that Joseph II would succeed in persuading Catherine to the same end.[121]

It was against this background that Harris visited London in late May 1787. He wanted additional funds to help the Orange cause and a declaration to France and the United Provinces, stating George III's determination to see the Dutch constitution restored, i.e. the authority of the house of Orange reinstated.[122] Harris pressed his case with both the Cabinet and Pitt. The Cabinet of 23 May was held after dinner at Thurlow's and Thurlow 'took the lead'. Harris took a minute that identified the views of individual participants, an unusual step, that is most valuable for the light it throws on the extent of debate within the ministry. Thurlow, 'in the most forcible terms that could be employed, declared against all half-measures', argued that Britain should prepare for war, cited the example of the War of American Independence as a warning against half-measures, hardly an encouraging point of reference for anything, and pressed for the raising of a German army 'equal to oppose that which France might march'. Thurlow did not mention Prussia, Austria or the Balkans. Richmond seconded Thurlow. Pitt was unenthusiastic and, in the face of advice from Harris and Stafford for action, argued that the ministry should consider whether it would not be wiser to preserve the peace, in order to best counter France by means of growing national prosperity. Harris opposed this argument, which was

[119] Beer (ed.), *Joseph, Leopold, Kaunitz*, p. 260.
[120] Montmorin to Choiseul Gouffier, 28 May, Choiseul Gouffier to Montmorin, 9 June 1787, AE CP Turquie 175 fols. 281, 303.
[121] Fitzherbert to Keith, 27 May 1787, BL Add. 35538 fols. 186–7; Ségur to Montmorin, 3 June, Montmorin to Belland, chargé at St Petersburg, 21 June, Montmorin to Choiseul Gouffier, 2 July 1787, AE CP Russie 121 fols. 73, 100–1, Turquie 176 fols. 10–11.
[122] Harris, 'Considerations to be employed with ministers to prevail on them to support the Republic of Holland', 19 May 1787, *Malmesbury*, II, 302–3.

the very one that Carmarthen had condemned to Keith, by stating that France would become stronger and that British inaction would have a bad impact in Europe.

The Cabinet broke up at midnight, agreeing only to read the papers produced by Harris. Carmarthen had made no material contribution, possibly because his views could be stated more successfully by Harris. Thurlow's position is controversial. Cobban suggested, and Ehrman agreed, that he was trying to kill the proposal for action by making it clear that it would entail expensive and politically contentious subsidies to German powers. George III's reluctance to sanction expenditure on the Dutch crisis would appear to support this interpretation, but it was not one that Harris or other contemporaries shared, and in the absence of evidence to suggest that a minister was being disingenuous it is possibly best to accept the views attributed to him. The pacific Eden did not agree with all of Thurlow's views, although he thought his reasoning 'on the Dutch business... able'. It is unclear how far the cautious position Thurlow adopted towards the prospect of war in September reflected his views that May. In December 1785 Thurlow had cautioned against Harris becoming involved 'faster and further' than his instructions suggested.[123]

On 24 May Harris met Pitt, who went over the Dutch issue carefully with him, 'felt strongly the importance of the object', and did not object to Harris' idea that Britain send a 'squadron of frigates' to Zeeland, a step that had been taken in 1747. On the 26th the Cabinet, with Harris in attendance, met again, this time in Whitehall. It agreed to suggest to George III that £70,000 be advanced to enable 'the well-disposed Provinces to maintain a sufficient force to counteract the immediate efforts of the Province of Holland'. Pitt informed George III that, as British assistance was restricted to money, the country was not over-committed, and he argued that, in light of the French financial situation, it was unlikely that France would 'embark on hostile operations'.[124]

Thus, as in the Balkans, a confrontation was drawing closer; while Britain, like Russia, was hopeful, in light of the weakness of her opponent, that she could achieve her goals without fighting. The intervention of

---

[123] Minutes of Cabinet, 23 May 1787, *Malmesbury*, II, 303–6. Ehrman's summary I, 526–7, fails to explain Thurlow's argument adequately. Cobban, *Ambassadors and Secret Agents*, pp. 132–3; Eden to Pitt, 23 Aug. 1787, *Auckland*, I, 185; Thurlow to Pitt, Sept., Thurlow to Stafford, 29 Sept. 1787, Sept., undated, PRO 30/8/183 fols. 174–5, 30/29/1/15, nos. 60, 63, 69; Thurlow to Carmarthen, 8 Dec. 1785, BL Eg. 3498 fol. 247; Pitt to Grenville, 7 Aug. 1787, BL Add. 59364 fol. 44.

[124] Malmesbury note, 24 May, Cabinet Minute, 26 May 1787, *Malmesbury*, II, 306–7, BL Eg. 3498 fols. 7–8, Aspinall, *George II* no. 367. *Malmesbury*, II, 307 gives the figure inaccurately as £20,000.

Prussia did not seem necessary. Indeed Harris in February had even hoped for an Austrian attack on Prussia, which he felt would lead to an Anglo-Austrian reconciliation that would further British interests throughout Europe, a foolish suggestion, in light of the views of Joseph II and George III, and one that reveals the difference between the views of Harris and George.[125] The ministry was widely believed to be divided over how far Britain should commit herself. On 7 July Ewart reported that three days earlier the Prussians had been definitely informed that the British government had decided 'not to interfere at all in Dutch affairs, in consequence of representations made by Mr. Pitt against it'. The normally well-informed *London Chronicle* claimed on 14 July, 'The Cabinet ... are warmly and earnestly divided upon the subject of Dutch affairs. Mr. Pitt and the Marquis of Stafford are stated to be against interfering with the present disputes in Holland, and every other member of the Cabinet is stated to have declared himself in support of the Prince of Orange', an assessment that was repeated in provincial papers, such as *Felix Farley's Bristol Journal* of 21 July. An anonymous report from London in the archives of the French Ministry of the Marine claimed that Thurlow was ascendant in the Cabinet and that Pitt had been successfully pressed by a majority of his colleagues to support William V. On 21 July the *London Chronicle* added, 'Mr. Pitt and the Lord Chancellor have been represented as differing materially on the subject of Dutch politics.' Government sources, however, stressed Cabinet unity.[126]

The situation was indeed becoming increasingly serious and unpredictable. As the province of Holland drifted into anarchy, the French government, itself absorbed by its own domestic problems, lost control both of its competing agents in Holland and of the Patriots. There was still a chance that France would intervene, and Carmarthen was anxious to find out whether Joseph II would allow a French army to pass through the Austrian Netherlands. A revolt there seemed imminent.[127] Dorset, who had wished to return home, was ordered to remain in Paris. Harris pressed for prompt payment of the money promised and more money, another £25,000 by 1 July.[128] The province of Holland, concerned about

---

[125] Harris to Carmarthen, 6 Feb. 1787, BL Eg. 3500 fol. 39.

[126] Ewart to Carmarthen, 7 July 1787, PRO FO 64/11 fols. 112–13; Copie d'une lettre de Londres, 19 July 1787, AN. AM. B⁷ 453; Hawkesbury to Cornwallis, 23 July 1787, BL Add. 38310 fol. 1; Aust to Liston, 15 Aug. 1787, NLS 5547 fol. 157.

[127] Carmarthen to Keith, 8 June 1787, PRO FO 7/13 fol. 165; Aust to Liston, 22 June 1787, NLS 5547; Colonel Charles Stuart to Hawkesbury, 30 July 1787, BL Eg. 3504 fol. 123.

[128] Carmarthen to Dorset, 15, 22 June 1787, KAO C168A; Harris to Pitt, 13, 15 June 1787, Winchester, Malmesbury 207, PRO 30/8/155 fol. 61.

the impact of British bribery on the loyalty of the Dutch army, and anxious because on 18 June the States General had decided to back William V's control over the army, decided on 23 June 1787 to call on France to mediate. The British ministry was therefore having to face the problem of deciding how it would act if France intervened, the question that had been avoided by Pitt in late May. George III, convinced that the army and navy were in no state to fight, the navy because it lacked sailors, argued that 'our line of conduct is perfectly clear. To try by temper and ability to show France we do not mean any open interference unless they drive us to it.'[129] Nevertheless, in early June, six warships were ordered to put to sea, a step that worried the French ministry. The British soon received news that the French were arming their fleet.[130] The problems that a possible diminution in Anglo-French tension might give rise to were indicated when Carmarthen felt it necessary to order Ewart to assure the Prussians that Britain had given no assurance to France about non-interference in the Dutch crisis, and, in response to Ewart's dispatch of 7 July, which he was ordered to contradict, the envoy was instructed to inform the Prussian government that 'although His Majesty would never set the example of foreign interference in the domestic concerns of the Republic, he could by no means see, with indifference, the attempts of any other power to destroy its independence'.[131] It is by no means clear what the British government would have done had the situation remained as it was in late June 1787, with the crucial additional complication of French intervention. There was considerable British disappointment about the cautious attitude of Frederick William II. Had the French government responded positively in late May to a Prussian approach for conciliation, then Britain might have found herself in diplomatic isolation, the crisis resolved in favour of Franco-Prussian co-operation. At that stage, however, the French saw no need for compromise, and were not willing to put pressure on the Patriots,[132] but in June 1787 the failure of British foreign policy appeared clear. Britain would either have to fight to protect her Dutch protégés or see them thwarted, and there was no German ally to do the fighting. Through Harris' involvement, she had helped to precipitate a crisis that she was unable to resolve. A French army was reportedly to be prepared at Givet by August, and Montmorin officially notified Eden on 1 July that it would be 12,000 strong. The

---

[129] George III to –, 30 June 1787, *McDowell and Stern Catalogue no. 27* (York, 1984), p. 5, item 25.   [130] Eden to Pitt, 1 July 1787, PRO 30/8/110 fol. 116.
[131] Carmarthen to Ewart, 26 June, 17 July 1787, PRO FO 64/11 fols. 100, 128.
[132] Dalrymple to Keith, 24 May 1787, BL Add. 35538 fols. 181–2; J. H. Rose, 'The Missions of William Grenville to The Hague and Versailles in 1787', *English Historical Review*, 24 (1909), 279; Cobban, *Ambassadors and Secret Agents*, p. 147.

Patriots had sought this step, though Brienne was worried about the cost. From Givet, a French army could avoid the Austrian Netherlands, and move through the Bishopric of Liège to Maastricht, as Richmond, using a map, showed the Cabinet on 23 May.[133] The British government had taken no steps to recruit the German force advocated by Thurlow and Richmond on that day, and it therefore risked a humiliating defeat. This would have arisen from chance, rather than design on the part of the French, but it would have vindicated the cautious line advocated by George III and Pitt. Richmond was to refer in 1788 to having considered the previous year 'the practicability of our taking the Texel and the Helder and stationing a fleet there to cut off all communication by sea with Amsterdam', but there was a hesitation in taking measures that led the Adjutant-General, Sir William Fawcett, to complain on 1 July, 'I have only to regret the almost insurmountable difficulties, which bold measures, however politic, or necessary they may be, for the interest of the Public, are sure to meet with in this country.' On 5 July 1787 Richmond outlined to Pitt the need to plan for war, also throwing light on the problems facing Britain in any policy of brinkmanship,

I have just seen the dispatches from Mr. Eden from which I think one may collect that Monsieur de Montmorin means more to take the advantage of negotiating with arms in his hands than to make any other use of them. The question now is whether as they have avowed preparations of their fleet, and the assembling a corps near Givet, we should trust to their assurances of not making any hostile use of them, or proceed to be equally prepared. Our great difficulty is that we cannot be preparing by degrees as they are, as such a measure on our side would be only defeating the means of a vigorous exertion if it should afterwards become necessary. For if our seamen are alarmed they will get on shore and hide themselves for fear of being pressed and thereby not only defeat our purpose of getting them when wanted but also deprive our trade in the meantime ... orders should be immediately sent to the Duke of Dorset to give the French ministry in the first place the most explicit assurances that our evolution squadron consists only of five or six ships and that it is not meant to reinforce it or to send it on any other service than that of manoeuvring; but also to inform them that arming twelve or sixteen sail of the line which ... they are doing, and collecting a corps of 12,000 men at the nearest part of their frontier to Holland while they are talking a language of conciliation is not the means of preventing at least the expense of preparations we both wish to avoid ... if a satisfactory answer is not immediately obtained I think we must directly press and fit out 20 sail of the line.
  It strikes me also that it would also be wise to take this opportunity of immediately entering into a treaty with the King as Elector of Hanover and with

---

[133] Eden to Carmarthen, 1 July, Carmarthen to Ewart, 3 July 1787, PRO FO 27/25, 64/11 fol. 109; Cobban, *Ambassadors and Secret Agents*, p. 146; Cabinet minute, *Malmesbury*, II, 304; Montmorin to Noailles, 2 July 1787, AE CP Aut. 353 fols. 7–8; *London Chronicle*, 10, 24 July 1787.

the Landgrave of Hesse and such other German princes as can be got, for a supply of an army of at least 50,000 men to be ready to march at a day's notice.[134]

The crisis was, instead, to turn out very differently, because on 28 June, en route to The Hague where she planned to rally Orangist support, Wilhelmina of Orange was stopped by a group of Free Corps and treated in a disrespectful fashion before she could return to Nymegen.[135] In light of the fate that Louis XVI was to suffer, the treatment of Wilhelmina was trivial, but it was a serious blow to the honour of her brother Frederick William II. This played a major role in the escalating crisis. On 6 July Holland formally sought French mediation, and on the 18th the invitation was accepted. There were also efforts to reduce tension by arranging a joint mediation. On 15 July Montmorin had suggested that Prussia and possibly even Britain could join France in a mediation, a conciliatory move in line with Eden's assessment of French conduct. Dorset, who thought that neither Britain nor France wanted war, believed that joint mediation was an option.[136]

Carmarthen, however, was not interested in such a move. Instead, he sought to encourage Frederick William II to act. Stressing British readiness for co-operation in the Dutch crisis, Carmarthen emphasised favourable international developments, especially the likelihood that Joseph II would not intervene. He mentioned not the crisis in the Balkans, the development of which was still unpredictable, but rather the disorders in the Austrian Netherlands. Anticipating the response to the French Revolution, Carmarthen suggested that the problems in the Low Countries could be the basis of Austro-Prussian co-operation 'whatever may be their separate objects in the Empire'. Harris urged Keith to tell the Austrian ministry that the troubles in the Austrian Netherlands and the United Provinces were linked. The French government felt obliged to assure Joseph that they had played no role in provoking the crisis in his dominions.[137] Opposition to Joseph II's reform policies had led to tension in the Austrian Netherlands, and, when Joseph rejected the

---

[134] Richmond to Harris, 13 May 1788, Winchester, Malmesbury 180; Fawcett to Cornwallis, 1 July 1787, PRO 30/11/138 fol. 157; Richmond to Pitt, 5 July 1787, PRO 30/8/170 fols. 81–2.

[135] Archibald Maclaine to [Sir Joseph Yorke?], 29 June 1787, Aspinall, *George III* no. 376.

[136] Eden to Pitt, 1, 6 July 1787, PRO 30/8/110 fols. 116–17; Carmarthen to Keith, 17 July 1787, PRO FO 7/13 fol. 192; Eden to Liston, 17 July, Dorset to Liston, 17 July 1787, NLS 5547 fols. 73, 79, KAO C184; Hawkesbury to Cornwallis, 23 July 1787, BL Add. 38310 fol. 1; Pitt to Cornwallis, 2 Aug. 1787, PRO 30/8/102 fol. 85; Cobban, *Ambassadors and Secret Agents*, pp. 155–63.

[137] Carmarthen to Ewart, 17 July 1787, PRO FO 64/11 fols. 129, 132; Harris to Keith, 24 July 1787, BL Add. 35538 fol. 306; Noailles to Montmorin, 7 July 1787, AE CP Aut. 353 fol. 16.

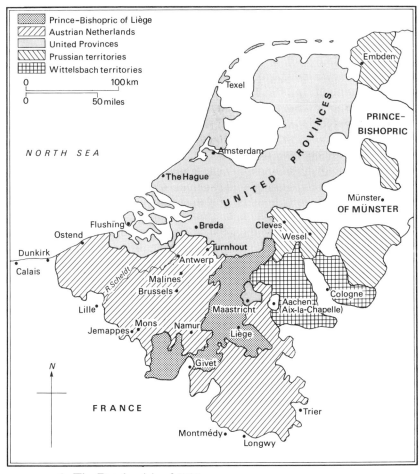

6. The Dutch crisis of 1787

concessions of the local government to the Estates of Brabant, preparations for armed resistance were made. Writing from the new Russian Black Sea port of Sevastopol, Joseph ordered Kaunitz to dispatch fourteen battalions and a cavalry regiment to restore order.[138] George III told Reviczky that, although, in general, he was in favour of the rights of the people, he supported Joseph in this crisis because he was a king, a

---

[138] J. Craeybeckx, 'The Brabant Revolution: A conservative revolution in a backward country?', *Acta Historiae Neerlandica*, 9 (1970); J. L. Polasky (ed.), *Revolution in Brussels 1787–1793* (Hanover, New Hampshire, 1987), pp. 55–9; Beer (ed.), *Joseph II, Leopold II und Kaunitz*, p. 266.

remark that throws light on the question of whether the British government could have made more of an effort in the 1780s to win the support of newly active political forces in Europe. The generally reactive nature of British foreign policy, and, in particular, its conservative support for established positions, suggests that there was scant chance of such an alignment. In 1787, the immediacy of confrontation with France took precedence over any consideration of the situation in the Austrian Netherlands. Keith was instructed to tell the Austrians that a French camp at Givet would threaten their position in the Austrian Netherlands.[139] As earlier with the Balkan crisis of 1783–4 and the Scheldt dispute, the British hoped to benefit from Austro-French differences. Now that Britain was coming to play a more active role, these differences seemed crucial to her success, even if they were not to lead to an Anglo-Austrian alliance.

Meanwhile, Frederick William was preparing to give substance to his diplomatic protests by assembling a substantial military force.[140] His grandfather, Frederick William I, had planned to attack the Dutch in the spring of 1733 as the result of a dispute over Prussian recruiting in Dutch frontier areas, but the invasion of 1787 was in fact the first movement of a Prussian army into the United Provinces. Logistically the task was not a difficult one. Much of the Dutch eastern frontier bordered or was very close to the Prussian dominions of East Friesland, Lingen, Tecklenburg, Cleves and Prussian Gelderland. The Prussian possession of Minden and the alliance of Hanover, Osnabrück and Brunswick further ensured that an invasion would not be too difficult, and, in Wesel on the Rhine in the Duchy of Cleves, Prussia had a nearby major base. On 20 July Ewart was told by the Prussian minister Count Finckenstein that on the 17th Frederick William had ordered the march of 23 battalions of infantry, 3 regiments of cavalry or dragoons, 10 squadrons of hussars, a corps of *jägers* (riflemen), 48 heavy cannon and about 50 field pieces. This force of about 25,000 was by 6 August to be on the march for the Dutch frontier in order to enforce the King's demand of satisfaction. The Austrian Envoy, Count Heinrich Reuss, had provided the valuable assurance that Joseph II would probably approve the Prussian line of conduct, and the British government had independently decided to sound the Austrians to the same end.[141] Pitt thought that the suspicion of a French role in the

[139] Reviczky to Kaunitz, 24 July 1787, HHStA EK 126; Carmarthen to Keith, 1 Aug. 1787, PRO FO 7/14 fol. 9.
[140] Pitt to Cornwallis, 2 Aug. 1787, PRO 30/8/102 fol. 85.
[141] Ewart to Keith, 21 July, Harris to Keith, 24 July, 1787, BL Add. 35538 fols. 293–4, 305–6; Pitt to George III, 17 July 1787, Aspinall, *George III* no. 378; Noailles to Montmorin, 24 July 1787, AE CP Aut. 353 fols. 46–7; Joseph II to Mercy, 28 July

troubles in the Austrian Netherlands was leading Joseph to adopt a more favourable role in the Dutch crisis. An absence of Austrian opposition was regarded as crucial. Although the Austrians were believed to have only 12,900 troops in the Austrian Netherlands, an estimate that rose to 14,900, their far more substantial forces in the hereditary lands were a potential threat to Prussia.[142]

Yet, Prussian policy, beset by ministerial feuds, wavered, and Frederick William's willingness to act was checked by contrary advice from Duke Carl August of Weimar and Duke Karl Wilhelm of Brunswick and by the prospect of joint mediation with France. Frederick William was persuaded that he should maintain his freedom of action and avoid becoming compromised with either Britain or France. Fortunately, for Britain, Carmarthen's instructions of 17 July and a revival in the influence of the anglophile minister Count Hertzberg, which Ewart attributed in part to 'the repeated favourable testimony given by His Majesty to the merit of that worthy and able minister, in his private correspondence with the King of Prussia' tipped the balance back in favour of co-operation with Britain. Lusi was overwhelmed by friendly attention from the British government and told by Pitt that the insult to the Princess of Orange gave Frederick William a golden opportunity for armed intervention.[143]

Prussia was not the only power to waver. The French government, affected by domestic political and financial problems and a likelihood that she would act alone, became more cautious. Unwilling to follow a French lead, the Patriots appeared a less attractive ally. Montmorin sought to avoid provoking either Britain or Prussia. At the same time as false reports were spread about preparations in Givet, Montmorin kept lines open via Dorset and Eden. They were assured that France would be pacific and reasonable.[144] The French hoped that Frederick William would be restrained from acting by signs of British passivity.[145] Uncertain

1787, Arneth and Flammermont, *Mercy*, II, 107; Carmarthen to Keith, 1 Aug. 1787, PRO FO 7/14 fols. 5–6.

[142] Pitt to Cornwallis, 2 Aug., Richmond to Pitt, 30 July 1787, PRO 30/8/102 fol. 86, 30/8/170 fol. 85; Stuart to Hawkesbury, 30 July, 6 Aug. 1787, BL Eg. 3504 fols. 121, 126.

[143] Ewart to Keith, 2 July 1787, BL Add. 35538 fols. 248–9; Ewart to Harris, 28 July 1787, *Malmesbury*, II, 344; Ewart to York, 1 Aug. 1787, Matlock CRO 239 M/O 759; – to Harris, 29 Aug. 1787, Winchester, Malmesbury, 150; Wittichen, *Preussen und England*, pp. 81–4; F. Luckwaldt, 'Die englisch-preussische Allianz von 1788', *Forschungen zur brandenburgischen und preussischen Geschichte*, 15 (1902), p. 67.

[144] Dorset to Carmarthen, 5, 12 July, 2 Aug. 1787, O. Browning (ed.), *Despatches from Paris, 1784–1790* (2 vols., 1909–10), I, 210, 214–16, 225; Eden to Pitt, 6 July 1787, PRO 30/8/110 fol. 117; Rayneval to Eden, 20 July 1787, *Auckland*, I, 176; Pitt to Cornwallis, 2 Aug. 1787, PRO 30/8/102 fol. 85.

[145] Montmorin to Falciola, chargé in Berlin, 11 Aug. 1787, AE CP Prusse 207 fol. 31.

about Prussian intentions, the British government prepared a small naval force and took steps to discover what was happening at Givet, but, at the same time, conciliatory instructions were sent to Paris, and on 27 July Pitt proposed a suspension of further armaments to the French envoy. Montmorin and Eden were able to negotiate an agreement, signed on 30 August, that neither would increase their naval armaments without informing the other. Assurances about French preparations were given, and, as an additional, though long-planned, positive step, Eden and Montmorin signed a convention settling differences over the rights of the French in Bengal, a measure that owed something to Castries' weaker position in the French government. Montmorin pressed Vérac on the need to avoid a Dutch civil war, which he feared the Patriots would lose and which might lead to a general European war. Vérac was finally recalled and Eden was told that his replacement would be more pacific.[146]

Prospects for peace were damaged by the Patriots' unwillingness to heed French advice that they apologise to Wilhelmina and accept foreign mediation,[147] and it became clear to both the British and Prussian governments that France could not further greatly the cause of peace in the United Provinces, although the prospect of a joint mediation had not been closed. William Grenville was sent to The Hague to check on Harris' reports. Arriving on 30 July 'completely tired with twenty four hours sea-sickness, and eight hours jolting in Dutch waggons', he soon confirmed the accuracy of Harris' analysis, an important step as Grenville was close to Pitt. Grenville reported that France was determined to support her Dutch protégés, albeit without going to war, and he suggested that Britain should respond in a similar manner, for example by enabling the States of Gelderland to hire foreign troops. He emphasised, however, the danger of encouraging the Orangists unless there was a prospect of Prussian assistance. George III was impressed by Grenville's reports.[148]

---

[146] Eden to Liston, 19 Aug., 3 Sept. 1787, NLS 5547 fols. 180–1, 5548 fol. 10; Carmarthen to Eden, 24 Aug., Eden to Pitt, 25 Aug. 1787, BL Add. 34426 fols. 23, 27; Pitt to Cornwallis, 28 Aug., Eden to Pitt, 2 Sept. 1787, PRO 30/8/102 fol. 77, 30/8/110 fol. 119; Declaration of 30 Aug. 1787, AE CP Ang. 561 fol. 134; Montmorin to Vérac, 9 July, 3, 6 Aug. 1787, AE CP Hollande 573 fols. 411–13, 574 fols. 17–18, 60–1; Eden to Pitt, 23 Aug. 1787, BL Add. 34426 fol. 8; G. C. Bolton and B. E. Kennedy, 'William Eden and the Treaty of Mauritius 1786–7', *Historical Journal*, 16 (1973), 694.
[147] Pitt to Cornwallis, 28 Aug. 1787, PRO 30/8/102 fols. 77–8.
[148] Carmarthen to Grenville, 27 July, Grenville to Pitt, 31 July, 1, 3, 4 Aug., Harris to Grenville, 18 Aug., Grenville to Harris, 23 Aug. 1787, HMC *Dropmore*, III, 408–16; Memorandum of points for Grenville, 29 July 1787, BL Add. 59070 fols. 3–5; Grenville to Marquis of Buckingham, 30 July 1787, HL STG. Box 39 (3); George III to Pitt, 5 Aug. 1787, CUL Add. 6958 no. 396; Pitt to Grenville, 7 Aug. 1787, BL Add. 59364 fols. 41–4; J. H. Rose, 'Missions of William Grenville', *English Historical Review*, 24 (1909), 285–6.

The French response to the Dutch crisis was greatly affected by their own domestic difficulties.[149] The British ministry was well-informed about these problems. Pitt was fully briefed on the parlous French financial situation by Calonne who had taken refuge in Britain, and Eden made the same point. Barthélemy reported that an awareness of French problems was having a major effect on British policy. On 19 August he dined at Hawkesbury's. Hawkesbury questioned him before dinner on French internal affairs, and at dinner itself the other guests, Pitt, Dorset and Grenville, devoted much attention to the same topic and, in particular, financial difficulties and the government's dispute with the *Parlement* of Paris. Calonne gave Carmarthen a copy of his work on French finances. A reduction of French influence in Amsterdam, one of the leading capital markets in Europe, would clearly weaken France further, not least because in recent years there had been considerable Dutch investment in France. Brunswick was confident that France could not afford a war, although he wanted 6,000 British troops sent to Holland.[150]

And yet, whatever the internal problems of the French and their assurances of pacific intentions, the very fact of real or rumoured French preparations obliged the British to keep step. For some while, British ministers and officials had expressed scepticism about the notion that French financial problems would prevent them from taking an active international role. Joseph II warned that the preparations of the various powers might well acquire a dynamic of their own and lead to war. Pitt informed Cornwallis that though the British government sought peace, it was necessary to prepare for war. The defences of Bombay were to be strengthened and, as control over Cape Town and Trincomalee was seen as crucial in any colonial struggle, Cornwallis was to seize the latter as

[149] Mirabeau to Calonne, July 1786, F. Salleo, 'Mirabeau en Prusse, 1786. Diplomatie parallèle ou agent secret?', *Revue d'histoire diplomatique* (1977), 347; Barthélemy to Montmorin, 14 Aug., Groschlag to Montmorin, 6 Sept. 1787, AE CP Ang. 561 fol. 55, Prusse 207 fol. 103; Montmorin to Luzerne, Ambassador in London, 7 Jan. 1788, Vaucher (ed.), *Recueil*, p. 544.

[150] Eden to Pitt, 6 July 1787, PRO 30/8/110 fol. 117; Barthélemy to Montmorin, 14, 20 Aug. 1787, AE CP Ang. 561 fols. 55, 72–3; Lansdowne to Cornwallis, 19 June 1787, PRO 30/11/138 fol. 143; Lansdowne to Abbé Morellet, 7 Aug. 1787, Beinecke, Osborn Files, Lansdowne; Hailes to Keith, 20 Aug., Pitt to Sir Archibald Campbell, 28 Aug., Dorset to Eden, 31 Aug. 1787, BL Add. 35539 fol. 81, 59364 fol. 68, 34426 fol. 69; Hawkesbury to Cornwallis, 23 July, Pitt to Cornwallis, 28 Aug., Carmarthen to Ewart, 21 Sept., Lieutenant-General James Grant MP to Cornwallis, 20 Dec. 1787, Cornwallis to Pitt, 6 Mar. 1788, PRO 30/11/138 fol. 164, 30/8/102 fol. 78, FO 64/12 fol. 40, 30/11/138 fol. 224, 30/11/175 fol. 1; Carmarthen to Dorset, 11 Oct. 1787, KAO C168A; J. C. Riley, *International Government Finance and the Amsterdam Capital Market, 1740–1815* (Cambridge, 1980), pp. 95, 179–85; Notes of conversation with Brunswick, 12 Aug. 1787, BL Add. 59364 fols. 48, 53.

soon as the first news of hostilities reached India. Thus, Britain would be well placed in any imperial conflict with France, at least in so far as the crucial question of protecting British India was concerned. In the longer term, the army in India was to be increased so that it would always be 'instantly' ready for 'offensive operations'. Dundas hoped that the crisis would leave Britain and the Dutch as allies with an agreement allowing Britain to use Batavia and the Cape in the event of war and an exchange of Trincomalee and Negapatam.[151]

At the same time as Montmorin negotiated with Eden the French continued their preparations to assemble troops at Givet[152] (though, in practice, as British agents reported, they amounted to little).[153] They did so because they hoped that belief in French military preparedness would give her a stronger position in international relations, and lead to concessions by other powers. The French were angry that while the British criticised the plans for Givet, they thought Prussian preparations acceptable. The bellicose Castries was prepared to fight, and on 16 August delivered a memorandum in the Council proposing that France act to defend the Dutch. His enthusiasm, however, was not shared by the bulk of the ministry, although Ségur, the minister of war, actively sponsored military preparations.[154] The British ministry was concerned about the increasing activity of French protégés in the United Provinces, who were not effectively under the control of Paris. The French government compromised their position and sowed doubt about their intentions by not totally ceasing to support the Patriots. They were sent artillerymen and money. Pitt was aware that it was necessary to win the struggle within the United Provinces as well as that on the international plane.[155] While the British and French governments hung back from hostilities, Frederick William II acted. As George III pointed out, by helping to keep France pacific through Eden's negotiations in Paris,

---

[151] Storer to Carmarthen, 11 Jan., Carmarthen to Keith, 27 July 1784, PRO 27/11 fol. 38, 7/9; Pitt to Cornwallis, 2 Aug. 1787, PRO 30/8/102 fols. 86–7; Dundas to Cornwallis, 22 July 1787, PRO 30/11/112 fols. 51–2, 68, 70; Pitt to Grenville, 7 Aug., Dundas to Grenville, 2 Sept. 1787, BL Add. 59364 fols. 43, 98.

[152] March details, 16 July 1787, AE CP Hollande 574 fol. 541.

[153] Stuart to Hawkesbury, 6 Aug. 1787, BL Eg. 3504 fols. 126–7; Pitt to Grenville, 7 Aug. 1787, BL Add. 59364 fol. 42; HMC Dropmore, I, 279, 285; Pitt to Campbell, 28 Aug., York to Richard Grenville, 17 Sept. 1787, BL Add. 59364 fol. 67, 70958.

[154] Montmorin to Barthélemy, 5, 12 Aug., Montmorin to Falciola, 6 Aug., Barthélemy to Montmorin, 7 Aug. 1787, AE CP Ang. 561 fols. 17–18, 47, Prusse 207 fols. 15–16, Ang. 561 fol. 22; Hardman, Louis XVI, pp. 100, 128–9; Comte de Ségur, Le Maréchal de Ségur (Paris, 1895), pp. 315–16.

[155] Carmarthen to Eden, 24 Aug., Harris to Eden, 31 Aug. 1787, BL Add. 34426 fols. 28, 72; Richmond to Pitt, 4 Sept. 1787, PRO 30/8/170 fols. 87–8; Cobban, Ambassadors and Secret Agents, pp. 145–6, 177; Pitt to Grenville, 1 Aug., Harris to Grenville, 4 Sept. 1787, BL Add. 59070 fols. 24, 107.

Britain left the field open to Prussia.[156] A Prussian ultimatum to Holland on 9 September had no effect, for the Patriots were determined to preserve their position, and were assured of French support by her representatives.

Frederick William was encouraged by the outbreak of war in the Balkans. Although Joseph II had made encouraging noises about the prospect of Prussian intervention in the Dutch crisis, he was not trusted. In the Scheldt dispute in 1784 the Austrians had displayed the ability of their military system to move troops to the Austrian Netherlands, where they possessed a force that could have been important in Dutch affairs. In 1787 this option was closed. On 14 August the Ottoman *divan* (Council of State) decided on war, on the 15th the Grand Vizier demanded formally from Bulgakow the return of the Crimea, and on the following day he was sent to the fortress of the Seven Towers, the traditional method of declaring war. The formal declaration was made by the *divan* on 19 August. The Turkish government decided to fight until the Russians had been driven from the Caucasus and the Crimea. A new Crimean Khan, Sahbas Giray, was appointed, and, after he was killed in Moldavia in 1789, Bahti Giray was appointed his successor, though he was killed in Moldavia in 1790. Under the terms of their alliance, Joseph, who had urged Catherine to be cautious, was obliged to help her if attacked. On 30 August he wrote promising aid, and he soon became absorbed by the prospects of gain and glory from war with the Turks. The actual Austrian declaration of war was delayed until 19 February 1788, in order to allow them to attempt a surprise attack on Belgrade. Mounted on 2–3 December, it was to be a failure, most of the Austrian force losing their way in the fog.[157] Nevertheless, from the end of August, Austrian military preparations were directed towards a Balkan war. On 14 September 1787 their envoy in Munich, Baron von Lehrbach, informed the Bavarian government that troops ordered to march to the Austrian Netherlands would instead go to Hungary. Next day Austrian troops camped near Schärding and Braunaw en route for the Rhine left for Hungary.[158]

---

[156] George III to Pitt, 3 Sept. 1787, Aspinall, *George III* no. 390.
[157] Fisher, *Annexation*, pp. 155–6; Aust to Liston, 11 Sept. 1787, NLS 5548 fol. 33; A. von Arneth, *Joseph II und Katharina von Russland: Ihr Briefwechsel* (Vienna, 1869), p. 300; Kaunitz's instructions for Stadion, H. Rössler, *Graf Johann Philipp Stadion: Napoleon's deutscher Gegenspieler* (2 vols., Vienna, 1966), I, p. 137; P. Bernard, 'The Emperor's Friend: Joseph II and Field Marshal Lacy', *East European Quarterly*, 10 (1976), 405–6; K. Roider, 'Kaunitz, Joseph II and the Turkish War', *Slavonic and East European Review*, 54 (1976), 538–54; Roider, *Austria's Eastern Question*, pp. 169–76.
[158] Chalgrin, French envoy in Munich, to Montmorin, 2, 15 Sept. 1787, AE CP Bavière 172 fols. 341, 349; Keith to Dorset, 14 Nov. 1787, KAO C191.

For many contemporaries, there was no doubt that Ainslie had persuaded the Turks to attack Russia in order to embarrass France and inconvenience Austria.[159] The outbreak of war was seen in government and diplomatic circles as very advantageous for Britain.[160] On 8 September Pitt wrote from Downing Street to his close friend and brother-in-law Edward Eliot, a Lord of the Treasury and MP, that 'last night brought accounts which seem authentic of war having been declared by the Porte... must add to the embarrassment of France'.[161] Foreign critics and the British opposition were to be more vociferous. William, Marquess of Titchfield, then staying at Bulstrode, the country house of his father Portland, wrote to Harris, 'The opinion here is that at our instigation the Porte has declared war against Russia... evidently most adverse to our real interest.' British denials had no effect and the claim that Ainslie was responsible for the war was oft repeated. It was to be pressed in the Commons by Fox during the debate over the Ochakov crisis in early 1791.[162] It was not surprising that many thought the cause or course of the French Revolution the result of 'Pitt's gold', when it was possible to believe that his ministry had engineered a major war entailing a fundamental defeat for French foreign policy in 1787.

Anglo-Prussian diplomatic support may have encouraged the Turks in 1787, but the immediate precipitants of the war were the absence in Egypt, in order to deal with a Mameluke uprising, of Gazi Hasan, the principal opponent of war, and news of troubles within the Austrian and Russian dominions. Ainslie saw 'the repeated refusal of Russia to retract her claims with respect to Georgia' as 'the immediate cause'.[163] As Ainslie was aware that his dispatches were opened in Vienna, it is clear that they have to be used with caution.[164] Diplomats did disobey orders and Constantinople was too remote for Ainslie to be easily checked upon. He could not be summoned home for consultation, as Harris was in 1787,

[159] Ségur to Montmorin, 8, 28 Aug., 12, 20 Sept., Montmorin to Ségur, 7 Sept., Noailles to Montmorin, 28 July, 1 Sept., Montmorin to Choiseul Gouffier, 23 Sept. 1787, AE CP Russie 121 fols. 213, 284–5, 122 fols. 48, 80, 14, CP Aut. 353 fols. 49–50, 103, Turquie 176 fol. 207; Herbert-Rathkael, Austrian envoy to Constantinople, 3 May, Testa, who reported during absence of Herbert-Rathkael at Kherson, to Kaunitz, 25 Apr., 25 May, 25 June 1787, HHStA Turkei II, 92/1 fol. 15, 92/2 fols. 73, 152, 250–2; Keith to Carmarthen, 29 Aug., Keith to Ainslie, 4 Sept., Ainslie to Carmarthen, 25 Sept., 24 Nov. 1787, PRO FO 7/14, 78/8 fols. 204, 251; Fraser to Liston, 11 Sept. 1787, NLS 5548 fol. 41; Vaucher (ed.), *Recueil*, p. 546.
[160] Buckingham to Pitt, 27 Sept. 1787, PRO 30/8/117 fol. 35.
[161] Pitt to Eliot, 8 Sept. [1787], Ipswich CRO HA 119 T108/39 no. 246.
[162] Titchfield to Harris, 15 Oct. 1787, Winchester, Malmesbury 169; Cobbett, 29, 64.
[163] Ainslie to Carmarthen, 17 Aug. 1787, PRO FO 78/8 fol. 159; Shaw, *Between Old and New*, pp. 25–8.
[164] Ainslie to Carmarthen, 10 Feb., 28 Dec., anon. marginal note in draft to Ainslie, 9 Oct. 1787, PRO FO 78/8 fol. 24, 281, 210.

while it was too far to send Grenville to check on the situation. It was suggested by Montmorin, Simolin and 'many others' that Ainslie had acted without instructions.[165] Such claims were not new. An earlier envoy, George, 7th Earl of Kinnoull (1730–6), had been accused in 1734–5 by Austrian, Dutch, Russian and Saxon diplomats of inciting Turkey to attack Russia, and thereby hampering the anti-Bourbon coalition, to which neutral Britain inclined, in the War of the Polish Succession. Kinnoull denied the charges, for which no conclusive evidence was advanced, but he was recalled by London.[166] In 1787 Choiseul-Gouffier also suggested that Ainslie was motivated by personal considerations, hoping that war would break out so that he could gain the profitable post of mediator and profit from dealings in munitions. Ainslie attributed the suspicion of his role to the jealousy his friendship with Turkish officials aroused in other diplomats.[167] Although it was not inevitable that Joseph would take a role in the Balkans, and his views on the Dutch crisis were encouraging for Prussia, Frederick William II was relieved to see his hands tied in the Balkans, as it both made it unlikely that Joseph would change his mind and weakened France diplomatically.

On the expiry of the Prussian ultimatum on 13 September, their army invaded the United Provinces. It was commanded by Karl Wilhelm, Duke of Brunswick, who had married George III's sister in 1764 and won praise from Frederick II when serving under him during the War of the Bavarian Succession. He advanced into Gelderland that day in order to await the reply of the States of Holland. That night, at Nymegen, Brunswick received the Holland declaration that Frederick William II had misunderstood Dutch events and its offer to dispatch two deputies to explain the situation. Judging this simply as an effort to gain time, Brunswick declared that he would advance into Holland to seek redress. The Prussians were supported by British military preparations. Fawcett, who had translated Frederick II's military regulations and had been sent to Germany to hire troops to help suppress the rebellious Americans, was on 29 August dispatched again, to hire troops from Hesse-Cassel, an agreement being signed on 28 September. George III was pressed by Pitt

[165] Montmorin to Ségur, 22 Mar., Montmorin to Choiseul-Gouffier, 22 Aug. 1787, AE CP Russie 123 fol. 42, Turquie 174 fol. 134; Browning, *Despatches from Paris*, I, 242.

[166] Robinson to Harrington, 8 May 1734, Harrington to Duke of Newcastle, Secretary of State for the Southern Department, 27 July 1735, PRO SP. 80/106 fol. 58, 43/87; Luigi Canale, Sardinian envoy at The Hague, to Antonio Solaro di Breglio, Sardinian envoy at Paris, 26 Nov. 1734, AST LM Francia 173; Prince Eugene, President of the Austrian War Council, to Count Philip Kinsky, Austrian envoy in London, 15 Dec. 1734, CUL Cholmondeley Houghton papers, correspondence no. 2375.

[167] Choiseul-Gouffier to Montmorin, 10 May, 10, 24 July, 3, 9 Aug., 25 Sept. 1787, AE CP Turquie 175 fols. 257–8, 176 fols. 24–5, 55, 66, 72, 210; Ainslie to Carmarthen, 9 Aug. 1787, PRO FO 78/8 fol. 155.

to prepare a Hanoverian force. The King, however, was less than helpful in reply, seeking information about how far Britain would pay and stating that he could not leave Hanover undefended. It was decided that the extra troops would be in British pay, and that the size of the British army would also be increased.[168] Naval preparations were stepped up, and it was made clear that if France intervened there would be war. As Eden could not be trusted to represent British views accurately,[169] Grenville was sent to Paris, where he arrived on 25 September, both to get France to declare her views and to smooth the ground for France to retreat.[170]

Patriot resistance collapsed, and Eden's claim that the Prussians would not be able to advance far because the dykes would be breached was disproved. The principal Patriot force, 7,000 strong under their Commander-in-Chief, the Rhinegrave of Salm, abandoned Utrecht on the night of 15–16 September. The fleeing army scattered, allowing the Orangists to enter the town on the 16th. Next day Gorcum fell after a short Prussian artillery bombardment, opening the way to The Hague. Dordrecht fell on the 18th, Delft on the 19th. William V re-entered The Hague on the 20th, the city having been taken over by the Orangist population on the 17th.[171] On 26 September the Dutch envoy informed the French government that Holland no longer sought French aid, which freed France from her engagements to the Patriots.[172] The last Patriot stronghold, Amsterdam, surrendered on 10 October. One of the most decisive campaigns of the century had finished. It indicated that *ancien régime* warfare was not axiomatically indecisive, as is all too often

---

[168] Draft of instructions for Fawcett, returned by George III, 26 Aug. 1787, BL Eg. 3498; Fawcett to Harris, 5, 28 Sept. 1787, Winchester, Malmesbury 152; Fawcett's papers in the Calderdale District Archive in Halifax add nothing; J. Black, 'Sir William Fawcett and the Publication of Military Works in the Mid-eighteenth Century', *Factotum*, 33 (1991), 10–13; Pitt to Stafford, 16 Sept., Carmarthen to Ewart, 16 Sept., Fawcett to Cornwallis, 30 Dec. 1787, PRO 30/29/384, FO 64/12 fol. 38, 30/11/138 fol. 234; ; Pitt to George III and reply, both 16 Sept. 1787, Aspinall, *George III*, no. 394, Manchester John Rylands Library Eng. Mss. 912 no. 37; anon., undated memo on Hessian subsidies, BL Add. 28068 fol. 254; Carmarthen to Ewart, 21 Sept. 1787, BL Add. 59364 fol. 128.

[169] Richmond to Pitt, 4 Sept., Buckingham to Pitt, 27 Sept. 1787, PRO 30/8/170 fol. 87, 30/8/117 fol. 35; Browning (ed.), *Memoranda of ... Leeds*, pp. 118–19.

[170] Grenville to Harris, 21 Sept. 1787, 3rd Earl, *A Series of Letters of the First Earl of Malmesbury, his Family and Friends* (2 vols., 1870), I, 490–2; Grenville to Pitt, 23 Sept. 1787, PRO 30/8/140 fol. 33; J. N. to Fox, 26 Sept. 1787, BL Add. 47562; Eden to Liston, 27 Sept. 1787, NLS 5548 fol. 105.

[171] Caillard, Secretary of the French embassy at The Hague, to Montmorin, 16, 18, 20 Sept. 1787, AE CP Hollande 574 fols. 416, 434–5, 450, 452; Eden to Liston, 14 Sept. 1787, NLS 5548 fol. 65; T. P. Pfau, *Geschichte des preussischen Feldzuges in der Provinz Holland im Jahr 1787* (Berlin, 1790) stresses the political dimension and R. Senckler, *Der preussiche Feldzug in den Niederlanden im Jahre 1787* (Berlin, 1893) has an operational focus. See also P. de Witt, *Une invasion prussienne en Hollande en 1787* (Paris, 1886).   [172] J. N. to Fox, 29 Sept. 1787, BL Add. 47562 fol. 105.

assumed, but that force could be concentrated and applied swiftly and successfully. British tourists found little damage: Thomas Brand, who travelled from Brunswick to The Hague via Utrecht, wrote,

the only marks of war which we saw were the destruction of a number of trees by the roadside to make batteries. Those of the Patriots were very neat; they had even painted some of their palisades. The princes were less so, but neither of them did any mischief. The sap of the trees was the only blood shed. In all the towns we passed ... were triumphal arches every 50 yards, with garlands of yellow flowers and a profusion of orange coloured ribbands and ornaments; and every soul wears the fortunate colour.[173]

Having told Eden on 13 September that France would support her Dutch allies and ordered Barthélemy to convey the same message to the British ministry, Montmorin ordered naval preparations, while the Amsterdam Patriots were promised a French army. The British government received reports of these preparations,[174] and there was concern that, although the speed of the Patriot collapse made French action pointless,[175] they might nevertheless find it impossible to back down. Discussing the possibility of war with Britain, Montmorin considered moving closer to the Austrians and Russians. Buckingham warned Pitt of the danger of a surprise French attack on Maastricht.[176]

In fact, France could do little. The appointment of Brienne as first minister on 26 August exacerbated ministerial rivalries. An angry Castries, who had sought the post, resigned (to the delight of Eden), and he took Ségur with him. The refusal of the *Parlement* of Paris on 13 August to ratify new taxes led to its exile to Troyes, and the provincial *Parlements* followed by also refusing.[177] Thus, the French government was handicapped by division and change at the moment when resolution and unity were required. Brienne's views on foreign policy are shadowy,

[173] Major-General James Murray MP to Harris, 1 Oct. [1787], Winchester, Malmesbury, 160; Brand to Wharton, 18 Oct. 1787, Durham UL Wharton papers.
[174] Pitt to George Rose, 16 Sept. 1787, BL Add. 42772 fol. 6; Eden to Liston, 14 Sept. 1787, NLS 5548 fol. 65; Carmarthen to Grenville, 21 Sept. 1787, BL Add. 59364 fol. 118; J. N. to Fox, 26 Sept. 1787, BL Add. 47562 fol. 104; *Recueil ... Hollande* III, 415; Montmorin to Barthélemy, 13 Sept. 1787, AE CP Ang. 561 fol. 193; George III to Pitt, 3, 16 Sept. 1787, J. H. Rose, *Pitt and Napoleon* (1912), p. 218; Cobban, *Ambassadors and Secret Agents*, pp. 192–4; Green, Consul in Nice, to Keith, 8 Oct. 1787, BL Add. 35539 fol. 175; Jackson, chargé in Turin, to Fraser, 10, 20, 27 Oct. 1787, PRO FO 67/5.
[175] Fraser to Liston, 24 Sept., Eden to Liston, 27 Sept. 1787, NLS 5548 fols. 90, 104.
[176] Anon. [Montmorin?] note, [c. 2 Oct. 1787], AE CP Russie 122 fol. 123; Buckingham to Pitt, 27 Sept. 1787, PRO 30/8/117 fol. 35.
[177] M. Price, 'The Comte de Vergennes and the Baron de Breteuil: French Politics and Reform in the Reign of Louis XVI' (unpublished thesis, Cambridge, 1989), p. 166; Eden to Dorset, 31 Aug. 1787, KAO C175; Egret, *Prerevolution*, p. 37; Ségur, *Ségur*, pp. 319–20; Castries, *Castries*, pp. 149–52; B. Stone, *The French Parlements and the Crisis of the Old Regime* (Chapel Hill, 1986), pp. 84–5.

but he was opposed to war in 1787 and held responsible for preventing direct action. France's domestic problems were apparent, Baron Groschlag's mission to Berlin to preserve Franco-Prussian links was unsuccessful, the Spanish government was unwilling to assist France, and British strength was obvious. Fawcett wrote from Hanover, 'Truly the French will b[eshi]t their breeches at the tremendous preparations you are making, to give them a drubbing.'[178] The British government ordered the preparation of 40 ships of the line, a formidable force. French forces did not move, and Dorset reported their Brest squadron as only having 12 of the line fit for service,[179] a reflection of the decline in military expenditure.[180] Staying with the Duke of Liancourt, Arthur Young noted 'the finances of France are in such a state of derangement, that the people best informed assert a war to be impossible'.[181] Though some aspects of the British military machine, such as the defences and garrison of Gibraltar, were in a weak state, in general it was clear that Britain was better prepared for war than France.[182] France backed down, a path eased by Grenville's mission to Paris.[183] Thurlow and Richmond had wanted France to be a party to the settlement in order further to guarantee it, but the speed of the Prussian triumph made that unnecessary. By means of a Declaration and a Counter-Declaration signed and exchanged at Versailles on 27 October the French government disclaimed any intention of seeking to intervene, and both powers agreed to place their navies on the footing of the peace establishment as it had been on 1 January 1787, the terms being those proposed by the British.[184] It was a mortifying step for the French to take and Eden only secured

---

[178] Hawkesbury to Cornwallis, 23 July 1787, BL Add. 38310 fol. 1; L.-P., Comte de Ségur, *Mémoires* (5th edn, 2 vols., Paris, 1843), II, 280–1; Ségur, *Ségur*, p. 316; Egret, *Prerevolution*, p. 42; Thurlow to Stafford, Sept. 1787, PRO 30/29/1/15 no. 63; Fawcett to Lewis, 16 Oct. 1787, Beinecke, 87.3.7.

[179] Dorset to Thurlow, 25 Oct. 1787, KAO C189.

[180] C. C. Sturgill, 'The French Army's Budget in the Eighteenth Century. A Retreat from Loyalty', in D. G. Troyansky, A. Cismaru and N. Andrews (eds.), *The French Revolution in Culture and Society* (Westport, 1991), p. 125.

[181] A. Young, *Travels during the years 1787, 1788 and 1789* (2nd edn, 2 vols., 1794), I, 72–3.

[182] Major-General Charles O'Hara, on the Gibraltar staff, to Nepean, Oct. 1787, Belfast, Public Record Office of Northern Ireland, O'Hara (Annaghmore) papers, T.2812/8/50; Sydney to Stafford, 29 Sept. 1787, PRO 30/29/1/15 no. 61.

[183] Carmarthen to Grenville, 21 Sept. 1787, BL Add. 59364 fols. 118–23, and subsequent correspondence in the volume; *Court and Cabinets*, I, 325–31; Rose, 'Grenville', 287–92.

[184] Pitt to Grenville, 23 Sept., Grenville to Pitt, 25 Sept., Grenville to Harris, 26 Sept. 1787, BL Add. 59364 fols. 153, 167, 173; Eden to Pitt, 27 Oct. 1787, PRO 30/8/110 fol. 125; Dorset and Eden to Carmarthen, 27 Oct. 1787, Declaration, Counter-Declaration; *Auckland*, I, 253–8; *Court and Cabinets*, I, 331–2; Pitt to Eliot, 30 Oct., Pitt to his former tutor, George Pretyman, 4 Nov. 1787, Ipswich CRO HA 119 T108/39 no. 287, 108/42 no. 256.

their concurrence with some difficulty.[185] Dorset, meanwhile, complained bitterly that Eden was usurping his position.[186]

Grenville had suggested that the crisis was 'one of the most important that this country [Britain] has ever seen', and another member of Pitt's circle, George Rose, wrote, 'The struggle is whether this country or France shall have the assistance of Holland in future contests; I do not scruple to say that almost our existence both at home and in the East Indies depend upon that.'[187] It is understandable that, under the pressure of events, British politicians should have made such statements. In fact, the crisis was crucial, not only because of the situation in Asia, where the gain of Dutch support made Britain clearly superior to France, but also thanks to the impact on France.[188] The French failure to act led to their diplomatic nullity of the late 1780s. From 1783 on, a number of influential ministers, including Calonne, Castries and Breteuil, had regarded alliance with the Dutch as very important, but in 1787 it had been lost. The Austro-French alignment had been devoid of much meaning in terms of co-operation and shared views for a number of years, but this was made clear in 1787. In addition, the crisis had an effect on French domestic developments. The strains produced by earlier participation in the competitive international system, especially the costs of war, meant that the French government had to achieve financial, and thus, in the context of the mid-1780s political, reform, but the likely consequences of such a process were far from clear and there was nothing pre-destined about domestic revolution. Arguably France could not have faced Britain and Prussia alone in 1787, but she had been defeated and humiliated in a crisis of brinkmanship. Had Louis XVI acted in 1787 and the Prussians not invaded, possibly he and the French monarchy would have achieved an aura of success and prestige that would have helped to counter the complex grievances of those years. In foreign policy terms 1787 marked the beginning of revolution, and of the first stage of revolutionary France's international position, one, of nullity and inconsequential diplomatic gestures, that was to last until 1791.

---

[185] Eden to Dorset, 2 Nov. 1787, KAO C175.
[186] Dorset to Carmarthen, 17, 25 Oct., Dorset to Pitt, 17, 18, 19 Oct., Pitt to Dorset, 22 Oct., Carmarthen to Dorset, 22, 30 Oct., Thurlow to Dorset, 22 Oct., Dorset to Thurlow, 25 Oct., Dorset to Hawkesbury, 17 Oct., Hawkesbury to Dorset, 23 Oct. 1787, KAO C172/66, 183, 168A, 189, 182.
[187] Grenville to Harris, 7 Sept. 1787, *Letters of ... Malmesbury*, I, 489; Rose to Wilberforce, 27 Sept. 1787, Bod. MS. Wilberforce d. 17/1 fol. 9.
[188] William Farquhar to Harris, 1 Jan. 1788, Winchester, Malmesbury 152; Murphy, 'Louis XVI and the Pattern and Costs of a Policy Dilemma: Russia and the Eastern Question, 1787–1788', *Consortium on Revolutionary Europe: Proceedings* (1987), 272.

4   To the banks of the Danube, 1787–1790

The happy change which a few years have produced in the circumstances of Great Britain, who is now incontestably in possession of
the balance of Europe, for the first time perhaps since the days of King
Henry the 8th.

Alleyne Fitzherbert, Envoy Extraordinary in The Hague, 1 January 1790[1]

I look only to the great and obvious features of our affairs, which are the
elevation of England from the downfall of her rival, and the pre-
ponderance of Prussia from the depression of Austria.

Daniel Hailes, Envoy Extraordinary in Warsaw, 1 January 1790[2]

A question of partners, 1787–1788

The Dutch crisis aroused little criticism in British political circles. The
government was assisted by the fact that the crisis took place during the
recess, the next session not beginning until 15 November 1787. Divisions
within the Cabinet did not, therefore, interact with parliamentary
politics, while it was possible to consider the difficult question of what
should be done if Prussia did not act and, subsequently, to arrange a
settlement that did not humiliate France too painfully, without having to
consider immediate parliamentary pressures. Opposition parliamentary
speakers were to point out that the confrontation with France hardly
accorded with Pitt's earlier statement about relations with that country in
the debate over the Eden Treaty, but such arguments had little political
resonance.[3] It was always open to government to adopt, in truth or
appearance, opposition views and thus to rob them of their arguments.
By allying with Austria in 1731 and declaring war on Spain in 1739,
Walpole had thus secured quiet parliamentary sessions in 1732 and 1740.

---

[1] Fitzherbert to Leeds, 1 Jan. 1790, BL Add. 28065 fol. 1. For the unprecedented
domestic harmony and naval strength of Britain, Barthélemy to Montmorin, 1 Sept.
1789, AE CP Ang. 570 fol. 338.

[2] Hailes to Ewart, 1 Jan. 1790, Matlock CRO 239 M/O 759.

[3] *London Chronicle*, 19 Jan. 1788; Fawkener to Elliot, 17 Oct., Aust to Liston, 2 Nov.
1787, NLS 12999 fol. 174, 5549 fol. 33; Sydney to Cornwallis, 4 Nov., General James
Grant to Cornwallis, 20 Dec. 1787, PRO 30/11/138 fols. 199, 224; John Hatsell to John
Hey, 2 Dec. 1787, Exeter, Devon CRO 63/2/11/2.

In the winter of 1786–7 the opposition leader in the Lords, the Duke of Portland, a relative of the prominent Orangist family, the Bentincks, had pressed for co-operation with Prussia in the United Provinces and effectual opposition to the French there. By acting firmly in 1787, the ministry had covered itself from any attack on the grounds of failing to defend national interests, while its successful co-operation with Prussia appeared to vindicate the government from the charge that it was unable to attract allies. Although over the previous two decades, ministers had generally preferred to seek the support of Austria and/or Russia, rather than the weaker and, under Frederick II, apparently more malevolent Prussia, there was considerable public support for the notion of a Prussian alliance. This stemmed essentially from the image of the Anglo-Prussian pact during 1756–61 (rather than its political reality), and was sustained by the developing mythical quality of the Seven Years War, Pitt the Elder and Frederick II, as well as by the continued attraction of the notion of a Protestant alliance.[4] Joseph II's schemes and the *Fürstenbund* seemed to demonstrate the continued relevance of such sentiments.

In the heady atmosphere of success after the Dutch crisis, it was easy to forget or downplay questions over the ministry's changing public statements about France, and the wisdom of committing Britain in Dutch affairs before being certain of Prussian assistance. Harris had many friends in the opposition, not least Fox, and they were unwilling to attack his achievement.[5] When the Pittite Thomas, Viscount Bulkeley told the House of Lords on 27 November 1787 that they had seen 'how all ranks of men pressed forward to support the exertions which the king of a free country alone can make when he reigns in the hearts and affections of his parliament and of his subjects', he was, albeit with the hyperbole adopted for the occasion, testifying to the singular *public* success of the British role in the denouement of the Dutch crisis. It had involved the humiliation of the national enemy, and had been quick, bloodless for Britain and, as was to be shown, not too expensive for her either.[6] The session began very well for the government, and in December Carmarthen thought it the quietest he could remember. Lord North, exhausted and ill in Bath, observed in January 1788, 'if

---

[4] Portland to his son, William, Marquess of Titchfield, 13, 20 Oct. 1786, 8 Feb. 1787, Turberville, II, 206–7; M. Schlenke, *England und das friderizianische Preussen 1740–1763* (Freiburg/Munich, 1963).

[5] Sydney to George III, Pitt to George, both 27 Nov. 1787, Aspinall, *George III* nos. 416–17; Philip Yorke to Philip, 2nd Earl of Hardwicke, 27 Nov. 1787, BL Add. 35383 fol. 263. On opposition support for vigorous governmental measures, London report in *Newcastle Chronicle*, 6 Oct. 1787.

[6] Eden to Liston, 10 Dec. 1787, NLS 5549 fol. 117.

Government are dissatisfied with the present House of Commons, they must have no great inclination to any Parliament whatsoever'.[7] Such a position was as important as the growing strength of government finances. The session was in fact to become far more difficult for Pitt, culminating in late June and early July when Sir William Dolben's bill to lessen crowding on slavers was pushed through the Lords despite the vociferous hostility of Thurlow and the more muted opposition of Sydney and Hawkesbury. In addition, Howe, the First Lord of the Admiralty, was obliged to resign as a result of a controversy over naval promotions, while a discontented 'third party' of former supporters emerged to oppose Pitt in the Commons. There was also a serious economic crisis, especially in the textile sector, with a substantial rise in bankruptcies.[8]

The likely diplomatic consequences of the Dutch crisis were unclear. Bulkeley, seconding the Address in the Lords, declared that the crisis would lead to 'the restoration to this country of her old and natural alliances', but it was by no means apparent that it would lead either to such an end, namely alliance with Austria and Russia, or that it would be followed by the negotiation of an alliance with Prussia, or the creation of an Anglo-Prussian alliance system. Within a year, the Triple Alliance of Britain, Prussia and the United Provinces, in fact a triangular alliance, as no single treaty bound the powers together, had been negotiated. The alliance with Prussia was to lead to poor relations with Austria and, more seriously, in 1791, to confrontation with Russia, the Ochakov crisis. The reversal of British policy in the spring of 1791 led to the collapse of the alliance. Thus, the period from the summer of 1787 to the spring of 1791 is given cohesion by this dynamic alliance, flanked, as it was, by two periods in which Britain was not part of an active alliance system; the Anglo-Dutch alliance in 1792–3 was reactive and truly defensive.

Although this chronology is accurate, it is important not to adopt a teleological approach to the development of Britain's alliance system, and to the subsequent course of the Anglo-Prussian alliance. As in 1725–6 and 1756–61, the Anglo-Prussian alignment reflected the failure of the British attempt to ally with Austria and/or Russia. The hesitant and halting progress of Anglo-Prussian relations in 1784–7 is worthy of note and the same ministers were in office in subsequent years.

And yet, there were also important reasons why the two powers should

---

[7] Carmarthen to Dorset, 7 Dec. 1787, KAO C168A; William Fraser to Liston, 6 Dec. 1787, NLS 5549 fol. 109; North to Sheffield, 29 Jan. 1788, BL Add. 61980 fols. 26–7.

[8] Sir L. B. Namier, *Monarchy and the Party System* (Oxford, 1952), pp. 22–4; J. Hoppit, 'Financial Crisis in Eighteenth-Century England', *Economic History Review*, 2nd ser. 39 (1986), 45–6, 51.

be drawn together. They were already united by a convention signed in Berlin on 2 October 1787 that formalised their agreement to cooperate in the Dutch crisis.[9] An Austrian alliance was not an alternative for Prussia. Joseph II had rejected the radical policy of reconciliation with Prussia, supported by Philip Cobenzl and Anton Spielmann, in favour of Kaunitz's stress on the continued threat from Prussia, and the consequent need for a Russian alliance, and his own interest in Balkan conquests.[10] Frederick William II was faced with the prospect of major Russian and Austrian gains at the expense of the Turks, without any equivalent for Prussia. Should the two powers then use the subsequent peace to pursue plans further west, for example a revival of the Bavarian Exchange scheme, a scheme that France or Joseph II were believed to be promoting in the winter of 1787–8,[11] then Prussia would be in a vulnerable position. The *Fürstenbund* had been a response to this situation, but in 1785–6 Frederick II had been unwilling to ally with Britain because, like Joseph II and Catherine II, he felt that she was weak and that it was more important to secure French support.[12] After the Dutch crisis, this was no longer the case. Britain had displayed determination and power, while France had been unable to support her protégés. In addition, there was now a legacy of division between France and Prussia. From late August 1787 Montmorin sought to improve relations between the two powers. This led to the dispatch of Groschlag to Berlin, but, in response to the Prussian invasion of the United Provinces, he received less accommodating instructions.[13] Prussian fears were not without substance: in November 1788 Catherine II suggested a joint attack on Prussia to Austria.[14]

For Britain there appeared to be more choice. The ministry could choose to opt for no formal alliance system, or, if it wished to adopt a more interventionist approach, it could pursue the Prussian option, see if the vigour that Britain had displayed offered the possibility of better relations with Austria and Russia, or heed French suggestions, eagerly reported by Eden, of co-operation.[15] Unwilling to lose the possibility of

---

[9] R. Lodge, *Great Britain and Prussia in the Eighteenth Century* (Oxford, 1923), p. 174.

[10] P. Bernard, 'Austria's Last Turkish War: Some Further Thoughts', *Austrian History Yearbook*, 19–20 (1983–4).

[11] Thurlow to Stafford, 1 Oct. 1787, PRO 30/29/1/15 no. 66; Ewart to Keith, 17 Nov., Charles Fraser, Secretary of Legation at St Petersburg, to Keith, 4 Dec. 1787, Robert Walpole, Envoy Extraordinary in Lisbon, to Keith, 20 Jan. 1788, BL Add. 35539 fols. 253, 282, 35540 fol. 25.

[12] Dalrymple to Liston, 24 Jan. 1786, NLS 5544 fols. 47–8.

[13] Cobban, *Ambassadors and Secret Agents*, pp. 176–7, 196.

[14] Aretin, 'Guarantor Power', 153.

[15] Barthélemy to Montmorin, 5 Oct. 1787, AE CP Ang. 363 fol. 75; Anon. minute, [Oct. 1787], *Auckland*, I, 245–9; Eden to Grenville, 10 Oct. 1787, HMC *Dropmore* III, 438.

better relations with Joseph II, Richmond had argued, before the Dutch crisis reached its height, that Britain should go no further with Prussia than a mutual guarantee in the event of being attacked as a result of the crisis. Thurlow was also cautious, and revealed his suspicion of alliances,

Every country should depend, as far as possible, on itself. It should therefore strive to put itself in a posture, which offers it no temptation to encroach upon others, and affords no opportunity for the encroachment of others. England seems to have gained that position to a considerable degree, within this island; if it could forget Ireland, I should have said in Europe... we stand firm in India... Defence is our single object; and that is supposed to be pretty much in our own power... I had rather not contract a defensive alliance with Holland; for this short reason, that we do not want their defence... nor can they give it, if they would, in the same extent.

Thurlow also criticised the idea of a Prussian alliance, on the grounds that 'it plunges us' into possible quarrels, and he revealed an opposition to the basis of the British role in the Dutch crisis, the notion that France had to be opposed for the sake of Britain's global interests: 'I very readily agreed, that the French pursuit in Holland meant annoyance to us. But I thought it the stone of sysiphus... to gain their [Dutch] places of strength... was too remote and chimerical.' In Thurlow's view, the fear of impracticable French operations in India was leading the British government into unwise commitments.[16] Carmarthen, characteristically, was still very suspicious of the French, arguing that they were still intriguing in the United Provinces.[17] Given that neither Britain nor France was interested in territorial gains in Europe, it might be suggested that their failure to develop a *modus vivendi* after the Dutch crisis, let alone the 'solid system of friendship and peace' advocated by Eden, and certainly of some interest to Pitt, was a mistake; not least because it obliged Britain to commit herself to Prussia, in short to become involved in the aggressive schemes of the central and eastern European powers. The French via Eden proposed co-operation in protecting the balance of power and in preserving the Turkish Empire from partition, by negotiating and then guaranteeing a peace on the basis of the *status quo ante bellum*. The French government, however, failed to reveal its own views and there was a fear that its use of any British declaration would harm British interests in other courts.[18] The failure in 1787–8 to take this

[16] Richmond to Pitt, 30 July 1787, PRO 30/8/170 fol. 85; Thurlow to Stafford, no date, PRO 30/29/1/15 no. 69.
[17] Carmarthen to Eden, 30 Oct. 1787, *Auckland*, I, 262.
[18] Eden to Carmarthen, 18 Oct. 1787, enclosing anon. French memorandum, PRO FO 27/26 fols. 225–30; Thurlow to Stafford, 1, 17 Oct. 1787, PRO 30/29/1/15 nos. 66, 68; Thurlow to [Pitt?], no date, PRO 30/8/183 fols. 189–91; Eden to Liston, 29 Oct. 1787, NLS 5549 fol. 27; Luzerne to Montmorin, 22 July 1788, AE CP Ang. 566 fols. 87–8.

approach further can thus stand as an instance of a more general inability of the western European powers to sink their differences, and, more specifically, as a continuation of the failure in Anglo-French relations prior to the crisis to translate favourable sentiments into real co-operation. In October 1787 Thurlow wrote to Dorset,

After what has passed, we certainly don't mean, if we can help it, to be baffled in Holland. Those states must not be interrupted in resettling their constitution. Beyond that, we have no cause of enmity or jealousy with France, or any other power.

Thurlow suggested to Eden that,

I think verily, if Monsr. Montmorin were possessed of our real sentiments, that, under his administration, at least, the two countries might approach to that cordiality and confidence, in which we place our best hopes of public happiness and prosperity. But of this prospect it is an essential part to make us easy for our external possessions, particularly India. While any trace of their late pursuit in Holland remains, there must be jealousy. While the French military is continually sliding into the provincial troops in Indostan, there must be jealousy. There may be explanations, local arrangements, and commercial intercourse, in the mean time; but too watchful an attention for cordial connection, will still remain.

Early the following month, Dorset proposed 'a kind of friendly intercourse' with France over the Balkan crisis 'especially as there is a disposition here to listen to anything that can tend to secure the peace and tranquillity of, *at least*, Europe'. Eden wanted 'a full and permanent system' with both France and Spain, while Tom Paine urged 'that this infamous business of perpetual wrangling between England and France might end'.[19]

Thurlow, however, had captured a central problem with Anglo-French relations. Like their Dutch, Portuguese and Spanish counterparts, but, unlike British relations with other powers, they were complicated, if not compromised, by colonial rivalry. Colonial differences were indeed to delay the successful negotiation of an Anglo-Dutch treaty after the Dutch crisis, and were to complicate relations between the two powers thereafter. British ministers sought, despite Dutch opposition, to gain control of Trincomalee, arguing that the port would then be better able to resist any French attack on British and Dutch possessions. If the Dutch were unwilling to cede Trincomalee, the

---

[19] Thurlow to Dorset, 22 Oct. 1787, KAO C189; Thurlow to Eden [9 or 12 Oct. 1787], BL Add. 28068 fol. 239; Dorset to Pitt, 8 Nov., Eden to Dorset, 22 Dec., 1787, KAO C183, 175; Paine to Lansdowne, 20 Nov. 1787, Bowood 60.

British at least wanted a garrison of their own troops.[20] In 1790 other colonial differences, less predictable than those between Britain and France in the Indian Ocean, nearly led to war between Britain and Spain in the Nootka Sound crisis. It was unlikely that any lasting Anglo-French agreement could be produced that would prevent colonial and maritime rivalry, and, indeed, sensitivity to the naval strength of both powers had been accentuated as a result of their armaments during the Dutch crisis. Just as the War of American Independence had dramatically increased British sensitivity about the strategic situation in Asia, so the Dutch crisis of 1787 had emphasised the possibility of war and the need to consider the defence of the British position. Anglo-French colonial and maritime rivalry continued, and helped to highlight the importance of the United Provinces and the value to Britain of tying her into an alliance system that would protect the constitutional position of the Prince of Orange, and thus the exclusion of the Patriots from power.

The Anglo-French convention on India signed in August 1787 did not allay British fears. Haidar Ali's successor, Tipu Sultan, was less enthusiastic than his father on co-operation with the French,[21] but the British were not aware of the tension in the relationship. Eden sought to reassure the British government about French intentions in the Indian Ocean,[22] but he had been discredited to a considerable measure by what was seen as a pro-French attitude during the Dutch crisis.[23] Montmorin gave similar assurances, while Dorset argued that domestic problems and the loss of their Dutch alliance, made it unlikely that France would pursue any hostile schemes in India. In 1788 the French government abandoned their Cochin China initiative.[24]

French envoys were convinced that British attitudes were strongly motivated by anxieties about their colonies; this was indeed a continuation of the generally reactive and defensive nature of British ministerial attitudes towards Anglo-Bourbon colonial relations throughout the century. On 1 April 1788 Barthélemy suggested that the Dutch alliance was still viewed as crucial to the defence of India, as it would close Trincomalee and Cape Town to the French, thus denying them the opportunity to attack Britain in any part of her vast Asian empire, 'dont

---

[20] Dundas to Grenville, 2 Sept. 1787, Harris to Grenville, 4 Jan. 1788, HMC *Dropmore*, III, 421, 443; Harris to Carmarthen, 15 Jan., Carmarthen to Harris, 4 Mar. 1788, BL Eg. 3500 fols. 48, 66; Harris to Pitt, 4 Mar., 25 May, 1, 4 July 1788, Winchester, Malmesbury vol. 207; Richmond to Pitt, 29 Aug. 1788, CUL Add. 6958 no. 534; Tarling, *Anglo-Dutch Rivalry*, pp. 17–50; Bassett, *Trade and Policy*, pp. 93–4.
[21] S. P. Sen, *French in India* (2nd edn, New Delhi, 1971), p. 517.
[22] Eden to Pitt, 18 Dec. 1787, PRO 30/8/110 fol. 132.
[23] George III to Pitt, 11 Dec. 1787, Aspinall, *George III* no. 420.
[24] Dorset and Eden to Carmarthen, 6 Jan. 1788, *Auckland*, I, 300; Dorset to Cornwallis, 10 Nov. 1787, PRO 30/11/138 fol. 201; Faure, *Français en Cochinchine*, pp. 147–84.

la conservation occupe aujourd'huy toute sa prévoyance'. The Chevalier de la Luzerne, sent to London as French Ambassador in January 1788, sought to end fears about French intentions in India, but he found British anxiety difficult to assuage. Pitt was informed in October 1787 that France was to send five regiments to the Indian Ocean and three to the West Indies. A concerned George III decided that month to send more troops to India. Reporting that France was to send less troops to the Indian Ocean than had been feared, Torrington, nevertheless, was 'still of opinion, as I ever have been, that something will happen in the East Indies, where France is in force by sea, and has vast advantages from her possession of Trincomalee, her numerous land forces, in the Isles of France, Bourbon, in the service of Tipu Sultan etc.' The Isles of France and Bourbon (Mauritius and Réunion) were seen as potential staging posts for any attack on India, while French schemes in Indo-China also aroused concern. In 1788 Tipu sent an embassy to France in search of military assistance.[25]

It is not surprising that concern about India did not cease with British success in the Dutch crisis. The likely extent and durability of the French domestic crisis were unclear. British success did not make French schemes inconceivable; only, by denying the prospect of Dutch bases and assistance, more difficult. The crisis of 1787 had revealed not that France was without forces, but that she was unwilling to use them in the circumstances of September 1787. France was believed to seek both revenge for her failure and an opportunity to reverse Britain's consolidation of her colonial position. That she would be unable to do so was certainly not clear in early 1788, when rumours both about France's Indian schemes and, less plausibly and seriously, about possible action in Europe circulated. It is striking that rumours and British concern about French plans in India did not disappear thereafter. In the summer of 1788, the French were questioned on the report that they had attempted to gain Trincomalee, and Montmorin provided fresh assurances of peaceful intentions. In September 1788, Grenville pressed Pitt on the need for Anglo-Dutch naval superiority over, and British equality with,

---

[25] Carmarthen to George III, 25 Jan., Pitt to George III, 1 Sept. and reply, 2 Sept. 1788, Aspinall, *George III* nos. 429, 477; Barthélemy to Montmorin, 1 Apr., Luzerne to Montmorin, 22, 29 Apr., 6 May, 20 June, Barthélemy to Montmorin, 12, 26 Aug. 1788, AE CP Ang. 565 fols. 4–6, 97, 110–14, 141, 300, 566 fols. 166–7, 240; Evan Nepean, Under-Secretary at the Home Office, to Pitt, 19 Oct. 1787, PRO 30/8/161 fols. 45–6; George III to Pitt, 12 Oct. 1787, Rose, *Pitt and Napoleon*, p. 129; Marianne, French naval agent in Rotterdam, to Luzerne, 31 Mar., instructions to St Priest, new envoy to the United Provinces, 14 May 1788, AN. AM. B⁷754; Torrington to Keith, 26 Apr., Straton to Keith, 19, 26 Aug., Pitt to Grenville, 29 Aug. 1788, BL Add. 35540 fol. 214, 35541 fols. 57, 75, 58906 fol. 44; Van de Spiegel, Dutch Pensionary, to Malmesbury, 2 Sept. 1788, Winchester, Malmesbury 180; Kennedy, 'Anglo-French Rivalry', p. 242.

France in the Indian Ocean, adding that Britain should 'never again' be exposed to the danger of losing the homeward-bound East India fleet, whose value, including the China trade, he estimated at £8 million. Until that October, the French government assumed, as a consequence of the strength of British forces in the Indian Ocean and the West Indies, that conflict with Britain was possibly imminent, and took precautions accordingly. In November 1788 Barthélemy complained that whatever France did she could not quiet British governmental fears about her plans for the Indian Ocean.[26] It was not until the breakdown of order in France in 1789 that they really eased, although in 1788 they had been less urgent than prior to the Dutch crisis and Carmarthen cited 'the internal condition of France' as a reason for his confidence that she would yield to British views in India.[27] The successful resolution of the Dutch crisis led Cornwallis, who in 1786 had been appointed Governor General and Commander in Chief in India, to press the East India Company's claim, under a 1768 treaty with the Nizam of Hyderabad, to the circar or fief of Guntoor (Guntur). The other five of the Northern Circars had been acquired by Robert Clive in 1766, and the sixth linked the area of British control to the Carnatic. With France weak, Cornwallis was certain that Tipu of Mysore would not oppose the claim and, therefore, that the Nizam would be compliant. Cornwallis, however, was determined to act firmly. He sent his aide-de-camp Captain John Kennaway, 'who is perfectly master of the languages, and who has already some knowledge of the Courts of Hindoostan', to Hyderabad, but also took pre-emptive action,

it will be most expedient that our troops should march into the Circar on Captain Kennaway's arrival at Masulipatam; and that our present Resident Meer Hussein should about ten days before inform the Nizam of our intention giving the most positive assurances that our design was entirely limited to the taking possession of the Circar as our undoubted right by treaty and that Captain Kennaway had orders to settle the account in the most fair ... manner.

The Nizam complied without resistance. The resolution of the Dutch crisis had, therefore, as had been forecast, improved the British position in India and yielded direct territorial benefit there, at the same time as

---

[26] Pitt to [Stafford], 14 July, 6 Sept. 1788, BL Add. 42772 fols. 8–9; Hailes to Carmarthen, 26 Aug. 1790, PRO 30/29/1/15 no. 80; Harris to Pitt, 22 July, Grenville to Pitt, 1 Sept. 1788, PRO 30/8/155 fol. 77, 30/8/140 fols. 35–6; Memorandum read to *Conseil d'état* by Count César-Henri de La Luzerne, Minister of the Marine and brother of the Ambassador in London, 14 Dec. 1788, Hardman, *The French Revolution*, p. 79; Barthélemy to Montmorin, 14 Oct., 11 Nov. 1788, AE CP Ang. 566 fols. 25, 121.

[27] Barthélemy to Montmorin, 4 Mar. 1791, AE CP Ang. 576 fols. 274–5; Carmarthen to Harris, 14 July 1788, PRO FO 37/23; Pitt to [Stafford], 6 Sept. 1788, BL Add. 42772 fol. 9.

Britain was reaping the diplomatic benefits in Europe. As a result of the acquisition of Guntur, British domination of India's eastern coast was strengthened.[28]

Cornwallis was able to report from Calcutta in December 1788 that relations with the French were good. A year later his concern over Tipu Sultan was eased by French weakness, and the French could do nothing to further their complaint that Britain had a larger naval force in Indian waters.[29] The Third Mysore War (1790–2) was made considerably easier for the British by the fact that the aggressive Tipu Sultan, who had attacked the Raja of Travancore, a British ally, on 29 December 1789, received very little foreign assistance. Concern that the French were supplying him with arms led both to threats of war in the British press and to a clash in November 1791 when Cornwallis' brother, Commodore William Cornwallis, searched French ships leaving their base of Mahé on the Calicut coast. An escorting French warship resisted and was captured after an engagement, leading to an angry French complaint, but the French were in no position to take the matter further.[30] Indeed, the report to the National Assembly of its Colonial Committee on France's Indian Ocean colonies, delivered on 7 January 1792, painted a picture of weakness and anarchy.[31] In November 1791 Ralph Payne noted the fear that British India would go the way of the Thirteen Colonies and that Cornwallis would lose to Tipu, but such anxieties were misplaced. Thanks in part to his reform of the army, Cornwallis was to be victorious and Tipu surrendered on 23 February 1792. He paid an indemnity, gave two of his sons as hostages and ceded a large amount of territory to the East India Company, including the Malabar coast, which Cornwallis hoped would be an 'extremely advantageous' source of spices, and the region of Salem from which the Carnatic could be attacked. Mysore was therefore cut off from the sea, a potential axis of French–Indian co-operation severed.[32]

---

[28] Cornwallis to Campbell, 12 Apr., Cornwallis to Nizam, 30 Apr., Nizam to Cornwallis, 2 Nov., Cornwallis to Pitt, 1 June 1788, PRO 30/11/159 fols. 123–4, 30/11/106 fols. 9–17, 30/11/175 fol. 3; Cornwallis to Kennaway, 16 June, Cornwallis to Directors of East India Company, 3 Nov. 1788, Ross (ed.), *Cornwallis* I, 537–42; Cornwallis to Lansdowne, 10 Nov. 1788, Bowood 40.

[29] Cornwallis to Dorset, 20 Dec. 1788, KAO C188/24; Aspinall (ed.), *The Correspondence of George Prince of Wales 1770–1812*, II (1964), pp. 50–1; Cornwallis to Campbell, 6 May 1788, PRO 30/11/159 fol. 131; Cornwallis to Lansdowne, 10 Nov. 1788, Bowood 40; Cornwallis to Pitt, 7 Mar. 1789, PRO 30/11/175 fol. 11; *Public Advertiser*, 19 Jan. 1792.

[30] *Newcastle Courant*, 5 Feb. 1792; *St James's Chronicle*, 5 Apr. 1792; Cornwallis to Dundas, 24 Dec. 1791, PRO 30/11/151 fol. 101.   [31] *AP* 37, 151.

[32] Payne to Malmesbury, 22 Nov. 1791, Winchester, Malmesbury 162; *Observer*, 4 Dec. 1791; R. Callahan, *The East India Company and Army Reform, 1783–98* (Cambridge, Mass., 1972), pp. 6–109; F. and M. Wickwire, *Cornwallis. The Imperial Years* (Chapel

Concern about India lent purpose to Britain's Dutch policy and made the long-term success of any reconciliation with France unlikely. The possibility of such a reconciliation was not, however, followed up. In January 1788 Pitt was interested in the idea of France ceding Mauritius and her Indian trading stations in return for 'some advantages on the side of the Levant', but there was no diplomatic momentum behind this suggestion,[33] and France was most likely to make gains at the expense of the Turks by co-operating with Austria and Russia, rather than with Britain. Luzerne's arrival in London did not herald a new entente in relations, Carmarthen noting, 'We have had a conference or two. He conducted himself in general well, full of general professions of friendship, but not disposed to enter into any particular subject which could lead further.' Whether France would have accepted an agreement that also committed her to passivity in the Indian Ocean is unlikely,[34] and any Anglo-French agreement in late 1787 would have had to face both domestic and diplomatic hurdles over the following three years. Montmorin pointed out to Eden that the constitution of Britain 'renders the dependance of others upon it precarious', but, despite French concern during the Regency Crisis, it was to be the Pitt ministry that was more solid than its French counterpart. The changes in the French government in 1787 made it a poor prospect for a lasting alliance, and this was to be further demonstrated with the fall of Brienne in August 1788, and then, more obviously, in 1789. In addition, any Anglo-French understanding would have faced serious problems over the future of the Austrian Netherlands in 1789–90, and during the Nootka Sound crisis in 1790. There were thus, as on earlier occasions, most obviously 1772–3,[35] good diplomatic reasons for a lack of British interest in co-operation with France, although, of course, it would also have exposed the Pitt ministry to internal division and to serious public criticism. Such co-operation would have marked the victory of Eden over Carmarthen and Harris, and would have been unworkable while the latter remained in their posts. It would also have ensured major parliamentary attacks. As such an alliance was not attempted, it is impossible to state precisely what would have prevented such a diplomatic revolution, but weight must be placed on opinion within Britain and on the susceptibility of the government to

Hill, North Carolina, 1980), pp. 98–173; Cornwallis to Dundas, 17 Mar. 1792, PRO 30/11/151 fol. 113.
[33] Pitt to Eden, 7 Jan. 1788, PRO 30/8/102 fol. 115; Eden to Liston, 11 Feb. 1788, NLS 5550 fol. 49.
[34] Carmarthen to Harris, 1 Feb. 1788, Thurlow to Eden, [9 or 12 Oct. 1787], BL Eg. 3500 fol. 523, 28068 fol. 239.
[35] Black, *Natural and Necessary Enemies*, pp. 75–9, and 'Anglo-French Relations 1763–1775', *Francia*, 18 (1991), 110–14.

the views both of its own supporters and of parliamentary independents who generally provided support. As with other aspects of foreign policy, the role of domestic considerations, therefore, emerges as of most importance in setting the parameters within which policy could be discussed, formulated and executed.

There were fewer domestic problems facing any attempt to improve relations with Austria, Prussia or Russia. The outbreak of war in the Balkans, however, reduced Britain's options. Not only was alliance with Austria or Russia now a far less attractive proposition, but it was unlikely, while the war lasted, that it would be possible to win the support of one of the two powers, either on its own or as a part of a wider alliance system including Prussia. In October 1787 Camden outlined to Pitt why he thought a Prussian alliance was now 'most desirable', and focussed first on the need to consolidate the Dutch triumph,

in the first place the safety and security of Holland will be most effectually accomplished by such a confederacy, and we shall be in no danger of losing that country again by any external attack, and this I hold to be of the first importance to England ... We have escaped miraculously from the most perilous situation we ever experienced and shall be mad if we [let] slip the opportunity of rooting out the French interest in that country for ever, which cannot be done but by building a wall of protection round it towards the land and that will be completely effected by a Prussian alliance.

The centrality of the United Provinces in British foreign policy was thus stated clearly. Camden continued by arguing that such an alliance would end Prussian 'dependency' on France, and that France 'being no longer secure against a continental war will not think it quite so safe to neglect her army by directing the whole exertion of her government to her navy'. He made it clear, however, that the idea of a Prussian alliance was being resisted, though he did not say by whom,

it is supposed this measure will throw France into a closer union with the Emperor, that she may be tempted to abandon Turkey – to unite with the 2 Imperial Courts – to beat the Turks out of Europe, and then agree to the German Exchange and get Flanders possibly for her share of the spoil.

Camden rejected these arguments, claiming that a stronger Austria was not in France's interest, and that the other suggestions were improbable and remote. He added a call for pragmatism, 'an unlikely and distant possibility can never be an argument against a present advantage'.[36]

And yet, there was reluctance about a formal alliance with Prussia. The agreement of 2 October 1787 related solely to the Dutch crisis, and from late September 1787 the Prussians pressed for a more wide ranging

---

[36] Camden to Pitt, 18 Oct. 1787, PRO 30/8/119 fols. 134–5.

alliance. The British reply was slow and cautious. George III wrote to Frederick William II about the benefit of closer relations, but there was concern about Prussian intentions, and it was initially unclear whether Britain should seek an alliance on its own or as part of a wider system.[37] The latter option faced serious difficulties. Although the Cabinet discussed the idea of an alliance system including Russia,[38] the Balkan crisis had embittered relations with her, the Ainslie affair reverberating throughout the winter of 1787–8. Catherine remained convinced that George III was secretly supporting the Turks, and was furious when the British government banned the hiring of British ships to transport Russian troops to the Mediterranean.[39] In addition, there seemed even less point than before in approaching Joseph II. Joseph indeed suggested to Catherine II a triple alliance, including France, that would have been in direct opposition to British interests. Poor Anglo-Austrian relations led to a decline in diplomatic correspondence. In January 1788 Keith complained that he had received no instructions since mid-September,

This is the fifty-third letter I have written to the office, since I have received one word in answer to any one. A silence so long and unprecedented can only prove that the variable, and even the inimical politics of this court have justly become matters of so much indifference to Great Britain, that they neither call for animadversion, nor for solid investigation. I likewise draw from the duration of your lordship's silence this equitable conclusion, that the king has at present no business to transact at Vienna, and that consequently my presence here is in no shape necessary for his service.

There were to be other long silences. Angry with Keith's complaints, Carmarthen granted his recall, though he did not leave until October 1788.[40] The Austro-French connection had not, as was hoped, disintegrated with the outbreak of war in the Balkans and Carmarthen used this to justify his silence.

It is much to be lamented that the continual reserve of the court of Vienna, towards England, has not only prevented every degree of useful, as well as friendly communication between the two powers, but has even furnished us with reasonable grounds of suspicion respecting the views of His Imperial Majesty ... His Imperial Majesty, I know, expresses himself as determined never to break

---

[37] George III to Frederick William II, 23 Nov. 1787, reply, 10 Jan. 1788, Aspinall, *George III*, nos. 351, 426; Ewart to Cornwallis, 1 Nov., Carmarthen to Ewart, 2 Dec. 1787, PRO 30/11/138 fols. 194–5, FO 64/12 fol. 199; Lodge, *Britain and Prussia*, pp. 177–81.

[38] Carmarthen to Thurlow, 23 Dec. 1787, BL Eg. 3498 fol. 250.

[39] Catherine II to Grimm, 24–5 Apr., 31 May 1788, *Sbornik imperatorskogo russkogo istoricheskogo obshchestva* (148 vols., St Petersburg, 1867–1916), 23, 445–8, 450; Marcum, 'Vorontsov', pp. 98–108.

[40] Keith to Carmarthen, 30 Jan., 3 May, Carmarthen to Keith, 12 Feb., 11 July 1788, PRO FO 7/15 fols. 36–7, 191, 53, 7/16 fol. 54; Keith to Carmarthen, 27 July, 13, 17 Sept., Carmarthen to Straton, 27 Aug. 1788, BL Eg. 3501 fols. 93–4, 100, 102, 96.

with France. That the security of his German, Italian, and Flemish dominions renders the friendship of that power absolutely necessary – implying at the same time the strongest suspicion of the intriguing spirit of the French government, and their readiness to thwart the views even of their best friends, when they are in any degree likely to render their own influence less necessary, or desirable. Such sentiments existing in the Emperor's mind, and the uniform conduct of the court of Vienna for many years past, so far as relates to this country, being considered, however friendly our disposition towards Austria may be, it appears to be totally impossible for you to receive any other than general instructions. No one measure that we could propose, would, in the present circumstances, be likely to succeed. Of course the very proposal would be liable to the disagreeable circumstance of either a direct refusal, or at best an evasive answer.

Carmarthen continued by expressing the hope that Austria would 'return to the ancient system',[41] but British policy was steadily moving towards Prussia and away from an Austria that was regarded as hostile. Given the domestic and international problems of the French government in 1787, it can be suggested that Joseph II failed to judge the shift of power in western Europe adequately. The support of the most active power there was gained by Frederick William II, and, although the Pitt ministry did not support Prussia's schemes for territorial rearrangements and for the independence of the Austrian Netherlands to the extent that Frederick William and his ministers desired, the Anglo-Prussian alliance gave added credibility and weight to Prussian pretensions and power. Arguably Joseph, offended by the *Fürstenbund* and unaware of Britain's new-found ministerial stability, failed to grasp the possibility of better relations. The failure of reform in France was, however, by no means predictable, Britain's disinclination to become involved in Balkan affairs had been made clear during the Crimean crisis of 1783, George III's poor relations with Catherine II made any triple alliance of Britain, Austria and Russia unlikely, and the eventual failure of the Anglo-Prussian alliance to meet Prussian expectations suggests that a British alliance might not have been particularly useful to Joseph.

By 1788 co-operation with Prussia was no longer sought by the British government simply in the United Provinces, and Carmarthen justified the eventual result, the Treaty of Berlin of 13 August 1788, for creating 'an alliance of so much importance to the mutual interests of both countries, and which may be the means of preventing the troubles which at present so unhappily exist from extending themselves more generally into other parts of Europe'. The consequence of the alliance was speedily apparent in Anglo-Austrian relations. Carmarthen replied in September

[41] Carmarthen to Keith, 11 Mar. 1788, PRO FO 7/15 fols. 95–6; Harris to Keith, 6 Mar. 1788, BL Add. 35540 fol. 112.

1788 to what appeared to be a tentative enquiry concerning the possibility of British mediation in the Balkans by informing Keith that Britain would do nothing without consulting her allies.[42]

Alice Carter argued that Prussia was no substitute for Austria, as Prussia's interest was 'to check, not to support, the guardian of the Southern Netherlands'.[43] Aside from making the questionable assumption that guarding the Austrian Netherlands from France was the central problem for British policy, her argument neglected the fact that in 1787–90 Prussia was better placed than Austria to intervene militarily in the United Provinces. The failure to negotiate an Anglo-Austrian alliance in 1787–8 is scarcely surprising given the nature of relations in 1784–6, but it also indicated the extent to which developing Anglo-Prussian links limited British options. Given the nature of Austro-Prussian relations in the 1780s, it was not plausible to try to add an Anglo-Austrian understanding to that between Britain and Prussia. Interventionism entailed commitments that limited options. Yet better Anglo-Prussian relations did not preclude an attempt to create a more extensive system. There were hopes of Sweden. In October 1787 the Swedish Ambassador in Copenhagen, Johann, General Baron Springporten, called on his British counterpart, Hugh Elliot, to suggest that the developing crisis in the Balkans was of wider importance, that a threat from Russia existed and that it should take a major role in the agenda of British foreign policy. Springporten

recapitulated the reasons which obliged the King of Sweden to consider every addition to the power of Russia, as dangerous to the safety of his own dominions. He also contended, that Denmark was almost equally interested to guard against the unsatiable ambition of a court, which, though now a powerful friend, might, in the sequel, prove an irresistible enemy. Count Springporten then applied (and I confess with great speciousness) the same train of reasoning to the interests of Great Britain, and added, that he expressly addressed me as the fittest person, both on account of my situation, and connexions at this court, to awaken its administration to a sense of the danger to which the independence of the Baltic will be finally reduced, if ancient prejudices prevent an union between two powers, whose weight and interest are annihilated by a mutual opposition, and who risk their existence, by listening to the dictates of ill-grounded jealousy, rather than to the evidence of reason and judgement. In speaking of the Turkish war, General Springporten made use of this remarkable expression, 'that his master considered the Ottoman Empire as the last remaining bulwark between Stockholm and Petersburg' ... he looked upon the present crisis, as the epoch in

[42] Carmarthen to Keith, 26 Aug., 24 Sept. 1788, BL Add. 35541 fol. 73, PRO FO 7/16 fols. 191–2.

[43] A. C. Carter, 'Britain as a European Power, from her Glorious Revolution to the French Revolutionary War', in J. S. Bromley and E. H. Kossmann (eds.), *Britain and the Netherlands in Europe and Asia* (1968), p. 133.

which the wavering politics of the nations of Europe, will be consolidated into fixed systems of friendship, or hostility.

Later that month Gustavus III paid a surprise visit to Copenhagen, in an unsuccessful attempt to win Danish support for a projected attack on Russia: a guarantee of her neutrality would guard Sweden's rear and destroy the Dano-Russian alliance. Gustavus also reinforced Springporten's approach. During a court ball, he told Elliot that there was little chance of co-operation between Denmark and Sweden, 'little hopes of any effective steps being taken to insure the independence of the Baltic, if Great Britain did not second his efforts for that purpose'. Gustavus also argued that French weakness both was bad for her allies, such as Sweden, and ensured that any league to confine Russia 'within just bounds' would have to spring from other powers. This initiative was supplemented by an approach by Nolcken, the Swedish envoy in London, to Carmarthen. He sought a 'Quintuple Alliance', including both Britain and Sweden.[44] The Swedish approach made strikingly clear, what was less immediately apparent in the case of relations with Prussia, that any alliance would entail commitments and rivalries in which it would be difficult for Britain to retain the initiative and her freedom of manoeuvre.

And yet Britain also faced problems that appeared to require the formation of a diplomatic system. Aside from guaranteeing the Dutch settlement, there was the danger that if Prussia was not secured she would ally with France. In addition, the winter of 1787–8 saw an upsurge in talk about the possibility of a new quadruple alliance, a union of the Franco-Spanish and Austro-Russian alliances, or at least a pact of France, Austria and Russia. In a major reversal of policy, the French ministry was willing to support the idea of Austrian and Russian gains at the expense of their traditional ally Turkey, as the price of an alliance with the two powers,[45] and there was speculation that France herself might benefit by gains in the Aegean, Crete, or Egypt. Carmarthen feared that the intentions of the alliance would not be restricted to the Balkans, and he noted the report that the Bavarian Exchange Scheme might be

[44] Elliot to Carmarthen, 27 Oct., 10 Nov. 1787, PRO FO 22/9 fols. 127–8, 136–9; Carmarthen to Thurlow, 23 Dec. 1787, BL Eg. 3498 fols. 249–50; Barton, *Scandinavia*, p. 155.
[45] Ségur to Montmorin, 6 Nov. 1787, AE CP Russie 122 fol. 211; Ewart to Keith, 17, 24 Nov., Harris to Keith, 4 Dec., 1787, Fraser to Keith, 31 May 1788, BL Add. 35539 fols. 252, 263, 279, 35540 fol. 249; Eden (sceptical) to Liston, 10 Dec. 1787, 11 Feb. 1788, NLS 5549 fol. 118, 5550 fol. 48; Pitt to Eden, 7 Jan. 1788, PRO 30/8/102 fol. 115; H. Ragsdale, 'Montmorin and Catherine's Greek Project: Revolution in French Foreign Policy', *Cahiers du monde russe et soviétique*, 27 (1986), 27–44; Murphy, 'Louis XVI … Policy Dilemma', 264–74; Marcum, 'Vorontsov', pp. 90–3.

revived.[46] The Russian government pressed France to gain advantages by joining in the Balkan conflict. Montmorin argued that as the Turks had acted without consulting France, she was free to do as she thought best, while Ségur, the envoy in St Petersburg, warned that if France did not win the alliance of Russia, Britain would.[47] The last was an argument frequently used by diplomats in this period, reflecting their sense that international relations was both competitive and, other than in that sense, unpredictable.

The British ministry received many reports about differences between the powers of the possible triple alliance, and Dorset offered encouragement on that head.[48] The government was also well aware that Spain was unhappy about Russian conquests at the expense of the Turks, and indeed the Spanish government rejected the idea of the alliance, while the French were unwilling to guarantee the existing status of Poland. There was, nevertheless, concern in Britain about the prospect of such an alliance, especially before it became clear that the Turks were still an appreciable military power and that France would not recover from the political and financial crisis of 1787 as was suggested. Ségur thought that an alliance of Austria, Russia and France would create fear in Britain and Prussia and be a brilliant revenge for the Dutch crisis.[49] Thus, although the Dutch crisis had resulted in a major triumph for Britain, it, in conjunction with developments elsewhere, especially the outbreak of war in the Balkans, had produced an international situation that was confused, frenetic and more urgent than that before conflict had begun. Carmarthen referred in December 1787 to 'the present unsettled state of the system of Europe', Keith the following month to 'irksome political perplexity... in short such a fog of mysterious forecast and doubtful conjecture, as has teazed me exceedingly'.[50]

---

[46] Ainslie to Carmarthen, 10 Nov., Elliot to Carmarthen, 22 Dec. 1787, PRO FO 78/8 fol. 243, 22/10 fols. 166–7; Storer to Eden, 14 Dec. 1787, *Auckland*, I, 453; Carmarthen to Eden, 4 Apr. 1788, NLS 5550 fol. 157.

[47] Ségur to Montmorin, 6, 23 Nov., Montmorin to Ségur, 7 Nov. 1787, AE CP Russie 122 fols. 218, 221, 263–5.

[48] Charles Fraser to Keith, 4 Dec. 1787, BL Add. 35539 fols. 281–2; *Court and Cabinets*, I, 401; Dorset to Stafford, 19 Dec. 1787, 17 Jan. 1788, PRO 30/29/1/15 nos. 74–5.

[49] A. Mousset, *Un témoigne ignoré de la Révolution: Le Comte de Fernan Nuñez, Ambassadeur d'Espagne à Paris 1787–1791* (Paris, 1924), pp. 188–92; Marcum, 'Vorontsov', pp. 92–3; Eden to Pitt, 29 Nov. 1787, CUL Add. 6958 no. 431; Ségur to Montmorin, 4 Dec., Montmorin to Ségur, 7 Dec. 1787, AE CP Russie 122 fols. 296, 308–9.

[50] Carmarthen to Ewart, 2 Dec. 1787, PRO FO 64/12 fol. 197; Keith to Frances Murray, 16 Jan. 1788, HL HM. 18940, p. 375; Harris to Keith, 6 Mar. 1788, BL Add. 35540 fol. 112.

The creation of an Anglo-Prussian alliance

The caution inspired by concern about Prussian intentions, which led to a stress on general co-operation but no urgency for an alliance, was matched by the wish to have something more concrete to rely on in such a volatile situation. Harris, characteristically, pressed hardest for action. Though he asserted his invariable wish 'to see the House of Austria as great and as powerful as success and wisdom can make it',[51] he used his private correspondence with Carmarthen to argue the case for an axis based on the successful partnership in the Dutch crisis. Keen to settle with the Dutch,[52] Harris also suggested that it would be possible to incorporate Russia into the new system,

I am satisfied that the moment England, Prussia and the Republic are allied, Russia will be very glad to become a fourth contracting party; that while the union is in suspence, she will waver between the two great partys in Europe and endeavour to keep her consequence by coquetting on both sides – Russia in fact is, only what the great powers in Europe chose she should be, and if in a congress, she was voted to Coventry,[53] she could not help going there. She knows this and acts accordingly. Vanity and a thirst for fame being the Empress' ruling passion, she always will lean towards the strongest side and the solid and formidable mass the three powers I mentioned above would form if intimately connected would be one to which I am sure she would be eager to join, the instant a favorable opportunity was held out to her to escape from the arms of the Emperor ... I am already for closing *immediately* with Prussia – I think we *could govern* that court now and if that is once ascertained I will be responsible for governing this [The Hague].

This was not an isolated example of Harris' bombastic exuberance. On 2 February 1788 he returned to the theme that a triple alliance would win the support of Russia, a view that Carmarthen hoped would be vindicated by events.[54] British diplomats could also argue that there was a 'natural connection' between Britain and Russia, and that this was being thwarted by a faction that would be replaced, especially as Grand Duke Paul was held to want change.[55] Harris' advice was that coming to the government from its most influential envoy, and indeed his influence was accentuated by Eden's removal from Paris to Madrid. Harris had served at St Petersburg and therefore his opinions seemed more significant. He was

---

[51] Harris to Keith, 1 Feb. 1788, BL Add. 35540 fol. 42.
[52] Harris to Carmarthen, 15 Jan. 1788, BL Eg. 3500 fol. 49.
[53] An English phrase meaning to be ostracised.
[54] Harris to Carmarthen, 29 Jan., 2 Feb., Carmarthen to Harris, 1 Feb. 1788, BL Eg. 3500 fols. 50–5.
[55] Charles Whitworth, Envoy Extraordinary in St Petersburg, to Leeds, 22 May 1789, PRO FO 65/17 fols. 117–18; Ewart to Cornwallis, 15 Aug. 1789, Williamwood 147.

indeed expressing the oft-held view that an alliance with Prussia or Russia would also win the other for Britain. It was a view that had been proved wrong in the past, and Harris' confident appraisal, both of Catherine and of how Russia could and should be treated, was dangerously simplistic and over-optimistic. It was to be the policy followed, though to a different end, towards Russia until 1791; namely that by developing a strong enough alliance system other powers could be persuaded to join, or intimidated into desisting from unwelcome steps.

And yet the problem of differing interests within the system was already apparent. It was soon to centre on the celebrated Hertzberg plan, the proposals of the relatively anglophile Prussian minister Count Ewald Hertzberg for major territorial changes in eastern Europe. Accepting that, as seemed likely, Joseph and Catherine would make gains at the expense of the Turks, Hertzberg suggested both that Prussia should not be excluded and that the opportunity existed to bring stability to eastern Europe. The first objective would be ensured by persuading Poland to cede Danzig and the province of Thorn (Torun) to Prussia, in return for regaining Galicia, ceded to Austria in 1772; the second by a guarantee for the rest of the Turkish Empire. A bold scheme, Hertzberg's plan was a revival of the diplomacy of the early 1770s when the interests of the partitioning powers had brought together the fate of Poland and the likely progress of the Russo-Turkish war that had begun in 1768. Hertzberg circulated his plan to Prussian envoys abroad and to most foreign envoys at Berlin. The skilled Austrian postal interception and decoding office acquired details of it in December 1787. Hertzberg sought to give his plan substance by persuading Russia to accept an Anglo-Prussian mediation of her conflict with the Turks.[56] Harris was as bold an arranger of international combinations as Hertzberg, but even he thought the Hertzberg plan dangerous,

I do not in my own mind like an accommodation that is to depend on the reciprocal aggrandizement of the belligerent powers and that of one of the mediating ones [Prussia]; it is establishing a principle of depredation ... and will I think stand in the way of that we are inclined to adopt.[57]

Harris' view was a sound one, and, though British policy became more anti-Russian in 1789–91, it was not lost sight of, for concern about establishing a system of collective security in eastern Europe and, in particular, interest in a viable Poland, were generally based on the notion of *status quo ante bellum*, not on 'reciprocal aggrandizement'. Never-

[56] W. Kalinka, 'La Politique prussienne en Orient à la fin du siècle dernier', *Revue des deux mondes*, 60 (1883), 666–70; A. T. Preuss, *Ewald Friedrich Graf von Hertzberg* (Berlin, 1909), pp. 138–48; Roider, *Austria's Eastern Question*, p. 179.
[57] Harris to Carmarthen, 2 Feb. 1788, BL Eg. 3500 fol. 54.

theless, Harris, as already pointed out, felt that the Prussian government could be 'governed', an assessment scarcely supported by the events of late 1786 and early 1787, and he was backed by Ewart, soon to be promoted, with Prussian support,[58] to be Envoy Extraordinary. Ewart argued that Frederick William II had 'hitherto formed no resolution whatever in this matter, and that his conduct will be entirely regulated by the course of events, and especially by the extent of the Emperor's operations'.[59]

Ewart was correct. Prussian policy was anything but fixed. The sensible device of maintaining competing groups within a government, that was so useful to determined monarchs, such as Louis XIV, or George II in 1742–4, who wished to retain control, was fatal if the monarch could not give direction. To a considerable extent this had been the case with the Emperor Charles VI and with Louis XV, but with Frederick William II it reached chronic proportions. Exacerbated by the politics of the boudoir, court factionalism under Frederick William made Prussian policy totally unpredictable and diplomats spent much time commenting on and speculating about the love life of the king, his support for favourites, such as Bischoffwerder, and the position of ministers. As Ewart pointed out, much depended on the play of international circumstances, which had become more volatile as a result of the outbreak of war in the Balkans. Schemes for aggrandisement and equivalents suddenly ceased to be simply matters of speculation.

It was not only Prussia whose conduct would be 'chiefly regulated' by the fortunes of war. The same was believed to be equally true of Russia[60] and Austria, and thus of the other powers seeking to play an active role in international relations. Thus, at the very moment that Britain was coming close to creating the diplomatic system that Carmarthen had sought since his appointment, that indeed had eluded his predecessors for a quarter century, war was helping to make any system both unpredictable in its course and likely to be under pressure from members that both had their own aggressive interests to pursue and felt them within their grasp.

Catherine rejected the Prussian mediation proposal. Visiting St Petersburg in July 1788, Titchfield reported to Harris on Russian attitudes towards the Turks: 'they talk here of extirpating that troublesome nation'.[61] However, as Ewart noted, Frederick William II was convinced that the course of events would make his interposition

---

[58] Harris to Carmarthen, 4 Mar. 1788, BL Eg. 3500 fol. 69.
[59] Ewart to Keith, 18 Feb. 1788, BL Add. 35540 fol. 66.
[60] Ewart to Keith, 8 Mar. 1788, BL Add. 35540 fol. 127.
[61] Titchfield to Harris, 25 July 1788, Winchester, Malmesbury 169.

unavoidable. Britain was thus having to consider alliance with a power that had not shelved plans for a territorial reordering of eastern Europe, and one where unpredictable factions played a major role in policy. George III lamented that Frederick William's mind was 'so easily wrought upon by deceiving men'.[62] Redrawing the map of Europe was not, however, the objective of the British ministry, and indeed Russian concern about the intentions of George III was scarcely borne out by the course of Anglo-Prussian relations in the year after the Dutch crisis. Reports of an army of 50,000 Hanoverians, Hessians and Brunswickers designed to support Prussia and paid for by a prussophile George III as Elector of Hanover were spread,[63] but Ewart stressed the limited objectives of his negotiations

to follow up the proceedings of last autumn respecting Holland, with more formal engagements between the two courts, to be contracted in order to confirm and guaranty the stipulations of their respective treaties with the Republic ... and particularly to inforce the permanency of the constitution and government as they have been at present reestablished.[64]

Nevertheless, George III had a bolder vision. He informed the Prince of Orange that he saw an Anglo-Dutch-Prussian system as a means to block the intrigues of Austria and France, and the Princess, who could be relied upon to pass on the message to her brother, Frederick William, that the system would be a means to oblige Austria and France to seek the continuation of the peace of Europe, and to that end to negotiate peace for Turkey.[65] A view of Britain as the European policeman was clearly suggested, and though nothing was said about Russia, she would be affected if the conflict between Austria and Turkey was ended. The prospect of Anglo-Prussian mediation being followed by a guarantee of Turkey and even her inclusion in a defensive alliance was raised. Schemes for territorial change, however, were neither countenanced nor condemned. Meanwhile, discussions continued between Britain and Prussia. Differing British and Prussian expectations concerning the long-term consequences of these negotiations complicated their progress. Prussian proposals in April 1788 for mutual defensive support outside the Dutch context were greeted with little warmth, to the anger of the Prussians, and Ewart warned that they might turn to France. Harris

[62] Ewart to Keith, 29 Mar. 1788, BL Add. 35540 fol. 171; George III to Carmarthen, 15 Apr. 1788, Aspinall, *George III* no. 450; Luzerne to Montmorin, 15 Apr. 1788, AE CP Ang. 565 fol. 77

[63] Luzerne to Montmorin, 13 May 1788, AE CP Ang. 565 fol. 160.

[64] Ewart to Keith, 22 Apr. 1788, BL Add. 35540 fols. 204–5.

[65] George III to Prince and to Princess of Orange, both of 6 June 1788, Aspinall, *George III* nos. 452–3; Luzerne to Montmorin, 27 June, Barthélemy to Montmorin, 4 Nov. 1788, AE CP Ang. 565 fols. 330–1, 567 fol. 104.

urged Pitt to ally with Prussia.[66] The defence of the United Provinces was clearly still a priority in governmental circles. Fawcett urged the re-establishment of the Scots Brigade as a reliable force in Dutch service; Richmond sent engineers to ascertain the practicality of seizing the Texel and Den Helder in the event of war and pressed Harris on the need to prevent their fortification, as it would limit the potential for successful naval action against a hostile United Provinces.[67]

The danger of closer Franco-Prussian relations led a Cabinet meeting on 31 May 1788, attended by Thurlow, Stafford, Howe, Pitt, Camden, Richmond, Sydney and Carmarthen, to decide that, although they wanted any Anglo-Prussian defensive system to be as extensive as possible, the need for a defensive alliance with Prussia was so fundamental that it should not be delayed if Frederick William II did not wish to wait for negotiations with other powers. That quintessential spirit of diplomatic perpetual motion, Harris, who had been recalled to London, was instructed to take advantage of Frederick William's forthcoming visit to his sister at Het Loo in the United Provinces in order to conclude such an alliance.[68] Given Harris' presence in London and the interest of George III in creating a new system, their influence can be implied as playing the major role in the Cabinet meeting and Harris' subsequent mission to Het Loo. In an interesting parallel to the situation a year earlier, when a more vigorous British approach to the Dutch crisis was determined upon, there seems to have been either a rejection of Pitt's caution, or he was persuaded to adopt a more vigorous attitude, for it was Pitt who had drafted the cool response to the proposed Prussian secret articles and who had preferred a larger league to a quick agreement with Prussia. Harris was instructed to assure Frederick William

of the King's earnest desire to cooperate with His Prussian Majesty in establishing such a system of mutual defence and assistance, as may, not only tend to the protection of the rights and possessions of the contracting parties themselves, but which may, from the weight and influence naturally belonging to it, contribute to the general tranquillity, by holding out such a force as may prevent the attempts of ambitious or intriguing powers from endangering the peace of Europe, or encroaching on the rights of individuals. With a view to render this very advantageous system complete, the accession of other powers must be desirable, and you will not fail to recall to the King of Prussia's recollection, the opening made on the subject, by the King of Sweden last winter,

[66] Ewart to Carmarthen, 12 Apr., Carmarthen to Ewart, 14 May 1788, PRO FO 64/13; Harris to Pitt, 22 Apr. 1788, PRO 30/8/155 fols. 67–8; Luckwaldt, 'Die englisch-preussische Allianz', pp. 105–6.
[67] Fawcett to Harris, 10 Mar., Richmond to Harris, 13 May 1788, Winchester, Malmesbury 152, 180.
[68] Cabinet minute, 31 May 1788, Aspinall, *George III* no. 450.

and the use that might be made of the proposals ... in endeavouring to prevail on the two northern crowns to accede to the confederacy.

The stress on the value of an extensive system was readily apparent. The ministry was proposing to revive the Stanhopian view, which had been so influential during the reign of George I, of Britain as a major partner in a continental collective security system, or, as Carmarthen put it on 10 June, 'a general alliance extensive enough to secure, in a great degree, the tranquillity of Europe'.[69] This was a very bold plan, one that revealed the now ambitious nature of British foreign policy. Little in the way of public debate lay behind the initiative, though, in the Commons debate on the Hessian subsidy on 5 December 1787, Pitt had stated that 'it was universally admitted that continental connections were beneficial and necessary to the country', while Burke for the opposition had declared that with Russia, Prussia and the Dutch as allies 'he should little care for the rest of the world'.[70]

Such bold talk was understandable in the aftermath of the Dutch crisis, but the Anglo-Prussian discussions in the summer of 1788 over the provisions for mutual military aid revealed a major shift from concern simply about the fate of the Dutch and their colonies. The prospect of war with France, Austria and Russia was mentioned, and, in facing this threat, considerable reliance was placed on assistance from other powers, such as Turkey and Sweden. Such an alliance system was to be compromised in British eyes by Prussia's pursuit of her own territorial goals, but it was also somewhat naive of the British ministry to believe that war could be discussed without her allies considering their own prospects for gain. Harris was informed 'that no alliance can exist without some mutual risk to each, of being engaged in war on account of the other's quarrels',[71] but Britain was to seek to define Prussian interests in an unrealistically circumscribed fashion, although, on the other hand, such tension was commonplace in alliances. Harris himself was reaching towards a new diplomatic order. He envisaged an international peace congress that would tackle not only Balkan and Baltic problems but also, as he suggested to Pitt,

all other subjects, which as far as human foresight can reach may lead in some future day to disturb the tranquillity of Europe ... the election of the King of the Romans – the fixing the nature of the Bavarian succession – the determining the doubtful points in the constitutions of Sweden and Poland, and various other less important objects which both in Germany and the North ought to be clearly and distinctly defined, in order that the great act of pacification should be a perfect

[69] Carmarthen to Harris, 6, 10 June 1788, PRO FO 37/23.
[70] Cobbett, 26, 1272, 1276.
[71] Carmarthen to Harris, 10 June 1788, PRO FO 37/23.

work, a kind of *new treaty of Munster*, which is certainly much wanted as the old one is quite obsolete.[72]

Little did Harris realise, that the Peace of Westphalia of 1648 was soon to be swept aside totally, not through negotiations but thanks to the revolutionary force, vigour and ideas of one of the two guarantor powers of 1648, France.

Harris left London on the evening of 6 June, and, after a long passage on a rough sea and in the face of contrary winds, he reached The Hague at 4 am on the 9th. After a quick stay in which he sought to counteract the efforts of the new French envoy, St Priest, to build up support, Harris reached Het Loo on the night of the 10th. His vigorous advocacy, and some skilful bribery of Frederick William II's *valet de chambre* to prevent his audience from being disturbed by Stein, a supporter of Franco-Prussian links, was crowned with success, a provisional Anglo-Prussian treaty being signed on the 13th. Frederick William II feared that it would drive Russia further into the arms of France and Austria, but Harris argued that there was no chance of detaching Catherine from Joseph, a reasonable view, and, more surprisingly, that it would be more advantageous to have the alliance of Sweden and Turkey, 'than the alliance of a country involved in a ruinous war, and whose resources appear to be exhausted at the outset'.[73] Harris' reassuring remarks revealed the dilemma of the architects of a collective security system that sought to harness the resources and further the interests both of the weaker powers in eastern Europe, Sweden, Turkey, and, soon, Poland, and, of the weakest of the three partitioning states, Prussia. Although the British government was not to welcome signs of chaos in the Austrian and Russian dominions as eagerly as its Prussian counterpart did, and was, indeed, to clash accordingly with her ally over the Austrian Netherlands, the British ministry was now in a position in which disorder in these dominions, as in France, was welcome, a situation that made it harder to envisage a reconciliation with Austria and Russia.

War in the Baltic

Frederick William told Harris on 13 June 1788 that he had no wish to aggrandise himself and did not wish the Anglo-Prussian mediation to be an armed one, but he made it clear that he did not want Joseph to benefit from the war in the Balkans.[74] The provisional treaty had to be ratified within six months, a provision that allowed Britain both to consider the

[72] Harris to Pitt, 29 Sept. 1788, PRO 30/8/155 fols. 85–6.
[73] Harris to Carmarthen, 13, 15 June 1788, PRO FO 37/23; Luckwaldt, 'Die englisch-preussische Allianz', pp. 114–16.
[74] Harris to Carmarthen, 15 June 1788, PRO FO 37/23.

terms for mutual assistance, a subject in which George III took a close interest,[75] and to investigate the possibility of a more extensive alliance. The outbreak of war in the Baltic, however, made the latter more dangerous. Any extension of the Anglo-Prussian system in northern Europe would centre on Gustavus III, for the Danish government was regarded as a Russian tool.[76] Gustavus, however, was not interested in any alliance that would prevent him from pursuing his schemes for aggrandisement, and had therefore in 1783 rejected Catherine II's proposal for a triple alliance to include Denmark.[77] Keen to exploit Russian involvement in war with Turkey, in order to win military glory and defeat Catherine II, the patroness of Finnish separatism and of domestic aristocratic opposition to him, Gustavus provoked war in June/July 1788. Swedish soldiers disguised as Russians staged a border incident at Puumala on 28 June, enabling Gustavus to declare war on 6 July 1788. He did so without consulting the Riksdag as he was obliged to do. Gustavus wished to break the threat posed by the Dano-Russian alliance in order both to annex Norway and, in changing decisively the international situation in the Baltic, to alter the domestic situation within Sweden in order to consolidate his authority.[78] Though, to some extent, Gustavus' aspirations prefigured those of the French revolutionaries in their drive for war with Austria in 1792, there were major differences, not least in the degree of control exercised by Gustavus and his consequent ability to decide when to launch a long-planned assault.

It was unlikely that the conflict would be a limited one. Denmark threatened to help Russia, which she was obliged to do by treaty, and Elliot reported, in the sort of language that reflected not only his own exuberant partisanship, but also the increasingly apparent tendency of British policy, that he feared that Russia and Denmark would defeat Gustavus' efforts 'to establish in the Baltic some degree of equilibre, and to raise a barrier against the insatiable ambition of the Czarina'. Camden warned Pitt that a Russian defeat of Sweden would make both her and Denmark dependencies of Russia, with detrimental consequences for Britain, and he argued that it was therefore necessary to secure the peace and tranquillity of the Baltic, while satisfying Russia that the British did not seek to take the part of Sweden,[79] a difficult task.

[75] George III to Carmarthen, 8 June 1788, Aspinall, *George III* no. 455.
[76] Elliot to Carmarthen, 7, 21 June 1788, PRO FO 22/10 fols. 100, 106.
[77] S. Oakley, *War and Peace in the Baltic 1560–1790* (1992), p. 162.
[78] A. Brückner, 'Russland und Schweden 1788', *Historische Zeitschrift*, 22 (1869), 314–402; H. A. Barton, 'Gustav III of Sweden and the East Baltic, 1771–1792', *Journal of Baltic Studies*, 7 (1976), 16, 24–5, and *Scandinavia*, p. 154.
[79] Elliot to Carmarthen, 14, 28 June 1788, PRO FO 22/10 fols. 103, 114; Camden to Pitt, 21 Oct. 1788, PRO 30/8/119 fols. 138–9.

Carmarthen wanted to solve the developing Baltic crisis by winning Denmark for the new alliance system, a familiar idea, for past anti-Russian schemes, most obviously those backed by George I, had relied heavily on the idea of a combination between the two Scandinavian states supported by one or more of Britain, France and the United Provinces. As in the past, it was all too easy to underrate differences between the two states and the impact of Russian power. In 1788 Elliot warned that Denmark would not join the new system, and that the only way to prevent her from supporting Russia was by threatening her with unspecified 'inconveniences'. He subsequently suggested the dispatch of a British fleet to the Sound.[80] Elliot's dispatches both were alarmist and revealed a disturbing analytical tendency. By seeing European international relations in terms of a confrontation between two systems, he ensured that specific changes, for example the possible overthrow of monarchical authority in Sweden, would be seen as of direct consequence for all other members of the system. Interventionism would therefore be not only advisable but necessary. Commitment to a particular domestic situation was scarcely novel: the British had spent most of the last seventy years supporting the Orangist position in the United Provinces. Nor was it novel for more distant Sweden, in whose internal politics Britain had intervened on a number of occasions from the mid-1720s onwards.[81] Nevertheless, as was to become clear in the sequel, Elliot's determination to prevent 'a total revolution in the government of that country' was to commit Britain, and, in a risky situation, far more than the government had anticipated. And yet, that stemmed from the stress on the strength of alliance systems in the European 'scale of power' that increasingly characterised British policy.[82]

The Baltic crisis made an extension of the British alliance system less likely, for a Sweden already at war was desirable as an ally only to other powers also at war with Russia. The crisis also made good relations with Prussia more necessary, if Britain wished to play a major role in an increasingly volatile situation. Harris had already reported that the Anglo-Prussian provisional treaty had improved Orangist morale, while the value of the alignment was further suggested by the willingness of the two powers to co-operate over the coadjutorship of the strategic prince-bishopric of Liège. The final Anglo-Prussian treaty, signed at Berlin on 13 August 1788, clarified their mutual military obligations in the event of

[80] Carmarthen to Elliot, 1 July, Elliot to Carmarthen, 19, 26 July 1788, PRO FO 22/10 fols. 138–40, 155, 157, 168.

[81] M. F. Metcalf, *Russia, England and Swedish Party Politics 1762–1766. The Interplay between Great Power Diplomacy and Domestic Politics during Sweden's Age of Liberty* (Stockholm, 1977); M. Roberts, *British Diplomacy and Swedish Politics, 1758–1773* (1980).   [82] Elliot to Carmarthen, 2 Aug. 1788, PRO FO 22/10 fols. 197–8.

war. The two powers also agreed to cooperate over the war in the Balkans.[83]

The developing Baltic crisis made conflict involving the new alliance seem unexpectedly close. The 'hare-brained heir and imitator of Charles XII of Sweden',[84] was to prove less successful in defeating a Russo-Danish challenge without foreign assistance than Charles had been in 1700. Gustavus' hopes of victory over Russia proved illusory. His army was not in good shape and a drawn naval battle off Hogland in the Gulf of Finland on 17 July, in which the Swedes were hindered by ammunition shortages, denied Gustavus the crucial control of the Gulf which he needed both for his military operations in Finland and if he was to carry out an amphibious attack on St Petersburg. An overland offensive on St Petersburg was then mounted without success. Gustavus was faced in August 1788 by conspiracy in his own army, the Pact of Anjala, and an appeal from the conspirators to Catherine.[85] In addition, in response to Catherine's request, an initially hesitant Denmark declared war and began operations at the end of August. The Danish government saw the Russian alliance as the sole guarantee against Swedish aims on Norway.

The powers of the new Triple Alliance sought to mediate between Denmark and Sweden, while the British government made it clear that any Danish attack on Sweden would make her a principal and an aggressor;[86] but British policy was taken further by Ewart and Elliot. They were to a certain extent encouraged from London, whence Harris sent a private letter to Ewart informing him that his instructions were based on the idea 'that the King of Sweden must not be crushed, or the balance of the Baltic overset'. Harris, who praised Gustavus' 'spirit and activity', outlined a very extensive diplomatic scheme, that would have committed Britain to the Baltic *status quo*,

If the three allies agree to mediate... it will be necessary in order to prevent Russia taking her revenge when an opportunity offers, to close the mediation by a guarantee of their dominions as regulated by the peace ... If the King of Sweden says he cannot make a separate peace from the Turks, the mediation may extend to them, and as a considerable space of time must elapse before such a resolution can be determined on, a suspension of arms should be agreed on in the interim and some assurances given that the Russian fleet does not leave the Baltic till an answer from Constantinople arrives.

[83] Harris to Carmarthen, 20 June, 18 July 1788, PRO FO 37/23; L. von Ranke, *Die deutschen Mächte und der Fürstenbund*, II (Leipzig, 1872), pp. 358–60.
[84] Keith to Ewart, 23 Aug. 1788, Matlock CRO 239 M/O 759.
[85] A. Brückner, 'Der Anjalabund in Finnland 1788', *Baltische Monatsschrift*, 19 (1870), 309–54; Barton, *Scandinavia*, pp. 157–9; Ewart to Keith, 30 Aug. 1788, BL Add. 35541 fol. 79.
[86] Pitt to Grenville, 1 Sept. 1788, BL Add. 58906 fol. 45; Carmarthen to Elliot, draft in Pitt's hand, 9 Sept. 1788, PRO FO 22/10 fol. 283.

Ewart also had a bold conception of what the situation called for. He wished to combine mediation of the Baltic and the Balkan crises, and he wrote to Elliot on 11 September 1788,

His Prussian Majesty enters roundly into our great view of employing a powerful and well concerted interference in order to secure the balance of the Baltic, in such a manner as to render the friendship of England, Prussia and Holland not only desirable but necessary and even *indispensable* to the three Northern Powers, whether considered separately or collectively. In regard to Russia, in particular, His Prussian Majesty is clear we ought to enforce our mediation with firmness and vigour, should it be necessary.[87]

Ewart approved a Prussian threat to the Danes that if they attacked Gustavus, Prussia would invade Holstein, and Britain would send a fleet. The Danes, however, invaded Sweden with 10,000 troops and advanced on Göteborg (Gothenburg). Having threatened the Danish government on 16 September with British and Prussian attack, Elliot, without instructions, left the next day for Sweden. Finding Gustavus, who was in a very weak position, on 29 September, Elliot eventually persuaded him to grant him powers to negotiate with the Danes on his behalf. He claimed to have told the King, 'Sire, give me your Crown; I will return it to you with added lustre.' Elliot then pressed the Danes to accept an armistice, which they did for eight days on 9 October. The threat of conflict with Britain and, crucially, Prussia led the Danes to prolong the armistice and accept a convention for the evacuation of Sweden which Elliot drew up on 6 November.[88]

Ewart's unauthorised 'answering for his Court as to active not defensive measures' aroused the anger of George III, who was determined to avoid war; while Elliot was criticised by the government, though praised by that of Prussia. Carmarthen, however, felt it necessary to defend Elliot to Vorontsov, arguing that he had acted in accordance with his instructions, which had been drawn up in light of the British policy of supporting the reestablishment of peace in the Baltic on a just and equitable footing.[89] The minister was not, however, called upon to justify anything similar to the *Fürstenbund*. George's views are instructive in light of the continued belief in his malevolent intentions held in pro-Russian circles. Elliot reported Bernstorff as saying 'that my conduct is

---

[87] Harris to Ewart, 16, 29 Aug., 9 Sept. 1788, Williamwood vol. 148, NLS 12999; Ewart to Elliot, 11 Sept. 1788, NLS 13022 fols. 166–8.

[88] Elliot to Carmarthen, 29 Nov. 1788, PRO FO 22/10 fols. 417–26. The letters from Elliot and his secretary Johnstone to Ewart are preserved in vol. 131 of the Williamwood collection.

[89] George III to Pitt, 19, 20 Oct. 1788, Aspinall, *George III* no. 485, Stanhope, *Pitt*, I, 484–5; Ewart to Elliot, 31 Oct. 1788, NLS 13022 fol. 188; Hawkesbury to Dorset, 23 Oct. 1788, KAO C182; Carmarthen to Vorontsov, 12 Nov. 1788, NLS 12999 fol. 219.

already fully justified by the court of Berlin, and the *Elector* of *Hanover*; adding, with a smile, that I might, therefore, be considered as having been better informed than the English cabinet'. There is, however, no evidence of any such royal *secret du roi*. George's letter to Pitt of 19 October makes it clear that he was opposed to war, and Pitt accepted that there was no need to commit Britain to go to war in support of Sweden. Hawkesbury, however, depicted a divided government,

I find that the King of Prussia is disposed to go all lengths in support of the King of Sweden and the Turks; and there are great dissensions in our Cabinet on the part we shall take in this business. The King declares against all measures, that shall involve this country in a war; and the Chancellor supports this opinion; and on the other hand Mr. Pitt and Lord Carmarthen are inclined to the Prussian system. Nothing is settled.[90]

The extent to which Elliot had risked committing Britain was therefore unwelcome but, as in the Dutch crisis, the situation had turned out unexpectedly well. Elliot's confidential report on this mission, endorsed 'most secret and not to appear in my official correspondence', made it clear, however, how unpredictable international developments could be. In a dispatch that included reference to the witches in *Macbeth*, he revealed that both Gustavus and the Danish commander, Prince Charles of Hesse, the husband of one of Christian VII's sisters, were adepts of 'mysterious arts', and Elliot claimed that, 'the Swedish and Danish war originated in a great measure from the fanatical, and occult principles of freemasonry combined with prophecy. The King of Sweden, as well as the Prince of Hesse, are both infatuated.' He reported the prophecy that the crimes of Gustavus III would be avenged by a man upon a white horse with a red coat, and noted that the Prince of Hesse chose to appear thus. Another prophecy, believed by both King and Prince, was that Gustavus would be saved by a stranger, a role Elliot appeared to fill. As he remarked, 'Finding myself thus armed with supernatural powers, I made the most natural use of them.'[91] Such belief in the occult was by no means unique, and it reflected the strength of what might be termed the dark side of the Enlightenment, were that not to imply that the movement should be seen, as its polemicists wished, as preeminently rational. The 1780s saw an increase in concern about the possible radical consequences of Freemasonry, a concern that stemmed in large part from fears aroused by the Bavarian Illuminati. This was one of a number of quasi-masonic organisations that arose, reflecting the popularity of the masonic form

---

[90] Elliot to Carmarthen, 29 Nov. 1788, PRO FO 22/10 fol. 423; Pitt to George III, 25 Oct. 1788, PRO 30/8/101 fol. 5; Hawkesbury to Dorset, 28 Oct. 1788, KAO C182.
[91] Elliot to Carmarthen, 29 Nov. 1788, PRO FO 22/10 fols. 450–60. Elliot's correspondence with Gustavus and Prince Charles is in NLS 13022.

and ideal and the absence of any effective supervisory body to control a movement that was both universal and prone to schism. Thus, the Valhalla Order, founded in 1780–1, a secret lodge with mystical rites, served to unite and inspire those interested in Finnish autonomy.[92] The suspicions the Illuminati engendered arose not so much from their beliefs, which were more utopian than revolutionary, as from their secrecy and their deliberate attempt to increase their influence in Bavaria, a state that was generally resistant to fashionable opinion. They were viewed in Bavaria as supporters of Joseph II. In 1785 all secret societies, including the Freemasons and Illuminati, were banned by Karl Theodor of Bavaria and in 1787 evidence that purported to demonstrate a plot by the Illuminati was published. The Bavarian Foreign Minister wrote of 'that abominable sect, which directly seeks to destroy religion and healthy morals and to overthrow the thrones of rulers'. Officials who were members were dismissed and the government persecuted the organisation.[93] Charles of Hesse was successively General Grand Master of the Hesse Illuminati and National Superior for all Scandinavia. He was also associated with the Rosicrucians and interested in alchemy, and led the future Frederick VI of Denmark to a passing 'interest in mystical religion and Freemasonry'.[94]

The Rosicrucians, who claimed, like the Freemasons, medieval and older antecedents, practised cabalism, astrology and sorcery. They were most influential in the 1780s both at the court of Frederick William II, a mystic as well as a bigamist, and in Russian masonic circles which came under their influence. Frederick William and two of the leading members of his entourage, Johann Rudolf von Bischoffwerder and Johann Christoph Wöllner, were members of the Rosicrucian Order. The Russian Rosicrucians were directed from Berlin, Nikolai Novikov publishing occult and Rosicrucian works in Russia, and attempts were made to recruit the heir to the throne, Grand Duke Paul. Already concerned about the Freemasons, Catherine II was worried about the possible revolutionary sympathies of the secret societies, and in the early 1790s their activities were limited, Novikov being imprisoned without a formal trial in 1792.

The role of the Illuminati and Rosicrucians in prefiguring concern about the part of conspiracies at the time of the French Revolution in developing the paranoid attitudes, style and discourse that was to be so

---

[92] Barton, *Scandinavia*, p. 137.
[93] Vieregg to Hallberg, 14 Aug. 1787, Munich, Bayr. Ges. Wien 730; M. Voges, *Aufklärung und Geheimnis* (Tübingen, 1987).
[94] C. Ingrao, *The Hessian Mercenary State. Ideas, institutions, and reform under Frederick II (1760–1785)* (Cambridge, 1987), p. 34; Barton, *Scandinavia*, p. 142.

important in the early 1790s, is apparent.[95] What is less clear is how far they should play a role in the discussion of international relations. In April 1789, for example, the French envoy in Berlin reported that 'le parti des illuminés et des Saxons' were under the orders of the British, and in the same dispatch he referred to the possibility of an Anglo-Prussian-Russian axis, an alliance that might be opposed to that of the Catholic powers.[96] Given the powerful role of a small number of individuals, their beliefs are of considerable importance, but the role of the occult and of mysticism in these are difficult to evaluate. They do not appear to have played any part in the personality of Charles of Hesse's first cousin, George III, a solid Anglican who preferred to use Herschel's telescopes for his star-gazing, though his mental collapse in the winter of 1788–9 was seen by some in non-medical terms. Frederick William II, Gustavus III and the future Paul I of Russia were, however, very different, and it is not clear how valid an explanation of international relations solely in 'rational' terms can be.

Whereas in the Dutch crisis the British government had kept control, and Harris had had to persuade the ministers to adopt a more vigorous policy, in the Swedish crisis of 1788 Ewart, and, still more, Elliot had interpreted British policy in a more cavalier fashion. Furthermore, Britain's ally, Prussia, had adopted a more assertive position, both than she had taken in 1787 and than that of Britain. The pattern was thus set for the course of Anglo-Prussian relations until their debacle in the Ochakov Crisis. Richmond pointed out to Pitt the need for 'more explicit communications' with Frederick William II, 'for unless we perfectly understand one another we shall be playing at cross purposes', but in fact the difference between the two powers arose, as during the previous Anglo-Prussian alliance during the Seven Years War, from divergent interests, rather than poor communications. The course of the alliance was to provide fresh proof for Keith's observation 'that in the general political state of Europe for the last forty years, *allied*, and *united* in point of common sense and reciprocal interests, have two very different significations'.[97] In addition, Catherine II had been further antagonised which had definitely not been the intention of the British ministry. Camden's

---

[95] J. J. Sheehan, *German History 1770–1866* (Oxford, 1989), p. 214; J. M. Roberts, *The Mythology of the Secret Societies* (1972).

[96] Esterno to Montmorin, 14 Apr. 1789, AE CP Prusse 120 fols. 92–3.

[97] Richmond to Pitt, 1 Sept. 1788, CUL Add. 6958 no. 536; Keith to Ewart, 21 Oct. 1788, Matlock CRO 239 M/O 759; P. F. Doran, *Andrew Mitchell and Anglo-Prussian Relations during the Seven Years War* (New York, 1986); K. W. Schweizer, *England, Prussia and the Seven Years War* (Lewiston, 1989) and *Frederick the Great, William Pitt, and Lord Bute. The Anglo-Prussian Alliance, 1756–1763* (1991).

hope that she could be reassured about British intentions was over-optimistic.[98] So was the argument in *Queries concerning the Conduct which England should follow in Foreign Politics*, a pamphlet written in October 1788 by Sir John Dalrymple, a senior Exchequer official. Dalrymple argued that Britain and Russia had mutual political and economic interests. He even claimed that Russia was fighting Britain's battle in her war with the Turks, as she was seeking to open up the trade of the Black and Caspian Seas. Dalrymple claimed that Prussia was weak, her success in the Seven Years War due to the talents of Frederick II, and that Britain could not depend on either Prussia or the United Provinces. He suggested that the situation was propitious for an alliance of Prussia, Denmark, Sweden, Russia, Austria and the Dutch, an alliance that would serve British interests by restraining France, but that Britain would not have to join. Dalrymple saw such an alliance as linked to territorial changes in which Prussia would gain Poland, the Dutch the Austrian Netherlands and Austria land from the Turks. He also claimed that the Anglo-Prussian treaty might involve Britain in a continental war, whereas his proposals would keep her neutral. Dalrymple's pamphlet, published in 1789, is interesting in that it revealed a desire for a new European system that would serve Britain's interests, but one that would be achieved without cost to her. This wishful thinking was indicative of unrealistic domestic expectations and overbold diplomatic speculations, problems that were to lead to the failure of British policy in 1791.

And yet, on the eve of the Regency Crisis in Britain, the international situation appeared increasingly propitious. The attraction of Britain as an ally was indicated not only by her Prussian alliance, but also by an approach in the autumn of 1788 from Karl Eugen, Duke of Württemberg via the Northite MP, Francis, Viscount Beauchamp, who met him in Stuttgart, and Harris, now ennobled as a reward for his success in the Dutch crisis and his negotiation of the provisional Anglo-Prussian treaty, as Lord Malmesbury. Karl Eugen's readiness to abandon his connections with France and Austria[99] was understandable. France was still suffering serious domestic problems and had not been able to mount a riposte to her Dutch defeat. The idea of a quadruple alliance of France, Spain, Austria and Russia had not been realised, while relations between France and the two last were not close.

In addition, the prospect of the war in the Balkans bringing rapid and, to the British, unwanted territorial shifts, possibly even the collapse of the Turkish Empire, had not materialised. As in 1690, when the Turks

---

[98] Camden to Pitt, 21 Oct. 1788, CUL Add. 6958 no. 536.
[99] Malmesbury to Pitt, 14 Nov., Beauchamp to Malmesbury, 14 Nov. 1788, PRO 30/8/155 fols. 89, 91–4.

under Grand Vizier Fazil Mustafa recaptured Nish and Belgrade, crushing hopes that their loss of Hungary would be followed by the fall of the Balkans, and 1738–9, when unsuccessful Austrian campaigns culminated in the Treaty of Belgrade, by which they ceded Belgrade, Little Wallachia and northern Serbia to the Turks, so in 1788, the Turks had proved more resilient than had been anticipated. The Austrians, deploying 140,000 troops, had hoped to conquer Belgrade, Serbia, Moldavia, Wallachia and most of Bosnia, but the Turks had concentrated their efforts against them, and not, as they had hoped, the Russians. Joseph II proved a poor commander-in-chief, disease debilitated the Austrian army and the Turks were able to put the Austrians onto the defensive. Invading the Banat in August, they captured the fortress of Mehadiye on 30 August and defeated the Austrians at Slatina on 20 September. An unsuccessful campaign, concern about Prussian intentions and a determination not to fight a war on two fronts, led Joseph to become interested in the idea of peace with Turkey. The interception in August 1788 of two letters from Hertzberg, suggesting combined Prusso-Turkish military operations against Austria, frightened Joseph, leading him to argue that, unless Catherine could specify an adequate degree of assistance that she would provide in the event of a Prussian attack, Austria should negotiate a separate peace. There was, nevertheless, scant prospect of peace. Both Catherine and Joseph wished to maintain their gains, while the Turks insisted on the return of the Crimea.[100] As British doubts grew, however, about the willingness of both Joseph and Catherine to fight on,[101] the government defined its attitude towards the possibility of being asked to mediate a settlement between them both and Turkey, or solely Austria and Turkey. Carmarthen insisted that the terms to be proposed by Joseph, and possibly Catherine, should be 'explicitly specified', but, more seriously, he stated that any overture would also have to be made to Prussia and the United Provinces, as George III would act only in concert with them.[102]

This was to be the British response throughout, most obviously to Austrian overtures at the beginning of 1790. If it ensured that Britain was thus tied to Prussia (for the United Provinces could be relied upon to follow the British lead), and thus lost a clearly independent and 'balancing' role, this seemed necessary if British views were to have the

[100] Shaw, *Between Old and New*, pp. 30–1; Roider, *Austria's Eastern Question*, pp. 177, 180–3; Joseph to Kaunitz, 15 Sept. 1788, Beer (ed.), *Joseph, Leopold, und Kaunitz*, pp. 318–19, 327.
[101] Keith to Ewart, 28 Sept., Ewart to Keith, 7 Oct. 1788, BL Add. 35541 fols. 115, 123; Charles Whitworth, Fitzherbert's replacement as Envoy Extraordinary in St Petersburg, to Carmarthen, 8 May 1789, PRO FO 65/17 fols. 104–5.
[102] Carmarthen to Keith, 24 Sept. 1788, PRO FO 7/16 fols. 191–2.

impact that seemed desirable. With reports from Vienna indicating increasing disorder in the Austrian government and rising discontent in the dominions of Joseph II,[103] an assertive role appeared increasingly likely to bring success.

The Regency Crisis

The Regency Crisis was to interrupt the rhythm of British diplomacy. On 17 October 1788 George III was taken ill, and, although he recovered sufficiently to take a levee on 24 October and Pitt wrote to him about Baltic developments on 25 October and 5 November, the King became delirious while at Windsor on 5 November. On 7 November 1788 it became common knowledge that George III was seriously ill, in fact, as modern scholarship has shown, incapacitated by an attack of porphyria, which to contemporaries appeared to betoken the onset of insanity. This had not been predicted, although age was obviously a factor in any system of hereditary monarchy. George was 50. His father, Frederick Prince of Wales, had died at the age of 44, while of George's six siblings, four died before the age of 50: Edward Duke of York (1739–67), Henry, Duke of Cumberland (1745–90), Frederick (1750–65) and Caroline Matilda, Queen of Denmark (1751–75). Conversely, William, Duke of Gloucester (1743–1805) and Augusta, Duchess of Brunswick (1737–1813) lived to over 60. The 1770s and 1780s were in general a period of long-lived monarchs. Louis XV, who died in 1774, had been born in 1715. Frederick the Great's dates were 1712–86, while those of Maria Theresa were 1717–80, Victor Amadeus III 1726–95, José I of Portugal 1714–77, and his heir Maria I 1734–1816, Augustus III of Saxony-Poland 1696–1763, Catherine the Great 1729–96, and Charles III of Spain 1716–88. By these standards, George III was not old in 1788, while average British male life expectancy at his age was over seventeen years. In addition, George's health recently had not been a serious cause for concern. He had survived an assassination attempt by the deranged Margaret Nicholson in August 1786; with the obvious exception of the case of Gustavus III, who was shot in 1792, eighteenth-century assassins were less successful than their successors during the anarchist movement. Although George III had been seriously ill in 1765, thereafter his health had been fairly good. In the spring of 1788 he had had a bout of ill health, but he had then spent a quiet summer at Cheltenham drinking the waters.

---

[103] George Hammond, commissary in Keith's absence, to Carmarthen, 5 Nov. 1788, PRO FO 7/17 fol. 16.

The serious and surprising breakdown of the king's health in late 1788 provoked a constitutional crisis in Britain.[104] Ill health had none of the certainty and finality of death, but it soon became apparent that while George III was ill it would be necessary to make provisions for a regency, and that this arrangement might have to last until the King's death, as his recovery seemed problematic. George's eldest son, George Prince of Wales, was, however, no friend to his father or his ministers, and thus the question mark that the reversionary interest posed against the policies and personnel of the governments in all the monarchies of the period, was dramatically highlighted in Britain in 1788. It had been a serious problem for the governments of both George I and George II, most obviously in 1717–20 and 1747–51, when their respective heirs had led opposition to them. The abrupt and sweeping differences that a new monarch could make had been demonstrated with the fall of the Tories after the accession of George I, and again when George III himself had succeeded to the throne in 1760. That had been followed by the fall of Pitt (1761) and Newcastle (1762), the end of the Old Corps Whig system, the reintegration of the Tories into national political life and a decisive break with continental interventionism and the alliance with Prussia.

George III had observed after Margaret Nicholson's attempt on his life, 'I have every reason to be satisfied with the impressions it has awakened in this country where perhaps my life is at present of more consequence than I could wish', the last a reference to his heir. It was assumed in late 1788 that when George, Prince of Wales became Regent he would dismiss the ministry and ask Fox to form a new one. It was also believed that this might affect British foreign policy, although commentators were less clear on this point. Two questions were raised. First, would a period of domestic political change, possibly turmoil, lessen the influence of British policy, whatever that might be. Hawkesbury reported on 28 October that the ministry was divided over foreign policy with nothing settled, and that the ministers could not see George III because of his illness.[105] *Felix Farley's Bristol Journal* claimed on 15 November 1788,

---

[104] J. W. Derry, *The Regency Crisis and the Whigs* 1788–9 (Cambridge, 1963); J. Brooke, *King George III* (1972), pp. 322–41; T. C. W. Blanning and C. Haase, 'Kurhannover der Kaiser und die "Regency Crisis"', *Blätter für deutsche Landesgeschichte*, 113 (1977) and, more extensively, 'George III, Hanover and the Regency Crisis', in Black (ed.), *Knights Errant*, pp. 135–50. Hawkesbury's letters to Dorset, which survive among the papers of the latter and were not used by Derry or Ehrman, offer a valuable perspective on the crisis.

[105] George III to Richard Grenville, 29 Aug. 1786, BL Add. 70957; Hawkesbury to Dorset, 28 Oct. 1788, KAO C182; G. Ellis, formerly secretary to Harris, to Malmesbury, no date, Winchester, Malmesbury, 151.

At no period whatever could the sickness under which his Majesty unhappily labours, have happened with greater danger to the general tranquility of Europe, than at the present. The negociations for peace, which are far advanced, and drawing to a favourable conclusion, will now probably be suspended, not indeed by our ministry, but by the foreign powers with whom we are treating. These, dreading a new government in this country, and not knowing whether it may pursue the same line of politics laid down by the present ministry, may hesitate to proceed any farther in the negociations now carrying on, until the recovery of his Majesty shall convince them that they may proceed with safety, or till they receive assurances from a new government that their political views and intentions are the same with those of their predecessors.

The following February, William Lindsay informed Malmesbury from The Hague that 'the stagnation of the English government seems to have caused a general suspension of foreign measures all over this part of Europe'. The next month Keith complained to Pitt that Carmarthen had not communicated with him officially for over four months.[106]

Aside from the general issue of stability, there was also the specific question of the impact of any new government on Britain's alliances with the United Provinces and, to a greater extent, Prussia. This question was highlighted not so much by the experience of the break with Prussia and the move from interventionism after the succession of George III, although a number of rulers and ministers, most obviously Catherine II, had been politically active in that period, as by the widespread belief that the current direction of British policy arose from the views of George III. This was thought to be especially true of the pro-Prussian and anti-Russian emphasis of British policy that was attributed in large part to George III, a *secret du roi* or royal private diplomacy, and Hanoverian influences. Thus, the interpretation of British policy held most strongly in St Petersburg and Copenhagen lent great emphasis on the views of George III and made the Regency Crisis appear of crucial importance in the field of foreign policy. The experience of the *Fürstenbund* suggested that this was an accurate view. As early as the beginning of December 1788, a change of policy was anticipated in St Petersburg, and later that month Vorontsov was sent instructions to approach Fox and Portland and to urge them to ensure that Britain abandon Prussia in favour of her 'true interests', namely, alliance with Russia. These instructions were repeated in March 1789.[107]

The Regency Crisis did not simply entail problems for British foreign policy arising from international doubts about the stability and continuity

---

[106] Lindsay to Malmesbury, 20 Feb. 1789, BL Add. 47568 fol. 259; Keith to Pitt, 20 Mar. 1789, PRO 30/8/149 fol. 37.

[107] Whitworth to Ewart, 12 Dec. 1788, Williamwood vol. 150; Marcum, 'Vorontsov', pp. 148–50, 153.

of that policy. There were also grave problems within the government itself. The important constitutional functions of the monarch in the field of foreign policy ensured that George III's incapacity disrupted and, in part, stopped the execution of policy. *Felix Farley's Bristol Journal* claimed on 22 November 1788:

Among other serious inconveniences arising from the Sovereign's indisposition, is that of a considerable interruption in the foreign correspondence; for, abstracted from the mere signatures of official papers, it is a fact that his Majesty was peculiarly assiduous in carrying on a very extensive communication with all the foreign courts in his own hand, and actually took upon himself the conduct of a great part of that business.

The surviving correspondence suggests that this statement was an exaggeration, but it indicates the importance attached to George III's personal links and initiatives. In addition, the King had played a major role in the formulation and conduct of policy, contributing his opinion, offering valuable advice and, to a certain extent, not so much arbitrating or policing – for that implies an antagonistic relationship – but controlling the situation in which both Carmarthen and Pitt played a major role, each suggesting ideas and drafting dispatches. The problems created by George's incapacity were felt by British envoys. In March 1789 Eden wrote from Madrid to Carmarthen:

Mere general assurances on our part, are insufficient, and the feelings, if not the answers, of foreign administrations, in return to such assurances, must be (justly and reasonably) that whilst we can take no measures, our conduct, cannot, to them, be a subject of either concert or counter-action, and that they wait to see what confidence may be due to us, when we are again restored to an executive system. The last mentioned sentiment has been repeatedly intimated to me by Count Floridablanca.[108]

George III's ill-health left the royal role in policy and politics unfulfilled, and obliged ministers, irrespective of the domestic political pressure to establish a regency, to consider how best to respond. On 6 November Richmond wrote from his seat at Goodwood to suggest to Pitt that if George III's condition deteriorated further,

it might not be improper to acquaint the Prince of Wales of what important concerns are going on with respect to foreign powers, and to ask his concurrence for pursuing them. I am aware of how delicate such a step may be, but it may become necessary, and it may be done without the least appearance of courting him improperly.[109]

It soon became clear that the situation was less under the control of the ministry than Richmond's proposal suggested, and the government was

---

[108] Eden to Carmarthen, 2 Mar. 1789, PRO FO 72/14.
[109] Richmond to Pitt, 6 Nov. 1788, CUL Add. 6958 no. 568.

not helped by the resumption of Parliament. The last session had ended on 11 July 1788, and had George fallen ill immediately afterwards the ministry would have enjoyed more leeway. However, the new session met on 20 November 1788. Indeed, for the Parliament elected in 1784, it was only for 1788 and 1789 that the new session began before Christmas, i.e. in the previous year: the new sessions in 1785, 1786, 1787 and 1790 did not begin until the respective Januarys, in every case between the 21st and 25th of January.

Parliament had to meet in order to deal with the constitutional crisis and inaugurate a regency, but the opening of the session would lead to new pressure on the ministry. In addition, it was far from clear that the ministry would remain united. The focus of unity – the King – was incapacitated, the means to achieve the purpose of government, the furtherance of royal policies in accordance with parliamentary views, suddenly unclear. Pitt's principal ministerial rival, Lord Chancellor Thurlow, who had quarrelled with Pitt over the abolition of the slave trade that summer, maintained an independent line throughout the crisis, although it is not clear what, besides his own interests, he hoped to further. Nevertheless, rumours about Thurlow's intentions circulated widely and helped to make the government's position appear more unstable.[110] The situation was further exacerbated by the unwillingness of the physicians, understandable in light of contemporary medical knowledge, to take any firm and consistent line on George III's prospects. It was unclear whether the King would recover, remain ill, or die, a range of options that left the field open for constitutional speculation. Although the Queen was mentioned, it was clear that, if there was to be a regency, the Prince of Wales would be Regent, and the ministry would therefore change. The extent of his powers was, however, unclear and that would have to be determined by Parliament.

Parliament met on 20 November, only to be adjourned for a fortnight while the politicians awaited developments in the King's health and the opposition sought to decide how best to proceed. When on 3 December the King's five doctors were examined before the Privy Council they disagreed as to whether he was likely to recover, though two days later a new doctor, Francis Willis, under whose attention George was to improve, first saw his new patient.

Meanwhile, the King's incapacity was both an obvious topic of diplomatic speculation and provided something for the diplomats to write about. British envoys were assured of continuity. Carmarthen wrote to Elliot on 5 December 1788,

---

[110] Hawkesbury to Dorset, 4 July 1788, KAO C182; Derry, *Regency Crisis*, pp. 40–3, 57–8.

Although the continuance of the disorder with which His Majesty is unhappily afflicted, renders it impossible to receive his royal commands at present, I flatter myself the system which His Majesty, in concert with the King of Prussia, has so happily established, will not in any degree suffer from this unfortunate occurrence.

Thus Elliot was given instructions as if nothing had changed. He was to try to bring Denmark 'to a close and cordial connection with England, and her Allies', and this was to help 'the settling the tranquillity of the Northern Powers, at the same time that the interests of Great Britain, and her allies, will gain an important accession of weight in the scale of Europe, by the accession of Denmark to their system'.[111] Delay, however, in Anglo-Dutch colonial negotiations, was attributed to the Regency Crisis, while Eden complained about a lack of instructions during the crisis, and argued that it jeopardised what he saw as a good opportunity to improve Anglo-Spanish, and thus harm Franco-Spanish, relations. He wrote to Carmarthen from Madrid on 11 January 1789,

I must regret that circumstances have delayed and prevented my having the means of instructing and improving that line of confidential intercourse which is described in my letters of the 11th and 12th of November and which had tended at least to weaken the connection between this court and that of Versailles.

Eden returned to this theme on 26 January, but it seems likely that Carmarthen, who disliked him and regarded him as a meddler, would have been wary of Eden's proposals anyway. Even when George was clearly recovering, Carmarthen still did not send Eden any specific instructions, and the previous August Eden had complained that he was not being kept informed about British foreign policy.[112]

The weight in Carmarthen's instructions to Elliot of 5 December 1788 was placed on Britain's alliance system, but it was by no means clear that a new government would not try to reconstitute it. Furthermore, the ambiguous nature of the phrase 'settling the tranquillity of the Northern Powers', which could be seen both in a reactive and in an interventionist, anti-Russian light, might take on a very different meaning if the alliance system was reshaped. The French envoys were very concerned about this point. Barthélemy argued that the principal change would be to the degree of government commitment to foreign policy, rather than to the direction of policy itself. He reported that the ministry would have to devote its attention to domestic affairs, that indeed there could be no

---

[111] Carmarthen to Elliot, 5 Dec. 1788, PRO FO 22/10 fols. 472–3.
[112] Carmarthen to William Gomm, Secretary in The Hague, 18 Nov. 1788, Eden to Carmarthen, 11, 26 Jan. 1789, 25 Aug. 1788, Carmarthen to Eden, 13 Feb., Duke of Leeds (Carmarthen's title from 23 March 1789) to Eden, 17 Apr. 1789, PRO FO 37/24, 72/13–14; Eden to Liston, 28 July, 7 Aug. 1788, NLS 5551 fols. 146, 171.

government whilst George III could not sign council resolutions, and that Thurlow was willing to serve the Prince of Wales. Barthélemy argued that because of Hanoverian interests and the influence of George III's favourite son, Frederick, Duke of York, British policy had been led by that of Prussia in recent years. He added that the Prince of Wales did not like Germans, but that he might be led to sustain the Anglo-Prussian alliance, both by its apparent success, and by the influence of his brother Frederick, who was close to the Prince. Luzerne noted criticisms in the opposition press of the anti-Russian consequences of Britain's Prussian alliance, but he shared the view that policy would be pro-Prussian, whether Pitt or Fox directed the ministry, as he argued that they both wanted to sustain 'le système intriguant' introduced by George III, in the hope of being able, if necessary, to divert France by a land war.[113]

Barthélemy of course was speculating, but that was the course forced on diplomats by continuing uncertainty as to the likely nature of developments in Britain. There was particular uncertainty as to whether a new ministry would maintain the Prussian alliance or whether it would seek to improve relations with Austria and/or Russia. In late 1788 the general consensus was that the alliance would continue, because of the influence not only of the Duke of York on his brother, but also that of Harris, ennobled that September as Lord Malmesbury, on Fox. Fox intended to return to the Foreign Office.[114] The Prussian Envoy Extraordinary, Philipp Karl von Alvensleben, was well pleased with what both the Prince of Wales and the Duke of York told him, though he informed Malmesbury that he thought it essential that British envoys at the crucial courts, St Petersburg, Stockholm, Warsaw, Constantinople and Madrid, should be reassured that the Prince of Wales would maintain the existing lines of foreign policy. Subsequently, the French envoy in Berlin was to argue that these links between Alvensleben and the Prince of Wales led the British government to turn against the envoy after the Regency Crisis, with the result that in August 1789 confidential discussions about the Low Countries were entrusted by Frederick William II to a special envoy, General Count Schlieffen. Luzerne was to stress the close links between Alvensleben and the Opposition, Barthélemy those between him and Malmesbury. Refreshed after his break that autumn in Switzerland, Malmesbury himself wrote to Ewart on 2 January 1789 to tell him that whatever happened he would continue at

[113] Barthélemy to Montmorin, 18 Nov., Luzerne to Montmorin, 9, 16 Dec. 1788, AE CP Ang. 567 fols. 139–42, 230–1, 271.
[114] Fox to Portland, 21 Jan. 1789, BL Add. 47561 fol. 96; Anne Willem, Baron Nagel, Dutch Envoy Extraordinary in London, to Van de Spiegel, 2 Dec. 1788, Bod. BB 50 fol. 185.

Berlin, as 'both sides' wanted him to succeed, and that there would be no change in British policy. Malmesbury made the same point in letters to Frederick William II and Hertzberg, as did the Prince of Wales in letters to Frederick William II, William of Orange and Wilhelmina of Orange, and in conversation with the Dutch envoy Nagel.[115] Ewart's contact with Malmesbury extended to providing him with the copy of at least one of his dispatches, and this copy was presumably passed on to Fox, as it survives in the latter's papers.[116] The accompanying letter referred to another dispatch that Ewart had sent Malmesbury. Ewart also enclosed a letter from Frederick William II to Malmesbury showing 'how much His Majesty continues to rely upon your assistance for enforcing the system so happily established', and made it clear that the Regency Crisis was having a serious effect on foreign policy,

those inconceivable delays which have so long interrupted the executive power … Count Simon Woronzow [Vorontsov]… has taken upon him to commit the names of both the Duke of Portland and Mr. Fox in a very unwarrantable manner, by writing in his letters to Petersburg, Copenhagen etc. that he was upon such a footing with them as to enable him to assure that they would immediately abandon Prussia and pay court to Russia. A letter of the Duke of Portland's to Lord Titchfield [his son], who communicated it to Elliot here, has already given a *dementi* to this impertinent assertion, but as I know that the Empress still relies much upon it and Woronzow still continues to write in the same style, I think it of the utmost consequence that he should be made to know how much the contrary is the fact, since nothing effectual can be expected at Petersburg so long as the hopes are entertained of separating us from Prussia.[117]

Alvensleben, Malmesbury and Ewart clearly cooperated closely and provided channels of communication between London and Berlin. Ewart, for example, wrote to Elliot on 24 February that 'Alvensleben gives every reason to expect that your instructions will be sent hither, should the other party come in, without delay, and drawn up in the manner we could wish.'[118] Ewart was not the only diplomat in touch with Malmesbury. William Lindsay, a 'particular friend' of Malmesbury,[119]

[115] Count Brühl, Saxon envoy in London, to Stutterheim, 12 Dec. 1788, Bod. BB. 50 fols. 168–9; Alvensleben to Malmesbury, undated, Malmesbury to Ewart, 12 Nov. 1788, 2 Jan. 1789, Winchester, Malmesbury, vols. 173, 157, 148; Esterno to Montmorin, 25 Aug. 1789, Luzerne to Montmorin, 9 July 1790, 9 Sept. 1791, AE CP Prusse 210 fols. 193–4, Ang. 574 fol. 30, 578 fol. 237; Francis Jackson, Secretary of Legation at Berlin, to Burges, 25 Feb. 1790, Bod. BB. 36 fol. 55; Prince of Wales to Frederick William II, no date, reply, 26 Feb. 1789, to Wilhelmina of Orange and to William of Orange, both 10 Feb., and letters from the two latter, 30 Jan. 1789, Aspinall, *Correspondence of George, Prince of Wales* I (1963), pp. 492, 494, 486–7, 456–7.
[116] Ewart to Carmarthen, 11 Feb. 1789, BL Add. 47568 fols. 257–8.
[117] Ewart to Malmesbury, 11 Feb. 1789, BL Add. 47568 fols. 255–6.
[118] Ewart to Elliot, 24 Feb. 1789, NLS 13022 fol. 196.
[119] Malmesbury to Ewart, 29 Aug. 1789, Williamwood vol. 147.

reported from The Hague that the Dutch were convinced that a change in the British ministry would not lead to any change in foreign policy. George Ellis, a former secretary to Malmesbury, reported to him from Paris that, after initial fears to the contrary, the French had come to the same conclusions.[120]

There was, however, uncertainty and room for sowing uncertainty. On 16 December 1788 Elliot's secretary Johnstone was told by Bernstorff that Frederick William II had recently shown 'a great deference' for Catherine II, 'This change is attributed partly to a belief that the Prince of Wales will adopt a different system from that of his royal father.' Catherine herself greeted the news of the crisis by having secret instructions sent to Vorontsov ordering him to make contact with Fox, who was regarded as pro-Russian, and Portland, and to inform them of her desire for a *rapprochement*. Charles Whitworth reported from St Petersburg the following March,

Much of their attention is ... taken up with what is passing in England, and they have been rather sanguine in their expectations that a change of ministers might produce a change of measures in their favour, and render the alliance with Prussia (the great effects of which is demonstrated by nothing more than by their dislike of it) of no avail.[121]

Ministers meanwhile were involved in parliamentary debates over the nature of the planned regency, especially over the powers of the Regent. The Commons' debates on 10 and 16 December were particularly bitter. The standard account, a first-rate study by John Derry, sees the ministry as triumphant, but that was not how it struck all its supporters. James, 2nd Earl of Fife, wrote to his Scottish factor William Rose on the 16th, 'Can anything describe the violence of the present times ... Mr. Pitt had only 64 of a majority. The House very full.' Though Hawkesbury thought it 'fully sufficient',[122] a majority of 64 in a house of 472 was indeed not very good, because in the absence of firm party groupings, the votes of many MPs were unpredictable, as indeed was indicated by the development of the so-called 'Armed Neutrality' group, led by the Duke of Northumberland. This group of about twenty peers and thirty MPs wanted Pitt to continue in office, but they opposed his policy of restrictions on the power of the Prince as Regent. It reflected in an organised fashion what had already been apparent in early 1784, namely

---

[120] Lindsay to Malmesbury, 20 Feb. 1789, BL Add. 47568 fol. 259; Ellis to Malmesbury, 25 Dec. 1788, Winchester, Malmesbury, 151.

[121] Johnstone to Fraser, 16 Dec. 1788, Whitworth to Carmarthen, 6 Mar. 1789, PRO FO 22/10 fol. 486, 65/17 fols. 65–6; Marcum, 'Vorontsov and Pitt', 51.

[122] Derry, *Regency Crisis*, p. 103; A. and H. Tayler (eds.), *Lord Fife and his Factor* (1925), pp. 194–5; Hawkesbury to Dorset, 19 Dec. 1788, KAO C182.

that at moments of constitutional tension there was a powerful tendency in favour of conciliation, compromise and coalition, and one that could look to leadership and membership among the independents. During the great crisis that began in late 1792, under the double threat of French success and domestic radicalism, this tendency was to benefit the government; and indeed it could be argued that any such movement would do so if it encouraged those who were unhappy with developments to seek to enlarge the ministry, rather than to overturn it by parliamentary defeat.

Yet, in the winter of 1788–9, the situation was worrying for Pitt, for his position could appear to be one of delaying the establishment of a regency, and thus of sustaining instability, while the focus of loyalty and order was now the heir to the throne, rather than the sick monarch. The longer the crisis lasted, the more obviously independents would adapt to the new situation, while ministerial cohesion would collapse as some ministers and place-holders sought favour in the emerging political order.

This situation had obvious consequences for one particular group of place-holders, British diplomats. Even if policy was not changed it was likely that many diplomats would be replaced, especially those in prominent embassies, and those, most obviously Eden, who had taken or been seen as having taken a clear political line. Dorset was anxious about the Paris embassy, and indeed Fox was uncertain about whether to keep him. The Duke was given hints that the Prince of Wales might retain his services. Hawkesbury, however, warned him that there was talk of replacing him by Malmesbury (with Thomas Grenville, who had been appointed to Paris by Fox in 1782, getting The Hague), and later, first, that the post had been offered to Mountstuart, and, subsequently, that it was to be given to the Earl of Jersey. In November 1788 Dorset wrote to Wraxall:

I see nothing but confusion if he [Pitt] is dismissed, a measure the nation will never long submit to. In regard to myself I am perfectly indifferent. If there is a general sweep I should like to go, but the moment I am recalled this country will look upon the views of England as *hostile*. This I have been *particularly* assured of at Versailles.

The following month, Dorset added, 'it is impossible to say how much this court wish to keep me, *that* the future ministers are to look to', and on 29 January the Duke wrote:

I suppose nous autres *place-men* shall soon know our fate. In regard to myself I have no hopes of being able to remain as they will want everything they can lay hold of for their friends ... whoever succeeds me will have a bad [berth?] of it for some time. Lord Malmesbury cannot be more disliked in England for his conduct than he is here.

On 5 February Dorset warned that whoever succeeded him, he would have a poor reception and 'if Lord Malmesbury should be appointed, the court will look upon it as little short of a declaration of war'. Stafford was also warned by Dorset about the danger of appointing Malmesbury. The cricket-loving and womanising Duke was also solicitous about the health of his monarch, sending a cure that reflects the extent to which in health, as in so much else, the notion of a division between a modernising, enlightened elite, and a marginal populace sunk in superstition, was, and is, misleading,

> I have always had little or no hopes of the King, I have sent however by this day's courier a remede which they tell me est sure. It is tout simplement the blood of a jack-ass which after passing a clear napkin through it two or three times is given afterwards to the patient to drink. I really hope Willis will try it.[123]

Dorset captured the uncertainty of the diplomatic situation, for it was difficult to believe that, even if the stated objectives of foreign policy remained the same, British policy would not be affected, in substance and detail, by the fact that it would be entrusted to new hands.

In addition, any stress on continuity was qualified by the extent to which policy was reactive, both necessarily and because the Pitt government sought defensive goals. In the winter of 1788–9 a series of new and developing questions arose. It was unclear how the conflicts in the Balkans and Baltic would develop, now that none of the combatants had achieved their objectives of a clear victory.[124] The extent to which internal problems in the Habsburg dominions, especially the Austrian Netherlands and Hungary, would develop, inhibit the policies of Joseph II and be amenable to external manipulation, was unclear, as were the consequences of growing reformism and anti-Russian pressure within Poland. The list could readily be extended. It was uncertain how far the Estates General would lead to a stronger France, to a reforming monarchy able to overcome opposing interests by using the revived assembly. It was not clear whether the accession of Charles IV, who became King of Spain on 13 December 1788, would lead to any changes in Spanish policy. If these situations and developments were uncertain, so also were the likely responses of other powers, including Prussia.

---

[123] Fox to Portland, [20 Jan 1789], BL Add. 47561 fol. 93; Derry, *Regency Crisis*, pp. 150–1; Hawkesbury to Dorset, 13 Jan., 3, 6, 20 Feb. 1789, KAO C182; Dorset to Wraxall, 27 Nov., 11 Dec. 1788, 29 Jan., 5 Feb. 1789, Beinecke, Osborn Files, Dorset; Dorset to Stafford, 11 Dec. 1788, 22 Jan. 1789, PRO 30/29/1/15 nos. 83–4; Dorset to Hawkesbury, 8 Jan. 1789, BL Add. 38471 fol. 224.
[124] Johnstone to Fraser, 20 Dec. 1788, PRO FO 22/10 fol. 491.

Thus, even if a new British government sustained the Anglo-Prussian alliance, it was far from clear what this would mean in practice, whether, in particular, Britain would support Prussian initiatives, especially in the increasingly volatile affairs of northern and eastern Europe.

The nature of Anglo-Prussian relations was unexpectedly thrown into prominence in early 1789 because of a surprising initiative by Joseph II. On 20 January 1789 Joseph II outlined his views on the position of Hanover in the Regency Crisis. He made it clear that as Emperor he would be responsible for the administration and regency of the Electorate, and that no Hanoverian envoy would be recognised at the Imperial Diet unless authorised by the Emperor. The following day Joseph clarified his position in instructions to Reviczky. He would help the Prince of Wales, but any regency for Hanover would require imperial approval. Joseph followed this up by seeking to suspend Hanoverian representation at the Diet.

The Prince of Wales responded firmly, assuming the regency of the Electorate, a step he had already discussed on 21 December, seeking the support of allies within the *Fürstenbund*, especially Frederick William II, and having Reviczky informed by Johann Friedrich Carl von Alvensleben, the head of the Hanoverian Chancery in London, that Joseph's interference would not be tolerated.[125] On 15 February 1789 Reviczky told Luzerne that he had informed Alvensleben that the consent of the Aulic Council and the Diet would be required for George, Prince of Wales, to become Regent of Hanover. Reviczky was surprised to discover from Alvensleben that he had already worked with George for a fortnight (in fact George had written to him on 3 February), that all orders for the Electorate were signed by George, that he was recognised as Regent and that instructions to the Hanoverian envoy at the Diet had been sent by George. Alvensleben was unable to explain the authority by which George had assumed this position. Meanwhile, the Emperor had decided to take a more cautious stance, and fresh instructions, sent to Reviczky on 20 February, presented the affair as a misunderstanding.[126]

Joseph's legalism is interesting given his eagerness to dispense with established forms in other contexts. It reflected in this case his opportunism, or rather the opportunism that understandably characterised international relations. George, Prince of Wales' position over

---

125   Blanning and Haase, 'George III', pp. 142–3; H. Furber (ed.), *The Correspondence of Edmund Burke*, IV (Cambridge, 1965), p. 431; Prince of Wales to Frederick William II, no date, and to Queen Charlotte, 6 Feb. 1789, Aspinall, *Prince of Wales*, I, 492, 486.
126   Luzerne to Montmorin, 16 Feb. 1789, AE CP Ang. 568 fols. 201–2; George, Prince of Wales to Alvensleben, 3 Feb. 1789, Blanning and Haase, 'Kurhannover', 443; Blanning and Haase, 'George III', p. 144; Lord John Russell (ed.), *Memorials and Correspondence of Charles James Fox*, II (1853), pp. 336–7.

Hanover reflected the same opportunism, or rather, in his case, pragmatism. Far from there being clear criteria on which the affairs of the Empire, still less those of Europe, were based, the situation was uncertain on numerous points, a prey to disputes in which opportunism and pragmatism played central roles. This indeed was the background against which such apparently new developments as the partitions of Poland and the diplomacy of the French Revolution were in part judged. Joseph II's conduct in early 1789 was foolish. His position in the Empire was too weak to permit him to bully Hanover: much had changed since the early 1780s. Joseph would have been better advised to try to woo the Prince of Wales, to offer help over Hanover and warnings about the direction of Prussian power. His failure to do so compromised any real chance of a major change in direction in British foreign policy.

The slaughtered jackass had been unnecessary. From early February 1789 George III began to improve, time enough to prevent the creation of a Regency, the formation of a Whig ministry and the fulfilment of the negotiations between Fox and the Armed Neutrality. On 19 February Thurlow informed the Lords that the King was in a state of convalescence, a situation already announced in the medical bulletin of the 17th. On 23 February the King resumed his correspondence with Pitt.

The Regency Crisis left George III angry with Joseph II and more convinced of the value of the Prussian alliance. When Reviczky presented Joseph's compliments on his recovery, the King was unimpressed, 'the Emperor's conduct in my late unfortunate indisposition has been contrary to the very Law of Empire and he does not therefore deserve more than bald civility'. Prussian diplomatic support had helped to strengthen the Prince of Wales' resolve to resist Joseph II's claims. The British and Hanoverian envoys in Berlin, Ewart and Ernst von Lenthe, who anyway lodged in the same house, held a joint supper and ball with illuminations to celebrate the convalescence of George III, the inscriptions displayed including 'George the sincere friend of Frederick William' and George 'the sure help of German liberty'. There was talk of George visiting Hanover for the first time in his life and of one of his daughters marrying the Prince Royal of Prussia. The alliance seemed in very strong shape.[127]

The crisis had not developed to a serious point, but it had been shown again that the interests of the rulers of Britain–Hanover on the Continent were apparently best served and defended by participation in a collective

[127] George III to ?, 5 Apr. 1789, *McDowell and Stern Catalogue* no. 27, p. 5; Reviczky to Leeds, 4 Apr., reply, 5 Apr. 1789, PRO FO 7/17 fols. 126, 128; Esterno to Montmorin, 9 May 1789, AE CP Prusse 210 fols. 114–15; Blanning and Haase, 'Kurhannover', 449 fn. 56.

security system involving co-operation with a major continental power. That was a central theme in British foreign policy during this period, but it was complicated by the interests of possible and actual allies. The problems presented by alliance commitments did not face Britain alone. It had faced Denmark in her relations with Russia, and was an issue for the Spanish government. Carmarthen may well have recognised common themes in Eden's report of 9 February 1789 on Floridablanca's views

continues to disavow all ideas of entering into a connection with the two Imperial courts, though he does not deny, that France has recommended and perhaps attempted such a measure. His reasons are, that alliances in general are inexpedient for great sovereigns and also attended with continual trouble and expense; and risks which are seldom compensated by the accession of apparent force and support – He thinks this position particularly true as to His Catholic Majesty, who having no combination to apprehend, nor any hostile ambitious projects to pursue, is sufficiently secured by the strength of his own dominions.[128]

In the spring of 1789 British policy in Europe and India faced not totally unrelated problems, for Cornwallis feared that pressure from the Marathas for a defensive alliance would lead his new allies deliberately to provoke an attack from Tipu of Mysore in order to obtain British assistance for the partition of Mysore. And yet, while resisting the pressure, Cornwallis was aware that he needed Mahratta support in the event of any war with Mysore.[129]

For the British government, the European situation was more pressing. Prussia was considering moves to ensure major changes in eastern Europe. The British response could appear more ambitious than the government intended. Whitworth, who distrusted the Russian government,[130] responded to the claim of Count Osterman, the Russian Vice-Chancellor, that 'the influence of the Court of London, in every quarter, [was] operating in a manner so contrary to her interest', by stating that 'it was not the practice of England to be an ally à demi'.[131] It was of course the task of envoys to persuade foreign powers that the alliance was firm, at the same time as the British ministry sought to define it in accordance with its views, but in 1789–90 the British government failed to keep sufficient control over its envoys, while certain envoys developed a disproportionate commitment to an ambitious conception of the Anglo-Prussian alliance. Thus, at the same time as there was a struggle for primacy within the alliance, there were also different pressures within British diplomacy. It was not a new situation for envoys to be advancing

128 Eden to Carmarthen, 9 Feb. 1789, PRO FO 72/14.
129 Wickwire, *Cornwallis*, pp. 128–9.
130 Whitworth to Carmarthen, 26 Feb. 1789, PRO FO 65/17 fols. 40–1.
131 Whitworth to Carmarthen, 20 Mar. 1789, PRO FO 65/17.

their own views and following their own heads. Harris had done so in the United Provinces and Eden in Paris. Elliot had conspicuously interpreted British foreign policy in his own fashion in late 1788, and Ainslie was alleged by some to have done so in 1787. And yet, Paris and The Hague were embassies from which envoys could be recalled for consultation, to which Grenville could be sent to supplement and check on diplomats, and with which correspondence could be regular and frequent. This was less true of Berlin and Stockholm, let alone Warsaw, St Petersburg and Constantinople. Distance brought dissipation of diplomatic control and a slackening in the intensity of diplomatic contact. Many other factors were involved, but the difference between the resolution of the crisis in the Austrian Netherlands in 1790 and that in eastern Europe reflected, to at least a small degree, the greater ability of the British government to comprehend and influence the diplomatic aspect of the former. The Regency Crisis, and the uncertainty over control of policy that stemmed from the *Fürstenbund* and had possibly been continued by a lack of clarity over the respective influence of Carmarthen and other members of the government, helped to produce a measure of confusion in British foreign policy, but the independent attitude of diplomats such as Elliot, Ewart and Hailes was also important. Daniel Hailes, from November 1788 Envoy Extraordinary in Warsaw, indeed stressed the problems facing envoys when he wrote to Ewart in May 1789, 'Our courts tell us sometimes the truth, but seldom or never the whole truth, and it is that that misguides their ministers and makes them after blamed for errors that they would, in fact, have been inexcusable in not committing.'[132]

Crisis in the Austrian Netherlands

In the summer of 1789 a new division was to develop in British views of the Continent. The outbreak of civil violence in Paris made the French crisis a matter of great attention for the British press and public at the same time as the ministry continued to be more concerned about problems further east. Indeed, British diplomatic activity in western Europe had already, prior to the storming of the Bastille, become markedly subdued. Eden had sought and been granted permission to escort his ill wife from Madrid to the French frontier. He was subsequently allowed to return to England because of her poor health. Having left Madrid on 2 June 1789, Eden never returned, although his recredentials were not sent until July 1790. Eden was promoted to the Irish peerage as Lord Auckland in November 1789, but did not replace Leeds, as had been rumoured. Charles Fraser was appointed Secretary of

---

[132] Hailes to Ewart, 31 May 1789, Matlock CRO 239 M/O 759.

Embassy and Minister Plenipotentiary to Spain in July 1789, but his instructions were not drawn up until the following February and he did not reach Madrid until May 1790. In the meantime the Consul, Anthony Merry, took charge of British affairs there. John Trevor was given leave of absence from Turin on grounds of health so that he could pass the summer in Switzerland.[133] The agenda of Anglo-French diplomatic exchanges was limited, restricted by mutual suspicion and a lack of common interest in eastern Europe. The French were not interested in the idea of co-operating with the British in seeking to mediate a settlement in the Balkans, because they feared it would hinder their attempts to improve relations with Austria and Russia.[134]

These powers themselves were in serious difficulties, and in the winter of 1788–9 both were willing to consider peace with the Turks on the basis of *uti possidetis*: current possession, in other words retaining their gains. Austria and Russia had found that it was easier to dominate international relations in peacetime than in war, for conflict brought defeats, or at least difficulties, and revealed the domestic limitations of strength. The last appeared in 1789 to offer the prospect of new international options. If Poland is treated as hitherto part of the informal Russian system, then it can be argued that both Catherine II and Joseph II found their authority under challenge in those areas of their dominions where it was anyway most precarious, in short that a war designed to enhance power was instead leading it to recede.

This was to place a major strain on the Anglo-Prussian alliance. When initially conceived, this had appeared most challenged by the prospect of French action in the United Provinces. Elsewhere in Europe it was possible to advance the reactive strategy of a return to the status quo prior to the Balkan war, or an acceptance of changes if made with the consent of Prussia and Britain. This goal, ambitious in itself, but, fortunately for Britain, not as yet too specific in its implications, was made more problematic first by the outbreak of war in the Baltic and secondly by the Prussian determination to exploit the difficulties facing Austria[135] and Russia, a determination that offers evidence of the ambitious nature of *ancien régime* diplomacy.

Far from deterring Joseph from adopting an aggressive position over Hanover during the Regency Crisis, war in the Balkans also did not stop him from taking provocative steps in the Austrian Netherlands. The refusal of the Estates of Brabant to accept Joseph's peremptory demands

---

[133] Leeds to Eden, 24 July 1789, PRO FO 72/15 fol. 37; *The Diary*, 8 July 1789; Leeds to Trevor, 1789, PRO FO 67/6.
[134] Montmorin to Noailles, 5 June 1789, AE CP Aut. 357 fols. 78–9.
[135] Hammond to Leeds, 17 June 1789, PRO FO 7/17 fol. 191.

for a new constitutional system as well as a permanent subsidy, led Joseph to annul all provincial privileges and declare that he would rule without the Estates, the firm policy that his brother-in-law, Louis XVI, did not adopt, but one that was not to be successful.

Those opposed to Joseph II appealed for foreign support. Henri Van der Noot, a Brussels lawyer who had played a major role in opposition to Joseph and gone into exile in London, appealed for aid first to the Dutch Pensionary Laurens Van de Spiegel, and then to the British government. Pitt refused to see him and Van der Noot moved to Breda in the United Provinces, from where he opened discussions with the Prussians.[136] The fate of the Austrian Netherlands was a very sensitive subject for the British government. The possibility of French intervention in the Dutch crisis of 1787 had raised anew the question of whether the Austrian Habsburgs, as allies of France, were, for Britain at least, the best rulers, and concern was heightened in 1788 by false reports that Joseph II had mortgaged or ceded part or all of the Austrian Netherlands to France.[137] If Austrian intentions were worrying, the prospect of a successful revolution in the Austrian Netherlands aroused even more concern. Such a revolution might be suppressed by Joseph, with a consequent unwelcome increase in Austrian power. It might also be exploited by France, either to help the rebels or to assist Joseph. An extension of French power was especially unwelcome, not least because of its consequences for the United Provinces. The revolution in France was blamed for the increased tension in the Austrian Netherlands. In August 1789 the Imperial Vice-Chancellor, Prince Franz von Colloredo-Mansfeld, told Noailles that the spirit of disobedience there was being fanned from France. Noailles replied with reason that disturbances had broken out earlier in the Austrian Netherlands,[138] but there was, nevertheless, the danger that they would be exploited either by the current French government or by the unknown quantity of a new one.

These problems came to play an increasingly prominent role in British governmental thinking in late 1789, indeed, in so far as the ministry was concerned with western Europe, it was largely with the Austrian Netherlands, not France. The issue was important, not simply because of the fate of the Low Countries, but also because it came to play a major role in Anglo-Prussian relations, providing an indication of the extent of Britain's willingness to support major changes in Europe. It thus played

[136] M. J. Post, *De Dreibond van 1788 en de Brabantse Revolutie* (Bergen op Zoom, 1961).
[137] Torrington to Keith, 18 Feb., William Augustus Miles, would-be and sometime British agent, to Keith, 18 Mar., Pitt to Grenville, 22 Sept. 1788, BL Add. 35540 fols. 67, 152, 58906 fol. 52; Barthélemy to Montmorin, 30 Sept. 1788, AE CP Ang. 566 fol. 318.   [138] Noailles to Montmorin, 12 Aug. 1789, AE CP Aut. 357 fol. 283.

a role similar to that of Anglo-Wittelsbach negotiations in 1729–30, for, as then, any acceptance of the sponsoring of the anti-Austrian interests of a minor power by Britain's principal ally (in 1729–30 France, now Prussia), would compromise Anglo-Austrian relations in the long as well as the short term and commit Britain simultaneously to her ally and to interventionism.[139]

In the summer of 1789 pressure from Britain's allies to take a role in the Austrian Netherlands steadily mounted. When Alleyne Fitzherbert, newly appointed as Envoy Extraordinary, reached The Hague in early July he was told by Van de Spiegel about a discussion he had held about independence for the Austrian Netherlands. Fitzherbert was unsympathetic, writing of 'a project, which to my apprehension appears wild and chimerical in the extreme', but he reported that the Prussian government was responsive. Fitzherbert resisted pressure from Van de Spiegel that he see representatives from the rebels in the Austrian Netherlands, as he feared that it would be encouraging the cause of revolution.[140] The British ministry soon had to define its policy in response to Prussian pressure for joint moves to exploit the situation. An anonymous British government memorandum of late August argued that

the end to which our measures ought to be directed with a view to the present troubles in the Netherlands seems to be to provide, that the Emperor should not acquire a degree of power in those provinces which might be dangerous to the present system of the Allies, nor France have an opportunity of forming a connection with them in the case, of their independency being established; and also to avail ourselves of events for procuring an accession of strength to our alliance.[141]

The last point was important, but ambiguous. The Prussian government was planning for war with Austria the following year, and thus the somewhat theoretical note struck by the British government clashed with the immediacy of opportunity sought by the Prussian counterparts. Frederick William II, like the Dutch, was interested in Van der Noot's proposal for a Belgian Republic under the protection of the Triple Alliance, but the British response was less warm. Aware, however, of the importance of the issue for the Anglo-Prussian alliance, Leeds was hopeful that he had talked round a Prussian special envoy, General Martin von Schlieffen, the anglophile governor of the strategic Prussian Rhineland base of Wesel,

[139] J. Black, 'Britain and the Wittelsbachs in the Early Eighteenth Century', *Mitteilungen des Österreichischen Staatsarchivs*, 40 (1987), 92–127.
[140] Fitzherbert to Leeds, 10 July, 14 Aug. 1789, PRO FO 37/26 fols. 22, 68.
[141] 'On the Proposal Respecting the Netherlands and Galicia', 27 Aug. 1789, BL Add. 28068 fol. 331.

in the conferences I had with M. de [General] Schlieffen, he seemed perfectly sensible of the difficultys [sic] which must attend any plan to be adopted, at present by the allied powers in respect to the supposed probable alteration in the government of the Austrian Netherlands.[142]

The reactive nature of British policy was clear. A cautious response to developments in the Austrian Netherlands was recommended,[143] coupled with the advice that it was sensible to see if the apparently imminent death of Joseph II led to changes in the situation. Malmesbury, now out of favour and office as a result of his conduct during the Regency Crisis, wrote to Ewart about 'the backward sort of system which has prevailed here', though he added, 'I consider it to proceed much more from a great inattention to business than from principle.'[144] And yet, the government was determined to prevent French intervention. The collapse of royal authority in France had been surprising, and it was worrying because of the support for Dutch Patriots shown by newly influential French politicians. It was also felt that the risings in Paris and the Austrian Netherlands were somehow linked. Those concerns were registered by British diplomats, especially Alleyne Fitzherbert, for the Anglo-Dutch relationship proved, as ever, responsive to developments further south. On 17 July Fitzherbert reported that the new French government, the short-lived royalist ministry that replaced that of Necker, had 'occasioned a very great and serious alarm among the leading people here, as two of the new ministers, the Baron de Breteuil, and the Duc de la Vauguyon, are known to entertain the most hostile dispositions against the constitution of this Republic'. Later in the month, he noted that exiled Patriots in Paris were seeking the support of the Estates General. Fitzherbert urged the Dutch government to keep an eye on the populace in disaffected towns, because he feared the impact of 'such an extraordinary fermentation' in France and the Austrian Netherlands, what he termed 'this contagion'.[145]

Fitzherbert's theme of the ready transferability and influence of radical sentiments, of the porousness of international frontiers and the dangers of revolutionary examples, was one that was to be repeated endlessly over the next few years. Other British diplomats noted that the same fears were held elsewhere. Anthony Merry, for example, reported that

---

[142] Leeds to Fitzherbert, 15 Sept. 1789, PRO FO 37/26 fol. 114; Esterno to Montmorin, 18, 25 Aug. 1789, AE CP Prusse 210 fols. 185–8, 192; Schlieffen to Lansdowne, 2 May 1789, Bowood 65; F. Salomon, *William Pitt Der Jüngere*, I (Leipzig, 1906), pp. 451, 453, 461. Through military service together, Schlieffen knew many prominent Britons.
[143] Leeds to Fitzherbert, 15 Sept. 1789, PRO FO 37/26 fol. 114.
[144] Malmesbury to Ewart, 29 Aug. 1789, Williamwood vol. 147.
[145] Fitzherbert to Leeds, 17, 31 July 1789, PRO FO 37/26 fols. 29, 47–8; Esterno to Montmorin, 18 Aug. 1789, AE CP Prusse 210 fol. 186.

Floridablanca was concerned about signs of Spanish support for developments in France.[146] These fears were to influence political responses. A strong sense of the interdependence of developments in different territories was obvious from the outset, and was demonstrated more clearly by the response to events in the Low Countries than to those in France. Discussion about foreign intervention was a natural product of a sense of interdependence. As soon as royal authority was challenged violently, there was talk of intervention in France. Merry reported a conversation with Floridablanca in which the minister 'after observing, that the case was highly interesting to all the sovereigns of Europe, hinted at some assistance which Spain might give to quell the disturbances'.[147]

It was, however, to be in the Low Countries that foreign powers first thought of intervening. The situation there was more volatile than in France where it proved possible to devise a new constitutional settlement without civil war, an obvious contrast to the United Provinces in 1787 and to the Austrian Netherlands. Disturbances soon spread from the Austrian Netherlands to the Prince-Bishopric of Liège. After rioting there from mid-August on, the Bishop fled at the end of the month and sought the support of the relevant imperial authorities in order to effect his return.[148] Of the three Directors of the Circle of Westphalia, the region of the Empire within which Liège was located, the King of Prussia, the Elector Palatine and the Archbishop-Elector of Cologne, only the first controlled a powerful military force. Thus, at the very time that the rebels in the Austrian Netherlands were seeking the support of 10,000 Prussian troops, there was also a prospect of Prussian intervention in Liège, although the Estates of the principality urged Frederick William not to act. Prussian intervention, were it to occur, would have different objectives: to restore order and support the status quo in Liège, to abet revolution and the creation of a new order in the Austrian Netherlands. That Frederick William and his ministers were willing to consider both indicated the flexibility of their thinking and the dominance of opportunistic, pragmatic calculations over ideological considerations. The opportunism that was to be noted over Prussian conduct towards Poland was already apparent in the Low Countries in 1789.

Faced by a developing crisis, the Dutch government decided to retain the Ansbach, Brunswick and Mecklenburg forces that they had hired. The Dutch army had been gravely weakened during the political disputes of the mid-1780s, and it had seemed necessary to hire German forces to

[146] Merry to Leeds, 10 Aug., Walpole to Leeds, 1 Aug., 19 Sept. 1789, PRO FO 72/15 fol. 81, 63/12; Noailles to Montmorin, 12 Aug. 1789, AE CP Aut. 357 fol. 283.
[147] Merry to Leeds, 27 July 1789, PRO FO 72/15 fol. 39.
[148] P. Harsin, La Révolution liègoise (Brussels, 1954).

protect the new government while it was reconstituted. This precaution was applauded by the British government, Leeds writing to Fitzherbert on 15 September 1789, 'you cannot too much encourage the very necessary precaution of having a competent body of foreign troops maintained by the Republic, to be in readiness in case of any emergency arising either from foreign or domestic enemies'.[149] The potency of the French example, 'the contagious spirit of innovation and discontent', appeared to be responsible for disturbances elsewhere, in, for example, the Habsburg territory of Anterior Austria, essentially the Breisgau, and the Electorates of Mainz and Trier, which, like Liège, were part of the Empire and therefore with 'forms of government... under the express guaranty and protection of the whole Germanic body'. Problems were also reported from the Erblande, the Habsburg hereditary lands in east-central Europe, for example from Styria.[150]

The maintenance of a pro-British government in the United Provinces was as important in 1789, as it had been in 1787 and was to be in 1792–3, and the first response of the British ministry to the developing crisis in France and the Austrian Netherlands was to concentrate on the security of the United Provinces. Indeed the government took a step to that end in September 1789. One of Schlieffen's objectives was to persuade the British government to give the British envoy at The Hague the power to summon the British-subsidised Hessian troops in case of any emergency affecting the United Provinces, without having to wait for orders from London which 'might be fatally delayed by the circumstances of wind and weather'. This proposal was accepted.[151]

Meanwhile the crisis in the Low Countries was becoming more serious. Brabant *émigrés* based at Breda in the United Provinces were organising revolutionary activity in Brabant, while the Bishop and the Estates of Liège both rejected the Prussian offer of mediation, leading the Prussians to prepare to enforce the decree of the Imperial court at Wetzlar and to restore the ancient constitution. The Dutch government made it clear that they would not permit the Austrians to infringe their territory in order to deal with the Brabant exiles, and reinforced frontier positions at Bois-le-Duc and Breda. The different anti-Austrian parties in the Austrian Netherlands, the Vandernootists and the more radical Vonckists, agreed to issue a declaration of independence on 24 October, the feast-day of the Archangel Raphael. This declared that Joseph II had lost his sovereign powers because he had infringed the liberties and

---

[149] Fitzherbert to Leeds, 18 Sept., 2 Oct., Leeds to Fitzherbert, 15 Sept. 1789, PRO FO 37/26 fols. 116, 152, 115.
[150] Hammond to Leeds, 2, 9, 19 Sept. 1789, PRO FO 7/17 fols. 267–8, 275, 283.
[151] Leeds to Fitzherbert, 15 Sept. 1789, BL Eg. 3500 fol. 79.

privileges of his subjects, who had the right to declare themselves sovereign. That day the revolutionary army marched from Breda in order to liberate the Austrian Netherlands. The 'army', supported by local villagers, defeated an Austrian force in a confused engagement in the village of Turnhout on 27 October. A lack of local support led to the abandonment of a march on Brussels, but in November an advance into Flanders led to the capture of Ghent and victories over Austrian forces.

Defeat and confusion led the Austrians to offer terms in December, but the promise to reinstate the privileges of Brabant came too late, rather like the conciliatory terms offered to the rebellious Americans by the British in 1778. On 11 and 12 December 1789 a popular revolt in Brussels drove the Austrians from the city, paving stones dropped from rooftops proving effective, as they had done at Turnhout. As in Genoa in 1746, a successful urban popular rising revealed the potential of a people's war. Regular forces seemed helpless, Robert Arbuthnot suggesting that rulers should 'all disband their regular troops, as we now find they are no match for a mob'. Joseph's authority in the Austrian Netherlands collapsed.[152]

The speed of the Austrian collapse took the Triple Alliance by surprise,[153] and underlined the unpredictability of international developments. In October 1789 Leeds had urged a cautious response towards approaches from the rebels on the grounds that the rebellion might collapse swiftly. He wrote to Fitzherbert on the same day as Turnhout:

Should the surrender of Belgrade, and other successes of the Emperor's arms against the Turks hasten the conclusion of peace between those powers, the military force of Austria might perhaps be employed to the westward, and the Flemish provinces of that power at least receive a considerable impression from such an army which it seems little likely the discontented part of them could resist.

How far France might become an object either of attention towards his sister [Marie Antoinette], or ambition for himself in the mind of the Emperor it is impossible to foresee, but each alternative being possible at least; both should be attended to.[154]

Leeds was wrong about the immediate scenario, but correct to discern primarily the volatility of developments, and secondly the reserves of power that Austria still possessed. In one light, Leeds' policy in the crisis over the Austrian Netherlands can be seen as a continuation of the austrophile attitude that he had shown as Foreign Secretary. In Leeds' eyes, Joseph II was foolishly neglecting Austria's vital interests and thus preventing the development of the natural and necessary Anglo-Austrian

---

[152] Polasky, *Revolution in Brussels*, pp. 112–29; Arbuthnot to Keith, 28 Dec. 1789, BL Add. 35541 fol. 367.
[153] Leeds to Fitzherbert, 24 Nov. 1789, PRO FO 37/27 fol. 24.
[154] Leeds to Fitzherbert, 27 Oct. 1789, PRO FO 37/26 fols. 201–2.

alignment. Joseph's refusal to accept this view had blocked such an alignment, and the logic of co-operation with Prussia had taken British policy in a very different direction, but it was not therefore in Leeds' view in the interest of Britain to see Austria fatally weakened. A similar theme can be found in earlier episodes of poor Anglo-Austrian relations.[155]

This view was given added force by French interest in the Austrian Netherlands, interest brought home clearly to the British ministry in the autumn of 1789 by the mission to London of Louis-Philippe, Duke d'Orléans (Philippe Égalité) the head of the junior branch of the French royal family, an anglophile who had visited London frequently and had close links with the Prince of Wales. Orléans, an opportunist, who flaunted his populism and opposed Louis XVI, left Paris after the October Days, in which he had played a questionable role. His 'empty diplomatic mission' has been presented as a form of exile engineered by Lafayette. In London Orléans pressed Pitt and Leeds on the threat to France posed by the move of any Austrian force into the Austrian Netherlands. Leeds felt that there was no basis for any confidential discussion with Orléans, and told him on 30 October that such an Austrian move was natural, and that Orléans should concentrate on helping restore order in France, without which, he claimed, she would not be heeded by other powers. George III was displeased by the mission.[156] Orléans was suspected by the British of having his own ambitions for those provinces, was indeed interested in becoming their sovereign, but his mission also drove home the danger that French concern about developments there, and the opposition of the people there to Austrian rule might lead to a potent alliance of the two revolutionary movements. Van de Spiegel warned that this would establish French power on the frontiers of the United Provinces, something that the Dutch had been seeking to prevent for generations.[157]

Given the threat from France, it was not surprising that the British ministry sought to preserve or rather recreate the status quo by hoping

---

[155] J. Black, 'On the "Old System" and the "Diplomatic Revolution" of the Eighteenth Century', *International History Review*, 12 (1990), 301–23.

[156] Hardman, *Louis XVI*, p. 173; Leeds to George III, 30 Oct. 1789, Browning (ed.), *Memoranda ... Leeds*, pp. 145–6; George III to Leeds, 19 Oct., Dorset to Hawkesbury, 24 Oct. 1789, BL Add. 27914 fol. 23, 38471 fol. 253; Leeds to Fitzherbert, 8, 11 Dec. 1789, BL Eg. 3500 fol. 101; Leeds to Lord Robert Fitzgerald, Minister Plenipotentiary in Paris 1789–92, 23, 30 Oct. 1789, PRO FO 27/33 A fols. 189, 207; Dorset to Hotham, 23 Oct. 1789, Hull UL DDHo/4/23; Luzerne to Montmorin, 23 Oct. 1789, AE CP Ang. 571 fol. 86; *Court and Cabinets*, III, 170; A. Britsch, 'L'Anglomanie de Philippe-Egalité, d'après sa correspondance autographe, 1778–1785', *Le Correspondant*, 33 (1926), 280–95.

[157] Vaucher (ed.), *Recueil*, pp. 558–63; Fitzherbert to Leeds, 10 Nov. 1789, BL Eg. 3500 fol. 103.

that it would be possible to broker a negotiated settlement in the Austrian Netherlands.[158] The unexpectedly rapid success of the revolutionaries made that proposal increasingly implausible, although it was a safer option than the commitments envisaged by the other members of the Triple Alliance, and one that had the advantage that it did not close the possibility of negotiations with either party. On 27 November 'the agent from the People of Brabant', Roode, saw Leeds and assured him that the Belgians were determined not to negotiate with Joseph, but also averse to any connection with France and resolved to keep the Scheldt closed. Postal interception revealed, however, that the last was not a point on which the Belgians were agreed.[159]

On 30 November 1789 the Cabinet met to discuss the situation. It was a different cabinet to that which had considered policy towards the United Provinces in May 1787. Pitt, Leeds, Thurlow and Camden still held the same posts, but Pitt's elder brother, John, 2nd Earl of Chatham, had replaced Viscount Howe as 1st Lord of the Admiralty in July 1788, while William Grenville, a first cousin to Pitt, replaced Sydney as Home Secretary the following June. The dominant note in the Cabinet minute was defensive, an obvious contrast to the boldness of Prussian planning:

> The main object which the allies ought to pursue appears to be the preventing the result of the present troubles in the Netherlands from raising up in that quarter a power formidable to our system; which might arise to the Emperor, supposing that Prince to succeed in overturning the constitution, or to France, in case the independence of those provinces was established in any mode which should connect them with that King.
>
> That the uncertain state of this business in the present moment does not seem to call upon any of the allies for immediate interference by force or by acknowledgement of the independence of the Provinces; because it is probable that whatever turn the events in that country may take, we shall be able to secure the main object of our policy ... and that with more advantage, by our not having pledged ourselves beforehand.

On the other hand, it was necessary to act to stop the spread of radical views in the Austrian Netherlands, not in order to create a *cordon sanitaire* for Britain, but because that would facilitate French influence. George III approved the minute because he felt that either the establishment of a democracy or the crushing of the revolution by Joseph, so that Imperial authority became absolute, would serve to unite the Austrian Netherlands more closely with France. Therefore, it was in

---

[158] Leeds to Keith, 13 Nov., Fitzherbert to Leeds, 13 Nov. 1789, BL Add. 35541 fol. 337, Eg. 3500 fol. 105.

[159] Leeds to Fitzherbert, 27 Nov., Fitzherbert to Leeds, 4 Dec. 1789, BL Eg. 3500 fols. 111, 121; J. Holland Rose, *William Pitt and National Revival* (1911), p. 514 mentions Pitt's refusal to see Roode, but not the meeting with Leeds.

the interest of Britain, as of the Dutch, to see the old constitution restored.[160]

The minute served as the basis for Fitzherbert's instructions. Leeds was clearly most concerned about the danger of French influence, as indeed he had been for a while.[161] The danger that France would recognise the independence of the new state, and thus acquire influence was stressed, but Leeds emphasised that the attitude of the Triple Alliance to the Austrian Netherlands should depend on their 'avoiding the excess of democratical principles' in their new constitution.[162] The problems of negotiating with a revolutionary government were emphasised by Thurlow in a perceptive letter, that also dwelt on the danger of Orléans' gaining a position comparable to the Prince of Orange:

> Without insisting upon the previous establishment of a complete form of government, it must at least be known, whom we converse with. The people? The army? who leads them? who has power and authority enough among them to answer for them? and, more particularly still, have the clergy, nobility, magistrates any common council, under the influence of which they are driving to any point, in which we can take an interest, and upon which we can rely; namely adherence to us, and detachment from our enemies?
>
> These are points to be secured, not by verbal promises, but by some actual system.[163]

Thurlow's response was symptomatic of that of the ministry to the revolutionary situation: hard-headed rather than ideological, but, more particularly, focussing largely on the international consequences. As with Leeds' instruction, democracy was undesirable because it would further French interests. Thurlow's point about the problem of deciding whom to negotiate with in a revolutionary situation was justified by the bitter differences between the traditionalists and the democrats in the Austrian Netherlands, while Fitzherbert reported that the independence cause was weak and poorly led.[164] Thus, the French threat continued to play a major role in the thinking of British ministers. The Anglo-Prussian alliance of 1788 arose from the need to protect the victory gained in the Dutch crisis of the previous year. Now the threat was if anything more potent: an intertwining of revolutionary movements in France and the Austrian Netherlands producing a domino effect in which

---

[160] Cabinet minute, 30 Nov. 1789, Bod. BB. 52 fol. 111; George III to Leeds, 1 Dec. 1789, BL Add. 27914 fol. 25.
[161] Leeds to Fitzherbert, 20 Nov., 4 Dec. 1789, BL Eg. 3500 fols. 107, 119; Leeds to Ewart, 9 Feb. 1790, PRO FO 64/17 fols. 53–4.
[162] Leeds to Fitzherbert, 1 Dec. 1789, PRO FO 37/27 fols. 38–9.
[163] Thurlow to James Bland Burges MP, Under-Secretary in the Foreign Office, 1789–95, 5 Dec. 1789, Bod. BB. 18 fols. 88–90.
[164] Fitzherbert to Leeds, 8 Jan. 1790, BL Add. 28065 fol. 23.

the Orangist position in the United Provinces was destabilised and then overthrown. 'Democratical principles' stood both for French influence and for unpredictability.

Unfortunately for the British government their cautious policy in the developing crisis was challenged not only by such principles, but also by Frederick William II, who was reported as resolved to attack Joseph II the following spring.[165] For the Prussians, the general international situation was both promising and frustrating. The continued resistance of Sweden and Turkey combined with evidence of mounting Russian and, in particular, Austrian difficulties,[166] gave rise to hopes of major changes in the European system, and, in the meantime, ensured that Prussia's relative power and influence increased. And yet, the situation was frustrating. Neither Russia nor Austria had collapsed hitherto, either domestically or on the battlefield. Indeed Sweden was in grave difficulties and Whitworth feared that Britain might have to take 'a decisive part' against Catherine in order to protect her.[167] In addition, the campaign of 1789 had been far more disadvantageous for the Turks than that of the previous year; especially with the loss of Akkerman (11 October) and Bender (14 November) to the Russians both without resistance, the Austrian victory at Mehadia (23 August), the victories of a joint Austro-Russian army at Fokshani (30 July) and, more importantly, at Martineshti (21 September also known as Battle of the Rimnick, and as Battle of the Boza or Buzau River), and the fall of Belgrade (8 October) and, without resistance, Bucharest (9 November) to the Austrians. Turkish morale collapsed.[168]

These victories made the revolt in the Austrian Netherlands very important for Prussia. Its success would justify the active anti-Austrian policy that had been pursued, and thus vindicate its proponents. It would encourage domestic opponents of the Habsburgs elsewhere, and create a new state that would need to look to Prussia for support. Hertzberg pressed for united action by the Triple Alliance, and Ewart warned that

the acknowledgement of the independence of the Netherlands, upon certain conditions, is the principle upon which the whole of the reasoning is founded, and that the revolution is supposed to be so completely accomplished as no longer

---

[165] Fitzherbert to Leeds, 27 Nov., 8 Dec. 1789, BL Eg. 3500 fols. 113, 128.

[166] Ewart to Cornwallis, 15 Aug. 1789, Williamwood 147.

[167] Whitworth to Ewart, 28 Aug. 1789, Liston, Envoy Extraordinary in Stockholm 1789–94, to Ewart, 22 Jan. 1790, Williamwood, 150, 148; Elliot to Pitt, 25 May 1789, PRO 30/8/132 fols. 202–3.

[168] Shaw, *Between Old and New*, pp. 36–9; A. Balisch, 'Infantry Battlefield Tactics in the Seventeenth and Eighteenth Centuries on the European and Turkish Theatres of War: the Austrian Response to Different Conditions', *Studies in History and Politics*, 3 (1983–4), 55–9.

to admit of any other alternative ... it would now be a very difficult matter to engage His Prussian Majesty to abandon his favorite idea of detaching the Netherlands entirely from the sovereignty of the House of Austria ... even formal conciliatory overtures, made by the Emperor to the Allies, or partial divisions among the provinces and different orders of the new states would no longer be considered as sufficient motives for reestablishing the Austrian government in any shape.[169]

Thus, the crisis in the Austrian Netherlands was pushing the British government to face the contradictions of its policy, of seeking an alliance to support a defensive anti-French position, but then having to appreciate the extent to which the views of her ally were incompatible with Britain's reactive and cautious stance. Diplomacy is the art of resolving contradictions, and they were and are always present in alliances. In the winter of 1789–90 the British position was eased by the extent to which fears of French intentions in the Low Countries became less urgent as France slipped further into obvious weakness with and after the October Days. Rather than Britain being forced to turn to German allies in order to protect a Dutch government threatened by French exploitation of the crisis in the Austrian Netherlands, the United Provinces had remained stable and there was no immediate danger of the new state turning to France. Discussion of the possibility of a reunion of the provinces of the Austrian Netherlands and the United Provinces[170] had no consequences, although it indicated the extent to which major changes were being discussed, as did the suggestion that Britain gain Ostend. The latter, made in October 1789 by a Belgian noble, Bethune, Comte de Charost, was of no interest to the British government.[171] On the other hand, as the able Fitzherbert pointed out, the defeat of Austrian forces in the Austrian Netherlands meant that it was no longer possible for Britain to arrange a settlement on the basis of concessions by Joseph II. There was now the danger that Joseph would reconquer the Austrian Netherlands or force the Triple Alliance to act against him.[172] In addition, the pressure created by Prussian expectations was a serious problem. Fitzherbert criticised Prussian promises of support to the Belgians.[173]

[169] Ewart to Leeds, 4 Jan. 1790, PRO FO 64/17 fol. 3.
[170] William Ritchie, in Utrecht, to 6th Earl of Kintore, 1 Jan. 1790, Aberdeen UL Keith of Kintore papers MSS. 3064 bundle 261.
[171] Fitzgerald to Leeds, 22 Oct., Charost to Burges, 14 Oct., Charost to Leeds, 15 Oct. 1789, PRO FO 27/33A fols. 187, 149–56; Rose, *Pitt*, p. 513.
[172] Fitzherbert to Leeds, 5, 22 Jan., Leeds to Fitzherbert, 12 Jan. 1790, BL Add. 28065 fols. 15, 47, 25.   [173] Fitzherbert to Leeds, 15 Dec. 1789, BL Eg. 3500 fol. 135.

Britain, Austria and Prussia in the winter of 1789–1790

Prussian schemes were not a new problem. Hertzberg's plans for eastern Europe had been disapproved of on previous occasions, most recently in June and September 1789. In October 1789 Leeds wrote to Keith, complaining of Hertzberg's desire for war, and adding 'His Prussian Majesty must be reminded that our connections with him are purely of a defensive nature.'[174] Other powers were aware of this tension,[175] and the reference in the National Assembly in January 1792 to the ambitious policies of Britain being based on using the Prussian army to intervene effectively in continental affairs[176] was misleading. In early 1790 Prussian pressure for the recognition of the independence of the Austrian Netherlands[177] was but part of what to the British government was very ambitious: Frederick William II's attempt to create a new alliance system, with Sweden, Turkey and Poland, in order to force Austria and Russia to accept Prussian views. The relationship between this new system and the Triple Alliance was unclear, because, although Frederick William sought to knit them together, for example by proposing a loan from the Triple Alliance to Gustavus III in early 1790, the extent to which objectives were shared varied; the whole was further confused by secretive and, at times, idiosyncratic Prussian diplomacy.

A reminder of the possibility of fresh directions came with separate Austrian and Russian approaches, via Reviczky and Vorontsov, for an alliance with Britain. Vorontsov communicated instructions from Catherine II in which she declared that she had no intention of annihilating the Turkish Empire and destroying the balance of power, revealed her peace terms, a frontier on the Dniester including Akkerman and Bender, and Bessarabia, Moldavia and Wallachia united as an independent Christian state, and sought British pressure on Sweden and Turkey to accept such terms. Leeds replied that the proposals would probably prolong the war, that the territorial changes envisaged would directly affect the interests of several European powers and that the British government could not support them. Leeds, instead, stated that the government sought a general peace based on moderate and equitable terms and would in concert with Britain's allies try to achieve one. Charles Whitworth, Envoy Extraordinary at St Petersburg, was instruc-

---

[174] Leeds to Keith, 16 Oct., Fitzherbert to Leeds, 18 Dec. 1789, Ewart to Leeds, 4 Jan. 1790, BL Add. 35541 fol. 317, Eg. 3500 fol. 137, 28065 fol. 9; Leeds to Whitworth, 25 Sept., 16 Oct., 1789, PRO FO 65/17 fols. 214–15, 7/18 fol. 18; Cunningham, 'Oczakow', 218–19.

[175] Esterno to Montmorin, 20 June, 11 July 1789, AE CP Prusse 210 fols. 150, 155.

[176] *AP* 37, 489.   [177] Ewart to Leeds, 4 Jan. 1790, PRO FO 64/17 f. 3A.

ted to persuade Russia to change her views and to accept an immediate armistice, and informed that the British government was ready to mediate on the basis of a peace 'without any material alteration' in the relative situation in which 'the belligerents had been before the war'. Catherine meanwhile remained convinced that British policy was being directed by Prussia.[178]

The Austrian approach was more realistic and sustained than that of Russia. It was part of a significant attempt by Joseph II, concerned about his poor health, the prospect of rebellion in Hungary and the danger of war simultaneously with Prussia and Turkey, to improve his negotiating position. This attempt also led to the dispatch of a special delegation to try to negotiate an armistice or peace with the Turks, and an approach to Prussia. Without informing Kaunitz, Joseph sent Johann Melchior Birkenstock to Berlin to discuss with Hertzberg a solution to the crisis. Unwilling to cede Galicia, Joseph was now ready to accept some territorial changes in accordance with Hertzberg's plan. Frederick William II, however, saw no need for compromise.[179] The Austrian approach to Britain followed a period when relations had been distant and cool.[180] Joseph was especially anxious about reports concerning Orléans' wish to become ruler of the Austrian Netherlands, and he felt that the prevention of this constituted an important shared interest that might serve to unite Britain and Austria. Reviczky made a declaration to Leeds concerning Joseph's pacific disposition, and Leeds assured him both that Britain would not recognize the Brabant agent and that she would be happy to assist in the negotiation of a settlement in the Austrian Netherlands.[181]

The Austrian and British governments, however, were not thinking only about the Austrian Netherlands.[182] On 6 December 1789 Kaunitz instructed Reviczky to obtain Britain's accession to the Austro-Russian alliance. He stressed the danger to Britain of Orléans' scheme and expressed the hope that Britain would not support Prussian schemes for major territorial changes in eastern Europe. Kaunitz added the claim that

[178] Catherine to Vorontsov, 19 Dec. 1789, Leeds to Vorontsov, 9 Feb, Leeds to Whitworth, 2 Apr. 1790, PRO FO 78/12B; Marcum, 'Vorontsov', pp. 157–61.

[179] K. Roider, *Baron Thugut and Austria's Response to the French Revolution* (Princeton, 1987), p. 77; H. Schlitter, 'Die Sendung Birkenstocks nach Berlin und der "grosse Plan" Hertzbergs', *Beiträge zur neueren Geschichte Österreichs*, 2 (1907), 25–9; A. von Vivenot, *Die Politik des österreichischen Staatskanzlers Fürsten Kaunitz-Rietberg unter Kaiser Leopold II* (Vienna, 1873), pp. 1–3.

[180] Keith to Ewart, 19 Dec. 1789, Williamwood vol. 148.

[181] *Mercy*, II, 274; Beer (ed.), *Joseph, Leopold, Kaunitz*, pp. 349–50; Leeds to Keith, 13 Nov. 1789, PRO FO 78/10 fols. 278–9; Leeds to Fitzherbert, 20 Nov. 1789, BL Eg. 3500 fol. 107.

[182] Leeds to Fitzherbert, 11 Dec. 1789, BL Eg. 3500 fols. 129–30.

as the Anglo-Prussian alliance was only defensive it did not prevent a defensive Anglo-Austrian alliance. Reviczky saw Leeds on 5 January 1790, but the Foreign Secretary told him that Britain needed to know the proposed terms of such an alliance before deciding whether to negotiate, that contracting a defensive alliance with a state actually at war was novel, and that Britain could not act without consulting her allies. Reviczky replied that Austria could not accept Prussian mediation, that Britain had often sought a renewal of her connection with Austria and that a strong Austria was useful to Britain as a counterbalance to France. In a remark that can be seen either as perceptive or as a poor addition to a weak hand, Reviczky added that France might still become formidable to Britain. Leeds replied that if so there would probably be sufficient time for Britain to consider how to act.[183]

This judgement might appear smug and foolish in light of the problems that were to face Britain at the end of 1792 as the triumphant forces of revolutionary France overran the Austrian Netherlands and threatened the Dutch. That situation, however, reflected the chance of military success. Leeds' view that if France became stronger then there would be time for Britain to adapt to the new situation, was a reasonable one if it was assumed that war, with its concomitant volatile changes, would not come at once. Leaving aside the intelligence of his argument, there was the simple fact that in January 1790 French power did not appear to be a major issue, that the British ministry had decided that bringing a stable peace to the rest of Europe was more important and that an Austria, weakened by an arduous war with Turkey and by domestic difficulties, was in no shape to confront France were it suddenly to become a major threat. Prussia was the only power likely to be able and willing to fulfil this role. In February Leeds was to compare 'the flourishing condition of the finances of Prussia [and] the state of its army', with the situation in Austria and Russia.[184]

On the other hand, Reviczky's point that Austria could be a valuable counterbalance to France was one that Leeds himself had been making in his early years as Foreign Secretary. By supporting the return of imperial rule to the Austrian Netherlands, albeit under conditions, the British government, among other aims, was seeking to retain Austria's value to an anti-French system. At Reviczky's request, Leeds put his thoughts in writing. He indicated a wish for better relations, but opposition to Kaunitz's proposal for a defensive alliance as inappropriate at the time, though much sought by Britain since the Seven Years War. Nevertheless,

[183] *Mercy*, II, 295; Leeds to Fitzherbert, 5 Jan. 1790, BL Add. 28065 fol. 13.
[184] Leeds to Ewart, 9 Feb. 1790, PRO FO 64/17 fol. 56.

Leeds made it clear that a joint effort by Joseph II and the Triple Alliance to bring peace to Europe was desirable. Nothing was said about the Austro-Russian alliance.[185] The Austrians did not give up. In the face of a serious crisis, convinced that the Turks were about to mount a major offensive, worried about food riots in Vienna and uncertain about Catherine II, Joseph II decided to make major concessions. By a rescript of 18 January 1790, the bulk of the legislation that had aroused discontent in Hungary was repealed, while by the end of the month the Emperor was pressing for an armistice with the Turks. This would obviously place major strains on the Austro-Russian alliance. The renewed approach to Britain was therefore part of a dramatic reversal of direction in Joseph's last weeks. On 12 February, Kaunitz wrote to Reviczky arguing that the present moment was most favourable for an Anglo-Austrian alliance, and offering to satisfy the grievances of the Austrian Netherlands and to ask for British mediation. His letter was communicated on 26 February, but Joseph died on the 20th.[186]

The British ministry was therefore in an interesting position in the winter of 1789–90: her support sought by Joseph II, at the same time as the views of Prussia were becoming more obviously unwelcome. The ministry chose to remain close to Prussia, although Joseph's approach doubtless encouraged a firm response to Prussian suggestions. It was a measure of Joseph's desperation and of the collapse of his respect for French power that he approached Britain before he died. On the other hand, the limited continental goals of British policy made her diplomatic support most appropriate for a power that wished to rescue itself from a difficult situation. This had been true of Gustavus III in late 1788 and was also true of Joseph II in the winter of 1789–90. It is not therefore surprising that in this period Britain was sounded out. An alliance, however, was not then plausible for either power. British would do nothing without her Prussian ally, whose army and finances both appeared strong, while a weak Austria was not an attractive alliance prospect. Conversely, British aims were not wholly welcome to Joseph. The British ministry did not view the Austro-Russian alliance with favour and was opposed to any settlement of the crisis in the Austrian Netherlands that would leave Joseph stronger.

Exploratory talks about the possibility of a reconciliation were to receive fresh impetus from the succession of Joseph's brother, the Grand

---

[185] Leeds to Reviczky, 11 Jan. 1790, PRO FO 7/19 fols. 19–21; Fitzherbert to Ewart, 19 Jan. 1790, Williamwood, 148.
[186] A. von Arneth (ed.), *Joseph II und Leopold von Toscona: Ihr Briefwechsel von 1781 bis 1790* (2 vols., Vienna, 1872), II, 280–95; Kaunitz to Reviczky, 12 Feb. 1790, BL Add. 28065 fols. 127–31; *Mercy*, II, 295.

Duke of Tuscany, as Leopold II. The main lines of British policy had already been set. Austria was, if possible, to be incorporated into an alliance system based on Prussia, not to replace it. The wisdom of this objective was to pose a question mark against British foreign policy in 1790–1, while an unexpected echo of the discussion between Leeds and Reviczky was sounded during the Nootka Sound crisis when France offered to come to the assistance of Spain. In fact, she was in no position to do so to any effect, and it is not clear that an Anglo-Austrian alliance would have deterred her from action, but the episode was, like the concern about Dutch stability in the autumn of 1789, a reminder that, alongside an agenda and cartography of British foreign policy dominated by eastern Europe, there was also a very different theme, that of concern about France.

The British ministry hoped that its negative reply to Austrian and Russian approaches would please the Prussian government, which had been informed of the former at the close of 1789;[187] but it was clear that it did not wish to accept Prussian direction, Leeds writing to Ewart on 9 February 1790 that,

the measures which His Prussian Majesty seems determined to adopt, with a view to force the two Imperial Courts to make peace with the Porte upon moderate terms not having been adopted in consequence of any concert between the Allies, cannot with justice be ascribed to the councils either of Great Britain or Holland; and whatever the consequences of so very active an interference may be, our system of defensive alliance cannot fairly be responsible for it.

Leeds suggested that Austrian and Russian weakness offered Prussia a prospect of success, but he added prudently that 'the event cannot be foreseen, and it may unfortunately happen that the war may be extended, instead of terminated'.[188] Similar caution was displayed in western Europe, where both Prussia and the Dutch sought British support for action on behalf of the Belgians. On 12 February 1790 Nagel, the Dutch envoy in London, presented Leeds with a letter from Van de Spiegel suggesting that Britain, Prussia and the Dutch should make preparations for the formation of an army of observation in order to safeguard the United Provinces and guarantee the independence of the Austrian Netherlands. Leeds thought the measure unnecessary and undeserved, and he reiterated his view that an independent state there would be fatal to British interests.[189]

---

[187] Ewart to Leeds, 4 Jan. 1790, PRO FO 64/17 fol. 3B.
[188] Leeds to Ewart, 9 Feb. 1790, PRO FO 64/17 fols. 55–6.
[189] William Gardiner, agent in Brussels, to Burges, 26 Jan. 1790, BB 35 fol. 4; Leeds to Fitzherbert, 12 Feb., Leeds to Ewart, 26 Feb. 1790, PRO FO 37/27 fols. 169–70, 64/17 fol. 107.

Meanwhile a new diplomatic horizon seemed to be opened up by the quintessential form of volatility in *ancien régime* international relations: not war, but death. Keith's servant bearing the news of Joseph II's death arrived in London on 3 March. Leeds' Under-Secretary, James Bland Burges, was not alone in looking 'forward to a new order of things'. Already on 26 February, Leopold had summoned John, Lord Hervey, the British Envoy Extraordinary in Florence, to a secret meeting, in order to inform him that Joseph's death had,

changed the way of thinking and the mode of acting of the court of Vienna; I am wholly inclined for peace, and on such a firm basis would I fix it, that I would agree to make any honourable sacrifice in order to attain it. An unfortunate alliance with Russia and an incomprehensible conduct of government have drawn on the state every possible calamity. To a natural friendship and alliance with England has been substituted jealousy and ill-humour, accompanied with the most indecent conduct that could mark it: every act of the court of Vienna has been against my opinion... A treaty of defensive alliance with England is an object I have most sincerely at heart. It cannot injure any other alliance, or even give umbrage to other courts, being calculated solely to insure the blessings of peace... could not account for the personal dislike of the Emperor towards England, unless led to it from his connection with Russia, whose jealousy proceeded from rivalry.[190]

This audience undermined the logic of the Anglo-Prussian alliance. Leeds had written to Ewart on 9 February that though Britain would take no part in a Prussian war, if Frederick William II felt obliged 'to draw the sword', a wonderfully traditional image, his success would 'be devoutly wished for by this country'.[191] But the sword would be drawn against Austria, rather than Russia; the former was more vulnerable and more tempting prey. Leopold's succession to the Habsburg dominions was to lead the British ministry to uncover the ambiguity in their earlier support of Frederick William II. His schemes could be seen as aimed against Austria and Russia, and, because the British government did not wish to participate in them, they had exerted no pressure on Prussia to make her plans more specific. With Joseph II's death this ambiguity ceased to be acceptable, as the British government sought to direct policy in an anti-Russian direction. There was an obvious parallel with the divergent interests in the Anglo-Russian agreement negotiated in late 1755. Whereas Czarina Elizabeth sought action against Prussia, George II and his British ministers wanted security against a possible Prussian attack on

[190] Burges to Keith, 5 Mar., Hervey to Leeds, 28 Feb., Hervey to Keith, 6 Mar. 1790, BL Add. 35542 fol. 53, 28065 fols. 177–9, 35542 fol. 67; A. Wandruszka, *Leopold II* (2 vols., Vienna, 1963–5), II, 353–69; Aretin, *Reich*, I, 251–62.
[191] Leeds to Ewart, 9 Feb. 1790, PRO FO 64/17 fol. 56.

Hanover. When the threat of the latter was ended by the Anglo-Prussian Convention of Westminster, the British expected the Russians to abandon their anti-Prussian goals, a change of policy that they were unwilling to accept.

The British response to Leopold's meeting with Hervey was eager. Fitzherbert warned Keith that an alliance was unlikely as the government wished 'to keep fair with Prussia', but Reviczky was given a message designed to please Leopold, and Keith was sent new instructions on 16 March 1790. He was ordered both to express pleasure at the moderate and pacific views expressed to Hervey, and to ascertain that the peace terms Leopold would accept were, as he had implied then, those of the *status quo ante bellum*, the situation prior to the outbreak of war. Leeds claimed in the instructions that such terms offered a better prospect of lasting peace 'than pacification founded upon an exchange of territory, or any alteration of relative power between the parties now at war could possibly produce'. Leopold was to be pressed to seek both a peace with Turkey, without waiting for Russia, and a settlement of the Austrian Netherlands 'with security of their constitution under the guaranty of the allies'.[192]

This approach was followed up. At the end of March, Keith was instructed to propose an immediate Austro-Turkish armistice to be followed by a peace congress, a parallel to the instructions sent to Whitworth on 2 April. Ewart was informed by Leeds that Leopold's disposition seemed different to that of Joseph, and he was therefore ordered to moderate the Prussian desire for war or territorial rearrangements in eastern Europe. Leeds argued that Hertzberg's agenda for a new-model eastern Europe was clearly no longer appropriate. He specifically criticised the notion that the Turks be urged to make territorial sacrifices to Austria in return for the Austrian cession of Galicia to Poland, a measure designed to lead to Polish concessions to Prussia. Leeds further claimed that forcing the acceptance of such changes would make it difficult to extend the Anglo-Prussian system, and he therefore ordered Ewart to persuade Frederick William II to set aside the unratified Prusso-Turkish alliance treaty concluded at Constantinople on 31 January 1790.[193] This treaty committed Prussia to fight in order to obtain satisfactory terms for the Turks, and specified the return of Ochakov and the Crimea. Ewart was also ordered to deny the idea circulating in Berlin that the British ministry had suggested the Austrian cession of Galicia on condition that the Austrian Netherlands were restored to the Habsburgs, an idea Auckland blamed on Ewart.[194]

There had been earlier attempts by the British ministry to distance itself from and restrain Prussian schemes, but this was the most clear-cut. The opportunities opened up by Austrian difficulties, by Russian loss of control over Poland and by Prusso-Turkish negotiations were to be closed, or rather exploited not in order to force through changes, but to bring a peace based on the British goal of the *status quo ante bellum*. This objective was to be achieved not simply through admonishing Prussia, but by active British negotiations. Thus, at the end of March, Leeds wrote to Captain Sidney Smith RN, who had placed his naval experience at the disposal of Gustavus III, 'The King of Sweden may be assured His Majesty's Government will never cease to pay the strictest attention to the situation of the northern powers, and the maintenance of that balance so necessary for their safety and prosperity.'[195] An international order based on territorial stability was thus clearly enunciated as British policy. It would therefore be mistaken to suggest that Britain did not have a pro-active policy in this period, but rather found that it had tied itself to a Prussian ally who had one, or any number of pro-active policies when any one did not work. A consideration of British policy in the spring of 1790 also suggests that it would be misleading to argue that a pro-active policy had been launched as a result of the Dutch crisis but derailed by the Regency Crisis, which had both brought policy making to a full stop, and caused the defection and removal of Malmesbury, the one man with the ability and energy to sustain such a policy. In such an analysis, Pitt apparently had too many other interests to give a consistent attention either to the formulation or to the implementation of foreign policy and therefore could not provide a firm and energetic controlling hand. By the late 1780s, this arguably also seems to have been true to some extent of Carmarthen, and there was no one else in the Cabinet in a position to control policy.

In fact, Leeds and Pitt were able in 1790 to devote considerable attention to foreign policy and the conception of the international situation that they advanced was a bold one, not least because it had to serve as the basis for an attempt to end a major war in which one power, Russia, had achieved considerable gains. It would therefore be wrong to suggest that after the Regency Crisis a policy vacuum existed in which a pro-active policy was continued, not from Whitehall, but by individual envoys, particularly Ewart and Elliot, freelancing and hoping to persuade

[194] Leeds to Ewart, 31 Mar. 1790, PRO FO 64/17 fol. 164; Auckland to Leeds, 7 Apr. 1790, BL Eg. 3504 fo. 210.
[195] Leeds to Smith, 31 Mar. 1790, BL Eg. 3504 fol. 204.

Pitt and Leeds to support them. Instead, the range of Whitehall's concern had greatly extended. During the Dutch crisis, Pitt had written to Grenville, 'we can hardly be engaged in any but a defensive war'.[196] Less than four years later, such a war was considered but in defence of much more ambitious goals. In notes for a speech drawn up after the Ochakov crisis, Pitt argued that it was the

general interest of a country in our situation, to prevent (if it can be done without too great effort or risk) any material change in the relative situation of other powers – particularly naval powers – and to diminish the temptation to wars of ambition.[197]

[196] Pitt to Grenville, 25 Sept. 1787, BL Add. 59364 fol. 171.
[197] Undated notes, PRO 30/8/195 fols. 49–50.

5   To the shores of the Pacific

Anglo-Spanish relations before the Nootka Sound crisis

Thus, in the spring of 1790 Britain was poised to take a more prominent role in the diplomacy of eastern Europe. In late January, however, a totally unexpected crisis touched off by events on the other side of the world came to occupy ministerial and public attention, and to take Britain to the brink of an unwanted war. Between 1702 and 1808, Britain and Spain were at war for all or part of forty-seven years. A highpoint of rivalry was reached in 1739–83, when the two powers were at war in 1739–48, 1762–3 and 1779–83. Theirs had truly been an imperial struggle, as control over the Caribbean, its islands and shores, the Philippines and the western Mediterranean was contested. And yet conflict was far from inevitable. There had been periods of co-operation between the two powers, most obviously the brittle alliance of 1729–33, and the more sustained relationship that had flourished in the aftermath of the War of the Austrian Succession and helped to keep Spain neutral in the early and middle years of the Seven Years War, a crucial period in the Anglo-French naval struggle. This relationship had been brought to a close when Charles III (1759–88) succeeded Ferdinand VI (1746–59), and there had been no such closeness after the Seven Years War. Instead, apart from a period in the early 1770s when relations improved, Britain and Spain were obvious rivals. The defeats of 1762 left Charles III with a desire for revenge, and this was heightened by a series of colonial disputes and by the survival after the war of the Franco-Spanish Family Compact of 1761. The French alliance was Spain's principal international commitment and in the 1760s it helped to sustain and accentuate Spanish opposition to Britain.[1]

[1] Sir Richard Lodge (ed.), *The Private Correspondence of Sir Benjamin Keene* (Cambridge, 1933); R. Pares, *War and Trade in the West Indies 1739–1763* (Oxford, 1936), J. M. J. Zamora, *Política mediterránea y política atlántica en la Españàa de Feijóo* (Oviedo, 1956); R. E. Abarca, 'Bourbon "Revanche" against England: The Balance of Power, 1763–1770' (unpublished Ph.D., Notre Dame, 1965); J. A. Lalaguna Lasala, 'England, Spain and the Family Compact, 1763–83' (unpublished Ph.D., London, 1968).

Anglo-Spanish colonial disputes arose both from specific issues and from a more general rivalry between the two powers. The maritime and colonial supremacy that Britain had gained in the Seven Years War challenged Spain's position in the New World. The actual British gain at Spain's expense, East and West Florida, was less serious, most of the territory being economically undeveloped and occupied by Native Americans, than the apparent vulnerability of the Spanish Empire to British power, demonstrated by the successful siege of Havana in 1762. British amphibious capability had clearly progressed greatly since the British failures in 1741–2. This vulnerability, however, helped to make the Spanish government hesitate about joining France in the War of American Independence, though a need to ensure that France shared Spanish objectives and concern about supporting a revolutionary example for the colonists of South and Central America were also important. Spain's eventual participation in the War of American Independence revealed the importance of her military forces, although their success was uneven. Minorca and West Florida were conquered, but Gibraltar successfully resisted a lengthy siege. Nevertheless, the subsequent peace, though delayed by her unsuccesful insistence on gaining Gibraltar, left Spain with West and East Florida, Minorca and limits on British operations on the Caribbean coast of central America. Spain remained an important naval power. Her fleet was increasing in size, and the naval shipyards, in both Spain and at Havana, in operating efficiency. Massive 112 and 120 gun three-deckers, as well as 74 gun two deckers of high quality were launched in the 1780s, though post-war cuts in naval estimates were followed by a substantial cut of 11 per cent in 1788. Training and seamanship improvements were begun in 1785.[2]

Specific differences between the two powers remained, but, more significantly, so also did the threat that Britain posed to the Spanish Empire. This was to be expressed with a new emphasis in the 1780s. In place of the former concentration on the Caribbean, its shores and nearby

[2] V. P. Atard, El tercer Pacto de Familia (Madrid, 1945); J. P. Merino Navarro, La Armada Española en el siglo XVIII (Madrid, 1981), 13–14; W. S. Coker and R. Rea (eds.), Anglo-Spanish Confrontation on the Gulf Coast during the American Revolution (Pensacola, 1982); J. A. Barbier, 'Indies Revenue and Naval Spending: The Cost of Colonialism for the Spanish Bourbons 1763–1805', Jahrbuch für Geschichte von Staat, Wirtschaft und Gesellschaft Lateinamerikas, 21 (1984), 179–81; C. Fernandez-Shaw, 'Participation de la Armada Española en la Guerra de la Independencia de Los Estados Unidos', Revista de Historia Naval, 3 (1985), 75–80; E. Manera, 'La Politica Naval Española del Rey Carlos III', Revista General de Marina, 211 (1986), 185–203; J. D. Harbron, Trafalgar and the Spanish Navy (1988), pp. 42–5, 86, 91–3, 106; J. Black, 'Anglo-Spanish Naval Relations in the Eighteenth Century', Mariner's Mirror, 77 (1991), 235–58; Eden to Carmarthen, 9 Feb. 1789, PRO FO 72/14; Eden to Sheffield, 26 Feb. 1789, BL Add. 45728 fol. 100.

regions, the energy devoted to the settlement of first Georgia and then the Floridas, the locus of British attention was increasingly to be the Pacific, and the base for British initiatives India, rather than the Atlantic seaboard of North America; though the notion of a conscious shift of policy, a 'swing to the East', advanced by Vincent Harlow, has been criticised. Britain was not alone in her Pacific interests. France, Spain, from her bases in Mexico and the Philippines, and Russia, from her colony in Alaska, all shared a wish to explore the ocean, and chart and establish claims to its coasts. This led directly to the Nootka Sound crisis of 1790, a crisis that prefigured many imperial clashes of the following century in that it arose from a place that had never been heard of by the statesmen of Europe and that most of them would have been unable to locate on a map.[3]

Anglo-Spanish rivalry was set against a background of Anglo-French hostility. Despite Spanish anger at France refusing to make peace conditional on the return of Gibraltar, relations between the two powers

---

[3] J. M. Ward, 'British Policy in the Exploration of the South Pacific, 1699–1793', *Royal Australian Historical Society*, 33 (1929), 25–49; J.-P. Faivre, *L'Expansion française dans le Pacifique* (Paris, 1953); V. T. Harlow, *The Founding of the Second British Empire, 1763–1793, I. Discovery and Revolution* (1952), chaps. 1–3; M. Roe, 'Australia's Place in the "Swing to the East", 1788–1810', *Historical Studies. Australia and New Zealand* 8 (1957–9), 202–13; G. Williams, *The British Search for the Northwest Passage in the Eighteenth Century* (1962); J. E. Martin-Allanic, *Bougainville Navigateur et les Découvertes de son Temps* (Paris, 1964); P. Marshall, 'The First and Second British Empires: A Question of Demarcation', *History*, 49 (1964), 13–23; J. Dunmore, *French Explorers in the Pacific. I. The Eighteenth Century* (Oxford, 1965); J. C. Beaglehole, *The Exploration of the Pacific* (3rd edn, 1966); G. Williams, *The Expansion of Europe in the Eighteenth Century: Overseas Rivalry, Discovery and Exploitation* (1966), chap. 7; M. E. Thurman, *The Naval Department of San Blas: New Spain's Bastion for Alta California and Nootka 1767 to 1798* (Glendale, California, 1967); D. Mackay, 'British Interest in the Southern Oceans, 1782–1794', *New Zealand Journal of History*, 3 (1969); E. S. Dodge, *Beyond the Capes: Pacific Exploration from Captain Cook to the Challenger, 1776–1877* (Boston, 1971); J. H. Parry, *Trade and Dominion: The European Overseas Empires in the Eighteenth Century* (New York, 1971); W. L. Cook, *Flood Tide of Empire: Spain and the Pacific Northwest, 1543–1819* (New Haven, 1973), pp. 65–396; C. I. Archer, 'The Transient Presence: A Re-Appraisal of Spanish Attitudes toward the Northwest Coast in the Eighteenth Century', *British Columbia Studies*, 18 (1973), 11–19, and 'Spanish Exploration and Settlement of the Northwest Coast in the Eighteenth Century', *Sound Heritage*, 7 (1978), 32–53; D. Mackay, 'Direction and Purpose in British Imperial Policy, 1783–1801', *Historical Journal*, 17 (1974); A. Frost, *Convicts and Empire: A Naval Question, 1776–1811* (Melbourne, 1980); P. J. Marshall and G. Williams, *The Great Map of Mankind. British Perceptions of the World in the Age of Enlightenment* (1982), pp. 258–98; M. Steven, *Trade, Tactics and Territory: Britain in the Pacific 1783–1823* (Melbourne, 1983); O. H. K. Spate, *Monopolists and Freebooters* (1983), pp. 299–307; D. Mackay, *In the Wake of Cook: Exploration, Science and Empire 1780–1801* (1985); O. H. K. Spate, *Paradise Lost and Found* (1988), pp. 151–60, 173–84; D. Howse (ed.), *Background to Discovery. Pacific Exploration from Dampier to Cook* (Berkeley, 1990); J. R. Gibson, *Otter Skins, Boston Ships, and China Goods: The Maritime Fur Trade of the Northwest Coast, 1785–1841* (Montreal, 1992), pp. 12–35.

remained close, although the Spanish government resented the manner in which it was treated by that of France.[4] Fearful of British colonial ambitions, Spain needed the alliance of France if she was to have any hope of thwarting them, and Liston's suggestions that Britain might take advantage of Franco-Spanish differences were somewhat unrealistic. Hailes' hint to Aranda, Spanish envoy in Paris in 1784, about unfriendly French intentions towards Spain elicited no response.[5] There were, nevertheless, points of common interest between Britain and Spain, most obviously their opposition to changes in the European system,[6] and more specifically their shared hostility to the growth of Russian power.[7] Two major bars to better relations did not seem insuperable. Gibraltar could be returned, possibly in return for colonial gains, an idea that worried French diplomats. The Spaniards, however, made it clear that they would not break their alliance with France for the sake of Gibraltar, while the British government essentially used the proposal as a diplomatic ploy in order to seek to weaken that alliance.[8] The anglophobe views of Charles III were regarded as a major difficulty, but he was aging, and was indeed to die in December 1788. George III was sufficiently lucid to tell Dr Willis on 4 January 1789 that he was not sorry for Charles' death as 'he was not friendly to this country'.[9]

And yet, Charles' death, shared interests in eastern Europe and the growing problems of Spain's ally France did not lead to an Anglo-Spanish alliance, despite Eden's efforts and French concern.[10] Floridablanca's retention of office and the continuation of the Franco-Spanish alliance were significant problems for Britain. Carmarthen had explained to Eden in September 1788 that George III was in favour of

the most intimate and friendly correspondence with Spain ... always supposing Spain to be ... independent ... the moment she becomes dependent on the

---

[4] Liston to Keith, 24 Oct. 1783, BL Add. 35530 fol. 120; J.-R. Aymes, 'Spain and the French Revolution', *Mediterranean Historical Review*, 6 (1991), 64.

[5] Bourgoing, French chargé in Madrid, to Vergennes, 14 Feb., Vauguyon, French envoy in Madrid, to Vergennes, 26 May 1786, AE CP Esp. 616 fol. 144, 617 fols. 83–4; Liston to Dorset, 8 Jan. 1785, KAO C184; Hailes to Carmarthen, 25 Nov. 1784, BL Eg. 3499 fol. 65.   [6] George III to Carmarthen, 30 Jan. 1786, BL Add. 27914 fol. 15.

[7] Carmarthen to Eden, 4 Apr. 1788, NLS 5550 fols. 157–8; Eden to Carmarthen, 10 June 1788, BL Add. 34428 fol. 75; Eden to Pitt, 12 Nov. 1788, PRO 30/8/110 fol. 141.

[8] Bourgoing to Vergennes, 21 Mar. 1785, Barthélemy to Montmorin, 7 Oct. 1788, AE CP Esp. 616 fol. 276, Ang. 567 fol. 15; Pitt to Carmarthen, 24 Jan. 1785, BL Eg. 3498 fol. 100; S. Conn, *Gibraltar in British Diplomacy in the Eighteenth Century* (New Haven, 1942), pp. 244–53; C. D'Alzina Guillermety, 'Puerto Rico y Gibraltar (1711–1788): una negociación frustrada', *Anuario de Estudios Americanos*, 47 (1990), 381–97.

[9] Liston to Mountstuart, 2 Jan. 1784, BL Add. 36806 fol. 57; Barthélemy to Montmorin, 7 Oct. 1788, AE CP Ang. 567 fol. 15; Tayler, *Fife*, p. 199.

[10] Montmorin to Lemarchand, 10 Apr. 1789, AE CP Esp. 626 fol. 283.

councils or subservient to the interests of France, she not only loses her own consideration and weight in the scale of Europe, but in every transaction wherein England is concerned must be considered in a very different light, from that in which her own natural resources, joined to the old characteristic of the Spanish Nation would indisputably place her. Count Florida Blanca, with an affectation of candour and sincerity, seems upon every occasion to treat this country and its government with a degree of suspicion, not less injurious in its nature than rude and unpolished in the mode of expressing it.[11]

This instruction expressed a central feature of British policy, namely a determination to deal with other powers individually, rather than negotiate with different alliances. Thus, there had been the determination to negotiate unilaterally with Russia in 1784 and with Austria in 1784–5, while Austria was again to be treated in this fashion in early 1790. Spain had to be separated from France for effective negotiations to take place; negotiations were designed to achieve this separation. The French *chargé* in Madrid, Bourgoing, claimed in 1786 that the favourite British aim was the splitting of the two major Bourbon powers.[12] He could have added the desire to divide Austria from France, and, though far less obviously, Russia from Austria. This British objective was unrealistic, unless the other power in question was in severe difficulties, as Austria was in early 1790, and, even then, it overestimated the willingness of other rulers to share the assumptions of British policy, to join the British diplomatic system and to set aside other actual or possible diplomatic links.

In the case of Spain, there was simply no need for her to align with Britain, even when her French ally became progressively weaker. Until the outbreak of the French Revolutionary War, there was no prospect of hostilities in Europe involving Spain, while she did not require British assistance for the furtherance of her North African interests. Spanish attacks on Algiers had been repelled in 1783 and 1784, and in 1786 Spain had been compelled to buy peace. The Spanish government did not propose to resume the conflict, which in its own way was as striking a testimony to the continued military vitality of non-European powers as Turkish resistance to Austria in 1788 or the campaigns of the rulers of Mysore, and indeed in 1792 Oran was evacuated by Spain. Had Spain, however, proposed to return to the attack then there is little doubt that the British government would not have wished to assist her. There were grave limits to Britain's willingness to act on behalf of allies, especially aggressively, but not only so: it is difficult to imagine the British helping to defend Oran. On the other hand, alliances of the period often excluded

[11] Carmarthen to Eden, 2 Sept. 1788, PRO FO 72/13.
[12] Bourgoing to Vergennes, 21 Mar. 1786, AE CP Esp. 616 fol. 276.

particular issues, and an Anglo-Spanish defensive agreement excluding Oran would have been possible.[13]

The British government's conception in 1788–91 of a British-led diplomatic system bringing peace and stability to Europe was superficially attractive to Spain, which had for long been concerned about the rise of Russia. In October 1788 Carmarthen instructed Eden to seek Spanish diplomatic support for the attempt by the Triple Alliance to mediate between Russia and Sweden, a measure also pressed on Eden by Pitt. The Spanish response was favourable.[14] And yet, the British objective had worrying implications. It was easy for Carmarthen to claim that 'it must necessarily be the interest of all impartial and neutral powers, not to see the independence or political consequence of Sweden annihilated',[15] but it was increasingly clear that any such mediation by the Triple Alliance might well lead to war. Furthermore, the notion of mediation to prevent change or protect a European system, always a somewhat imprecise if not nebulous goal, could be extended from Sweden to Turkey and Poland, which would also increase the risk of conflict. The following autumn British and Prussian diplomats spoke of the need for those powers that wished to support the balance of power in Europe to act to prevent the destruction of Sweden.[16]

When, in the early years of the Pitt ministry, the British government had sought better relations with Spain, Britain had been isolated and apparently weak, an undesirable ally, even if, for a power that was essentially 'satisfied' and not seeking gains, such as Spain, British objectives were not a cause for concern. After 1787, however, Britain was stronger, but her desire for stability in Europe carried with it a much stronger risk of war. At the end of 1789, Robert Walpole, Envoy Extraordinary in Lisbon, favoured the idea of closer links between Britain, Spain and Portugal, but Lúis Pinto de Sousa Coutinho, the Portuguese Foreign Minister, felt that Spain would not wish to be 'brought into difficulties' in case the Anglo-Prussian alliance became involved in a conflict, and Walpole soon reported the failure of the approach. Floridablanca gave Anthony Merry, the Consul in Madrid who had been left in charge of relations in Auckland's absence, some pertinent advice on 6 January 1790. He suggested that given the problems of Catherine II and Joseph II, especially the latter, the terms of a Balkan peace could be safely left to them, that if Britain took 'an open part ... it

[13] J. Sabater Galindo, 'El Tratado de Paz Hispano-Argelino de 1786', *Cuadernos de Historia Moderna y Contemporánea*, 5 (1984), 57–82.
[14] Pitt to Eden, 27 Oct., Eden to Pitt, 12 Nov. 1788, PRO 30/8/110 fols. 136, 141.
[15] Carmarthen to Eden, 15 Oct. 1788, PRO FO 72/13.
[16] Ségur to Montmorin, 4, 8 Sept. 1789, AE CP Russie fols. 4, 24.

would be impossible to tell where the flame would stop', and that she and Spain would be best advised to concentrate on economic improvement.[17] This advice was in accord with Floridablanca's general approach. In early 1789 he had explained his opposition to the idea of a quadruple alliance with Austria, France and Russia, in terms of a minimalist view of foreign policy:

His reasons are, that alliances in general are inexpedient for great sovereigns and also attended with continual trouble and expense; and risks which are seldom compensated by the accession of apparent force and support. He thinks this position particularly true as to His Catholic Majesty, who having no combination to apprehend, nor any hostile ambitious projects to pursue, is sufficiently secured by the strength of his dominions.[18]

Yet the French Revolution did lead to an opening for improved Anglo-Spanish relations. In September 1789 they had been upset by Spanish concern about a reported plan for the dispatch of a British fleet to the Caribbean and by British worries about Spanish naval preparations. There was also tension in the Bay of Honduras.[19] The following month, however, Floridablanca proposed better relations, and in early November Leeds instructed Merry to assure the minister of the British desire to listen to Spanish proposals to that end. Floridablanca told Merry that he would first need to hear from France,[20] but it was already clear that the Spanish government was very concerned by developments there.

Neither Floridablanca nor Merry appreciated that their interesting discussions about the European situation and the prospect for better relations between the two powers would soon be replaced by the language of protest and intimidation. Indeed, a certain lack of perception can be glimpsed in Merry's dispatch of 7 January. Having allowed Floridablanca to talk and then finding him impatient to continue his work, Merry 'thought it prudent to defer to another opportunity, to speak to him about the capture of the English vessel at Nootka'. When he did introduce the matter, Merry found Floridablanca unwilling to discuss it at length.[21] This was scarcely surprising given the difficulty of ascertaining what had actually happened on the other side of the world. This remained the case for a number of months.

---

[17] Walpole to Leeds, 5, 10, 24 Dec. 1789, Merry to Leeds, 7 Jan. 1790, PRO FO 63/12, 72/16 fols. 14–16.   [18] Eden to Carmarthen, 9 Feb. 1789, PRO FO 72/14.
[19] Merry to Leeds, 17 Sept., 29 Oct., Leeds to Merry, 9 Oct., 25 Dec. 1789, PRO FO 72/15 fols. 178–80, 270, 232, 375–86.
[20] Merry to Leeds, 12 Oct., 7 Nov., Leeds to Merry, 3 Nov. 1789, PRO FO 72/15 fols. 243–4, 310, 277.
[21] Merry to Leeds, 7, 15 Jan. 1790, PRO FO 72/16 fols. 14–16, 64.

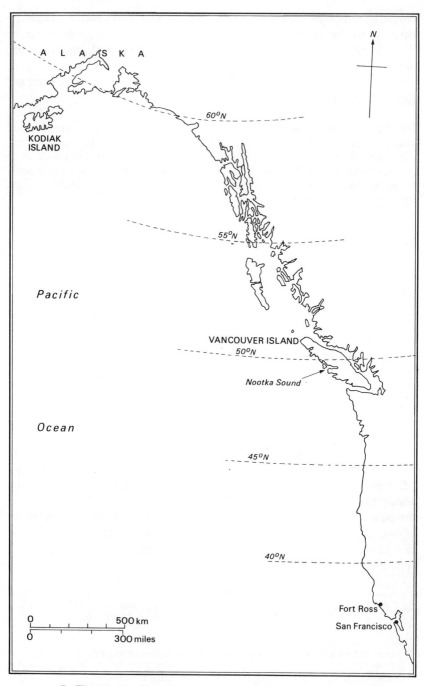

7. The Nootka Sound crisis

The Nootka Sound crisis

The clash that led to the dispute had occurred the previous year. The publication in 1784 of the narrative of Cook's last voyage, which included his account of his voyage along the north-west coast of North America, appears to have inspired three very similar British projects for developing the fur trade with the Orient from that coast and also for searching for a north-west passage. In June and August 1786 separate expeditions reached Nootka (Nutka) Sound on Vancouver Island; that under John Meares wintered on the shores of Prince William Sound. He returned in the summer of 1788, obtained permission to use a plot of land at Friendly Cove on the side of Nootka Sound from the local Indians and established a trading depot there.

The new base and the prospect of profits from trade on this 'new' coast excited both mercantile and official interest, but, as bold plans were being devised and executed, they were prevented by Spanish action designed predominantly to block a reported Russian plan to occupy Nootka. In 1784 the Russians had established a permanent base on Kodiak Island, and, thereafter, started to expand their activities along the coast. In February 1789 Eden wrote from Madrid, 'Accounts have been received here from Mexico of several settlements of Russians being made on the coast of California between the 49 and 68 Degrees.'[22] The Spanish government had already decided to act. On 6 May 1789 a Spanish warship anchored in Nootka Sound and over the following weeks it asserted Spain's right to the area. Subsequent printed accusations do not provide an adequate basis for establishing exactly what happened, but, after treating the first four British ships he encountered with some civility, though seizing one as a prize, the Spanish commander, Don Estaban Jose Martínez, responded on 5 July to a claim by Captain James Colnett that he was taking possession of Nootka Sound on behalf of George III, by arresting the captain and his crew, and subsequently sent the three British ships there to a Spanish base. The British flag was pulled down, and Martínez proclaimed that the coast from Cape Horn to 60° North was possessed by the Spanish crown; the coast further north being left to Russia.[23]

[22] Eden to [Sheffield], 26 Feb. 1789, BL Add. 45728 fol. 99.
[23] J. Meares, *Voyages made in the Years 1788 and 1789, from China to the North West Coast of America* (1790); V. T. Harlow, *Second British Empire* II (1964), pp. 425–6; W. R. Manning, 'The Nootka Sound Controversy', *Annual Report of the American Historical Association for the Year 1904* (1905), 279–478; L. Mills, 'The Real Significance of the Nootka Sound Incident', *Canadian Historical Review*, 6, (1925), 110–22; F. W. Howay, 'A List of Trading Vessels in the Maritime Fur Trade, 1785–1794', *Proceedings and Transactions of the Royal Society of Canada*, 3rd series, 24 (1930), 111–34; G. V. Blue,

News of the incident reached London, via Merry, on 21 January 1790. Leeds and the Cabinet adopted a firm line, Leeds writing to Merry on 2 February of 'our right to visit for the purposes of trade, or to make a settlement in the district in question; to which we undoubtedly have a complete right, to be asserted and maintained with a proper degree of vigour, should circumstances make such an exertion necessary'.[24] In a letter handed five days later to the Spanish Ambassador, the Marquis Bernardo del Campo, Leeds pressed for the immediate release of the British ship reportedly seized at Nootka, and insisted that it had to come before any discussion of territorial rights. On 10 February 1790 Campo in turn formally complained, demanding that the British government act to prevent future infringements of Spanish territorial rights. Pitt was not happy with Leeds' move, feeling that he had acted precipitantly before the facts had been ascertained, and that he had neglected to consult the Cabinet adequately.[25]

Pitt therefore decided to take a more active role and on 26 February a reply was sent to Campo. The return of the seized property and compensation were demanded, but, on a more conciliatory note, it was argued that more information would be required before other issues could be discussed.[26] Though the makings of a serious dispute were already present, neither government sought to push the matter. Instead, both waited for information and for the response to their demands, though, in accordance with a Cabinet decision of 23 February, the British made plans for an expedition to Nootka to establish what had happened, found a settlement and, if necessary, demand immediate satisfaction. On 22 February Floridablanca told Merry that the seized ship would be restored, but on 27 March the minister struck a more anxious note:

He dwelt much on the circumstance of our demanding satisfaction before any discussion had taken place of the matter of right on either side, and said from this, and above all, from the manner of our expressions he could draw no other conclusion than that it must be our wish to make the affair in question, a ground for quarrelling.

'Anglo-French Diplomacy During the Critical Period of the Nootka Controversy', *Oregon Historical Quarterly*, 39 (1938), 162–79; C. de Parrel, 'Pitt et l'Espagne', *Revue d'histoire diplomatique*, 64 (1950), 58–98; J. M. Norris, 'The Policy of the British Cabinet in the Nootka Crisis', *English Historical Review*, 70 (1955); L. Marinas Otero, 'El Incidente de Nutka', *Revista de Indias*, 27 (1967), 335–407; Cook, *Flood Tide of Empire*, pp. 119–30; R. Cole Harris (ed.), *Historical Atlas of Canada* I (Toronto, 1987), p. 167; Spate, *Paradise*, pp. 309–21; V. González Claverán, 'Malaspina, New Spain and the Northwestern Otter', paper given at the Vancouver conference on Exploration and Discovery, 1992.   [24] Leeds to Merry, 2 Feb. 1790, PRO FO 72/16 fols. 87–8.
[25] Del Campo to Leeds, 10 Feb., Pitt to Leeds, 23 Feb., Leeds to Pitt, 23 Feb. 1790, PRO 30/8/341 fols. 64–5, 30/8/102 fol. 170, 30/8/151 fol. 43.
[26] Leeds to Campo, 26 Feb. 1790, PRO FO 72/16 fols. 136–7.

Floridablanca threatened that this would force Spain 'to an under-standing with other powers'.[27] Such a threat lacked substance. Florida-blanca had already voiced his fears about developments in France and his concern about the progress of Russian arms. The minister suggested an alliance of Spain, France, Denmark, Russia and Sweden, and there was talk of another of France, Spain, Austria and Russia, but Merry reported his doubts that Spain would fight.[28] On 17 April Floridablanca told Merry that he hoped that Britain would not make Nootka an object of serious dispute,[29] but that month the British adopted a more aggressive line, a result both of fears aroused by Spanish naval preparations and of the publication of Meares' case.

Merry had reported Spanish preparations since mid-February, but had seen them initially solely as a small 'fleet of exercise'.[30] In April he noted increased preparations, reporting on 15 April that fourteen ships of the line were to be fitted out for immediate service, a dispatch received in London on 3 May. Two days later, Floridablanca assured him that these preparations were designed not against Britain, but because it was feared that French sedition would lead to a revolt in the Spanish West Indies. Merry repeated these assurances in his dispatches of 19 and 29 April, and he further reported that, although the Spanish fleet was arming fast, it would be unable to recruit sufficient sailors.[31] Floridablanca did not change his tone about the destination of the armament until the beginning of May, but the British government was already concerned as it had been receiving reports of Spanish naval moves from a number of sources, including Robert Walpole at Lisbon.[32]

Meares, the entrepreneur largely responsible for the British presence at Nootka, returned to London in early April and provided the first complete account from a British viewpoint of the events of the previous summer. In particular, Meares reported that more than one British ship had been seized, that the crews had been imprisoned and mistreated, that Martínez had formally claimed the coast, and that all this had been done despite the presence of a British settlement flying the flag built on land purchased from the local Indian chief, the latter's acknowledgement of British overlordship, the Indian agreement that the British should enjoy

[27] Mackay, *Wake of Cook*, pp. 87–93; P. Webb, 'The Naval Aspects of the Nootka Sound Crisis', *Mariner's Mirror*, 61 (1975), 134; Merry to Leeds, 22 Feb., 29 Mar. 1790, PRO FO 72/16 fols. 113, 238; Manning, 'Nootka Sound', 369–73.
[28] Merry to Leeds, 25 Feb., 29 Mar., 5, 12 Apr. 1790, PRO FO 72/16 fols. 118, 239–40, 245–6, 257.   [29] Merry to Leeds, 19 Apr. 1790, PRO FO 72/16 fol. 272.
[30] Merry to Leeds, 18 Feb. 1790, PRO FO 72/16 fol. 109.
[31] Merry to Leeds, 15, 19, 29 Apr. 1790, PRO FO 72/16 fols. 261, 270, 294–5; memorandum on Spanish naval preparations, Apr. 1790, BL Add. 59279 fol. 9.
[32] Merry to Leeds, 3 May, Walpole to Leeds, 28 Apr. 1790, PRO FO 72/17 fol.3, 63/13.

the exclusive right to trade and Meares' prior claim to territory on behalf of George III. Meares presented his report to Grenville, who, as Home Secretary, was responsible for colonial issues, and it was published on 5 May. It was soon supplemented by two pamphlets by John Etches, *An Authentic Statement of the Facts relative to Nootka Sound* and *A Continuation of An Authentic ...* Meares' account was unreliable. He was seeking compensation and found it easy to strike traditional themes of Spanish cruelty to achieve his aims. A summary of the *Memorial* was the first item in the *Gentleman's Magazine* for June 1790, but the editor still thought the issue in dispute somewhat obscure.[33] Nevertheless, in the absence of any other British report, the government had to take Meares' claims seriously, not least because he was a naval officer and stressed that he had acted in the name of George III, and it was also necessary to consider the possible domestic resonance on the eve of a general election.[34] In addition, the Spanish answer presented by Campo on 20 April promised to free the British crews, but made no mention of redress, while Spanish rights were reasserted. The release was presented as an act of courtesy, not satisfaction for a wrong.[35]

The British government responded with firm measures. On 30 April the Cabinet decided to demand satisfaction and to fit out a fleet to support the demand. On 1 May the Admiralty was ordered to fit out a fleet of forty of the line to be assembled at Spithead as soon as possible, and on 3 May a press for sailors was authorised, while on 6 May Pitt asked the Commons for supplies.[36] The small proposed expedition to the north-west coast of America was shelved, replaced by the prospect of fleet action in European waters where British naval power could be brought to bear most effectively. The defensive nature of British intentions and preparations was, however, stressed: Leeds informing Merry that a fleet was being prepared to protect British subjects 'from further encroachments' and to support the negotiation over the Nootka dispute, adding

At the same time that it is the sincere wish of His Majesty to arrange every difficulty by fair and friendly negotiation, yet the language of Count Floridablanca, and the very extraordinary preparations in the Spanish ports, render it incumbent on His Majesty to be prepared, in case the Spanish ministers should

---

[33] *Authentic Copy of the Memorial of Lieutenant John Meares to the Right Honourable William Wyndham Grenville, dated 30th April 1790; Gentleman's Magazine*, 60 (1790), 487–90, ed. comment, 487.
[34] Norris, 'Policy', 572–5; Webb, 'Nootka', 135, but see Ehrman, *Pitt* I, 559 fn. 1.
[35] Campo to Leeds, 20 Apr. 1790, PRO FO 72/16.
[36] Cabinet Minute, 30 Apr., Grenville to George III, 1, 2 May, George III to Grenville, 1, 2 May, Grenville to Earl of Westmorland, Lord Lieutenant of Ireland, 3 May 1790, HMC *Dropmore*, I, 579–80; Pitt to George III, 4 May 1790, Aspinall, *George III* no. 589; George III to Pitt, 5 May 1790, Rose, *Pitt and Napoleon*, p. 221.

prevail upon their sovereign to adopt measures of a hostile nature towards Great Britain, in preference to a candid discussion of the several points now at issue.

Merry was ordered to state that the base at Nootka had been purchased by a British subject and that it had flown the British flag, in short that Spain had acted against a rightfully established settlement. Merry was also authorised, in order 'to convince Count Floridablanca that our real object is justice not resentment', to read the minister a confidential instruction stating that George III would reduce his forces to a peace establishment 'when he shall be satisfied that similar measures will be taken by the Court of Spain, and when he shall have obtained an adequate reparation, and sufficient security for the future',[37] the last a very ambiguous, and for Spain worrying, demand. The potential for forcible re-evaluation of Britain's position in the Pacific was made abundantly clear by Pitt when he told the Commons that Spanish claims would prevent Britain from extending its navigation and fishery in the Pacific.[38]

Having adopted a firm line in Parliament, the ministry was now obliged to seek more than the restitution of ships and crews that it could probably have achieved with relative ease. As a result, it was decided to send a higher-ranking diplomat to Madrid, and Fitzherbert, the most experienced diplomat available, was appointed as Ambassador. His instructions made it clear that the ministry saw any struggle as likely to involve France, while the new envoy was also ordered to report on the military and political position in the Spanish American colonies.[39] In the event of war, the British government was clearly hoping to realise oft-held aspirations to support revolution in Spanish colonies. On 6 May Pitt and Grenville, who had been responsible since February for plans to send a secret expedition to Nootka in order to protect British citizens and establish a settlement, had a meeting with Francisco de Miranda, a Spanish American seeking British support for an independent federated empire in Spanish America. There were to be several more meetings over the next month, and, like much British planning, they indicated the extent to which Britain was willing to envisage major changes if war broke out. There was also consideration of using the Vermont separatists and other American frontiersmen, especially those of Kentucky, in order both to prevent the United States from joining Spain and to attack the Spanish colonies along the Caribbean coastline of North America.[40]

[37] Leeds to Merry, 3, 4 May 1790, PRO FO 72/17 fols. 11–12, 16–19, 185/6.
[38] *Parliamentary Register*, 27, 564–5.
[39] Instructions to Fitzherbert, 7 May 1790, PRO FO 72/17 fols. 35–46.
[40] F. J. Turner, 'English Policy towards America in 1790–1791', *American Historical Review*, 7 (1901–2), 711–12; W. S. Robertson, *The Life of Miranda* (2 vols., Chapel Hill, 1929) I, 97–112; Ehrman, *Pitt*, I, 385–6; Frost, 'Nootka Sound and the Beginnings of

Grenville subsequently argued that the possibility of Indians and 'American back settlers' being used to attack Spanish colonies had been exaggerated, but, in a glance at the possible volatility of developments in the New World, he emphasised the need for Britain to retain their help in case of an American attack on British positions, 'It is unquestionably true that the Americans have for these last two or three years been meditating attempts against our posts.'[41]

At the same time as it was considering military options, the British government was also negotiating for the maintenance of peace, not just with Spain, but with France also. The two countries were still united by the Family Compact, and there were also suggestions that war might be welcome to some political circles in France, especially the Crown, as it might serve to unite the country. The notion of solving domestic problems by launching a foreign war was commonplace in the eighteenth century. The British ministry did not want war with France. Although the country was vulnerable, and war would have offered the opportunity to reverse the defeats of the War of American Independence, such a struggle would have been unpredictable, not least in its influence on the volatile Low Countries. Britain's principal ally, Prussia, was in no position to help, while the prospect of a naval and colonial struggle with both France and Spain was not welcome: had war with France broken out, it would have been necessary to shelve many plans for operations against Spain. On 7 May 1790 Leeds sent orders to Lord Robert Fitzgerald at Paris to explain why Britain was arming her navy, to stress her wish for a peaceful settlement and to repeat assurances that George III wished to preserve good relations with France. Two days later, Montmorin told the Spanish envoy, Fernan Nuñez, that a peaceful settlement would be best, that if necessary the National Assembly would be informed of French obligations to her ally, but also that fulfilling these would encounter opposition.[42] Fitzgerald communicated his instructions to Montmorin, who replied that British conduct was precipitate, that Spain was not hostile over Nootka, and that Spanish naval armaments were a response to their British counterpart. Fitzgerald saw differing pressures for French armaments, from those who really sought counter-

Britain's Imperialism of Free Trade', paper given at Vancouver conference on Exploration and Discovery, 1992; S. F. Bemis, 'The Vermont Separatists and Great Britain, 1789–1791', *American Historical Review*, 21 (1916), 547–60, but also see fn. 23 on p. 154 of C. R. Ritcheson, *Aftermath of Revolution: British Policy Towards the United States* (Dallas, 1969) as well as pp. 98–106, 111–15, 160–3; J. L. Wright, *Britain and the American Frontier, 1783–1815* (Athens, Georgia, 1975), pp. 50–65.

[41] Grenville to Hawkesbury, 14 Jan. 1791, BL Add. 38226 fol. 42.

[42] Leeds to Fitzgerald, 7 May 1790, PRO FO 27/34; A. Mousset, *Un témoin ignoré de la Révolution française: Fernan Nuñez, ambassadeur d'Espagne à Paris, 1787–1791* (Paris, 1924), pp. 201–2.

revolution and from the 'popular party', keen to prevent Britain or Spain from seizing French colonies.[43]

Fitzherbert reached Paris en route for Madrid on 11 May 1790 and had an important discussion with Montmorin the following afternoon. His report is of course filed in Foreign Office, Spain, and its location illustrates the folly of studying bilateral relations solely from the obvious series. Montmorin assured Fitzherbert that France would offer her good offices to settle the dispute, but in a way that was satisfactory to Britain. He added that the French decision to arm fourteen ships of the line was a reluctant response to British armaments, leading Fitzherbert to reply that, as Britain was arming in response to Spain, the French step would be considered very threatening, and would in turn lead to fresh British preparations. When writing to the President of the National Assembly on 14 May, in order to inform him of Louis XVI's decision to arm fourteen of the line, Montmorin noted that the British government had informed him that their preparations were aimed only against Spain and that George III wished both to settle the dispute by negotiation and to preserve good relations. Nevertheless, he made it clear that France must match any British armament, and he added that it was necessary to show Europe that domestic developments had not destroyed France's ability to deploy her forces. The Assembly was assured, however, that Louis XVI would try to settle the dispute by negotiation.[44] On 16 May Leeds set out British terms in an instruction for Fitzherbert. In addition to reparation for the seizures at Nootka, the government pressed for such security as would prevent such episodes in future and end disputes between the two powers. The British would not accept the Spanish claims to American territories that they did not occupy and to the exclusive navigation of the Pacific, and the instruction stated the ministry's concern to protect their Pacific whale and seal fishery.[45]

As Spain was not actually in occupation of the American coastline north of San Francisco, where a base had been founded in 1776, the British position opened up a large extent of coastline to settlement, especially if it could be made clear that Spain had no right to Nootka Sound. Even more clearly, Spain ruled few of the island groups in the Pacific, with the exception of the Philippines, Marianas and Carolines. The British position, though presented as a defensive step designed to prevent future clashes, was pregnant with possibilities for new British establishments, and this was serious given current and recent British

---

[43] Fitzgerald to Leeds, 16 May 1790, PRO FO 27/34.
[44] Fitzherbert to Leeds, 15 May 1790, PRO FO 72/17 fols. 52–3; Montmorin to Luzerne, 17 May 1790, AE CP Ang. 573 fols. 115–16; *AP*, 15, 510–11.
[45] Leeds to Fitzherbert, 16 May 1790, PRO FO 72/17 fols. 55–9, 84–7.

interest in the Pacific. Furthermore, in rebutting Spanish claims, both to the American mainland and to the exclusive navigation of the Pacific, the instruction referred to the 'principles of the Law of Nations', as well as 'the plain sense' or 'fair construction' of existing treaties, a disruptive thesis. Spanish fears over many years of British colonial intentions thus seemed to be realised, and it has been claimed that the British argument gave 'a gloss of respectability to a ruthless act of expropriation'.[46]

A defiant Spanish response, to be effective, however, would require the support of other powers. The diplomatic situation was not propitious for her. This was due not so much to Floridablanca's caution in European affairs since the War of American Independence, as to the difficulties now facing both Spain's ally France and other powers opposed to Britain. The situation thus echoed Britain's during the War of American Independence to a certain extent, in that her isolation then owed more to the circumstances of the conflict and period, than to her earlier policies in 1763–74. Though Spain approached Austria, Russia, Denmark and Sweden, the response was poor. They had more pressing problems, while Russia's ambitions on the Pacific coast of North America were themselves a source of concern to Spain. There is no evidence for John Trevor's suggestion that Russia was in some way behind Spanish action,[47] though it indicated the depth of hostility towards Catherine II circulating in British diplomatic circles. The United States of America offered a better prospect for Spain, because of poor Anglo-American relations. Spain and the United States, however, were in dispute, especially over the frontier of West Florida.[48] In addition, Anglo-American relations were eased by suggestions about the possibility of an alliance. George Beckwith, a British agent in New York, though not an accredited minister, explored the possibilities in discussions with Alexander Hamilton, the Secretary of the Treasury. The two powers, however, had different views about the fate of any conquests from Spain, especially of New Orleans.[49]

Spain's principal hope was France. The effect of the French decision to arm fourteen of the line was, however, greatly lessened on 22 May by the resolution of the National Assembly, after bitter debates, that the

[46] Norris, 'Policy', 580.
[47] Trevor to Keith, 12 June 1790, BL Add. 35542 fol. 244. Hailes shared this suspicion, Hailes to Jackson, 23 Oct. 1790, PRO FO 353/66.
[48] A. P. Whitaker, *The Spanish-American Frontier, 1783–1795: the Westward Movement and the Spanish Retreat in the Mississippi Valley* (Boston, 1927).
[49] H. C. Syrett (ed.), *The Papers of Alexander Hamilton*, 7 (New York, 1963), pp. 70–4; J. P. Boyd, *Number 7, Alexander Hamilton's Secret Attempts to Control American Foreign Policy* (Princeton, 1964), pp. 4–13; Ritcheson, *Aftermath of Revolution*, pp. 103–4, 112–15.

King could not declare war without its approval. These debates reflected a profound division as to the nature of the political community centring on the struggle between different ideas about the relationship between crown and nation, which developed into a clash of royal versus national sovereignty, with particular reference to the right of declaring war. The eventual decision was a compromise, as it had been argued by some that the monarch should lose the right completely, while speakers such as Barnave had condemned the idea of an armament. Spanish policy had also been criticised bitterly by, among others, Charles de Lameth and Robespierre.[50]

This decree was praised on moral grounds in the British press. The *Times* of 26 May argued that it was clear from history that the most harmful conflicts 'originated in the injustice, the animosity, or the capricious passions of individuals', a statement that was misleading as far as Louis XV and Louis XVI were concerned, and that certainly failed to anticipate the role of popular assemblies, the Legislative Assembly and the National Convention, in leading France to war in 1792 and 1793. The *Morning Herald* of 31 May 1790 saw the National Assembly's decree as

the very essence of true philosophy! a death's wound to despotism, arbitrary power, and false prerogative of ambitious, cruel, bloodthirsty tyrants ... and the total extirpation of that radical disease of the French Cabinet aspiring to universal dominion! ... may be said to form a new epoch in the annals of the world, tending to spread universal amity ... this great and beatific revolution!

History rarely conforms to the broad sweeps of 'true philosophy', whether ostensibly polemical or the apparently subtler product of systems builders. Diplomats assessed the decree of the National Assembly in terms of present advantage. It appeared to demonstrate that not only France's strength (and therefore the response of other powers to her), but also her very process of foreign policy formulation, had been changed dramatically by the Revolution. French diplomats, such as Luzerne, were very concerned by the decree, which, conversely, was greeted with delight in Britain. British diplomats were convinced that it would oblige Spain to keep the peace.[51]

[50] *AP* 15, 518, 530, 559; B. Rothaus, 'The War and Peace Prerogative as a Constitutional Issue during the First Two Years of the Revolution 1789–91', *Proceedings of First Annual Meeting of the Western Society for First History 1974*, pp. 120–38. This is based on Rothaus' thesis 'The Emergence of Legislative Control over Foreign Policy in the Constituent Assembly, 1789–91' (unpublished Ph.D., Wisconsin, 1968); E. Lemay, 'L'Intérêt de la "nation" dans le débat sur le droit de déclarer la guerre ou la paix à l'Assemblée constituante (15–22 mai 1790)', unpublished paper. I would like to thank Edna Lemay for sending me a copy of her paper.
[51] O. Ranum, 'Louis XV and the Price of Pacific Inclination', *International History Review*, 13 (1991), 331–8; Hammond to Keith, 4 June, Trevor to Keith, 10 June 1790,

The Spanish government was even more concerned by the apparent sign that France would not provide support. On 16 June a formal demand for French assistance was made, but, in reply, Spain was informed that Louis XVI must submit the request to the National Assembly. Nothing was in fact done until late August, and until then it appeared that Spain would receive no aid. Indeed, the National Assembly was more concerned about the consequences of the crisis for French politics, not least the alleged views of the French envoy in Madrid, Vauguyon, who appealed to Louis XVI for permission to justify himself before the Assembly from charges of having incited the crisis.[52]

The Spanish government claimed that they could find other allies,[53] but in practice they could hope for no more than mediation, which the French and Portuguese governments were both willing to offer.[54] This was not seriously considered by the British ministry, an obvious contrast to the demand that Britain should play a role in bringing peace to eastern Europe. Portugal, whose government supplied Britain with information on Spanish naval armaments,[55] would have still posed problems as a mediator. She was vulnerable to Spanish pressure, but, more seriously, her own colonial position was based in part on historic claims to tracts of unoccupied territory (unoccupied by Europeans which was the issue in European diplomacy), and there were specific colonial disputes between Britain and Portugal. France could not be seen in Britain as an impartial mediator, and it would have been foolish politically even to have explored the idea. In addition, the terms communicated by Spain suggested that mediation would not serve British interests. Walpole reported in June that the Spanish government was ready for mutual disarmament, but also wanted Gibraltar.[56]

The path to a diplomatic settlement through the good offices of other powers was not attractive for the British government. Instead there would have to be a settlement directly with Spain, though it was unclear whether it would involve war. By early June, the British were certainly prepared for war, Burges writing:

Though we have not yet received any formal answer from the Court of Spain, I still incline to hope that peace will be the end of this negotiation. As matters of this sort however are liable to many variations, we continue our preparations with

BL Add. 35542 fols. 219, 237; Luzerne to Montmorin, 31 May 1790, AE CP Ang. 573 fols. 197–200.
[52] Parrel, 'Pitt et l'Espagne', 74–5; Vauguyon to Montmorin, 2 June 1790, AE CP Esp. 629 fols. 7–19.   [53] Walpole to Leeds, 20 June 1790, PRO FO 63/13.
[54] Montmorin to Luzerne, 28 May, Luzerne to Montmorin, 8 June 1790, AE CP Ang. 573 fols. 194, 253; Walpole to Leeds, 9 June 1790, PRO FO 63/13.
[55] Walpole to Leeds, 26 May 1790, PRO FO 63/13.
[56] Walpole to Leeds, 20 June 1790, PRO FO 63/13.

unceasing activity, and have already an immense naval force, ready for any contingency, and certainly superior by many degrees to any that Spain can be able to send forth.[57]

Dutch support had been secured. When first approached, Van de Spiegel had stressed the difficulties that this entailed: the problems of recruiting sufficient sailors, the exhausted finances of the Republic, the threat to Dutch trade in the Mediterranean, the absence of any obvious benefit for the Dutch, and the difficulty of taking any initiatives given the nature of the Dutch constitution. The Dutch fleet was, however, regarded as a valuable force, nearly forty of the line, of which over half were in a very good state. Auckland, who had replaced Fitzherbert at The Hague, was able to persuade the Dutch to help, and the British government indicated a willingness to pay. In the end, at their own expense, the Dutch armed a squadron of ten of the line fast and sent it to join the British fleet in early July.[58] The Prussians responded positively to the British request for support.[59]

Thus, the situation seemed very propitious for Britain, although there were a number of imponderables, including the likely response of France and the United States to the outbreak of war. There were also questions over British tactics. On 2 June Leeds wrote to Pitt to express his concern. He feared that Spain would try to delay matters, might give satisfaction for the incident at Nootka Sound, but avoid the wider question of rights, and added,

I cannot possibly approve of any measure short of a direct unqualified satisfaction for the insult, without a single engagement on our part of tendering the probable event of a future discussion, of any one of the objects in dispute, by way of purchasing the compliance of Spain with the satisfaction demanded... in all probability Spain will not give way, we however must not relax. War of course must result. Supposing however for arguments sake they give the satisfaction, I do not think the question of Nootka Sound determined... I can by no means approve the idea of Mr. Fitzherbert the moment he has received the satisfaction demanded instead of giving the Spanish Minister time to breathe, following up his blow (for a pretty sharp one the obtaining the satisfaction will be) with cramming down Floridablanca's throat, either a formal cession of Nootka Sound, or the admission of our fishing vessels to the southward, the mode of negotiation I disapprove of and the offensive impression it ought to create might perhaps invalidate the terms of the satisfaction as well as annull any forced advantages which compulsion could desire for us, in respect to our fishery, perhaps an object of full as much importance in point of national advantage as any stipulation

---

[57] Burges to Keith, 2 June 1790, BL Add. 35542 fol. 215.
[58] Auckland to Leeds, 12, 15 May, Leeds to Auckland, 18 May, Auckland to Pitt, 22 May 1790, PRO FO 37/29 fols. 21, 30, 50, 30/8/110 fol. 165; Auckland to Keith, 15 June 1790, BL Add. 35542 fol. 254.
[59] Leeds to Ewart, 7 May, Ewart to Leeds, 15 May 1790, PRO FO 64/17 fols. 215, 236.

respecting Nootka Sound ... After what has passed, Spain I think ought to go to war by refusing the satisfaction, it may however perhaps be her object to gain time, and therefore she may postpone hostilities till we come to ... the fishery. War I think must be the result of our present discussion with that power, and I do not see how it can be avoided without disgrace to one of the parties.

Leeds' letter and, more generally, his policy throughout the crisis, have been criticised,[60] but the minister was correct to argue that both powers were now in a situation where, unless one backed down, war was unavoidable and that, if that happened, it would represent a compromising of views that would bring disgrace. If Spain was unwilling to yield, and there was no sign that the situation was otherwise, then the logic of military and diplomatic possibilities suggested that Britain should act speedily. Expeditions would have to be sanctioned, prepared and dispatched to distant corners of the globe, all of which would take time, and it was also sensible for Britain to act while France was weak and there was the hope that problems in eastern Europe could be solved without war. There was also the need to act before domestic criticism of naval inaction[61] became too strong, and the need to have something definite, either war or a settlement, to present to the forthcoming session of Parliament. The claim that the firm British line was influenced by pressure from public opinion and the imminence of a general election has been queried on the grounds that there is no evidence that Pitt held such fears and that his policy can be accounted for without them. Nevertheless, Luzerne felt that the domestic context was significant. He argued that the Spanish proposal for mutual disarmament prior to negotiations was unacceptable, because no British ministry would dare to do it in light of the agitation over the issue, which Luzerne had reported fully. He also thought the proximity of elections was important. Furthermore there is little doubt that enthusiasm for war, or at least the expectation of a diplomatic triumph, was widespread. A British caricature published on 14 July 1790, *The British Tar's Laughing-stock, or The Royal Quixote*, an attack on Charles IV, included the verse,

> Our British tars shall crop your ears,
> And drive your Fleets to hell.[62]

During June and July diplomatic exchanges between Britain and Spain, especially Floridablanca's reply of 4 June, continued to be

---

[60] Leeds to Pitt, 2 June 1790, PRO 30/8/151 fols. 45–6; Ehrman, *Pitt*, I, 560; Norris, 'Policy', 575.

[61] Henry, 2nd Viscount Palmerston to Benjamin Mee, 12 May 1790, Aspinall, *George III* no. 589 fn. 1; Luzerne to Montmorin, 4 June 1790, AE CP Ang. 573 fol. 240.

[62] Norris, 'Policy', 572–5; Webb, 'Nootka', 135; Ehrman, *Pitt* I, 559 fn. 1; Luzerne to Montmorin, 8, 15 June, 13 July 1790, AE CP Ang. 573 fols. 253, 274–5, 574 fols. 43–4; Syrett (ed.), *Hamilton*, 7, 137.

unsatisfactory from the British point of view.[63] Richmond was expressing the general opinion when he argued that the Spaniards were determined to exclude Britain from the Pacific and the American coast, and that their offer to make reparation conditional on a settlement of those points was therefore worthless. In light of this, Leeds' statement that Britain wanted an alliance with Spain, but must have satisfaction first, was less relevant than his attempt to find out if Portugal would allow the British navy to use Lisbon as a base.[64] Both powers continued to arm. The British were fully informed of the build-up of a large Spanish fleet at Cadiz.[65] Montmorin feared that, despite their talk of peace, the British ministry would be driven towards war by an over-confidence created by their own armament and a conviction of French weakness,[66] and indeed Pitt was under pressure from bellicose colleagues convinced that Spain would not yield to diplomatic pressure, and confident about the prospects of war. Thus, the parliamentary recess did not end pressure for action. Taking the waters at Tunbridge Wells, Camden wrote:

I saw plainly there could be but one opinion in the present conjuncture. War as I always thought was inevitable and to temporize impossible. The jealousy of their court gave the first provocation, and their pride refuses satisfaction. The consequence is evident. We have no choice, for the outrage at Nootka cannot be a subject of discussion. I trust in the spirit of the kingdom and your wisdom and good fortune.[67]

Domestic pressure, the strength of the British naval armaments and a sense that negotiations hitherto had made no progress,[68] led to the dispatch on 5 July to Fitzherbert of firm instructions, drafted by Pitt. Immediate and full reparation was demanded, although this was not to preclude any subsequent discussion of Spain's right to claim unoccupied territory.[69] In an accompanying letter, Burges made it clear that domestic considerations were of weight. He noted that the instructions revealed that the views of the Cabinet were unshaken, an important indication to Fitzherbert of the source of policy, and continued:

[63] Fitzherbert to Burges, 16 June 1790, Bod. BB. 38 fol. 120; Pitt to Stafford, 27 June 1790, PRO 30/29/1/15 no. 96; Fawkener to Hawkesbury, 28 June 1790, BL Add. 38225 fol. 261; Auckland to Pitt, 17 July 1790, PRO 30/8/110 fol. 168.
[64] Richmond to Pitt, 22 June 1790, CUL Add. 6958; Leeds to Walpole, 29 June, – June 1790, PRO FO 63/13.
[65] State of the Intelligence, 13, 26 June, Fitzherbert to Leeds, 16 June 1790, PRO FO 95/7 fols. 330, 391–4, 381; list of the fleet at Cadiz, 29 July 1790, BL Add. 59279 fols. 11–12; Webb, 'Nootka', 139.
[66] Montmorin to Luzerne, 15, 26 June 1790, AE CP Ang. 573 fols. 289, 312.
[67] Camden to Pitt, 29 June 1790, PRO 30/8/119.
[68] Earl of Pembroke to Malmesbury, 19 July 1790, Winchester, Malmesbury 163.
[69] Leeds to Fitzherbert, 5 July 1790, PRO FO 72/18.

The more indeed this affair is considered, the more impossible it appears to put up with anything short of the satisfaction originally demanded, previous to anything like a negotiation on the question of right. I consider therefore the representation now sent as the ultimatum of our court, to which a specific as well as immediate answer from that of Spain will be extremely desirable on every account; as delay can only serve to keep the public in a state of painful suspense, and oblige us to maintain an armament at full as great an expense as if we were actually at war, while we derive no advantage from it, and while faction will daily be growing strong by a state of inaction, the true motives of which are not known, while ideal ones are easily fabricated.

Burges was convinced that Spain would not yield on the Pacific fisheries and therefore intended to amuse Britain by delays. He also noted that the continuation of the British armaments for any length of time would be financially ruinous.[70] The following day, Floridablanca made it clear to Puyabry, the French *chargé d'affaires* in Madrid, that, in his view, the French position was crucial to British and Spanish attitudes. The minister claimed to be sure of French good intentions, but to have grave doubts about their capability. Puyabry argued that, although it was now impossible in France to assemble an army, because of political fears of a counter-revolution, no such domestic factors precluded a naval armament;[71] an interesting parallel to contrasting British attitudes throughout the eighteenth century towards a strong army and a strong navy, which had recently played a role in the defeat of Richmond's fortifications plan.

Isolated, and intimidated by British naval preparations, Spain gave way. On 24 July Floridablanca signed a Declaration virtually identical with that sent to Fitzherbert on the 5th, and the envoy signed the Counter-Declaration he had been sent. Spain agreed to reparations without jeopardising the discussion of their right to Nootka; Britain accepted the reparations without abandoning their right.[72]

The central issues thus remained unsettled, though the British government was hopeful that, having demonstrated their naval strength and forced Spain to back down, it would be possible to arrange them to their satisfaction.[73] To achieve this end, the British kept their fleet prepared, and rejected a Spanish proposal for mutual naval disarmament. On 17 August, Fitzherbert was sent fresh instructions. The Spanish claim of sovereignty over the coast of America must be dropped as part of a settlement in which Britain and Spain agreed those limits of latitude

[70] Burges to Fitzherbert, 5 July 1790, Bod. BB. 38 fol. 121.
[71] Puyabry to Montmorin, 7 July 1790, AE CP Esp. 629 fols. 112–14; memorandum on French preparations, 29 July 1790, BL Add. 59279 fols. 15–16.
[72] English texts in Cobbett, 28, 914–16; Manning, 'Nootka Sound', 404–6.
[73] Auckland to Burges, 11 Aug. 1790, Bod. BB. 30 fols. 47–8.

and territorial waters within which British merchants could not settle or trade freely, while outside those limits they should have the same rights of navigation, fishing, and settlement on unoccupied territory. Fitzherbert was told to suggest territorial waters of five, or at the most ten, leagues from the coast, and the latitudes of 31°N–45°S, from Little California in modern Mexico to the fjord coastline of modern southern Chile. If necessary, 40°N was to be accepted: about 170 miles north of San Francisco. This would still have left the coastline of modern Canada and the Pacific North West of the United States open to British settlement.[74] There were high hopes about the economic possibilities of the region, especially in terms of the long sought North West passage. One of the major purposes of Commander George Vancouver's voyage to the north eastern Pacific, which began when he sailed from Falmouth on 1 April 1791, was to discover such a passage.[75] Robert Liston wrote of a possible North West passage from near Nootka to Hudson's Bay and of a large inland sea like the Baltic or the Mediterranean, adding 'if the coasts of this new Mediterranean are of a rich sort, producing shiptimber, and peopled with a race of men wishing to exchange furs for our woollens and other manufactures, we cannot give up such an extensive prospect for the increase of our trade'.[76] The southern boundary was of importance because of a clash over the extent of British whaling, an industry that was regarded as important by the government. In April 1789 two London ships had been detained sealing on Penguin Island, off Puerto Deseado, some 200 miles north of Santa Cruz, in Patagonia. Despite their claim that they had had to put in for repairs and water, the vessels were ordered to depart and their seal skins were seized. The issue was serious as the British claimed that Spanish sovereignty did not extend over the uninhabited coastline, a proposition denied by the Spaniards. Prior to the news of the Nootka incident reaching London, the Spanish position on the Southern Fishery had thus already caused concern.[77]

Fitzherbert presented the proposals on 8 September 1790, but, by then, the situation had changed, thanks to the unexpected decision of the French National Assembly on 26 August to press Louis XVI to negotiate

---

[74] Leeds to Fitzherbert, 17 Aug. 1790, PRO FO 72/18.
[75] Williams, *British Search for the Northwest Passage*, pp. 221–6, 235–45; Mackay, *Wake of Cook*, p. 83. On Vancouver, B. Anderson, *Surveyor of the Sea* (Seattle, 1960).
[76] Liston to Auckland, 14 Sept. 1790, BL Add. 34433 fol. 117; *Gentleman's Magazine*, 60 (1790), 664, 61 (1791), 404–6.
[77] Ehrman, *Pitt* I, 344–51; Harlow, *Second British Empire*, II, 315–21; Mackay, *Wake of Cook*, pp. 37–41; G. Jackson, *The British Whaling Trade* (1978), p. 103; St Helens to Grenville, 15 June 1791, BL Add. 59022 fol. 23. For concern about Austrian interest in whaling, Carmarthen to Keith, 20 Dec. 1785, BL Add. 35535 fol. 307.

a 'national treaty' between France and Spain and to authorise the arming of forty-five ships of the line and a proportionate number of frigates. The latter step was taken in light of the armaments of other unnamed powers and to provide security for French trade and colonies; Spain was not mentioned. However, the congruence of the authorisation of the armament with the advice for a national treaty, and the nature of Anglo-Spanish relations, made the objective of the measure readily apparent. The decision was ratified by Louis XVI on 28 August, and on 1 September Montmorin ordered Puyabry to inform Floridablanca that Louis XVI would order the naval armaments as soon as possible, although he added that only thirty of the line could be armed. Montmorin also sought to begin the negotiation of the new national treaty.[78]

The French moves suggested the possibility of war between Britain and the two Bourbon powers,[79] and when Luzerne told Pitt that French armaments were purely defensive, Pitt replied that after the decree of 26 August they could not be seen in that light. When Luzerne communicated the decree to Leeds on 7 September, he told him that it was simply a precautionary measure and that Spain sought a peaceful solution to the crisis. Luzerne reported that the decree had produced a big effect on the British ministry, who, he argued, had been convinced that France would not act,[80] but the response was in fact more one of scepticism about France's ability to mount the naval armament that had been promised. It was argued that France lacked the necessary funds and that the measure was simply for effect. This impression was corroborated by British naval observation of Brest, by French ministerial assurances about their intentions, Montmorin telling the new British envoy, Earl Gower, that the work in the dockyards would proceed very slowly,[81] and by obscure contacts with politicians, popular in the Assembly. The progress of the latter is still unclear, unsurprisingly so given the important role of William Augustus Miles, Britain's answer to Hertzberg, a would-be British diplomatic agent of great fertility in speculation and problematic reliability who was ever ready to claim great successes. Miles was sent to Paris by Pitt in July, Hugh Elliot, a friend of Mirabeau, following in late

---

[78] Decree, 26 Aug., Montmorin to Puyabry, 1 Sept., Montmorin to Fernan-Nunez, Spanish envoy in Paris, 1 Sept., Puyabry to Montmorin, 13 Sept. 1790, AE CP Esp. 629 fols. 235, 231–2, 236–7, 264.

[79] Luzerne to Montmorin, 3 Sept. 1790, AE CP Ang. 574 fol. 210.

[80] Aust to Auckland, 7 Sept., Burges to Auckland, 7 Sept. 1790, BL Add. 34433 fols. 73, 75; Luzerne to Montmorin, 7, 10, 14 Sept. 1790, AE CP Ang. 574 fols. 210, 242–50, 263.

[81] Webb, 'Nootka', p. 144; Auckland to Burges, 1 Sept. 1790, Bod. BB. 30 fol. 55; Van de Spiegel to Auckland, 1 Sept., Burges to Auckland, 7 Sept., Ewart to Auckland, 15 Sept., Leeds to Fitzherbert, 1 Sept., Auckland to Grenville, 4 Sept. 1790, BL Add. 34433 fols. 23, 75, 119, 28066 fol. 241, 58919 fol. 12; Gower to Leeds, 29 Aug. 1790, Browning (ed.), *The Despatches of Earl Gower 1790–92* (Cambridge, 1885), p. 29.

October. Miles made approaches to Talleyrand, Mirabeau and Lafayette, was elected a member of the Jacobin Club and seems to have succeeded in lessening suspicion of Britain among the popular politicians. Elliot worked to the same end and, as a more distinguished, though still unofficial agent, appears to have had more success.[82]

In the meantime, the problem for Britain was that the decree of the National Assembly might offer vital encouragement to the Spanish government,[83] and encourage her to refuse to accept the British terms. As the summer slipped away, the prospect of any successful naval operations in 1790 receded, and the British ministry was left with the problem of a rapidly approaching parliamentary session. Were nothing to have been achieved, then the government would be criticised for the expense and lack of action of the naval armament, the same dilemma that had faced the Walpole ministry in 1729.

Floridablanca's reply on 15 September to Fitzherbert's proposals was not satisfactory. Though the proposals were accepted in principle, British fishermen were not to be allowed to make landings on the American coast, while nothing definite was said about Nootka.[84] Landings by fishermen were seen as a means to conduct contraband trade with Spanish colonists, something that the Spanish government had long sought to stamp out, and the prospect of Britain seeking to incite the native Indian population to throw off Spanish rule was also unacceptable.[85] The reply was dismissed by the British ministry, and Burges was not alone in thinking that there would be war.[86] Tension continued to rise. Luzerne warned Montmorin that Britain was also after French colonies in West Indies, and that the French should reinforce them. In addition, he claimed that the British had secret agents in the most important colony, Saint-Domingue (Haiti).[87] Pressure for action against Spain was also rising within Britain. As on the eve of the War of Jenkins' Ear which broke out in 1739, there was talk of Spanish atrocities against

---

[82] Leeds to Burges, 29 Aug. 1790, Bod. BB. 37 fol. 25; Gower to Pitt, 22 Oct. CUL Add. 6958 no. 858; Pitt to George III, 25 Oct. 1790, Aspinall, *George III*, no. 631; Pitt to Elliot, – Oct., Elliot to Pitt, 26 Oct. 1790, PRO 30/8/102 fols. 121–5, 30/8/139 fols. 123–8; C. P. Miles (ed.), *The Correspondence of William Augustus Miles on the French Revolution 1789–1817* (2 vols., 1890), I, 150–71; Rose, *National Revival*, pp. 578–81; H. V. Evans, 'William Pitt, William Miles and the French Revolution', *Bulletin of the Institute of Historical Research*, 43 (1970), 196–8.

[83] Auckland to Burges, 1 Sept., George Rose MP, Secretary to the Treasury, to Auckland, 2, 24 Sept. 1790, Bod. BB. 30 fols. 55, 27, 159.

[84] Fitzherbert to Leeds, 16 Sept. 1790, PRO FO 72/19.

[85] Puyabry to Montmorin, 26 Oct. 1790, AE CP Esp. 629 fol. 351.

[86] Leeds to Fitzherbert, 2 Oct., Burges to Auckland, 30 Sept. 1790, BL Add. 28066 fol. 285, 34433 fols. 198–9; Charles Townshend MP to Lord Middleton, 27 Sept. 1790, Guildford CRO Brodrick MSS 1248/11 fol. 184; A. and H. Tayler (eds.), *Fife*, p. 220.

[87] Luzerne to Montmorin, 21, 28 Sept. 1790, AE CP Ang. 574 fols. 282, 294–5.

British sailors, one story being 'taken up with a high hand' by the opposition newspapers.[88] There was also call for bold action against Spain from newspapers that were not opposed to the government. By 8 October Howe's fleet at Spithead consisted of forty-three ships of the line, ten frigates and ten smaller craft. In response to a reported Spanish reinforcement of the West Indies, the British sent more forces thither. Fourteen ships of the line, twelve frigates and four smaller craft were reported as ready for sea at Brest.[89]

The British ministry responded to the Spanish reply by sending two drafts of a possible treaty which was to be accepted within ten days.[90] The ultimatum reached Fitzherbert on 12 October and he presented it the next day. Although Floridablanca was willing to accept the terms in essence, his ministerial colleagues met in the Junta de Estado (Cabinet)[91] and on 25 October decided for war. They feared that British claims jeopardised the logic of the Spanish imperial system. Floridablanca, however, brokered a solution by producing a compromise on territorial limits. Territorial waters were to be ten leagues from the coast; the idea of a clear boundary in the south was discarded in favour of an earlier British suggestion that neither power should make settlements in the unoccupied areas there unless to block settlement by a third power; the possible latitudinal limit in the north was rejected, in favour of allowing free settlement to the north of the areas occupied by Spain in April 1789, which included most of the coast of modern California. The land Meares had purchased and the buildings he had constructed were to be returned, and compensation was to be paid for the loss of British effects. British whalers and traders were to be able to operate 'in the Pacific Ocean or in the South Seas, or in landing on the coasts of those seas in places not already occupied, for the purpose of carrying on their commerce with the natives of the country or of making establishments there'. Terms acceptable to Fitzherbert and Floridablanca were presented on 23 October, Charles IV accepted them on the 24th and on the 28th Fitzherbert and Floridablanca signed a Convention, the Junta not being consulted.[92]

Spain had backed down, not least in clearly signing under pressure.

[88] Burges to Auckland, 24 Sept. 1790, BL Add. 34433 fol. 162.
[89] *Public Advertiser*, 1 Nov. 1790; Webb, 'Nootka', 147; Aspinall, *George Prince of Wales* II (1964), no. 535.
[90] Leeds to Fitzherbert, 2 Oct. 1790, BL Add. 28066 fol. 285, PRO FO 72/19.
[91] On this institution, G. Bernard, *Le Secrétariat d'État et Le Conseil Espagnol des Indes (1700–1808)* (Geneva, 1972), pp. 55–7; J. A. Escudero, *Los orígenes del Consejo de Ministros en España* (2 vols., Madrid, 1979), I, 330–52; J. Lynch, *Bourbon Spain 1700–1808* (Oxford, 1989), pp. 301–2.
[92] Convention, Cobbett, 28, 916–18, Manning, 'Nootka Sound', 454–6.

The rights of the British to settle along the coast between Alaska and California and to fish in the Pacific were now established. Pitt, who had feared that Spain would not 'without a struggle give way far enough to meet our demands',[93] was delighted, writing on 4 November:

The decisive answer arrived this morning and is perfectly satisfactory. The Spanish Minister at last agreed on the 24th of October to a project of a Convention containing all we wish ... The terms will I believe be found to secure all that we could demand in justice or had any reason to desire.

That day Howe was ordered to cease his preparations.[94] The British government, however, had not gained all the points it had advanced in the negotiations. British merchants were not to be allowed to trade directly with Spanish America and the British demand for specific borders had been avoided. In May 1791 Floridablanca pressed Fitzherbert, who had been raised to the Irish peerage as Lord St Helens as a reward for negotiating the Convention, to ensure that the former prohibition was respected, revealing at the same time his concern about his domestic position:

the Spanish Minister is the more anxious that the British vessels now on their way to the South Seas should be effectually restrained from touching at any bona fide Spanish settlement, as it is a matter in which he has himself a kind of personal interest; for, amongst the violent attacks made upon him as author of the late Convention it was particularly urged that he had thereby opened a door to an illegal intercourse between Great Britain and the Spanish colonies.[95]

Furthermore, reparation for losses at Nootka was not granted until January 1794, despite considerable British irritation at a delay made necessary in part by the need to establish what had happened. The Opposition was to criticise the terms, as well as the expense of the armament. The rising Whig MP, Charles Grey, later the 2nd Earl Grey who was to play such a prominent role over the First Reform Act, complained in the Commons on 14 December 1790 that British rights to settle were still 'uncertain'. Fox condemned the limits on what the whalers could do. Newspaper criticism of the Convention came from a number of angles. Ayre's *Sunday London Gazette and Weekly Monitor* of 21 November 1790 was sceptical about the reported commercial benefits. The paper argued instead that it would be very expensive to fish in Pacific

[93] Pitt to Stafford, 20 Oct. 1790, PRO 30/29/1/15 no. 97.
[94] Pitt to Pretyman, 4 Nov., Pitt to Edward Eliot, 4 Nov. 1790, Ipswich HA 119 T108/42 no. 265, 108/39 no. 227; Pitt to Addington, 12 Nov., Hood to Addington, 28 Nov. 1790, Exeter, Devon CRO D152/MC1790/OZ 2, 17; Auckland to Pitt, 10 Nov. 1790, PRO 30/8/110 fols. 172–3; Buckingham to Grenville, 9 Nov. 1790, HMC *Dropmore*, I, 611; Dr. Charles Blagden to Henry, 2nd Viscount Palmerston, 22 Nov. 1790, Beinecke, Osborn Shelves C 114.
[95] St Helens to Grenville, 16, 25 May 1791, BL Add. 59022 fols. 18, 20.

waters and that the export market for British manufactures would be very small.[96]

And yet, the resolution of the crisis was seen as a triumph for the British government. It reflected the very successful naval mobilisation, which was a measure of Britain's recovery from the Anglo-Bourbon struggle of 1778–83, and the diplomatic situation. Britain's allies had stood by her, conspicuously so in the case of the Dutch fleet, while Spain had been unable to obtain reliable assistance. Not only was France a weak ally, her problems revealed by discontent in the major dockyard at Brest, but she was also a potential source of subversion, and this was a present threat to mainland Spain that the Spanish government was increasingly concerned about. Puyabry's reports conveyed a sense of the alarm that the Spanish ministry felt about the possible spread of radical sentiments. Frenchmen were expelled or arrested, measures taken to prevent the spread of French works and ideas.[97] The impact of this concern on Spanish foreign policy is unclear. Members of the Junta were clearly willing to continue to defy British claims, whatever the status of their French ally. Keith pointed out in October 1790 that 'as to France the wisest man is *least able* to foresee what will happen there',[98] and this imponderable clearly affected Floridablanca, both in the short term concerning the likely extent of French assistance, and in the longer term relating to the possible influence and impact of French domestic developments.

Given these doubts, it might be suggested that there was something anachronistic about the British triumph. As with the Falklands crisis of 1770, it arose both from the successful British naval mobilisation and from the French failure to fulfil promises to support their Spanish ally.[99] The repetition of this triumph in 1790 concealed the extent to which the Franco-Spanish alliance was being dissolved by Spanish concern about domestic French developments and by the determination of French politicians to redefine French foreign policy and to gain control of it from the crown. Thus the dynastic link between France and Spain became of less importance, and a triumph over it of less moment. Far from threatening Britain's colonial and maritime position, the Franco-Spanish alliance was to be swept aside as a consequence of the changes within France. The two powers were to go to war on 7 March 1793, Spain being

[96] Jackson, Secretary of Legation in Madrid, to Grenville, 29 Dec. 1792, PRO FO 72/25; Spate, *Paradise*, pp. 318–20; Jackson, *Whaling*, pp. 104–5; *Gazeteer*, 6 Feb. 1792; *Gentleman's Magazine*, 61 (1791), 47.
[97] Puyabry to Montmorin, 24, 29 Sept., 26 Oct., 2 Nov. 1790, AE CP Esp. 629 fols. 283, 296–7, 355, 376.   [98] Keith to Auckland, 9 Oct. 1790, BL Add. 34433 fol. 272.
[99] N. Tracy, 'The Falkland Islands Crisis of 1770: Use of Naval Force', *English Historical Review*, 90 (1975), 40–75.

encouraged to this step by British approaches for an alliance. Indeed, Auckland suggested as early as December 1790 that developments in France might lay the basis for better Anglo-Spanish relations.[100]

Thus, the British triumph at Nootka can be seen as anachronistic, one of the last acts of a world of *ancien régime* diplomacy that was soon to be remoulded under the impetus of revolutionary change and challenge. Such a perspective is not, however, terribly helpful. If the dynamics of the Anglo-French-Spanish 'sub-system' were changing, they had never been constant, and it is anyway not appropriate to judge the events of 1790 from the perspective of a hindsight predicated on the basis that the French Revolution changed the world, that it broke out in 1789, that the *ancien régime* elsewhere was thereafter living on borrowed time, and that European international relations should have altered fundamentally in response to the Revolution.

It was French nullity, rather than the threat from France that was crucial in 1790, and this enabled Britain to overawe Spain. Far from that confrontation being regarded as an anachronistic *ancien régime* episode, it can instead be suggested that the race for influence in the Pacific was one of the most important aspects of the politics of this period, one that France's domestic problems made her unable to play a significant role in. France's earlier activity in the Pacific, which was greatly motivated by political and economic considerations,[101] was not sustained at the former level, and, partly as a result, British influence in this, to Europeans, increasingly important ocean grew greatly in this crucial period. In the waters of the south-west Pacific, the British added to their empire Lord Howe Island (1788), the Chatham Islands (1791) and Pitt Island (1791). Captain William Bligh made intelligible charts of Fiji, the Banks group and Aitutaki in the Cooks, Captain Lever discovered the Kermadecs and Penrhyn Island, Captains Gilbert and Marshall discovered the islands that bear their names, and in 1789 Lieutenant John Shortland coasted the shores of Guadalcanal and San Cristobal. The Vancouver expedition explored part of the coast of New Zealand, discovered the Chathams and charted the Snares. The French expedition that set off under D'Entrecasteaux in 1791 circumnavigated Australia, named the Kermadecs, discovered the D'Entrecasteaux islands and explored the Solomans, but the energy that had characterised French activity in the mid-1780s was not maintained, and this activity was cut short by the Revolutionary

---

[100] Auckland to Burges, 21 Dec. 1790, Bod. BB. 30 fol. 89.
[101] Dunmore, *French Explorers*; S. L. Chapin, 'Scientific Profit from the Profit Motive: The Case of the LaPerouse Expedition', *Actes du XIIe Congrès International d'Histoire des Sciences* (Paris, 1971), XI, 45–9, and 'The Men from across La Manche: French voyages, 1660–1790', in D. Howse (ed.), *Background to Discovery*, pp. 81–127.

Wars. The French added nothing to their empire in the south-west Pacific.[102]

It is not an idle question to speculate as to what would have happened had war broken out between Britain and Spain in 1790, because the issue helped to shape the position of both powers. British firmness owed much to a conviction of victory. Auckland, one of the more pacific of British diplomats, wrote of the prospect of war with Spain, 'she may hurt us by her obstinacy, but I *know* that a war would be utter ruin to her both here and in South America, exclusive of the circumstance of our naval superiority'. Fitzherbert was convinced that that superiority had helped him, and referred to his 'negotiating with 60 sail of the line at one's back'.[103] On the other hand, British campaigns against France in the West Indies during the Revolutionary war indicated the problems posed by seeking colonial conquest.[104] In 1790 Britain was prepared for a naval war, rather than a full-scale assault on the Spanish Empire, though plans for the latter were being made right to the end of October. Concern about the situation in Canada and India meant that few troops could be spared from either for amphibious operations. Had the Bourbons obliged by offering their fleets for full-scale naval engagements then the British navy would probably have won these: the Spanish navy, though good and too often underrated, was a smaller force, while its French counterpart was affected by the problems and disorder of the French state. If no such major actions had taken place, then the situation was less favourable for Britain. If the Spanish navy stayed in its bases, principally Cadiz, Ferrol, Cartagena and Havana, then these would have to be blockaded or closely watched, neither an easy task in the days of sail. Dispersing British naval forces in order to support amphibious operations would have made these operations, and their supporting units, vulnerable to a concentration of Spanish naval strength, and thus much of the British navy would have had to be deployed to guard against this risk. The situation would have been exacerbated by the possibility of French intervention, for even if France, as in 1739–40, refused to act on behalf of her Spanish ally, it would be necessary to plan for such action, and thus to keep a large fleet in Channel waters.

The situation was therefore less propitious than might appear. The structure of the Spanish maritime empire could have been disrupted,

---

[102] Beaglehole, *Exploration of the Pacific*, pp. 318–22, and *The Discovery of New Zealand* (2nd edn, Oxford, 1961), pp. 72–3.

[103] Auckland to Burges, 2 Oct., Fitzherbert to Burges, 22 Nov. 1790, Bod. BB. 30 fol. 65, 38 fol. 131.

[104] D. Geggus, *Slavery, War and Revolution: The British Occupation of Saint-Domingue 1793–1798* (Oxford, 1981); M. Duffy, *Soldiers, Sugar and Seapower. The British Expeditions to the West Indies and the War against Revolutionary France* (Oxford, 1987).

but, given the naval technology and capability of the period, it was not practical to plan for control of the seas.[105] The Pitt ministry was fortunate that it was not necessary to go to war, although, had a struggle for colonial mastery been the principal British goal, French weakness meant that 1790 offered one of the best opportunities for success in the eighteenth century. Trevor argued that if Britain had 'listened only to motions of ambition and even interest, every circumstance might induce her to wish for war'.[106] Yet, war to achieve this aim was not the government's objective, and, once the Convention had been signed, pro-ministerial newspapers warned of the hazards and costs of war,[107] in face of opposition criticism that not enough had been gained. Pitt took a major role in the crisis and deservedly reaped much of the credit. The Opposition were unable to capitalise on the dispute, and those ministers who were unhappy about policy, whether in general or specific points, were not vindicated by the successful resolution of the crisis. The lack of a clear Opposition case was indicated by Lady Palmerston's question, 'we want to know *why* we ought to dislike the King's speech'. The government was successful in the Commons debate on 14 December 1790 by a substantial majority: 247–123.[108]

And yet, the Nootka Sound crisis did have some unfortunate effects for British foreign policy. To a certain extent it distracted and delayed attention from the crisis in eastern Europe, for, unlike the situation during the Falklands crisis of 1770, the British ministry had already committed itself heavily to a prospectus for continental international relations. The successful facing down of Spain also left the ministry with an exaggerated sense of British power, which led them to an unsuccessful confrontation with Russia. Auckland observed in November 1790, 'It remains to finish the Turkish business, and to adjust the affairs of the Netherlands.'[109] Like the rest of the government, he anticipated success in both. They were to be proved wrong, and the failure of British

---

[105] HMC, *Dropmore*, I, 587; Dull, 'Why did the French Revolutionary Navy Fail?', *Consortium on Revolutionary Europe. Proceedings*. 1989, II, 121–37; M. Kimbrough, 'The Revolutionary French Navy', *Transactions of the Seventh International Congress on the Enlightenment* (3 vols., cont. pag., Oxford, 1989), 346–9; A. B. Rodger, *The War of the Second Coalition 1798 to 1801* (Oxford, 1964), p. 5; J. Black, 'British Naval Power and International Commitments: Political and Strategic Problems, 1688–1770', and 'Naval Power, Strategy and Foreign Policy 1775–1791', in M. Duffy (ed.), *Parameters of British Naval Power 1650–1850* (Exeter, 1992), pp. 42–6, 93–120.

[106] Trevor to Keith, 8 Nov. 1790, NLS Acc. 9769 72/2/63.

[107] *Public Advertiser*, 10 Nov. 1790.

[108] Ehrman, *Pitt*, I, 570–1; Auckland to Pitt, 10 Nov. 1790, PRO 30/8/110 fol. 172; Lady Palmerston to Malmesbury, 26 Nov. 1790, Winchester, Malmesbury 162; E. A. Smith, *Lord Grey 1764–1845* (Oxford, 1990), pp. 31–2.

[109] Auckland to Pitt, 30 July, Auckland to Burges, 9 Nov. 1790, PRO 30/8/110 fol. 170, Bod. BB. 30 fol. 76.

diplomacy in 1791 helped to weaken the resistance to revolutionary France when war broke out the following year.

In another direction, the Nootka Sound crisis was less favourable than is generally appreciated. The fate of the Pacific coast of modern Canada was still unclear. Indeed, it has with reason been argued that British policy was motivated by a concern to vindicate British principles of colonial sovereignty rather than to secure new dominions.[110] Trade, rather than territory, was most at stake for the British in the Pacific. In 1788 the East India Company had drawn up a project for an agreement with the Spanish Royal Philippine Company, in which Manila was to become a free port enabling the British both to trade indirectly with South America and, as a result, to obtain silver that could be used in the China trade. The company had pressed the government on the matter in 1785 and negotiations were conducted for some time, being resumed after the Nootka Sound crisis in 1793.[111] Although the British flag was hoisted at Nootka when the Spaniards handed over the site of Meares' house in 1795, the position was left to the Indians. Spanish pretensions had been challenged successfully on the coast of modern Canada, but in 1812 the Russians leapfrogged to the south and established Fort Ross 100 kilometres north of Spanish-held San Francisco. In the face of British and American protests, Tsar Alexander I claimed all the coast down to 51°North in 1821. This thinly populated Russian empire was to be shortlived. An Anglo-Russian convention in 1825 fixed the southern limit of Russia's claim at 54°40'.[112] Fort Ross was sold in 1841, Alaska in 1867. Yet, this episode was a reminder of the far-flung nature of Russian power. The range of this power exerted a grip on the imagination. In 1790 it was believed that Catherine II might send a fleet to the Red Sea via Madagascar and Ainslie was instructed to warn the Turks accordingly.[113] In 1791 Russian intentions and power were to be the central issue in British diplomacy and public debate over foreign policy.

---

[110] Mills, 'Real Significance', 122.
[111] Carmarthen to Pitt, 17 Jan. 1785, BL Eg. 3498 fol. 96; B. Atkins, 'Australia's Place in the "Swing to the East"', 1788–1810: Addendum', *Historical Studies. Australia and New Zealand* 8 (1957–9), 316.   [112] Spate, *Paradise*, pp. 320–2.
[113] Leeds to Ainslie, 8 Jan. 1790, PRO FO 78/11; BB. 55.

6   The failure of Britain's continental policy, 1790–1791

when I am to seek the motive of the war in Ochakov; the principle of the war in the rigorous exaction of the status quo against the nation which was first attacked, and the expediency of the war in risquing our fleets in the Baltic against all the difficulties of that sea and without the alliance of any of the powers of the Baltic, and finally the certain and enormous expense to which we shall be immediately subject exclusive of resulting contingencies which by possibility might overset not only the Turkish but the Prussian Empire; and in the present temper of mankind extend the calamity to our own country; I confess to you that I look with astonishment at the levity with which some people urge the war: and all because they say that the national dignity is engaged: I have no idea of national dignity as opposed to national wisdom.

Auckland to Burges, 19 March 1791.

The young Gentleman's easy victory over the cats of Nootka Sound, seems to have induced a propensity for continuing to play with the feline genus; but if I am not much mistaken the old Russian tabby will scratch him harder than he expects.

Dr Campbell, 31 March 1791

… His Majesty, whose uniform views are directed to the preservation of peace, and to the maintenance of the present relative situation of the principal states of Europe. And this principle you will distinctly state to the Emperor as the great and leading object of the policy of this country …

Instructions to Earl of Elgin, 19 April 1791[1]

The settlement of Austro-Prussian differences

The strains in the Anglo-Prussian alliance in early 1790 and the prospect of a new departure in Anglo-Austrian relations indicated both the difficulty of responding to developments when allies were bound together by few shared interests, and the unpredictability of international

---

[1] Auckland to Burges, 19 Mar. 1791, Bod. BB. 30 fol. 136; Campbell to Mylord, 31 Mar. 1791, Preston CRO DDCa 22/19/2; Instructions to Elgin, 19 Apr. 1791, PRO FO 7/23 fol. 94.

developments. The last, in the shape of the succession of a seemingly friendly Leopold II, offered an opportunity to deal with a number of apparently urgent problems that concerned the British government: the situation in the Austrian Netherlands and, therefore, more generally in the Low Countries; the crisis in eastern Europe, or rather the interlocked crises that spanned Europe from the Black Sea to the Balkans; and the strains in the Anglo-Prussian alliance. All were apparently soluble if Austria became more friendly and amenable. That would, it was hoped, ensure that Habsburg authority was re-established in the Austrian Netherlands on terms acceptable to Britain and the Dutch, and also to the local population, so that they were not driven to look for support from France; for, whether the French government was radical or not, such support would be harmful to what were generally seen as British interests. In eastern Europe, a change in Austrian policy would, it was hoped, facilitate the negotiation of peace between her and the Turks, and thus isolate Russia, encouraging her to do likewise. A more reasonable ruler of Austria would also abandon Joseph II's aggressive advocacy of Imperial pretensions. This would ensure that peace in the Balkans would not be followed by an increase in tension in the Empire, which had been a potential problem. It would also serve to reduce Austro-Prussian tension. Thus, Britain would not find herself pressed by her Prussian ally to support aggressive steps: there would no longer be the need or the opportunity for Prussia to act thus.

The complex diplomacy of the spring and summer of 1790 was to leave Britain without an Austrian alliance, but the prospect of an unwelcome war between Austria and Prussia was averted. On some occasions in the spring this did not, however, seem possible. Despite British pressure for an armistice and negotiations on the basis of the *status quo ante bellum*,[2] Prussia continued to prepare for war, hopeful both of Polish support and that the Turks would continue to fight. Leopold wrote to George III on 3 April 1790 seeking his mediation over Belgium and writing of natural links and true interests,[3] but expectations that Leopold's succession would be followed by a dramatic improvement in relations were disappointed, and indeed Leopold was very critical of Britain in letters to his sister Marie Christine. Keith found Austrian policy unsettled and Austria unwilling to abandon Russia. He accused Kaunitz of blocking good relations. On 4 May 1790 Cobenzl told Keith that Austria needed Russia, that Russia alone could defend herself against Prussia and Turkey, but that if Russia abandoned Austria the latter would be in the

---

[2] Leeds to Ewart, 30, 31 Mar. 1790, PRO FO 64/17 fols. 157–61, 164.
[3] Leopold to George III, 3 Apr. 1790, PRO FO 7/20 fol. 43; Aust to Liston, 16 Apr., 5 May 1790, NLS 5567 fol. 73.

'utmost danger'. Russian help was more necessary because Austria could no longer count on her ally France.[4] On 5 May 1790 Montmorin informed Noailles that if Prussia attacked Austria, France would be placed in a very difficult position. He could not see where she would be able to find troops and money to help Austria, an interesting comment on the practicality of French help to Spain in the Nootka Sound crisis. Montmorin was also aware that France could not hope to be asked to mediate a peace in the Balkans. She had close links with both Austria and Turkey and had been responsible for the terms of the last peace treaty between the two powers, the Peace of Belgrade of 1739. And yet France was obviously not able to play a comparable role in the Balkans in 1790, and her role was being taken by Britain. Montmorin understood this, accepted that Austria would have to turn to British mediation, and wrote of 'l'état de nullité' in which France found herself.[5]

Leopold's succession led to British pressure on Turkey to negotiate peace, and on Austria to agree to a preliminary armistice.[6] Separately, Leopold had written to Frederick William II on 25 March 1790, saying he sought peace without territorial gains from the Turks; and in his reply on 15 April the King of Prussia made his willingness for negotiations clear. The British were aware of this direct correspondence. On 26 April the Austrian Conference of ministers agreed that peace had to be concluded with Turkey as soon as possible, and that if Prussia insisted on the *status quo ante bellum* as the basis for this peace it should be accepted.[7] The following month Prussia proposed that Austria accept either the *status quo ante bellum* as the basis for an Austro-Turkish settlement, or the Hertzberg exchange scheme, and on 25 May Leopold indicated his preference for the first. The British ministry continued to stress the value of the *status quo ante bellum*, despite a warning from Van de Spiegel that it would be difficult to persuade Austria and Russia to return their gains.[8] This objective was seen as the best way to secure the collective security system that the British government believed would be the soundest guarantee of peace and stability. It offered also the opportunity, first of integrating Turkey into the international system on terms that would not

---

[4] Keith to Leeds, 6 Apr., 5 May 1790, NLS Acc. 9769 72/2/73, PRO FO 7/20 fols. 146–8; Keith to Ewart, 4 May 1790, Williamwood, 155; Auckland to Keith, 29 June 1790, BL Add. 35542 fol. 279.
[5] Montmorin to Noailles, 5 May 1790, AE CP Aut. 359 fols. 255–7.
[6] Ainslie to Keith, 8 May, Ainslie to Leeds, 8 May 1790, BL Add. 35542 fols. 177–9; Leeds to Keith, 23 May 1790, PRO FO 7/20 fol. 181.
[7] Wandruszka, *Leopold*, II, 265; Ewart to Major General Richard Grenville, Comptroller and Master of the Household to the Duke of York, 19 May 1790, Williamwood 147; Kalinka, 'Politique Prussienne', 674–5; Roider, *Austria's Eastern Question*, p. 188.
[8] Auckland to Burges, 26 May 1790, Bod. BB. 30 fol. 24; Kalinka, 'Politique Prussienne', 676.

leave her simply as a potential victim, secondly the basis for a Russo-Swedish settlement that did not involve Swedish concessions, and thirdly a means to win the alliance of Poland without having to accept any complex territorial exchanges that would be bound to leave dissatisfied powers.

The British position was made clear in a lengthy instruction to Ewart sent on 21 May 1790, one in which Pitt's close interest is indicated by the draft in his papers. British support for the *status quo ante bellum* was presented as in Prussia's interest, more so than Hertzberg's plans; while the possibility of such terms were seen as the product of the intervention of the Triple Alliance, an intervention that did not require participation in the conflict. As with the concurrent crisis with Spain, the threat of action was to be preferred to the use of force, the purpose of diplomacy being seen as giving direction and effect to that threat. Ewart was instructed that

the war should be terminated on such grounds as may leave both the Porte [Turks] and Sweden in a posture to be useful allies, and to contribute to the security of Prussia against any attempts from the courts of Vienna and Petersburg. On this ground His Majesty wished to prevent any considerable change being produced in the relative situation of the belligerent powers, and we thought, that notwithstanding the successes of Austria and Russia against the Porte yet considering the other embarrassments of those courts, and the evident interest of the allies as well as the weight arising from the situation, it was reasonable to propose the status quo as the basis of negotiation.

These objectives were seen as counteracted by the Prusso-Turkish treaty negotiated by Diez, the Prussian envoy in Constantinople, but not yet ratified by Frederick William II. Concluded on 30 January 1790, this exceeded Diez's instructions in committing Prussia first to use force against Austria and Russia and secondly to the Turkish aim of recovering the Crimea.[9] In addition, Prussian policy towards the Austrian Netherlands was seen as unacceptable. If, however, Prussia was reasonable, and Austria and Russia refused an armistice as a preliminary to negotiations, then

His Majesty will be ready in that case, as far as the actual circumstances of his situation may then admit, to take measures for preventing, or resisting any attack from France and Denmark, and to endeavour to give countenance and support to the measures of the Court of Berlin.[10]

Ehrman claimed that the mention of support against any attack by France or Denmark, when the most likely assailants were Austria and

---

[9] Kalinka, 'Politique Prussienne', 671–3; Bagis, *Ainslie*, p. 75.
[10] Leeds to Ewart, 21 May 1790, PRO FO 64/17 fols. 249–53. Draft, PRO 30/8/338.

Russia, was 'in effect a discouragement', and he did not discuss the last clause cited above. There is no doubt that the British government wished to discourage Prussia from starting hostilities, but, in the event of Austria and Russia, rather than Prussia, being unreasonable in British eyes, the situation would be different. A British offer of support against France and Denmark was not without value. They were still allied to Austria and Russia respectively, and, were Prussia to concentrate all her forces against those powers, then her western provinces would be vulnerable to French and Danish attack. Other than in the form of naval action, Britain could do little militarily to harm Austria and Russia, but British land support was not necessary if Prussia could count on Sweden, Poland and Turkey.

Undertaking to endeavour to give countenance and support meant keeping Britain's options open, a reasonable goal in the spring of 1790, especially given uncertainty over Leopold II's intentions. Options were further kept open by stating Britain's support for 'the status quo [ante bellum] or such just and moderate alternative as may be substituted by general consent', an ambiguous phrase, though it was made clear that Hertzberg's plan for exchanges centred on the acquisition of Galicia by Poland was too much. Nevertheless,

if an arrangement could be effected which without involving Prussia in a war, might rescue the Porte from its present difficulties at the expense of only moderate concessions, and at the same time in some degree indemnify even Turkey itself by increasing the power of those to whom it must look for future protection, and by procuring the guaranty of the Allies for its remaining possession; such an issue, with a view even to the Turkish interest might be preferable to the risking the continuance and extension of hostilities by insisting strictly on the status quo.[11]

Frederick William continued his military preparations and on 20 June 1790 ratified the Prusso-Turkish treaty. If the ratification made no mention of the Crimea and left Prussia's agreement to fulfil the terms dependent on her ability to do so,[12] it was, nevertheless, a provocative step, not least because of the customary uncertainty about secret clauses. As with the limited British endorsement of Prussian policy, so the qualifications of Prussian support for Turkey were less apparent to most diplomatic observers than the fact of their alliance. Bagis suggests that Frederick William II may have been influenced by the possibility that ratification would make it easier to persuade the Turks to make territorial concessions to Austria, in return for which elements of the Hertzberg

---

[11] Ehrman, *Pitt*, I, 550 fn. 3; Leeds to Ewart, 21 May 1790, PRO FO 64/17 fol. 255.
[12] Bagis, *Ainslie*, p. 86.

plan could be proposed; by the danger that otherwise Russia and Turkey, who had conducted negotiations, would reach a separate agreement; and by the impending end of the period laid down for ratification.[13]

Unlike Gustavus III, the Turks were to make no separate peace in 1790, and this left the Triple Alliance, most obviously Prussia, with an important role. The readiness of Leopold II, less than happy about the unwillingness of Russia to offer military support against a possible Prussian-inspired Polish invasion of Galicia, to treat without his ally, the restraining hand of Britain on Prussian aggressiveness[14] and problems with Prussian mobilisation, which led the relevant minister to commit suicide,[15] encouraged a move towards negotiations in June 1790 and on 27 June Prusso-Austrian talks began in the Silesian village of Reichenbach. Ewart was initially excluded, because Frederick William still hoped to gain Galicia, but he, and his Dutch counterpart, insisted on playing a role as envoys both of members of the Triple Alliance and of mediating states. Ewart pressed firmly for the option of the *status quo ante bellum*, albeit with possible small and mutually agreed modifications, rather than any bolder scheme, and, in doing so, conformed closely to the wishes of the British government.[16] The terms of the Convention of Reichenbach, signed on 27 July 1790, corresponded to British wishes. Austria was to negotiate peace with the Turks on the basis of the *status quo ante bellum*; if any modifications were made for the security of the Austrian frontier they should be by mutual consent; and Prussia should be compensated by Austria for any acquisitions the latter might make. Belgium was to return to Habsburg rule, but with the pre-Josephine constitutions of the different parts of the Austrian Netherlands. Britain and the United Provinces were to act as guarantors of the Convention. In certain respects this was a triumph for Britain: her principal ally had been dissuaded from a war that was definitely not in Britain's interests. Yet the terms were essentially those outlined by Leopold II in his correspondence with Frederick William II before the negotiations, and, once Prussia had agreed to negotiate, there was little prospect of any others being agreed to. Leopold II was not interested in the opportunism and risk of the Hertzberg scheme.

The Convention of Reichenbach left Britain with four major problems. The first was facilitating peace between Austria and Turkey and this was

---

[13] Ibid., pp. 87–8.
[14] Leeds to Ewart, 25 June 1790, PRO FO 64/18 fols. 55–6; Kalinka, 'Politique Prussienne', 677.
[15] Noailles to Montmorin, 21 July 1790, AE CP Aut. 360 fol. 67; Bernard, 'Austria's Last Turkish War', p. 31.
[16] Leeds to Ewart, 20, 23 July 1790, PRO FO 64/18 fols. 123–6, 137–8.

to be a lengthy and troublesome business. Selim III, whose forces were preparing to attack in Wallachia, considered himself betrayed by Prussia. A number of his ministers thought it worth fighting on, but the news of the Russo-Swedish peace led the Turkish government to decide to negotiate with Austria on the basis of the Convention of Reichenbach. Though a nine-month truce was agreed at Giurgevo on 19 September, envoys of the two powers did not meet under the mediation of the Triple Alliance at Sistova, a Bulgarian town with limited facilities for diplomats, until 31 December 1790, and the treaty was not concluded until 4 August 1791. Secondly, there was the question of how best to persuade Russia to accept the prospect of a similar peace with the Turks. Thirdly, it was necessary to consider how Belgium was to return to being the Austrian Netherlands. Fourthly, and linked to all these problems, was the question of defining an acceptable relationship between Britain and Prussia.

Austria or Prussia?

It is abundantly clear that the Anglo-Prussian alliance was in major difficulties long before the Ochakov Crisis, that in short the domestic aspects of the latter cannot alone explain the collapse of the alliance. There is an obvious echo of the failure of the Anglo-French alliance in 1731 and its Anglo-Austrian successor in 1733.[17] British governmental correspondence in the summer of 1790 about the Prussian ally was very harsh. Her policies were presented as contradictory, her attitudes towards the Turks as dishonourable, her treatment of Britain as dishonest, especially in the ratification of the Prusso-Turkish treaty, despite promises to the contrary.[18] In addition, the Prussian desire to prevent in some way a reintroduction of the Habsburg authority in the Austrian Netherlands on the basis of the *status quo ante Josephus II* was seen by the British ministry as meddlesome, provocative and dangerous.

The problems in the Anglo-Prussian relationship were masked by the successes of the summer of 1790: the avoidance of war, and the settlement at Reichenbach on satisfactory terms. And yet there is evidence of ministerial concern about the direction of British policy. Leeds wrote to Burges, with whom he had a close and confidential relationship, about his 'doubts of the necessity of our hurrying on a general peace in the present

---

[17] J. Black, *The Collapse of the Anglo-French Alliance 1727–31* (Gloucester, 1987); J. Black, 'Anglo-Austrian relations, 1725–1740', *British Journal for Eighteenth Century Studies*, 12 (1989), 29–46.

[18] Auckland to Pitt, 17 July, Leeds to Ewart, 23 July 1790, PRO 30/8/110 fol. 168, FO 64/18 fols. 134–6; Burges to Auckland, 20 July, Burges to Jackson, in charge in Berlin in Ewart's absence in Reichenbach, 23 July 1790, Bod. BB. 47 pp. 5, 13.

moment'.[19] The decision, nevertheless, to press on and seek to incorporate Russia into the Anglo-Prussian system, if necessary by intimidation and even hostilities, can be seen as flawed from the outset, dependent on co-operation with an ally that was both unreliable and interested in different objectives. It could be suggested that this problem was overlooked because the ministry was preoccupied by the crisis with Spain, or even that the need to secure the support of her principal ally during that crisis led to insufficient pressure being exerted on Prussia to conform to British wishes in eastern Europe.

These criticisms are possible but it was still plausible in the late summer of 1790 to feel first that the Anglo-Prussian alliance was working successfully and secondly that there was no acceptable alternative. War had been avoided, the preliminaries of a peace, substantially on the basis of the *status quo ante bellum*, arranged between Austria and Turkey, and there were promising signs that Poland could be brought into the system, her differences with Prussia settled and Prusso-Polish territorial and commercial arrangements secured that would facilitate a major expansion in British trade with Poland. British policy can be explained as an understandable reaction to ambitious Prussian objectives, an attempt to secure a less disturbing British solution first.[20]

In addition, if Britain was to play a major role on the Continent, then it was not clear that there was any better power to ally with. Catherine II did not accept British objectives and was hostile to George III, and this left the choice of Prussia or Austria. Leopold II had already proved a frustrating ruler to negotiate with, and he faced a number of major problems. In mid-July 1790 Cobenzl told Noailles that Austria had never been in a more dangerous situation, not even at the outset of the War of Austrian Succession, when Maria Theresa's succession had been challenged by so many powers, because, he claimed, the degree of internal discontent that faced Leopold II and was fomented by Prussian agents, was much greater than that which had existed in the early 1740s.[21] The situation was of course not completely unprecedented, but it was necessary to look to distant precedents. Harris had compared The Hague in August 1787 to Paris during the Fronde (1648–52),[22] a period of great disorder, and the challenges facing Ferdinand II at the outset of the Thirty Years War (1618–48) were greater than those confronting

[19] Leeds to Burges, 27 June 1790, Bod. BB. 37 fol. 23.
[20] Leeds to Ewart, 20 July, Leeds to Hailes, 23 July 1790, PRO FO 64/18 fols. 127–9, 62/3 fols. 137–8.
[21] Noailles to Montmorin, 14 July 1790, AE CP Aut. 360 fols. 49–50; R. Gragger, *Preussen, Weimar und die ungarische Königskrone* (Berlin/Leipzig, 1923).
[22] James to Gertrude Harris, 21 Aug. 1787, Merton, Malmesbury F.3.3.

Leopold II. Leopold was to overcome speedily the problems he inherited, in large part by abandoning the more foolish of his brother's policies, and by astute political management. It is, therefore, all too easy to overlook the weak state of Austria in the summer of 1790. The Austrian Netherlands had not been regained; peace talks with the Turks under the Reichenbach Convention had not yet begun. It was far from clear that Leopold would be able to restore order in his dominions, especially Galicia and Hungary. The Hungarian Diet was interested in the idea of a Prussian guarantee of Hungarian rights. Austrian finances had suffered both from the Turkish war and from the breakdown of order. Weaknesses in the Austrian army had been revealed both in the war with Turkey and in the confrontation with Prussia in the first half of 1790.

Aside from the weaknesses of Austria as a potential ally, it was also by no means clear that Leopold II would be willing to act against Russia. A strong Russia was Austria's best guarantee against Prussia and Turkey, even more so thanks to French weakness. Given Kaunitz's complaint in July 1790 about the despotic and vehement tone of the British and Prussian envoys, it is unlikely that pressure to take action against Russia would have been welcomed, and the following year Leopold was to show that he would not yield to such pressure. On 25 September 1790 Kaunitz even told the Prussian envoy, Jacobi, that, despite Reichenbach, the Austrians had the right to help Russia if the latter was attacked by Prussia.[23]

Thus, for the British ministry there was no question of switching from Prussia to Austria. Concern about Kaunitz's continued influence made Hertzberg appear less exceptional as a problem. There was of course the possibility of better relations between the three powers, Britain, Prussia and Austria. They resulted from Reichenbach, and played a major role in British calculations in late 1790, and in the spring of 1791, but the British were to be disappointed during the crisis with Russia. The Austrians sought reconciliation with Britain,[24] but they no more wanted to surrender the initiative and follow where she might lead, than the British did with Prussia, or, as the British were to discover the following summer, than the Prussians did with them.

The return of Belgium to Habsburg rule

The Convention of Reichenbach encouraged the British ministry to clarify its position over the Austrian Netherlands. In May 1790 Burges had urged the agent from the Estates of Brabant to accept the favourable

[23] Vivenot, *Kaunitz*, p. 7; Keith to Ewart, 26 Sept. 1790, Malmesbury 148; Elgin to Pitt, 27 Dec. 1790, PRO 30/8/132 fol. 165.   [24] Vivenot, *Kaunitz*, p. 9.

terms offered by Leopold.[25] The success of the negotiations at Reichen-bach led the Triple Alliance to accept the return of Habsburg rule, Leopold promising to restore the constitutional situation under Maria Theresa. The British government was convinced that an independent Belgium would be a vulnerable state, demanding costly protection, and, subsequently, a commercial and possibly political rival. It sought the return of Habsburg rule and, though hopeful that this would be peaceful, was willing to contemplate it occurring through invasion.[26] There was no sense of support for self-determination, no departure from pragmatism and self-interest in the attitude of the British ministry; but it was at least more consistent than that of Frederick William II, who excused his abandonment of the cause of independence by pleading political necessity. His attitude towards the Belgians was to prefigure the greater Prussian betrayal of the Poles in 1791–3. In the face of British opposition, the Prussians abandoned their suggestions of Belgian–Austrian negoti-ations in Berlin and Prussian support for the Belgians in the negoti-ations.[27]

The British and Dutch urged the Belgians to send envoys to negotiate on the terms of the return of Habsburg authority at The Hague, and the Belgians asked the Triple Alliance to prevent an Austrian invasion while negotiations proceeded. The British wanted Leopold to invite the Triple Alliance formally to co-operate in negotiating a settlement and to agree that, even if force had to be used, the 'ancient constitution' should still be restored.[28] The possibility of a peaceful settlement was, however, lost because of the unwillingness of both sides to settle. The Belgians, affected by the pressures of their serious internal divisions, were unwilling to offer any terms until 21 November 1790, the day after Leopold's deadline, while the Austrian position was strengthened by the armistice with the Turks, which allowed the move of troops towards Belgium.

British concern about developments in the area was increased by rumours about French interest. Auckland reported in September 1790 that the National Assembly had intimated to its Belgian counterpart that it would send 60,000 troops to help resist any Austrian advance.[29] There was, of course, even less chance of it doing so than of it arming forty-five ships of the line, but one of the major reasons for British willingness to

[25] Burges to Keith, 23 May 1790, BL Add. 35542 fol. 197.
[26] Leeds to Auckland, 27 July 1790, PRO FO 37/30 fols. 75–6.
[27] Ewart to Leeds, 1 Sept. 1790, BL Add. 34433 fol. 21; Jackson to Elgin, 25 Dec. 1790, Broomhall 60/23/43.
[28] Leeds to Keith, 16 Aug. 1790, PRO FO 7/21 fols. 111–14.
[29] Auckland to Burges, 11 Sept. 1790, Bod. BB. 30 fol. 58.

see Habsburg authority restored was their concern to see the region stabilised, and possible French moves thereby blocked. That was also the reason for the stress on the restoration of the 'ancient constitution', which, it was assumed, would assuage Belgian grievances. On 21 November 1790 the Belgians suggested a compromise, the traditional resort of *ancien régime* diplomacy, a dynastic expedient: that Leopold's second son become hereditary Grand Duke of Belgium. Leopold was not interested in such a compromise. His troops invaded Belgium on 24 November, their divided and disheartened opponents putting up very little resistance. One Belgian force was under a half-pay British officer, John Money, who had been appointed a major-general by the Belgians. The Austrian representative at the Conference in The Hague, Count Mercy, told the envoys of the Triple Alliance that Leopold no longer accepted their intervention. Brussels fell on 3 December.

The secret instructions for Thomas, 7th Earl of Elgin, ostensibly sent to congratulate Leopold on his coronation as Emperor, but also ordered to explain the British attitude towards Belgium and to press for a peaceful restoration of Habsburg authority, were thus rendered irrelevant before he even left London.[30] Belgium had become the Austrian Netherlands again, having put up even less resistance than the Dutch Patriots in 1787, although the situation was still far from stable. The Austrian reliance on force rather than negotiation was not welcomed by the British. Auckland protested, but the crisis was resolved, first by the speedy success of the invasion, and secondly by the willingness of Leopold to agree to the restoration of ancient rights and privileges. Ewart successfully pressed Frederick William II to accept the Austrian move. By a convention signed at The Hague on 10 December 1790, this new settlement was guaranteed by the Triple Alliance.[31] Leopold, however, refused to ratify the Hague Convention.

Changing international relations

The way for the Austrian invasion of Belgium had been cleared by the Prussian acceptance of Leopold's position at Reichenbach and by French weakness. Resistance had been perfunctory. And yet the invasion was of considerable importance. It appeared to represent a major check to forces for change throughout western Europe, to encourage the sense that

[30] Leeds to Elgin, 29 Nov. 1790, PRO FO 7/23 fols. 3–7; Aust to Alexander Straton, 29 Nov. 1790, Ipswich HA 239/2/74. There is nothing relevant in S. Checkland, *The Elgins 1766–1917* (Aberdeen, 1988).
[31] Auckland to Pitt, 3 Dec., Ewart to Pitt, 2 Dec. 1790, PRO 30/8/110 fols. 176–7, 30/8/133 fol. 272; Straton to Leeds, 4, 8, 11, 15 Dec. 1790, Ipswich HA 239/2/1; Auckland to Grenville, 15 Dec. 1790, BL Add. 58919 fol. 13.

French radicals could be defeated in a similar fashion. The invasion was also an aspect of what Britain was trying to achieve in Europe: a return to stability, the freezing of structures, frontiers and constitutions. And yet, the reimposition of Habsburg control both reflected and contributed to an aspect of greater volatility in international relations, namely the growing strength and independence of Austria in 1790–1. The ending of the conflicts and confrontations in eastern Europe created a situation of greater unpredictability, of a questioning of objectives and alliances, and of new alignments. It was this that was to be responsible both for the Second and Third Partitions of Poland (1793 and 1795), and for the ability of Prussia and Austria to act in western Europe.

The 'decisive and permanent shift in the configuration of power in Europe' which Blanning dates to 1787–92, and the reconstruction of eastern Europe which he somewhat confusingly dates to 'the period after 1787' (apparently up to 1795 for he includes the Third Partition),[32] were in fact chronologically very much a two-stage process, and each stage pointed in very different directions. The first stage was that, variously, of confrontation and conflict between the Austro-Russian alliance, and the Triple Alliance, plus Turkey, Sweden and Poland. Though it was marked by serious defeats for Turkey and Sweden, it culminated in major military and diplomatic setbacks for Austria and Russia, and the serious weakening of their alliance.

It was the very different second stage that saw Poland partitioned and the major changes referred to by Blanning. This period was distinct from the first stage, made different by the end of the automatic hostility between Prussia and Austria–Russia that had given cohesion not only to the years 1787–90, but also to the whole of the 1780s. This hostility had given other smaller powers room for manoeuvre, rather as Bourbon-Austrian opposition had provided opportunities for the Wittelsbachs, Hanover, Prussia and Savoy-Piedmont for much of the first half of the century. The end of such opposition had resulted in major changes, the Treaty of Aranjuez of 1752 bringing 40 years of stability to Italy and ending the opportunity for important initiatives by Savoy-Piedmont (Kingdom of Sardinia).[33] Franco-Austrian understanding played a major

[32] Blanning, 'French Revolution and Europe', 187–8.
[33] Livet (ed.), *Recueil... Cologne* (1963), lxii; J. Black, 'The Development of Anglo-Sardinian Relations in the First Half of the Eighteenth Century', *Studi Piemontesi*, 12 (1983), pp. 58–9; D. Kosary, conclusions for the session on 'Les "Petits Etats" face aux changements culturels, politiques et économiques de 1750 à 1914', Comité International des Sciences Historiques, *XVIe Congrès International des Sciences Historiques, Actes III* (Stuttgart, 1986), p. 182; J. Black, 'The Problems of the Small State: Bavaria and Britain in the Second Quarter of the Eighteenth Century', *European History Quarterly*, 19 (1989), 26, 30.

role in keeping the Empire peaceful in 1764–77. Similarly, from 1792 better relations between the partitioning powers, their increased understanding and co-operation, transformed Poland from reality to aspiration, and helped to ensure that, with that important exception, eastern Europe changed far less than the western half of the continent in that revolutionary decade. It is possible to see the second stage as a continuation of the first, or indeed not to differentiate between them, but this is misleading, a failure to note the distinct nature of specific conjunctures. British diplomats were to be aware of major changes in central and eastern Europe between early 1790 and mid 1791, of a transition from rival power blocs to a more ambiguous and shifting situation. In early 1790 Britain had a major role to play as a prominent member of one of the two alliances that provided structure to the affairs of Europe. By mid 1791 her voice was not heard and a year later she was clearly isolated.

Having addressed above the question of whether the British ministry should have sought the alliance of Austria rather than Prussia, there is therefore the additional question of whether it should have realised in 1790 that the entire situation was changing out of all recognition, with potentially important consequences for Britain, that the issue of what type of policy Britain should pursue was to be pushed to the forefront of attention by developments over which she had no control. The more familiar way to approach this question is to ask whether the British government over-emphasised its capacity for intimidating Russia in the Ochakov crisis, and, by backing down, destroyed the Anglo-Prussian alliance, leading to British isolation. Yet, this crisis can be seen as a symptom both of the wider problem of the tension between action and passivity, interventionism and isolation in British policy, and of the more specific problems confronting Britain as the major central and eastern European powers interacted and responded to developments in 1790–2.

British ministers and diplomats were to have a very divided response to the Ochakov crisis, and their discussions about the advisability and practicality of confronting Russia reflected wider questions about the purposes of British policy. At the same time, the general direction of that policy, towards the creation of an all-encompassing collective security system, based on stability and the preservation of the *status quo*, in essence a repetition of the Stanhopian defence of the Utrecht system in 1716–21 and Newcastle's policies in 1748–55,[34] was being undermined by the changes outlined above. Freed from the threat of Prussian attack,

---

[34] J. Black, 'The British attempt to preserve the peace in Europe 1748–1755', in H. Duchhardt (ed.), *Zwischenstaatliche Friedenswahrung in Mittelalter und Früher Neuzeit* (Cologne, 1991), pp. 227–43.

Austrian policy was characterised by independence and unpredictability: Leopold II refused to become simply a member of the new system. However, while Prussia remained opposed to Russia, there was no prospect of a return to the partitioning system. The British government could still use the Prussian alliance to put pressure on Russia, but, in doing so, they were working on the assumption that an enforced Russo-Turkish peace, on terms acceptable to the Triple Alliance, would have cemented the collective security system. In fact, by giving Russia and Prussia fresh options and opportunities, it would have undermined that system, arguably as speedily as the actual British abandonment of Prussia during the Ochakov Crisis.

These problems were not clear during the summer and autumn of 1790. Instead, there was concern about the extent to which pressure on Russia would be weakened by unexpected developments, especially the surprising separate Russo-Swedish peace, and the need to concentrate Anglo-Dutch naval strength on a possible war with Spain. No more a believer in limited wars than his contemporaries, Gustavus III had decided to try to seize St Petersburg in 1790, and to that end sought to gain control of the Baltic and the Gulf of Finland. He was unsuccessful, attacks on Russian squadrons on 2 and 4 May, the second under the personal command of Gustavus, both failing. A major engagement in the Gulf of Finland on 23 May was inconclusive. The Swedish cannon had been heard in St Petersburg, but, after the battle, the Russians were able to blockade the Swedes in Vyborg. On 28 June a major galley engagement took place off Sveaborg. The Russians were defeated, but the cumulative toll of recent battles on the Swedish fleet was considerable and Gustavus wanted peace. Auckland commented accurately after the victory: 'His Swedish Majesty rises greatly in the opinion and respect of Europe, though I fear in spite of all his brilliant exertions and perseverance, that he is still on the brink of ruin.'[35]

A man of absolutes, Gustavus saw little point in fighting if he could not win. The Triple Alliance wished to see him remain at war with Russia, because that would put pressure on Catherine II to yield to the threat of action on behalf of the Turks. In addition, it was felt important that the eventual Russo-Swedish peace should be part of a general peace settlement for eastern Europe mediated by the Triple Alliance, and thus under its guarantee. This would, it was hoped, bring stability, as well as peace, to eastern Europe and maintain the importance, and thus cohesion, of the Triple Alliance. In place of the Westphalian settlement, with its guarantor role for France and Sweden, and the Teschen agreement, with

[35] Auckland to Burges, 29 July 1790, Bod. BB. 30 fol. 46.

its role for Catherine II, there was to be a more comprehensive peace arranged and presided over by the Triple Alliance.

One of the major problems with such a schema was that it required all disputes to be arranged according to an agenda and time-scale laid down by the alliance, but Gustavus III was not willing to conform to this. British reluctance to pay subsidies was a contributory factor, though the Prussian government was informed that, if absolutely necessary, Britain would join with Prussia in providing money.[36] However, the financial issue was but a symptom of the wider failure of the Triple Alliance to meet Gustavus' expectations. By not attacking Austria in 1790, a move that would have activated the Austro-Russian understanding about mutual defence and complemented the Turkish attack on Russia in 1787, Prussia had ensured that the campaigning season of 1790 would pass without any new military pressure on Russia. Furthermore, there was the danger that a negotiated peace encompassing Russia would spring from the train of negotiations begun, amidst scenes of rural squalor, at Reichenbach. This would leave Gustavus III isolated, or, if he was included in the peace, it would be on the basis of the *status quo ante bellum*. Catherine II was willing to grant him such terms, without his having to risk another year of expensive and unpredictable conflict, and the campaign of 1790 did not encourage Gustavus to feel that he would be able to obtain better terms, especially as Russia was not under military pressure from Turkey.

To fight on in order to be included in a possible collective security system, offered certain cost and the uncertain prospect of a nebulous gain. Direct negotiations at Verela in Finland led to a treaty signed on 14 August 1790. The treaty was based on the *status quo ante bellum*, the general British goal, and, by recognising the new Swedish constitution of 1772 and renouncing intervention in Swedish politics, Catherine had also accepted Gustavus III's monarchical revolution, and thus abandoned the Russian policy of keeping Sweden weak by supporting constitutional limitations on governmental authority. This new policy of non-intervention bore fruit in Catherine's instructions to the new Russian envoy in Stockholm.[37] And yet, the peace was greeted by her with delight as removing one of her enemies from the war, and that without the humiliating mediation of the Triple Alliance. The treaty showed that it was not necessary to turn to that alliance in order to obtain acceptable peace terms. Conversely, British ministers and diplomats reacted angrily, accusing Gustavus III of letting down both the Turks

---

[36] Leeds to Ewart, 21 May 1790, PRO FO 64/17 fol. 257.
[37] H. A. Barton, 'Russia and the Problem of Sweden-Finland, 1721–1809', *East European Quarterly*, 5 (1972), 450.

and the Triple Alliance.[38] On 11 July 1789 Gustavus had signed a treaty with the Turks, in which, in return for subsidies, he had promised not to make a separate peace. Indeed, Burges feared that there was some truth in reports that Spanish gold had persuaded Gustavus to settle with Catherine. Her success in freeing herself from one of her enemies might well, it was thought by some, discourage Britain from fighting over Nootka. The Spaniards had indeed played a role in opening channels of communication,[39] but the terms reflected shared Russian and Swedish interest in peace, not Spanish bribery. The reports, however, indicated that belief in conspiracy and bribery was not restricted to revolutionary and counter-revolutionary circles; rather, it pervaded the whole of *ancien régime* diplomacy and was inherited by the politicians and commentators of the age of revolution.

The Treaty of Verela, yet another example of the emergence from obscurity of minor settlements that characterised the peace-making process in eastern Europe, lessened both the pressure on Catherine II and the prospect of any successful concerted action by the Triple Alliance. Whereas Prussia could strike at Russia across Poland, with which a defensive treaty was signed on 29 March 1790, Britain could only act by the use of naval force. Though the dispatch of a squadron to the Black Sea, where Russian and Turkish fleets had been in conflict for several years, was discussed, this posed formidable logistical problems; also the Black Sea was unknown to the British navy. In practice, naval action would mean a British fleet in the Baltic, a step pressed by Whitworth, but such a fleet would depend heavily on local bases for replenishment and repair. That had been the pattern of British operations when the navy had last been deployed in the Baltic, during the reign of George I, and the technological situation had not changed.[40] Given the close relations between Denmark and Russia, this policy had assumed that support would be provided by Sweden; while the shallow waters of

---

[38] Auckland to Grenville, 4 Sept. 1790, BL Add. 58919 fol. 12; Leeds to Burges, 6 Sept. 1790, Bod. BB. 37 fol. 26; Gabard, *chargé* in Vienna, to Montmorin, 11, 15 Sept. 1790, AE CP 360 fols. 173–4, 178.

[39] Burges to Auckland, 21 Sept. 1790, BL Add. 34433 fol. 147; Whitworth to Ewart, 16 Apr. 1790, Williamwood vol. 148; A. M. Schop Soler, *Die spanisch-russischen Beziehungen im 18. Jahrhundert* (Wiesbaden, 1971), p. 153.

[40] Whitworth to Ewart, 1 Apr. 1790, Williamwood vol. 148; D. Aldridge, *Admiral Sir John Norris and the British Naval Expeditions to the Baltic Sea* 1715–1727 (Ph.D., London, 1971); Aldridge, 'The victualling of the British naval expeditions to the Baltic Sea between 1715 and 1727', *Scandinavian Economic History Review*, 12 (1964), 1–25; Webb, 'Sea Power in the Ochakov Affair of 1791', *International History Review*, 11 (1980), p. 21; Aldridge, 'The Royal Navy in the Baltic', in W. Minchinton (ed.), *Britain and the Northern Seas* (Pontefract, 1988), pp. 75–9; R. C. Anderson, *Naval Wars in the Baltic during the sailing ship epoch 1522–1850* (1910).

much of the Baltic and the strength of Russian galley forces ensured that it would also be valuable for the British to be supported by the Swedish galley fleet.

Swedish neutrality did not, however, end the issue of the dispatch of a British fleet to the Baltic. As when last pressed by Prussia, during the Seven Years War,[41] this was seen as both militarily and politically crucial. Militarily, it would protect the Prussian coast from Russian naval attacks and cover the flank of any invasion of Livonia. Politically, a British fleet would be tangible proof of Britain's commitment to her ally and would overawe Denmark. And yet, there were problems, as Leeds made clear in a secret instruction to Ewart of 14 August 1790. This conveyed George III's approval

of the measure adopted by the King of Prussia of again recommending to the Empress of Russia a pacification with Sweden and the Porte, on the terms of the status quo; and also of the determination taken by His Prussian Majesty to collect troops towards the Russian frontier, for the purpose of giving weight to his representation ... the King will renew his instructions to his minister at St Petersburg to cooperate with that of Prussia, and will also take measures for assembling a squadron ready to sail at a short notice for the North Seas, should circumstances render such a proceeding necessary ... His Majesty however is desirous that the King of Prussia should, if possible, avoid actual measures of force, especially as in the present advanced season of the year, and in the uncertainty of what may be the issue of his negotiations with Spain, His Majesty cannot answer for being able actually to send a squadron into the Baltic.[42]

Ewart was not instructed to say that Britain would be unable to send a fleet as soon as the ice cleared the following spring, and, to that extent, his instructions helped to mislead the Prussians, but, as yet, the government had not decided that it would not send a fleet. Instead, it was reacting to circumstances, necessarily so, in naval terms, given the uncertainty about the possibility of hostilities with Spain and France. Such an *ad hoc* policy sat ill with the clearly defined aim of enforcing peace on the basis of the *status quo ante bellum*, but it was not only necessary, but also seemed sensible to British diplomats who were optimistic about the chances of Catherine II agreeing to such terms. Francis Jackson, Secretary of Legation at Berlin, reported,

All that is required here is that Russia may not be allowed to employ her naval force against the coasts of Prussia, and that a declaration should be made at Petersburg to that purport, and supported, *if necessary*, by the appearance of a fleet in the Baltic; of this, however, the necessity appears very doubtful; as the

---

[41] J. Black, 'Naval power and British foreign policy in the age of Pitt the Elder', in Black and Woodfine (eds.), *Naval Power*, pp. 100–3.
[42] Leeds to Ewart, 14 Aug. 1790, PRO FO 64/18 fols. 216–17.

very idea of such an apparition will probably suffice to frighten the Russians into almost any terms that may accompany it.[43]

Such remarks might appear over-optimistic, but, as Robert Liston pointed out from Stockholm, 'one can hardly imagine that in her present exhausted condition, she will hazard a contest with Prussia, Poland and Britain, in addition to the Turkish quarrel'.[44]

Catherine was indeed keen to end the war with the Turks. In secret discussions with them in the autumn of 1789 the Russians had demanded the acknowledgement of former gains, including the Crimea, an advance of the frontier from the Dnieper to the Dniester, the creation of an independent state of Dacia from Moldavia, Wallachia and part of Bessarabia under Catherine's grandson Constantine, peace with Joseph II, and the exclusion of Gustavus III from the settlement, which would have left him vulnerable to Russian action. Such demands would have been whittled down in negotiations, but on 24 October 1789 the new Sultan, the young and energetic Selim III, had proclaimed a Holy War, and thus ended the negotiations.[45] The following spring, her growing problems led Catherine to try again. In March 1790 she authorised Potemkin to abandon the Dacian plan and the idea of an independent Moldavia for Constantine, and thus to offer terms that more realistically reflected the progress of the war and the need for compromise as part of the peace process. The following month, Potemkin suggested terms that would leave the Turks Wallachia, Moldavia, Akkerman and Bender. Catherine would promise not to intervene in Georgia. Selim, however, still confident of the benefits of Prussian and Swedish intervention that he mistakenly anticipated, rejected the terms.[46] These negotiations paralleled discussions over possible terms elsewhere in Europe. The Russian government rejected the British proposal of an armistice on the grounds that the Turks would use one in order to trick Austria and Russia. Subsequently, Vorontsov proposed a Dniester frontier to the British, arguing that the arid and uncultivated nature of the land between there and the Bug ensured that its acquisition would not augment Russian strength or diminish that of the Turks. Leeds replied in June to the Russian demand to be informed of what terms would be deemed acceptable by stating that these would be either the *status quo ante bellum*

subject, however, to some reasonable modifications, or one founded upon such exchange between the different powers, and those immediately in their

---

[43] Jackson to Burges, 4 Aug. 1790, Bod. BB. 36 fol. 60; Ewart to Auckland, 1 Sept. 1790, BL Add. 34433 fol. 19.
[44] Liston to Auckland, 10 Sept. 1790, BL Add. 34433 fol. 82.
[45] Madariaga, *Catherine*, p. 410.
[46] Shaw, *Between Old and New*, p. 57; Madariaga, *Catherine*, p. 414.

neighbourhood, as may tend to conciliate their different interests and pretensions, and, at the same time, prevent any material alteration on the while, in the Balance of Power in the North and East of Europe.

The following month, Leeds informed Vorontsov that the Russian proposal of a frontier on the Dniester would not satisfy the Turks. In August Vorontsov was sent fresh instructions. A Dniester frontier was presented as a barrier that would ensure a permanent peace. The Russians sought Anglo-Prussian pressure on the Turks to accept Potemkin's proposals. The British government rejected these terms in October, arguing that they conformed neither to the interests of the Turks nor to the general basis on which Britain wanted the negotiations founded.[47]

The war continued, but it was clear that Catherine wanted peace, and that it was therefore a good opportunity for the Triple Alliance to offer assistance in securing it. The British government was concerned about the possibility of a separate Russo-Turkish peace,[48] though Leeds told Vorontsov that it was willing to accept one, provided that the Porte was willing to join the system of the Triple Alliance afterwards.

The Prussian and British governments were, however, unwilling to rely on separate Russo-Turkish negotiations, although that was both the wisest policy, and, in the end, such negotiations were to end the conflict. Both governments feared that such a peace could only be obtained on terms that would centre on substantial Turkish territorial concessions, which would consolidate the Russian position on the northern shore of the Black Sea. From the Prussian point of view, any territorial changes in eastern Europe that were not matched by an equivalent for Prussia were unacceptable, as they would lead to a relative decline in Prussian power. This had been the Prussian position during the last Russo-Turkish conflict, that of 1768–74, and it had provided the rationale for Frederick II's search for an equivalent at the expense of Poland, a search that had led to the First Partition. Indeed, in 1790–1, at the same time that Prussia prepared for a war with Russia in which Polish co-operation would be important, she was interested in a repetition of just such an arrangement, again at the expense of Poland.

---

[47] Osterman to Vorontsov, 1, 26 May, 27 Aug., Leeds to Whitworth, 15 June, Leeds to Vorontsov, 17 July, 9 Oct. 1790, PRO FO 78/12B.

[48] 'The account of Count Lusi's conference with the Grand Vizir … seems to have removed every apprehension of Prince Potemkin's being able to succeed in his endeavours of bringing about a peace without the intervention of the Allies', Leeds to Ewart, 10 Sept. 1790, PRO FO 64/18 fol. 246.

The Polish question

The Polish question was to play a major role in the development of British governmental attitudes towards Russia in 1790–1.[49] For the British government, substantial Russian gains at the expense of Turkey were unacceptable, not so much because of the threat to the security and future integrity of the Turkish Empire, although that was a factor, as because such gains would threaten the entire basis of recent British diplomacy, with its stress on the *status quo ante bellum*. They would make the successful conclusion of an Austro-Turkish peace difficult, because Austria might demand significant territorial gains; and they would also increase Prussian dissatisfaction with British diplomatic restraint and lend fresh impetus to her desire for gains. Under the Convention of Reichenbach, Khotin and other Austrian gains in Moldavia and Wallachia were to remain in Austrian hands until the end of the war between Turkey and Russia. A peace that left Russia with territorial gains might leave Austria reluctant to fulfil her agreement. The Prussian position in late 1790 was unusual, for, as a result of the Reichenbach Convention and thanks to British pressure, she was not actively pursuing territorial gains. Peace would cement this stability. Possibly the British were naive in thinking that this situation could last for any length of time, though, in fact, Prussia had gained no territory since 1772. It would certainly not last if Russia made major gains. Thus, Russian acquisitions would reactivate that ever adaptable diplomatic *perpetuum mobile* of the period, Hertzberg's exchange scheme, except that it would be more clearly a device for equivalent gains. The obvious sphere for Prussian expansion in eastern Europe after the Convention of Reichenbach was Poland, the power with which she had the longest frontier. Russian gains from Turkey would also threaten Poland's south-eastern frontier and block hopes for an expansion of Polish trade via the Black Sea.

Positive interest in Poland at the highest reaches of the British government was new. During both the War of the Polish Succession (1733–5) and again in the early 1750s, when the Polish succession became an issue, the British government had taken the attitude that Poland was a long way away, and that British interests there, in the shape of keeping the Bourbon candidate out, were best served by Britain's allies. Britain did not take a role in the Polish royal election of 1764. This has been seen as a failure to appreciate the importance of the election for the alliance

---

[49] R. H. Lord, *The Second Partition of Poland. A Study in Diplomatic History* (Cambridge, Mass., 1915); J. Lojek, 'The International Crisis of 1791: Poland between the Triple Alliance and Russia?', *East Central Europe*, 2 (1975), 1–63; J. Lojek, 'British Policy toward Russia, 1790–1791, and Polish Affairs', *Polish Review*, 28, 2 (1983), 3–17.

diplomacy of the period after the Seven Years War.[50] That is true, but it reflects a criticism of British foreign policy that exaggerates Britain's capacity for manoeuvre. This emerged clearly at the time of the First Partition of Poland in 1772. The military and diplomatic problems that any British response would have encountered were considerable, not least in terms of co-operation with France. Despite feelers towards such co-operation, in particular on the part of George III, the decision not to act reflected a sensible response to Britain's international and domestic position.

And yet, Poland was not so remote or so unimportant to Britain, that the government could not be stirred. Frederick II's attempt to follow up his gains in the First Partition, by annexing Danzig [Gdansk] or at least crippling its trade, led to British diplomatic action and moves against Prussian exports to Britain. Harris, then envoy in Berlin, observed:

our national honour as well as our national interests will not allow us to be infatuated by his politics or intimidated by his strength, and for our honour it becomes us at this moment to risk something rather than to suffer him to exercise such outrageous and wanton acts of oppression, unnoticed.

Danzig though was exceptional. It was Poland's leading port and Britain enjoyed a considerable trade with Poland and one characterised by a favourable balance of trade. Danzig had also been a major supplier of timber for the British navy during the Seven Years War. Concern for Danzig and its trade did not extend to the rest of Poland, although the brutal exercise of power by a strong neighbour that was at stake in the case of Danzig was scarcely confined to that city. Successive British ministries remained concerned about Danzig.[51] In 1783 Fox tried to co-ordinate opposition to a possible Prussian annexation, encouraging himself with the reflection that Frederick II would not act if such a step was to be widely disapproved of. Lord Dalrymple, the envoy in Warsaw, suggested, however, that neither Austria nor Russia would observe their guarantees of Polish frontiers after the First Partition, and that the notion of equivalence would lead to a loss of territory, 'if the Emperor attempts to make any conquests, on the side of Turkey, the King of Prussia will immediately enter this country'.[52]

[50] Scott, *British Foreign Policy*, p. 64.
[51] Ibid., pp. 197–202; Harris to Keith, 3 Jan. 1773, BL Add. 35504 fol. 209; W. F. Reddaway, 'Great Britain and Poland, 1761–1772', *Cambridge Historical Journal*, 4 (1934), 223–62; W. Konopczyński, 'England and the First Partition of Poland', *Journal of Central European Affairs*, 8 (1948), 1–23.
[52] Fox to Keith, 21 Sept. 1783, PRO FO 7/7; Dalrymple to Keith, 11 Nov. 1783, BL Add. 35530 fol. 173; Alexander Gibson, Consul in Danzig, to Dorset, 17 Feb. 1784, KAO C188/18.

Aside from Danzig, Poland scarcely featured in the foreign policy of British governments in the late 1770s and early 1780s. Carmarthen might look widely for potential allies in 1784, but there was little to be gained from Poland, and, given the Foreign Secretary's lack of interest in commercial issues, it is not surprising that Alexander Gibson, Consul in Danzig, complained in 1788 about his failure to respond to Gibson's attempt to interest him both in the fate of the town and in regulating Prussian tolls on the Vistula so that Anglo-Polish trade could increase. Three years earlier, Pitt had suggested 'complying with the wishes of Russia' over Danzig in order to help Anglo-Russian relations. British envoys to Poland, such as Charles Whitworth (1785–8), received few instructions. Poland was dominated by Russia; indeed Noailles observed in 1784 that Poland was like a Russian province, adding that it was possible to exaggerate Russian power in all respects except for her influence in Polish affairs.[53]

That influence was to collapse dramatically within five years. As with the crisis of 1768–72, it was the outbreak of a Russo-Turkish conflict that loosened the Russian grip on Poland, though Prussia played a major role in encouraging Polish opposition to Russian dominance in 1788. The Polish Diet that met on 6 October 1788 saw a decisive rejection of this dominance. The Polish system of government, guaranteed by Russia, was dismantled, a Russian offer of alliance rejected. The Diet was to ignore the Russian-supported plan for only a modest increase in the army, which numbered 18,000 in 1788 and which the partitioning powers wished to restrict to a maximum at 30,000, and instead to approve a plan for an army of 100,000 under its own control and supported by general taxation. Such a force would be able to hinder any attempt to reimpose the Russian quasi-Protectorate, especially if the Poles were supported by Prussia and the Russians at war with the Turks. By April 1790 Hailes was able to report that the Polish army was already 44,000 strong and well equipped, though badly disciplined.[54]

---

[53] Gibson to Harris, 26 Feb. 1788, Winchester, Malmesbury 175; Pitt to Carmarthen, 15 Sept. 1785, BL Eg. 3498 fol. 130; A. W. Ward and G. P. Gooch (eds.), *The Cambridge History of British Foreign Policy, 1783–1919*, I (Cambridge, 1922), p. 179; J. H. Clapham, 'The Project for an Anglo-Polish Treaty (1782–1792)', *Baltic and Scandinavian Countries*, 1 (1935), p. 33; Noailles to Vergennes, 4 Aug. 1784, AE CP Aut. 348 fol. 9.

[54] Hailes to Keith, 5 Apr. 1790, BL Add. 35542 fol. 111; D. Stone, 'Patriotism and Professionalism: The Polish Army in the Eighteenth Century', *Studies in History and Politics*, 3 (1983–4), pp. 64–5; J. Lukowski, *Liberty's Folly. The Polish-Lithuanian Commonwealth in the eighteenth century, 1697–1795* (1991), pp. 239–44. On Hailes, D. Stone, 'Daniel Hailes and the Polish Constitution of May 3, 1791', *Polish Review*, 26 (1981), 51–63, and Z. Libiszowska, *Zycie polskie w Londynie w XVIII wieku* (Warsaw, 1972), pp. 114–37, which emphasises the flawed basis of the idea of an Anglo-Prussian-

This shift had been encouraged by Prussia, keen both to weaken Russia and to obtain an ally against her. It therefore represented a gain for the Triple Alliance, and this encouraged British interest. George Hammond wrote: 'The revolution which has taken place in the sentiments of that nation, and the almost total annihilation of the Russian influence, are very favorable to the views of those powers, who are desirous of rendering more equal the balance of power in the North.'[55] There was no necessary reason for British interest. The affairs of Poland could have been left to Prussia, rather as those of Portugal were left to Britain. There was indeed for the Poles a danger that in place of Russian dominance they would simply gain that of Prussia,[56] and the Prussians, who definitely did not want reform in Poland, worked secretly to prevent her from becoming stronger. On 29 March 1790 a defensive treaty was signed with Prussia, by which she promised to support the new constitution and to assist by force in preventing any foreign power from intervening in Polish domestic affairs in accordance with a previous guarantee of the former constitution. This was clearly aimed at Russia and led to Russian plans for a pre-emptive invasion in order to block Prussian use of Poland, as well as a scheme for the occupation of the western Ukraine.[57] Frederick William II hoped that, in the event of war, Polish gains from Russia, possibly a reversal of the Truce of Andrusovo, the 1667 territorial settlement confirmed by the Treaty of Eternal Peace of 1686, that had seen Russia acquire Kiev, the eastern Ukraine, Smolensk and much of White Russia, would leave Poland willing to cede territory to Prussia. Such hopes, like those of Gustavus III and Hertzberg, are a reminder not only that influential contemporaries did not see a static international system, but also that the plans made earlier in the century for a reversal of Russia's position in eastern Europe still had a strong echo towards its close.

Prussia was not only a dangerous ally for Poland; she also sought some of her territory, especially Danzig and Thorn. Though the Hertzberg plan was designed to win international and Polish support, by obtaining an equivalent for Poland in Galicia, there was no doubt of Prussian territorial ambitions. It was therefore sensible for the Poles to take an interest in British policy, especially as the active British envoy in Warsaw, Daniel Hailes, was keen to encourage his government to take a

Dutch-Polish alliance against Russia. Hailes argued that Prussian territorial claims threatened the possibility of co-operation with Poland: Hailes to Jackson, 12 Nov. 1790, PRO FO 353/66.
[55] Hammond to David Hartley, 26 Nov. 1788, Reading CRO D/EHy F96.
[56] Montmorin to Esterno, 19 Mar. 1789, AE CP Prusse 210 fol. 67.
[57] Madariaga, *Catherine*, p. 412.

reciprocal interest, and this was supported in the highest quarters, by Pitt himself, who saw Poland potentially as a trading partner of great importance; in some measure a substitute for Russia, with whom commercial negotiations had failed, and at least a partner that would reduce the need to please Russia for commercial reasons. In addition, he hoped that Poland would play a role in the collective security system he envisaged.[58]

Pitt's interest in Poland was a facet not only of his own interest in commercial expansion and negotiations, but also of a more general European sense that areas of great economic opportunity existed in the hinterlands of eastern Europe and that these could be readily exploited. Hungary and southern Russia were the obvious examples, both in large part closed to Britain. Emigration to these areas had been considerable, as had been internal colonisation, agricultural improvement and better transportation. If agricultural changes were generally quantitative, and therefore less disruptive of traditional practices, rather than qualitative, they were still of importance. The agricultural improvers had less impact than they sought, but across much of Europe the peasantry and the landowners produced more. This was particularly apparent in Hungary and the Ukraine, and is arguably related to the greater international strength of Austria and Russia. The pattern of industrial activity and change in eastern Europe was somewhat different, though, as in agriculture, the growth in eastern European production was one of the striking features of the century. There was no correlation between areas of agricultural and industrial production. Hungary, Moldavia, Wallachia and the Ukraine did not witness industrial growth comparable to that of their agriculture. Most Polish industry was small scale, and the country did not experience development comparable to that in neighbouring regions, such as Bohemia and Silesia. The Polish grain trade did not produce skills, techniques and forms of organisation that would aid industrialisation and it led to little manufacturing activity bar milling. Eastern European industrial growth was largely found in Russia, especially the metallurgical industries of the Urals, and in the area of east-central Europe composed of Bohemia, Saxony and Silesia, the cockpit of European conflict in 1740–63.[59]

[58] Lojek, 'British Policy', 7; Ewart to Pitt, 16 Nov. 1790, PRO 30/8/133 fols. 263–6.

[59] H. Freudenberger, 'Industrialisation in Bohemia and Moravia in the Eighteenth Century', *Journal of Central European Affairs*, 19 (1960), 347–56, 'The Woollen-Goods Industry of the Habsburg Monarchy in the Eighteenth Century', *Journal of Economic History*, 20 (1960), 383–406, *The Waldstein Woollen Mill: Noble Entrepreneurship in Eighteenth-Century Bohemia* (Boston, 1963), 'An Industrial Momentum Achieved in the Habsburg Monarchy', *Journal of European Economic History* 12 (1983), 339–50; A. Klima, 'Mercantilism in the Habsburg Monarchy – with Special Reference to the

Poland, therefore, was not in a position to compete industrially with Britain. Instead, its economy was complementary, and this was especially valuable given the problems that protectionism was placing in the way of British exports in northern Europe. A stress on commercial negotiations and the ethos of free trade in this period can be misleading, as mercantilist thinking and protectionist legislation were more common.[60] Ever since his arrival in Berlin, Ewart had been interested in better commercial relations with both Prussia and Poland. He argued that Britain would be the principal market for Prussian and Polish exports, and that, if Prussia lowered her often crippling transit duties, Britain would be able to export manufactured goods not only to her, but also to Poland and Saxony. Interest in the possibility of a new commercial role for Poland was further aroused by James Durno, Consul in Memel, a timber merchant who spent over six months in Britain in 1789 and influenced the government with his ideas for a new focus on Anglo-Polish relations.[61] Once returned to Poland, Durno began to correspond directly with Pitt,[62] while the evolution of British policy was seen in the new pressure on Prussia to arrange a satisfactory commercial arrangement with Poland. Leeds wrote to Ewart in July 1790 concerning

points in which the interest of this country, and its future security in a connection with Prussia is very deeply concerned: and with a view to which His Majesty has been desirous ... to contribute to a commercial arrangement between Prussia and Poland, under such a system of transit duties as would secure the free importation into Poland of British manufactures and the free exportation from thence of those articles which are produced in the dominions of the Republic, and in the countries bordering upon it. We should have a very direct and material interest in support of the independence of that country, and in keeping it out of the hands of Russia, to whom it would, in that case, be a powerful commercial rival; and the facility of drawing our naval stores and other materials of manufacture from thence instead of from Russia, would render the friendship of the latter less important to us in fact, and much less an object of attention with the public in this country.[63]

Bohemian Lands', *Historica*, 11 (1965) 95–119; D. F. Good, *The Economic Rise of the Habsburg Empire, 1750–1914* (Berkeley, 1984); A. Kahan, *The Plow, the Hammer, and the Knout: An Economic History of Eighteenth-Century Russia* (Chicago, 1985); P. Clendenning, 'The Economic Awakening of Russia in the Eighteenth Century', *Journal of European Economic History*, 14 (1985), 443–72; J. Komlos, *Nutrition and Economic Development in the Eighteenth-Century Habsburg Monarchy. An Anthropometric History* (Princeton, 1989), pp. 167–73.
[60] H. P. Liebel, 'Free Trade and Protectionism under Maria Theresa and Joseph II', *Canadian Journal of History*, 14 (1979), 355–73.
[61] Ewart to Fraser, 5 Dec. 1786, BL Eg. 3501 fols. 57–8; Gerhard, *Aufstieg Russlands*, pp. 292–308; Ehrman, *Commercial Negotiations*, pp. 118–20, *Pitt*, I, 507–8.
[62] Durno to Pitt, 26 May, 3 Aug. 1790, CUL Add. 6958 nos. 808, 842.
[63] Leeds to Ewart, 20 July 1790, PRO FO 64/18 fol. 127.

Leeds' last point was very interesting: it is obvious that the government realised the sensitivity of relations with Russia at the outset of the confrontation with her, and were concerned to influence the terms of the public debate. In addition, Leeds made it apparent that the ministry did not wish Polish trade to be forced 'into those channels which depend entirely on Russia', and it was further made clear that Polish territorial cessions to Prussia were supportable only

as a part of a Commercial Treaty to which the three allies and Poland should be parties, and in which they should mutually guaranty to each other the stipulations of the Treaty, that is to say, to Prussia the possession of Danzig and Thorn, to Poland the right of carrying on its commerce through Prussia on moderate transit duties, and to Great Britain and Holland, the right of free import and export of such articles as shall be agreed upon on such duties.[64]

Thus, in place of territorial gain, the basis of Prussian schemes for equivalence, the British government sought commercial equivalents as both ends in themselves and the basis of closer links. In addition, improved trade with the Turkish Empire attracted some British commentators. Trevor wrote of 'the Levant trade – a great object, which will open two millions of commerce to us, who have a right to Turkish gratitude'. A commercial treaty with the Turks was considered. It was rumoured in January 1791, though without cause, that the Turks would cede Cyprus to Britain, and thus provide her with a major commercial base in the eastern Mediterranean.[65] And yet, territory was not absent from British plans. In February 1789 Durno had written to Carmarthen on the need to obtain the Russian restoration of Ochakov and Bessarabia to Turkey, in order to prevent Russia from dominating the Black Sea, with consequences for both Turkey and Polish trade. This theme became more insistent the following year as British diplomacy focused increasingly on the notion of the *status quo ante bellum*. That notion had not precluded modifications, as the negotiations for an Austro-Turkish peace indicated, but there was less chance of this valuable element of flexibility playing a role in any Russo-Turkish peace mediated by the Triple Alliance. First, Catherine II was distrusted by both the Prussian and the British governments to a far greater extent than Leopold II. The death of Joseph II had had a cathartic effect for the alliance's relations with Austria; there had been no equivalent change in relations with Russia.

---

[64] Leeds to Ewart, 20 July, Leeds to Hailes, 23 July 1790, PRO FO 64/18 fols. 127–8, 62/3 fols. 137–8; Ewart to Pitt, 24 Nov. 1790, Williamwood vol. 147.

[65] Trevor to Keith, 8 Nov. 1790, NLS Acc. 9769 72/2/63; Ehrman, *Commercial Negotiations*, pp. 140–4; *Gentleman's Magazine*, 61 (1791), 85; Anon., *A Comparative Estimate of the Advantages Great Britain would derive from a Commercial Alliance with the Ottoman in preference to the Russian Empire* (1791), pp. 5–7.

Secondly, the Polish issue played a major role in the crisis. Polish access to the Black Sea would be prevented by Russian gains in the area, and a stress on a strictly interpreted *status quo ante bellum* seemed more pertinent as the idea of extending the collective security system to include Poland and Turkey became more attractive to the British ministry, or at least to Pitt and Ewart. Ewart pressed the need, 'in contracting defensive engagements' with the Turks, 'to stipulate a naval assistance sufficient for protecting their coasts, and particularly for overawing Russia in the Black Sea', scarcely a modest goal.[66] Recuperating from illness in Bath and corresponding directly with Pitt, Ewart was at pains to present such a system as a natural product of the Anglo-Prussian alliance:

The ideas I had communicated respecting your intention of combining Poland and Turkey with the system of the allies produced great satisfaction at Berlin and the interposition of this country in the affairs of Poland was considered by the best judges as the most effectual means of fixing the fluctuating politics of that Republic.

Ewart's interpretation of the motives and likely policy of the Prussian government was generally too optimistic, and he was overly optimistic about the chances of Catherine II backing down. Ewart believed it necessary for Britain to follow a forward policy in eastern Europe in order to thwart Hertzberg's attempt to negotiate a Russo-Prussian understanding on the basis of Russian support for the acquisition of Danzig and Thorn by Prussia. His proposals included the expenditure of 'a few thousand pounds' in order to help in 'acquiring the direction of' Poland, and support for the cession of Danzig to Prussia in return for concessions. Ewart argued that Prussia could easily overrun Livonia, but he saw the crisis as a likely repeat of that of 1787 in which Russia, like France then, would back down. Referring to Ewart, Van de Spiegel wrote of 'ces vastes génies dont la sublime politique embrasse l'univers entier'.[67]

Although, however, the Prussians were delighted to see Poland break free from the Russian orbit, and were pleased at the prospect of Polish assistance if they wished to attack Austria or Russia, they no more wished to see a strong and independent Poland than the other partitioning

[66] Ewart memorandum, 'Considerations on the expediency of combining Poland, Turkey and one of the inferior Baltic powers with the defensive system of the Allies', Nov., Ewart to Pitt, 24 Nov., 13, 22 Dec. 1790, PRO 30/8/332, 133 fols. 264, 274–5, 278.
[67] Ewart to Pitt, 16, 24 Nov., 2, 13 (quote), 22 Dec. 1790, 15 Jan, 14 Feb. 1791, PRO 30/8/133, fols. 263, 267–8, 271, 273, 278, 282, 294; Van de Spiegel to Auckland, 31 Jan. 1791, BL Add. 58919 fol. 40. Hailes pressed for spending 'a few paltry crowns' to gain Poland, Hailes to Jackson, 8 Jan. 1791, PRO FO 353/66.

8. Ochakov and the Black Sea

powers did. To the extent that their policies in eastern Europe involved support for such a Poland, both Pitt and Ewart were being unrealistic. The divergence between Prussian and British policy in 1788–90 had centred on the tension between the pursuit of generally aggressive objectives and those that were more pacific, but in the winter of 1790–1 the Polish issue emerged as a specific difference. Just as Prussian support for Belgian insurgents had threatened the stability of an area that was judged to be of vital importance for British interests, so British support for a resurgent Poland challenged the Prussian position, though the British government failed to see the situation in that light. It allowed its general optimism about the possibility of guiding and restraining

Prussian policy, both in the short and in the long term, to affect its assessment of the prospects for persuading the Prussians to accept the British conception of Poland's role and future development. If it was intended to supersede Russia as a commercial partner by Poland, so it was also possible that a stronger Poland would make Prussia a less attractive alliance partner, or at least reduce her room for manoeuvre in negotiations. In addition, were a stronger Poland to ally in a subsequent confrontation or conflict with Austria and/or Russia, then Prussia would find herself in a weaker position. Thus, when in January 1791 the British government offered to bring Poland into the Triple Alliance they were stressing the possibility of closer Anglo-Polish relations and a shift of emphasis within the alliance.

Ochakov

At the same time, the British ministry was increasingly focusing attention on Ochakov. The retention of this fortress by the Russians seemed to be the major bar to any peace with the Turks on the basis of the *status quo ante bellum*, and the British government chose to see this as a major infringement that could not be comprehended by any notion of modifications, as well as increasingly the central issue in the negotiations. The wisdom of this step was and has been questioned. Ochakov was described by a pamphlet critical of British policy as 'a solitary fortress, situated in the midst of an uncultivated country, on the borders of the Black Sea, between the rivers Nieper and Niester'. The British government had been informed by the Austrian minister Cobenzl in early 1790

that Ochakov was not of sufficient importance to be the cause of hostilities on our part. The district was a desert... the Empress would undoubtedly never suffer the works [fortifications] to subsist... The river Dnieper... was unfit for the purposes of preparing armaments, and even if it were... vessels could pass into the Black Sea without coming within reach of the fort.

Cobenzl added that Catherine II looked upon the retention of Ochakov as a point of honour, and that Constantinople was anyway threatened from Sevastopol, not Ochakov. That December Spielmann told Elgin that Ochakov 'was an object of no manner of importance'.[68] It is striking that the British ministry was to delay until the winter of 1790–1 before checking these points, in particular the question of whether Ochakov

[68] Anon., but written by Vorontsov's secretary Joly (see Marcum, 'Vorontsov', p. 183), *Serious Enquiries into the Motives and Consequences of our Present Armament against Russia* (1791), p. 12; Elgin to Leeds, 24 Jan. 1790, BL Add. 34430 fol. 62; Elgin to Pitt, 20 Dec. 1790, PRO 30/8/132 fol. 158.

controlled the entrance to the Dnieper. This suggests that the government was more concerned about the Russian retention of Ochakov as
being an exception to the *status quo ante bellum* rather than as posing a
threat to the Turks, and also that it did not appreciate early enough that
it would be obliged to face significant public criticism on the issue.
Ochakov is on the northern shore of the Dneprovskiy Liman, a nearly
landlocked section of the Black Sea into which the estuaries of both the
Bug and the Dnieper open. Ochakov is situated at the narrow strait which
forms the seaward entrance of this section or bay. As a confusing factor,
however, the term Ochakov was often taken in the diplomacy of the
period to include not just the fortress, but, in addition, what was also
termed the district of Ochakov: the lands between the Bug, which had
marked the Russo-Turkish frontier under the Peace of Kutchuk–
Kainardji of 1774, and the Dniester, whose mouth is about 70 miles from
Ochakov. The Dniester was seen as a possible route from Poland to the
Black Sea. At its southernmost point, the Polish province of Podolia, part
of the western Ukraine, was only about 100 miles from the mouth of the
Dniester. Alexander Straton, Secretary of Legation in Vienna, wrote to
Leeds in February 1791 about,

Ochakov and its district ... it would render her [Russia] mistress of the mouths of
all the rivers which run into the Black Sea, and of course of almost the whole
commerce of the southern part of Poland, several articles of which, such as hemp,
pitch, timber etc. are of infinite consequence to a maritime power. Besides, thus
situated relative to Poland, Russia might so far cramp the trade, and have such a
local influence over the former, as to make her feel that a connection with the
Empress, might be more advantageous to the Republic, than an alliance with
Prussia.[69]

The Ochakov region was, therefore, apparently crucial to British hopes
of a stronger Poland. Whether it could be feasibly preserved in Turkish
hands was less clear, and this issue was to be raised. Writing to Keith in
January 1791, Auckland, who was aware of the limitations of naval power
and had become the leading sceptic in diplomatic service about the
direction of British policy, referred to the objective of avoiding

any material dismemberment of the Turkish Empire: There is a strong
disposition on this side of Europe to consider the cession of Ochakov and its
district as such a dismemberment. I wish you would take occasion to ... tell me
your opinion of the real value and importance of Ochakov; both in respect to the
Sultan's means of defence, and also with respect to the commerce of the Black
Sea.

[69] Straton to Leeds, 9 Feb. 1791, PRO FO 7/24 fol. 88, Ipswich HA 239/2/1; Leopold to
Kaunitz, 17 Feb. 1791, Beer (ed.), *Joseph, Leopold, Kaunitz*, p. 398; Gerhard, *Aufstieg
Russlands*, p. 331.

Auckland's scepticism became more marked after he obtained the expert opinion of the Dutch Admiral, Kingsbergen, who had served in the Russian navy and knew the Bug–Dnieper estuary.[70] The envoy's scepticism was further justified in part by the way in which Ochakov, and indeed other major Turkish fortifications, had delayed but not prevented Russia's advance in this and previous conflicts. Ochakov had fallen rapidly to Marshal Münnich in July 1737, although that owed something to the explosion of the powder magazine. The Russian garrison, however, then lost 20,000 men due to disease, and in 1738 the fortress was destroyed and abandoned to the Turks, as Auckland, who had been reading a history of that war, pointed out to Pitt in February 1791. The Turks rebuilt the fortress, only to have it stormed by Potemkin in December 1788. Anapa, the major Turkish fort on the Black Sea near the Kuban, was to fall, with Sheikh Mansur inside it, on 22 June 1791, after a siege of sixty-one days. The vulnerability of Turkish fortresses in that war was demonstrated when Bucharest, Gadzhibey, Akkerman and Bender fell in September, October and November 1789, followed by the Danube forts, Kilia, Tulcha, Izakchi and Izmail, in October–December 1790. These successes, and especially the fall of the last on 10 December, were the backdrop to the diplomacy of early 1791, to the negotiations at Sistova and to Russian firmness. The fall of Izmail was widely noted. Under a local byline, the *Glocester Journal* of 7 February 1791 devoted two paragraphs to developments, past and possible, in the Balkan war. They included a brief account of the siege of Izmail and discussion of how its fall might make that of Constantinople more likely.

In addition, when the Turks had retained their fortresses on or near the coast that had not prevented Russian advances across the upper reaches of the Bug and Dniester. Thus, as was pointed out in 1791, in the war of 1768–74 the Turkish retention of Ochakov and Akkerman had not prevented Golitsyn from advancing to Khotin on the upper Dniester in 1769, nor Rumyantsev moving down the Pruth to the Danube in 1770 and across that river in 1774.[71] Though of great importance, sieges, nevertheless, generally played a less important role in campaigns than battles, especially outside heavily fortified zones, such as the Low Countries. The leading generals of the mid and late eighteenth century, Saxe, Frederick II and Rumyantsev, concentrated on wars of manoeuvre. Fortifications were no substitute for a field army. They could not win a

[70] [Eden/Auckland], *Four Letters to the Earl of Carlisle* (2nd edn, London, 1779), p. 53; Auckland to Keith, 11 Jan. 1791, NLS Acc. 9769 72/2/6; Auckland to Grenville, 29 Jan. [1791], BL Add. 58919 fol. 33; Auckland to Burges, 1, 9 Mar. 1791, Bod. BB. 30 fols. 129, 133; Auckland to Elgin, 18 Mar. 1791, Broomhall 60/1/99; *Auckland* II, 382–3; Gerhard, *Aufstieg Russlands*, p. 327.
[71] Auckland to Pitt, 2 Feb. 1791, BL Add. 58919 fol. 38; Anon., *Serious Enquiries*, p. 17.

war and for their defence to be successful they depended on substantial garrisons and supporting forces.

The importance attacked to Ochakov might therefore seem surprising. Were it to be restored, it was likely that it would fall again swiftly in the next conflict. Even if it did not, there was no guarantee that Turkish retention of the fort would affect the war. It could be outflanked by land and by sea. The Russians had not needed Ochakov in order to gain the Crimea and their development of that acquisition, especially the creation of a naval base at Sevastopol, made Ochakov somewhat irrelevant.

The British government can therefore be criticised for risking confrontation, indeed war, with Russia for no reason of consequence. And yet, the decision can be defended. The general need to maintain as strict an interpretation of the *status quo ante bellum* as possible was seen as central to the British objective of facilitating a stable general peace, not least in order to avoid Austrian claims at Sistova and Prussian demands for equivalent gains. In addition, Ochakov was seen as important, and the reasons given are interesting, because of the relative rarity of any discussion of geopolitical and strategic considerations in British diplomatic instructions. In December 1790 Elgin warned Spielmann that the fall of Ochakov might well be followed by that of Constantinople, and that the consequent growth of Russian power might threaten Austrian interests,

Who could say where the Court of Petersburg would stop if, after forming a solid footing, not only in the Crimea, but in other parts, of the Black Sea, and striking there at the vitals of the Ottoman Porte, (and Ochakov alone was perhaps sufficient) she should seize some unlucky moment, when the rest of Europe was unable to assist that country, and erect her standard in Constantinople? – If once there, the Unna might prove a weak barrier: and Belgrade and Orsova more troublesome neighbours.[72]

Two months later, Straton wrote to Leeds about the report of a Russian plan involving Greeks in the Turkish Empire to throw the Turks out of Europe, 'Russian money has been plentifully distributed, in the islands of the archipelago and a flotilla on the coast of Dalmatia is to supply the Greek inhabitants with arms.' In April 1791 he added the report that a Russian fleet was to sail from Sevastopol to Constantinople.[73] In January 1791 Leeds wrote to Francis Jackson, who had taken charge in Berlin in Ewart's absence, concerning a conversation Jackson had had with General Möllendorff, who had been selected to command the Prussian forces in the forthcoming campaign:

[72] Elgin to Pitt, 20 Dec. 1790, PRO 30/8/132 fol. 158. On the precarious nature of the Turkish position, Shaw, *Between Old and New*, pp. 46–7.
[73] Straton to Leeds, 9, 16 Feb., 16 Apr. 1791, PRO FO 7/24, Ipswich HA 239/2/1.

It seems to be true, that the cession of Ochakov and its district by the Turks might afford to Russia the means of commanding a trade from Poland by the Black Sea, which would be contrary to the interests both of England and of Prussia. It would also enable the Russians in future to make a much more effectual use than they have hitherto done of the Crimea, in any offensive operations they might carry on against Turkey, and it would besides remove the delay, which has taken place in the present and former wars, from the siege of Ochakov.

Leeds also referred to 'the advantage Russia must possess in any future operations against Constantinople itself, by being possessed of that district'. Ewart, who claimed to have consulted 'military men', advanced the same view in response to Auckland's claim that Turkish safety would not be affected.[74] These arguments were not without value. In 1788 Ochakov had occupied the major Russian army and their Black Sea fleet for the entire campaign. Potemkin's force began the siege in June; the fortress was not finally taken, and then by storm, until 17 December. Though battles were generally more important than sieges, as Narva (1700) and Poltava (1709) demonstrated, fortresses did play a major role in eighteenth-century conflicts in northern and eastern Europe; many campaigns revolved around them. Sieges could delay plans, occupy a large number of troops and require formidable quantities of supplies, forcing generals to devote more of their resources to protecting their supply lines. Sieges were not necessarily inconsequential alternatives to battle. Fortresses performed the crucial strategic function of securing lines of supply and communication, and were also significant as a concrete manifestation of control over an area, where armies might otherwise manoeuvre inconsequentially. Fortifications stabilised the inchoate borders of eastern Europe and were the signs and sources of political control in an area of multinational empires and no firm historical boundaries.[75]

The gain of Ochakov consolidated Russian control over their acquisitions in 1774 and their position in the Crimea. By threatening the mouth of the Dnieper, Ochakov had limited the extent to which the Russians could use their new shipyard and naval supply base at Kherson, as well as the fortress at Kinburn. Ochakov was also, in Turkish hands, a military and naval base from which these positions, as well as the Crimea, could be threatened. Indeed, in 1787 the Turks had planned to use it as

---

[74] Leeds to Jackson, Jan., 8 Jan. 1791, PRO FO 64/20 fols. 23, 21; Ewart to Auckland, 14 Feb. 1791, PRO 30/8/133 fol. 291; Jackson to Auckland, 8 Feb., Ewart to Auckland, 12 Feb., Ewart to Jackson, 18 Mar. 1791, Williamwood vol. 148.
[75] J. Black, *A Military Revolution? Military Change and European Society 1550–1800* (1991), pp. 53–7.

a base from which to seize Kherson and Kinburn and to reconquer the Crimea. Given their failures in the subsequent conflict, this might appear ridiculous, but in fact they were able to launch attacks on the Kinburn peninsula in 1787, and both Catherine II and Potemkin were worried about the situation. The Russian government argued that their retention of Ochakov was essential for security reasons and complained that their interests were being ignored.[76]

Confrontation with Russia

Ochakov was therefore not without consequence, but it is very doubtful that its return to the Turks merited the threat of war between Britain and Russia. Yet, it was in that direction that Pitt was directing British policy. He was influenced by Ewart, who had gone to Bath for his health in November 1790 and been summoned thence to London. Ewart criticized Hertzberg and his plan,[77] but also warned Pitt of the danger of losing Prussian support and thus wrecking 'the strength and permanency of the actual system of politics' of Britain, by failing to take a firm line towards Russia.[78] With other diplomats, such as Alexander Straton in Vienna, reporting rumours of a lack of British support for such a line,[79] it was clear that the matter had become an issue of confidence in the Anglo-Prussian alliance on the part of Prussia and other European powers. Ewart warned Pitt that Catherine sought a Russo-Danish-Swedish alliance designed 'to shut the Baltic whenever they may judge it necessary', and also tried to influence policy by writing to Thurlow.[80] On 8 January 1791 the British government acted in order to confirm the alliance with Prussia and to settle hopefully the disagreement with Russia. Jackson was instructed to reassure the Prussians, but it was also made clear that any decision to increase the British role would depend upon the response of other powers. Jackson was informed that the British government could not pledge to send a fleet to the Baltic if Catherine II refused terms, until the sentiments of other powers were ascertained, and Leeds added,

---

[76] Undated notes by Pitt, PRO 30/8/195 fol. 51; Madariaga, *Catherine*, p. 397; Osterman to Vorontsov, 31 Oct. 1790, PRO FO 78/12B.

[77] Ewart to Pitt, 24 Nov., 28 Dec. 1790, 11 Feb. 1791, Williamwood vol. 147, PRO 30/8/133 fols. 279, 287.

[78] Ewart to Pitt, 13 Dec. 1790, 15 Jan., 11 Feb. 1791, PRO 30/8/133 fols. 273–4, 282, 288; Jackson to Auckland, 8 Feb., Ewart to Auckland, 12 Feb., Ewart to Auckland, 12 Feb. 1791, Williamwood vol. 148.

[79] Straton to Leeds, 22 Dec. 1790, 8 Mar. 1791, PRO FO 7/24 fols. 45–6, Ipswich HA 239/2/1; Hailes to Jackson, 19 Jan. 1791, PRO FO 353/66.

[80] Ewart to Pitt, 28 Dec. 1790, PRO 30/8/133 fol. 281; Thurlow to Ewart, 17 Jan. 1791, Williamwood, 148.

it is evident that the difficulty of executing such a measure, or at least the expense of the execution, might under possible circumstances, and without those lights which we may expect very speedily to obtain, prove greater than the object in question (important as it is) would justify.[81]

The ministry was hopeful of Spanish diplomatic support, both because relations had improved in the aftermath of the Nootka Sound crisis and because the Spaniards had long expressed concern about Russian conquests at the expense of the Turks.[82] Austrian diplomatic support was also sought, with the argument that if Russia gained Ochakov that would increase Russia's relative power, and that would be bad for Austria.[83] Diplomatic support was useful, though in the case of Austria this meant essentially that Austria should not fulfil her treaty obligations to help Russia in the event of her being attacked. This was important as there had been warnings that Austria might give Russia an equivalent in money to the number of troops stipulated in their treaty, and suggestions that there was even support for war with Prussia.[84] When Spielmann suggested to Elgin that Leopold II co-operate with Britain in settling the crisis, he made it clear that Austria was willing to accept the Russian retention of Ochakov. This was unacceptable to the British government, while co-operation with Austria would have angered Prussia.[85]

A spate of despatches was sent on 8 January 1791. Dutch support was sought, while the Poles were offered both a commercial treaty and accession to the Triple Alliance, the latter a step not welcome to Prussia. In any confrontation with Russia involving the British navy, the attitude of Denmark and Sweden would be crucial, a conclusion that was to be vindicated by the dependence of British naval operations in the Baltic in 1808–12 on Swedish forbearance. The peace between Russia and Sweden had been followed by closer relations between the two powers and it was hoped that this would lead Denmark to turn to the Triple Alliance. The opening of their ports to the British navy was the desired consequence.[86] It was also hoped that pressure on Sweden, if necessary the offer of a subsidy of £100,000, would lead Gustavus III to be neutral or even helpful. The British government was willing, however, to consider more

[81] Leeds to Jackson, 8 Jan. 1791, PRO FO 64/20 fol. 22.
[82] Leeds to Jackson, 8 Jan. 1791, PRO FO 64/20 fol. 20.
[83] Leeds to Elgin, 8 Jan. 1791, PRO FO 7/23 fols. 31–2.
[84] Straton to Leeds, 27 Dec. 1790, PRO FO 7/24 fol. 52; Elgin to Pitt, 27 Dec. 1790, PRO 30/8/132 fols. 165–6; Auckland to Grenville, 13 Feb. 1791, BL Add. 58919 fol. 43.
[85] Elgin to Pitt, 20 Dec. 1790, PRO 30/8/132 fol. 158.
[86] Drake, envoy in Copenhagen, to Liston, 13 Nov. 1790, NLS 5567 fol. 115; V. R. Ham, 'Strategies of Coalition and Isolation: British War Policy and North-West Europe, 1803–1810' (unpublished D.Phil., Oxford, 1977), pp. 298–9; A. Ryan, 'An ambassador afloat: Vice-Admiral Sir James Saumarez and the Swedish court, 1808–1812', in Black and Woodfine (eds.), British Navy, pp. 237–58.

blatant pressure, to be applied by the Prussians on the German possessions of Denmark and Sweden, 'Pomerania must answer for Sweden, and Holstein for Denmark; and the event of both being active against us is scarcely probable',[87] a return to the approach adopted by Ewart and Elliot in the Dano-Swedish crisis of 1788, but this time one that was government policy.

British policy was therefore to be conditional on the approval of other powers, but this approval was to be sought actively. Seeking the approval of other powers was sensible, while delay would allow time for naval preparations and for a breaking of the Baltic ice, and it would also ensure that action, if any, would take place after Parliament had risen. Prussia would be satisfied, while time was still left for Russia to open serious negotiations. Auckland appreciated this point,

the mere idea and report of the activity and energy of our Cabinet will have an excellent effect. Among the other excellencies of the new measures I think it not the least that it gives and secures a few weeks for negociation and deliberation:- for I... looked with considerable affright at M. de Hertzberg's project of a memorial which tended to commit us.[88]

Auckland hoped that deliberation would lead to caution, as he did not believe it was necessary or prudent to fight Russia.[89] Pitt was, however, being pressed with the argument that a confrontation was necessary to support British policy. Back at Bath, Ewart wrote stressing that Frederick William II doubted the British willingness to help, and argued that if the British backed down they would lose their influence in Prussia and northern Europe 'which would make it impossible to maintain the present system long, and still more so to extend it'. In the winter of 1790–1 interest in the extent and intention of British naval preparations was widespread. Both Leopold II and Spielmann pressed Elgin on the matter in December 1790.[90] Ewart urged the need to tell Prussia when the British fleet was to sail for the Baltic, a point underlined by reports, for example from Vienna, that Britain would not send a fleet to the Baltic.[91] The British press reported Prussian complaints about the

---

[87] Leeds to Jackson, 8 Jan. 1791, PRO FO 64/20 fols. 16–19. Jackson, who hoped that British approaches to Austria, Denmark and Spain would influence Gustavus III, also suggested that Britain should hold out 'the prospect of conquests to be made in Finland', Jackson to Liston, 20 Jan. 1791, PRO FO 353/88.

[88] Auckland to Burges, 10 Jan. 1791, Bod. BB. 30 fol. 93.

[89] Auckland to Grenville, 4 Sept., 31 Dec. 1790, Auckland to [Burges?], 29 Jan. 1791, BL Add. 58919 fols. 12, 14–15, 33; Auckland to Pitt, 22 Dec. 1790, PRO 30/8/110 fol. 179; Auckland to Burges, 13 Jan. 1791, misfiled in 1793 papers, BL Add. 34447 fol. 24.

[90] Ewart to Pitt, 15 Jan. 1791, PRO 30/8/133 fol. 281; Elgin to Pitt, 20 Dec. 1790, PRO 30/8/132 fol. 159.

[91] Ewart to Pitt, 15 Jan., 11, 15 Feb. 1791, PRO 30/8/133 fols. 281, 287, 289; Straton to Leeds, 22 Dec. 1790, Ipswich HA 239/2/1.

government's attitude.[92] Ewart's arguments appear to have influenced Pitt, though he was doubtless aware anyway that he needed Prussian support for his diplomatic strategy, but a measure of scepticism about Ewart's fervent advocacy would have been in order. In February 1790 he had argued that Anglo-Austrian negotiations and a refusal to acknowledge Belgian independence would so anger Prussia as to leave him unable to answer for anything, and had been subsequently proved wrong. Now, Ewart claimed that if Russia was obliged to back down 'the whole force of Prussia' would be 'always at our disposal'.[93]

Meanwhile in London, ministers and diplomats looked at the weathervanes, for strong westerlies were a major problem in early 1791, delaying posts from the Continent,[94] and waited anxiously for the replies to the instructions sent on 8 January 1791. Propinquity ensured that reports from Auckland at The Hague and Drake at Copenhagen had a particular impact; especially the latter, as hopes had been placed on winning Danish support. Drake, however, reported first that the influence in Prussia of Hertzberg, a source of considerable irritation but regarded at least as an anglophile, was declining, and secondly that the envoys of the Triple Alliance in Copenhagen had thought it pointless to attempt to divide Denmark from Russia and had therefore decided not to do so. Russian assurances had quietened Danish concerns about Russo-Swedish relations.[95] It was clear that the Danes would remain neutral, although they offered to approach Catherine II in order to sound her on a possible settlement.[96]

A different way to reach a peaceful agreement was suggested by Leopold II. This idea, conveyed in Elgin's dispatch from Vienna of 9 January 1791, was not in reply to the British initiatives launched on 8 January, but it obliged Leeds to clarify the government's thinking while it waited for the replies. Leopold had suggested 'a system of defensive alliances between Great Britain, Prussia, and the two Imperial Courts, for the purpose of preventing as far as possible, any future interruption of the public tranquillity'.[97] Leeds understandably found it imprecise and inopportune, but he emphasised British interest in a defensive

[92] *Gentleman's Magazine*, 60 (1790), 945.
[93] Ewart to Leeds, 11 Feb. 1790, BL Add. 28065 fol. 121; Ewart to Pitt, 15 Jan. 1791, PRO 30/8/133 fol. 282.
[94] Auckland to Burges, 13 Jan., Auckland to Pitt, 2 Feb. 1791, BL Add. 34447 fol. 24, 58919 fol. 38; Nagel, Dutch envoy, to Greffier Fagel, 4 Feb. 1791, Bod. BB. 50 fol. 191.
[95] Drake to Burges, 25 Jan., 1 Feb. 1791, Bod. BB. 34 fols. 3, 5.
[96] Drake to Leeds, 4 Feb. 1791, PRO FO 22/13; Auckland to Burges, 13 Feb. 1791, Bod. BB. 30 fol. 124; Auckland to Drake, 8 Mar. 1791, BL Add. 46822 fol. 166; Ewart to Pitt, 15 Feb. 1791, PRO 30/8/133 fols. 289–90.
[97] Elgin to Leeds, 9 Jan., Leeds to Elgin, 8 Jan., PRO FO 7/23 fols. 33–8, 31–2; Elgin to Pitt, 27 Dec. 1790, PRO 30/8/132 fol. 165.

system of the major powers designed to keep the peace. Keen to see Austria included, Leeds argued that Russia could join only when peace had been restored with the Turks. Once Russia had joined, her territories would be guaranteed and, therefore, Leeds argued, she would have less reason to fear the Turkish retention of Ochakov.[98]

The instruction was interesting because it revealed clearly what the British government hoped to achieve once the confrontation with Russia was over. The plan was simultaneously bold and very conservative. A system incorporating all the major powers was aimed at and yet it was to be 'directed to the future preservation of the established and subsisting balance between the different powers of Europe'. That was a design open to all powers, including France once her government was settled. The British ministry sought not only peace but the fixing of the *status quo ante bellum*, the only basis of sustaining current power relationships that was likely to be widely acceptable. Elgin told Spielmann 'that the Allies and particularly Great Britain, could have no interest, but the general interest of Europe'.[99]

Leeds' instruction to Elgin was vague as to how these objectives were to be secured and, as was usual with British discussion of international relations, sought the *status quo* in Europe without making mention of extra-European territories, despite the fact that these clearly affected European power relationships. On the other hand, Leeds did address one of the major threats to the projected system, Austro-Prussian animosity, which he attributed to 'ancient prejudices'. He wrote of the need to bring both powers 'to a permanent system of good understanding and friendship'.[100] This was obviously true in the short term. No attempt to coerce Russia or, subsequently, to bring her into the projected system could work if the two powers were bitter enemies and acting accordingly. In the long term, Leeds' objective reflected the need for good relations between the major powers if the system was to work harmoniously. Paradoxically, such understanding and friendship was to be achieved soon, but it was done without British participation. Nevertheless, the Austro-Prussian system directed against revolutionary France fulfilled the earlier British objective of defending the *status quo*, although the stress of the two powers on indemnification and their gains at the expense of Poland made the self-interested and partial nature of their policy obvious.

Whatever the future prospect for an Austro-Prussian understanding, in February 1791 Austria was one of the powers that gave an un-

[98] Leeds to Elgin, 4 Feb. 1791, PRO FO 7/23 fols. 65–7.
[99] Elgin to Pitt, 20 Dec. 1790, PRO 30/8/132 fol. 158.
[100] Leeds to Elgin, 4 Feb. 1791, PRO FO 7/23 fols. 71–2.

satisfactory reply to the suggestions of the Triple Alliance. When the Prussian envoy Jacobi, whom Leopold II disliked, pressed the Emperor, Leopold told him that Catherine II would accept neither a dictated peace nor the *status quo ante bellum*, that she was in a strong position and that he would fulfil his treaty obligations to her.[101] Straton was also pessimistic, reporting that Austria was trying to stir up anti-Prussian activity in Poland, and that Leopold had been prevailed upon by his ministers to support Russia. To the concern of the British, the Austrians became less co-operative at Sistova, a location that Keith had found inconvenient, as he had anticipated. Distrust of Austrian policy and concern about its inconsistency increased. Straton argued that the recovery of order after the collapse of Joseph II's last years was making Austria less accommodating.[102] The situation elsewhere was also unsatisfactory for the British government. The Dutch were unwilling to risk war with Russia, Spanish diplomatic support did not amount to much, the unreliable and distrusted[103] Gustavus III demanded a massive subsidy, as well as command of the allied naval force, and the Russians were uncompromising. Indeed, the joint Prusso-British demand that Catherine restore all her recent conquests had been rejected in an uncompromising fashion.[104]

Auckland read all the British diplomatic correspondence that passed through The Hague under flying seal, and he became steadily more sceptical about the wisdom and likely success of British policy. He suggested that pressure might lead Catherine to demolish the fortifications of Ochakov and even possibly to leave the district neutral, but he felt certain that a demand for restitution would lead to an unnecessary war. With reason, Auckland was unconvinced of the stability of the Prussian government and suspected that Frederick William II did not want war with Russia.[105] Auckland was also dubious about the prospect

---

[101] Leopold to Kaunitz, 17 Feb. 1791, Beer (ed.), *Joseph, Leopold, Kaunitz*, p. 398.

[102] Straton to Leeds, 27 Dec. 1790, 15, 25 Jan., 19, 23, 26 Feb, 8, 9, 12, 23 Mar., 2 Apr. 1791, Keith to Straton, 10, 22 Feb., 8, 15, 18, 29 Mar., 6, 12 Apr. 1791, Ipswich HA 239/2/1, 2/165, 170, 175–7, 179, 182, 184; Straton to Leeds, 19, 26 Feb., 2 Mar. 1791, PRO FO 7/24 fols. 95–104; Hailes to Jackson, 24 Sept., 19 Oct. 1790, PRO FO 353/66; Keith to Liston, 20 Oct. 1790, NLS 5567 fol. 102; Elgin to Pitt, 20, 27 Dec. 1790, PRO 30/8/132 fols. 159, 164–5; Auckland to Elgin, 18 Mar. 1791, Broomhall 60/1/99. Keith's reports from Sistova are in PRO FO 7/25–7. Roider, *Austria's Eastern Question*, pp. 190–2 offers a sympathetic portrayal of Austrian policy, but it is possible to argue that he neglects its opportunism.

[103] Jackson to Ewart, 6 Mar. 1791, Williamwood 148.

[104] Whitworth to Leeds, 8 Jan. 1790, PRO FO 65/20; Rose, *Pitt and National Revival*, pp. 597–8.

[105] Auckland to [Ewart], 2 Feb., Auckland to Grenville, 29 Jan., 8 Feb., Auckland to Pitt, 2 Feb. 1791, PRO 30/8/110 fol. 184; 30/8/110 fols. 34, 42, 38. Hertzberg was distrusted by other diplomats, Jackson to Hailes, 8 Feb. 1791, PRO FO 353/66.

of Austrian, Danish and Spanish support,[106] though he was not aware of Hertzberg's suggestion to the Russian envoy that Russia retain Ochakov in return for the Prussian gain of Danzig and Thorn. Auckland suggested to London that Catherine be left 'the dismantled district of Ochakov' and that the Turkish frontier be jointly guaranteed by Britain, Prussia and Spain. Unlike the ministry, he was sensibly searching for a compromise that would gratify Catherine without leaving her significantly more powerful.[107]

Auckland became appreciably more concerned in March 1791 as the prospect of a peaceful settlement appeared to recede. He was convinced that the Danish government was devoted to Russia and worried about Swedish subsidy demands, not least because they might serve to strengthen a ruler who could turn against Britain. Auckland feared that alliance with her would entail supporting Swedish hopes for gains from Russia, abandoning principles and concurring in 'a war of conquest'. Auckland was also concerned about the cost of subsidising Hanoverian forces. Fearing 'an abyss of debts and difficulties', Auckland also struck a note that was otherwise singularly absent from the crisis, the need for *ancien régime* states and societies to preserve their strength in the face of revolutionary challenge, the 'general fermentation in the world', which, he argued, challenged the existence of all 'civilized' states. The lack of justice of the British position and the risks that it entailed both worried Auckland, and he still sought to suggest compromises. On 22 March 1791 Auckland wrote to Drake arguing that Ochakov and its district should be ceded to Russia

with a stipulation however that the fortress shall never be re-established and that no town or fortress or settlement shall be made on the eastern banks of the Dniester and consequently that the navigation of the river shall remain liberated from all coercion or interference on the part of Russia.[108]

Such a suggestion, which would have required the guarantee of the Triple Alliance, was not unprecedented. Rights of navigation and, in the case of Azov, demilitarisation had played a major role in Russo-Turkish negotiations over the previous century. Auckland's concern with the navigation of the Dniester was interesting, given the role that the free navigation of the Scheldt had played in the early 1780s and was to play

---

[106] Auckland to Grenville, 29 Jan. [1791], BL Add. 58919 fol. 33.
[107] Auckland to Burges, 13, 19, 26 Feb. 1791, Bod. BB. 30 fols. 124–7; Auckland to Grenville, 8 Feb., 23 Apr., Auckland to Drake, 25 Feb. 1791, BL Add. 58919 fols. 42, 53, 46822 fol. 164; Rose, *Pitt and National Revival*, p. 597.
[108] Auckland to Burges, 5 Mar. 1791, Bod. BB. 30 fol. 132; Auckland to Grenville, 5 Mar. Auckland to Drake, 22 Mar. 1791, BL Add. 58919 fol. 46, 46822 fol. 168. On Auckland's efforts to counteract Ewart: Ewart to Jackson, 24 Mar. 1791, Williamwood 148.

again in 1792–3. Far from seeing his proposal as an example of an
antiquated diplomatic world that was soon to be swept aside by the force,
or at least forces, of revolutionary justice or, more accurately, power, it is
clear that it reflected both the attempt to move beyond territory as a basis
of compromise, and a wish to incorporate into the treaty the interests of
a third party, Poland, for whom the free navigation of the Dniester was
important.

The Danish government, with its links to both Russia and Britain, was
a possible intermediary between the two powers, but suggestions of a
new conciliatory approach designed to negotiate a compromise, had little
weight with the ministry in London. Pitt and Leeds were becoming
impatient for action, but crucial impetus was provided by Prussian
pressure. The Dutch, on the contrary, were very unenthusiastic, and not
inclined to see the crisis as a dispute that really involved them.[109] On 11
March 1791 Frederick William II personally wrote to Count Redern, his
envoy in London, to demand a definite declaration on whether Britain
would join with Prussia in forcing Russia to an acceptable settlement. If
not, he warned that they would have to accept the Russian gain of
Ochakov, and the King claimed that it was clear that this would give
Russia a superiority over Turkey that was very prejudicial even to British
interests.[110] This Prussian approach reflected Bischoffwerder's mistaken
belief that in his secret mission to Vienna the previous month he had
persuaded Leopold II to accept the notion of an Austro-Prussian alliance
aimed against Russia and designed to facilitate the Prussian gain of
Danzig and Thorn in return for commercial concessions to the Poles.
This would leave Prussian territory unbroken from Memel to Magde-
burg. Frederick William II would achieve his first territorial gains, and
the prize of Danzig which had eluded his uncle. Firm action against
Russia now seemed possible, for, whatever Leopold's view on Prussian
gains in Poland, it seemed unlikely that he would send military assistance
to Catherine. Well aware of divisions within the Prussian government,
Jackson nevertheless felt able to write on 11 March that 'the business is
now in its old train'.[111]

In response to the Prussian message, the Cabinet met on 21 March and
then again at greater length the following day. Pitt, Thurlow, Chatham,
Leeds, Grenville, Stafford, Camden and Richmond were present on the
22nd and they decided on action. Thirty-nine ships of the line and a

[109] Ewart to Jackson, 24 Mar. 1791, Williamwood 148; Fawkener to Grenville, 29 Apr.
       1791, BL Add. 59023 fols. 12–13.
[110] Frederick William to Redern, 11 Mar. 1791, Rose, *Pitt and National Revival*, p. 608;
       Jackson to Leeds, 6, 11 Mar. 1791, PRO FO 64/20.
[111] Jackson to Ewart, 11, 15 Mar. 1791, Williamwood 148.

proportionate number of frigates were to be sent to the Baltic towards the end of April, on the supposition that the Danes would not obstruct the passage of the Sound and would permit the use of their ports. Ten or twelve of the line were to be prepared for the Black Sea. In the meantime, a joint Anglo-Prussian ultimatum was to be presented to Catherine II, demanding a Russo-Turkish peace on the basis of the *status quo ante bellum* within a fixed period. Gustavus III was to be offered a joint subsidy in return for neutrality and the use of his ports. Poland and Turkey were to be pressed to accede 'to the general system of defensive alliance' and Dutch co-operation was to be obtained.[112] Vice-Admiral Hood was confident that he could evade Danish control of the Sound by sailing through the Belt.[113] Ewart, who attended the Cabinet on the 22nd, wrote that evening to Jackson, with whom he had a confidential correspondence:

Thank God, everything is settled *at length* in the most glorious manner – Auckland's pretty dispatch with [Admiral] Kingsbergen's report were given to me to refute ... Auckland ... is now completely knocked up ... I have just sent to Mr. Pitt the projects of two Conventions to be sent to you, one for the plan of vigorous co-operation and the other for a preliminary arrangement respecting the cession of Danzig ... I never fought so hard a battle as with our Principals.

Two days later he wrote again, revealing that he was clearly planning for war,

Everything goes on to a wish ... The Baltic fleet will consist of 35 sail of the line ... and the *necessary fire ships*, for I have strongly urged the expediency and ease of burning all the B-'s [sic] ships and docks should she be obstinate. I have likewise represented that the moment our fleet has the command of the Gulf of Finland, it would be very easy to transport ten thousand Prussians across and debark them within a few miles of Petersburg, which could thus be taken *d'emblée* [at once], as the Russians would naturally turn all their efforts towards Livonia. Do talk Moellendorff over upon this ... the Black Sea ... there is no doubt but that all their naval force and establishment there could be easily destroyed.

Ewart was confident that a British fleet in the Baltic and the prospect of a Prussian invasion of Pomerania would lead Gustavus III to accept a subsidy treaty, and he thought that he would join in the attack on Catherine II as soon as she was in difficulties. Ewart was also hopeful of a corps of 30,000 Poles and on the 25th he suggested that the British fleet and fireships could burn both Cronstadt and Revel. On the 27th Ewart wrote, 'I'll answer for it that the Crimea shall be restored to the Porte, should things be pushed to extremities', and that day he gave Pitt a plan

---

[112] Cabinet Minute, 22 Mar. 1791, Aspinall, *George III* no. 663; O. Browning (ed.), *The Political Memoranda of Francis Fifth Duke of Leeds* ... (1884), pp. 150–2.
[113] Ewart to Jackson, 27 Mar. 1791, Williamwood 148.

of operations for the Poles and the Turks.[114] Meanwhile, the Turks were being encouraged by the British and Prussian envoys at Sistova to act offensively in order to retake Wallachia.[115]

Pitt, Leeds and Chatham, the First Lord of the Admiralty, saw George III on 23 March and on the 25th the ultimatum to Russia was drawn up, the original in Pitt's handwriting. A dispatch of 24 March from Redern reached Berlin a week later and brought news of the British ultimatum and the decision to have fleets in the Baltic and Black seas. On the 25th a proclamation was issued in London to encourage recruitment for the navy. Able seamen were offered £3, ordinary seamen £2 and able landsmen £1. On 27 March Frederick William II ordered the deployment of 88,000 troops on the Livonian frontier, while instructions were sent to British envoys. Jackson was informed of the Cabinet's decision, presented as designed to induce Catherine to conclude a peace 'on terms more consistent with the general interests of Europe'. Frederick William was to be informed of British naval plans, though their reliance on an assurance of Danish neutrality and the use of Danish ports was to be stressed. Leeds observed that 'these exertions on our part, combined with the movement of the Prussian troops into Livonia may, it is to be hoped, induce the Empress to listen to reason'; in other words the Prussians, but not the British, were actually to begin hostilities, though, once sent, it was accepted that a fleet might readily become involved in action. Leeds also stressed the need to get both Poland and Turkey to join the system of the Triple Alliance, as it would 'render the whole system still more respectable' and 'be the surest method of contributing both to the prosperity and tranquillity of those two countries in particular'. Such a step had been pressed by Ewart and resisted by Auckland. Pitt accepted Ewart's idea of 'a powerful naval guarantee' to Turkey and the dispatch of British naval officers and seamen 'to put their naval force on a proper footing'. A joint Anglo-Prussian declaration was to be made at St Petersburg. While the system was to be extensive it was not to be motivated by 'ambition or aggrandisement', and, therefore, it was necessary that the objective of Anglo-Prussian interference should be clearly ascertained. Leeds stressed that neither power should seek acquisitions for itself, a measure that Ewart was certain Austria and Spain would never accept, but that their gain should be procuring a 'still greater degree of security for the Porte on the Black Sea'.[116]

---

[114] Ewart to Jackson, 22, 24, 25, 27 Mar. 1791, Williamwood 148.
[115] Keith to Straton, 10 Feb. 1791, Ipswich HA 239/2/165.
[116] Leeds to Jackson, 27 Mar. 1791, PRO FO 64/20 fols. 181–92; Ewart to Jackson, 24 Mar., 14 Apr. 1791, Williamwood 148; ultimatum in Leeds to Whitworth, 27 Mar. 1791, PRO FO 65/20; Jackson to Straton, 2 Apr. 1791, Ipswich HA 239/2/234.

Given Prussian ambitions, this was unrealistic, though, as Straton reported, if Russia retained Ochakov or Prussia gained Danzig and Thorn, Austria would want an equivalent. Jacobi had already told Spielmann that if war broke out and Prussia was successful, she would be entitled to ask for gains to recompense her for her armament.[117] The difficulties that the British government had had with its Prussian ally led it to underline the pacific intentions, if not now methods, of the alliance. In a letter sent to accompany the instruction, Burges, whom Ewart referred to that day as 'my most cordial friend',[118] wrote,

it is extremely desireable that the end of our interference ... should be clearly and precisely ascertained, in order to avoid misconceptions, should hostilities arise, as to the terms on which, according to different contingencies, a pacification may be afterwards acceded to.[119]

Given the domestic storm that was to envelop British policy, it is worth noting that on 27 March the government sought to limit its objectives for diplomatic reasons, not because it was concerned about the possible domestic response.

Crisis in London

On 28 March 1791, the government took its dispute with Russia to Parliament, a measure it had earlier sought to avoid. Indeed Ewart had written to Pitt of the latter's 'wish to have the session of Parliament over before taking any decisive steps'. Now, however, Pitt presented to the Commons the King's message on the need for further naval armaments, George's approval having been obtained the previous day.[120] The message declared that the failure of British efforts to end the Russo-Turkish war led to the need to lend weight to diplomatic representations by strengthening the navy. The Commons were assured that the expenditure was 'for the purpose of supporting the interests of His Majesty's kingdom, and of contributing to the restoration of general tranquillity on a secure and lasting foundation'. In a brief exchange, Fox made it clear that the issue would be treated as one of confidence in the ministry, and that he felt that Parliament was receiving insufficient information about the causes of the crisis.[121]

The following day, 29 March 1791, the issue was debated in both houses. In the Lords, the government case was presented not by Leeds,

117 Straton to Leeds, 6 Apr. 1791, Ipswich HA 239 2/1.
118 Elgin to Pitt, 20 Dec. 1790, PRO 30/8/132 fol. 160.
119 Ewart to Jackson, 27 Mar. 1791, Williamwood 148.
120 Burges to Jackson, 27 Mar. 1791, Bod. BB. 49 fol. 3.
121 Ewart to Pitt, 11 Feb. 1791, PRO 30/8/133 fol. 288; Grenville to George III, 27 Mar. 1791, BL Add. 58856 fol. 24.

who was not an assiduous debater, but by the Home Secretary, Grenville. He had become leader of the Lords in November 1790, and was clearly close to Pitt. A report that Grenville might succeed Leeds had been mentioned to the latter by Burges on 4 March. Since succeeding to the duchy in March 1789, Leeds had talked openly of his wish to resign. On 29 March 1791 Grenville gave the Lords no details beyond presenting the armament as the natural consequence of 'the system of continental alliances that had been entered into' in order to establish and secure 'a solid pacific system over all Europe'.[122] In reply, Earl Fitzwilliam moved to specifics. He accepted that Britain must support her alliances, but he queried the need to act aggressively in early 1791. Drawing attention to the defensive nature of Britain's obligations, Fitzwilliam stated that there was no danger of any attack upon Prussia, and he argued that if Russia retained Ochakov and Akkerman, which would have given her control over the mouth of the Dniester, that that would not pose any problems. Fitzwilliam, therefore, moved an amendment making support conditional upon Parliament receiving information to show that an increase in the navy was necessary in order to achieve diplomatic success.[123] The government did not regain the initiative in the Lords. Its case was poorly prepared and supported; Grenville argued that it was essential not to give replies that might be prejudicial to the public interest. Lord Porchester attacked this silence, the likely economic consequences of war and the foolish ambition of government policy. The Earl of Carlisle argued that Russia was Britain's natural ally and that it was wrong for the ministry to expect parliamentary support without explanation and 'upon confidence merely'.

Stormont claimed that Britain and Prussia were about to transform a defensive into an offensive alliance, by an aggressive armed mediation on behalf of a power that had began the war. Having argued that British policy was more aggressive than that of Louis XIV, the touch-stone of *ancien régime* depravity, had ever been, Stormont stated that Russian retention of Ochakov and Akkerman would have no detrimental consequences. He drew attention to the failure of British naval pressure on Peter the Great, and claimed that Britain had adopted the French policy of supporting Turkey against Russia. Stormont attributed the crisis 'to the imperative and haughty language held by the minister to Russia', and suggested that had naval action been necessary it should have been pursued while Sweden was hostile to Russia. Richmond, who personally did not support the direction of British policy, replied briefly on behalf of the government, arguing that they were seeking only an

[122] Cobbett, 29, 31–3.
[123] *Political Memoranda of Leeds*, p. 148; HMC *Dropmore*, I, 526; Cobbett, 29, 33–4.

augmentation of naval power in order to give weight to negotiation, and claiming that it was wrong to state that Catherine II wanted only Ochakov and Akkerman. He, however, explained neither what else she was supposed to want, nor the seriousness of her demands.

Loughborough, for the opposition, argued that Richmond's argument was different from that of Grenville, who, he claimed, had suggested that Britain was preparing to intervene in the war.[124] Loughborough referred to the calamities of war, the obscurity of the issue at stake, the propensity of the government to become involved in disputes, the proposed aggression against a natural ally, the arrogance of the British negotiating position, the lack of clarity as to how Russia was to be attacked and the failure of the British ministry to emulate the French National Assembly in avoiding unnecessary conflicts. For Loughborough, the French Revolution offered not simply an opportunity for Britain both to reduce her military establishment and to enjoy the benefits of peace, but also a standard of conduct in foreign policy that Britain should seek to emulate.[125]

Loughborough was answered by his legal rival Thurlow, who reiterated the need for ministers to have the ability to decide what it was safe to disclose, and, thus, stated that the issue was a matter of confidence. Nevertheless, he continued by arguing that defensive treaties had to be interpreted in order to support the interests of allies, that Russian conquests on Polish frontiers would give Russia an ascendancy in Poland that threatened Prussia, and that Russia was not the natural ally of Britain, or at least, if so, was acting in a very unnatural manner. Thurlow's remarks are of considerable interest given his close links to George III, and his willingness to challenge publicly what he acknowledged was the common opinion that Russia was Britain's natural ally. In January 1791 Thurlow had corresponded with Ewart, approving the plans of the latter, but criticising the conduct of policy by the government, particularly the delay in confronting Russia and making 'proper arrangements... with the Porte, Poland, and Sweden' and noting his own lack of influence.

Lansdowne replied to Thurlow in a lengthy and wide-ranging speech that included an attack on the willingness of the ministry to risk war with Spain over Nootka Sound, a stress on the strength of Russia as an enemy, a discussion of the lack of support Britain would receive from any power bar Prussia, and of the costs of war, and reference to the 1st Earl of Chatham's hostility to the idea of an alliance with the Turks. Lansdowne, who mentioned Chatham twice, had been his protégé, and he, like other

[124] Cobbett, 29, 34–5.   [125] Cobbett, 29, 35–45.

opposition speakers, referred to the former minister in order to demonstrate that his son, William Pitt the Younger, had abandoned the policies of the great war-leader. Lansdowne, like Loughborough, brought up the example of France, praising the decision of the National Assembly that the right of making peace and war was 'in the nation', and its condemnation of views of ambition and conquest, while arguing that if the British government foolishly risked war and higher taxes, that might produce a national bankruptcy and revolution. The Earl of Fife who was present, and who thought that Thurlow spoke very well, argued that Lansdowne spoke 'quite on the principles of the National Assembly. He wishes confusion and anarchy'. In reply, Leeds simply stated the need for ministers to maintain secrecy. The opposition amendment was defeated, and the Address then carried by 97 to 34. George III thought the division 'must give confidence abroad from showing the support given'.[126]

Pitt was more forthcoming in the Commons than any of the ministerial speakers in the Lords. He argued that Britain was seeking to prevent any alteration in the relative strength of the European states, as that would weaken the system of defensive alliances, and that if concern with the affairs of the Continent and therefore an alliance system were judged necessary, such a policy was essential. If Turkey became weaker, Pitt claimed, that would affect Prussia and, therefore, Britain. Thus the war between Russia and Turkey did not simply affect those powers.[127]

He was answered by Lansdowne's son, the much-travelled Earl Wycombe, who complained about a lack of information, the detrimental political and commercial effects of conflict with Russia, and the fact that hostilities were intended although Russia had neither attacked the interests of Britain nor those of any ally. An amendment, criticising government policy and stressing the value of peace, was introduced by Thomas Coke and seconded by William Lambton. Lambton argued that ministers might have pledged themselves to Frederick William II to engage in war with Russia, but that the nation was not obliged to ratify such engagements. Though this argument was one that accorded with the views advanced in the National Assembly the previous year, it was also a traditional claim of opposition. By advancing this argument, Lambton evaded the question of the impact of such a defeat on Britain's foreign standing as a possible ally. He then proceeded on safer ground by arguing that the fleet would lack friendly ports in the Baltic.[128]

---

[126] Cobbett, 29, 45–52; Thurlow to Ewart, 17 Jan. 1791, Williamwood 148; Fife to Rose, 30 Mar. 1791, Aberdeen UL Tayler papers 2226/131/855; George III to Grenville, 30 Mar. 1791, BL Add. 58856 fol. 26.   [127] Cobbett, 29, 52–5.
[128] Cobbett, 29, 55–9.

The opposition case was further supported by James Martin and Robert Vyner, who emphasised the need to provide Parliament with information, before being answered by Richmond's protégé, Thomas Steele, a Treasury official, who pointed out that Catherine II had revealed her hostility at the time of the Armed Neutrality and argued that Britain's situation with respect to her allies required her to prevent Catherine from gaining territory from Turkey. John Sommers Cocks returned to the charge of a lack of information, and was followed by Fox who delivered a lengthy attack on the ministry. Russia was presented as a natural ally, who had not attacked Britain's ally Prussia, for, declared Fox, advancing an argument that was to become more important when Franco-Dutch relations became an issue in those between Britain and France in the winter of 1792–3, had such an attack been made, Britain would have been obliged immediately to support her ally. Fox drew attention to British support for the Russian fleet during the Russo-Turkish conflict of 1768–74, and to her refusal to act against Russia when she annexed the Crimea, argued that there was no reason to change policy, and claimed that Britain and Prussia had inspired the Turkish attack on Russia in 1787. He asserted further that the government was inconsistent in not bringing up the supposed threat from Russia in the sessions of 1788, 1789 and 1790, that Ochakov was of little significance, that the British treatment of Russia was arrogant, that the ministry adopted different standards in India and Europe, that a Russian entry into the Mediterranean would challenge Britain's Bourbon enemies, that Russia was an important commercial partner, and that British policy should be based on an alliance with Russia and either Austria or Prussia. Poland did not feature.[129]

Pitt retorted that the Prussian alliance was the consequence of the Anglo-Dutch connection, and that if Russia triumphed over Turkey, Prussia would be obliged to concentrate on defending herself not the Dutch. The commercial value of Poland was stressed, but Pitt also discussed the general objective of British policy, namely the creation of a collective security system that would be able to compel other powers to abandon schemes of ambition and conquest.[130]

Burke closed the debate, attacking the confidence required by the government from Parliament, asserting that Turkey had never previously been considered part of the European balance of power, and was a savage and un-Christian power, and claiming that Ochakov was not material to the balance. His eloquent speech focussed on the morality of helping the Turks, which he termed an anti-crusade, but he also, with good cause,

[129] Cobbett, 29, 59–70.   [130] Cobbett, 29, 70–75.

asked fairly whether it was necessary, in order to preserve the balance, that no power should make territorial gains. Burke skilfully mingled moral and practical considerations in order to argue that helping the Turks was very different from intervening to prevent France from gaining control of the United Provinces in 1787. Fox had raised up the issue of different standards towards the conflicts in southern India and between Russia and Turkey, and it was clear that differences between Christian and non-Christian powers posed a problem in adopting a consistent approach towards the morality of international relations.[131]

The ministry defeated the amendment by 228 to 135, the tellers for the opposition being North's son, George, and Charles Grey. George III was pleased by what he saw as a 'very handsome majority', which he felt would give energy to government policy,[132] but the cohesion and confidence of the government had been badly damaged by the parliamentary debates. The policy of maintaining a bold front and hoping that Russia would back down, outlined by Pitt on 28 March when he wrote to Stafford 'I feel that we have nothing for it, but to go on with vigour and to *hope for the best*', was not enough for Parliament. There were clearly serious problems with the conduct of government business and the presentation of policy, problems in which the complexity and seriousness of the diplomatic situation interacted with a lack of confidence amongst the ministers and an absence of a sure grasp for the management of both houses over the issue. Leeds recorded a visit from Thurlow on 2 April in which 'he lamented with me our being *gagged* in the debates, and thought as I did that it would be better to come forward in both Houses in respect to the measures we were pursuing in our present discussion with Russia'. A fortnight later, Henry Addington, the Speaker of the Commons, made the same point. There was also a failure to manage public opinion. The previous year, Lord North had told Luzerne that he had never seen a government strong enough to ignore press attacks without risking its popularity. Luzerne commented that the ministerial maxim in Britain was in general 'faire mob contre mob', to respond to Opposition attempts to lead the people against the government by leading them in the opposite direction. That was not to happen in 1791. The government's failure to provide sufficient justification of its policy, its surprising and damaging silence, reflected the extent to which the ultimatum to Russia was directed in part at restraining Prussia from a shift of policy towards possibly either reconciliation with Russia or an aggressive destabilising war of territorial aggrandisement. This could not

[131] Cobbett, 29, 75–9.
[132] George III to Pitt, 30 Mar. 1791, Aspinall, *George III* no. 666.

be publicly admitted, both because it would offend Prussia and also because to do so would nullify the impact of the ultimatum and hence thwart both objectives of British policy.[133]

Popular agitation against war with Russia developed rapidly, encouraged by Vorontsov and the Russia Company. Vorontsov, who had threatened Leeds with stirring up a popular outcry that would block ministerial schemes, played a major role in a busy press campaign against government policy. He also provided opposition speakers such as Fox with arguments about the danger of war, and encouraged the Russia Company to act.[134] In contrast, the ministerial press was confused and circumspect. There were articles defending government policy, for example the London piece in the *Newcastle Courant* of 15 January 1791 which misleadingly claimed that British naval action in 1719 had driven Peter the Great to make peace with Sweden and thus 'the ambition of Russia was checked by the power of Great Britain'. Uncertain, like the ministry, as to what would happen, the pro-government press was hesitant. It was difficult to explain a policy designed both to lead to the intimidation of Russia, but not war with her, and to retain Prussia as an ally, but also to restrain her. The expectations and nuances affecting foreign policy at this juncture were difficult to convey in a positive fashion, especially as an unwanted war came to seem more likely.

It was Parliament, however, where the crucial pressure was brought to bear on the government. The ministry could try to rely on its majority in both houses providing support on the grounds of confidence, but that majority was unreliable and the government was split. Fife noted on 31 March, 'We had a very disagreeable debate yesterday in the House of Lords and not so well for ministers as usual; they also lost 6 in the House of Commons on the debate on the address.' The majority was to crumble alarmingly in April 1791, but already there were signs of concern. The government's reduced majority was noted in diplomatic circles and abroad. The absence of some ministerial supporters from the debates was attributed to their reluctance to support the government.[135] The multifaceted and somewhat unfocussed nature of the opposition attack

[133] Pitt to Stafford, 28 Mar. 1791, PRO 30/29/384; *Political Memoranda of Leeds*, pp. 159, 167; Luzerne to Montmorin, 31 May 1790, AE CP Ang. 573 fols. 202–3.

[134] Anderson, *Britain's Discovery*, pp. 143–85; Marcum, 'Vorontsov and Pitt', 51–3; *Public Advertiser*, 23, 29 Feb. 1792; [J. Currie], *A Letter, Commercial and Political, Addressed to the Right Hon. William Pitt* (Dublin, 1793), p. 45; Lord, *Second Partition*, p. 186; A. G. Cross, *"By the Banks of the Thames". Russians in Eighteenth-Century Britain* (Newtonville, Mass., 1980), p. 26; Ehrman, *Pitt*, II, 25–6; Marcum, 'Vorontsov', pp. 180–4.

[135] Fife to Rose, 31 Mar. 1791, Aberdeen UL Tayler papers 2226/131, 855a; Luzerne to Montmorin, 1 Apr. 1791, AE CP Ang. 577 fol. 88; Auckland to Drake, 5 Apr. 1791, BL Add. 46822 fol. 170.

ensured that the views and anxieties of different peers and MPs were catered for, whether concern about the costs of war and consequent taxation, or the loss of the Russia trade, or geopolitical and strategic considerations. Opposition arguments appealed both to those who had doubts about the value of continental interventionism, and to those who supported the idea but did not like the direction given it by the ministry. The debates on 29 March were important because they helped to lead to a change in policy; whereas those in April influenced a government already in retreat, and reflected that retreat. The debates of the 29th were also significant because, as Fox pointed out that day, the Opposition had substantially supported the ministry over the Dutch and Nootka Sound crises,[136] or at least had found it inexpedient to press home their criticisms.

The ministry had been unsettled for a while. Grenville's promotion to the Leadership of the Lords in November 1790 reflected Leeds' failure as Leader in the 1790 session and the continued poor relations between Thurlow and Pitt, and, in turn, exacerbated matters. These bad relations between the two leading ministers in the government were not a secret. Thurlow informed Leeds, who also did not feel consulted by Pitt, that it had been rumoured that the Duke of Montrose would become Foreign Secretary. In distant Sistova Keith feared to see the ministry 'in some measure *unhinged* by the removal of the Chancellor'. Grenville himself was clearly concerned about the strength of the ministry, for on 8 March 1791 he threw out the idea of a coalition to his Foxite brother Thomas to raise with Fox. Thomas took up the matter with Fox, and in Thomas' papers there is an undated project for a new coalition Cabinet. It was assumed that Stafford and Camden would resign and Leeds be 'removed'. Chatham was to be First Lord of the Treasury, Thurlow and Richmond would remain in the Cabinet, Pitt be Secretary of State, presumably for the Home Office, Grenville and Fox be either the other Secretary of State or First Lord of the Admiralty, and Portland, Lord

[136] Cobbett, 29, 61. On the importance of trade with Russia, H. H. Kaplan, 'Russia's Impact on the Industrial Revolution in Great Britain During the Second Half of the Eighteenth Century: The Significance of International Commerce', *Forschungen zur osteuropäischen Geschichte*, 29 (1981), 7–59, and 'Anglo-Russian Commerce during the 1790s', *Consortium on Revolutionary Europe Proceedings 1986*, 227–234. For the strength of Anglo-Russian commercial links, customs statistics are in Ehrman, *Commercial Negotiations*, pp. 216–21, and a state of the trade in Edward Forster, Governor of the Russia Company to Hawkesbury, 29 June 1791, BL Add. 38226 fols. 255–7. Memoranda on Russian trade in 1785–6, AN. AM. B^7 451; Genet, French envoy in St Petersburg, to Montmorin, 30 Oct. 1789, Barthélemy to Montmorin, 31 Dec. 1790, AE CP Russie 130 fol. 137, Ang. 575 fol. 378; Anon., *Serious Enquiries into the Motives and Consequences of our present Armament against Russia* (1791), pp. 25, 40, 44.

John Cavendish and either Fitzwilliam or Stormont would gain office and enter the Cabinet. Fox was interested and thought a coalition possible, but he was unwilling to see Pitt remain as head of the government in the Commons and the difficulties of selecting a new Cabinet led Thomas Grenville to drop the proposal. It probably helped, however, to create a sense of uncertainty and to encourage Fox to press home the attack over Ochakov.[137]

In light of the government's majorities in Parliament, Lojek has argued that it was a Cabinet split that was crucial. The government was already split over the wisdom of risking war with Russia. Grenville, Richmond and Stafford were unenthusiastic, Thurlow unwilling to support Pitt, though also apparently unwilling to take a strong stand. And yet, there had been considerable tension in the ministry for a while. Having just dined with Leeds, Hawkesbury had complained in July 1789, 'Mr. Pitt goes on triumphantly and communicates with neither the Chancellor, the Duke of Leeds, nor myself, nor anyone with whom I have any connection.' George III had had to press Thurlow in November 1789 to settle his differences with Pitt. Close to Grenville, Dundas and Chatham, whose promotion he worked for, Pitt's relations with the ministerial group of 1784 (if that term does not suggest a misleading coherence) were generally cool. Such division did not matter greatly while the parliamentary and international situation was favourable, for then ministers did not air or press their doubts about Pitt; but the parliamentary storm on the 29th revealed that this was no longer so, and there was no compensatory good news from abroad. The parliamentary situation appeared crucial. Richmond told Leeds on the 30th that 'the country would not support' confrontation with Russia. When Leeds threatened next day that he would resign if policy changed, Pitt stressed the loss of support in the Commons, a theme he returned to on 4 April. The argument that confidence had to be placed in the ministry had been unconvincing; Opposition arguments about the inadvisability or danger of confronting Russia powerful.[138]

---

[137] *Political Memoranda of Leeds*, pp. 148–9, 159–60; McCahill, *Order and Equipoise*, pp. 134–5; Keith to Straton, 28 Dec. 1790, Ipswich HA 239/2/153; memorandun, 'Project of Facilities 1791', Aylesbury, Buckinghamshire CRO, Grenville papers D56 1/1b; P. Jupp, *Lord Grenville 1759–1834* (Oxford, 1985), pp. 123–4; *London Packet* 30 Mar. 1789.

[138] Lojek, 'British Policy', *Polish Review*, 14; Hawkesbury to Dorset, 2 July 1789, KAO C182; Pitt to Rose, 8 Nov. 1789, BL Add. 42772 fols. 20–1; George III to Thurlow, 22 Nov., reply c. 23 Nov. 1789, *Bonham Books Catalogue*, 15 Apr. 1991, lots 165–6; George III to Pitt, 21 Nov. 1790, Stanhope, *Pitt*, I, 491–2; Luzerne to Montmorin, 17 Mar., 28 Aug. 1789, 5 Oct. 1790, AE CP Ang. 568 fols. 338–9, 570 fol. 312, 575 fols. 6–7; John Hinchliffe, Bishop of Peterborough to Duke of Grafton, 7 Dec. 1790, Bury St Edmunds CRO Grafton papers 423/741; Thurlow to Ewart, 17 Jan. 1791,

When the Cabinet met on 30 March, Grenville, Richmond and Stafford expressed doubts. On the 31st Camden was unenthusiastic and Leeds expected a major change of policy at the Cabinet that evening. Grenville, Richmond and Stafford repeated their doubts there, but an expedient allowed Pitt to paper over the rifts in the ministry. In light of a dispatch from Drake, which arrived on 27 March, conveying a suggestion from Bernstorff that a compromise about the boundaries of the Ochakov district, that would leave the lower Dniester under Turkish control, would be accepted by Catherine II, the Cabinet decided to pursue the suggestion with the Danish ministry, while urging the Prussians to delay the projected moves against Russia. Jackson was instructed to tell the Prussian government that British naval preparations would continue, but he was not to act on the joint ultimatum to Russia or any other projects until he received further instructions.[139] Ewart and Burges were contemptuous about the Danish proposal, and Leeds unconvinced of its merit, while, among British diplomats, both Straton and Keith pressed for firmness towards Russia. Leeds, however, eventually agreed to pursue the proposal.[140] Nevertheless, Leeds was very unhappy about developments, and on 9 April he wrote to Pitt that he could not approve of the Danish proposals 'forming the basis of our *retreat*', not least because he distrusted Denmark as pro-Russian. Ewart was to make the same point about Denmark to Pitt. Leeds added, 'My opinion is unshaken; we ought to proceed upon our first plan. The language of opposition confirms me in the necessity of not giving way to their clamour at home, or the effects of it abroad.' Leeds stated that he had heard no satisfactory reasons for abandoning the plan which he warned would wreck the reputation of the government and establish 'a Russian party in the House of Commons'. Ewart shared his views.[141] In hindsight, it is clear that a turning point had been reached and that was apparent to ministers at the time. The approach to Denmark represented the search for compromise urged earlier by Auckland, who ironically on 30 March wrote of Ewart's 'complete triumph' over him.[142]

The decision to delay matters while such a search was made was a fatal one. It led to two different time-scales in early April, one, the diplomatic,

Williamwood 148; *Political Memoranda of Leeds*, pp. 152–4, 160; Pitt to Ewart, 24 May 1791, PRO 30/8/102 fols. 127–33.
[139] *Political Memoranda of Leeds*, pp. 152–8; Leeds to Jackson, 31 Mar. 1791, PRO FO 64/20 fols. 202–3.
[140] Ewart to Jackson, 27 Mar. 1791, Williamwood, 148; Straton to Leeds, 26 Mar., Keith to Straton, 8, 12, 22 Apr. 1791, Ipswich HA 239/2/1, 2/183–4, 187; Leeds to Jackson, 31 Mar. 1791, PRO FO 64/20 fols. 202–3.
[141] Leeds to Pitt, 9 Apr. 1791, PRO 30/8/151 fol. 47, BL Eg. 3498 fol. 173; Ewart to Pitt, 14 Apr. 1791, Williamwood, 148.
[142] Auckland to Burges, 30 Mar. 1791, Bod. BB. 30 fol. 138.

characterised by waiting and hesitation, the other, the domestic, marked by growing criticisms of government policy and rapid moves towards a crisis. The Cabinet decision was secret. While Pitt waited for the replies from the Continent, he was in touch with Ewart, first by post, and subsequently in person. He wrote to him on 6 April that 'events have taken a turn here, which seem to have little or no chance of pushing our plan to its original extent'.[143] Ewart was at the spa of Buxton at the beginning of April and he wrote thence to Burges to warn him that delay would lose Britain Prussia, Poland and Turkey. Ewart was also concerned about the success of Opposition arguments,

I fear Opposition is too busy and too successful, in spreading insidious reports all over the country, in order to alarm the public on the subject of the armaments and their object. I therefore hope that your pen is employed in refuting their misrepresentations, and I am just going to write some remarks ... [144]

Returning to London, Ewart found Pitt on the 11th still convinced of the correctness of British policy, but now sure that a majority of the Commons were against him and unwilling to support a Vote of Credit. Ewart reported Pitt as being very upset, with tears in his eyes, confessing his mortification, and much affected by the recent parliamentary debate. Pitt still intended to keep the fleet ready to sail, and he hoped that a compromise could be negotiated, the line taken by the Cabinet on 12 April 1791, though Leeds, who had taken little share in the Cabinet deliberations on 10 April, now declared that he could not sign the proposed new instructions to Ewart. Ewart was to return to Berlin to preserve the alliance. Pitt accepted Ewart's point of the need for 'immediately making the most public and positive overtures to Poland and Turkey, for the formation of the most intimate alliance, with a powerful naval guarantee to the latter, and the assistance of English officers and seamen to put their naval force on a proper footing', but all was now to be overshadowed by the quest for compromise with Russia.

After the Cabinet on the 12th, Leeds asked Ewart to dine with him alone, and in the latter's words

made a declaration of his principles, which struck me with equal admiration for his vigour of mind and talents, and regret that he should have so seldom exerted them ... I urged to him especially the difference there was between Mr. Pitt's having flinched and varied in any respect in his own mind, and his being driven by the most mortifying necessity to himself to alter his line of conduct.

On the 13th, according to Ewart, Pitt agreed to delay sending the messenger to Jackson for another two days, while Leeds 'seemed

---

[143] Pitt to Ewart, 6 Apr. 1791, Williamwood 157.
[144] Ewart to Burges, 5, 7 Apr. 1791, Bod. BB. 34 fols. 142–4.

disposed to agree to remain in office, provided he did not sign'. However, Ewart added in his letter to Jackson of the 14th,

> Mr. Pitt was extremely affected by the violent opposition in the House of Commons on Tuesday [12 April], has been much agitated since, and appears much embarrassed towards me – Lord Grenville is very much with him, which I do not like, for he will do all the mischief he can.[145]

On 12 April, clearly scenting an opportunity, the Opposition had raised British foreign policy in the Commons. Grey moved eight resolutions which represented cumulatively a major attack on this policy, as both misdirected and inconsistent. The fifth resolution stated that British interests were not likely to be affected by Russian gains on the shores of the Black Sea, while the sixth and seventh drew attention to Britain's obligations to her allies as defensive and argued that no such case then applied. The habits of eighteenth-century political debate, the fashion for 'enlightened' opinion and the convenience of being in Opposition – if not irresponsibility then at least non-responsibility – combined to allow Grey to set a moral tone. He argued that the maxims of policy which ought to govern foreign policy were clear and evident, that the only just cause of war was self-defence, and certainly not political expediency, that self-defence comprehended responding to an unjust attack on an ally, but not being bound to support the other engagements of Frederick William II, and, Grey claimed in an intelligent use of the parliamentary argument, that Parliament would never have accepted the Anglo-Prussian treaty had it been offensive. He continued by arguing that Russian gains did not affect the balance of power or the interests of Britain, that Constantinople was more threatened from the Crimea, that Ochakov did not control the Dnieper, and that a Russian advance into the Balkans did not require control of Ochakov. The value of Russian trade, the lack of British commercial interest in the Black Sea, and Chatham's unwillingness to send a fleet to the Baltic in 1759 were all cited.[146]

The first resolution, that it was at all times, and especially in the present circumstances, the interest of Britain to preserve peace was then put, and seconded by Major Thomas Maitland. Maitland essentially repeated Grey's points, though they lost none of their force by repetition, adding only the somewhat unnecessary statement that Britain ought not

---

[145] *Political Memoranda of Leeds*, p. 162; Ewart to Jackson, 14 Apr. 1791, Williamwood 148. Ehrman, *Pitt*, II, 25 fn 1 dates the meeting between Pitt and Ewart as occurring after the 12th, but the reference to Pitt being very affected by the debate on that day occurs after the account of the interview. On Grenville's views, E. D. Adams, *The Influence of Grenville on Pitt's Foreign Policy, 1787–1798* (Washington, 1904) pp. 11–13; Jupp, *Grenville*, pp. 122–7; Duffy, 'Pitt, Grenville and the Control of British Foreign Policy in the 1790s', in Black (ed.), *Knights Errant*, pp. 152–4.

[146] Cobbett, 29, 164–77; Smith, *Grey*, p. 34.

to fight even if the Russians took Constantinople; and the more interesting claim that the government was proposing to fight to support an ideal balance of power, never previously entertained. Maitland, who had served in India, further stated that Prussia could never be obliged to help Britain to the same extent that Britain had to be ready to act on her behalf. Though he thus ignored the crucial question of Prussian willingness to help defend the United Provinces, Maitland was essentially correct in implying that European powers could provide little assistance to furthering Britain's extra-European goals.[147]

The first speaker for the government was the relatively inexperienced Robert, Viscount Belgrave, later 1st Marquis of Westminster, a Lord of the Admiralty but only 23 years old. Belgrave again advanced the need for confidence in the ministry, an argument that gained no force by repetition, but he also brought up the 'Eastern Question'. If Catherine II was allowed to pursue her 'career of victories', she would conquer the European portions of the Turkish Empire, and then possibly Egypt, which would give Russia superiority in the Mediterranean and make her a formidable commercial and maritime rival to Britain. The following year, Pitt outlined the danger that, once in control of the Black Sea, Russia would become a more powerful naval power. He emphasised 'the jealousy natural against the first existing naval power [Britain]', and 'rivalship with our interests in the East Indies', which he saw as stemming from 'Russia being in possession of the sovereignty on the Black Sea and the countries adjacent'. Richard Willis had warned Pitt that Catherine had 'long arms' and might 'instigate the Tartar nations at the back of India to give *us* a blow that might be felt for a century'. Willis recalled successful earlier invasions of India, most recently that of Nadir Shah in 1739, and claimed that George Bogle, who had been sent on a mission to Tibet by Warren Hastings in 1774–5, had thought such an invasion practicable. This thesis, like, for example, British fears of Russian activities in Iran, greatly exaggerated Russian capabilities while minimising the difficulties facing her. Just over a century later, the Ochakov crisis was to be put in this misleading context by Montagu Burrows, Chichele Professor of Modern History at Oxford, and a former captain in the Royal Navy. A great searcher after continuity, he claimed that Turkey had been saved by Pitt, but that the opportunity to confront Russia had been 'lost, and the Crimean War was required ... to save the East Mediterranean'.[148]

[147] Cobbett, 29, 177–9.
[148] Cobbett, 29, 179–81; undated notes, PRO 30/8/195 fols. 50–1; Willis to Pitt, 31 Jan. 1791, CUL Add. 6958 no. 910; Atkin, *Russia and Iran*, p. 36; M. Burrows, *The History of the Foreign Policy of Great Britain* (1895), vi, 158–9.

Charge provoked counter-charge as the lengthy debate continued, historical precedents and geopolitical speculations both appearing. Both power politics and moral issues were raised. The Foxite Samuel Whitbread argued that the expulsion of the tyrannical Turks from Europe, a move far more radical than any the French revolutionaries were to attempt the following year, would be of universal benefit. It would lead to an economic revival of the Balkans that would help every commercial state. In addition, Whitbread claimed, in an interesting reversal of customary attitudes, that the extension of Russian power to the south would weaken her, that large empires could not subsist and that if a Russian state stretching from the Pacific to the Balkans did, it would have to devote its attention to domestic problems. Frederick, Earl-Bishop of Derry, had already anticipated Whitbread's first point. Whitbread further criticised British policy as immoral when he claimed that opposition to Russia sprang from her hostility to British-supported Prussian ambitions for the gain of Danzig and Thorn. Sheridan made a similar point. And yet, Whitbread also struck a practical note, referring to the commercial consequences of war with Russia and the example of George I's failure to coerce Peter the Great.[149]

Sir William Young, a firm Pittite, in reply, reiterated Belgrave's point about the danger of Russia as a Mediterranean power, an example of the propensity of ministerial speakers to seek the supposed general threats posed by Russia's advance, while their rivals, though willing to range widely in criticising the direction and morality of British foreign policy, tended to focus on the supposed advantages to Russia that would arise from the gain of Ochakov and its district. The problem facing parliamentarians, discussing the commercial and strategic aspects of remote districts, was mentioned by Sheridan who referred to Young as having 'expatiated with as much familiarity concerning the Dnieper and the Danube, as if he had been talking of the Worcestershire canal'. Young also traced a path from Britain's maritime and colonial position to the Black Sea, via the United Provinces and Prussia, that matched the development of British foreign policy over the previous seven years. The need for a naval ally had led to the United Provinces, her security was provided by Prussia and Prussian strength required that Russia should not be stronger. This was indeed true in terms of consequences, though, as Sheridan pointed out, these were unintended, not part of a determined system.[150]

The ministry won the division by 253 to 173, a majority of 80.[151] Luzerne claimed that, having counted on a majority of 150, Pitt was

---

[149] Cobbett, 29, 181–204; B. Fothergill, *The Mitred Earl* (1974), pp. 137–8.
[150] Cobbett, 29, 204–214.   [151] Cobbett, 29, 217.

astonished and embarrassed by the vote. The government could survive such a victory, had indeed overcome worse parliamentary upsets, but after the division on 13 April, Fox declared not only that Pitt must be convinced by the vote that war would be unpopular and that the country was roused from a lethargic state, but also that Pitt must expect to see his majority whittled away by daily motions. After a weak reply by Pitt, a Foxite MP, William Baker, gave notice that he would bring the subject before the Commons in a new shape on 15 April.[152]

The British backdown

This was the sort of parliamentary pressure that could crack a badly divided ministry. It was underlined by heightened public interest in the debates. The *Leeds Intelligencer*, in its issue of 17 May, reported on the votes of the county MPs on Grey's motion, an unusual step. Walpole had abandoned the Excise bill in similar circumstances in 1733. The domestic situation led Pitt to change the direction of British policy. The Commons adjourned after Baker's motion at 3.30 am on 16 April, the division being 162–254,[153] but already, before that debate, Pitt had began to draft dispatches that would signal a change. There was to be no ultimatum to Russia, then or in the future, though an appearance of firmness was to be maintained. Nevertheless, conciliation was to be the policy, compromise the objective. New instructions were drawn up for Ewart, and, with Leeds unwilling to sign them, were presented to the Cabinet on 16 April by Grenville, who was to replace the Duke as Foreign Secretary after Leeds resigned. The Duke had already told George III on the 15th that he would resign, though he proposed to wait until the day of adjournment for the parliamentary recess. On 21 April Leeds delivered up the seals of his office. That day George III sent them to Grenville, who formally added responsibility for foreign affairs to his position as Home Secretary. On 8 June Grenville resigned the latter post in order to become Foreign Secretary on a permanent basis. Burges was subsequently to blame him for the backdown. Leeds was treated better than Sherif Hasan Pasha, the Grand Vizier, shot at Shumla on 14 February 1791 as a result of Turkish failures that winter.[154]

The British government sought to rescue the Prussian alliance and the peace offensive in eastern Europe from its climbdown, and to negotiate

---

[152] Luzerne to Montmorin, 15 Apr. 1791, AE CP Ang. 577 fol. 142; Cobbett, 29, 217–18.
[153] Cobbett, 29, 218–49; Fawkener to Hawkesbury, 16 Apr. 1791, BL Add. 38226 fol. 127.
[154] *Political Memoranda of Leeds*, pp. 162–73; Pitt to George III, 1791, PRO 30/8/101 fol. 29; Fawkener to Hawkesbury, 17 Apr. 1791, BL Add. 38226 fol. 130; Grenville to George III, 19 Apr., George III to Grenville, 19, 21, 30 Apr. 1791, BL Add. 58856 fols. 32–9; Jupp, *Grenville*, p. 127; Burges, memo, Bod. BB. 74 fol. 30.

peace 'on such terms as may not in their effect too much endanger the security of the weaker country, or alter in too great a degree the relative situation of those nations in the East of Europe whose situation forms so material a part in the general balance of power'. Ewart was ordered to return to his post in order to tell Frederick William II that the opportunity provided by the possibility of Danish mediation and the domestic storm within Britain about the prospect of war had led the government to prefer the course of peaceful compromise; that Elgin had been ordered to sound Leopold II and there was no need for Prussian jealousy; and that the British ministry now sought a modification of the *status quo ante bellum* that might 'not be wholly inconsistent with the security of the Porte'. Ochakov and its district could be ceded if the fortress of Ochakov was demolished and none other built, and if the Russians were not to settle their acquisition. The Russians were to be kept away from the Dniester, in order to prevent them from controlling the river and thus influencing Poland. To that end a frontier east of the river, possibly Lake Telegel (Tiligul'skiy) was suggested. This would have left the future town of Odessa in Turkish hands. Ewart set off for Berlin though he was very pessimistic about the prospects for the new policy and found it personally 'dreadful'.[155]

Though Grenville and Auckland distrusted Leopold II, the new approach was to be supported by an attempt to use Austria as an intermediary with Russia, necessarily so, as it seemed increasingly likely that Leopold would not settle with the Turks until he was certain that Catherine would. Elgin was instructed to ask the Emperor to press Russia to accept peace and to offer Leopold a treaty of defensive alliance that would incorporate him, the powers of the Triple Alliance, and, after peace was signed, Turkey. This was seen as likely to help Austria by guaranteeing the Austrian Netherlands, checking Russian progress against the Turks, ending Austro-Prussian animosity and renewing her 'ancient connection' with Britain and the United Provinces.[156] The Austrians were also to be pressed to complete the negotiations with the Turks at Sistova on the basis of the Reichenbach engagements. In an interesting use of the revolutionary ferment then affecting so much of Europe, Grenville argued that any delay in settling the conflict would

[155] Grenville to St Helens, 19 Apr., Auckland to Grenville, 16, 19, 23 Apr. 1791, BL Add. 59022 fol. 11, 58919 fols. 48, 50, 52–3; Grenville to Ewart, 20 Apr. 1791, PRO FO 64/21 fols. 7–19; Ewart to Burges, 21 Apr. 1791, Bod. BB. 34 fol. 146; Ewart to Jackson, 19 Apr., Pitt to Ewart, 24 Apr. 1791, Williamwood 148, 157.
[156] Grenville to Auckland, 1 May 1791, BL Add. 58919 fol. 61; Auckland to Straton, 22 Apr. 1791, Ipswich HA 239/2/275; Instructions to Elgin, 19 Apr. 1791, PRO FO 7/23 fols. 92–4; Elgin to Leopold II, 11 May, Ewart to Elgin, 19 Apr. 1791, Broomhall 60/1/85, 95.

only encourage Leopold's domestic opponents.[157] Such an argument reflected a common habit of considering external and domestic commitments as competitive, but it is also interesting to note that the task facing Leopold was seen in terms of reimposing order within his own dominions, rather than intervening in other states to the same purpose. In addition, Elgin's instructions spoke of the British government's prime concern as being that of maintaining the relative position of the principal states. There was no suggestion that this could be influenced by domestic developments within them (as opposed to territorial gains), nor that the structure of collective security that Leopold was to be offered should be designed to act against such developments. Thus, at the same time that the British ministry was offering the somewhat utopian hope of a collective security system to prevent international territorial changes, except by general agreement, it was also failing to consider the possible implications of developments within France. Given that the collective security system was designed to serve fundamentally conservative and reactive goals, British policy as a whole can be seen in that light.

At the same time, British policy can be seen as poorly advised in a narrower perspective. Any solution to the crisis in eastern Europe would clearly require better relations between Austria and Prussia in the first instance, and Prussia and Russia thereafter, as well as stability for Poland and peace for Turkey, but the British ministry failed to appreciate the degree to which such better relations would lead both to a reduction or even collapse of British influence, and to a related search for such relations at the expense of Poland and Turkey. Commenting on Elgin's instructions, which he saw as they went through The Hague under flying seal, Auckland wrote of the proposed expansion of the collective security system: 'the extension of the connection, if it were probable that so wise a measure both for Austria and Prussia could be effectuated cordially and solidly, such a result would compensate fully for all the other mortifications of the moment'.[158] Instead, Austria and Prussia were to ally, but within a new system, designed to serve goals that were not those of the British government; indeed the short-term mortifications of the Ochakov climbdown were to pale into insignificance beside the collapse of the British diplomatic system later in 1791. Such a collapse, though not the form it took, had been anticipated by Ewart, Leeds and Pitt from the moment at which the impetus of the British confrontation with Russia slackened, and to that extent they were vindicated by subsequent diplomatic developments. Similarly, relations between Britain and Morocco suffered when the settlement of the Nootka Sound crisis led the

[157] Grenville to Straton, 19 Apr. 1791, PRO FO 7/24 fol. 152.
[158] Auckland to Ewart, 23 Apr. 1791, Matlock CRO 239 M/O 759.

British government to retract its earlier support for a planned Moroccan attack on Spanish-held Centa and, instead, to press Morocco against such an attack.[159]

On the other hand, it can be argued that an eventual collapse of the British diplomatic system was inherent in the very nature of the Anglo-Prussian alliance, especially given the different aims of the two powers, that, in short, Anglo-Prussian co-operation in 1787–91 repeated the pattern of the last period of such co-operation, during the Seven Years War. And yet the skill of diplomacy consists in part of taking advantage of adverse circumstances, of winning benefits from precarious alignments, of turning the contingencies of the specific moment to profit. The British ministry had succeeded in doing so in 1787, and from that had stemmed the Triple Alliance. In trying to make that system permanent, Pitt and Ewart can be faulted. Their language of permanent alliance and a widely spread collective security system failed to take sufficient note of the play of circumstance. This was despite the fully reported rifts within the Prussian government, the tergiversations of its policy and the inconstancy of Frederick William II; as well as the *volte-face* of Swedish policy in 1790.

The new British policy defined in mid-April 1791 was to be presented by Ewart in Berlin, Elgin with Leopold II then in Florence, and by a special envoy, William Fawkener, at St Petersburg. It was backed up by efforts to win Austrian, Danish, Dutch and Spanish diplomatic support,[160] though Grenville based his hopes mostly on Fawkener and on war-weariness on Catherine's part. Fawkener, the senior clerk in the Privy Council Office, had little diplomatic experience. He had served as Envoy Extraordinary and Plenipotentiary in Lisbon, but had been sent there simply to negotiate on commercial matters, had assisted an already well-established envoy, Robert Walpole, and had served for only a brief period, from 25 October 1786 to the following January. Fawkener's great advantage for his new posting was that he had not been involved in the anti-Russian policies of recent years. Though Leeds approved of the choice of Fawkener, who was an old friend, he was also reported to be very close to Pitt, and had indeed worked closely with him on commercial negotiations. In addition, he had already revealed in late February that he was both critical of Prussia and felt that the Anglo-Prussian alliance had pushed matters too far.[161]

[159] ? to Consul James Matra, 14 Nov. 1790, BL Add. 51705 fols. 4–5.
[160] Pitt to Ewart, 24 May 1791, PRO 30/8/102 fols. 130–1; Grenville to St Helens, 19 Apr. 1791, BL Add. 59022 fols. 7–12.
[161] Grenville to Fawkener, 26 Apr., 24 May 1791, PRO FO 65/20, BL Add. 59023 fol. 14; *Political Memoranda of Leeds*, p. 162; Barthélemy to Vergennes, 3 Oct. 1786; Barthélemy to Montmorin, 25 Feb. 1791, AE CP Ang. 558 fol. 5, 576 fols. 223–5.

Initial signs were favourable. Ewart reached Berlin at the end of April and found his reception by Frederick William II 'far surpassed my expectation... His Prussian Majesty expressed the highest regard for you, and entered into your feelings as well as your reasonings on the present unfortunate disappointment'. Frederick William and his closest advisor Bischoffwerder were both eager to see Austria join the system and Ewart was told that Prussia would co-operate with Elgin in his negotiation to that end.[162] The need to forward this negotiation was pressed by the British government. Pessimistic about the chances of bringing Russia into the alliance system, the ministry hoped, nevertheless, that Austrian support would help establish Poland on a secure footing, settle Austro-Turkish differences and help produce an agreement with Russia. Thus, the opportunities offered by the death of Joseph II were to be pressed home again; Austrian help to be a substitute for the intimidation of Russia.[163] Ewart was still pressing the case for intimidation, arguing that Britain could only preserve the Prussian alliance and defend Constantinople if it sent a squadron to the Black Sea, a move sought by Frederick William. Ewart's failure, despite a recent visit to Britain, to appreciate the current sensitivity of anti-Russian moves was readily apparent. Temperamentally forceful, Ewart also argued 'that nothing but the certainty of this Court [Prussia] being able to act with vigour' would lead to a settlement at Sistova. Still there, Keith wanted a firm approach towards Austria and the dispatch of the British squadrons.[164]

Although the fleet that had been prepared was not demobilised till August, naval action, however, was no longer an option, as Chatham explained to Ewart when he wrote on 24 May about the plan for an expedition to the Black Sea:

the undertaking would be rather an arduous one, the navigation being so little known, and the prevalence of particular winds in the summer months, rendering the passage up the canal of Constantinople very precarious, but these obstacles are to be surmounted, and I should see no objection as a military operation to this step, but on the contrary considerable advantage, were vigorous measures in question, but... this plan has not been approved here from the consideration that the sailing of a squadron for the Black Sea would be considered, as tending to immediate hostility, and would renew all those alarms and discussions which

[162] Ewart to Pitt, 30 Apr. 1791, BL Add. 58906 fol. 102; Ewart to Burges, 7 May, Jackson to Burges, 6 May 1791, Bod. BB. 34 fol. 147, 36 fols. 68–9; Pitt to Ewart, 24 May 1791, Williamwood 157, PRO 30/8/102 fol. 132.
[163] Grenville to Elgin, 23 May 1791, PRO FO 7/23 fols. 125–7.
[164] Ewart to Grenville, 6, 17 May 1791, PRO FO 64/21; Ewart to Burges, 7 May 1791, Bod. BB. 34 fol. 147; Ewart to Straton, 25 June, Keith to Straton, 1, 6 July 1791, Ipswich HA 239/2/237, 212, 214.

have to a degree subsided, only from the persuasion that the business was in a train of negociation. It is also feared that it might discourage at present, the favorable dispositions that seem to manifest themselves in the Court of Spain, and the old objection besides of expense recurs ... [165]

Grenville argued in early July that 'the situation of this country' meant that it could not act offensively.[166] Instead, the ministry was searching for a compromise. Grenville suggested that the future security of Turkey, a goal that Ewart pointed out had been regarded hitherto as indispensable,[167] would depend more on a system of guarantee than on the exact location of the frontier.[168] Fawkener made the same point.[169] Grenville further argued that despite Prussian pressure no fleet could be sent to the Baltic, because it would be inconsistent with the new line of policy, and would be unacceptable domestically. Grenville had already suggested that the Hessian subsidy treaty signed in 1787 not be renewed for financial reasons, and had indicated that, 'desireable as it certainly would have been to us in every point of view to have raised up a commercial rival to Russia', schemes for the development of Poland in this light had been dropped.[170] Ewart, who still sought to 'give the impulsion and direction' to Prussian policy, no longer felt informed of Pitt's 'private sentiments'.[171]

Fawkener's instructions were drawn up in this context. There was hope that such a system of guaranty could be created, that Russia could be influenced more successfully with Austrian assistance than that of the British navy and the Prussian army. Fawkener was accordingly instructed to seek a compromise: Ochakov and its district were to be left neutral and uninhabited, Russian and uninhabited, or Russian and demilitarised but with the frontier east of the Dniester. These hopes were to prove illusory, because the response to British approaches was unsatisfactory both at St Petersburg and in Italy. Fawkener reached The Hague on 29 April and St Petersburg on 24 May 1791, but found Catherine II unwilling to accept the British proposals. The Russians argued that they needed a certain and distinct frontier, and could not accept demilitarised status as it would not prevent a Turkish attack.[172] Catherine was hopeful both of

[165] Chatham to Ewart, 24 May 1791, Williamwood 157.
[166] Grenville to Ewart, 6 July 1791, *Dropmore*, II, 124.
[167] Ewart to [Grenville?], no date, BL Add. 58906 fol. 106.
[168] Grenville to St Helens, 19 Apr. 1791, BL Add. 59022 fols. 9–10.
[169] Fawkener to Hawkesbury, 18 June 1791, BL Add. 38226 fol. 246.
[170] Grenville to Ewart, 25 May 1791, PRO FO 64/21 fols. 126–31; Grenville to Auckland, 1 May 1791, Grenville to Lord Henry Spencer, 27 Mar. 1792, BL Add. 58919 fols. 61–2, 34441 fol. 508.   [171] Ewart to Pitt, 4 Aug. 1791, PRO 30/8/133 fol. 297.
[172] Fawkener to Hawkesbury, 16 Apr., 18 June 1791, BL Add. 38226 fols. 127, 246; Whitworth and Goltz memorial, 26 May, Osterman to Whitworth and Goltz, 6 June, Whitworth, Fawkener and Goltz memorial, 29 June, 22 July, Osterman to Whitworth,

further military success against the Turks, and of winning the support of Leopold II. The Emperor was indeed unreceptive to Elgin,[173] despite the latter's hopes,[174] and by mid-June it was clear from what he had told the Earl and from what Count Stadion, the Austrian envoy in London, had told Grenville, that Leopold was not ready to enter the British system, despite Auckland's hope that need for British help over the Austrian Netherlands and the possibility of Austrian action against France might lead him to do so. The Austrian government rejected all idea of a guarantee of Turkey, and pushed claims for territorial gains at the expense of the Turks. At the same time the Austrian envoys at Sistova continued to adopt an unhelpful attitude.[175] Grenville was reduced to hoping that Bischoffwerder would be more successful.[176] Ostensibly sent to support Elgin, he reached Milan where Leopold was on 10 June 1791. Uncertain about Austrian intentions, Grenville had to face the danger that the talks at Sistova would break down, that the failure to intimidate Catherine would lead to the unravelling of the Reichenbach agreement. He was keen on Turkish flexibility in the frontier negotiations, but, if Austria renewed the conflict and war broke out as a result between Austria and Prussia, Grenville was aware that Britain would be obliged to help her ally, scarcely a welcome prospect in either the domestic or the international perspective. He told Stadion that Britain would fulfil her commitments as a guarantor of the Reichenbach convention.[177]

Given the fact that Austria and Prussia were to sign a preliminary convention at Vienna on 25 July 1791, Grenville's fears can appear foolish, but they indicate the British government's strong anxiety about continental commitments, an anxiety which had been both focussed and accentuated as a result of the climbdown over Ochakov. Bischoffwerder found Leopold II initially cool towards his approach for an alliance, but on 12 June news arrived that Leopold's brother-in-law Louis XVI was about to flee Paris. This provided a new focus for Leopold. Austrian attention, which in 1787 had swung from the west to the east, was to swing back. Instead of fighting the Turks again, it now appeared

Fawkener and Goltz, 20 July 1791, PRO FO 78/12B; Grenville to Richmond, 29 July 1791, BL Add. 58937 fol. 136.
[173] Auckland to Elgin, 12 July 1791, Broomhall 60/23/20.
[174] Elgin to Ewart, 11 Mar. 1791, Williamwood 148; Sir John Macpherson, with Elgin, to Straton, 12 May, Elgin to Straton, 20 May 1791, Ipswich HA 239/2/249–50.
[175] Keith to Straton, 4 June, Ewart to Straton, 21 June 1791, Ipswich HA 239/2/201, 236; Ewart to Elgin, 30 May, 7, 25, 29 June, Straton to Elgin, 9, 16, 27 June 1791, Broomhall 60/1/61, 60/23/5, 60/23/1; Auckland to Grenville, 27 May 1791, BL Add. 58919 fol. 85; Ewart to Pitt, 4 Aug. 1791, PRO 30/8/133 fol. 297.
[176] Grenville to Ewart, 14 June 1791, PRO FO 64/21 fols. 168–9.
[177] Grenville to Ewart, 7 July, Grenville to Keith, 7 July 1791, PRO FO 64/21 fols. 217–30, 7/27 fol. 35; Ainslie to Ewart, 18 July 1791, PRO FO 261/7 p. 61.

important to settle with them, and to win Prussian support against France. Whereas Elgin wished to direct Austrian attention so as to facilitate an acceptable settlement of the Russo-Turkish conflict, Leopold was able, thanks to Bischoffwerder's limitations as a diplomat, to negotiate an agreement with him that entailed no such commitments.[178] Elgin did not have full powers to enter into a treaty of defensive alliance with Leopold, and the British government was unwilling to send either such powers or instructions for negotiating an alliance until Leopold had fulfilled his obligations under the Reichenbach agreement. Elgin indeed was criticised for seeking 'official instructions relative to the affairs of France'; a step he was pressed to take by Bischoffwerder.[179] On 22 July 1791 a Cabinet meeting of Dundas, Grenville, Pitt, Richmond and Thurlow approved the draft of a letter from George III in answer to one from Leopold II, indicating the extent to which ministers were consulted on such correspondence, and

agreed that His Majesty's minister at Vienna should be instructed in his conversations on the subject... to insist strongly on the necessity of the conclusion of the negotiations for peace at Sistova previous to any further explanation on other subjects – That in conformity to the tenor of the King's letter he should not hold out the expectation of assistance from this country in the plan of interference in France and that he should keep in view the necessity of arranging the business of the Convention respecting the [Austrian] Netherlands previous to explanations on the subject of France, or of the conclusion of the alliance.[180]

This cautious attitude, which was accompanied by an instruction to Keith to do nothing without Prussian concurrence,[181] reflected understandable British doubts about Leopold's intentions, as well as the importance attached to the Low Countries; but it led the government to miss an opportunity to probe the possibilities for better Anglo-Austrian relations. On the other hand, it was not realised that a new alignment was being created, that, in short, Britain had to define her position anew.

Bischoffwerder's unilateral diplomacy left Britain isolated, and encouraged the already marked move towards a policy of caution. Ainslie was instructed to urge the Turks to negotiate directly with the Russians and to avoid giving any commitments of British support. In instructions of 19 August 1791, Grenville specifically ordered him to give no assurances about any guarantee of Turkish possessions after a peace had been negotiated.[182] Auckland was unsure whether the new Austro-

[178] Vivenot, *Politik des ... Kaunitz*, pp. 176–81; Lord, *Second Partition*, pp. 210–11.
[179] Elgin to Pitt, 15 June 1791, Broomhall 60/23/24, PRO 30/8/132 fol. 172.
[180] Cabinet minute, 22 July 1791, BL Add. 59306 fol. 1.
[181] Grenville to Keith, 7 July 1791, PRO FO 7/27 fols. 46–8.
[182] Bagis, *Ainslie*, pp. 122–3.

Prussian alignment would have lasting consequences, or be as ephemeral as the Prusso-Turkish offensive treaty negotiated by Diez in January 1790, but he predicted correctly that if the former this would lead to the end of the Anglo-Prussian alliance. Never a fan of the Prussians, Auckland was happy to voice his criticism of their conduct, though he added a comment that was both indicative of his superiors' views and explained why the new focus of diplomatic activity excluded Britain and the negotiations had had to be unilateral,

It is also highly indecorous, for the instructions to Bischoffwerder and Lord Elgin were mutually communicated; their commission and its object were one and the same: but it now appears that there was a secret instruction and that we were outwitted, if one man can be said to outwit another, when the outwitting consists in a surprize contrary to good sense and fair expectation. As to the French business, I sincerely hope and trust that for the present at least we shall remain quiet spectators.[183]

The new alignment was to last long enough to influence developments in many quarters of Europe. Leopold's concern with France led to a new moderation in the demands of his plenipotentiaries at Sistova,[184] and a treaty was signed there on 4 August 1791. The frontier modifications were modest, and Keith was delighted by the settlement.[185] The relative neglect of the British by the Austrians was indicated by the fact that the Prussian envoy, not Keith, was given one of the few early copies of the map depicting the new frontier.[186] It proved easier, however, to draw a map than to settle the new frontier on the ground. Disputes over delimitations were not settled by the boundary commissions until late 1795.

There was to be no general guarantee for the Austro-Turkish agreement, no more than for the Russo-Turkish peace that came surprisingly quickly. Russian victories over the Turks in advances across the Danube at Babadag (14 June) and Machin (10 July), revealed the vulnerability of Selim III, his army was largely destroyed, and he now knew that he could not count on a Prussian diversion or on British naval support in the Black Sea, where on 11 August the Russian fleet successfully engaged the Turks off Cape Kaliakra, south of Varna.

That day peace preliminaries and an armistice were agreed at Galatz. Russia gained Ochakov and the territory to the Dniester, though she had to agree not to fortify it. The annexation of the Crimea was silently

[183] Auckland to Keith, 23 Aug. 1791, NLS Acc. 9769 72/2/7.
[184] Auckland to Elgin, 10 July, Keith to Elgin, 26 July 1791, Broomhall, 60/23/20, 22.
[185] Keith to Frances Murray, 14 Aug. 1791, HL HM. 18940 p. 401; Keith to Straton, 29 July, 2, 12, 14 Aug. 1791, Austro-Turkish Convention, Ipswich HA 239/2/222–51, 135.   [186] Keith to Grenville, 5 Aug. 1791, PRO FO 7/27 fol. 167.

accepted. Anapa was to be returned to the Turks. In subsequent negotiations, the Turks failed to persuade the Russians to accept a frontier to the east of the Dniester, and Potemkin failed to obtain a substantial indemnity, Anapa and an independent Moldavia. These preliminaries became the basis of the Treaty of Jassy of 9 January 1792, and Russia did not have to accept the humiliation of mediation by third parties and the limitations posed by the prospect of their guarantes. The terms were better for the Turks than had seemed possible during much of the war,[187] and British officials consoled themselves with the thought that this was due to the intervention of the Triple Alliance.[188] The Russo-Turkish peace was to be shortlived, as was the Dniester frontier. In 1802 Russia gained the right to control the appointment and dismissal of the hospodars of Moldavia and Wallachia. In 1806, Selim's close relations with Napoleon led to a Russian invasion of Bessarabia, Moldavia and Wallachia. The war was ended by the Treaty of Bucharest of 1812, by which Russia gained Bessarabia.[189] The Russian frontier thus reached the Pruth and the Danube. The Russians captured Anapa in 1828, during the Russo-Turkish war of 1828–9, and by the Treaty of Adrianople (Edirne) of 1829 the Turks agreed to give up their possessions and claims in Anapa and on the Circassian coast.

International guarantes would have scarcely prevented these gains. The vulnerability of the Turkish position was already obvious in 1792. In June of that year Captain Sidney Smith was sent on a secret mission to Constantinople in order to report on the Turkish military position and 'to consider the means which the Russians may appear to him to have of making an impression upon Constantinople, or any other part of the Turkish Empire, by any attack made from the Black Sea, either by their naval force, or by an army landed near to Constantinople, and acting in concert with their fleet; and the means by which such an attack might best be resisted'. The following year, George Monro sent Burges a lengthy account of the Turkish position in Europe in which he argued that it was impossible for the Turks to retain it unless they received foreign assistance or totally changed their system of government.[190] Ochakov no longer seemed relevant, but the 'Eastern Question' had certainly emerged.

The new Austro-Prussian alignment clearly affected Britain. What-

---

[187] Grenville to George III, 14 Aug. 1791, BL Add. 58856 fol. 66.
[188] George III to Grenville, 14 Aug. 1791, BL Add. 58856 fol. 67, Bod. BB 52 fol. 125; Whitworth to Grenville, 24 Jan. 1792, PRO FO 65/23 fol. 9; undated notes, PRO 30/8/195 fol. 51.
[189] G. F. Jewsbury, *The Russian Annexation of Bessarabia* (Boulder, Colorado, 1976).
[190] Grenville to Smith, 19 June 1792, Monro to Burges, 11 Apr. 1793, Bod. BB. 41 fol. 6, 67 p.1.

ever his earlier failings, the sickly and stressed Ewart had obviously displayed an uncertain grasp of the diplomatic situation since his return to Berlin in April 1791. Two months later he wrote to Burges, who simultaneously enjoyed the confidence of many diplomats and, as Under Secretary, offered them the possibility of influencing affairs, that Britain 'might again get possession of the reins, and be greater than ever'; but he added that if Prussia submitted to Austria, the British system would be ruined.[191] In fact, the Prussian approach to Leopold was but another instance of the propensity for secret unilateral diplomacy that had led Prussian ministers to seek negotiations with Catherine II the previous winter at the same time as they prepared for war with her.[192] Frederick William II was temperamentally inconstant, but he also had no intention of allowing his ally to control his options, and the British determination to do so had left him very irritated.[193] The Prussian negotiations with Austria were soon followed by neglect of Britain in other respects. British diplomats, such as Straton, complained that their Prussian counterparts both neglected and were reserved towards them.[194] Ewart's influence in Berlin collapsed, as Malmesbury noted when he visited the city for the Duke of York's wedding.[195] Ewart sought leave of absence from Berlin on grounds of health, and became concerned about the size of his pension.[196] His successor, Morton Eden, a very experienced diplomat, complained the following January of a lack of 'free and friendly communication' from the Prussian government.[197]

At the same time, the British envoys to Catherine II and Leopold II felt that they lacked the confidence of their host states. Straton wrote from Vienna, 'As to poor old England, the Austrian Ministry as well as their Master appear to have forgotten that such an island exists.'[198] Fawkener's impact in St Petersburg was lessened by the independent attitude of envoys from other states that he had thought would support

---

[191] Ewart to Burges, 20 June 1791, Bod. BB. 34 fol. 156.
[192] On the 'fluctuating' nature of Prussian policy, Keith to Straton, 24 May 1791, Ipswich HA 239/2/198.
[193] Leopold II to Kaunitz, 27 June 1791, Beer (ed.), *Joseph, Leopold, Kaunitz*, p. 413; Jackson, mémoire for Grenville, Aug. 1791, Bod. BB. 61 p. 31.
[194] Straton to Grenville, 10, 11, 17 Aug. 1791, PRO FO 7/24 fols. 265–71; Ewart to Burges, 17 July, 8 Sept. 1791, Bod. BB. 34 fols. 163, 165; Ewart to Pitt, 4 Aug. 1791, Williamwood, 148; Grenville to Auckland, 7 Nov. 1791, BL Add. 58920 fol. 32.
[195] Malmesbury to Portland, 14 Oct. 1791, *Malmesbury*, II, 441; Malmesbury to Prince of Wales, 3 Oct. 1791, Aspinall (ed.), *George, Prince of Wales* III (1964), no. 623.
[196] Ewart to Pitt, 4 Aug., 9 Sept., 7 Oct. 1791, PRO 30/8/133 fols. 298–301; Grenville to Ewart, 25 Aug. 1791, Williamwood 157; Burges to Grenville, 10 Sept. 1791, BL Add. 58968 fol. 13.
[197] Eden to Auckland, 6 Jan., 3 Mar. 1792, BL Add. 34441 fols. 102, 401; Grenville to Eden, 27 Mar., Keith to Grenville, 18 Apr. 1792, PRO FO 64/24, 7/29.
[198] Straton to Eden, 11 Dec. 1791, Broomhall 60/23/1.

British goals, by the arrival of Robert Adair, an agent of the Whig Opposition, on 17 June 1791, and by the fact that Britain's views were no longer of great relevance for Russo-Turkish relations. Ewart predicted correctly that Fawkener would have little effect, and indeed his mission was seen as humiliating. Adair, in contrast, was received very well by Catherine II, unsurprisingly so as he argued that Pitt was unable to coerce Russia. Catherine also ordered a marble bust of Fox. A bronze copy that was made of it was placed on the colonnade at her palace of Tsarskoye Selo. Not all of Fox's allies approved. Frederick, 5th Earl of Carlisle, wrote, 'It was an egregious folly in Fox sending a Mr. Adair... to counteract Mr. Fawkener.'[199]

The Russian ministers were still suspicious of Ainslie and convinced that he was trying to keep the Turks in the war. The Vice-Chancellor, Count Osterman, told Fawkener in late July that Ainslie had recently told the Turks that British fleets would be sent to the Black and Baltic seas. Fawkener and the Prussian envoy had to accept the settlement offered by the Russians in July 1791: it left Russia with Ochakov and the territory to the east of the Dniester, though free navigation on the river was agreed.[200] These terms formed the basis of the Russo-Turkish peace.

The attempt to respond to Russian power had proved harder to sustain in domestic terms than in 1719–20 when, under Peter the Great, this power appeared to be a new and threatening development. By 1791, the British political nation was accustomed to Russian domination of eastern Europe, and to viewing her rivals, Sweden, Poland and Turkey, as pro-French. The novel views in 1791 were the positive assessment of an anti-Russian Poland and the argument that the fate of Pontic Europe was of crucial consequence for Britain, but these did not appear to be a convincing reason for a reinterpretation of traditional opinions, any more than the maintenance of the Prussian alliance appeared to justify war with Russia. Though support for what Adair later termed 'the ancient and wise alliances of my country', which he claimed he had upheld at St Petersburg, namely alliance with Austria, Russia and the United

[199] Ewart to Elgin, 29 June 1791, Broomhall 60/23/5; *Letters from the Continent; Describing the Manners and Customs of Germany, Poland, Russia, and Switzerland, in the Years 1790, 1791, and 1792* (1812), p. 122. For identification of the author, G. de Beer, 'An Anonymous Identified: Lionel Colmore', *Notes and Queries* (1967), 303–4; A. G. Cross, 'British Sources for Catherine's Russia: 1) Lionel Colmore's Letters from St Petersburg, 1790–1', *Study Group on Eighteenth-Century Russia Newsletter*, 17 (1989), 17–19; Fawkener to Grenville, 1, 12, 28 July 1791, BL Add. 59023 fols. 19–26; Frederick, 5th Earl of Carlisle, 'Anecdotes about numerous people' Castle Howard, J14/65/2.

[200] Fawkener and Whitworth to Grenville, 21, 27 July 1791, PRO FO 65/22; Fawkener to Grenville, 28 July 1791, BL Add. 59023 fols. 25–6; Whitworth, Fawkener and Goltz memorial, 22 July 1791, PRO FO 78/12B.

Provinces,[201] had been affected by events since 1755, they were still seen as more natural than any system designed to coerce Russia. In 1791 Miles questioned whether it was in Britain's interest to permit Catherine to conquer the Turks.[202] Two years later, he claimed that 'the advantages that would have resulted from a measure no less politic than just, were too remote and collateral to be generally known in a country unaccustomed to consider the Muscovite as an enemy'.[203] By abandoning his policy,[204] Pitt rode out the political storm, but the lesson was a clear one that would not have surprised ministers who in 1733, 1753 and 1763 had displayed little interest in heeding suggestions that they involve themselves in Polish affairs. It appeared best to leave these matters to favourably-disposed continental powers, and to restrict commitments to allies in these circumstances. Direct intervention might have unpredictable results, both domestically and diplomatically. A stress on the need for limited objectives for British foreign policy had indeed characterised the public agitation against war with Russia. The provincial press was used to try to establish acceptable goals and to spread a message of concern about British policy. Thus, the *Newcastle Courant* of 30 April 1791 carried the following notice,

At a general, most numerous, and respectable Meeting of the Inhabitants of the town and neighbourhood of Manchester, convened (at the requisition of many considerable Merchants, Manufacturers, and others) by public Advertisement, in both the Manchester Papers, for the purpose of considering the present alarming Situation of Affairs between this Country and Russia, and held at the Exchange, in Manchester, this 19th day of April, 1791 THOMAS WALKER, Esq. Boroughreeve, in the Chair,
It was resolved,

1. That in the present alarming situation of affairs between this country and Russia, it is highly necessary for the people of Great Britain to take into consideration the evils of an impending war.

2. That in the opinion of this Meeting no nation can be justified in engaging in war, unless for reasons, and upon principles strictly defensive.

3. That a commercial Country like Great Britain, whose taxes are so heavy, and whose debt is so enormous, ought to be particularly cautious of engaging in any war, unless upon the most urgent and evident necessity.

---

[201] A. W. Ward and G. P. Gooch (eds.), *The Cambridge History of British Foreign Policy 1783–1919* I (Cambridge, 1922), p. 211; Lord John Russell (ed.), *Memorials and Correspondence of Charles James Fox* (2 vols., 1853), II, 387.

[202] [Miles], *An Enquiry into the Justice and Expediency of Prescribing Bounds to the Russian Empire* (1791), pp. 20, 40.

[203] Miles, *The Conduct of France towards Great Britain Examined* (1793), p. 24.

[204] Derry, who is overly sympathetic to Pitt in his account of the crisis, argues that 'it is exaggeration to talk about the collapse of Pitt's foreign policy', but it is difficult to see how such a conclusion can be avoided, J. Derry, *William Pitt* (1962), p. 89.

4. That it is not clear from theory, or experience, that the pretext of maintaining the balance of power in Europe, is a sufficient reason for plunging the inhabitants of this island into the manifold evils attendant on war; and that all treaties of alliance which tend to involve Great Britain in the quarrels and disputes of the nations upon the Continent, are injuries to the interests of this country.

5. That although the power of declaring war is vested in the Crown of Great Britain, yet as the honour of the nation is concerned in the justice of it, and as the labour and industry of the people must be taxed to support it, they have a right to full and satisfactory information of the grounds and reasons on which war is at any time to be declared.

6. That it does not appear to this Meeting that any sufficient reason has yet been assigned for involving this country in a war with Russia – and that it is the duty of our Representatives in Parliament to with-hold their assent to any burthen being imposed on the people, till the justice and necessity of it shall be fully shewn.

7. That these Resolutions be signed by the Chairman, and transmitted to the Members for the county of Lancaster; and that they be requested to vote in support of the principles expressed therein.

8. That the foregoing Resolutions be published in some of the London, and in the Manchester, Liverpool, Birmingham, Leeds, Norwich, and other provincial Newspapers.

Walker, a Whig who had collaborated with Wedgwood in opposition to the Irish commercial propositions of 1785, had also bitterly criticised the Eden Treaty.[205] On 7 May 1791, the *Newcastle Courant* reported,

A protest to the resolutions made at Manchester ... is entered into by a numerous body of other inhabitants of that town, who say, 'that although they feel in common with their fellow subjects, the evils attendant upon a war, yet they think an interference of that nature highly improper on a subject which the constitution hath wisely lodged in the hands of the executive power.'

Meetings have been held at Wakefield and Norwich, and resolutions entered into similar to those inserted in our last from Manchester, relative to the expected war with Russia.

'May all the nations of Europe renounce ambitious schemes of war and conquest', was one of the toasts given at a meeting of the 'Gentlemen of the Hampshire Club, established for the support of public liberty' held in Winchester on 22 July 1791.[206]

If British policy seemed in late 1791 increasingly irrelevant to the continental powers, this, however, owed much to the new diplomatic

---

[205] J. Money, *Experience and Identity. Birmingham and the West Midlands 1760–1800* (Manchester, 1977), pp. 44–5.
[206] *Salisbury and Winchester Journal*, 1 August 1791.

agenda that developed in the summer of 1791, rather than to the new absence of a British role in eastern Europe, and, specifically, the Polish and Turkish questions. Instead, the decision of the British government not to become involved in a developing crisis that it could indeed have played a role in, the confrontation between revolutionary France and her neighbours, and rather, as Hawkesbury put it, to 'wait for events' and avoid obligations, was to prove crucial. On 23 May 1791 Pitt sent Elgin a private note written in his own hand that explained his attitude clearly:

I wish only to mention, with respect to the subject of French politics, that it would certainly seem to me very desireable that we should derive the full benefit of any impression which they may make on the Emperor's mind, to dispose him to enter cordially into a system for the general tranquillity, but that at the same time we wish wholly to avoid committing ourselves in any degree to any thing, which can show any disposition to encourage any sort of interference in the internal affairs of France.[207]

[207] Hawkesbury memo, – Aug. 1791, Bod. BB 61, p. 10; Pitt to Elgin, 23 May 1791, Broomhall 60/2/16; Pitt to Ewart, 2 Sept. 1791, Williamwood 157. Hawkesbury's view was supported by others including Frederick Earl-Bishop of Derry, B. Fothergill, *A Mitred Earl* (1974), p. 137, and Liston, Liston to Drake, 10 Jan. 1792, BL Add. 46822 fols. 213–14.

By the turn which affairs take upon the Continent I should hope for peace, and then the French may hang one another as much as they please.

Charles Townshend MP, August 1790[1]

Anticipating crisis and change: the situation prior to the Estates General

Anglo-French relations diminished in importance once it became clear that France would not respond militarily to the British-supported Prussian invasion of the United Provinces. Concern about French intentions in India led to rumours of war between the two powers in the summer of 1788,[2] but the crisis passed, both because the hostility of these intentions was exaggerated and because France was clearly not in a state to fight a war. The British government was more concerned about the developing crisis in eastern and northern Europe, its French counterpart with domestic problems. Yet, there were signs of continued tension and the British remained anxious not only about French colonial schemes, but also about their hopes for the Low Countries. It was also known that France had sought to consolidate its existing links into a quadruple alliance of France, Spain, Austria and Russia. Such an alliance could have been aimed only against the Triple Alliance.

Such schemes appeared hopelessly out of line with France's internal crisis. 'The situation of France' was cited in October 1788 as a reason why Frederick William II felt that the position was propitious for a confrontation with Russia, and similar attitudes underlay the developing role of the Triple Alliance in the affairs of eastern Europe. France was losing her allies. In 1787 she had lost the Dutch, while Joseph II had given a marked eastern orientation to Austrian policy and one that reflected the greater importance of his alliance with Russia over that with France. In the mid-1780s it was unclear whether Joseph would prefer his

[1] Townshend to Lord Midleton, 19 Aug. 1790, Guildford, Surrey CRO Brodrick Mss 1248/11.   [2] Straton to Keith, 26 Aug. 1788, BL Add. 35541 fol. 75.

Russian ally or the 'alliance of 1756'; in 1787 the decision was clearly taken. France was a traditional ally of Sweden, and she had supported Gustavus III in the international crisis that followed his coup in 1772. In 1788, however, France was in no shape to offer him effective assistance, and it was the Triple Alliance that came to the help of Gustavus in his conflict with Denmark. The British sought, though with less success, to improve relations with Spain.[3] France's surviving alliances, with both Austria and Spain, were increasingly without meaning.

This development was not solely due to French domestic problems. It can be seen as a continuation of the general slackening of French diplomatic influence that had characterised international relations since the 1680s, and more markedly since the mid-1750s, not least because French diplomacy had faced more intense competition from new or relatively new great powers: Britain, Russia, Prussia. It also reflected shifts in 1787–8, especially the revived importance of Austro-Turkish and Russo-Turkish relations. Nevertheless, domestic circumstances were seen as crucial, as well as providing an apparently obvious indication of French strength. Keith observed in October 1787: 'I hear much of French anger and of their plans of revenge, but I know that France has at this moment, a deadly fit of the gout, and is debilitated in her legs and arms.'[4] This stress on domestic circumstances was traditional. The French Revolution in its early or pre-revolutionary stages was seen not as a new development, a product of spreading radicalism, but rather as a conventional political crisis, in which a ruler faced serious domestic problems, primarily aristocratic factionalism and financial difficulties. These appeared to affect France's international capability, her ability to wage war or sustain a military confrontation, her stability as an ally, but they were not novel in type, did not therefore necessarily appear insuperable or likely to provoke a change in the French political system, and it was possible to envisage a revival of French strength. This was to come, eventually, through revolutionary change, but in 1788 and early 1789 it appeared instead that a revival, producing a more effective monarchy, would come either through a solution to the political crisis achieved by traditional means or by means of institutional reform and constitutional revival that focussed on a new partnership between crown and nation, a path predicted by Tom Paine in his pamphlet *Prospects on the Rubicon* published on 20 November 1787. This was certainly what was sought by the French government and political nation.

---

[3] Ewart to Keith, 7 Oct. 1788, BL Add. 35541 fol. 123; Carmarthen to Eden, 2 Sept. 1788, PRO FO 72/13.
[4] Keith to Ewart, 1 Oct. 1787, Matlock CRO 239 M/O 759; Dorset to Stafford, 19 Dec. 1787, PRO 30/29/1/15.

This possibility raised fears in Britain. The option of reform, or at least altered circumstances, bringing renewed strength was never far from the mind of at least some British commentators. In November 1787 Dorset sent Pitt a memorandum warning of the danger that an Estates General might be called, 'the consequence of which might be productive of a total change in the constitution'. Conversely, Hawkesbury feared that any insurrection in France would be crushed, making its government stronger, and he therefore hoped that the people would remain discontented, keeping the government weak and unsettled, but would not revolt. The historian William Robertson, however, welcomed the prospect of France adopting British constitutional principles, and thus becoming stronger.[5] Luzerne reported in May 1788 that Pitt had told him that the conduct of the French Parlements seemed irregular and unreasonable, but that the summoning of the Estates General might strengthen French government. Four months later, after disturbances in Dauphiné, the convoking of the Estates General for May 1789, the suspension of payments from the heavily indebted Treasury (16 August), the resignation of Brienne (25 August) and the reappointment of Necker (25, 27 August), a measure actively supported by the Austrian envoy; Barthélemy, noting great British interest in French developments, reported that there were widespread hopes, shared by George III, that the forthcoming Estates General would be 'l'époque d'un desordre sans remède'. Yet, he also discerned a fear that the Estates General would lead to a revival of French strength as a result of royal power being more solidly based.[6] Pitt was certainly concerned that the return of Necker, who had a formidable reputation as a financial expert, would lead to an improvement in French finances, though in fact Necker had no plan but for the hope that the Estates General would somehow produce a solution.[7] Grenville sent Pitt an interesting analysis of the French situation and suggested that an opportunity existed to improve relations with her:

[5] Paine to Lansdowne, 20 Nov. 1787, Bowood 60; A. O. Aldridge, 'Thomas Paine, Edmund Burke and Anglo-French Relations in 1787', *Studies in Burke and his Time*, 12 (1971), 1859; Dorset to Pitt, 8 Nov. 1787, Hawkesbury to Dorset, 26 May 1788, KAO C183, 182; Auckland to Grenville, 4 Sept. 1790, BL Add. 58919 fol. 12; R. B. Sher, '1688 and 1788. William Robertson on Revolution in Britain and France', in P. Dukes and J. Dunkley (eds.), *Culture and Revolution* (1990), p. 101.

[6] Luzerne to Montmorin, 13, 20 May, Barthélemy to Montmorin, 2, 9, 23 Sept. 1788, AE CP Ang. 565 fols. 156–7, 184–6, 566 fols. 252, 268, 306; Egret, *Necker* (Paris, 1975), pp. 210–12.

[7] Pitt to Grenville, 29 Aug. 1788, BL Add. 58906 fol. 43; Price, *Vergennes and ... Breteuil* 317. The literature on Necker, as on most topics associated with the French Revolution other than foreign policy, is extensive. J. Egret, *Necker: Ministre de Louis XVI, 1776–1790* (Paris, 1975), and R. D. Harris, *Necker: Reform Statesman of the Ancien Régime* (Berkeley, 1979) are especially valuable.

The advancement of Necker is certainly ... a relief to the French government in the important point of their finances, and may retrieve their credit from a blow that seemed likely to overwhelm it. But I cannot help thinking that the example of two ministers driven out in little more than a year by the effects of popular clamour or public resentment will not tend much to establish the authority of the crown.

I am by no means sure that ... I see the change in as unfavourable light as you do to our interests. An actual bankruptcy in France would have been severely felt by many persons in this country and might to a degree have operated to the disadvantage of our own public credit. Necker is a pacific minister by system, and must be so now from necessity. He has also his own popularity to maintain that being evidently the only support on which he can depend. This must make him very reluctant to do anything that may increase the burdens of the people beyond the most urgent and present necessity, and the consequence will I trust be, that some check will be given to that sort of intrigue and restlessness which keeps us in hot water, even while we are most confident of the impossibility of any serious effects from their schemes ... I should be much inclined were I in your situation to find some channel of sending a message to Necker of individual and personal compliment. The similarity of situations and a variety of other topics which cannot escape you, afford a sufficient opening for this, and some good might result from it ... A renewal of the wish to live in a better understanding with that government ... *without abandoning our respective political systems in Europe*, and a wish that this understanding might be the means of restoring and maintaining peace as formerly in the time of Fleury [1726–43] ... might I think in proper hands afford the subject of a communication that might produce much solid good.[8]

The following month, however, Grenville stressed the value to Britain's international position of French weakness. Indeed, in terms of the percentage of the French budget spent on the military in 1712–88, 1788 was the low point. Post-war demobilisation in the army from 1783 was followed by a fresh reduction, and morale was affected badly. France truly was less of a threat, and less viable as an ally.[9] Though Pitt had told Luzerne about his wish for better relations, the British government was more concerned about the alliance with Prussia, and was, anyway, soon to be absorbed by the Regency Crisis.

The notion that the British government was frightened that a national assembly could help revive French strength led to the suspicion that Britain would intervene in order to prevent such an eventuality. Such an idea did not spring from the disturbances of 1789, but was already present the previous autumn, when Barthélemy suggested that once the Estates General met, the British, who, he claimed, always had a large number of subjects in France observing all aspects of French affairs, would then both have more and would use them to foment trouble by

---

[8]   Grenville to Pitt, 1 Sept. 1788, PRO 30/8/140 fols. 34–5; Ellis to Malmesbury, 10 Dec. [1788], Winchester, Malmesbury 151.

[9]   *Court and Cabinets*, I, 429–30; Sturgill, 'French Army's Budget', pp. 125, 127, 132.

underhand methods. Suspicion was mutual. John Trevor reported in March 1789 that 'in the present inability of France to act ostensibly, her usual meddling part, her secret intrigues are the more to be apprehended', though he was writing not about the French subversion Harris had reported from the United Provinces, but about French influence on Spanish policy.[10] In late 1788, however, there was still a general conviction that domestic problems would prevent France from thwarting Britain's diplomatic schemes.[11] Concerned about the extent of discontent in the United Provinces, Lord North was, nevertheless, not so worried about the promises of French assistance for the dissidents, 'there I hope we are secure for some time and that Monsieur Necker's abilities great as they are, will not be able to put that kingdom soon in a condition to disturb the public tranquility'.[12]

The Regency crisis that winter appeared to alter the relative position of Britain and France, though Hawkesbury was consoled by the thought that France was still in a 'worse state'.[13] Echoing the view of British diplomats on French problems, Luzerne argued that the crisis would not make the present, or any future British government, pro-French; but that the period of domestic uncertainty would weaken its international position.[14] At the same time, Joseph II and Catherine II both seemed more beset by problems than they had been two years earlier. France did not appear to be in as poor shape relative to other powers as she had been in 1788. She seemed more stable in early 1789 than she had been in the summer and autumn of 1788. The possibility that the Estates General, formally summoned on 24 January 1789, would bring renewed vigour to France was credible. It might be able to produce political and fiscal solutions that would offer a guarantee for the national debt. The Count of Aranda, formerly Spanish envoy in Paris, could suggest to Montmorin in January 1789 that the third estate would support the crown, in order not to be crushed by the other two estates. He felt sure that the wealth and numbers of this estate would be of great consequence; in short that the crown could create a powerful new constituency of support.[15] Gustavus III had had considerable success in Sweden in seeking the support of the third estate against aristocratic opponents. Hawkesbury

[10] Barthélemy to Montmorin, 7 Oct. 1788, AE CP Ang. 567 fol. 13; Trevor to Carmarthen, 21 Mar. 1789, PRO FO 67/6.
[11] Barthélemy to Montmorin, 18 Nov. 1788, AE CP Ang. 567 fol. 139; Hawkesbury to Dorset, 23 Oct. 1788, KAO C182; George Hammond, Commissary in Vienna, to David Hartley, 29 Apr. 1789, Reading, Berkshire CRO D/EHy F97/40.
[12] North to Sheffield, 22 Sept. 1788, BL Add. 61980 fol. 36.
[13] Hawkesbury to Dorset, 20 Jan. 1789, KAO C182.
[14] Luzerne to Montmorin, 16, 23 Dec. 1788, 13 Jan. 1789, AE CP Ang. 567 fols. 272–5, 312, 568 fol. 37.
[15] Aranda to Montmorin, 16 Jan. 1789, AE CP Esp. 626 fol. 27.

was certain that Necker would be unsuccessful and suggested prophetically that 'nothing but a great military character who could head their
troops in case of any insurrection could carry them through their present
difficulties'.[16] An anonymous British pamphlet of 1789 indicated both
the extent of belief in the possibility of French revival and its public
nature:

France will not be quiet. To men who form opinions concerning future events,
by connecting together the chain of causes and effects which produce them,
nothing can be more provoking than the present blindness, both of the great and
of the little in England, with regard to France. They say France is on the verge
of ruin, at the very time when she is on the verge of greatness. Either, one event
must happen relating to the finances of France within six months or another
probably within eighteen; and whichever of them casts up, will exalt the wealth
of the government of France above that of England. For, the present disorders in
the finances of France must soon end in one of two ways: either the Noblesse and
the Church will consent to pay taxes in common with the rest of the subjects, or
they will not. If they do, the debts of France will be consolidated, and one regular
provision made for the payment of their interests, and another for a sinking fund
to extinguish their principals, in the same way, as is done in England. In which
case, the public credit of France, from the superior natural resources of the
country over those of England, will start up in an instant far superior to that of
England. Or if the Noblesse and Church will not consent to pay taxes in common
with the rest of the subjects; then the Government of France will, nay must,
declare a bankruptcy; because, without the aid of new taxes produced by that
consent, Government has not revenues sufficient to pay the interest of its debts.
In this last case, there will be a convulsion, perhaps for a year; while those who
subsisted formerly on the employment given them by the creditors of the public,
will be obliged to look for it from other persons; but the convulsion will subside
when that employment is found, which never can be long lost in a country full of
an industrious people, and of natural advantages. The government of France will
then rise, like a phoenix, more vigorous from her own ashes as she did after the
Mississippi;[17] and starting, when clear of debt, with a credit which she could not
have got when in debt, and with a revenue which is now thirty millions sterling,
will in every money market in Europe, beat England with a revenue not half so
large, and loaded with above 250 millions debt.

If either of these two events happen (and one of them must happen, because no
third can), then the French will fall either on England alone, or on the House of
Austria alone, or upon both; because they have always done one or other of those
things, whenever they could with a prospect of success.[18]

Thus, alongside the more optimistic response to developments within
France, the fear that French renewal would lead to a more aggressive

---

[16] Hawkesbury to Dorset, 3 Feb. 1789, KAO C182.
[17] A reference to the French financial crisis in 1720. H. Lüthy, *La Banque Protestante en
France de la Révocation de l'Edit de Nantes à la Révolution, I, Dispersion et Regroupement,
1685–1730* (Paris, 1959).
[18] Anon., *Considerations on the Prussian Treaty* (1789), pp. 17–19.

foreign policy was voiced publicly. It was this strand that was to be most marked in governmental thinking, more so than concern about the domestic example of French changes. Such concern took a while to develop, and did not play so prominent a role in government thinking.

The crisis of the summer of 1789

After elections in early 1789, the Estates General convened at Versailles on 5 May 1789, at the same time as armies from the Adriatic and the Black Sea to the Gulf of Finland prepared for the campaigning season. Louis XVI's opening speech was interrupted by repeated cries of *Vive le Roi*.[19] In the opening session Necker pressed the case for reform, but division, over the issue of common voting, a measure that would lessen aristocratic influence and that was supported by Necker, or separate voting, by estate, was serious from the outset.[20] Dorset, an instinctive conservative who had scant sympathy for reform, had little sense of impending crisis, and was indeed devoting much of his efforts to cricket. It is scarcely surprising that the attention of the British government continued to be focused on eastern Europe. On 14 May 1789 Dorset observed,

there is fine confusion amongst the deputies aux Etats generaux and the nobility and Tiers état are at daggers drawn. How it will end nobody can foresee, some people think they will be obliged to separate without doing anything, which will be a lucky circumstance for the King who seems in a manner to have descended from his throne and resigned all his prerogatives into the hands of the nation. All unquiet in the town, but the guards and patroles are as numerous as ever, reinforcements of troops are also arriving every day, and the smallest disturbance is suppressed with an incredible activity.[21]

Dorset saw the divisions as advantageous to Britain.[22] The third estate refused to accept the system of orders, and on 10 June 1789 voted for the common verification of credentials. Heady oratory, pressure of circumstances and a growing sense of crisis led the Third Estate to declare themselves the National Assembly and to claim a measure of sovereignty on 17 June.[23] The government countered by planning a 'Royal Session'

---

[19] Dorset to Leeds, 7 May 1789, PRO FO 27/32 fol. 5.
[20] J. M. Roberts (ed.), *French Revolution Documents* I (Oxford, 1966), pp. 98–101.
[21] J. Goulstone and M. Swanton, 'Carry on Cricket: the Duke of Dorset's 1789 tour', *History Today*, 39/8 (1989), 18–23; Dorset to Wraxall, 14 May 1789, Beinecke, Osborn Files, Dorset. On troop movements, Dorset to Leeds, 7 May 1789, PRO FO 27/32 fol. 4.
[22] Dorset to Wraxall, 21 May 1789, Beinecke, Osborn Files, Dorset; Dorset to Leeds, 11 June 1789, PRO FO 27/32 fol. 135.
[23] Dorset to Leeds, 7 May 1789, PRO FO 27/32 fol. 4; Roberts, *Revolution Documents* I, 106–7.

to reassert the authority of Louis XVI, and Dorset thought that if the King turned to the nobility and army he would succeed. In London Calonne stated that Louis would dissolve the Estates General.[24] The preparatory prohibition of any meetings by the Estates, however, led the angry deputies, wrongly concluding that a dissolution was intended, to assemble on 20 June in an indoor tennis-court and pledge themselves not to disperse until reform was complete and France had a new constitution. Eventually held on 23 June 1789, the Royal Session was a failure.[25] Louis XVI's proffered reforms were no longer sufficient, and the Third Estate refused to disperse. Louis backed down, while public order collapsed in Paris. On 27 June the King bowed to the crisis and instructed the clerical and noble orders to join the National Assembly.

Meanwhile, the French government had turned to Britain for help. Midsummer was always a period of difficulty in the *ancien régime* economy: the period before the new harvest was that in which food stocks were at their lowest, concern and rumours about the food supply at their most acute. After the poor harvest of 1788, grain prices climbed in the second half of 1788 and continued to do so into 1789. Necker had sought to employ governmental controls over the grain trade in order to keep the volatile population of Paris, which had already rioted on 27–8 April 1789, quiet. This led to shortages in other provinces, producing bread riots across northern France in May 1789,[26] and, although the situation was eased by imports from England, America, Spain, Italy and Turkey,[27] uncertainty led to stockpiling. In June the situation grew worse and on 25 June Necker wrote to Pitt to seek the assistance of the British government.[28]

The flour that Necker sought could be obtained only if the British government suspended the corn laws. In order to maintain the domestic supply in Britain, the export of wheat or flour was prohibited when the price of wheat climbed to 44 shillings a quarter. In June–July 1789 the price was considerably higher. The French request was considered by the Committee of Trade on 2 and 3 July 1789, Pitt being present at both sessions. The request was rejected and on 3 July Pitt wrote accordingly to Luzerne, citing the present situation of the corn supply in Britain and

[24] Dorset to Leeds, 18 June 1789, PRO FO 27/32 fols. 155–6; Hawkesbury to Dorset, 5 June 1789, KAO C182.
[25] Dorset to Leeds, 25 June 1789, PRO FO 27/32 fols. 186–90; Roberts, *Revolution Documents*, I, 109–11, 115–23.
[26] Dorset to Leeds, 7 May 1789, PRO FO 27/32 fol. 4; F. Aftalion, *The French Revolution. An Economic Interpretation* (Cambridge, 1990), p. 42.
[27] Dorset to Leeds, 21 May, 11 June 1789, PRO FO 27/32 fols. 89–90, 137.
[28] Necker to Pitt, 25 June, Luzerne to Pitt, 28 June, Dorset to Leeds, 25 June, 6, 9 July 1789, PRO 30/8/161 fols. 23–4, FO 27/32 fols. 191, 230, 260; Dorset to Pitt, 9 July 1789, KAO C183.

uncertainty about the forthcoming harvest.[29] This decision was criticised, both at the time and subsequently. Luzerne reported criticism of the ministerial decision as lacking in generosity and indeed it was attacked in the Commons on 6 July by, among others, Wilberforce. The historian, J. Holland Rose, was to claim that 'the gift of 20,000 sacks of flour outright would have been the best bargain of Pitt's career ... would have ... brought about a genuine *entente cordiale*'.[30] There is no evidence for this, though such a move might have lessened what was soon to be a widely held conviction in France that the British government was instigating disorder there.[31]

The situation in Britain was not propitious for such exports. After the mediocre harvest of 1788, grain stocks were low, and prices were rising in London and the south-east. The bulk of mercantile and political opinion was against the measure, and the grain trade was a sphere in which it was dangerous to intervene. Hawkesbury, who had been present at the relevant meetings of the Committee of Trade and who had written to Dorset that 'we have had the wettest summer that was ever known', later told Luzerne that government action was motivated by fears of famine. The mistrustful Luzerne stated that nobody believed that reason,[32] but Pitt's reply had been predictable, and indeed a measure of Necker's lack of confidence in an approach to Britain was that he made it so late. It is unclear how far Pitt's response reflected a desire to weaken France. Ehrman has suggested that Pitt was responsible for an initial desire to help the French, but it did not amount to much. Pitt had already revealed concern at the prospect of Necker strengthening France and, on 13 July 1789, he does not appear to have been sorry to see royal power weakened in France.[33] Earlier that day, Grenville had presented a Bill for the further regulation of grain exports. On 26 August Necker complained 'in strong terms' to Eden, then passing through Paris on his way back to London from his Spanish embassy, both that Pitt had not supplied the requested flour and that he had failed to respond personally to Necker's letter. Eden himself ascribed the shortage of bread in Paris at that stage

[29] Pitt to Luzerne, 3 July 1789, PRO 30/8/102 fol. 180.
[30] Luzerne to Montmorin, 7, 28 July 1789, AE CP Ang. 570 fols. 76, 173; Cobbett, 28, 226–30; Andrew Stewart to Sir William Pulteney, 19 July 1789, CUL Add. 6958 no. 695; Rose, *William Pitt and National Revival*, p. 544. Ehrman disagreed, but saw Pitt as insensitive, *Pitt*, II, 45–6.
[31] Luzerne to Montmorin, 29 Oct. 1789, AE CP Ang. 571 fol. 98; Dr Charles Blagden to Palmerston, 29 Jan. 1790, Beinecke, Osborn Shelves C 114; Trevor to Leeds, 3 Feb. 1790, PRO FO 67/7.
[32] Hawkesbury to Dorset, 16 July 1789, KAO C182; Luzerne to Montmorin, 1 Jan. 1790, AE CP Ang. 572 fol. 3.
[33] Ehrman, *Pitt*, II, 45 fn. 3; R. Blunt (ed.), *Mrs Montagu, 'Queen of the blues', her letters and friendships from 1762 to 1800* (2 vols., 1923), II, 237.

not to any problems with the harvest, but to a breakdown in the distribution system arising from the political crisis.[34]

On 6 July 1789 Pitt told the Commons of the decision. Three days later, Dorset wrote to Pitt, arguing that a refusal to supply flour might have fatal consequences. The crisis in France was soon, indeed, to reach its first peak, though grain prices were only one factor in the cauldron of confusion. Dorset thought that a counter-revolution and recourse to the army was the only remedy left to Louis XVI, and the king was indeed pressed to attempt this. On the 11th Necker was dismissed, as was his ally Montmorin. They were replaced by a ministry under Breteuil whose intentions are unclear. Traditionally, it has been argued that Louis intended to reassert royal authority by force, only to be forestalled by rebellion in Paris, but it has recently been suggested that Breteuil sought a settlement to the crisis through negotiations with the National Assembly. These tentative negotiations were, however, rendered redundant by a popular uprising in Paris. Anger at the Royal Session combined with anxiety about the troops massing near Paris. On 14 July the price of grain peaked in Paris and the Bastille was seized in an outburst of popular action. Dorset thought that 'Nothing could exceed the regularity and good order with which all this extraordinary business had been conducted.'[35] Louis XVI was advised that he could not rely on his troops to suppress the Parisians, who had rallied to the support of the National Assembly; and on 17 July his brother, the Count d'Artois, later Charles X, the leading opponent of reform, left Versailles for the frontier.

The overthrow of royal authority was generally applauded in Britain. Newspapers, both ministerial and opposition, proclaimed the establishment of liberty and the collapse of tyranny.[36] France was seen as emulating Britain in constitutional terms,[37] and the violence of the changes could be excused by reference to similar episodes in British history.[38] At the same time, it was generally believed that the thwarting of what was seen as a royalist counter-revolution marked the success and thus end of the revolution,[39] an indication of the limited and conventional goals that were then seen as constituting a revolution. Louis XVI visited the Hôtel de Ville on 17 July to announce that Necker had been recalled

---

[34] Eden to Pitt, 27 Aug. 1789, PRO 30/8/110 fols. 1478.
[35] The traditional account, P. Caron, 'La tentative de contre-révolution de juin-juillet 1789', *Revue d'Histoire Moderne et Contemporaine*, 8 (1906–7), 5–34, 649–78, has been challenged by that of M. Price, 'The "Ministry of the Hundred Hours": A Reappraisal', *French History*, 3 (1990), 317–39; Dorset to Pitt, 9 July, Hawkesbury to Dorset, 5 June, 10 July 1789, KAO C183, 182; Dorset to Leeds, 16 July 1789, PRO FO 27/32 fol. 308; ? to ?, 19 July 1789, PRO 30/29/1/15 no. 86.
[36] *Diary*, 7, 28 July, *Times*, 17 July 1789.   [37] *Diary*, 13 July 1789.
[38] *Oracle*, 6 Aug. 1789.
[39] Dorset to Leeds, 16 July 1789, PRO FO 27/32 fols. 330–1.

the previous day and that troops were withdrawing. Pitt and Grenville had already thought 'the Revolution in France ... in substance decided' on 13 July. A week later, after the news of the fall of the Bastille and of Louis XVI's visit to the Hôtel de Ville arrived, Grenville wrote to his elder brother, the Marquess of Buckingham, 'the whole seems now to be completely given up, and the Duke of Dorset's expression of the Revolution being actually concluded appears not to be too strong'.[40] The more prescient Hawkesbury predicted further trouble, and pointed to the British example of the restoration of the 'old government' after the rule of 'one bold man at the head of an army [Cromwell]'.[41]

The major consequence for Anglo-French relations appeared to be French unhappiness about the British attitude, specifically that of Dorset. His known attachment to the Queen and to courtiers opposed to reform posed a problem,[42] but this was exacerbated by the publicity given to an intercepted letter from Dorset to Artois congratulating him on his escape. Dorset argued that he had written nothing that was incriminating, but, as he pointed out, 'it was sufficient the being spread abroad that I had written to the Comte d'Artois to make me an object of public attention'. On the grounds that there was no essential business of 'a public nature', the Duke also sought permission to take a leave of absence already granted him.[43] He was sent this on 31 July. Luzerne was certain that Dorset wished to create trouble and thought it likely that he was intervening in French politics.[44] Luzerne was also convinced that the British government wished to cause problems for France abroad in order, if possible, to exacerbate her domestic difficulties.[45] Dorset was accused of distributing large sums of money in order to foment disturbances; and, in response to attacks in the National Assembly on 24 and 25 July, Dorset, concerned about his own safety and that of his compatriots, wrote to Montmorin on the 26th in order to refute the accusations made against him and to state that Britain favoured good relations. Montmorin communicated the letter to the President of the National Assembly, who read it out publicly on the 27th.[46] The atmosphere of rumour and paranoia in Paris was noted next day by Martha Swinburne, who recorded reports 'that England was going to

[40] Blunt (ed.), *Montagu*, II, 237; Grenville to Buckingham, 20 July 1789, HL STG. Box 39(5).   [41] Hawkesbury to Dorset, 24 July 1789, KAO C182.
[42] Dorset to Leeds, 17 July 1789, PRO FO 27/32 fol. 331; Charles Sackville to Hotham, 31 July 1789, Hull UL DDHo/4/23.
[43] Dorset to Leeds, 28 July 1789, PRO FO 27/32 fols. 403–4.
[44] Luzerne to Montmorin, 14, 25 Aug. 1789, AE CP Ang. 570 fols. 229–30, 302.
[45] Luzerne to Montmorin, 31 July 1789, AE CP Ang. 570 fol. 180.
[46] Dorset to Leeds, 27, 28, 30 July, Dorset to Montmorin, 26 July 1789, PRO FO 27/32 fols. 390–3, 402, 423.

declare war and had already distributed 20 French millions in Paris –
such nonsense could only have gained credit with the mob, but then it is
King Mob that governs ... The merest trifle is enough to inflame the
populace who never consider but take fire at the first word.'[47]

French criticism of the British attitude aroused a response. On 30 July
1789 Leeds complained to Luzerne that a member of the Estates General
had claimed that the British were sending money to France in order to
further intrigues. The envoy replied that, with so many members,
anything could be said.[48] Next day, Leeds urged the need for British
tourists to be careful not to give offence to any of the French political
groups.[49] Meanwhile, Dorset, who had already suggested that tourists
should be warned of rising lawlessness, had pressed Leeds on the need to
state British good will officially, and, in light of Leeds' reply of 31 July,
the Duke was able on 3 August to send Montmorin an assurance that the
British government wished to cultivate good relations. This was read at
the National Assembly next day, but it had little impact. A belief in Pitt's
malevolent intentions towards France was widely held, though un-
warranted by the actual record of clandestine British activity.[50] Montmorin had already ordered Luzerne to find out if the money circulating
among soldiers and the Parisian populace was provided by the British.[51]
Dorset left Paris on 8 August 1789 and returned to Britain, to become
Lord Steward of the Royal Household that October. He was to hold the
post until shortly before his death in 1799. Dorset's diplomatic career
thus ended in embarrassment, but, for him, the appeal of the Paris
embassy was lost with the outbreak of the Revolution, and the post of
Lord Steward was preferable.

Anglo-French relations in late 1789

On 12 August 1789, the French *Conseil d'Etat* discussed a memorandum
by Luzerne's brother, the Secretary of State for the Marine, in which he
reiterated fears he had expressed repeatedly since the beginning of May
about the purpose of British naval armaments and the impact on any
likely French response of financial problems. He noted the danger of a
British attack both on Brest and on France's colonies. The *Conseil*

[47] Political Extracts from Mrs Swinburne's letters, BL Add. 33121 fol. 15.
[48] Luzerne to Montmorin, 31 July 1789, AE CP Ang. 570 fols. 180–1.
[49] Leeds to Lord Robert Fitzgerald, 31 July 1789, PRO FO 27/33A fol. 4.
[50] Dorset to Leeds, 28 July, Leeds to Dorset, 31 July, Dorset to Leeds, 6 Aug., Dorset to
     Montmorin, 3 Aug. 1789, PRO FO 27/32 fols. 403, 461, 487, 494; Pierre Etienne
     Dumont to Lansdowne, 24 Nov. 1789, Bowood 14; A. Cobban, 'The British Secret
     Service in France, 1784–92', *English Historical Review*, 69 (1954), 226–61.
[51] Montmorin to Luzerne, 3 Aug. 1789, AE CP Ang. 570 fol. 201; Vaucher (ed.), *Recueil*,
     p. 558.

decided, however, that the resources for any French defensive armament were lacking.[52] Two days earlier, Montmorin had congratulated the Ambassador Luzerne on his reply to Leeds on 30 July, aired the possibility that Britain would attempt to cause trouble in French colonies and instructed Luzerne to keep an eye on links between *émigrés* and the British government. Luzerne responded accordingly by drawing attention to claims in Britain that it was a suitable opportunity to gain revenge for French intervention in the American War of Revolution, and to seize French colonies.[53] This theme was to vie with that of alleged malign neglect on the part of the British ministry, in the reports of French diplomats over the following three years. An absence of hostile British moves was not seen as any proof of good intentions, for the French envoys were convinced of the opposite.[54] What they tended to underestimate was the degree to which the British government, like its Austrian, Prussian and Russian counterparts, was more concerned about developments in eastern Europe.[55] Such an emphasis was not restricted to ministerial circles. Nearly all German newspapers devoted more space in 1789 to the Austro-Turkish war than to events in France. In Britain there was more public attention to French domestic developments,[56] but, at governmental level, such developments were of importance largely as they affected or were believed likely to affect French foreign policy. Concern was definitely aroused about the possibility of French intervention in the Austrian Netherlands: from the outset the Revolution was seen, both within and outside France, as for export, though what that entailed in late 1789 was very different from what it was to entail three

[52] Memorandum, 12 Aug. 1789, Hardman, *French Revolution*, p. 79.
[53] Montmorin to Luzerne, 10 Aug., Luzerne to Montmorin, 25 Aug., 22, 29 Sept., Barthélemy to Montmorin, 15 Sept., Esterno to Montmorin, 9 Sept. 1789, AE CP Ang. 570 fols. 301–2, 571 fols. 11, 33, 570 fols. 367–70, Prusse 210 fol. 213.
[54] Memorandum of Secretary of State Luzerne, 2 Oct. 1789, based on information from his brother, the Ambassador, Hardman, *French Revolution*, p.80; Montmorin to Luzerne, 4 Oct. 1789, AE CP Ang. 571 fol. 42; M. Le Brasseur to ?, 2 Oct. 1789, AN. AM. B⁷ 454.
[55] Whitworth to Leeds, 16 Oct. 1789, PRO FO 65/17 fol. 226.
[56] R. E. Begemann, 'The English Press and the French Revolution' (unpublished Ph.D., Emory, 1973); J. Black, 'The British press and the French Revolution', in M. Vovelle (ed.), *La Révolution Française* (4 vols., Paris, 1989), I, 371–9, 'La Presse Britannique et la Révolution Française', in P. Retat (ed.), *La Révolution du Journal*, 1788–1794 (Paris, 1989), pp. 309–19; J. Black, 'The British Press and Eighteenth-Century Revolution: the French case', in P. Dukes and J. Dunkley (eds.), *Culture and Revolution* (1990), pp. 110–20. For the press of the period, L. Werkmeister, *A Newspaper History of England, 1792–1793* (Lincoln, Nebraska, 1967); I. R. Christie, 'British Newspapers in the Later Georgian Age', in Christie (ed.), *Myth and Reality*, pp. 311–33; J. Black, *The English Press in the Eighteenth Century* (1987), esp. pp. 277–91; K. W. Schweizer and R. Klein, 'The French Revolution and Developments in the London Daily Press to 1793', in Schweizer and Black (eds.), *Politics and the Press in Hanoverian Britain* (Lewiston, 1989), pp. 171–86.

years later. And yet, French intentions were not at the forefront of British ministerial concern at this point, any more than they were for Austria, Prussia and Russia. The crisis in the Low Countries was less intense and sustained than that in eastern Europe, and, at this stage, the British government was more concerned about its Prussian than its Dutch ally, although it is clear that the Prussian alliance was to a considerable degree seen as part of a commitment to the United Provinces that was fundamentally anti-French in its orientation. In late 1792 Britain and France were to move apart over the French refusal to accept the principle of respecting former agreements. Three years earlier this had also seemed to Fitzherbert an important issue in Anglo-Belgian relations; the new republic had to be anchored in the international system: 'The great object seems to be to oblige this new Republic to recognize the more important articles of subsisting treaties, and to enroll ... that recognition amongst the fundamental points of their constitution.'[57] At that stage, there was no question about France being in a position to burst the mould of international obligations asunder.

It was not surprising that in late 1789 the British government failed to share the degree of concern of a number of other powers about the possible danger from the spread of French radicalism and the example of revolution. This worried the Dutch, Sardinian and Spanish[58] governments, and there was already in late 1789 the possible basis of an anti-revolutionary alliance. Opposition to revolution was not the same however as a wish to take action to suppress it in France. The Spanish government considered the idea, but in October 1789 Victor Amadeus III of Sardinia told John Trevor that he was unwilling to help the royalist émigrés because he wished to see France weak; indeed he declared that he was against France always being 'the domineering power of Europe'.[59] Thus, the French Revolution was seen, in part, in ideological terms, but the differing Spanish and Sardinian responses reflected the continuation of ancien régime diplomatic attitudes, the differing views of France's allies and enemies. The British response was very much in line with that of Sardinia.

Trevor's reports from Turin did, however, also draw attention to another potential problem arising from developments in France. Changes in policy towards frontier regions might alter France's relations with other powers or at least create problems for the latter. Thus, in November 1789 Trevor reported that France might sell Corsica, purchased as recently as 1768, back to Genoa, and that it might, thereafter, be bought

[57] Fitzherbert to Leeds, 15 Dec. 1789, BL Eg. 3500 fol. 136.
[58] Merry to Leeds, 17, 24 Sept., 29 Oct. 1789, PRO FO 72/15 fols. 182, 192, 271.
[59] Trevor to Leeds, 15 Oct. 1789, PRO FO 67/6.

by Russia or the Spanish Bourbons. He also suggested the possibility of British purchase or of an independent Corsica under British protection.[60] The acquisition of the island by one of the branches of the Spanish Bourbons was not too serious a threat for Britain: with the loss in 1782 of Minorca, the value of which had been questionable,[61] her role in the western basin of the Mediterranean had lessened and thus become less vulnerable to changes there. Russian interests in the Mediterranean were, however, already a cause for concern.[62] Trevor's reports came to nothing, but they were a reminder that, even if the export of revolution was excluded from consideration, changes in French policy could be of considerable consequence.

The thwarting of the royalist 'counter-revolution' and the return of Necker brought neither order nor stability to France and her politics. Eden, then in Paris, sent Pitt on 27 August an account of a society in a state of dissolution, a political chaos with no Leviathan in sight:

The anarchy is most complete; – The People have renounced every idea and principle of subordination; The Magistracy (so far as there remains any traces of magistracy) is panic-struck; the army is utterly undone, and the soldiers are so far freed from military discipline that on every discontent and in the face of day, they take their arms and knapsacks and leave their regiments. The Church which formerly had so much influence is now in general treated by the people with derision; the revenue is greatly and rapidly decreasing ... even the industry of the labouring class is interrupted and suspended ... and it is sufficient to walk into the streets and to look at the faces of those who pass to see that there is a general impression of calamity and terror. – such a state of things must come soon to a crisis and the anxiety to be restored to order and security would soon tend to establish in some shape an executive government; but there is cruel want of some man of eminent talents to take the lead.[63]

Necker could not take this role, nor, more crucially, could Louis XVI, and, as yet, there was no Napoleon in sight. Eden reported from Paris on 3 September that the National Assembly was divided, the government without money and France unlikely to be a threat to other states for some time.[64] His assessment was confirmed the following month. The October Days made it clear that the revolution was not over, and that suggestions

---

[60] Trevor to Leeds, 17 Nov., 2 Dec. 1789, PRO FO 67/6; Trevor to Keith, 12 Dec. 1789, BL Add. 35541 fol. 354.
[61] D. Gregory, *Minorca, the Illusory Prize. A History of the British Occupation of Minorca between 1708 and 1802* (1991), pp. 206–17.
[62] A. Bode, *Die Flottenpolitik Katharinas II und die Konflikte mit Schweden und der Türkei 1768–92* (Munich, 1979); F. Venturi, *The End of the Old Regime in Europe 1768–1776. The First Crisis* (Princeton, 1979), pp. 3–153.
[63] Eden to Pitt, 27 Aug. 1789, PRO 30/8/110 fols. 147–8; Eden, from November 1789 Lord Auckland, to Sheffield, 6 Jan. 1790, BL Add. 45728 fol. 107.
[64] Eden to Leeds, 3 Sept. 1789, PRO FO 27/33A fols. 68–9.

that order would be restored and 'an executive Government' established, were premature. Louis XVI's reluctance to accept reform, and rumours of preparations for a counter-revolution, led on 5 October to a march on Versailles by a Parisian crowd, including many women, determined to bring Louis to Paris. After the Queen's apartments were stormed by a section of the crowd, the King, under pressure, went to the Tuileries palace next day. Versailles was abandoned, the volatile metropolis even more the centre of power and politics. Montmorin tried to put the best gloss he could on the October Days,[65] but diplomats, visitors to Paris and other commentators saw royal power as exploded and, as yet, no solid alternative to it.[66]

To a certain extent, the developing crisis in the Austrian Netherlands in late 1789 redirected the attention of the British government from eastern to western Europe and made the intentions of French politicians, both in and out of office, appear important. In addition, the mysterious but related visit of Orléans to London excited attention. French policy was, however, considered from the outside. No attempt was made to consult the French government on the situation in the Low Countries[67] or indeed on anything else. This can be seen as a mistake. Given the argument advanced in the winter of 1792–3, as the two countries moved towards war, that the British government could not negotiate with unaccredited French diplomats, or with those whose credentials were not recognised, it is interesting to note that when that had not been a problem there had been little in the way of negotiation. Arguably, negotiations in the winter of 1789–90 would have served little purpose. There was no common ground over the situation in the Low Countries, the French envoys in London would have probably represented any approaches in a negative light, and the French government appeared far from stable. Luzerne certainly responded with suspicion to George III's expression of goodwill towards Louis XVI.[68]

Yet, the failure to use the diplomatic channels available can be seen as mistaken, not least because it lessened the chances of an avoidance of confrontation during the Nootka Sound crisis, a crisis in which there was little reason for revolutionary France to support Spain. There were indeed interests that Britain and France shared: the re-establishment of

---

[65] Montmorin to Noailles, 11 Oct., Genet to Montmorin, 27 Nov. 1789, AE CP Aut. 358 fol. 106, Russie 130 fols. 203–4.

[66] Colonel William Gardiner to Dorset, 13 Nov. 1789, Bod. BB. 63 fols. 2–4; Green, Consul in Nice, to Keith, 14 Dec., General Conway to Keith, 15 Dec. 1789, BL Add. 35541 fols. 356–8; William Ritchie to 6th Earl of Kintore, 1 Jan. 1790, Aberdeen UL MS. 3064 bundle 261.

[67] Luzerne to Montmorin, 5, 8, 15 Jan. 1790, AE CP Ang. 572 fols. 16–17, 26–7, 67–8.

[68] Luzerne to Montmorin, 22 Sept. 1789, AE CP Ang. 571 fols. 10–11.

peace in Europe and the maintenance of the Turkish Empire.[69] The French could have done little to further these ends in 1790, but diplomatic support for Britain would not have been harmful. Instead, Dorset's departure was followed by a downgrading of the embassy, a step criticised by Eden. Seeking the post himself, he made the point that French affairs 'must in all events bear the first importance' for Britain, and that therefore 'experience and activity' were required. Dorset, however, was replaced by Lord Robert Fitzgerald, a nephew of Richmond's without diplomatic experience, and Fitzgerald was given the rank of Minister Plenipotentiary. In September 1788 Richmond, who sought to favour Fitzgerald's career, made it clear to Pitt that he was inexperienced, and suggested that it was best if he acquired the diplomatic 'trade' by serving in a court without 'very important business'. Fitzgerald's mission was not to be a distinguished one. When his relationship with a married woman ended with her death, he left Paris without leave. Fitzgerald received very few instructions in early 1790; one of the few ordered him to destroy all 'the cyphers and decyphers in your Lordship's possession which might be endangered upon any sudden commotion arising at Paris'. All the encyphered letters Fitzgerald received from any other British envoy were to be sent to London to be decyphered.[70] In effect, the embassy was to be a listening post, not a base for negotiations.

No Ambassador was appointed to Paris in 1789. Such an appointment might have appeared inappropriate in light of the unsettled nature of the French government,[71] but it was also significant that no diplomat of any experience was sent to Paris. In November 1788, for example, it had been rumoured that Eden or Malmesbury (Harris) would replace Dorset, and Eden had certainly sought the post then. He was disappointed not to replace Dorset the following year.[72] In 1790 Eden, now Lord Auckland, was to go to The Hague, Fitzherbert to Madrid; whereas the in-experienced George, Earl Gower, went to Paris, an appointment that had taken a considerable time to make and that was criticised. Gower (1758–1833), the eldest son of the Marquis of Stafford, had travelled widely and was an MP, but he had no diplomatic experience. His youth,

[69] Luzerne to Montmorin, 8 Jan., Montmorin to Luzerne, 12 Jan. 1790, AE CP Ang. 572 fols. 27, 49–50.
[70] Eden to Pitt, 3 Oct. 1789, PRO 30/8/110 fol. 149; Richmond to Pitt, 29 Aug., 1 Sept. 1788, CUL Add. 6958 nos. 534, 536; Richmond to Grenville, 4 Feb. 1792, BL Add. 58937 fol. 154; Leeds to Fitzgerald, 5 Mar. 1790, PRO FO 27/34; Barthélemy to Montmorin, 9 Sept. 1788, AE CP 566 fol. 269.
[71] *Glocester Journal*, 11 Jan. 1790.
[72] Payne to Keith, 1 Nov. 1788, BL Add. 35541 fol. 128; Eden to Pitt, 12 Nov. 1788, 3, 5, 6 Oct. 1789, PRO 30/8/220 fols. 144, 149–53.

however, would not have been a bar in Pitt's eyes.[73] The British government's attitude towards France was not unique. French diplomats elsewhere complained of neglect, and Montmorin was aware of the extent to which domestic problems both precluded an active foreign policy and lessened the consideration paid to France.[74]

The nature of Anglo-French relations in the winter of 1789–90 in one respect mirrored those of the summer of 1787 and prefigured those of 1792. They were dominated by the situation in the Low Countries. The need to thwart French intentions or to prevent the development of a situation there that might favour France then or in the future was stressed by the British government.[75] There seemed little point discussing the issue with the French government because promises of non-intervention would be of no permanent value. In addition, the diplomatic situation in early 1790 appeared propitious for Britain. Joseph II approached her for better relations and, shortly afterwards, died, to be succeeded by the apparently more favourable Leopold II. Discussing the fate of the Austrian Netherlands with the French would not please Austria. If the French government was not trusted by the British, those termed the 'demagogues', the radicals of the time, appeared undesirable as allies in the winter of 1789–90 as they were supporters of an independent Belgium and opposed to the position of the House of Orange in the United Provinces. As yet the 'French demagogues' appeared too weak to be 'able to master a sufficient force to obtain a superiority in the Netherlands',[76] but their interest in and possible plans for this region made them suspect.

The Nootka Sound crisis

That was the position in Anglo-French relations when the news from the distant Pacific seaboard of North America raised the danger of conflict between Britain and Spain, and made the issue of France's likely role the central, and for many the only, topic in relations. What was striking about the situation hitherto was the relative lack of sympathetic interest shown by the British government towards developments in France, either in support or in opposition to them. Louis XVI had not been close

[73] Leeds to Fitzgerald, 21 May 1790, PRO FO 27/34; Trevor to Keith, 12 June 1790, BL Add. 35542 fol. 246.
[74] Montmorin to Noailles, 22 Jan., 13 Feb., Noailles to Montmorin, 24 Feb., 24, 27 Mar. 1790, AE CP Aut. 359 fols. 33, 111–12, 139, 170, 173–4; Kaunitz to Mercy, 17 Feb. 1790, *Mercy*, II, 295.
[75] Leeds to Elgin, 26 Feb., Gardiner, agent in Brussels, to Leeds, 26 Feb. 1790, BL Add. 28065 fols. 163, 171; Burges to Auckland, 12, 16 Mar. 1790, Bod. BB. 30 fols. 9, 11.
[76] Dorset to Hawkesbury, 16 Feb., Ewart to Leeds, 11 Feb., Fitzherbert to Leeds, 2 Mar. 1790, BL Add. 38225 fol. 42, 28065 fols. 121, 184.

to George III, nor was he in any way related. France had humiliated Britain during the War of American Independence. By early 1790 it seemed increasingly clear that changes across the Channel could not be presented as readily as hitherto as a French version of the 'Glorious Revolution': the creation not of a constitutional monarchy, for that already existed, as Noailles pointed out to Kaunitz, but of a monarchy whose constitution was acceptable both to the social elite and to fashionable opinion, the political system toasted in New York by John Jay on 6 February 1790 at the dinner for the twelfth anniversary of the Franco-American treaty.[77] Fitzgerald referred in April 1790 to 'the alarming prospects of the dissolution of all government'. The fragmentation of political authority the previous year encouraged in France a response to violence as a means to further ends.[78] There was, nevertheless, relatively little sense of concern in Britain, either amongst the ministry or in the press, though Auckland and Dorset sounded an alarmist note.[79] In response to a letter of Dorset's, Hawkesbury wrote to the Duke on 10 February 1790 about 'a supposed intercourse between some of our Dissenters and persons at Paris; there was no suspicion of this before, and it will now be particularly attended to. It is wished, that the name of any person in France with whom any such correspondence is likely to be carried on could be procured.' Hawkesbury noted his suspicion of interest among the Whigs in 'some proposition calculated to introduce the principles of the French Revolution here … makes it more important to attend to every sort of intercourse that is passing between the two countrys'. Dorset, in turn, pressed Hawkesbury and Pitt on the need to thwart the dissemination of revolutionary ideology from France.[80]

British radicals were known to be in correspondence with their French counterparts,[81] but there was nothing to match the efforts of the Spanish and Russian governments to prevent or limit the circulation of news about developments in France.[82] Trevor warned Leeds that the French would try to create 'some disturbance or confusion' in Britain,[83] but that was not the language of his superiors in London. The government was,

---

[77] Noailles to Montmorin, 7 Apr., Otto, French envoy in the United States, to Montmorin, 7 Feb. 1790, AE CP Aut. 359 fol. 204, Etats Unis 35 fol. 47; Begemann, *English Press*, p. 172.
[78] Fitzgerald to Leeds, 23 Apr. 1790, PRO FO 27/34; S. F. Scott, 'Problems of Law and Order during 1790, the "Peaceful Year of the French Revolution"', *American Historical Review*, 80 (1975), 862–88.
[79] Auckland to Ewart, 22 July 1790, Williamwood 155.
[80] Hawkesbury to Dorset, 10 Feb. 1790, KAO C182; Dorset to Hawkesbury, 9 Apr. 1790, BL Add. 38225 fol. 147.   [81] *Glocester Journal*, 4 Jan. 1790.
[82] Merry to Auckland, 4 Jan. 1790, BL Add. 34430 fol. 20.
[83] Trevor to Leeds, 3 Feb. 1790, PRO FO 67/7.

however, having to define its attitude to the French domestic situation in response to requests for assistance from the French *émigrés*, and foreign supporters of their cause. In December 1789 Artois appealed to Pitt for help for the *émigré* cause. He argued that if the French government declared a bankruptcy, it would become a threat to Britain, and that if the Revolution continued there would be a danger of a general war and of the wrecking of the balance of power. Artois sought a British lead in encouraging other powers to discuss the French situation and suggested an alliance of Britain, Prussia and France once royal authority was restored, with Britain compensating herself for her efforts with French colonial possessions. Pitt did not reply. On 28 March 1790 George III gave a cautious response to an approach from Spain. Pitt was allowed to be explicit about no money having been used to sustain disorder in France, but the King continued:

In the present posture of affairs with Spain, I do not see we can take any step towards that Court, but, should that storm blow over, there cannot be any objection to assure her of our resolution not to prevent the French Constitution from being reestablished on terms conformable to the sentiments of the Comte d'Artois.[84]

Tacit support for the cause of counter-revolution was equivalent to offering none: there was no prospect of Britain coming to the aid of the revolutionaries in any civil war, but they would have to be displaced. Given the situation in 1790, this seemed likely to require foreign assistance. In his cautious response that March, George III sketched out what would become, under the pressure of foreign pressure, an increasingly clear British response. No assistance would be provided unless vital British interests were affected. The British government would have gone to war with France in 1790, but the cause would have been French support for Spain over Nootka, not ideology, and the decision would have been taken irrespective of the complexion of the French government. Indeed, far from the Revolution dividing the two countries, Lafayette saw Britain as a possible ideological and political ally for France. He felt able to tell Fitzgerald that he wanted a division of landed property to create a 'more perfect equality ... among men', and that, on a future occasion, France would join Britain in weakening Spain by encouraging revolution in Spanish America, 'for that it was the sincere wish of this country to see a similar revolution to the present one take place all over the world and the national cockade universally worn'.[85]

---

[84] J. H. Rose, 'The Comte d'Artois and Pitt in December 1789', *English Historical Review*, 30 (1915), 322–4; George III to Pitt, 28 Mar. 1790, CUL Add. 6958 no. 782.
[85] Fitzgerald to Leeds, 4 June 1790, PRO FO 27/34.

It can be suggested that the British governmental response to French policy in 1790 prefigured that of 1792–3: it was not the ideological challenge (or response) that made the vital difference, although both were indubitably far clearer by 1792; instead, it was the challenge to interests. In 1790 the French reaction to the Anglo-Spanish confrontation was problematic, delayed and never came to fruition. In 1792 the contest was more direct, in terms of the issues at stake and the measures taken by France, and both powers were acting in a volatile situation in which it was difficult to back down, not just thanks to domestic pressures but because what was at stake was indeed very important; although, as will be argued, ideological considerations also played a major role, not least by crucially exacerbating mistrust.

The crisis of 1790 can appear as both the last gasp of the Anglo-Bourbon *ancien régime* confrontation and a foretaste of the post-1815 struggles between imperial powers for trans-oceanic territory and colonial trading rights, struggles arising from competing interests not ideologies. Yet it also revealed the state of uncertainty and flux in interests, objectives and alignments that arose from the revolution in France. Alongside the traditional Anglo-Bourbon element in the confrontation, there were cross-currents suggesting different concerns that might lead to other alignments, joining Britain and Spain or Britain and France. Spanish governmental concern over developments within France and the possible impact of French revolutionary ideology helped to induce both hesitation about turning to France and post-crisis interest in better relations with Britain. Concern about French ideology and the revolutionary example had existed since the previous autumn. It was therefore credible for Floridablanca to tell Anthony Merry in April 1790 that Spanish naval preparations were designed to prevent a French-inspired revolt in the Spanish West Indies, and possible for Merry to believe it.[86] Montmorin suspected that the British were trying to divide the Bourbon powers, but by playing on French, not Spanish, fears, a process aided by the emergence of the National Assembly as an alternative basis for power to the royal court. Certain that Pitt wished to split the Franco-Spanish alliance, Montmorin suspected that he was trying to arouse suspicions about Spanish intentions in the National Assembly, specifically that Spanish armaments were designed to reverse the Revolution. Luzerne reported that the British were trying to detach Spain from her French alliance.[87]

Such anxieties played a role both in diplomatic calculation and in the

---

[86] Merry to Leeds, 19, 29 Apr. 1790, PRO FO 72/16 fols. 270, 295.
[87] Montmorin to Luzerne, 30 Apr., 21 Aug., Luzerne to Montmorin, 17, 20 Aug. 1790, AE CP Ang. 573 fols. 50, 173, 163, 168.

domestic politics of the states involved; indeed the latter were to be a focus of the 1790 crisis, as speculation about French intentions and capability helped to determine its course and chronology. A central feature of the Nootka Sound crisis was the strain created by the transition from the Bourbon Family Pact to an alliance reflecting the changes in power within France. French developments affected both the content and the medium of diplomatic activity, with the National Assembly assuming an important, though unpredictable, role. In addition, and the distinction was crucial, the National Assembly was separate from the royal government and able to advance different policies to an extent that in 1790 bore no comparison with Parliament. As the Ochakov crisis the following spring was to indicate, Parliament was scarcely under government control, or, rather, the crisis revealed the limitations of control, but in 1790 foreign diplomats were certain that in negotiating with Britain they need only negotiate with the Pitt government. The rapid speed of change in France and the absence of sufficient time, trust and shared views to permit the development of stable constitutional conventions and techniques of parliamentary management, helped to keep the relationship between the royal government and the National Assembly unsettled, but so also did differences over policy. Above all, there was a crucial lack of trust, a justified sense that, if he was able to dispense with it, Louis XVI would not accept the role of the Assembly. George III made it clear to foreign diplomats, including Barthélemy, that he did not think that the new French political system could last.[88]

Fitzgerald reported in May 1790 that the 'popular party' took the British side in the Nootka Sound crisis, and indeed that month both Montmorin and Nuñez expressed their conviction that several deputies in the National Assembly were taking bribes from the British government.[89] In response to the crisis, the British government developed links with politicians in the Assembly, what Leeds called 'a double negotiation; *official* with the Court, and *private* with the leaders of the assembly'.[90] The latter, which Gower's official position made him unsuitable for, led to Hugh Elliot's discussions in October 1790. Elliot emphasised that he could not commit his 'more intimate conversations' to paper, but his letter of 26 October 1790 to Pitt provided sufficient detail to make it clear that he saw the crisis as an occasion not only to use the French 'popular leaders' to block French assistance to Spain, but also as a means for establishing an Anglo-French understanding. In a private conference with Antoine Barnave, Menou and Emmanuel

[88] Barthélemy to Montmorin, 4 Mar. 1791, AE CP Ang. 576 fols. 267–8.
[89] Fitzgerald to Leeds, 21 May 1790, PRO FO 27/34; Rothaus, 'War and Peace', p. 122.
[90] Leeds to Burges, 29 Aug. 1790, Bod. BB. 37 fol. 25.

Fréteau, a deputation from the Diplomatic Committee of the National Assembly, Elliot explained the conduct of the British government and persuaded them, in the event of Spain failing to accept British terms, to agree to take no further measures against Britain until after they had had further discussions with him, which would give Elliot an opportunity to influence French policy. Elliot denied that the British government was seeking revenge for French intervention in the War of American Independence, the exploitation of the Revolution or the gain of the French West Indies. He also sought to interpret British politics in a way likely both to win the support of his hearers, and to suggest that, in so far as the political struggles within France were of wider import, part of a more general struggle, the Pitt ministry was on the same side as the French 'popular' leaders. Pitt, in fact, had not shared Fox's exuberant delight in the outbreak of the Revolution.[91] He was most concerned about its likely impact on French strength and had greeted Necker's resignation on 3 September 1790 by noting that it would 'certainly not diminish the confusion'.[92]

Elliot, nevertheless, quoted Mirabeau as having argued in July 1790 that Pitt was 'the choice of the People, confirmed by the favour of His Sovereign, resisting the combination of an aristocratic party'. Elliot 'also enforced the comparison between our own opposition and the aristocratic party in France', and suggested that Spain, rather than Britain, was resorting to covert diplomacy by arguing that she sought war 'in concert with the French malecontents, in order to draw on a crisis, which might raise insurmountable barriers against the progress of that glorious revolution' in France. Elliot further argued that, whereas it was necessary for the British government via himself to negotiate secretly in France with those who were not in the ministry, the French should not do the same in Britain,

I proved how much it was the interest of the popular leaders here to discourage all connections with party or private associations in England; that Government alone in Great Britain could serve their cause and that hitherto it had taken no step whatever to prove either hostility or ill-will towards their growing happiness.

Always an optimist about his own achievements, Elliot claimed that he had been completely successful, that 'the popular party' had shown him 'unbounded confidence', and that he was 'more master of the secret springs of action here than anybody else could have been'. He was also confident that the drift in French politics was towards Britain, that the popular orators favoured her and the Pitt ministry, and that French

[91] Fox to Richard Fitzpatrick, 30 July 1789, BL Add. 47580 fol. 139.
[92] Pitt to Edward Eliot, 9 Sept. [1790], Ipswich HA 119 T108/39 no. 273.

politicians would like to see peace between Britain and Spain and 'a subsequent advantageous connection' between France and Britain.[93]

In 1792 French foreign policy was to be notorious for confusion, as envoys and agents followed separate lines of policy and contradicted each other. This was not, however, an innovation of revolutionary government. In the confused diplomacy of Frederick William II envoys were sent to the same court, Podewils and Jacobi at Vienna for example, but given different instructions, as personal diplomacy superseded and complicated the official diplomacy of the government. French policy in the United Provinces in 1787 had been complicated by the differing views and connections of their various agents there. Keith complained in 1792: 'in the actual state of the Austrian Chancery for Foreign Affairs, a Minister who has any business to transact there runs the risk of receiving three different answers on the same head, if he puts a question successively to Prince Kaunitz, Count Cobenzl and Baron Spielmann'. In the British case, Miles tended to chart a solitary and different course to accredited British diplomats, but this was not true of Elliot. His discussions with French politicians were carried out with the full knowledge and approval of the British envoy, Gower.

Gower was clearly impressed by Elliot, but he also argued that the French government was unstable, which made it more important to seek support in the National Assembly. He reported that Elliot's relationship with Mirabeau had produced 'an easy means of maintaining a good understanding' between the British government and 'the prevailing party in the National Assembly', and, after Elliot's meeting with the deputation, he enthusiastically sketched out the prospect for good relations:

Mr. Elliot has brought the prevailing party in this country to act according to their true interest; and, if they meet with proper encouragement from you, they seem ready to go any lengths towards inforcing our claims with regard to Spain, and they are, I believe, sincere in their desire to promote a real and effectual good understanding between the two countries. I shall be extremely happy to cooperate with Mr. Elliot in a negotiation which appears to me to be so desirable.[94]

That letter was written six days before the publication of Burke's *Reflections on the Revolution in France*. It serves as a powerful reminder both of the challenge Burke faced in attempting to redefine radically Anglo-French relations, and of the extent to which diplomatic, political and ideological alignments appeared unsettled in late 1790, and thus

[93] Elliot to Pitt, 26 Oct. 1790, PRO 30/8/139 fols. 123–8; Evans, 'Miles', *Bulletin*, 197.
[94] Keith to Grenville, 14 July 1790, PRO FO 7/30; O. Browning (ed.), *The Dispatches of Earl Gower* (Cambridge, 1885), pp. 38–40; Gower to Pitt, 22, 26 Oct. 1790, PRO 30/8/139 fols. 121, 129.

open to new departures. The suggestion of an alliance can be dismissed. Elliot was an enthusiast and somewhat of a maverick, Gower, who Lord Camelford criticised as overly sympathetic to the Revolution,[95] was inexperienced and over-impressed by the charismatic Elliot. Both took the immediate task, of seeking to develop links with members of the National Assembly in order to prevent French support for Spain, further than the British government had intended. Discussion of common interests and shared objectives was a necessary adjunct of more specific negotiations, but the latter did not need to lead to anything more. Reporting to George III on Elliot's discussions, Pitt mentioned the possibility that they might help to preserve peace, or at least prevent France from helping Spain, but not the idea that they could lead to better Anglo-French relations.[96] He was similarly cautious in what he wrote to Elliot:

whatever confidential communications may take place with the Diplomatic Committee for the sake of bringing them to promote our views, no ostensible intercourse can be admitted but through the medium of accredited Ministers or the Secretary of State for Foreign Affairs, and that in the name of the King. The second point which is of still more importance is that no assurances shall be given directly or indirectly which go farther, than that this country means to persevere in the Neutrality which it has hitherto scrupulousy observed with respect to the internal dissensions of France, and from which it will never depart unless the conduct held there should make it indispensible as an act of self defence; and that we are sincerely desirous of... a friendly intercourse and good understanding between the two Nations.

Unwilling to take any steps that might help any French 'political party', Pitt also stated that Elliot should use no language that suggested that Britain was ready to negotiate an alliance, 'which even if such a thing should be really wished in France, various events might make it impossible for us to accede to'. Pitt and Leeds, who was kept informed of the correspondence by him, were agreed on the need to steer 'quite clear of anything like cringing to France'.[97] Having returned to London, Elliot kept Pitt informed of his subsequent correspondence with French politicians, and pressed Barthélemy on the value of an Anglo-French alliance,[98] but the ending of the confrontation with Spain led to a decline in British governmental interest in France, her politics and policies. Even had the British ministry sought more, the French situation was too

[95] For Camelford, A. Cobban and R. A. Smith (eds.), *The Correspondence of Edmund Burke*, VI (Cambridge, 1967), p. 390.
[96] Pitt to George III, 25 Oct. 1790, Aspinall, *George III* no. 631.
[97] Pitt to Elliot, Oct. 1790, PRO 30/8/102 fols. 124–5; Pitt to Leeds, Oct. 1790, BL Add. 33964 fol. 21; Evans, 'Miles', *Bulletin*, 198.
[98] Barthélemy to Montmorin, 25 Feb. 1791, AE CP Ang. 576 fol. 228.

unsettled to make negotiations aimed at anything other than immediate objectives worthwhile. Furthermore, whatever her government, France could offer little assistance to Britain in her foreign policy. Leeds had referred in April 1790 to 'the present reigning anarchy', Anthony Storer that September to 'a state of perfect impotence'.[99] For a power preparing to confront Russia, France was not so much likely to be an uncertain ally as one so weak as to have no weight in diplomatic combinations. French weakness indeed had considerably lessened the danger that she would be able to intervene in the Low Countries.

And yet, the suggestion of better relations has to be considered seriously, not least because, by refusing to follow it up, the British government helped to increase doubts about its intentions in French 'popular' circles, and to encourage them to turn towards opposition and radical groups in Britain, a choice that Elliot had discerned. Arguably such a move reflected anyway the increasingly radical direction within French popular politics, and it was certainly encouraged by the hostile French response to the appearance of Burke's *Reflections*. The Dutch crisis of 1787, as well as the American War of Independence, however, had shown that ideology did not have to provide the key to alliances, and French popular politicians were able to differentiate between Britain, with its limited government and its participatory political system, and other *ancien régime* states. Furthermore, as British governmental relations with both the French court and ministry, and the *émigré* princes were poor, a failure to develop links with the popular party ensured not only that the British government was left with no allies in France, but also that it had no reliable channels of communication open that could be used in any future crisis. The failure to follow up Elliot's lead was a serious discouragement, and the option was further restricted when Mirabeau died on 2 April 1791. Miles felt that an opportunity for negotiating an alliance had been lost. The political position of those pressing for better relations with France was, however, hardly an encouragement to resort to such a policy. On 26 November 1790 Earl Stanhope told the Lords that France was now friendly and that 'an alliance between Great Britain and that great and free state would be so powerful, that nothing could stand that was intended to defeat our professed pacific intentions',[100] but Stanhope did not reflect majority opinion in the Lords.

In light of the new direction that was to be given to European diplomacy by the Austro-Prussian reconciliation in the summer of 1791 and their subsequent policy of active hostility towards revolutionary

[99] Leeds to Fitzgerald, 16 Apr., Storer to Auckland, 28 Sept. 1790, BL Add. 28065 fol. 277, 34433 fol. 185.   [100] *Senator*, I (1791), p. 26.

France, any intervening improvement in Anglo-French relations could only have eventually posed serious problems for the British government. Not only, therefore, would any improvement in relations in the winter of 1790–1 have been very unlikely to ease Anglo-French tensions in late 1792, when both the international and domestic French situations were very different, but, in addition, it would not have survived the altered diplomatic position in the summer of 1791. Without by then any powerful ally, the Pitt ministry did not wish to escape from isolation by joining with France.

Burke and the Revolution

France in the summer of 1791 was still a weak and unpredictable power, but, in addition, the flight of Louis XVI from Paris on 20 June, the subsequent crisis in France and the sense of crisis in Britain, which led to the loyalist 'Church and King' anti-Priestley riots in Birmingham in July, seemed to vindicate earlier warnings that developments in France threatened not only the fabric of society in France, but also the peace of Britain. That argument derived much of its force from Edmund Burke. There had been little difference along party lines in the reporting of the early stages of the Revolution by the British press.[101] This was largely because the Revolution, though seen as newsworthy, was not regarded as significant in terms of British politics. Debate over British political issues, and, in particular, the Dissenters' campaign for the repeal of the Test Act, was generally without reference to French developments. There were, however, exceptions, and Burke did not originate the idea of using the Revolution as a means of condemning domestic developments that he disliked. One contributor to the *Leeds Intelligencer* of 2 March 1790 attacked the idea of repealing the Test by noting:

Since last year, a reinforcement of reasons *for laying all things open* has been imported from France, and we are reproached with falling so far short of the liberality of sentiment displayed in that Kingdom. I love liberty as well as any man, but not that particular species of it, which allows only seven minutes to prepare for death, before one is hanged up by fish-women at a lamp iron; and though superstition be a very bad thing, I hope never to see the British National Assembly possessed by the spirit of Voltaire.

That day, in a Commons attack on the proposal for a repeal of the Test and Corporation Acts, Burke suggested that the Dissenting ministers

---

[101] Garbett to Lansdowne, 23, 24, 25, 31 July, 3, 5, 6 Aug. 1791, Bowood 18; R. B. Rose, 'The Priestley Riots of 1791', *Past and Present*, 18 (1960), 68–88; G. M. Ditchfield, 'The Priestley Riots in Historical Perspective', *Transactions of the Unitarian Historical Society*, 20 (1991), 3–16; Begemann, *English Press*, p. 73.

were recommending the same attack on the church as had happened in France. Fox, in contrast, praised the example of French moves towards toleration.[102] The language of rights which played such a major role in French politics influenced the situation in Britain. Dissenters no longer sought repeal as a privilege and favour; they were proclaiming their rights. In his sermon 'On the Love of Our Country', delivered on 4 November 1789, the prominent Dissenting minister Richard Price praised the Revolution as God's work. Indeed, demand for repeal raised the political temperature and the hostile reaction to it was to assist Burke's cause. Competing meetings, for and against repeal, were matched by newspaper comment. The *Daily Gazetteer*, a paper that supported parliamentary reform and repeal of the Test and Corporation Acts, had already favourably compared French changes with the British position in its issue of 12 January 1790.[103]

Events in France, however, played no real role in the general election of 1790, which was a major success for the government,[104] despite the relative sophistication of opposition organisation.[105] In March 1790 Major-General Richard Grenville, Comptroller and Master of the Household to the Duke of York, wrote to Ewart expressing his conviction that the elections would go well and adding: 'I hope the example we have before our eyes of the misery and ruin attending a total subversion of all order and government, may check any spirit of that kind which may lay lurking amongst us'.[106] The development of domestic radicalism was to prove him wrong, but, at least as far as the general election was concerned, it was striking to see how few parallels were drawn at this stage. A report in the *Ipswich Journal* of 21 August 1790 on the election campaign included the observation, 'I blushed to hear a gentleman... advert to France as an example of freedom, worthy of the imitation of the electors of Suffolk.' Such comments appear to have been rare.

It was Burke's *Reflections* that made France a central topic of British political debate by linking developments in the two countries in a

[102] Debrett, *Parliamentary Register*, 27, 178–87; Cobbett, 28, 388, 397; Hatsell to Henry Addington, 17 Sept. 1789, Exeter, Devon CRO D152 M/C 1789 OZ5; R. A. Smith, 'Walpole's Reflections on the Revolution in France', in W. H. Smith (ed.), *Horace Walpole, Writer, Politician, and Connoisseur* (New Haven, 1967), pp. 92–3, 111.
[103] J. Fiske (ed.), *The Oakes Diaries I. Business, Politics and the Family in Bury St Edmunds, 1778–1800* (Woodbridge, 1990), pp. 262–3; G. Ditchfield, 'The Campaign in Lancashire and Cheshire for the repeal of the Test and Corporation Acts, 1787–1790', *Transactions of the Historic Society of Lancashire and Cheshire*, 126 (1977), 132.
[104] Pitt to Edward Eliot, 9 July 1790, Ipswich HA 119 T108/39 no. 293; R. G. Thorne (ed.), *The House of Commons 1790–1820* (5 vols.), I, 115–26.
[105] D. E. Ginter, 'The Financing of the Whig Party Organization, 1783–1793', *American Historical Review*, 71 (1966), 421–40, and *Whig Organization in the General Election of 1790* (Berkeley, 1967).
[106] Grenville to Ewart, 25 Mar. 1790, Williamwood 147.

polemical fashion, and, by and in doing so, changed the nature of this political debate.[107] If his ideas were not new, his prominence and the controversy that he aroused made them widely discussed. Not only conservatives applauded Burke. John Courtenay, a Foxite MP, sent a copy to his former patron, George, 1st Marquess Townshend, adding that it was 'universally read, and universally admired, as it well deserves to be, as the finest composition in the English language, and (bating a few exceptionable passages) inculcating the soundest constitutional doctrine, the true philosophy of human nature, and the best and purest morals'.[108] The conservative Earl of Fife thought it should be printed in gold.[109] The *Reflections* touched off a pamphlet debate, although the press was of crucial importance, both in printing excepts from the writings of Burke, his supporters and his critics, and in commenting upon them, all often at some length. Burke's analysis of *ancien régime* France was contested, but it was the progress of radical thought in Britain and the consequences of the Revolution for British politics that aroused most interest in the political debate. In one sense the Revolution *per se* became relatively unimportant from late 1790 in so far as this debate was concerned. It was its implications for British politics that were generally discussed, a situation that persisted until 1792, when the outbreak of war on the Continent and the possibility of Anglo-French conflict helped to increase interest in French developments.

Burke's conscious statement of a conservative ideology and his use of it to attack British and French radicalism helped to create a partisan division in British press reporting of France. If French developments were to be used to castigate British radicalism, then radicals were going to rally to their defence, a process aided by the relative absence of Anglo-French diplomatic tension between late 1790 and late 1792. The depiction of similarities between British and French developments in the press, especially the opposition press, was not new. It was based on the

---

[107] B. Fontana, *Rethinking the Politics of Commercial Society: the Edinburgh Review 1802–1832* (Cambridge, 1985), pp. 26–7; The literature on Burke, the *Reflections* and the subsequent controversy is vast. F. P. Lock, *Burke's Reflections on the Revolution in France* (1985) and S. Blakemore (ed.), *Burke and the French Revolution* (Athens, Georgia, 1992) are good recent introductions. The most recent edition can be found in L. G. Mitchell (ed.), *The Writings and Speeches of Edmund Burke. 8: 1790–1794* (Oxford, 1989), though Philippe Raynaud's introduction to the Hachette edition is also very valuable, while the best guide to the works produced on the controversy is G. T. Pendleton, 'Towards a Bibliography of the *Reflections* and *Rights of Man* Controversy', *Bulletin of Research in the Humanities*, 85 (1982), 65–103. A crucial topic is covered in J. T. Boulton, *The Language of Politics in the Age of Wilkes and Burke* (1963).

[108] Courtenay to Townshend, 4 Nov. 1790, Beinecke, Osborn Shelves, Townshend Box 5.

[109] Fife to William Rose, 25, 27 Nov., 3 Dec. 1790, 4 Jan. 1791, Aberdeen UL 2226/131; John Hatsell, Chief Clerk of the House of Commons, to Henry Addington, the Speaker, 6 Nov. 1790, Exeter CRO D. 152 MC. 1790/OZ 25.

view that national character, far from being immutable, could alter as a result of social and political changes, such as the spread of corruption. Thus, over the previous century, opposition newspapers had argued that Britain could readily follow the example of the Continent and that the British Revolution Settlement of 1689–1701 had failed to safeguard Britain against despotism, because no event or constitution could preclude the consequences of misrule. Europe had been presented as a stage depicting what would happen to Britain were it to be misgoverned; the price of liberty was eternal vigilance.[110]

When change came in France it became for conservative British commentators a stage depicting what could happen to the country were it run by the opposition, or, even more worryingly, by their radical allies. Conversely, opposition writers were driven to defend their cause, and, by extension, the situation in France. Under the stimulus of Burke's *Reflections*, opinions about the Revolution and its implications became more defined, a process encouraged by the extent to which Burke's attitude provided ministerial writers with a valuable opportunity to divide the opposition. In addition, the determination of radicals to organise and proselytise underlined Burke's insistence that the cause of revolution was indeed universal in its intentions and threat, though he failed to draw attention to the differences between indigenous and French radicalism.

The partisan division in the press over French developments, which began in late 1790, though it had been prefigured earlier, lasted into the period of Anglo-French conflict, becoming more defined and bitter with time. The charge in the ministerial press that opposition newspapers were pro-French became more serious as developments within France became more marked and as the two countries moved towards conflict. The leading opposition papers, in particular the *Morning Chronicle*, were accused of links with French envoys. The revolutionary government placed high hopes on James Perry, owner-editor of the *Morning Chronicle*, who had gone to Paris in 1791 in the capacity of a 'deputy' of the English Revolution Society, in order to send back reports that would give the paper the edge in its coverage of the Revolution.[111]

These changes and developments in the British public debate over France, Anglo-French links and British politics were to be important for

---

[110] Begemann, *English Press*, p. 122; J. Black, 'Ideology, History, Xenophobia and the World of Print in Eighteenth-century England', in Black and J. Gregory (eds.), *Culture, Politics and Society in Britain 1660–1800* (Manchester, 1991), pp. 203–4.

[111] I. R. Christie, 'James Perry of the Morning Chronicle, 1756–1821', in Christie (ed.), *Myth and Reality in Late Eighteenth Century British Politics* (1970), pp. 344–5; I. S. Asquith, 'James Perry and the "Morning Chronicle" 1790–1821' (unpublished Ph.D., London, 1970), pp. 18–19.

relations between the two countries, but, in the short term, the controversy sparked off by the publication of Burke's book was superseded, to a certain extent, in public attention by the confrontation with Russia. Furthermore, this confrontation dominated governmental consideration of foreign policy in the winter of 1790–1 and in the following spring. Far from Burke providing a clarion call for action, the public debate over the *Reflections* was without consequence for a government concerned about more distant horizons, more immediate problems. In addition, Elliot's successful discussions suggested that the 'popular party' in France were not only pro-British, but also manageable, that they might accept a pro-Pittite view of British politics, as well as a conception of international relations that suited Britain. From that standpoint, Burke's analysis appeared both irrelevant in general and wrong in specifics.

In one important respect, the idealism of the Revolution directly accorded with British foreign policy. The most important French statement on foreign policy in 1790 was the renunciation of offensive war by the National Assembly on 22 May.[112] The undertaking of war for the purpose of making conquests was formally rejected. This was not an isolated expression of opinion, or even an opinion restricted to the public sphere. A month earlier France's leading diplomat, Noailles, had written from Vienna to suggest that Europe would be more tranquil if rulers accepted what they had inherited, and concentrated on domestic problems instead of territorial aggrandizement.[113] It would be easy to dismiss such statements as a consequence of French weakness, to suggest that the objectives, agenda and course of international relations were essentially set by the distribution and use of power. From this perspective, France did not play an active role when her relative power declined, but in 1792 she returned to play a major part in a system in which she had played a minor role since 1787, and a limited one since the Seven Years War. Such an interpretation, however, is too mechanistic and simplistic. Objectives were clearly framed in light of relative capability, but they also reflected the conception of the international system held by those who comprised the government. In this respect, as in much else, there was considerable continuity between the policies of the *ancien régime* French state and those of the politicians of 1789–91. France had essentially abandoned an aggressive continental foreign policy in mid-century, not in 1789 or 1787. Her forces had not campaigned in the Low Countries since 1748, nor had Louis XV or Louis

[112] *Archives Parlementaires de 1787 à 1860 : Recueil complet des débats législatifs et politiques des chambres françaises* (127 vols., Paris, 1879–1913), 15, 663.
[113] Noailles to Montmorin, 21 Apr. 1790, AE CP Aut. 359 fol. 237.

XVI made or sought any territorial gains at the expense of the Austrian Netherlands. A similar situation prevailed on France's eastern border where the sole major gain, the Duchy of Lorraine in 1766, was a product of a reversionary settlement agreed in the Third Treaty of Vienna of 1738, rather than of subsequent action. At Utrecht (1713), Louis XIV had abandoned his possessions east of the Alps, and, although France attacked Austrian Italy in the Wars of the Polish (1733–5) and Austrian Succession (for France 1741–8) these interventions were not designed to lead to French conquests, while, thereafter, the Austro-French alliance kept the peace in Italy. The defensive and reactive character of French foreign policy became more pronounced during the eighteenth century. It had played a role in Louis XIV's reign, with his concern about the vulnerability of France's eastern frontier and his anxiety about the Spanish Succession and the prospect of a recreation of the empire of Charles V. The projected Habsburg–Lorraine union, finally realised with the marriage of Maria Theresa in 1736, played a major role in encouraging France to confront Austria in the early and mid-1730s. French governments were also unhappy about possible changes that might affect the interests of her allies, for example the Imperial Election Scheme of the early 1750s, and entered the European sphere of the Seven Years War in response to an act of aggression, the Prussian attack on Saxony and Austria.[114]

After 1763, this reactive tendency became more marked. France ceased to seek European territorial gains, making none after the purchase of Corsica in 1768. Instead frontier treaties based on stabilisation and equity, rather than aggrandisement and force, were negotiated with her neighbours.[115] At the same time, her diplomacy focussed not on developing alliances that could be used against powers with which she was, or was likely to be at war, but rather on creating an alliance system that would bring stability to the Continent and, specifically, counter Russian power. Thus, instead of seeking eastern European support against the Habsburgs, as she had done prior to 1756, French diplomacy

---

[114] J. Black, 'Louis XIV's Foreign Policy Reassessed', *Seventeenth-Century French Studies*, 10 (1988), 199–212, 'French Foreign Policy in the Age of Fleury Reassessed', *English Historical Review*, 103 (1988), 359–84; O. Ranum, 'Louis XV', *International History Review* (1991).

[115] P. de Lapradelle, *La Frontière: étude de droit international* (Paris, 1928), p. 45 fn. 1; J. F. Noel, 'Les Problems des frontières entre la France et l'Empire dans la seconde moitié du XVIIIe siècle', *Revue historique*, 235 (1946), pp. 336–7; G. Livet (ed.), *Recueil ... Trèves* (Paris, 1966), cxix-cxx, cxxxiii-cxl, 58, 228–46, 249, 254–6, 265–75, 278–93; Murphy, *Vergennes*, p. 454; D. Nordman and J. Revel, 'La Formation de l'espace français', in J. Revel (ed.), *Histoire de la France, I, L'Espace français* (Paris, 1989), pp. 29–169; P. Sahlins, 'Natural Frontiers Revisited: France's boundaries since the seventeenth century', *American Historical Review*, 95 (1990), 1423–51.

was designed to maintain a static territorial system in eastern Europe, one that would complement the status quo that her alliances with Austria and Spain had brought to the Low Countries, the Rhineland and Italy.[116] Burke then supported such a system. He criticised the First Partition and Britain's failure to oppose it, though by 1793 he was to argue that Britain had to accept the Second Partition in order to help in the unification of Europe against Jacobinism.[117]

The static eastern European territorial system proved unable to cope either with Russian strength or with the schemes of the partitioning powers, and it finally collapsed in 1787–91 with French views on eastern Europe treated as irrelevant, by allies and rivals alike, and thus Montmorin's moves towards a different attitude towards eastern Europe, one that was prepared to co-operate in major territorial changes,[118] were without consequence. The essential objective of French foreign policy over the previous half-century, of a stable Europe without aggressive wars, was inherited by the government of Revolutionary France. This was not surprising. At least initially, the Foreign Minister, Montmorin, and many of the diplomats were unchanged; indeed the diplomatic corps was not seriously affected by the changes of 1789. It was safer and less contentious to further a view of French interests in London or Constantinople than in Paris. In addition, a powerful draught of revolutionary enthusiasm contributed to the same end. Aggressive war was as one with feudalism: neither had their place in the best of all possible worlds being created with such alacrity and naivety, and both could be safely condemned.

This idealism accorded with the underlying principles of British foreign policy towards the Continent in 1789–91. There was a similar hostility towards aggrandisement and war in Europe, an identical suspicion of the intentions of the rulers of the powerful continental states. British policy might appear compromised by her Prussian ally, and by her desire to see Austrian power re-established under Leopold II, but the British government both sought to restrain Prussia and wished Leopold to regain control of the Austrian Netherlands on the basis of a

---

[116] Hailes to Carmarthen, 11 Nov. 1784, BL Eg. 3499 fol. 58; E. Boutaric (ed.), *Correspondance secrète inédite de Louis XV sur la politique étrangère...* (2 vols., Paris, 1866); Duc de Broglie, *Le Secret du Roi* (2 vols., Paris, 1878); D. Ozanam and M. Antoine, *Correspondance Secrète du Comte de Broglie avec Louis XV* (2 vols., Paris, 1956, 1961); Murphy, *Vergennes*; H. M. Scott, 'Russia as a European Great Power', in R. Bartlett and J. M. Hartley (eds.), *Russia in the Age of the Enlightenment* (1990), pp. 20–2.

[117] G. L. Vincitorio, 'Burke and the Partition of Poland', in Vincitorio (ed.), *Crisis in the 'Great Republic'* (New York, 1969), pp. 33–45.

[118] H. Ragsdale, 'Montmorin and Catherine's Greek Project', *Cahiers du Monde Russe* (1986).

recognition of their earlier privileges. Compared to the new-modelling objectives of the revolutionaries by late 1792, British policy in 1789–91 was itself reactionary, most obviously in the opposition to Belgian independence and in the support of the House of Orange, but in terms of French policy at the time the contrast was less marked.

Burke's analysis was therefore positively misleading as to international relations. When he was writing the *Reflections* and when they were published, the British government, its French counterpart and the dominant party in the National Assembly shared a hostility to aggrandisement and a desire for territorial stability in Europe that clearly marked them out from the Prussia of Frederick William II and the Russia of Catherine II; it also separated them from Austrian policy under Joseph II, though not under his successor. Territorial stability was not the same as constitutional rigidity: domestic change was not unacceptable to the British and French governments, though views varied. Most French politicians sought, though to very varying degrees, change within France; the British ministry was keen to see governmental reform and national regeneration in Poland, though not the Low Countries. The strong sense that the Revolution would spill over France's frontiers, the fears that had led to British governmental concern over the future of the Low Countries in late 1789 and to Floridablanca sounding the British, was less apparent and urgent by the winter of 1790–1. In June 1790 the Sardinian government sounded Trevor on its fears about French intrigues in neighbouring Savoy, which was part of the kingdom of Sardinia, the possibility of it 'being debauched' from its allegiance and therefore acquired by France. The Foreign Minister added, 'to the great honour of His Majesty, practices of the same sort in the Low Countries are said to have been rendered abortive by His Majesty's powerful interference'.[119]

Such fears proved premature, and in 1789–90 the British government felt under no need to protect France's neighbours, no obligation to act as a policeman along France's frontiers, preventing the debauching of the subjects of others; with of course the inevitable exception of the Low Countries. Even there, the fears of late 1789 abated. Thus, in 1790 British policy towards France was relatively unconstrained by continental commitments or problems, and it can be argued that a rare occasion existed for the relaxed development of a closer working relationship. This helped to make the revival of older tensions in the Nootka Sound crisis so serious, as indeed did the longevity of the crisis. The crisis called forth all the force of traditional British polemic. On 4

[119]   Trevor to Leeds, 2 June 1790, PRO FO 67/7.

November 1790, the same day in which it carried another extract from Burke's recently published *Reflections*, the *Public Advertiser*, a London daily paper, declared,

The French change their white flag for a flag of British colours, blue, white and red. The reason is obvious; the white flag has become a dirty flag; it has frequently been compelled to fall before the blue, red, and white of England, which they wish now to imitate; but British sailors will not fear to meet them – they will glory in tearing down the colours they have assumed, and mount over them British true blue.

At the same time French fears about British intentions gained new energy. Both Luzerne and Barthélemy were convinced that the British ministry was delighted to see France weak and wished to seize her colonies, and such reports continued after the Nootka Sound crisis was over.[120] The absence of British naval demobilisation after the crisis, as Britain prepared for confrontation with Russia, stoked these fears. The French envoys were convinced that the government was both in touch with *émigrés*, who allegedly frequently met Pitt and Hawkesbury, and sponsoring sedition in Paris. In the National Assembly on 28 January 1791, Mirabeau referred to the latter. Such worries were mistaken, and reflected both the paranoid nature of French politics and public debate at this point, as well as a self-centredness that could only see preparations against Russia as obviously designed against France.

Similarly, British concern about French strength (as opposed to the example of French radicalism), was somewhat ridiculous. The anonymous pamphlet, *A Letter from a Magistrate to Mr. Rose, of Whitehall, on Mr. Paine's Rights of Men* [sic] of 1791, mostly devoted to a lengthy attack on Paine, expressed unhappiness about French developments, including a lack of conviction about 'their pacific intentions towards us until the harbour of Cherbourg is demolished and the Family Compact is dissolved'.[121] The debate over Burke's *Reflections* was more important in defining attitudes towards France than any informed discussion of France's international position, and this debate developed while the government was engrossed with the confrontation with Russia. Burke and/or his book had been attacked not only by radicals outside Parliament, but also by Foxite Whigs from its appearance. Earl Stanhope, who attributed the Convention with Spain to the National Assembly, rather than the British government, abused Burke in the Lords, while Fox and Sheridan disapproved of the *Reflections* 'as favoring tory

120 Luzerne to Montmorin, 3, 14 Dec. 1790, 5 Apr. 1791, Barthélemy to Montmorin, 31 Dec. 1790, 7, 14, 28 Jan., 11, 18, 25 Feb. 1791, AE CP Ang. 575 fols. 247, 309, 577 fols. 104–5, 575 fols. 381–5, 576 fols. 16, 43, 93, 123, 190, 227.
121 *A Letter from a Magistrate*, p. 7.

principles'. Never one to avoid exaggeration, Barthélemy claimed that the book had united the entire nation against French developments, but he was more accurate in reporting that it had made its author acceptable at Court.[122]

The publication of the *Reflections* and Burke's political prominence were responsible for the discussion of French developments in the parliamentary session of 1791, a marked contrast to the previous session, when France had been largely ignored. The extent to which French weakness left the government free to pursue other objectives was a major theme. In the Lords' debate on 29 March 1791 on the royal message about the war between Russia and Turkey, Lord Porchester, for the opposition, 'said, he was almost tempted to wish that France had at present recovered her vigour, that she might have been able to have opposed some check to the career of Pitt's ambition'. Stormont argued that Britain had taken over France's role, an interesting observation in light of their shared interest in preventing territorial change, not that that was Stormont's point:

the languid state of France: instead of taking the advantage of the cessation of her intrigues, which pervaded every court, they were actually doing what France herself would have endeavoured to have done, namely to make Russia the enemy of England, and to support the Turk against Russia.

Loughborough brought France into the debate, but adopted a different tack, directing attention to the resolution of the National Assembly on 22 May 1790:

surely their magnanimous and truly political declaration, that they would for ever avoid wars on speculative and theoretical points ought to have suggested to us a wiser and more elevated system ... The revolution in France presented to us the means of reducing our establishments, of easing the people, and of securing to them for a length of years, the blessings of peace.

Loughborough, in short, saw French developments only in terms of Anglo-French relations and was unconcerned about the wider international dimension. This indeed was to be the dominant response in British public debate, Stormont's alternative response, like his learned discussion of the past history of Franco-Turkish relations, being unusual, a consequence of his diplomatic background. Hitherto in the debate, the ministerial speakers had made no reference to France, but Loughborough's praise brought a response from his arch-rival in the legal

---

[122] Fife to Rose, 27 Nov. 1790, Aberdeen UL 2226/131/830a; John Hinchliffe, Bishop of Peterborough, to Duke of Grafton, 7 Dec. 1790, Bury St Edmunds CRO, Grafton papers 423/741; Barthélemy to Montmorin, 4, 11, 18 Feb. 1791, AE CP Ang. 576 fols. 122, 156, 192.

profession, the conservative Thurlow. He offered a view of manly diplomacy and contrasted the political calculation of speculative schemes, such as Hertzberg's, although he did not mention it, with a wise, moral and true policy: 'France had never assumed a bold, a manly, or a political aspect. They were, in his mind, a tissue of political fopperies, as distant from true wisdom, as from morality and honour.' Thurlow continued by condemning the use of the Turks by *ancien régime* France, an example of the extent to which conservative British politicians were still critical of the past foreign policy of that power. Lansdowne, in turn, praised the National Assembly for determining that the right of making peace and war came from the nation, not the crown, and he urged the British government to follow the example of trusting the people, by giving them more information.[123] In 1788 Harris had written that the francophile Lansdowne had 'principles and opinions' that should not be communicated 'to a foreigner let him be ever so well disposed as can be'. In the autumn of 1789, Lansdowne believed that nothing could stop the 'regeneration' of French government. He would have been a fine model for the fictional English nobleman who Samuel Rogers, a banker and poet from a Dissenting background who supported the cause of reform in Britain, had seen on the Parisian stage the previous month. He uttered 'the noblest sentiments and assures the people, that the English are not their enemies, but their rivals in glory and draws his sword in their cause'.[124]

The Commons debate on 29 March 1791 began with little reference to France, Pitt ignoring her, while Fox indicated the extent to which traditional concepts of Anglo-French relations retained their vitality. He asked why Britain should assist the Turks in preserving their control of the Black Sea, as it would only 'give to France, our rival, the monopoly of the Levant trade, a monopoly not derived from the cheapness of her merchandise or its superiority over ours, but from the open and avowed partiality and kindness of the Turkish government to the French'.[125] There was no reference to a new diplomatic order created or made possible by the Revolution. Burke's lengthy speech was not devoted to the Revolution, but he adopted a moral approach to the Balkan crisis and Britain's role in it that reflected his views of French developments, and his curious mixture of sage reflection and eloquent histrionics.

France played only a minor role in parliamentary debates until the Commons debate on 12 April of Grey's motion criticising the prepara-

---

[123] Cobbett, 29, 35, 38, 44, 46, 51.
[124] Harris to Carmarthen, 15 Jan. 1788, BL Eg. 3500 fol. 48; Garbett to Lansdowne, 22 Nov. 1789, Bowood 17; Samuel Rogers to his sister, 4 Feb. 1791, Beinecke, Osborn Files, Samuel Rogers.   [125] Cobbett, 29, 68.

tions for a war with Russia. Grey's first resolution, 'that it is at all times
... the interest of this country, to preserve peace', echoed the National
Assembly of the previous year. He also made a point familiar in
opposition discourse over the previous century, when he stated that
ministerial demands for parliamentary support over sensitive foreign
issues, demands made without discussing policy, but resting on the
theory of confidence in the government, and the practice of using its
majority, 'converted the House of Commons into what was little better
than the parliament [sic] of Paris before the late revolution'.[126] Grey
made no mention of a more pointed contrast, the current situation.
Indeed, French weakness was taken for granted. George, Lord North,
later 3rd Earl of Guilford, the son of the former first minister, told the
Commons that

whoever attended to the state of France, would not expect much harm from her,
at least while she remained in her present situation. However they might disagree
about the calamities she must undergo in passing from despotism to liberty, they
must all subscribe to the truth ... that no government could be established in that
country, which would not prove more favourable to the tranquility of Europe
than their old one.

Far from pressing a course of colonial conquest, North urged peace and
a reduction in the armed forces. Sheridan, however, criticised the Pitt
ministry for taking 'up the little, busy, tattling spirit of intrigue, that
worst part of the character of France', and said that this led him 'to
lament the loss of French enmity', as it left the government free 'to
pursue other schemes'.[127] Though interesting, these points were of little
consequence in the debate compared to the time devoted to the affairs of
Pontine Europe; this was scarcely a discussion conducted in the shadow
of the *Reflections*.

In the Commons debate on 15 April 1791 over Baker's motion
respecting the armament against Russia, John Cocks criticised the idea of
war with Russia over Ochakov, and praised the apparent changes that the
Revolution had brought to French foreign policy:

There was one principle in the French revolution which could not be doubted,
and that was that war should not be entered into unless for the purpose of self
defence. This was not an age when ministers, or king's favourites, or king's
mistresses, or the mistresses of ministers ... could make war merely for their own
will and pleasure: that age was past, and he trusted that this country would never
engage in a war, from blind confidence in any minister.

The following speakers did not take up the French theme until
Lansdowne's much-travelled son, Earl Wycombe 'earnestly entreated

---

[126] Cobbett, 29, 177, 175.   [127] Cobbett, 29, 187–8, 214.

the minister to consider that the late revolution in France had expanded
the minds of the people of this country to more enlightened principles of
freedom, and that it would not be safe, at this moment, to irritate the
nation, by plunging it into a precarious and expensive war'.[128]

It was Fox who developed the theme that the Revolution had totally
changed Britain's international situation,

He had been a strenuous advocate for the balance of power, while France was that
intriguing, restless nation which she had formerly proved. Now, that the
situation of France was altered, that she had erected a government, from which
neither insult nor injustice was to be dreaded by her neighbours, he was
extremely indifferent concerning the balance ... No man could say that Russia
was the successor of France in this respect ... He entered into a comparison of the
present state of France with its former condition, both as it respected the politics
of Europe, and the happiness of the people, for the purpose of showing that those
who detested the principles of the revolution had reason to rejoice in its effects.[129]

Burke sought to reply, but it was past 3 am and the MPs preferred to vote
on the motion. What was apparent from the debates was that, although
developments within France were of considerable interest, political
relations with that country were not a subject of much contention. On the
other hand, it was also clear that a sufficient number of parliamentarians
regarded the Revolution as a propitious development for Britain, either
because they approved of the changes within France or because they saw
them as likely to prevent France from following hostile policies, to make
any support for counter-revolution very contentious. Burke's arguments
might enjoy support in the abstract and appear persuasive in light of
concern about radicalism, whether British or French, but that was quite
a different matter both from the notion of a counter-revolutionary
crusade and from the specific problems that any negotiations designed to
counter the Revolution in the international sphere would encounter.
The *émigrés* in Britain did not enjoy the confidence (as opposed to the
sympathy) of the government,[130] but it was the British response to
the views of other powers that was crucial.

The British government and the Declaration of Pillnitz

The European reaction to the Revolution changed considerably during
the summer of 1791, thanks first to a crisis in the position of Louis XVI
and secondly to the transformation of the situation in eastern Europe and
the associated regaining of the initiative by Austria. Disenchantment
with and concern about his position within France led Louis XVI to heed

[128] Cobbett, 29, 223, 234.   [129] Cobbett, 29, 247–8.
[130] Pitt to George III, 14 July 1791, Aspinall, *George III*, p. 690 fn. 1.

the advice from his wife and others that he should flee Paris. He intended to escape to Montmédy in Lorraine, near the frontier with the Austrian Netherlands and in an area where the military commander, the Marquis de Bouillé, was willing to offer protection, and then to pursue a negotiated restoration of his authority. It is unclear how far Louis planned to seek international assistance in re-establishing his position. Leopold II was initially cool about his brother-in-law's plight, but his attitude changed as the situation deteriorated and as it became clear that Louis would try to flee, thus forcing a crisis. If the King escaped, it would place him in a better position to demand help for counter-revolution from both within and outside France. George III, who thought the attempt to escape understandable, observed, 'should they providentially get out of France, it will bring to the test whether the nobility, clergy and law will join the regal cause'; more obviously it would bring relations between France and Leopold II to a head, and thus threaten the stability of the Low Countries and the Empire. If Louis failed, his position would be perilous, which would also exacerbate relations. Louis escaped from the Tuileries on the night of 20–21 June 1791, but was recognised at Sainte-Ménehould on the evening of 21 June and stopped at Varennes. Although 100 soldiers subsequently arrived to assist his flight, they were outnumbered by a large and hostile crowd.[131] He was returned to Paris, where Thomas Pelham MP found the situation surprisingly 'quiet',[132] but the problem of a monarch out of sympathy with developments in his country had not been solved. Had Louis XVI been able to take a different attitude, and the problems at that juncture were clearly not all on one side, then the international crisis that France was to be the centre of over the next nine months might well have taken a different course.

Leopold II responded to the Flight to Varennes on 6 July 1791, by issuing the Padua Circular, an appeal to Europe's rulers for concerted action to restore the liberty of the French royal family.[133] Such a policy required Austro-Prussian co-operation. Catherine II and the virulently anti-revolutionary Gustavus III, who agreed on 18 October 1791 to act against France, were not in a position to do much, and Spain and Sardinia were too weak to act effectively. Frederick William II had already displayed an ability to intervene militarily in western Europe, and it was also clear that Leopold II would be able to act there only if assured of Prussian support. On 25 July the two powers reached a

---

[131] George III to Grenville, 23, 25, 27 June 1791, BL Add. 58856 fols. 48, 53, Bod. BB. 52 fol. 117; accounts of Varennes episode, BL Add. 59064 fols. 2–16; Hardman, *Louis XVI*, pp. 185–97.

[132] Pelham to Malmesbury, 21 June 1791, Winchester, Malmesbury 163; Pelham's extensive travels in France in 1791 can be followed in BL Add. 51705.

[133] Vivenot, *Politik ... Kaunitz*, pp. 185–7.

preliminary agreement. In August the two monarchs met at Pillnitz, the summer palace of the Elector of Saxony near Dresden, and on the 27th, urged to action by Artois, they issued the Declaration of Pillnitz, which sought to give added force to the principles set forth in the Padua Circular.

The monarchs, however, made it clear that they would act to secure the position of Louis XVI only if they gained the support of their fellow sovereigns; Leopold II was clear that this must include Britain.[134] Her government, though, had already decided that it would adopt a cautious approach. On 26 July 1791 Grenville ordered Straton not to hold out any expectation of assistance for Leopold's 'plans of interference in the affairs of France'. The British government would not approve of Austrian intervention in France, for fear of fresh troubles in the Austrian Netherlands. On the other hand, such assistance was not to be refused outright, and Straton was not to imply that the ministry would support 'the Democratical party in France'. Auckland placed an interesting gloss on the new policy, that indicates how it could be interpreted, but that reflected his own views, rather than those of the ministry:

I am glad that we take the line of not entirely discouraging his Imperial Majesty's views in regard to France: If his conduct is handsome and fair toward the Allies, in respect to the pacification of Sistova, the Convention of the Hague, and the farther explanations which may arise as to Poland and Russia, it may be in our power to lend him essential service in the French enterprize, both for the sake of royalty, and for the re-establishment of popular subordination and good government in Europe.

Grenville observed presciently that any clash between Leopold and revolutionary France would affect the Low Countries.[135] During the last two wars between Austria and France, the Austrian Netherlands had remained neutral in 1733–5 and in 1741–4, though Louis XV had invaded in 1744. The political situation was, however, very different by 1791. French reluctance to invade in the 1730s and 1740s had reflected a concern with the likely response of Britain and the United Provinces. In addition, the Austrians had then seemed as vulnerable in Italy and the Empire as in the Austrian Netherlands. By 1791 it was clear that priorities would be different. An offensive war by revolutionary France would be likely to focus on the Low Countries, because of both the opportunities presented by political tensions and government weaknesses there and proximity to Paris, and because campaigns in the Empire and Italy, as earlier in the century, had required both a strong professional

[134] Vivenot, *Politik ... Kaunitz*, pp. 234–43.
[135] Grenville to Straton, 26 July, Grenville to Keith, 19 Sept. 1791, PRO FO 7/24 fols. 246–7, 7/28; Auckland to Elgin, 29 July 1791, Broomhall, 60/23/20.

French army backed up by a reasonable logistical system, and the support of allies; both were now absent. Thus, Grenville pointed out that if Leopold acted the National Assembly was likely to respond by seeking 'to raise fresh troubles in the Netherlands'.[136] That would obviously pose difficulties for Britain, not least as a party to the, as yet unratified, Hague Convention on the Austrian Netherlands. In one respect, 'the late events in France' served British interests, for they were seen as an inducement to Leopold II to offer reasonable terms at Sistova. Indeed, it was rumoured that the French were bribing the Turks to fight on, a false report that indicated the prevalence of conspiracy theories. The British government was more concerned in the summer of 1791 with securing a settlement of the Balkan war that would ensure the 'future security of the Porte' than with the plight of the French royal family or the schemes of the émigrés. Pitt felt able to write in August 1791, 'Our different business [sic] on the Continent is on the whole tolerably well over.'[137] Ewart thought the plans for a counter-revolution, and the Declaration of Pillnitz ridiculous and argued that Britain should stay aloof. More seriously, Gower argued that foreign intervention would only unite France against Louis XVI, who he presented as a cowardly, blundering fool, and lead to the creation of a stronger French state. Hawkesbury claimed that 'If the French monarchy is not restored, France is not likely to be our enemy, unless we provoke her to it.'[138]

The British were unclear as to Leopold and Frederick William's determination to secure a counter-revolution, and doubts on this head were also expressed to Louis XVI. Straton was assured that Leopold sought intimidation, not action.[139] The attitude of the British government was very cautious, reflecting their new priority on watching events rather than intervening to shape their course.[140] Of all the powers, Britain was best placed to act against France at this stage. The substantial fleet that Pitt had visited at Spithead in late July was not ordered to disperse until 17 August. It was not to act against France until 1793. Mercy's mission

---

[136] Grenville to Straton, 26 July 1791, PRO FO 7/24 fol. 247.
[137] Trevor to Keith, 7 June, Auckland to Keith, 23 Aug. 1791, NLS Acc. 9769 72/2/64, 7; Grenville to Keith, 29 July 1791, PRO FO 7/27 fols. 128–31; Pitt to Pretyman, 24 Aug. 1791, Ipswich HA 119 T108/42 no. 237; Dundas to Grenville, 15 Sept. 1791, HMC Dropmore II, 193.
[138] Ewart to Burges, 8 Sept. 1791, Bod. BB. 34 fols. 165–6; Ewart to Elgin, 8 Sept. 1791, Broomhall 60/23/5; Gower to Grenville, 1 July 1791, BL Add. 59021 fol. 1; Hawkesbury, mémoire, Aug. 1791, Bod. BB. 61 p. 6.
[139] Anon., 'Observations on the speech proposed to the King', [early Sept. 1791], A. Freeman (ed.), The Compromising of Louis XVI. The 'Armoire de Fer' and the French Revolution (Exeter, 1989), p. 79; Straton to Grenville, 29 July 1791, PRO FO 7/24 fols. 254–5; Keith to Ainslie, 11 Sept. 1791, NLS Acc. 9769 72/2/66.
[140] Pitt to Ewart, 2 Sept. 1791, Williamwood 157.

to London in August to seek British support was unsuccessful, as was that the following month of the Chevalier de La Bintinaye, the agent of the *émigré* princes. Mercy reported that Pitt and Grenville were uncommunicative on all diplomatic matters and he concluded that the British government had decided to observe French developments in a passive fashion, remaining free from all engagements. Mercy also noted both the wealth of the country and signs of radicalism which, he felt, indicated that Britain faced the same dangers as the other European monarchies. He discussed the subject with Burke who, not surprisingly, shared this perspective. Mercy also met Dorset.[141]

The Chevalier had lost his right arm fighting the British in 1780. He was given by Aust on 23 September a letter from George III to 'Monsieur', Louis XVI's brother the Comte de Provence, later Louis XVIII, stating that Britain would maintain an exact neutrality. Grenville ordered Aust to tell La Bintinaye that British neutrality extended to 'not influencing in any manner' the decisions of other powers. Later that month, Grenville gave the same message to the Chevalier in person.[142] In August 1791 Keith was ordered to express, but only in general terms, George III's wishes for any event that might help Louis XVI. The additional reference to George's hope for 'any opportunity of establishing with the court of Vienna such a system of good understanding and concert as may tend to promote and maintain the general and permanent tranquillity of Europe'[143] was very vague, and George had already written to Leopold to state that he would not take a role in French internal affairs.[144]

The reference to a concert for promoting peace offered in theory the basis for a league against Revolutionary France, but, aside from Grenville's caution in restricting his instruction to good intentions, it was clear that such a league would be aimed rather at preventing change outside France's borders than at effecting a counter-revolution within them; in short it would serve British ends in the Low Countries, not Austrian ends in France. Nevertheless, the creation of a security system aimed against France was not, at this stage, a priority for the British ministry; France did not appear a threat and such a goal would be hopelessly compromised by the interest of other powers in counter-revolution. They increasingly saw such a counter-revolution as crucial to stability in western Europe. In the short term they were wrong: although French instability threatened her neighbours and was increasingly to

[141] Mercy to Kaunitz, 4 Sept. 1791, HHStA Frankreich Varia 44 fols. 23–5.
[142] George III to Monsieur, 19 Sept., Grenville to Aust, 20 Sept. 1790, PRO FO 90/17, 27/37.   [143] Grenville to Keith, 19 Aug. 1791, PRO FO 7/27 fols. 182–3.
[144] George III to Leopold II, 23 July 1791, Broomhall 60/1/93.

come to do so, a counter-revolution effected by foreign troops could not but be bloody, and might not be successful. On the other hand, the passive British response offered little guarantee of western European stability. When the Sardinian envoy in London told Grenville that Leopold II was seeking the support of Victor Amadeus III against France, the minister told him:

of His Majesty's intention not to take any part either in supporting or in opposing the measures now in agitation for re-establishing the French monarchy. I at the same time added that if the new circumstances which may hereafter result from the events to which these measures may give rise should be of a nature to affect the interests of His Majesty's subjects, His Majesty would in that case feel no difficulty in entering into the fullest explanations on that subject with the different powers of Europe, who may also be concerned.[145]

Not only was this hardly the language of Burkean reaction; it was also not a position that had much appeal for a vulnerable neighbour of France. It was as much the cautious response of the British government to French developments, as her exclusion by the eastern powers from the diplomatic process in eastern Europe, that ensured that Britain became increasingly isolated. The French, characteristically, distrusted British motives, Barthélemy reporting that the government wanted to see France the victim of anarchy, in order that it should be best placed to seize her West Indian possessions, a charge repeated by Vorontsov but denied by Grenville. Barthélemy's reports stressed continuity: British avidity for colonial gains, Pitt's propensity for intrigue, the sinister schemes of Malmesbury. Barthélemy was also certain that the British government was responsible for the Austro-Prussian reconciliation.[146] He was, in fact, much mistaken; the major problem for Anglo-French relations posed by misleading reports from French envoys and agents long preceded the crisis in relations in the winter of 1792–3. Indeed it represented an obvious continuity between *ancien régime* and revolutionary France.

In reaction to the Declaration of Pillnitz, Grenville, who was taking a more prominent role in foreign policy than Leeds had done in his last years as Foreign Secretary, and who was sceptical about the willingness of Leopold and Frederick William to act, spelled out British policy on 19 September 1791: non-intervention and concern with France only in so far as national interests were involved. There was no sense of the compromises and exigencies of alliance politics,

---

[145] Grenville to Trevor, 2 Sept. 1791, PRO FO 67/8.
[146] Barthélemy to Montmorin, 9, 16, 23 Sept. 1791, AE CP Ang. 578 fols. 230–8, 249–58, 281–2; Marcum, 'Vorontsov and Pitt', 54; Gower to Grenville, 26 Aug., Grenville to Gower, 31 Aug. 1791, BL Add. 59021 fols. 9–10.

During the whole course of the troubles which have so much distracted the kingdom of France, His Majesty has observed the most exact and scrupulous neutrality, abstaining from taking any step which might give encouragement or countenance to any of the parties which have prevailed there, or from mixing himself in any manner whatever in the internal dissensions of that country. It is His Majesty's intention still to adhere to this line of conduct, unless any new circumstances should arise by which His Majesty should be of opinion that the interests of his subjects would be affected, and even in that case any measures to be taken by His Majesty would be directed to that object only. With respect to the concert which has been proposed to His Majesty and to other powers by the Emperor, or to the measures of active intervention which appear to have been in contemplation for the restoration of the French monarchy, either on its former footing, or at least in a state of more dignity and authority than at present, the King has determined not to take any part either in supporting or in opposing them.

This was very much Grenville's policy, and it was also supported by Dundas, whose growing influence was not restricted to Indian affairs. Similar remarks were made in the press, while Grenville supplemented his instructions to Keith by stating that George III was not willing to give advice as it might influence the conduct of other rulers.[147]

British policy was not to change essentially until late 1792. In the last months of 1791 the press war about events in France and their British echoes was not matched by diplomatic efforts. Caution led the ministry to discourage the idea of a mutual guarantee of governmental system by the United Provinces and the Austrian Netherlands.[148] Disenchantment with Leopold II, suspicion about the possible consequences of his French policy and caution about foreign commitments, combined to restrict the ministry's willingness to accept new undertakings. A Dutch guarantee of the situation in the Austrian Netherlands might lead to war between France and Austria spreading to include the Dutch and their ally Britain. Yet, by deterring the Dutch, who did not wish to follow the British lead on this matter, from such a guarantee and now showing little interest in the Austrian Netherlands, the British government was sending out a confused message about the extent to which its commitment to the Low Countries included the Austrian Netherlands.[149] The British position was neither to satisfy the Austrians nor to deter the French.

[147] Grenville to Keith, 19, 27 Sept., Grenville to Walpole, 18 Oct. 1791, PRO FO 7/28, 63/14; Grenville to Dundas, 14 Sept., reply 15 Sept. 1791, BL Add. 58914 fols. 178–9, 182–3; Auckland to Sheffield, 7 Sept. 1791, BL Add. 45728 fol. 124; Times, 23 Sept., London Chronicle, 24 Sept. 1791.
[148] Grenville to Auckland, 29 Oct., Richmond to Grenville, and reply, both 5 Nov. 1791, BL Add. 58920 fols. 26–7, 58937 fols. 151–2; Grenville to Keith, 1 Nov. 1791, PRO FO 7/28.
[149] Grenville to Auckland, 17, 19 Dec. 1791, BL Add. 58920 fols. 42–3, 48.

Arguably, neither could have been done, but the government did not explore the possibilities, nor did it clarify its attitude towards the region that was in fact to provide the occasion for the outbreak of war between Britain and France.

British policy was seen as hostile by the French, and unsatisfactory by the European monarchs increasingly concerned about France but keen to share the burden of confronting her. Hanoverian conduct was also criticised in Vienna.[150] Britain was not alone in her cautious approach to any such confrontation. Conscious of Spain's military weakness, her government was also unwilling to do much in practice.[151] Yet, despite the desire to improve relations with Spain,[152] the British ministry no more sought to explore common ground with like-minded rulers than to join the Pillnitz powers. Louis XVI's formal acceptance of the new constitution on 13 September 1791, a move about which he had little choice after his unsuccessful flight, led to a repetition of British government wishes for good relations with France, but care was taken not to commend the step.[153] Signs of French aggression and instability – the annexation of the Papal territory of Avignon in September 1791 and the growing calls for war against Austria and the German protectors of the *émigrés*, the tension between Louis XVI and the new Legislative Assembly which followed his vetoing of the decree against the *émigrés* passed on 9 November 1791 – did not meet with a response from the British ministry, though the British press devoted more space to French news, as a result of both the ending of hostilities in eastern Europe and the heightened tension of French politics. On 5 October 1791, the first issue of the *Newark Herald* referred to 'the affairs of France' as 'having for some time past been the subject of general conversation'. Pitt and his colleagues, however, kept a non-commital attitude towards the growing tension between France and the Empire over the shelter given to the *émigrés* by rulers such as the Elector of Trier.

This was but part of a marked shift in policy and mood from the interventionism and confidence of a year earlier. There had also been a change of personnel. Ewart, who left what was for him a now unhappy embassy at Berlin, after the marriage of the Duke of York and Frederica, Princess Royal of Prussia on 29 September 1791, retired to Bath. From there he complained about the direction of British policy and the influence of Auckland.[154] Ewart was now, however, a forgotten voice or

---

[150] Keith to Grenville, 31 Dec. 1791, PRO FO 7/28.
[151] Merry to Liston, 10 Oct. 1791, NLS MS. 5568 fol. 44; Aymes, 'Spain and the French Revolution', 65.   [152] Cabinet minute, 6 Aug. 1791, BL Add. 59306 fol. 5.
[153] Grenville to Gower, 5 Oct. 1791, PRO FO 27/37; George III to Grenville, 6 Oct. 1791, BL Add. 58856 fol. 100.
[154] Ewart to Burges, 28 Nov. 1791, Bod. BB. 34 fols. 173–4.

at most an embarrassment to Pitt. He died at his brother's house in Bath on 27 January 1792. There was no truth in the rumour that he had been poisoned by a Russian agent. The fate of Ewart's papers became involved in the politics of justification as individuals and politicians sought to make political capital out of the Ochakov crisis or to avoid condemnation. Ewart had complained that Morton Eden had refused to let him have documents he wished to keep. Ewart's brother returned to Burges the letters he had written Ewart, and whose return Burges had sought. Eden, however, was still concerned about the papers. He informed Auckland that summer that the opposition had sought to purchase them from his widow, but that she had refused to dispose of them in a way that might harm the ministry. Eden suggested that the government should seek to obtain them, though Auckland was less concerned, and the papers stayed with the family, so that today they are held at Williamwood by a direct descendant.[155]

Leeds was no longer a figure of consequence in foreign policy. He was to speak on 20 February 1792 in the Lords debate over the Ochakov Crisis, but, although the debate attracted distinguished speakers including Hawkesbury, Grenville, Guildford, Stormont and Elgin, it was very much an examination of the past, not a discussion of present or future policy. This was also true of Grey's motion in the Commons on the same day. Opposition politicians argued that the government had been foolish and unsuccessful, but the ministry won the divisions, that in the Commons on 1 March 1792 by 244 to 116.[156] Leeds' successor, Grenville, sought peace and prosperity, was distrustful of the major powers and unwilling to commit Britain to any bold initiatives. Isolation did not seem to concern him. When First Lord of the Treasury during the 'Ministry of the Talents' in 1806–7, Grenville followed an 'isolationist policy', preferring to adopt a distant attitude to the Third Coalition and to plan colonial expeditions, rather than to trust Prussia and send forces to northern Europe.[157]

In 1792 war on the Continent seemed increasingly likely but French defeat was regarded as very probable. Other than for the fallout of the Ochakov affair, there seemed little for British politicians to do over foreign affairs; even less for the ministers to do as far as foreign policy was concerned. A government that had devoted so much effort to trying to bring peace to the Balkans did not stir to prevent war in western

[155] Ewart to Burges, 28 Nov. 1791, John Ewart to Burges, 29 Jan. 1792, BB 34 fols. 173–4, 179–80; Burges to John Ewart, 28 Jan. 1792, Williamwood 147; Morton Eden to Auckland, 14 Aug., Auckland to Grenville, 21 Aug. 1792, BL Add. 34444 fol. 73, 58920 fol. 153.   [156] Cobbett, 29, 849–1000.
[157] *Court and Cabinets*, III, 196; Jupp, *Grenville*, pp. 150–1, 282–3; Ham, *Strategies of Coalition*, pp. 296–7.

Europe. That it could have done little was a measure of diplomatic failure – the collapse of Britain's alliance system after Ochakov – but this was also a product of a wider change of mood in the British ministry, a repetition of the caution and circumspection that had caused and followed the fall of Townshend in 1730 and, more obviously, the collapse of the Anglo-Prussian alliance in 1762. The cost of the Nootka and Ochakov armaments was probably also a factor encouraging Pitt and Grenville to adopt a circumspect approach. The Ochakov crisis had led the government to caution, to a marked reaction against earlier policies. This was both prudent, in light of uncertainties about continental developments, not least within France, and yet it also limited Britain's options. Not being part of a powerful alliance system, she was unable to bring much influence to bear, other than by acting negatively. On the other hand, the experience of her involvement in eastern European diplomacy suggested that British influence could be no more than precarious, subject to the exigencies and expedients of others.

> I have indeed long been of opinion that Great Britain has already alliances enough – that an extension of her connections is more likely to excite jealousy, and provoke counter-associations than add to her power or increase her security.
>
> Robert Liston, Envoy Extraordinary in Stockholm, 10 January 1792[1]

> The affairs of the Low Countries naturally form a part of every consideration of the present state of France.
>
> Lord Grenville, Foreign Secretary, 20 March 1792[2]

The winter of 1791–2 witnessed a marked deterioration in Franco-Austrian relations, one that was to culminate in April 1792 with both powers taking steps to lead to hostilities, although it was actually France that declared war first: on 20 April. The move towards war reflected incompatible views on the rights of German princes, both in Alsace and in harbouring French *émigrés* near France's borders, but these were made more serious by a mutual lack of sympathy and understanding and a shared conviction that the other power was weak and would yield to intimidation. Brissot and other Girondin leaders saw war as a means to unite the country behind them.[3] Relations between revolutionary France and Austria were more acute than those between the former and other powers, not so much because of their common frontier in the Low Countries, as because of the fact that the ruler of Austria, Leopold II, was both Emperor and brother-in-law of Louis XVI. In his former role he had to protect the frontiers of the Empire and the interests of the princes threatened by revolutionary France, whether because they claimed rights in Alsace or, more seriously, sheltered *émigrés*. On 29 November 1791 the National Assembly called upon Louis XVI to insist that Leopold II and

---

[1] Liston to Drake, 10 Jan. 1792, BL Add. 46822 fol. 213.
[2] Grenville to Keith, 20 Mar. 1792, PRO FO 7/29.
[3] L. Ranke, *Ursprung und Beginn der Revolutionskriege, 1791 und 1792* (Leipzig, 1879); H. A. Goetz-Bernstein, *La Diplomatie de la Gironde. Jacques-Pierre Brissot* (Paris, 1912); N. Hampson, *Danton* (1978), p. 68.

the Elector of Trier disperse the *émigré* forces on their territories. The pressure from the Revolutionaries was more acute because it followed a half-century during which French governments had largely ceased to press on their German neighbours, had certainly abandoned the opportunistic expansion of Louis XIV in favour of conciliation and negotiation, best expressed in a series of border treaties designed to settle disputes and establish a permanent peace. The French reached settlements with the Austrian Netherlands (1738, 1769, 1779), the Republic of Geneva (1749, 1752, 1763), the Prince of Salm (1751), the Duke of Württemberg (1752, 1786), the Prince of Nassau-Saarbrücken (1766, 1783, 1786), the Bishop of Liège (1767, 1772, 1773, 1778), the Canton of Berne (1774), the Prince of Nassau-Weilbourg (1776), the Elector of Trier (1778) and the Bishop of Basle (1779, 1785). If the right of the strongest had then still played a major role in the fixing of frontiers, an entirely different principle had also appeared, that of strict equality between the parties, whatever was the degree of their relative power, both in the course of the negotiations and in the final agreement. In contrast, there was no element of compromise either in the French demands of late 1791 or in their subsequent policy.[4]

Many of the Rhenish principalities appeared vulnerable not only to external pressure, but also to domestic agitation and insurrection. The collapse of the Prince-Bishopric of Liège and of the Habsburg position in the Austrian Netherlands was a salutary warning, because most of the Rhenish principalities appeared even weaker than the government of the latter. Habsburg territorial interests in the region were also important. Aside from the Breisgau in Swabia and the county of Falkenstein in the Palatinate, both possessions of Leopold, the Archbishop-Elector of Cologne was his brother Max Franz; while the Elector of Trier, Clemens Wenzeslaus, was a member of the Electoral family of Saxony, whose support Leopold sought. He had also provided his nephew Artois, who

---

[4] A. Tratchevsky, 'La France et l'Allemagne sous Louis XVI', *Revue historique*, 15 (1881), pp. 50–82; G. Grosjean, *La Politique rhénane de Vergennes* (Paris, 1925); M. Braubach, 'Frankreichs Rheinpolitik im Zeitalter der französischen Revolution', *Archiv für Politik und Geschichte*, 8 (1927), 172–86; B. J. Kreuzberg, *Die politischen und wirtschaftlichen Beziehungen des Kurstaates Trier zu Frankreich in der zweiten Hälfte des 18 Jahrhunderts bis zum Ausbruch der französischen Revolution* (Bonn, 1932); A. Sprunck, 'Die französischen Emigranten im kurfürstentum Trier', *Kurtrierisches Jahrbuch*, 6 (1966), 133–42; J. Tulard, 'La Diplomatie française et l'Allemagne de 1789 à 1799', in J. Voss (ed.), *Deutschland und die französische Revolution* (Munich, 1983), pp. 43–8; E. Oberländer, '"Ist die Kaiserin von Russland Garant des Westphälischen Friedens?" Der Kurfürst von Trier, die französische Revolution und Katharina II 1789–1792', *Jahrbücher für Geschichte Osteuropas*, 35 (1987), 219–22; E. Buddruss, 'Die Deutschlandpolitik der Französischen Revolution zwischen Traditionen und revolutionärem Bruch', in K. O. Aretin and K. Härter (eds.), *Revolution und Konservatives Beharren. Das Alte Reich und die französische Revolution* (Mainz, 1990), pp. 145–50.

had arrived in Koblenz in June 1791, with the nearby chateau of Schönbornlust. Koblenz had become the centre of *émigré* activity. The third Archbishop-Elector, Friedrich Karl of Mainz, had appealed for Imperial support against French infringements of his rights, especially his metropolitan rights over the bishoprics of Basle, Speyer and Strasbourg, guaranteed by the Peace of Westphalia, but taken from him by the decrees of the National Assembly. In response to French pressure, Clemens Wenzeslaus agreed to expel the *émigrés*, but Leopold decided that a firm Austrian stance, supported by the threat of military force, seemed the best way to protect the principalities in the region from external and internal threats. He rejected the National Assembly's position on Alsace, and on 21 December 1791 Kaunitz informed the French envoy that if France acted against Trier, Austria would send military assistance from neighbouring Luxemburg. Armand Gensonné, presenting the report of the Diplomatic Committee to the National Assembly, argued that the Austrian step reflected Leopold's determination to dominate the French government.[5]

In fact, Leopold's role as brother-in-law of Louis XVI was somewhat ambivalent. Although he did not despise him in the robust fashion of Joseph II, he had only limited sympathy for the unfortunate monarch. In addition, support for Louis' position was hindered if not compromised by the myriad rivalries among the agents of the royalist cause and by the understandable inconsistencies of Louis' position, exemplified by his switch from flight to Varennes to acceptance of the new constitution.

The manner in which misleading expectations about the likely response of the other led both powers to war in April 1792 has recently been skilfully described and dissected by Blanning.[6] It was a process in which Britain played no role, other than the important course of inaction. This was itself instructive. There had been no major war in the Low Countries and on the eastern frontier of France since the end of the War of the Austrian Succession in 1748. That conflict itself had been the last in a series, that had started during the reign of Louis XIV with the Dutch war (1672–8), in which the Austrian Habsburgs, allied to other German rulers and to one or both of the Maritime Powers (Britain, United Provinces), had resisted France in both northern Italy and from the Alps to the North Sea. Initially, Britain had not played an active role. She had not resisted Louis either during the Dutch war of 1672–8, or subsequently during the attempts to thwart his *réunions* policy of territorial

---

[5] *Recueil ... Trèves*, pp. 310–14; *Recueil ... Mayence*, pp. 270, 274–5; *AP* 37, 410–11.
[6] Blanning, *Origins*, pp. 96–123. See also J. H. Clapham, *The Causes of the War of 1792* (Cambridge, 1892); P. Howe, 'Belgian Influence on French Policy, 1789–1793', *Consortium on Revolutionary Europe 1986*, 213–22.

aggrandisement.[7] The situation changed dramatically after the Glorious Revolution. The accession of William III committed Britain to an active armed intervention in the struggle to resist Louis on the Continent, and Britain played a major role in the Nine Years War and the War of the Spanish Succession. Thereafter, the Low Countries was not troubled by hostilities until 1744: during the Anglo-French alliance of 1716–31, successive French ministries did not pursue Louis XIV's aspirations for territorial gain, while in the War of the Polish Succession (1733–5) and in the opening stages of the War of the Austrian Succession (1741–3), France, though at war with Austria, did not attack her most vulnerable territory, the Austrian Netherlands, because she did not want to provoke the full-scale intervention of the Maritime Powers. Her eventual attack, in 1744 in response to the Dettingen campaign of George II, produced a major struggle in which Britain played the leading role in resisting France. The eventual peace, that of Aix-la-Chapelle in 1748, was followed by over fifty years in which France ceased to press militarily on the Low Countries; indeed she largely abandoned European territorial aggrandisement. Combined with the Franco-Austrian alliance and with the decline in Anglo-Dutch good relations, both of which were related to this shift, these changes helped to remove the Austrian Netherlands from the focus of British attention. The very process by which coalitions were assembled to guarantee and protect the territory from French attack ceased to be relevant or familiar.

The Revolution brought changes of great consequence to the tone of French policy. The sense of caution that had led to the wish to limit British and Dutch hostility, and therefore to limited territorial objectives in 1733–5 and 1741–3, was no longer present to the same extent. Instead, confidence in France's ability to confront and overcome the world of established privilege was expressed fervently in the somewhat millenarian atmosphere of the debates in the National Assembly. For over a century, French foreign policy had focussed on the need to avoid the development of a powerful opposing coalition. Some French politicians and diplomats still urged this course in 1792: they hoped to win the support or at least neutrality of Britain, Prussia and the United Provinces. Brissot claimed in January 1792 that the collapse of the Austro-French alliance was a guarantee of Prussian neutrality, and also suggested that

[7] For recent accounts with somewhat different emphases, J. Black, 'The Revolution and the Development of English Foreign Policy', in E. Cruickshanks (ed.), *By Force or By Default? The Revolution of 1688–1689* (Edinburgh, 1989), pp. 135–58, and 'British Foreign Policy and International Affairs during Sir William Trumbull's Career', *British Library Journal* 19 (1993), pp. 199–217; J. Miller, *Charles II's Foreign Policy* (Royal Stuart Papers 38, Huntingdon, 1991).

France had no reason to fear a hostile coalition as she could unite with the powers of the Triple Alliance. He urged his audience to recall the Anglo-French alliance of 1716, which, he claimed, had been negotiated easily.[8] Brissot's speech was but one instance of the common habit of speakers in the National Assembly of ranging widely over French foreign policy that century with little suggestion that past episodes were irrelevant because of subsequent international or domestic changes. Louis, Count of Narbonne, the minister of war from December 1791 to March 1792, an illegitimate son of Louis XV, and Charles-François Dumouriez, Foreign Minister from 15 March to 13 June 1792, both sought to win Prussian neutrality.

The *new* nature of the discussion, formulation, and execution of French foreign policy ensured, however, that the suggestion that allies should be sought was not pursued consistently, that it was compromised by attempts to inspire political change elsewhere, if not also political and social radicalism, and that the new universalist rationale of the French polity, its mission and ideology, made *ad hoc* attempts at compromise and at the retention of aspects of the *ancien régime* diplomatic system unconvincing. Once they were unconvincing, there was little mileage in them, for a degree of certainty about the intentions and consistency of a partner in negotiation was as important as the apparent nature of these intentions. The decrees of the National Assembly in November 1792 destroyed British acceptance of both aspects of French policy. It appeared not only unacceptable in content, but also inconsistent and unpredictable in intention. This was a crucial challenge to any last-minute negotiations. It was not the case that the British government simply responded in a hostile fashion to the development of French policy, but rather that in November 1792 the French ignored what the British thought they earlier had made clear to be their position on the Low Countries. This led to war. The loyalist move in British public culture in late 1792 and the weakening of the parliamentary opposition were very important, but British governments had displayed over the previous century a willingness to go to war even if the political nation was not united about means and objectives.

On 9 July 1791 the *London Chronicle* published an article from Paris about a rumoured British landing in Brittany on behalf of the *émigrés*. It was false. As western Europe moved towards war, both the public and the private voice of British government urged caution and non-intervention, and expressed considerable scepticism about the intentions of the *émigrés* and their crowned sponsors. Auckland, the most important

[8] *AP* 37, 470.

British envoy, wrote to Keith, his most significant colleague, in August
1791:

I have no great idea of the proposed crusade against France; there exist few
examples in history of these leagues against particular nations having produced
anything like the end for which they were instituted, and for this plain reason that
the parties concerned in such leagues are subject to every impression that can
tend to disunion, and the party attacked becomes on the other hand more united
than ever.[9]

Such scepticism reflected in part the disenchantment with other powers
that the events of 1791 had provoked. Although Britain had in fact let
Prussia down, British ministers were most conscious of a sense of being
betrayed by Leopold II. Nothing had come from his talk of alliance,
there had been delays at Sistova, and the Austro-Prussian reconciliation
of the summer had involved a deception of Britain by both powers.
British distrust of Leopold was demonstrated by the dispatch of
instructions to Keith to work for better relations after news of the
Emperor's death on 1 March 1792 reached London.[10] The cause of
counter-revolution was compromised further by the unreliability of its
other two principal monarchical sponsors. Gustavus III had abandoned
his allies in 1790, and had a very poor reputation with British ministers.
Catherine II was seen as anti-British, an impression accentuated and
epitomised by the recent Adair mission to St Petersburg, and there was
considerable suspicion about her intentions. On 31 January 1792 Charles
Whitworth reported that Russia was to invade Poland that spring with an
army of 130,000, and that Catherine was ready to gain Austrian and
Prussian consent by offering a partition. The following month he
suggested that the scheme was related to secret Austro-Prussian
negotiations.[11] The perceptive Whitworth saw a partition of Poland as
the essential objective of any league designed apparently only against
France.[12]

Britain was not willing to join any such alliance. An implicit, let alone
explicit, exchange of Austro-Prussian support against French schemes in
western Europe, in return for British acceptance of or even connivance in
Austro-Prussian-Russian action against Poland was neither possible nor
acceptable in early 1792. Such a situation was to pertain once Britain
went to war with revolutionary France, but that reflected wartime

[9] Auckland to Keith, 23 Aug. 1791, NLS Acc. 9769 72/2/7.
[10] Straton to Elgin, 28 Jan. 1792, Broomhall 60/2/21; Lord Henry Spencer, Minister
Plenipotentiary in The Hague, to Grenville, 7 Feb. 1792, BL Add. 59022 fols. 134–5;
Grenville to Keith, 20 Mar. 1792, PRO FO 7/29.
[11] Whitworth to Grenville, 31 Jan., 10 Feb. 1792, PRO FO 65/23 fols. 11–12, 21.
[12] Whitworth to Grenville, 24 Feb. 1792, PRO FO 65/23 fol. 34.

exigencies and was not an agenda for peacetime diplomacy. Such an exchange had existed earlier in the century. Britain had accepted Russian action during the War of the Polish Succession and encouraged the move of Russian troops towards the Rhine in 1735. In 1748 such a move had been subsidised, and in the 1740s and early 1750s Britain had accepted a Russian dominance of eastern Europe as a natural consequence of the Anglo-Austrian and Austro-Russian diplomatic alignments.

British reluctance to accept, still less encourage, Catherine's Polish schemes can therefore be seen not only as foolish, given the dangers of isolation, but also as at variance with policy earlier in the century. Yet, if better Anglo-Russian relations are judged to have been necessary, it is still clear both that the basis for any negotiation was absent and that, having abandoned a 'forward' policy in eastern Europe the previous year, the British government was not about to take up another such policy, even if its likely sponsors made its success more probable. In March 1792 Grenville wrote of 'the reserve which the Court of Petersburg observes towards this government on all affairs of any importance'. Morton Eden was instructed to

omit no favourable opportunity of conveying the sense, which is here entertained, of the infinite danger to the interests of Prussia from leaving the Court of Petersburg at liberty to act without restraint in that quarter, while the Austrian and Prussian forces may be engaged on the side of France, and of the Netherlands.

The following month Grenville suggested to Whitworth that Austria and Prussia would probably seek to persuade Russia to be more conciliatory towards Poland. This offered a possible opening to Britain, and Grenville had already written of the desirability of an Austro-Prussian concert to restrain Russia over Poland, but he did not envisage a role for Britain:

it is not His Majesty's intention that you should take any share in any measures which the Prussian minister may adopt on this subject; and if he makes any application to you for that purpose, you will content yourself with stating, that you are too little apprized with the views of his court, to be able in any manner to second or cooperate with them, as your disposition and general instructions would otherwise lead you to do.[13]

Thus, it was not simply a reluctance to become involved in a second partition of Poland that led Britain to keep a distance from Austria, Prussia and Russia; there was, irrespective of their policies, a more fundamental suspicion of these powers.

Far from deciding how best to negotiate an understanding with the partitioning powers, the British ministry was faced in early 1792 with the

[13] Grenville to Whitworth, 27 Mar., 20 Apr., Grenville to Morton Eden, 27 Mar., Grenville to Keith, 20 Mar. 1792, PRO FO 65/23 fols. 55, 96–7, 64/24, 7/29.

question of how best to respond to a French approach. The general context was one of a relative lack of ministerial concern about the situation on the Continent, and a new scepticism about British capability that was especially associated with Grenville. As he shared these views with Auckland, their relations were closer than those between Auckland and Leeds, and to a certain extent Auckland's influence revived. This also owed much to Ewart's fall from favour and to the continued exclusion of Malmesbury from the diplomatic corps. Auckland took care to cultivate Grenville. Another reason for Auckland's rising influence was that with the collapse of the Anglo-Prussian alliance, the only important power with whom Britain had close relations was the United Provinces, and the Ambassador, Auckland, was the relevant expert. In January 1792 Grenville signalled his wish not to become involved with the Austrian Netherlands and his view that it would be possible to distinguish British commitments to the Austrian Netherlands and the United Provinces. He wrote of,

his doubts as to the prudence of our mixing ourselves in such a scene of folly and bad conduct as the Austrian government in the Netherlands. Surely if mere military force is sufficient to maintain the Emperor's sovereignty his 50, or 60,000 men will answer that purpose without trouble or expense on our part, and without committing the Republic and us with the Enragés of France. If there is such a rooted hatred to the Emperor's government there, that not even that army can keep them quiet, will 20 or 30,000 men from England and Holland do it? Or if not why should we have the disgrace of being involved in his failure? ... I feel very strongly that this is not a time for embarking in gratuitous or unnecessary guarantees, particularly of forms of Government – still more particularly in the case of a Government wholly destitute both of wisdom and honesty.[14]

This was a reversal of the British position in late 1789. The prospect of a pro-French government in the Austrian Netherlands, while not welcome, would not be resisted. The instability of the Austrian Netherlands was blamed on Leopold's mistaken policies.[15] In short, the government had abandoned not only its role in eastern Europe, but also the earlier policy towards the Austrian Netherlands. This was not a shift to please the Dutch, already concerned about French preparations and the likely British response. For the British government, participation in any Austrian-led league was not only undesirable because it would involve the need to support her position in the Austrian Netherlands militarily. There was also the question of what such a league might entail. In February 1792 Morton Eden reported from Berlin 'that the Austrian and Prussian courts were desirous of seeing a restitution of Avignon take

---

[14] Grenville to Auckland, 17 Jan. 1792, BL Add. 34441 fol. 162.
[15] Spencer to Auckland, 24 Jan. 1792, BL Add. 34441 fol. 217.

place, and of its becoming a point of general concern'. It was thus clear that a policy of *status quo ante* revolution would involve in practice a considerable degree of intervention in what were now in effect internal French affairs. The following month Eden reported that, in the event of war, Austria and Prussia would probably seek to retain Alsace-Lorraine as indemnification for their expenses.[16]

Against this background, a French mission, whose most prominent member was Talleyrand, arrived in London on 24 January 1792. It was designed to prevent Britain from joining Austria and to investigate the possibility of better relations. The chances of meaningful negotiations, however, were compromised by Talleyrand's credentials which presented him as a person well informed of French policy with whom it was hoped Grenville would discuss matters, rather than as someone with a diplomatic character. Grenville also complained that Talleyrand's conversation was general, not specific.[17] Talleyrand was more optimistic. He reported that Britain was less hostile than was generally believed in France, and that it was essential that France insist on a declaration of neutrality, if necessary intimidating Britain into what it was her interest to offer. The notion of intimidation, specifically of arming a squadron at Brest, was, however, rejected in Paris, where it was argued that Britain would act through conviction and interest, not fear.

Amidst talk of the possibility of an Anglo-French alliance, there was the growing problem of how Britain was going to respond to the outbreak of war on the Continent. Talleyrand's protestations and British neutrality both probably contributed to Pitt's mood when, in the Commons on 17 February 1792, he predicted fifteen years peace: 'there never was a time in the history of this country when from the situation of Europe we might more reasonably expect fifteen years of peace than we may at the present moment'. Two days earlier, Talleyrand had suggested to Grenville a mutual guarantee of European and colonial territories. He argued that only prejudice could separate the two countries: that their natural interests dictated alliance.[18] Such arguments were not new, the product of a reassessment of foreign policy as the *ancien régime* tumbled. They

---

[16] Morton Eden to Grenville, 21 Feb., 3 Mar. 1792, BL Add. 34441 fols. 357, 403.
[17] Grenville to Spencer, 31 Jan., Grenville to Gower, 10 Feb. 1792, BL Add. 34441 fol. 258, PRO FO 27/38; Auckland to Grenville, 17 Jan. 1792, Auckland to Pitt, [1792], BL Add. 58920 fol. 59, PRO 30/8/110 fol. 215; *St James's Chronicle*, 24 Jan., *Gazetteer* 6 Feb. 1792. On Talleyrand being ill received, Sir Ralph Payne to Malmesbury, 17 Feb. 1792, Winchester, Malmesbury, 162.
[18] Talleyrand to Lessart, 27, 31 Jan., 3, 7, 17 Feb., Lessart to Talleyrand, 15 Feb. 1792, AE CP Ang. sup. 29 fols. 189–95, 219–20, 202–6. Much has been printed in G. Pallain, *La Mission de Talleyrand à Londres en 1792. Correspondance inédite de Talleyrand avec le Département des Affaires Étrangères...* (Paris, 1889); Cobbett, 29, 326.

echoed the suggestions made by Vergennes and Rayneval in 1786, but, as then, it was easier to suggest such an alignment than to appreciate how it would work in practice or to forsake old rivalries. Talleyrand continued to press for a naval armament in order to intimidate Britain,[19] an idea that suggested he understood neither the state of the French navy nor the motivation of British policy. Talleyrand discerned an essential division in British policy between Pitt, Grenville and Dundas, allegedly favourable to reconciliation with France, and Camden, Thurlow, and, in particular, George III, who were totally against such a policy.[20] This accorded with a tradition of seeing George III as a malign force, but there is no evidence for such a division in the spring of 1792. A comprehensive formal understanding with France was not on the agenda, but Grenville lost nothing in expressing good wishes, as he did to Talleyrand on 1 March.[21] Attacking the government's policy, Fox was to tell the Commons on 15 December 1792 that British diplomatic action might have prevented the outbreak of hostilities, but this was wishful thinking and a political ploy, rather than a realistic assessment of the situation. Grenville's cautious response to Talleyrand's approach was vindicated as Austria and France moved closer towards hostilities, though the British government was convinced that the inclinations of Leopold and Frederick William II were pacific, which was true of the former, but not of the latter.[22]

Grenville replied to Talleyrand's suggestion of a treaty of mutual guarantee by arguing that as he had no official authority to treat on the matter, negotiations could not take place. Instead, Grenville offered a bland assurance of good intentions, that it was not the intention of the government to foment or prolong disorder in France in order to serve British interests. Charles, 3rd Earl Stanhope, a radical peer, attempted, in conjunction with Talleyrand, to persuade the British government to arbitrate Austro-French differences, but Grenville was cool and Stanhope's brother-in-law, Pitt, rejected the idea. Nevertheless, Talleyrand reported on his return to Paris in March that it was highly probable that Britain would be neutral if war broke out. Gower was instructed that he was only to reply to French approaches about Britain's position if war broke out, specifically whether she would be formally neutral or mediate, if they came from the minister of foreign affairs and if he said he was instructed to make them. If so, Gower was to reply that he did not know, but that he was ready to transmit any application made to him in writing.

[19] Talleyrand to Lessart, 21 Feb., Feb. 1792, AE CP Ang. sup. 29 fols. 222, 229.
[20] Talleyrand to Lessart, 2 Mar. 1792, AE CP Ang. sup. 29 fol. 240.
[21] Talleyrand to Lessart, 2 Mar. 1792, AE CP Ang. sup. 29 fol. 239.
[22] Grenville to Keith, 20 Mar. 1792, PRO FO 7/29.

The British position was therefore a very cautious one. The stress on what Grenville termed 'regular official channels' was explained in part by reference to the need for accurate communications, but the insistence on written applications reflected mistrust as much as caution. Such applications fostered precision, but they were also designed to enable the British government to clarify and defend its position if necessary. And yet, in the volatile state of France, where denunciation of rivals was a means as well as an end of politics and where ministers held office at the mercy of a fortune more fickle and deadly than that of a monarch's smiles, such a clarification on the French part was hazardous. Grenville ordered Gower not to begin any discussion about the British position nor even to do anything that might appear to lead to one.[23]

Such a position was understandable because too pliable an attitude might serve to increase French demands, because the terms of any Anglo-French understanding might lead to difficulties with Austria, especially if Britain undertook to act as a mediator, and because the British government did not wish to further the French objective of creating an alliance system directed against Austria. As ever, it is misleading to consider Anglo-French relations simply in bilateral terms. This was not their context in 1792, nor indeed in many respects their vital dynamic. For French ministers and politicians, relations with Britain were necessarily subordinate to the more urgent and important question of the fate of the Franco-Austrian struggle. Good relations with Britain and Prussia were sought in order to limit the possibility of a successful Austrian-led counter-revolution.

The British government neither wished nor thought it prudent to serve this purpose. Arguably the ministry could have used the French need for good relations or an understanding, in order to make its views on the Low Countries clearer, but it was difficult to do so without running the risk of committing itself in the Franco-Austrian struggle. Grenville was opposed to what he termed 'gratuitous and unnecessary guarantees'.[24] The Austrian government was indeed reported by Keith to be very suspicious of British intentions[25] and this left the British government little room for manoeuvre. The decision to treat the territorial integrity of the United Provinces, an ally, differently to that of the Austrian Netherlands, was central to the unwillingness to subordinate British

[23] G. P. Gooch and G. Stanhope, *The Life of Charles, Third Earl Stanhope* (1914), pp. 117–19; L. M. Porter, 'Anglo-French Relations, August 10th 1792 to February 1st 1793. A Study of Great Britain and France in the six months prior to the outbreak of war' (unpublished Ph.D., York, 1973), p. 59; Grenville to Gower, 9 Mar. 1792, PRO FO 27/38.   [24] Grenville to Auckland, 17 Jan. 1792, BL Add. 58920 fol. 62.
[25] Keith to Grenville, 8 May 1792, PRO FO 7/30.

policy to the Franco-Austrian struggle. Elgin, back in Britain, was dubious that a counter-revolution could work, and pointed out the pointlessness of establishing a form of government unless it enjoyed popular support. He added 'Peace and plenty is the sum of our politics.' This was an accurate summary of Pitt's policy. The Hessian subsidy was not renewed and the naval estimates were cut by 2,000 seamen.[26]

The sudden death of Leopold II on 1 March 1792 appeared to offer an opportunity for new approaches, in an international situation that was becoming increasingly volatile, as the French and Polish crises moved simultaneously to a head and the campaigning season came closer. The British response was to seek to define a new relation with Austria, not France, a crucial decision, but one that the volatility, weakness and isolation of France pointed towards. The instructions to Keith on 20 March and to Morton Eden on 27 March crucially sought information on how the accession of a new Habsburg ruler, Leopold's eldest son, Francis II, was likely to affect Austrian and Prussian policy.[27] It was difficult to frame initiatives without reliable information and yet that was to be the British situation throughout the crisis of 1792. The government, however, was to make more efforts to establish the views of France's enemies than those of France herself. Dumouriez, nevertheless, sought to strengthen relations with Britain by replacing Yves Hirsinger, the *chargé d'affaires* left in charge after Luzerne had died on 14 September 1791 and Barthélemy had left London at the end of December 1791, by an Ambassador, the Marquis de Chauvelin. Chauvelin's efforts were supplemented by a second mission by Talleyrand.

Van de Spiegel, the Dutch Grand Pensionary, suggested that Britain should make a declaration to France stating her determination to be neutral, but emphasising that she could not see the Austrian Netherlands invaded. Grenville replied by complaining about a lack of Austrian and Prussian confidence in Britain over the Austrian Netherlands, whose affairs had finally been settled without reference to Britain, and by suggesting that he did not regard French defeat in any war as inevitable:

the interest which both Great Britain and the Republic have in preserving the tranquillity of those provinces, is certainly of great weight: but much difficulty would be felt here in contracting any new engagement on that subject with the Court of Vienna, unless the views of that Court, as to the affairs of France, were most unequivocally and satisfactorily explained. The mischief of our being committed in that dispute, even in defence of the tranquillity of the Netherlands, would be extremely serious, and might lead, both here and in Holland, to those

---

[26] Elgin to Straton, 16 Mar. 1792, Ipswich HA 239/2/274.
[27] Grenville to Keith, 20 Mar., Grenville to Morton Eden, 27 Mar. 1792, PRO FO 7/29, 64/24.

very consequences, which our interference in the affairs of the Netherlands would be principally intended to avert.[28]

The likely British response to a French conquest of the Austrian Netherlands was still unclear when war broke out less than a month later on 20 April 1792. The National Assembly voted that day for war with Austria. Eight days later, and before the news had reached Vienna, the Austrian Council of State decided to attack France, Frederick William II following that summer. Though the British press expected a speedy Austrian victory, the possibility of British intervention in response to a French invasion of the Austrian Netherlands was mentioned.[29] Grenville made clear his unhappiness about such a prospect to Chauvelin.[30] The Austrian government said that it could not defend Ostend, a port from which British control of the North Sea could be challenged, if France sent a large force to attack it.[31] French troops did in fact advance on 28 April towards Tournai, but they withdrew in a disorderly fashion in the face of an Austrian unit and murdered their commander, General Théobald Dillon. A force sent on 29 April to attack Mons also turned back and retreated in panic. In June, the Armée du Nord tried again. Under its new commander, Marshal Luckner, it captured Menin and Courtrai on 19 June, only to abandon them both on the 30th as it retired to Lille. These setbacks appeared to vindicate both Burke's portrayal of France as so tending towards anarchy that even its army was incapable of acting other than as a force of bandits,[32] and the sense that the war would have a foregone conclusion. William Gardiner reported from Brussels that the military situation had stabilised satisfactorily, and Lord Camelford, who was there that summer, did not fear a French advance.[33]

At the same time, the outbreak of war immediately cut short any possibility that the accession of Francis II could serve as an opportunity to explore the prospect for better Anglo-Austrian relations, as that of Leopold II had done. Austria was both at war and had been attacked by France; this was seen as an insuperable bar to any alliance given the British determination to remain neutral.[34] It would be misleading to see

[28] Spencer to Grenville, 23 Mar., Grenville to Spencer, 27 Mar. 1792, BL Add. 34441 fols. 496, 509–10.   [29] *Times* 25 Apr., *St James's Chronicle* 28 Apr. 1790.
[30] Chauvelin to Dumouriez, 1 May 1792, AE CP Ang. 580 fol. 263.
[31] Keith to Grenville, 8 May 1792, PRO FO 7/30.
[32] *Public Advertiser*, 7 May 1792; Francis Moore, visiting Paris, to Burges, 4 Aug. 1791, BL Add. 58968 fol. 3; George III to Grenville, 4 May 1792, BL Add. 58856 fols. 154–6; J. A. Lynn, *The Bayonets of the Republic. Motivation and Tactics in the Army of Revolutionary France 1791–94* (Urbana, 1984), pp. 4–6.
[33] Gardiner to Burges, 16 May 1792, Bod. BB. 35 fol. 11; Gardiner to Dorset, 17 May 1792, KAO C180; Camelford to Harris, 12 June 1792, Winchester, Malmesbury 146.
[34] Keith to Grenville, 8 May 1792, PRO FO 7/30.

this as too serious a mischance. The prospect of such an alliance was limited. Austrian concern about Russian plans in Poland were hardly going to lead her to turn to a power now determined to do nothing to help Poland. More pertinently, from the British point of view, the Austrian government was already committed before the death of Leopold II to an anti-French policy that was more threatening and active than anything the British government wished to support. Had Britain negotiated an alliance with Austria in the winter of 1791–2 then she would have risked war in the event of any outbreak of hostilities between France and any of the neighbouring German rulers, a true surrender of the initiative.

The nadir of Anglo-Austrian relations was indicated by Keith's request for his recall in early May. He was not well, but he stressed, as his reason, his despair of any prospect for an improvement in relations. Similarly, the Prussian communication of the Austro-Prussian alliance met with a bland and delayed British response.[35] British policy towards France was hardly going to improve matters. On 24 May Grenville sent Chauvelin an official note promising neutrality as long as France respected Britain's obligations and rights under her existing treaties. In his report, Chauvelin pointed out that this would mean respecting the territorial integrity of Prussia and the United Provinces. He saw the note as offering an opportunity for better relations, though he stressed the need both to stop press attacks on the British government and to persuade the National Assembly to distinguish between enemy and neutral powers, in other words to replace the discourse of opposition to a hostile social and political order by a measured discussion of the realities of international relations.[36]

There was force in Chauvelin's observations; it has been too easy in the past to present him as foolish. And yet, at the very moment that he was warning of the danger of a presentation of relations in an ideological fashion, the British government was taking a step that appeared to justify such an analysis. On 21 May 1792 a Royal Proclamation against seditious meetings and publications was issued. This was not an isolated episode. It took place against the background of rising concern within the social and political elite about signs of increasing domestic radicalism.[37] On 31 May, the Prince of Wales, giving his first speech in the Lords, spoke in favour of the Proclamation. Widespread concern was reflected in more

---

[35] Keith to Grenville, 8 May 1792, PRO FO 7/30; George III to Frederick William II, 18 May, Grenville to Morton Eden, 18 May 1792, PRO FO 64/25.
[36] Chauvelin to Charles-François Dumouriez, Foreign Minister 15 March–13 June 1792, 28 May 1792, AE CP Ang. 581 fols. 86–9.
[37] Auckland to Grenville, 14 Mar. 1792, BL Add. 58920 fol. 77. The most recent valuable treatment is M. Philp (ed.), *The French Revolution and British Popular Politics* (Cambridge, 1991).

vitriolic press attacks on domestic radicalism, as well as on French developments, and in moves towards a fundamental political realignment that would unite the ministry, its independent supporters and the conservative Whigs behind the government.[38]

Such a move, which would have divided the Whig party down the middle, was not necessary for parliamentary reasons: there was no doubt of Pitt's control of both Houses and Whig divisions ensured this further without any need for realignment. Instead, these discussions reflected a potent sense of unease about public tranquillity. Political calculation, however, played a role, and when, with George III's permission, Pitt sought Portland's support in checking any attempt that might threaten public order,[39] he was aware of how this would help him politically. The crisis within the government created by Pitt's successful demand that he or Thurlow, who was opposing Pitt in both the Lords and the Cabinet, go,[40] was also important, as Pitt wished to ensure that any reconstitution of the ministry was satisfactory from his point of view. Social links prepared for and reflected new allegiances, as so often in this period, when who dined with whom was, and was seen as, a crucial indicator of affiliation. Having not spoken to Burke since his disrespectful speech on the Regency Bill, the ultra-loyalist Earl of Fife was so pleased by his attacks on radicalism that he had him over for dinner and drank a bumper to Burke and the British Constitution. The Sardinian envoy, Marquis St Martin de Front, saw the attempted reconstitution of the government as a move to create a stronger ministry able, without fear of opposition, to negotiate continental alliances that could both enable Britain to play a role and allow her to check the ambitious schemes of the partitioning powers. This suggestion reflects the tendency among diplomats to search for an explanation in terms of foreign policy of what was generally explicable in domestic terms.[41]

Chauvelin warned of the danger of exaggerating the strength of British radicalism and of attacking the British political system. He was especially scathing at the expense of the French press, which he had criticised earlier in the spring, and denounced the habit of presenting Britain as

---

[38] Loughborough to Auckland, 4 May 1792, PRO 30/8/153 fol. 67; H. Butterfield, 'Charles James Fox and the Whig Opposition in 1792', *Cambridge Historical Journal* 9 (1949); L. G. Mitchell, *Charles James Fox and the Disintegration of the Whig Party 1782–1794* (Oxford, 1971), pp. 153–93.

[39] Pitt to Portland, 9 May, Portland to Pitt, 9 May 1792, PRO 30/8/102 fol. 222, 30/8/168 fol. 72; Front to Victor Amadeus III, 22 June 1792, AST LM Ing. 93.

[40] Pitt to George III, 16 May 1792, PRO 30/8/102 fol. 178; Dundas to George III, 16 May 1792, Aspinall, *George III* no. 754; *Bonham Books*, 15 Apr. 1991, lots. 169–70.

[41] Fife to William Rose, 10 May 1792, A. and H. Tayler (eds.), *Fife*, p. 235; Front to Victor Amadeus, 13 July 1793, AST LM Ing. 93.

both on the brink of revolution and as divided between the partisans of privilege and the friends of the people. Instead, he warned that the bulk of the population was generally indifferent to all political discussions, and was instead attached to the constitution by habit, prejudice, prosperity and comparisons with the situation elsewhere. Chauvelin recommended that France concentrate on good relations with the government rather than supporting opposition to it, and he also presented the ministry as divided, rather than a hostile monolith. He depicted a royal 'parti', headed by Thurlow and Hawkesbury, a rival group headed by Pitt, who was supported by Chatham, Grenville and Dundas, and a middle group, of Camden, Richmond and Stafford, that moved first one way and then the other. Far from this being dangerous for France, Chauvelin argued that the situation was becoming more satisfactory for her, because Thurlow's departure had helped to cement the triumph of Pitt and Grenville who were determined to stop Britain entering the war.[42] In response to Pitt's pressure, George III had decided on 16 May that Thurlow must go, though, in order to cause the minimum disruption to legal business, he remained Chancellor until 15 June 1792.[43]

Chauvelin's account of British ministerial politics is debatable. Thurlow and Pitt had long been rivals, but their quarrels in early 1792 had apparently been over the slave trade and financial measures,[44] not over foreign policy. There was a hint that ministerial disputes over whether Britain should join Austria were responsible for Thurlow's resignation,[45] but there is no conclusive evidence. It is more reasonable to focus attention on the clear occasion of the final crisis, Thurlow's public opposition to the Sinking Fund Bill in the Lords on 14 May 1792, which nearly led to the defeat of the Bill. However, although Chauvelin may have been inaccurate on the details of ministerial disagreements, his essential analysis of British politics and society was reasonable, as was the obvious conclusion that France had to rely not on social or political revolution, but on working with the existing power structure, not on subversion but on negotiation, not on a foreign policy of the people but on the diplomacy of courts and cabinets, not on manifestos but on the 'regular official channels' sought by Grenville.

It is probable that, had this advice been followed, war between Britain and France could have been avoided, at least in the short term, that in short the domestic political situation in France, with its inflammatory, if

---

[42] Chauvelin to Dumouriez, 23 May 1792, AE CP Ang. 581 fols. 44–6.
[43] George III to Dundas, 16 May 1792, Stanhope, *Pitt*, I, 437; George III to Thurlow, 17 May 1792, Aspinall, *George III* no. 755; *Court and Cabinets*, III, 207.
[44] Ehrman, *Pitt*, II, 174–5; McCahill, *Order and Equipoise*, p. 135.
[45] *St James's Chronicle* 19 May 1792.

not bellicose, consequences for the nature as much as content of diplomacy, was in large part responsible for the war, or at least for the failure to undertake serious negotiations towards a satisfactory settlement of differences. The domestic situation in France was more important than that in Britain, as it is difficult to show that the style and content of British foreign policy was dramatically changed by domestic circumstances in late 1792.

The failure of the French advance into the Austrian Netherlands and the British declaration of neutrality brought an easing in Anglo-French relations. Having earlier been worried about a French advance into Flanders, Auckland could adopt a more relaxed attitude by late July. In mid-June, George III had himself told Front that a corps of 4,000 Dutch Patriots had assembled at Dunkirk. Had this attacked the United Provinces and been supported by the French, then Front was certain that war would break out. He soon, however, reported that British fears about this Patriot force had been eased by fresh reports about its composition and intentions.[46] Furthermore, Grenville told Chauvelin that George III had principally the United Provinces in view when he referred to his allies and that his commitments were only defensive, so that Prussia, which had come to Austria's assistance, was not comprehended. Chauvelin also pointed out that Britain was not obliged to come to the defence of the Austrian Netherlands as the Convention of The Hague of 10 December 1790 had not been ratified by Austria,[47] but this was no longer apparently an important issue. As the focus of attention switched to France's eastern frontier there was a marked relaxation in the pace of British diplomacy. The Portuguese Foreign Minister pointed out that circumstances had not altered sufficiently for Britain to have to abandon her neutrality. In both Turin and London, the Sardinian government pressed the British on an alleged French scheme to sponsor a popular rising in Genoa, and then attack Piedmont, but Grenville's response amounted to nothing more than fair words. Front told Grenville that the French government was of such a nature that even if circumstances did not permit it to display its malevolent nature by attacking, there was always the danger that an attack would be mounted as soon as a favourable occasion was discerned. Grenville saw the force of this argument. Grenville and Burges both, however, refused to respond to reiterated approaches from Front for the dispatch of more British warships to the Mediterranean to protect the Italian states against

[46] Auckland to Burges, 20 July 1792, Bod. BB. 30 fol. 172; Front to Victor Amadeus, 19, 22 June, 6, 21 July 1792, AST LM Ing. 93.
[47] Chauvelin to Dumouriez, 5 June, Chauvelin to Chambonas, 18 June 1792, AE CP Ang. 581 fols. 130, 177–8.

possible attack. A Tuscan approach to George III to the same end was also unsuccessful. Front concluded that Britain would only come to the assistance of the Dutch.[48]

Indeed, a different problem suggested itself, a stronger France within the system of the partitioning powers. Morton Eden reported in June that if Austria, Prussia and Russia succeeded in re-establishing order and good government in France, she would probably be invited to join in an alliance with them. The previous year, Hawkesbury had pointed out that a restored Louis XVI would be more attached 'to his ancient allies... than ever'.[49] Some alliance would obviously be likely, for, as after the reimposition of Orangist control in the United Provinces in 1787, it would be necessary to guarantee the new order, while the foreign powers that had intervened would wish to receive a political benefit. From the British point of view, this was, however, a very alarming possibility. France had been the most consistently opposed of the western European states to the notion that the partitioning powers could redraw the map of eastern Europe. She had only shifted tack under Montmorin, when already obviously weak and then in a clearly and unsuccessfully opportunistic fashion. And yet, the prospect of a quadruple alliance of France, Spain, Austria and Russia had worried British ministers in 1787–8. In 1792 such a system would be even more threatening. It would comprehend Prussia, and, therefore, Austria would not be challenged in the Empire. Poland and Turkey would be cowed, Sweden part of the system; the Continent, in short, would be united in a system in which Britain played no role, while its members would have no reason for gratitude to her. Furthermore, the purpose of such an alliance might not be defensive. The prospect of a new partition of Poland illustrated the aggressive and active potential of such a league. A combination of Catherine II's boldness and Prussian fertility in redrawing boundaries was worrying, especially if applied to western Europe or the Turkish Empire. In the former, it was the Holy Roman Empire that was most at risk from territorial reorganisation. The prospect of a Bavarian exchange scheme unopposed by Prussia, and even with Prussia making gains herself, was worrying, and the possibility of change in the Empire was in fact demonstrated in 1791 when Frederick William II acquired the principalities of Ansbach and Bayreuth from the Margrave, who having married the much-travelled and somewhat notorious Elizabeth, Lady Craven, went to live in Brandenburg House, Hammersmith and in

---

[48] Walpole to Grenville, 9 June 1792, PRO FO 63/15; Front to Victor Amadeus, 1, 8 June, 13, 21 July 1793, AST LM Ing. 93.
[49] Morton Eden to Grenville, 19 June 1792, PRO FO 64/25; Hawkesbury, mémoire, Aug. 1791, Bod. BB 61, p. 4.

Berkshire. These fairly extensive gains, which had a combined population of over 400,000, took Prussian power into the central regions of the Empire, and demonstrated the extent to which territory could change hand by traditional means. The subsequent attack on the legal rights of the Imperial Knights in these new possessions[50] revealed, however, the impatience with inherited privilege that was such an obvious feature of governments throughout Europe in this period, though only in France was it extended to an attack on the crown.

The new Austro-Prussian alignment had been a matter of irritation rather than concern to British ministers and diplomats since its inception, but in July 1792 Scipion-Louis-Joseph, Marquis de Chambonas, the new French Foreign Minister, suggested to Chauvelin that by destroying the balance in the Empire it threatened the independence and liberties of the Empire, both of which were of concern to Britain.[51] The apparent danger to the Turkish Empire was indicated by the report of Sidney Smith on his secret mission. The notion that the co-operation of the partitioning powers threatened British interests was argued by Chambonas and Chauvelin for obvious reasons. Chauvelin hoped that Britain would take a more active role in order to prevent the loss of French territory to Austria and Prussia or the return of an *ancien régime* government in France which, he stated, had alone been the cause of all the wars which had divided the two nations for so long. He also pointed out the contrast between British willingness to fight over the barren wastes of Pontine Europe, and her impassivity over closer and more urgent issues, a contrast to the comparisons that were to be drawn between the British responses to the Second Partition of Poland and to French advances after Valmy. Chauvelin's language was also interesting precisely because he revealed conservative ideas, in favour of the preservation of an international system apparently threatened, as Europe had been since 1772, by the revolutionary union of the partitioning powers. He wrote of it being in Britain's interest both to conserve 'the old balance of Europe, as it is established by treaties', and to see France and Poland settle their own internal affairs.[52] On 6 July Guillaume de Bonnecarrère, who had been appointed as Director General of the Political Department of the Foreign Ministry by his friend Dumouriez, secretly approached Gower and told him that he would be ready to negotiate better Anglo-French relations if he received suitable encouragement from the British government. Having consulted Pitt, Grenville replied favourably: Gower was to investigate what could be

[50] Gagliardo, *Reich and Nation*, pp. 228–9.
[51] Chambonas to Chauvelin, 2 July 1792, AE CP Ang. 581 fols. 218–19.
[52] Chauvelin to Chambonas, 10, 14 July 1792, AE CP Ang. 581 fols. 254, 277–8.

obtained. It is not clear how far Bonnecarrère's approach was related to other French diplomatic initiatives. Chambonas made approaches to Prussia and, though to a lesser extent, to Austria, in an effort to limit, if not end, the war. They met with no response, although it is clear from Morton Eden's reports that the alliance with Austria and the projected invasion of Prussia were unpopular in influential Prussian circles. In May Dumouriez had also instructed the newly accredited envoy to Naples to seek Neapolitan neutrality, but this initiative was unsuccessful. An approach had also been made to the Elector of Mainz, with warnings of the threat that the Austro-Prussian alliance posed to the rest of the Empire. Before defecting, Lafayette negotiated with the Austrians via Brussels.[53]

Bonnecarrère's opening was to be swept aside in the agitation and disruption that engulfed France from late July. Bonnecarrère lost his post with the fall of the monarchy the following month. The Chauvelin–Chambonas correspondence might appear ridiculous, the exchange of improbable hopes by men fearing that France was about to suffer its most serious defeat in modern history, aristocratic officials of a world that was about to be swept aside. Chambonas, the third Foreign Minister so far that year, lost his job on 23 July; there were to be another two in 1792. Paris was already filling with armed volunteers, keen to fight against the enemies of the Revolution, and increasingly ready to identify them with the occupants of the Tuileries. Louis XVI's dismissal on 13 June of the Girondin ministers appointed on 10 March had both created a sense of new diplomatic possibilities and helped to unite and radicalise his opponents. Marseilles' volunteers marched into Paris on 30 July singing the *War Song* written by Rouget de Lisle, the threatening battle hymn that was to be linked thereafter with them. Elsewhere, meanwhile, other

[53] Gower to Grenville, 6 July, Grenville to Gower, 13 July 1792, BL Add. 59021 fols. 31–3; Front to Victor Amadeus, 29 June 1792, AST LM Ing. 93. On this important official see G. Bonnecarrère, *Exposé de la conduite de Bonne-Carrère depuis le commencement de la Révolution* (Paris, 1794) and J. Baillou (ed.), *Les Affaires Etrangères et le Corps Diplomatique Français* (2 vols., Paris, 1984), I, 285. On French approaches, A. Mathiez, 'L'Intrigue de Lafayette et des généraux au début de la guerre de 1792', *Annales Révolutionnaires*, 13 (1921), 89–105; G. Wolf, 'Le Marquis Scipion de Chambonas, Ministre des Affaires Etrangères de Louis XVI', *Annales historiques de la Révolution Française*, no. 259 (1985), 25–45, 'Le Dernier Ministère Feuillant et la politique étrangère du Marquis Scipion de Chambonas', *Actes du 110ᵉ Congres National des Sociétés Savantes, Montpellier 1985. Hist. Mod. et Cont.* (Paris, 1986), I, 265–71, 'Juin 1792: Faut-il négocier avec la Prusse ou avec l'Autriche?', *L'Information historique*, 49 (1987), 191–3, 'Un oublié de la diplomatie sous la Révolution Française. Le Marquis Scipion de Chambonas', *Bulletin de la Société des Sciences Historiques et Naturelles de l'Yonne*, 123 (1991), 76–9; Morton Eden to Grenville, 19 June, 10, 17, 28 July 1790, PRO FO 64/25; G. Grosjean, 'Les Relations diplomatiques de la France avec Les Deux-Siciles de 1789 à 1793', *La Révolution française*, 15 (1888), 28–31; *Recueil... Mayence*, pp. 283–4.

forces were being marshalled; troops that bore no comparison with the volunteers were preparing for action. Robert Jenkinson, later, as 2nd Earl of Liverpool, the head of the ministry at the time of Waterloo, saw the review of the Prussian troops at Koblenz, and wrote to his father, Hawkesbury, that, 'the celerity and precision with which all their movements are performed, are inconceivable to those who have not seen them. Every operation they go through is mechanical.'[54]

By 19 August, when these men crossed the French frontier, the Bourbon monarchy had been swept aside in France. There may seem to have been an inevitability in the changes gathering pace that summer, an almost mechanical shifting of gears towards a bloody culmination of the developing international and domestic crises, one that made the correspondence already referred to pointless. And yet it is a pointed reminder that the eventual course and configuration of the struggle was far from inevitable; that, as Gardiner suggested, 'we live in an age when such extraordinary events arrive, that all reasonable foresight is totally derouted'.[55] The outbreak of war narrowed the range of options for combatants, but the very nature of the conflict made the situation more than ordinarily uncertain to contemporaries. This was true not only of the unpredictability of international developments, variously demonstrated by the death of Leopold II, the assassination of Gustavus III, who died on 29 March 1792 having been shot at a masked ball on the 5th, and the surprising failure of the Prussian invasion of France, but also of the role of domestic changes in France. Grenville observed on 4 August: 'I expect no resistance or next to none to the progress of the troops; but what can restore good government and good order in that country, and who is to do it, and under what form ... any man deserves to be laughed at who pretends to pierce through.'[56] The poisonous effects of paranoia had already brought denunciations and violence to Paris. On 25 July the Prussian commander, the Duke of Brunswick, had issued a declaration setting out the aims of Frederick William II and Francis II. They claimed to seek the re-establishment of Louis XVI's legislative authority and to that end Brunswick warned that Paris would be subject to exemplary vengeance if the king was harmed. Fears had been expressed that Louis would be killed or forcibly removed to Bordeaux if Brunswick neared Paris, and on 8 August Breteuil, now an *émigré*, wrote to both Pitt and Grenville pressing for a British declaration on behalf of the personal safety of the royal family supported by a threat of George III's vengeance

---

[54] Jenkinson to Hawkesbury, 25 July 1792, Bod. BB. 37 fol. 62.
[55] Gardiner to Dorset, 17 May 1792, KAO C180.
[56] Grenville to Auckland, 4 Aug., Pitt to Grenville, 9 Aug., Auckland to Sheffield, 24 July 1792, BL Add. 58920 fol. 148, 58906 fol. 129, 45728 fol. 138.

if this safety was infringed. Four days earlier, Gower had sought permission for a formal statement about the royal family's safety. The British government responded cautiously to these suggestions, not wishing to take a step that would compromise either Louis or Britain.[57] News of Brunswick's declaration reached Paris on 1 August and aroused outrage, as Gardiner had feared it would.[58] The news helped to precipitate the crisis on 10 August. The Tuileries was stormed on 10 August, their largely Swiss garrison being mostly slaughtered by the forces of the insurrectionary commune. The monarchy was suspended by the Legislative Assembly, and on 13 August Louis XVI was in effect imprisoned in the Temple keep. The theory, and, to a limited extent, practice of popular sovereignty was thrust to the fore. The stress of war had thus led to the sweeping away of the French monarchy, but that itself increased concern about Brunswick's likely response. Fear mounted as the Prussians invaded, initially meeting scant resistance. They crossed the French frontier on 19 August, and the French frontier fortresses fell rapidly. Civilian pressure on the garrisons led to the surrender of Longwy on 23 August and Verdun on 3 September. Lafayette had already fled to the Allies on 19 August, having failed, four days earlier, to persuade the troops he commanded at Sedan to take an oath to Louis XVI. The revolution seemed both threatened and betrayed. On 28 August and 2 September Danton called on the Assembly for war en masse.[59] On 17 August 1792 a special tribunal was established in Paris to try those accused of political crimes. Four days later the guillotine began its abrupt labours. Several thousand suspected traitors were arrested and between 2 and 7 September over a thousand were killed, victims to so-called people's justice as the prisons were purged. Montmorin was one of those killed, as was his successor as Foreign Minister, Lessart.

Foreign diplomats had been accredited to Louis XVI. The collapse of his government led to a break in formal diplomatic relations, not least because it was unclear who was now wielding authority in Paris and what the effect of Brunswick's advance would be. The British, Danish, Dutch, Polish, Spanish, Swedish, Swiss and Venetian envoys left. The removal of executive power from Louis XVI ensured that diplomatic credentials were no longer valid. The Cabinet met on 17 August, Pitt, Chatham,

[57] H. A. Barton, 'The Origins of the Brunswick Manifesto', *French Historical Studies*, 5 (1967), 146–69; Front to Victor Amadeus, 27 July 1792, AST LM Ing. 93; Breteuil to Pitt, 8 Aug., Breteuil to Grenville, 8 Aug. 1792, BL Add. 59064 fols. 18–22; Gower to Grenville, 4 Aug. 1792, PRO FO 27/39; J. T. Stoker, *William Pitt et la Révolution française 1789–1793* (Paris, 1935), p. 116.

[58] Gardiner to Dorset, 12 Aug. 1792, KAO C180.

[59] A. Chuquet, *Les Guerres de la Révolution I: La Première Invasion Prussienne* (Paris, 1886); Hampson, *Danton*, p. 81.

Dundas, Hawkesbury and Richmond being present, and decided to recall Gower, in part because of the danger to his life: his Swiss guard had been killed. The British government had been horrified by the accounts it had received from Paris. That from Gower's messenger Morley was more grisly than the Earl's dispatch. It referred in the storming of the Tuileries to the mob 'industriously' disfiguring the faces of its victims 'by roasting them' in fires and to an indiscriminate massacre without distinction of age or sex. The Cabinet met twice and sent two agents to Paris to acquire information, but it was Gower's recall that was crucial.[60] Despite concern that he had been stopped en route for the Channel, Gower reached London on 1 September, the Secretary of Embassy, William Lindsay, following a week later, after his threat to leave anyway and to let the French take the consequences if he was detained or killed led to his finally receiving his passport.[61]

The recall of Gower was, according to Grenville, who had returned to London from a summer and honeymoon absence, 'most conformable to the principles of neutrality' on which British policy was based. The British ministry would not therefore be required to recognise any new French government, a step which would alienate Prussia and Austria, and also deviate from the course that the Dutch government had already outlined. In addition, it would be easier, if relations were broken, to maintain a cool response to French approaches, such as that from Chauvelin in mid-August for British interposition to persuade the invaders to leave France. The British ministry thus trod a path in which the Prussian invasion and the developments in Paris made her neutrality clearer, and accentuated her distance from the combatants. On 21 August Grenville explained the new policy towards Chauvelin, who had initially condemned the events of 10 August,[62] and then persuaded Pitt to return the note he had delivered. Chauvelin was not to be expelled, but the government had decided

not to consider ... as official, any communications except in the usual form and through the usual channel of a Minister accredited by His Most Christian Majesty, nor to receive any new minister having credentials from any other authority or power in that Kingdom erected on the suspension or abolition of the

---

[60] Burges to Grenville, 15 Aug., 3 Sept., Dundas to George III, 17 Aug., Burges to Grenville, 15, 17 Aug., Dundas to Gower, 17 Aug., Burges to Auckland, 17 Aug. 1792, BL Add. 58857 fol. 18, 58968 fols. 29, 31, 54, 34444 fols. 88, 90; Burges to Elgin, 17 Aug. 1792, Broomhall 60/2/22; Auckland to Burges, 21 Aug. 1792, BB. 30 fol. 179.
[61] Aust to Grenville [27 Aug. ?] [28 Aug. ?], 8 Sept., Burges to Grenville, 1, 8 Sept. 1792, BL Add. 58968 fols. 41, 47, 58, 51, 60–1; Pitt to Edward Eliot, 31 Aug. 1792, Ipswich HA 119 T108/39 no. 279; Auckland to Burges, 21 Aug., Lindsay to Burges, 3, 5 Sept. 1792, BB. 30 fol. 179, 45 fols. 118, 120.
[62] Chauvelin to Grenville, 16 Aug. 1792, HMC Dropmore, III, 460–1.

Monarchy.... it is by no means the King's intention to depart from the line of neutrality which he has observed, or to interfere in the internal affairs of France or in the settlement of the future government of that kingdom.

A similar position was adopted by the Neapolitan government,[63] though such distinctions appeared academic as the Prussians, supported by Austrian, Hessian and émigré units, advanced on Paris from the east. Meanwhile the French were seeking better relations with Britain. The new French government, with the intelligent but unreliable and politically weak former journalist Pierre Lebrun as the Foreign Minister, was reasonably content, as Lebrun informed the Legislative Assembly on 23 August, with British inactivity and decided to retain Chauvelin in London and to not allow 'miserables querelles d'etiquette', in the form of retaliation for Gower's recall, to harm relations. Jean-François Noël, an unfrocked priest sent as a special agent to supplement and check on Chauvelin, was instructed not to seek to inspire domestic opposition to the Pitt government, for the radical party of the Friends of the People was seen as paralysed. There was thus no immediate shift to a revolutionary foreign policy, a diplomacy of insurrection. Noël was ordered to press for the consolidation of a natural union between Britain and France, by means of a modification of the Eden Treaty into a treaty of defensive alliance. In return for British government assistance with a loan of £3–4 million, the cession of Tobago was to be offered, though, in a new note, the consent of its inhabitants was seen as necessary. A crucial distinction was also drawn between the Austrian Netherlands and the United Provinces. Recognising British concern about the latter, Lebrun sought to be conciliatory, not to intimidate. Noël was to say that neither the Belgian 'Patriots' nor their French patrons supported the cause of Dutch revolution, and was to announce that the Batavian Legion of Dutch 'Patriot' exiles was to be dissolved.[64] Noël's instructions were at once naive – there was no chance of a British loan – and perspicacious in their appreciation of British sensitivity over the United Provinces. They were followed up by the foolish suggestion that Chauvelin encourage Britain to mount a colonial war on Spain.[65] Though unrecognized, he was to stay

[63] Grenville to Auckland, 21 Aug., Rose to Auckland, 20 Aug. 1792, BL Add. 34444 fols. 114–15, 107; Grosjean, 'Relations', 32.
[64] Chauvelin to Lebrun, 28 Aug., Lebrun to Noël, 29 Aug., 11 Sept. 1792, AE CP Ang. 580 fols. 39–42, 46–52, 113; J. T. Murley, 'The Origin and Outbreak of the Anglo-French War of 1793' (unpublished D.Phil., Oxford, 1959), pp. 36–7; Murley's work is more detailed than another relevant unpublished thesis, L. M. Porter, 'Anglo-French Relations 10 August 1792 to 1 February 1793: a study of Great Britain and France in the six months prior to the outbreak of war' (York, 1973).
[65] Lebrun to Chauvelin, 14 Sept., Lebrun to Noël, 18 Sept. 1792, AE CP Ang. 582 fols. 137, 167; Porter, 'Anglo-French Relations', pp. 132–53.

in London, his initial recall rescinded, the only creditable agent among the demi-monde of would-be French diplomats that proliferated that autumn.

By that stage, the state of France was such that any British move towards her was very improbable. The September Massacres were unacceptable even to Fox, and the response of commentators and politicians less sympathetic to the Revolution and less understanding of the revolutionary process was far more strident. Searching the classical world for comparisons, the Earl of Dalkeith thought they outstripped 'the massacres of Rome in its most abandoned style' and revealed an 'innate love of blood'. He wrote of 'the hell devils already celebrating their orgies at that great cauldron of the world', adding, 'May God of his infinite mercy direct some Prussian hussar's sabre to Dr. Priestley's and Paine's necks.' George III, horrified anyway by developments in Paris, including the report that Marie Antoinette was to be put on trial, pointed out that there was no solid government in France. Aust told Payne that Louis XVI would 'be tried, and would probably be beheaded in imitation of Charles 1st'.[66] Indeed, the British government departed to a certain extent from its path of neutrality by warning that if Louis XVI was treated with violence, those responsible would not receive asylum in Britain. When Gower was recalled, it was argued that to hope for the safety of the royal family did not entail any abandonment of the neutral British position towards the 'internal government of France'. Burges wrote of the British warnings:

They contain as much as the line of conduct adopted here can admit of; and, if anything can restrain the course of Parisian horrors, they will do it; for I do not know where such miscreants can now look for refuge, or where they can expect to be received when stained with such crimes as they undoubtedly meditate.[67]

Even so, the ministry took care to adopt a cautious position. It has been argued that it took the step as a result of Austro-Neapolitan pressure,[68] and both Brunswick and Mercy had certainly sought British intervention on the matter. Mercy had asked Elgin to suggest that the British government guarantee amnesty to those 'now in authority' in Paris if they avoided harming the French royal family;[69] but it is clear that the

---

[66] Morton Eden to Auckland, 24 Oct. 1792, BL Add. 34445 fol. 138; Dalkeith to Malmesbury, 29 Sept. 1792, Winchester 149; George III to Grenville, 3, 4 Sept. 1792, BL Add. 58857 fols. 30–1; Payne to Malmesbury, Friday, Winchester, Malmesbury 162.

[67] Dundas to Grenville, 17 Aug. 1792, BL Add. 59064 fols. 36–7; Burges to Elgin, 21 Sept. 1792, Broomhall 60/2/32.   [68] Ehrman, Pitt II, 203.

[69] Dundas to Major General Sir James Murray, 12 Sept., Elgin, Envoy Extraordinary in Brussels, to Grenville, 16 Sept. 1792, PRO FO 26/19; Grosjean, 'Relations', 43.

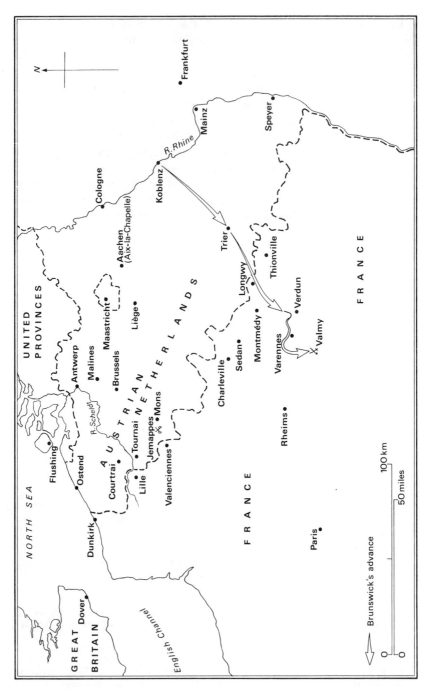

9. The opening stages of the French Revolutionary War

ministers organised the approach[70] in order to be able to take some step but without deviating from its general line of non-intervention. George III agreed.[71] Nevertheless, the British government had clearly revealed an attitude that was not likely to please its French counterpart; there was already a marked lack of sympathy even though, in September, there did not yet appear to be any clash of interests. This attitude was not sufficient to please the *émigrés*, who might soon compose the government of France, or, more seriously, their monarchical supporters. And yet, the British government wanted Brunswick to succeed, and feared the consequences of failure. In response to a discussion between Brunswick and Major-General Sir James Murray, who was reporting on his advance to the British government, Dundas sent Murray instructions on 12 September that reflected his views and those of Pitt and the absent Grenville. In line with British neutrality, Murray was to seek the views of the invading powers, but he was also informed of British hopes

that the result of the present interference of the powers of Germany may be the re-establishment of such a government in France, as, on the one hand, would protect other powers from a renewal of that spirit of restlessness and intrigue, which had so often been fatal to the tranquillity of Europe, and, on the other hand, secure to the executive government such a degree of energy and vigour, as might enable it to extirpate those seeds of anarchy and misrule, which had so peculiarly of late characterised the whole transactions of that distracted country.[72]

Brunswick, who sought a more committed British position, found the instructions unsatisfactory. At the same time Elgin was defending Britain's continued neutrality to Count Franz von Metternich, father of the great minister and Mercy's replacement as Minister Plenipotentiary of the Austrian Netherlands. Metternich had argued that the abolition of the monarchy had changed the situation, not least because, he claimed, no constitution was legal unless acknowledged by neighbouring powers.[73]

Brunswick's slow progress gave rise to concern among British commentators,[74] and the Duke indeed encountered serious problems with the intractable terrain of the Argonne, logistics, the effect of rain on the roads, and sickness, especially dysentery, in his army. More seriously, French resistance did not collapse as that of the Dutch Patriots had done

---

[70] Stadion and Prince Castelcicala to Grenville, 20 Sept., and reply of 21st, 1792, Ipswich HA 239/2/298–9.
[71] Grenville to George III, 21 Sept., reply 22 Sept. 1792, BL Add. 58857 fols. 34–6; Grenville to Elgin, 21 Sept. 1792, PRO FO 26/19; *Court and Cabinets*, III, 217.
[72] Dundas to Murray, 12 Sept. 1792, PRO FO 26/19.
[73] Auckland to Grenville, 12 Sept., George III to Grenville, 7 Oct. 1792, BL Add. 58920 fol. 157, 58857 fol. 52; Murray to Grenville, 27 Sept., Elgin to Grenville, 28 Sept. 1792, PRO FO 26/19.
[74] Auckland to Elgin, 25 Aug. 1792, Broomhall 60/1/106; *Court and Cabinets*, III, 217.

in 1787. Brunswick's army was not prepared for a major campaign and it was arguably too late in the year to attempt one.[75] Thus, the very fact of French resistance, irrespective of its seriousness, was sufficient to check Brunswick, an echo of George Washington's success in thwarting British strategy during the War of American Independence by keeping the Continental Army in being.[76] On 20 September 1792, at Valmy, his force was outnumbered by about 34,000 to 52,000 and Brunswick turned back without a full-scale engagement. There was scant hand to hand fighting, the French artillery decided the day and the Prussians failed to dislodge the French defenders.[77] Brunswick was about 108 miles from Paris, but only 20 from the valley of the Marne and 35 from Rheims, both of which offered easy routes to the metropolis.

Brunswick's failure to press forward and his subsequent retreat, which began on the 30th,[78] were so surprising that there were reports of secret purposes on the part of Frederick William II, and indeed negotiations between Dumouriez and the Prussians for a cessation of arms began on 23 September and lasted for a month. Elgin kept London informed of these negotiations, and accurately predicted their eventual failure.[79] The 'retreat of the finest army that ever was collected together and commanded by the most famous general in Europe, from the presence of an undisciplined horde of volunteers without officers and ill furnished in all respects' was very worrying, not least because it was assumed that Austria could not afford a second campaign and that Prussia might abandon the war. The French government indeed hoped for a separate Franco-Prussian peace as a possible prelude to a quadruple alliance of the two powers, Britain and the Dutch. The attacks on Montmorin in the Legislative Assembly from 22 until 31 August had centred on his failure in 1791 to take advantage of what was seen as a good opportunity to negotiate a Franco-Prussian alliance. Clearly, the revolutionary credentials of the new government would require it to seek such an alliance. Whatever the possible diplomatic consequences of Valmy, the immediate

[75] Gardiner to Dorset, 24 Aug. 1792, KAO C180; Reports from Murray to Elgin, Broomhall 60/1/162, PRO FO 26/19; Burges to Grenville, 3 Sept. 1792, BL Add. 58968 fol. 53 reporting views of Jenkinson.

[76] J. Black, *War for America. The Fight for Independence 1775–1783* (Stroud, 1991), pp. 57, 112, 144, 176, 247.

[77] Reports by John Money, BL Add. 59279 fols. 29–34, HMC *Dropmore*, III, 467–9; J.-P. Bertaud, *Valmy, la démocratie en armes* (Paris, 1970); S. F. Scott, *The Response of the Royal Army to the French Revolution* (Oxford, 1978), pp. 171–2; E. Hublot, *Valmy ou la défense de la nation par les armes* (Paris, 1987); J. Lynn, 'Valmy', *Military History Quarterly*, 51 (1992), 88–97.

[78] Murray to Grenville, 2 Oct. 1792, PRO FO 26/19.

[79] Burges to Grenville, 11 Nov. 1792, BL Add. 58968 fol. 74; Hampson, *Danton*, pp. 92–3; Elgin to Grenville, 2 Oct. 1792, PRO FO 26/19; Stephen Rolleston, Clerk in the Foreign Office, to Aust, 19 Oct. 1792, BL Add. 51705 fols. 58–9.

military results were worrying enough. Grenville thought the retreat 'truly unfortunate in every point of view', while Burges initially consoled himself with the thought that it was a device to lure the French into open country.[80] Auckland was fearful that Valmy had opened a new chapter in the social, and thus political, context of military power:

In the experience which I have had of life, I never recollect any event which occasioned so great and so general an astonishment – it is a severe blow to the cause – to put it in the power of the Jacobin clubs to say that an undisciplined rabble of new republicans greatly inferior in honour, has foiled the greatest armies and best generals in Europe.[81]

The full extent of the imminent crisis was not yet, however, apparent. The campaigning was apparently drawing to its close, autumn being a season of mud, damp and ailments stemming from rain, rather than mists and mellow fruitfulness. The French had not yet revealed any capacity for mounting a successful offensive. Their debacle in the Austrian Netherlands was scarcely an auspicious example and since then their government appeared to have collapsed. Thus, in early October there were signs of a possible new international situation, whose course and configurations could not be predicted, but not of an imminent crisis caused by the unexpected advance of French armies.

[80] Auckland to Spencer, 8 Oct. 1792, BL Add. 34445 fol. 29; Auckland to Elgin, 4, 9, 18, 23 Oct. 1792, Broomhall 60/1/106; Auckland to Burges, 9 Oct. 1792, Bod. BB. 30 fol. 192; George III to Grenville, 7 Oct., Grenville to Richmond, 11 Oct., Burges to Auckland, 9 Oct. 1792, BL Add. 58857 fol. 52, 58937 fol. 164, 34445 fol. 48; B. Rothaus, 'Justice from the Fall of the Monarchy to the September Massacres: the case of the Count of Montmorin', *Proceedings of the Annual Meeting of the Western Society for French History*, 14 (1987), 154–7.
[81] Auckland to Straton, 9 Oct. 1792, Ipswich HA 239/2/283; Trevor to Grenville, 29 Sept. 1792, PRO FO 67/10.

> The English assassins of the Jacobin faction are working hard to corrupt the public mind in favour of their brother murderers in France – and not *one* person, either on the part of government, or opposition makes the slightest effort, of any kind, to prevent the ill effects of these poisons. I am, I confess, sick at heart from all these horrors and perfectly disgusted with the conduct or rather no conduct of both parties, at a time when neutrality does not nor cannot produce neutral effects.
>
> Burke to Malmesbury, 10 September 1792

Before the news of Valmy reached London, the French had already advanced. On 22 September 1792 the Army of the Alps under Montesquiou invaded Savoy, seizing Montmélian. The poorly prepared, outnumbered and dispersed defenders retreated in confusion across the Alps into Piedmont and on the 24th the French occupied Chambéry. Nice, then part of the kingdom of Sardinia (Savoy-Piedmont), fell to the Army of the Var under Anselme, supported by a naval squadron under Truguet on 29 September. Victor Amadeus III hired Austrian troops, but he also sought British assistance.[1] The reply was negative, for the British government did not have a defensive treaty with Sardinia and wished to retain its freedom. Pitt changed the reply in draft in order to make it 'more general, and [to] leave it clearly to ourselves to determine what consequences are too important to let us remain spectators'. Grenville, meanwhile, was unresponsive to approaches from the Genevan envoy. Chauvelin was able to report that Britain would make no opposition to French advances into Savoy and the independent city republic of Geneva.[2] Italy appeared in 'imminent danger', in the words

---

[1] An earlier treatment of this subject appeared in *Francia* 20/2 (1993); Burke to Malmesbury, 10 Sept. [1792], Winchester, Malmesbury 145; Trevor to Grenville, 24, 27 Sept., 1 Oct. 1792, PRO FO 67/10; Trevor to Auckland, 1 Oct. 1792, BL Add. 34445 fols. 3–4; Trevor to Elgin, 8 Oct. 1792, Broomhall 60/1/182; Palmerston to Malmesbury, 9 Oct. 1792, Winchester, Malmesbury 162.

[2] Pitt to Grenville, 16 Oct. 1792, BL Add. 58906 fol. 141; Grenville to Front, 18 Oct. 1792, PRO FO 67/10; Chauvelin to Lebrun, 31 Oct. 1792, AE CP Ang. 583 fol. 139; Anon. corresp. in Geneva to Elgin, 8, 12 Oct. 1792, PRO FO 26/19.

of John, Lord Hervey, Envoy Extraordinary in Florence. Tuscany seemed defenceless, the people ready to rebel. A British naval captain reported that the French were claiming that they would invade the island of Sardinia and thence proceed to Civitavecchia, Rome, Naples and Sicily, while another force invaded the Milanese.[3] Neutral powers, such as Genoa, were placed under considerable strain by their fears and the contrasting demands of the combatants.[4]

Elgin had reported that Brunswick wanted to take winter quarters at Verdun and had suggested that he might capture Thionville, Metz, Montmédy and Sedan before the onset of winter,[5] thus creating an eastern barrier to French advances, and a strong basis for a march on Paris the following spring. Brunswick, however, retreated from France, abandoning such gains as Verdun on 8 October and Longwy on 22 October. The siege of Thionville was raised. Meanwhile, French forces advanced on Brunswick's flank, and overran the middle Rhine. Speyer fell to Custine on 30 September, followed by Worms (4 October), Mainz (21 October) and Frankfurt (22 October). Resistance was initially minimal.[6] On 23 October the celebratory salvoes of the cannon of General Kellermann's Army of the Moselle proclaimed that all foreign troops had been driven from the Republic.

Most seriously for Britain, the French followed up Valmy by invading the Austrian Netherlands again, a step proposed by the Executive Council on 6 October. Lebrun did not see this as a necessary cause of Anglo-French differences. He was interested in the possibility of a quadruple alliance of Britain, France, Prussia and the Dutch. Arguing that France and Prussia had a shared interest in an independent Austrian Netherlands not under Austrian control, and that Pitt might be willing to second Prussian schemes, Lebrun informed Chauvelin that France was willing to support independence and to promise not to annex any of the Austrian Netherlands. The British government was also to be reassured about French intentions towards the Dutch.[7]

Such speculations offer interesting evidence of the attitudes of participants. In the case of the revolutionaries they can be seen as demonstrating a willingness to consider new ideas or as proof of an absence of realistic assessment of the situation, but the pace of events made them redundant anyway. The Austrian siege of Lille had been

[3] Hervey to Straton, 6, 30 Oct. 1792, Ipswich HA 239/2/383, 387; Trevor to Grenville, 28 Oct. 1792, PRO FO 67/10.
[4] R. Boudard, *Gênes et la France dans la deuxième moitié du XVIIIe siècle, 1748–1797* (Paris, 1962), p. 165.
[5] Elgin to Grenville, 6 Oct. 1792, PRO FO 26/19; *Court and Cabinets*, III, 219.
[6] T. C. W. Blanning, *Reform and Revolution in Mainz 1743–1803* (Cambridge, 1974), pp. 274–5.   [7] Lebrun to Chauvelin, 31 Oct. 1792, AE CP Ang. 583 fols. 133–4.

unsuccessful. Mounted with inadequate forces and directed at one of the strongest sets of fortifications in western Europe, it was raised in early October, the fortifications unbreached. Elgin, now Envoy Extraordinary in Brussels, reported from mid-October that an invasion was expected and that the defences were weak, Flanders in particular being vulnerable. As signs of popular discontent increased in late October, the French pressed on the frontier.[8] Nevertheless, Elgin was sent no particular instructions, bar to deny reports that George III had been responsible for Brunswick's retreat.[9]

Dumouriez, who had been appointed commander of the Armée du Nord on 17 August, supported by Belgian and Liègeois patriot forces, invaded the Austrian Netherlands on 3 November. Three days later, at Jemappes near Mons, Dumouriez, with an army of 45,000, defeated the main Austrian field force in the Austrian Netherlands, an army of only 13,200, an example of what Grenville termed 'the amazing superiority of [French] numbers'. After a lengthy cannonade by the greatly superior, massed French artillery, a vigorous attack, by troops who advanced in columns and deployed back into line at close range, carried the day. The effectiveness of the French mobile field artillery was a testimony to the success of Gribeauval's reforms, which had been introduced from the 1760s, a product of *ancien régime* innovation.[10] The Low Countries were open. The Austrian Netherlands were to fall to the French far more rapidly than when last attacked by them in 1744. Then they had acted as a buffer for the United Provinces, which had not been invaded until 1747. In 1744–7, however, much of the resistance had been mounted by British, Dutch and Anglo-Dutch subsidised forces, while, though some towns and fortresses had fallen rapidly, for example Bruges, Brussels and Ghent, others, such as Ostend, had delayed the French advance. The situation was very different in 1792. There were no British, Dutch or Anglo-Dutch subsidised units. The fortifications were mostly suffering from over forty years of neglect. After Jemappes, the Austrian government left Brussels, its forces, poorly led by Duke Albert of Saxe-Teschen, moved towards the Rhineland, abandoning the Austrian Netherlands and exposing the Dutch frontier. Brussels fell on 13 November, Dumouriez entering the city the following day. A French warship entered Ostend without resistance on 16 November, and Malines fell on the 17th. Only isolated posts, principally the citadels in Antwerp

[8] Elgin to Grenville, 16, 19, 26, 31 Oct. 1792, PRO FO 26/19.
[9] Grenville to Elgin, 26 Oct. 1792, PRO FO 26/19.
[10] *Court and Cabinets*, II, 230; B. P. Hughes, *Firepower. Weapons effectiveness on the battlefield, 1630–1850* (1974), p. 15; W. H. McNeill, *The Pursuit of Power* (Oxford, 1983), pp. 170–1; Lynn, *Bayonets*, pp. 211, 255; C. de la Jonquière, *La Bataille de Jemappes* (Paris, 1902), pp. 141–78..

and Namur, were left. They surrendered on 29 November and 2 December. On 27 November the French entered Liège.[11]

This was an unprecedented crisis for the Dutch and their British allies. There was no time for political calculation and diplomatic negotiation, nor indeed for moving troops to the United Provinces. On the day of Jemappes, Grenville had written personally to Auckland, reiterating his conviction that neutrality was the best policy. He observed of the Dutch:

> Their local situation, and the neighbourhood of Germany, Liege, and Flanders may certainly render the danger more imminent, but it does not I think alter the reasoning as to the means of meeting it – and those means will I think be always best found in the preservation of the external peace of the Republic, and in that attention to its internal situation which external peace alone will allow its government to give to that object.

Grenville also made the sensible observation that intervention in French affairs was likely to be counter-productive, a view also taken by Auckland:

> I cannot but remain in the persuasion that the re-establishment of order in France under any form can be effected only by a long course of intestine struggles, and that foreign intervention, while it retards the free course of the principles now prevalent in France, and their natural operation on the people there, serves the cause of anarchy, by giving both an excuse for its disorders, and the means of collecting military force to support them.[12]

Valmy had revealed the failure of a counter-revolutionary strategy. Had Britain been a member of the Austro-Prussian league, then France would have been in a parlous state, blockaded and subject to colonial losses and amphibious attacks on her mainland, but it is doubtful that this would have altered the fate of the struggle on her eastern frontier. The course of the Revolutionary War after Britain's entry in 1793 certainly points to this conclusion,[13] as does the Seven Years War, for the Anglo-French conflict in Westphalia then was not determined by the maritime struggle. Brunswick's failure led Grenville to congratulate himself on British neutrality. On 7 November he revealed his thoughts in a letter to his older brother. Predicting the continuation and spreading of the war, Grenville was also confident that Britain would not be involved and that

---

[11] A. Chuquet, *Jemappes et la Conquête de la Belgique* (Paris, 1890); S. Tassier, *Histoire de la Belgique sous l'occupation française en 1792 et 1793* (Brussels, 1934).

[12] Grenville to Auckland, 6 Nov. 1792, BL Add. 34445 fol. 197, 58920 fols. 162–3; Auckland to Sheffield, 7 Sept. 1791, 28 Sept. 1792, BL Add. 45728 fols. 124–5, 143.

[13] P. Mackesy, *The Strategy of Overthrow 1798–1799* (1974) and *War without Victory. The Downfall of Pitt, 1799–1802* (Oxford, 1984).

neutrality was the best policy for her.[14] Despite rumours arising from the Prussian conferences with Dumouriez, there seemed little real prospect of a settlement between the combatants, let alone a new alignment that excluded Britain. Elgin reported at the beginning of November that Mercy and the *émigré* Breteuil were both convinced 'that there was no possibility of negociating with France: even granting, what did by no means appear, that such terms had been offered by that country as could have been accepted by the Combined Powers'.[15] The lack of panic in London was indicated by the absence of Grenville and Pitt in early November. On 1 November Keith found no Under Secretary at the Foreign Office.[16]

Yet, if Valmy indicated the unpredictabilities of international developments and the consequent hazards of interventionism for Britain, the collapse of the Austrian Netherlands was to indicate the dangers of the opposite policy. On 7 November Elgin reported that Flanders was to be evacuated, and the government to leave Brussels for Ruremonde.[17] This in fact was but a stage, for the government was not to cease in its flight until the Austrian Netherlands had been abandoned. It was to prove impossible for Britain, in a situation made volatile by military developments and the pressures of domestic French politics, to establish a satisfactory compromise with France, or, as Auckland wished, negotiate a truce,[18] while British isolation and events elsewhere in Europe hindered the creation of new and effective diplomatic links directed against France.

In response to pressure in early November from the Dutch envoy, Nagel, Pitt sought to follow a policy of diplomatic deterrence, a promise of support to the Dutch that it would not be necessary to fulfil. On 12 November the news that the Austrian government had left Brussels reached London. Next day, Grenville responded with a series of initiatives. The Dutch government was sent a public assurance of support in the event of invasion or any attempt 'to disturb its government', the latter an interesting testimony to fears of French subversion. Grenville wanted the message to be known in France as soon as possible, though, to that end, he relied on 'ordinary channels of communication' via The Hague, rather than the direct message suggested to Pitt by Nagel, and advocated by Burges. Grenville also adopted

---

[14] Grenville to Buckingham, 7 Nov. 1792, *Court and Cabinets*, II, 222–4; Grenville to Auckland, 6 Nov. 1792, BL Add. 58920 fols. 161–2.
[15] Elgin to Grenville, 2 Nov. 1792, PRO FO 26/19.
[16] Keith to Straton, 2 Nov. 1792, Ipswich HA 239/2/321.
[17] Elgin to Grenville, 7 Nov. 1792, PRO FO 26/19.
[18] Auckland to Grenville, 9 Nov. 1792, BL Add. 58920 fol. 165.

Auckland's idea of approaching Austria and Prussia in order to establish their views and thus assess whether there was a basis for possible co-operation. The Prussians were informed of French intrigues in Berlin. Auckland urged Straton to show the declaration he had presented to the States General on the 16th to the Austrian government, as he hoped this would lead to a full exchange of views. Grenville was confident that the declaration of British support would have its effect on France, but, if not, he knew Britain was 'committed'. At the same time, Burges sought to put pressure on France by urging the Dutch to emulate Britain's ban on grain exports. He defended the ban as a response to the policies of 'modern Frenchmen', their attempts to produce crises by intervention in domestic affairs; in short Burges had no doubt that the nature of international relations was altering in response to revolution.[19]

The decisive move towards war was therefore made in mid-November. The British government had indicated publicly that it was ready to fight in a contingency that it knew might occur in a matter of weeks, if not days. The relationship between this crisis and the response to domestic radicalism is problematic. Concern over the latter had been rising rapidly. Radicalism was believed to have been revived and encouraged by Valmy, and Valmy and its consequences doubtless played a role in this belief, creating a sense of unease and unpredictability. Worried by Brunswick's failure, Portland wrote, 'I do believe there is no other mode of preventing the dissemination of the French doctrines but by force of arms and convincing them by those means only that such a state of government, if I may so call what now exists in France, is incapable of giving any protection to the members of it against the attempts of any invader.' Some of the leading Whigs were so concerned that they were willing to offer the government support in 'strong measures', and there was renewed interest in Whig ranks in a coalition designed to produce unity against radicalism.[20] Reports reaching the ministry from around the country spoke of a rising tide of agitation, before which the local authorities were often helpless. There was an increasing sense that the

---

[19] Grenville to Auckland, 13 Nov., Grenville to Straton, 13 Nov., Grenville to Morton Eden, 13 Nov. 1792, PRO FO 37/41, 7/31, 64/26; Auckland to Straton, 16 Nov. 1792, Ipswich HA 239/2/286; Auckland to Grenville, 9 Nov., Grenville to Auckland, 13 Nov., Burges to Auckland, 13 Nov. 1792, BL Add. 34445 fols. 253–6, 58920 fols. 166, 168; Auckland to Burges, 16 Nov. 1792, Bod. BB. 30 fol. 197; Pitt to Stafford, 13 Nov. 1792, Stanhope, *Pitt*, I, 456.

[20] Portland to Windham, 13 Oct. 1792, BL Add. 37845 fol. 5; Portland to Malmesbury, (quote) 21 Oct., Darnley to Malmesbury, 21 Oct. 1792, Winchester, Malmesbury 179, 149; *Court and Cabinets*, II, 227–8; William Windham to Thomas Grenville, 14 Nov. 1792, Bod. MS. Eng. Lett. c. 144 fol. 306; Grenville to Richmond, 11 Oct., Pitt to Grenville, 18 Nov. 1792, BL Add. 58906 fol. 146, 58937 fol. 164; Payne to Malmesbury, 7 June 1791, Palmerston to Malmesbury, 9 Oct. 1792, Winchester, Malmesbury 162.

issue would come to one of force. Already, before Valmy, Samuel Garbett had written from Birmingham, 'our working people are become extremely turbulent and licentious since they discovered their power by the riots of the last year, and saw the difficulty of convicting and punishing them legally ... our Police is so insufficient that we are often in terror'. Garbett pressed the need for 'arms in the hands of Persons of Property'. Such concerns became more insistent after Valmy. On 11 November, Pitt, worried by reports from South Shields and the 'want of force' on the part of the authorities, suggested that it might soon be necessary to call out the militia. On the same day George, Marquess Townshend, the Lord Lieutenant of Norfolk, offered an echo of the baronial past:

The method I took on a late occasion and shall endeavour to apply again on any similar, was to summon immediately the high constables and others, and to collect tenants and neighbours to suppress any tumults and riots, to read first the Proclamation and warn them of the consequence of persevering. I armed my tenants and attendants; 3 or 4 especially about me with short swords in case of any personal assault.[21]

The relationship between the aristocracy and military power is not the most obvious theme in eighteenth-century British, especially English, history; though as recently as the War of American Independence the domestic correspondence of Lord Amherst, who was in effect Commander-in-Chief of the British army 1778–82, gave the impression of a society in which aristocratic Lords Lieutenant played a major military function, while the readiness of pro-Hanoverian aristocrats to raise regiments had been a feature of the '45.[22] The American, and then the French, Revolution had led to fresh consideration of constitutional issues and political strategies. In 1789 Richmond had agreed with Grenville on the importance of the 'aristocratical' part in the British constitution. Three years later Dundas, concerned about the situation in Perth, Dundee and Montrose, warned Pitt that 'if the spirit of liberty and equality continues to spread with the same rapidity' that it had done since Valmy, then it would be impossible to suppress sedition by force

---

[21] Garbett to Hawkesbury, 5 Sept. 1792, BL Add. 38228 fol. 45; Pitt to Grenville [11 Nov. 1792], BL Add. 58906 fols. 144–5; Townshend to John Blofeld, 11 Nov. 1792, Bod. Ms. Eng. Lett. c. 144 fol. 274.

[22] This theme does not emerge in the fine study by I. F. W. Beckett, *The Amateur Military Tradition 1558–1945* (Manchester, 1991), but on Amherst see War Office corresp. 34 in PRO, on 1745, P. Luff, 'The Noblemen's Regiments: Politics and the 'Forty-Five', *Historical Research*, 65 (1992), 54–73, and on the post-1793 situation 'The Strategic Context', unpublished paper by John Cookson. I would like to thank him for providing a copy.

only. He added, 'the safety of the country must I am persuaded depend on the body of the well effected to the Constitution, (which with few exceptions is every body of property or respect) in some shape or other taking an open, active and declared part'.[23] In the crisis of late 1792 the government of a British state that was weaker than John Brewer's recent survey might suggest, was to turn in many directions as it sought to recruit support. If reliance on the landed elite might appear conservative, the attempt to encourage a mass movement of loyalism revealed a willingness to turn to, and an ability to use, the public politics of the present.[24]

The domestic situation pointed to the need for continued peace. Grenville had outlined the relationship in his letter to Auckland on 6 November 1792, and Jemappes and its consequences had not altered that. He wrote to Buckingham that war and resulting taxation would jeopardise the domestic situation, but that 'from policy and good faith' the British were obliged to defend the Dutch. Grenville hoped that if a few months 'could be tidied over' 'the bubble of French finance' would burst, but he pointed out that such hopes had been deceptive in the past. He was concerned about the spread of radical clubs in Britain, and the situation in Ireland.[25]

And yet, despite the domestic situation, the British government had indicated its willingness to fight. It was not ready to abandon the Continent, to leave its Dutch ally, and the decision seems to have been taken with no difficulty and with little discussion. It was clear that the domestic situation pointed in an opposite direction, but this does not seem to have deterred Pitt or Grenville. They hoped to reconcile competing pressures by relying on deterrence, but they were aware that it might not work, and that prudence might suggest a more passive course.

As Ehrman has pointed out, the pace of communications helped to

---

[23] Richmond to Grenville, 14 Sept. 1789, BL Add. 58937 fol. 108; Dundas to Pitt, 22 Nov. 1792, PRO 30/8/157 fols. 142–3.

[24] *Court and Cabinets*, II, 227–9; C. Emsley, 'The Home Office and its Sources of Information and Investigation 1791–1801', *English Historical Review*, 94 (1979), 561; J. Brewer, *The Sinews of Power. War, Money and the English State 1688–1783* (1989); R. Dozier, *For King, Constitution, and Country. The English Loyalists and the French Revolution* (Lexington, Kentucky, 1983); H. T. Dickinson, 'Popular Loyalism in Britain in the 1790s', in E. Hellmuth (ed.), *The Transformation of Political Culture: Germany and England in the Late Eighteenth Century* (Oxford, 1990), pp. 503–34; D. Eastwood, 'Patriotism and the English State in the 1790s', in M. Philp (ed.), *British Popular Politics*, pp. 146–68. On the use of the press, Bod. BB 74 fol. 22; H. R. Winkler, 'The Pamphlet Campaign Against Political Reform in Great Britain, 1790–1795', *Historian*, 15 (1952), 23–40; J. J. Sack, *From Jacobite to Conservative. Reaction and Orthodoxy in Britain, c. 1760–1832* (Cambridge, 1993), pp. 12–14.

[25] Grenville to Buckingham [16 Nov. 1792], HL STG. Box 39 (6).

increase tension.[26] On 13 November 1792, Grenville's instructions were sent to Auckland, who wanted discussions with the French government.[27] News of them had not reached Paris by 16 November when the Executive Council decreed that the Austrians should be pursued wherever they retreated, a threat to neutrals such as the Elector of Cologne and, more particularly, the Dutch, and that the estuary of the Scheldt was to be open to navigation, a clear breach of the Peace of Westphalia. Four days later, and with the French still unaware of British policy, these decisions were ratified by the National Convention. It is unclear whether an earlier British communication of their views, or a direct one initiated on 13 November would have made any difference. The logic of their new ideas and their rejection of the past made the French radicals unwilling to accept the apparent denial of the natural right of the Belgians to trade enforced by the closure of the Scheldt. Lebrun did not anticipate the British response and argued that he was not seeking to harm the rights of the Dutch, but that the Belgians were not obliged to maintain engagements made by their former Habsburg masters, whose yoke had now been rejected.[28] In light of Joseph II's well-known attitude towards the Scheldt, Lebrun's argument was weak, but it indicated his wish to dramatise the breach between *ancien régime* and revolutionary diplomacy. Lebrun had already revealed in his attitude to the cession of Tobago a concern with the rights of inhabitants that was at variance both with *ancien régime* diplomacy and with the practice of the government of revolutionary France. The dispatch of warships up the Scheldt would also enable the French to put pressure on the garrison in Antwerp.

British hesitation in dealing directly with Paris reflected an unwillingness to accept the position of the French government. This was prudential rather than ideological. On 6 November Grenville indicated to Auckland that, if pressed, the British would refuse to acknowledge the republican government of France, but in terms that would not preclude later recognition if it became firmly established, 'in which case', he added, 'it must at last be sooner or later recognized by all the other countries of Europe, as those of Switzerland and Holland have been, and as the revolutions of this country [1688] and Portugal [1640] are now even by France and Spain' respectively.[29] Three years earlier, Leeds had been willing to maintain direct, though informal, links with the Belgian insurgents. They were rebels against a ruler with whom George III had diplomatic relations. He had written to Fitzherbert, 'it will be highly

[26] Ehrman, *Pitt*, II, 208.
[27] Auckland to Grenville, 15, 16 Nov. 1792, BL Add. 58920 fols. 171–2.
[28] Lebrun to Chauvelin, 23 Nov. 1792, AE CP Ang. 583 fol. 302; Murley, 'Anglo-French War', 142.   [29] Grenville to Auckland, 6 Nov. 1792, BL Add. 34445 fol. 197.

expedient for the Allies to keep up (though privately) a direct intercourse with the Insurgents, so as to establish the most favourable impression on their minds of the importance of our friendship'. On the other hand, the context was different to that in late 1792. Leeds had been concerned that Britain should not lose the chance of influence in Belgium to other powers, while he was also hopeful that she might be able to mould the new Belgian constitution. He had therefore suggested the dispatch of agents to Ghent and Luxemburg.[30]

There was no ideological hostility on Grenville's part to dealing with a republican France, but he wanted it to be stable and he did not wish to move out of line with the other European powers. Both attitudes were sensible: on 13 November Grenville launched an attempt to improve relations with Austria and Prussia, as well as one to deter France. And yet, in the circumstances of late 1792, such a position provided little basis for preventing a deterioration in relations between the two powers. Grenville replied coolly to Chauvelin's attempts to discuss matters, asking Chauvelin to explain first what he wished to discuss, a demand Chauvelin rejected.[31] The contrast with the Dutch crisis of 1787, when the two powers had last come close to war, was instructive. Then British diplomats had remained in Paris, negotiating actively, there had been diplomatic negotiations in London and Grenville himself had gone on a special mission to Paris. These negotiations had helped to ease the path for a crucial backdown on France's part, but British success in the crisis was due ultimately to Prussian action. In late 1792 the future security of the United Provinces would clearly depend in part on Prussia being willing to fulfil her defensive obligations under the 1788 treaty, and on an acceptable solution to the situation in the Austrian Netherlands. While Austria and Prussia were at war with France, such co-operation was not going to be eased by a British recognition of the Republic.

The French decrees of 16 November directly threatened the Dutch. That day Auckland reported fears of a French amphibious attack on Zeeland and Emden. The message reached London on the 20th. On 17 November Gideon Duncan wrote from Ostend that France was to send warships up the Scheldt in order to aid in the attack on the citadel of Antwerp. He also reported that it was thought that the French would attack the Dutch. Ostend fell, without resistance, to units of the French National Guard from Dunkirk. They were joined by the Batavian

[30] Leeds to Fitzherbert, 1 Dec. 1789, PRO FO 37/27 fol. 38–9; Fitzherbert to Leeds, 8, 15 Dec., Leeds to Fitzherbert, 15 Dec. 1789, BL Eg. 3500 fols. 127–35.
[31] Chauvelin to Grenville, 19, 22 Nov., Grenville to Chauvelin, 21 Nov. 1792, BL Add. 34445 fols. 352–6; Grenville to Auckland, 23 Nov. 1792, PRO FO 37/41; *Correspondence of Miles* I, 352–3.

Legion, Dutch Patriots, who made no secret of their intention to invade the United Provinces. Duncan added a warning of the unpredictability of the revolutionaries, a worrying feature for the British ministry, one that threatened both aspects of the phrase diplomatic calculation. He noted Batavian claims, 'that should England attempt to interfere, in a few months more they will hoist a Cap of liberty on the Tower of London. This shows the madness of these Democrates, and who knows how far their enthusiasm may carry them, for they have no order, or command among them.'[32] The French had taken the crucial decisions that were to bring relations with the Dutch and British to a crisis point, but they also continued to issue decrees that individually and collectively helped to raise tension and increase suspicions. On 19 November, in response to appeals for help from radicals in Zweibrücken and Mainz, the National Convention passed a decree declaring that the French people would extend fraternity and assistance to all peoples seeking to regain their liberty.[33] As a general principle, this was subversive of all international order; it was also unrealistic and was revoked by the Convention on 14 April 1793, Danton pointing out that it would oblige the French to assist a revolution in China. In specific terms the decree challenged the Dutch government, for Dutch Patriot refugees in Paris continually pressed for action on their behalf, and Lebrun was soon writing of freeing the Dutch.[34] The decree also threatened the British position in Ireland. Eight days later Savoy was incorporated into France, a positive consequence of the decree of 19 November and a worrying augury for the fate of the Austrian Netherlands; on 3 December the decision was taken to try Louis XVI, a major extension of the competence of the National Convention, and on 15 December a decree to ensure that the *ancien régime* be swept away in territories occupied by French forces was promulgated. Elections were to be held to create a new order, but the electorate was restricted to adult men ready to swear an oath to be 'faithful to the people and the principles of liberty and equality'. Military success would thus lead to a new political order and it was anticipated that people thus 'freed' would supply French forces and seek 'reunion' with France.

While pro-government British newspapers suggested that French moves might lead to war,[35] despite the wish of the British ministry to maintain its neutrality, Grenville sought to avoid an alarmist response.

---

[32] Auckland to Grenville, 16, 20 Nov. 1792, PRO FO 37/41; Duncan to Aust, 17, 21, 22 Nov. 1792, BL Add. 34445 fol. 348, PRO FO 26/19.

[33] *AP* 53, 472–4. M. Bouloiseau, 'L'Organisation de l'Europe selon Brissot et les girondins, à la fin de 1792', *Annales historiques de la révolution française*, 57 (1985), 290–4 is of interest.   [34] Murley, 'Anglo-French War', pp. 127–30.

[35] *Diary*, 21, 24 Nov., *Times*, 24, 29 Nov. 1792.

On 23 November he ordered Auckland to inspire 'confidence and resolution' into the Dutch government, but he added:

I am strongly inclined to believe, that it is the present intention of the prevailing party in France to respect the rights of this country and of the Republic, but it will be undoubtedly necessary, that the strictest attention should be given to any circumstances, which may seem to indicate a change in this respect.[36]

Two days later, Grenville suggested that Duncan's reports of French plans were exaggerated, and revealed that he was less than keen to send British frigates to Flushing in order to forestall a possible French attack, a move that had been made in 1747.[37] On the 25th, there were still encouraging signs of a French willingness to keep the peace. Chauvelin had approached Grenville, and, more acceptably, Emmanuel de Maulde, a protégé of Dumouriez who was French envoy in The Hague, had visited Van de Spiegel and opened up a channel for negotiations aimed at probing the possibility of Anglo-Dutch mediation in the conflict. Acknowledging 'the vapouring and bravado so naturally to be expected' in public from the French, Grenville was keen on talks via Maulde as they would avoid the necessity of receiving a French envoy in London. He thought that the fate of the Austrian Netherlands would be the most delicate issue, itself a sign of a lack of concern about the Dutch situation, and did not understand how any equivalent could be made to Francis II for that loss.[38] Such an argument might appear anachronistic in the new dawn of the principles of international conduct being enunciated in France, but in fact equivalents were to be the basis not only for the diplomacy surrounding the Second and Third Partitions of Poland, but also for the redrawings of the map of Europe over the following twenty-three years, by both France and her rivals. Pitt agreed as to the value of responding to the French approach, but George III was more sceptical:

I feel the advantage of a General Peace if it can be effected to the *real* satisfaction of the various parties concerned, but at the same time not less forcibly a disinclination to France gaining this point and perhaps laying a foundation to encourage other countries to attempt the same game; for it is peace alone that can place the French Revolution on a permanent ground as then all the European states must acknowledge this new Republic ... I am far from sanguine either that the French General [Dumouriez] will venture to speak out or that if he would we can manage the business in a manner to satisfy the various courts concerned, or even escape blame from an appearance of being the first to acknowledge the French Revolution.[39]

---

[36] Grenville to Auckland, 23 Nov. 1792, PRO FO 37/41.
[37] Grenville to Auckland, 25 Nov. 1792, PRO FO 37/41.
[38] Grenville to Auckland, 25 Nov., Auckland to Grenville, 3 Dec. 1792, BL Add. 34445 fol. 382, 58921 fol. 3; Murley, 'Anglo-French War', pp. 230–1.
[39] Grenville to George III and reply, both 25 Nov. 1792, BL Add. 58857 fols. 57–9.

George III was properly sceptical about the likely success of negotiations; but the alternative, as he recognised in his letter, was bleak, and Auckland was authorised to take part.

On 26 November, the day on which a French warship sailed from Ostend for the Scheldt, the news of the Scheldt decree and of the decision to allow Dumouriez to pursue the Austrians onto Dutch territory reached London, and a now worried Grenville changed his tone abruptly. These moves were seen as aimed against Britain as well as the Dutch. War seemed imminent, diplomacy a matter less of averting it than of ensuring that it broke out under the most propitious circumstances. That day he wrote to Auckland:

If the French are determined to force us to a rupture, it seems of little moment what is the particular occasion that is to be taken for it, except with a view to the benefit of standing on the most advantageous ground, with respect to the public opinion in the two countries. But it is a much more material question to determine to what degree it would be more or less advantageous to us, or the French, in point of our respective state of preparation, that things should come to their crisis now, or a short time hence, supposing that such a crisis cannot ultimately be avoided.

Negotiations to gain time seemed a prospect, but Auckland was also informed that naval preparations had been put in train. He was asked to find out from the Dutch, who traded actively with France, what the state of naval preparations at Brest were.[40] Thus, war was definitely seen as on the cards from 26 November, and all subsequent negotiations took place against this background, though various figures, such as Auckland and Van de Spiegel still pressed for peace.[41] Meanwhile, the situation in the Low Countries continued to deteriorate. Austrian forces persisted in retreating with apparently no limits to their flight, while French warships entered the Scheldt estuary. Auckland argued that the navigation of the Scheldt was a point of little real importance, but he accepted that Dutch rights on the matter were indisputable.[42]

On 29 November the Cabinet met and Grenville saw Chauvelin. No minutes of the former appear to have survived, but support seems to have been given to a policy of firmness and naval mobilisation. A squadron was to be dispatched to help the Dutch if required, underlining the promises of support that were sent to The Hague, in response to Nagel's request.[43] The danger of war led Grenville to abandon the position he had taken on

[40] Grenville to Auckland, 26 Nov. 1792, PRO FO 37/41, BL Add. 34445 fols. 396–7, 58920 fol. 176; Grenville to Buckingham, 26–7 Nov. 1792, HL STG. Box 39(7).
[41] Auckland to Grenville, 26 Nov., Van de Spiegel to Auckland, 27 Nov. 1792, BL Add. 58920 fols. 178–80.
[42] Auckland to Grenville, 28 Nov. 1792, BL Add. 58920 fol. 186.
[43] Minute of Nagel meeting with Grenville, 29 Nov. 1792, PRO FO 37/41.

21 November, and, instead, a week later, to seek a meeting with Chauvelin. Grenville told Chauvelin that British non-intervention in French affairs had always been part of a policy centring on the maintenance of the rights of Britain and her allies, a point that was indeed borne out by what Chauvelin had been told earlier in the year. Chauvelin was more diffuse. He told Grenville that the French Republic was solidly established, governed by immutable principles, such as eternal reason, and more concerned with reality than with forms. He defended the opening of the Scheldt in an uncompromising fashion, but found Grenville unwilling to discuss the issue. Having complained about the distant attitude of the British government over the past year, Chauvelin told Grenville that France did not want war. Grenville replied that it would be the fault of France if it broke out.[44]

The inviolability of treaties was the sticking point. Lebrun ordered Chauvelin to explain the opening of the Scheldt to Pitt, but he did so in language that would not be acceptable. France, Lebrun declared, would examine treaties by the light of the eternal principles of the law of nature and nations; the navigation of the Scheldt belonged to the Belgians by the indefeasible laws of universal justice.[45] Meanwhile other links were being established and tested as the various French agents in London man-oeuvred for position. The differences between French agents can be blamed on the confusion of revolutionary politics, the subordination of administration to politics, but the *secret du roi* and French policy in the Dutch crisis of 1787 indicate that *ancien régime* diplomacy had given rise to similar situations. In late 1792 the French agent Jean-François Noël was especially keen to displace Chauvelin, while a number of British officials, politicians and would-be politicians were ready to lend an ear to French approaches. On 30 November, for example, Charles Long MP, the joint Secretary of the Treasury, saw Jean-Scipion Mourgue, a French agent who had been educated in England, while William Smith MP, a Pittite Dissenter, met Hugues-Bernard Maret, a senior official from the French foreign ministry, who arrived in England on 10 November 1792. Mourgue was a protégé of Maret and a friend of Miles, through whom the approach was arranged. Long told Miles according to the latter, 'that if France would enter into a negotiation with the Court of Vienna and surrender at least a portion of its conquests, and consent to a general pacification, the Republic would be acknowledged – the not insisting on the opening of the Scheldt to be always understood'.

[44] Minutes of a conference with Chauvelin, 29 Nov. 1792, BL Add. 34445 fols. 441–3; Chauvelin to Lebrun, 29 Nov. 1792, AE CP Ang. 583 fols. 349–58; Murley, 'Anglo-French War', p. 254.
[45] Lebrun to Chauvelin, 30 Nov. 1792, AE CP Ang. 583 fols. 361–3.

Mourgue, however, 'insisted on the rights of the Republic, and on the "immutable laws of nature"'. Unlike Mourgue, Maret was conciliatory. He explained that France could not back down over the Scheldt, as it would discredit the government with the Belgians, but he added that she was not stirring up sedition in Britain and that the decree of 19 November referred only to Germany.[46]

The last point was of consequence for the ministry was becoming increasingly concerned about the domestic situation and the extent to which it might be manipulated by France. In a hand-written letter sent to Auckland on 27 November, Grenville suggested that there was 'a concerted plan to drive us to extremities, with a view of producing an impression in the interior of the country'.[47] This echoed the ministerial response to the last period of subversion, the Jacobite period, when foreign war had been seen as serving Jacobite ends. In 1792 a poor harvest was steadily working through into higher prices and this was leading to rising social discontent. Much of it was not politically specific, but some was, and the spread of radical agitation led to concern at every point.[48] Political clubs, such as the London Corresponding Society, were growing in size and prominence. The Society pressed for universal male suffrage, annual parliaments, a British reform convention and a programme of public economy. The Perth Society of the Friends of the People was formed on 14 August, the Society of the Friends of the Constitution in Dundee on 17 September. Some clubs were in touch with the National Convention.[49] Congratulatory addresses were dispatched prominently.[50] None of the means or media of public politics employed

[46] *Correspondence of Miles* I, 357–63; Smith, notes on interview, 30 Nov. 1792, CUL Add. 7621; Maret to Lebrun, 2 Dec. 1792, AE CP Ang. 584 fol. 19; Murley, 'Anglo-French War', pp. 259–65.

[47] Grenville to Auckland, 27 Nov. 1792, BL Add. 34445 fol. 401, 58920 fol. 184.

[48] Ehrman's chapter '1792: The Dimensions of Unrest', *Pitt*, II, 91–171, is an excellent introduction to this subject.

[49] A. W. L. Seaman, 'Reform Politics at Sheffield, 1791–97', *Transactions of the Hunter Archaeological Society*, 7 (1957), 215–28; C. Jewson, *Jacobin City: A Portrait of Norwich in its Reaction to the French Revolution, 1788–1802* (Edinburgh, 1975); A. Goodwin, *The Friends of Liberty: The English Democratic Movement in the Age of the French Revolution* (1979); M. Thale (ed.), *Selections from the Papers of the London Corresponding Society 1792–1799* (Cambridge, 1983); H. T. Dickinson, *British Radicalism and the French Revolution 1789–1815* (Oxford, 1985); J. Stevenson, 'The "Friends of France": The English Provinces and the French Revolution 1789–93', *Franco-British Studies*, 6 (1988), 61–70; J. Brims, 'From Reformers to "Jacobins": The Scottish Association of the Friends of the People', in T. M. Devine (ed.), *Conflict and Stability in Scottish Society 1700–1850* (Edinburgh, 1990), p. 36.

[50] Duncan to Elgin, 5 Dec. 1792, PRO FO 26/19; Murley, 'Anglo-French War', pp. 153–4; Goodwin, *Friends of Liberty*, pp. 241–62, 507–14; D. V. Erdman, *Commerce Des Lumières. John Oswald and the British in Paris, 1790–1793* (Columbia, Missouri, 1986), pp. 150–3.

by the radicals in late 1792 were new, but they were alarming for three reasons. First, they were definitely focussed on non-parliamentary, rather than parliamentary, action, and thus represented a rejection of existing constitutional mechanisms. Secondly, they were focussed on a foreign power, the traditional national enemy, a formidable military force that had beaten Britain in the last war and was currently demonstrating its military strength. Thirdly, the very volatility of international, especially French, developments made the situation in Britain appear more precarious.

Discontent and agitation was not restricted to England; much of Scotland and Ireland appeared unstable, though Hanover was peaceful. The immense pressure mounted by the Catholic Committee in Ireland forced Pitt, concerned about 'the present state of the world', to overrule the Lord Lieutenant, the Earl of Westmorland, and the wishes of the Protestant Ascendancy and led him to placate the Catholic agitation by granting them the vote in early 1793. Dundas instructed Westmorland on the need 'to connect all lovers of order and good government in a unity of resistors to all the abettors of anarchy and misrule'. The British ministers were determined to prevent any alliance of Catholics and radical Presbyterians.[51]

After Valmy, the domestic position became more acute, and from 26 November on the prospect of an imminent war with France made the situation especially alarming. This played a role in both the willingness of Pitt and Grenville to see French agents and in the decision to send Charles Long to Paris in order to begin discussions with the Executive Council. The army was too small to cope with insurrection, defend Britain from invasion and campaign in the Low Countries. When last tried in 1745, it had proved necessary both to bring back most of the army from the Low Countries and to send for Dutch and Hessian forces. The

---

[51] Auckland to Pitt, 14 Dec. 1791, [1792], PRO 30/8/110 fols. 203, 215; Pitt to Westmorland, 10 Nov. 1792, quoted in T. Bartlett, *The Fall and Rise of the Irish Nation. The Catholic Question 1690–1830* (Dublin, 1992), p. 155. Dundas to Westmorland, 7 Jan. 1793, quoted in Bartlett, 'The Origins and Progress of the Catholic Question in Ireland, 1690–1800', in T. P. Power and K. Whelan (eds.), *Endurance and Emergence. Catholics in Ireland in the Eighteenth Century* (Blackrock, 1990), p. 14. The extensive relevant literature on Ireland includes E. O'Flaherty, 'The Catholic Convention and Anglo-Irish Politics, 1791–3', *Archivium Hibernicum*, 40 (1985), 14–34; Bartlett, *Catholic Question*, pp. 124–72; C. J. Woods (ed.), *Journals and Memoirs of Thomas Russell* (Blackrock, Ireland, 1992). On Scotland, H. W. Meikle, *Scotland and the French Revolution* (Glasgow, 1912); Furber, *Dundas*, pp. 78–84; T. M. Devine, 'The Failure of Radical Reform in Scotland in the late Eighteenth Century', in Devine (ed.), *Conflict and Stability*, pp. 51–64; M. Fry, *The Dundas Despotism* (Edinburgh, 1992), pp. 159–76. On Hanover, G. Schneider (ed.), *Das Kurfürstentum Hannover und die Französische Revolution. Quellen aus den Jahren 1791–1795* (Hildesheim, 1989); R. Oberschelp (ed.), *Die Französische Revolution und Niedersachsen 1789–1803* (2 vols., Hildesheim, 1989).

margin of safety was far tighter by the end of November 1792, although political disaffection in the army was far less than feared. Concerned about the situation in Britain, George III refused to send any troops thence to Ireland.[52] In response to the threat of insurrection,[53] the government moved troops nearer to London and on 1 December embodied parts of the militia, a step that obliged it to summon Parliament within a fortnight. On 19 December a bill to regulate the arrival and conduct of aliens was introduced. It would affect Chauvelin, no longer recognised as a diplomat. The development of loyalist associations was more encouraging for the government, and suggested that, in Grenville's words, the government would be able 'to assert its true situation in Europe'.[54] On 20 November The Association for Preserving Liberty and Property against Republicans and Levellers was launched at a meeting at the Crown and Anchor Tavern in London. It was encouraged by the government, though far from dependent on its support. On 28 November John Hatsell, Clerk of the Commons, wrote:

I wish every county was like Devonshire – but I fear, that in Ireland, Scotland, the manufacturing parts of Yorkshire and particularly in London, there is a very different spirit rising ... the Society at the Crown and Anchor. This appears to me a better plan than trusting to the soldiery and brings the question to its true point – a contest between those who have property and those who have none – If this idea is followed up generally and with spirit, it may, for a time, secure us peace *internally*.[55]

Much of the press was harnessed to spread a message of loyalty and order. Burges played an active role in the foundation of the *True Briton* and the *Sun*. Provincial papers vigorously provided the same message, marginalising radicals and suggesting that the nation was united behind the government. Thus, for example, *Wheeler's Manchester Chronicle* of 22 December 1792 published accounts of loyalist anti-Painite demonstrations in Pendleton, Preston and Stockport, attacked Paine itself and asserted Lancastrian loyalty,

It is extraordinary with what industry blazoned accounts have been sent to the London papers, of riots that never existed in this town ... the bent of the people is peaceable, with a satisfied continuance at those employments which their

[52] Brims, 'Reformers to "Jacobins"', pp. 37–9; C. Emsley, 'Political Disaffection and the British Army in 1792', *Bulletin of the Institute of Historical Research*, 48 (1975), 245; George III to Grenville, 26 Nov. 1792, BL Add. 58857 fol. 62.

[53] Burges to Grenville, 4 Nov. 1792, BL Add. 58968 fol. 72; C. Emsley, 'The London "Insurrection" of December 1792: Fact, Fiction, or Fantasy', *Journal of British Studies*, 17 (1978), 66–86.   [54] *Court and Cabinets*, III, 232.

[55] Hatsell to John Ley, 28 Nov. 1792, Devon CRO 63/2/11/1/53; A. Mitchell, 'The Association Movement of 1792–3', *Historical Journal*, 4 (1961), 56–77; D. E. Ginter, 'The loyalist association movement of 1792–3', *Historical Journal*, 9 (1966), 179–90; Dozier, *For King, Constitution and Country*, pp. 56–9.

various duties call them to ... the People, all over the kingdom, have spontaneously made the principles of the present constitution, the standard of their affection, with a determined resolution to reject wild theories, and support that kind of Government, which is so happily calculated to protect their persons and property in return.

Auckland called for a programme of indoctrination in order to achieve an acceptable politicisation of the country:

every possible form of Proclamations to the People, orders for Fast Days, Speeches from the Throne, Discourses from the Pulpit, Discussions in Parliament etc. I am sure that we should gain ground by this. The prosperity and opulence of England are such, that except the lowest and most destitute class, and men of undone fortunes and desperate pursuits, there are none who would not suffer essentially in their fortunes, occupations, comfort, in the glory, strength and well-being of their country, but above all in that sense of security which forms the sole happiness of life, by this new species of French disease which is spreading its contagion among us ... the abandoning of religion is a certain step towards anarchy.

This mixture of national identity, economic interest, religious conviction and a 'sense of security' was to prove very potent. Loyalism was to sweep the country, though many were not touched. By 4 December, Dundas could suggest 'that the chief danger at home is over for the present'. It has been claimed that about 1,500 loyalist associations, involving about 15,000 active members, were formed between November 1792 and February 1793.[56] It was far from the case that everyone was a loyalist, it proved difficult to sustain the level of engagement, and the relationship between government and loyalism could be ambiguous, but, nevertheless, in much of the country a network of loyalist associations was established and this provided a crucial prop to the government. It was one that the French underrated, for their agents in London mostly stressed the vitality and French sympathies of British radicalism. They failed in the basic task of diplomats, revolutionary or otherwise, which was the provision of information, for, aside from misrepresenting the situation in London, they made no effort to visit the rest of the country: the coffee-houses of London were preferred to the manufacturing towns of Yorkshire. Gideon Duncan claimed that 'the French are induced to be insolent, from the addresses they receive from some of our insignificant clubs in England, who give themselves as the voice of the nation'.[57] Thus, the French government deluded itself as to the likely consequence

---

[56] Auckland to Grenville, 26 Nov. 1792, BL Add. 58920 fols. 178–9; Stanhope, *Pitt*, I, 458; Dozier, *For King, Constitution and Country*, p. 62. Dozier's figures are based on extrapolation from an inadequate sample of provincial newspapers.
[57] Duncan to Elgin, 5 Dec. 1792, PRO FO 26/19.

of any war with Britain, while its British counterpart was encouraged by signs of loyalist vitality.[58]

Relations, however, continued between the two governments. Pitt agreed to the suggestion that he meet Maret and the two met on 2 December. Pitt presented the Scheldt resolution as likely to lead to war with first the Dutch and then the British, and argued that the resolution of 19 December was a hostile act. Maret, who saw Pitt as an opponent of war and its supporters, whom he grouped around Hawkesbury, told him that France wanted good relations with both Britain and the United Provinces, but that French public opinion was ready to demand British diplomatic recognition of the republic, and he urged Pitt to treat with France publicly. Maret repeated what he had told Smith about the Scheldt and 19 November decrees. Pitt's desire for negotiations emerged clearly from the discussions, as did his determination to keep them secret. Grenville concluded from the meeting that the French would probably send someone to open 'a communication', and that it was therefore unnecessary for Charles Long to go to Paris in order to negotiate there, as had been planned after Grenville's meeting with Chauvelin on 29 November. George III thought this prudent as it would be easier to control discussions in London, but, he added, that any negotiation would probably fail and that, in light of this, it was necessary not to allow the French to embarrass the British government by revealing how far they might have been willing to make concessions.[59]

Two days after the meeting between Maret and Pitt, came news of a fresh provocative French step, the demand that Dumouriez's army be granted passage through the Dutch possession of Maastricht. The British government urged the Dutch to refuse such a breach of their neutrality which it saw as provocative to the Austrians and likely to lead to fresh demands. As the Austrians retreated eastwards, French forces had advanced to occupy Aachen, whence they threatened nearby Maastricht as well as a possible advance to the Rhine.[60] Convinced that the French were relying on sowing subversion in Britain, and encouraged by 'rising' loyalism, Grenville was sure that firmness was the best policy.[61] Certainly public negotiations with the French could only have

[58] Grenville to Auckland, 4 Dec. 1792, 15 Feb. 1793, BL Add. 58921 fols. 10, 107.
[59] Maret to Lebrun, 2 Dec. 1792, AE CP Ang. 584 fols. 20–2; Grenville to Auckland, 4 Dec. 1792, PRO FO 37/41; Grenville to George III, 2 Dec., reply, 3 Dec. 1792, BL Add. 58857 fols. 69–71; undated instructions for Long, PRO FO 27/40; Murley, 'Anglo-French War', pp. 265–9; Evans, 'Miles', 201–2.
[60] Grenville to Auckland, 4 Dec. 1792, PRO FO 37/41; Anon. report from Aachen in Grenville's papers, 19 Dec. 1792, BL Add. 59279 fols. 37–8.
[61] Grenville to Auckland, 4, 18 Dec., Auckland to Grenville, 4 Dec. 1792, BL Add. 34446 fols. 32–3, 58921 fol. 28, 34446 fol. 43.

discouraged the loyalists. In addition, whatever the messages from individual French agents, French policy and pretensions continued to be unacceptable. On 5 December Lebrun outlined a policy towards the Dutch that was totally unacceptable to Britain. He argued that the Dutch had the right to have the most advantageous form of government, and that no other power should intervene to maintain the old constitution. Chauvelin was instructed to explain that any guarantee by which a power sought to submit a people to a destructive system of government was a blow against the eternal rights of the nation and therefore null and void. Anglo-Prussian support for the Orange dynasty and the attitude of the partitioning powers towards Poland were cited as examples.[62]

Such arguments were regarded not only as subversive of all international order, but also as bogus, for self-interest was seen as the central objective of French policy, force as its *modus operandi*. The hostile French treatment of neutrals, such as the imperial free city of Frankfurt, was commented on, and invasion, rather than self-determination, was believed to be their plan for the Dutch. On the 3rd a somewhat excited William V of Orange told Auckland that Dumouriez, who indeed wanted an immediate invasion, was to attack through Breda 'as a signal for insurrection', that the Princess was to be killed, and that 'he would resist to the utmost, and die upon the spot'.[63] In fact, William survived the French conquest of the United Provinces in 1795. Dying heroically was more fashionable in both Neo-classical and Romantic iconography than it was in practice for the monarchs of the period; but William's language indicated that it was not only the French who were being excitable.

Absorbed by the trial of Louis XVI, the strains of which made compromise in foreign policy very difficult, and affected by the rhetoric and experience of success, the French government failed to appreciate the impact of its policies and statements on neutral powers. On 9 December Lebrun expressed his conviction that a wish to tackle domestic problems would keep Britain peaceful and he linked this to Pitt's readiness to see Maret. Lebrun saw the calling out of the militia as a sign that the government was very worried about the internal situation.[64] In fact, a rising tide of loyalism, support from prominent opposition politicians, concern about French intentions and the need to consider Austrian and Prussian attitudes, were pulling the British government in an opposite direction, as Chauvelin warned Lebrun on the 7th.[65] That

---

[62] Lebrun to Chauvelin, 5 Dec. 1792, AE CP Ang. 584 fols. 51–2.
[63] Auckland to Grenville, 5 Dec. 1792, PRO FO 37/41.
[64] Lebrun to Chauvelin, 9 Dec. 1792, AE CP Ang. 584 fol. 92.
[65] Chauvelin to Lebrun, 7 Dec. 1792, fols. 67–77; Loughborough to Pitt, 9 Dec. 1792, PRO 30/8/153 fol. 71.

426   British foreign policy, 1783–1793

day, the Austrian envoy, Stadion, reported that Grenville had urged him on the 6th on the need for a collective security system designed to block French aggression.[66] Such a move left little room for easing Anglo-French tensions. Lebrun, though over-confident about the British response, was aware of the need to prevent war with her, but he was under pressure both from the prevailing mood in the Convention and from the Jacobin charge that the government was seeking to betray the Revolution by compromise abroad and by sparing the life of Louis XVI. Maret was instructed to tell Pitt that the French wanted good relations, but a clear preference for formal negotiations with Chauvelin and thus recognition of his credentials from the republican government was expressed.[67] Lebrun's instructions to Chauvelin did not address British concerns. A promise not to attack the Dutch was linked to the expectation that Britain would not intervene in Dutch affairs and would not protect the 1787 Orangist settlement, which would entail not only abandoning the Anglo-Dutch treaty of 1788, but also vital British concerns in foreign policy in both Europe and Asia. Chauvelin was to declare that there was no chance of France changing her position over the Scheldt, a position dictated by natural law. The 19 November decree was only to apply to powers France was at war with, but the dignity of the republic precluded any acceptance of Pitt's wish for secret negotiations. Chauvelin therefore was to take Maret's place in any discussions with Pitt.[68]

On 12 December 1792 Noël returned to London, after a trip delayed by adverse winds and bad roads. He resumed contact with the British government via Miles and Smith. On the 12th Noël told Miles that France was justified over both the Scheldt and the right to pursue the Austrians into the United Provinces. He also warned that, if war broke out between the two powers, Britain would not benefit from seizing French colonies, as the contagion of revolution would spread from them to the British colonies. That afternoon Noël and Maret saw Smith. Despite Noël's tone, his report to Lebrun urged caution. He noted that the people had become markedly loyalist and on the 14th Noël, Maret and Chauvelin all sent warning reports: France must not live in false security. Noël argued that the French would be foolish to count on disorder in Britain. Maret saw Pitt that evening, but the minister, who argued that Chauvelin was not accredited as an envoy, kept the meeting short and did not enter into negotiations with Maret. Nevertheless, Maret's report stressed the necessity of avoiding any step that led the British ministry to think that France was conniving with the opposition.

---

[66] Vivenot, *Quellen zur Geschichte...* II, 393.
[67] Lebrun to Maret, 9 Dec. 1792, AE CP Ang. 584 fols. 96–7.
[68] Lebrun to Chauvelin, 9 Dec. 1792, AE CP Ang. 584 fols. 92–5.

Chauvelin, who on the 7th had reported that the British government was in a weak position, now stated that his instructions over the last fortnight had been inappropriate for the maintenance of peace. He reported that the British government would not recognise the French republic as a preliminary to negotiations, that rising loyalist feeling was encouraging the ministry to take firmer steps and that it would not treat the opening of the Scheldt as anything other than an aggressive measure. Chauvelin also argued that the execution of Louis XVI would increase support for war with France. Four years earlier, when it had been widely believed that Joseph II had ceded or mortgaged the Austrian Netherlands to a then unrevolutionary France, Miles himself had written that if France opened the Scheldt 'adieu to the commerce and power of Britain – she has both doors of the British Channel, and we shall be at her mercy'.[69] Sheridan had earlier warned Chauvelin that the Whigs would support Pitt if France invaded the United Provinces or interfered with British domestic affairs, although he also stated that they would attack Pitt if he went to war over the Scheldt.[70]

Chauvelin also focused on a major problem that was of rising importance as the weather deteriorated: the impact of delayed communications. Noël's letter of the 13th, for example, did not reach Paris until the 18th, the reports of the 14th did not arrive until the 20th. Chauvelin argued that distance and contrary winds combined with a volatile situation, which rendered any general instruction impossible, to ensure that by the time a dispatch was replied to, the situation had changed markedly.[71] There were many other occasions that winter when wind delayed the packet boats.[72] Storms in the Bay of Biscay impeded correspondence with Lisbon and Madrid, while French advances disrupted postal services in the Austrian Netherlands and Germany. Grenville's letters to Ostervald of 29 December 1792 and 8 January 1793 did not reach Lisbon until 22 January. Communications were scarcely a new problem: they had posed major difficulties for the British government during the Ochakov crisis. In addition, the Calais–Dover route posed fewer problems than the Helvoetsluys–Harwich crossing. The former was shorter and less subject to interruption, especially to the westerlies that stopped the Harwich passage.[73] Yet, in the frenetic

[69] Chauvelin to Lebrun, 14 Dec., Maret to Lebrun, 14 Dec., Noël to Lebrun, 14 Dec. 1792, AE CP Ang. 584 fols. 157–65; Evans, 'Miles', 202; Miles to Keith, 18 Mar. 1788, BL Add. 35540 fol. 152.
[70] Chauvelin to Lebrun, 3 Dec. 1792, AE CP Ang. 584 fol. 34.
[71] Chauvelin to Lebrun, 14 Dec. 1792, AE CP Ang. 584 fols. 156–7; Evans, 'Miles', 203.
[72] Duncan to Aust, 22 Nov., Duncan to Elgin, 10 Dec. 1792, PRO FO 26/19.
[73] Keith to Straton, 2 Nov. 1792, Ipswich HA 239/2/321; Ostervald to Grenville, 23 Jan. 1793, PRO FO 63/6; W. Fraser to Pitt, 24 Dec. 1787, PRO 30/8/137 fol. 31.

atmosphere of the last weeks of 1792, when differences were great and discussions possible, distance and delays between London and Paris were major problems.

This was demonstrated in mid-December. The cautious reports sent on 14 December had obviously not reached Paris by the next day, when Lebrun wrote to Chauvelin ordering him to obtain from the British government a firm explanation of their conduct towards France, though he did offer a conciliatory clarification of the 19 November decree. The Dutch would not be attacked while they remained neutral, indeed on the 13th Dumouriez had been ordered into winter quarters; but Lebrun was firm over the Scheldt, which he argued should be decided by justice and reason. Lebrun claimed that the issue was not very important and that if the British government treated it otherwise it was clear that it wanted war. Lebrun added prophetically that it was foolish to fight over the Scheldt as Britain would lose the Dutch, and that the war might not go as well as the British expected. Chauvelin was ordered to spread knowledge about his new instructions, though not to give them great publicity. The principle of appealing to the British nation against its ministry in the event of war was advanced, as a threat that could be made if the British government's response was unsatisfactory. Also on the 15th the Convention passed a decree on the occupied territories which swept away their existing social order and subordinated their governments to the task of supplying French forces. This made peace with Austria and Prussia less likely and also made it clear that Belgium (and the United Provinces if conquered), were to be incorporated into the French system. Any political settlement acceptable to the Republic would guarantee continued French influence over Belgium, a threat to Britain that was much more pointed than the Scheldt decree. News of the decree reached London on 19 December and had a considerable effect.[74]

Against this background, the continuing informal discussions in London seemed pointless, as did Stanhope's attempt to persuade Grenville of France's 'friendly disposition'. On the 18th the British government received a report from Francis Wilson, who had been left in Brussels after Elgin's departure, stating that French troops were moving towards the Dutch frontier.[75] Duncan, meanwhile, noted the general belief that the French had decided to invade in order to preempt British actions.[76] Smith went to see Noël on the 16th, told him that France must

---

[74] Lebrun to Chauvelin, 15 Dec. 1792, AE CP Ang. 584 fols. 177–8; Evans, 'Miles', 203.
[75] Stanhope to Grenville, 19 Dec. 1792, Stanhope, *Pitt*, I, 461–2; Wilson to Burges, 11 Dec. 1792, PRO FO 26/19. Wilson's papers can be consulted in the Public Record Office of Northern Ireland in Belfast, T2761.
[76] Duncan to Elgin, 8 Dec. 1792, PRO FO 26/19.

not attack the Dutch or press the Scheldt issue and warned him that the nation would rally round the government if convinced that the outbreak of war was the work of France. Lansdowne, one of the few peers who still sympathised with the Revolution, was also clear that it was up to the Republic to avoid war.[77] Noël's report reached Paris on the 21st, but the previous day Chauvelin was sent instructions to insist on the recognition of his credentials and to find out officially if Britain saw the Scheldt and 19 November decrees as a cause of war.

This attempted resort to public diplomacy was unwise if the Republic wished to keep the peace. Recognition was an extremely sensitive issue at this point because of the trial of Louis XVI. In addition, the opening of the parliamentary session on 13 December and the consequent opportunities for opposition attacks made the government vulnerable if it negotiated publicly, and this was emphasised further by suspicions, fanned by Miles, of links between the Opposition and prominent French republicans.[78] Though greatly exaggerated, these were given some substance by the discussions of a few prominent figures with Chauvelin. It was unlikely that Fox was not informed of his meetings with Sheridan. The prospect of the French informing the Opposition of the progress of negotiations was dangerous, an unwelcome echo of Vorontsov's conduct during the Ochakov crisis. The risks of negotiating with the French were demonstrated on 19 December when, probably as a result of rising political concern about British naval armaments,[79] Lebrun told the National Convention that discussions had taken place and had been initiated by Pitt. Adopting an aggressive approach, he declared that British naval armaments were unimpressive, threatened to turn to the British people and insisted that their government should not defend the Dutch *status quo*. Lebrun's diatribe was applauded enthusiastically by the Convention.[80]

Thus, while the Dutch decision not to resist the passage of French ships up the Scheldt and the French order of 13 December to Dumouriez to respect Dutch neutrality and to move into winter quarters served to defuse immediate tension over Dutch security and, therefore, to prevent an immediate outbreak of war between France and Britain, the general context was one not only of a failure to settle or negotiate major differences, but of a number of steps that made the general tenor of relations worse, and the atmosphere more charged and bitter. British moves to block grain exports to France, particularly an Order in Council of 13 November, were resented, not surprisingly given the sensitivity of

[77] Noël to Lebrun, 16 Dec. 1792, AE CP Ang. 584 fols. 183–4.
[78] Sheffield to Auckland, 3 Jan. 1793, BL Add. 34446 fol. 442.
[79] Murley, 'Anglo-French War', p. 300.   [80] *AP* 55, 164–5.

food supplies. The Aliens Bill, introduced by Grenville on 15 December, also aroused anger, while the French were concerned about British military preparations. The issue of relations with France played a major role in Parliament, and increased divisions among the Whigs. When the session began on 13 December, Fox attacked the ministry for failing to negotiate with France, and drew attention to the fate of Poland. His amendment was, however, defeated by 290–50 because on 11 and 12 December meetings of prominent Whigs at Burlington House had agreed not to oppose the address. Portland had already approved via Loughborough the draft of the royal speech that he had been shown, finding the section on British foreign policy 'particularly satisfactory'. Fox was left to rage impotently 'that there was no address at this moment Pitt could frame he would not propose an amendment to, and divide the House upon'; a statement that vindicated earlier press claims to the same effect. Fox was convinced that the Revolution had taken an unfortunate path because it had not been allowed to develop without external threats; he saw France's enemies as united in a crusade of despots seeking to suppress liberty; and he viewed George III in this light. These views enjoyed little support within the political elite. On 15 December Fox's motion to send an envoy to Paris to negotiate with the French government was defeated in the Commons without a division.[81] The *Morning Chronicle*, an opposition paper, of 20 December stated that the

only difference between Mr. Pitt and Mr. Fox, is that Mr. Pitt is doing secretly, by means of confidential secretaries, who assumed no diplomatic character, what Mr. Fox is for doing publicly by an Ambassador ... Mr. Fox's mode could only fail of success from the determination of the French to concede none of the points in dispute: Mr. Pitt's may fail on a mere point of punctilios ... for the sake of a mere ceremony.

Whatever the merits of this argument, Fox's call for negotiations had both further marginalised him among the Whigs and been received in a very hostile fashion 'out of doors', in other words outside Parliament.[82] As he was probably aware that discussions were going on anyway and had also agreed that the Dutch had to be assisted if attacked,[83] Fox's conduct has been discussed in terms of 'criminal folly' and 'faction'.[84] There is force in these charges. In addition, any moves towards France would

[81] *Malmesbury corresp.* II, 473–6; Loughborough to Pitt, 9 Dec. 1792, PRO 30/8/153 fol. 71; Malmesbury to Hawkesbury, 4 Dec. 1792, BL Add. 38228 f. 157; *Public Advertiser*, 14, 20 Jan. 1792; L. G. Mitchell, *Fox and the Disintegration of the Whig Party*, pp. 202–4; L. G. Mitchell, *Charles James Fox* (Oxford, 1992), pp. 125–30; Brims, 'Reformers to "Jacobins"', pp. 39–40.   [82] *Malmesbury corresp.* II, 476.
[83] *Malmesbury corresp.* II, 474.   [84] Murley, 'Anglo-French War', pp. 340–1.

probably have been both unsuccessful and seen as a sign of weakness. Yet, if there was to be any chance of avoiding war, negotiations had to take place. Given the problems associated with dealing with the variety of French agents in London, of which the recognition of Chauvelin was only one, it would have been best to send a British agent to Paris. On the other hand, not least in light of the international context, specifically Britain's relations with other powers, this would have had to be an unofficial mission. By calling publicly for an embassy, Fox was jeopardising any such course of action.

The French demand for recognition forced a crisis in Anglo-French relations which Dumouriez' inactivity had postponed, but the situation was becoming more serious anyway both because of attempts to improve British relations with powers opposed to France and because of a growing mutual mistrust. Pitt refused to see Chauvelin in late December. On 27 December the British government received Chauvelin's demand for recognition transmitted in accordance with Lebrun's instructions of the 20th. Grenville considered Chauvelin's paper 'both in form and substance wholly unsatisfactory'.[85] Auckland thought the 'terms so violent and so menacing that it is difficult not to suppose an intention to declare war against us'.[86] The response was hostile. Chauvelin was not to see Pitt or Grenville; that seemed to be too like a *de facto* recognition. Instead, after a delay that was indicative of the sense that war could not be avoided and that covered a period when the Foreign Office was sending off appeals for foreign co-operation, Grenville sent Chauvelin a note on the 31st. The French claim to annul treaties on the basis of a natural right that they alone were to judge was presented as destructive to all relations. France must abandon her expansionist schemes in the Low Countries. These essentials were seen as more important than French assurances that the decree of 19 November did not apply to neutrals and the promise that the Dutch would not be attacked if they remained neutral. Both that decree and French conduct towards the Dutch were condemned in Grenville's note. The threat of an appeal to the British people was rejected with the statement that monarchy and people were linked together and that therefore only communications addressed to the government would be acknowledged.[87]

Meanwhile, on the 28th and 29th, Grenville had given new energy to the attempt to create an anti-French system. The hostile aspect of this policy was indicated by the instruction sent to Ostervald, the Secretary of Legation at Lisbon, on the 29th: he was to urge the Portuguese to arm

[85] Grenville to Whitworth, 29 Dec. 1792, PRO FO 65/23 fol. 271.
[86] Auckland to Straton, 1 Jan. 1793, Ipswich HA 239/2/281.
[87] Grenville to Chauvelin, 31 Dec. 1792, BL Add. 34446 fols. 389–92, PRO FO 95/100.

their navy.[88] Such a measure was clearly intended as a preparation for the deployment of a large British fleet in the Mediterranean that was seen as desirable, not least by potential allies, in order to counteract French naval activity. The arrival of such a fleet would, in particular, encourage Spain, a power whose support Britain was now seeking. In order to permit such a move, it was necessary for Britain and her allies to be clearly superior to France in home waters, and Grenville became increasingly interested in obtaining information on French naval preparations. The Dutch government was asked via Auckland to obtain reports of the situation in Brest through commercial channels. Thus, negotiations were giving way to war, diplomats were serving the ends of the forthcoming struggle. Indeed, on 27 December the Cabinet decided to send warships to Flushing in order to help the Dutch against any attack on their territory or ships, the last an obvious prospect if they sought to enforce the closure of the Scheldt, a measure the British government clearly wished them to take. Grenville argued that 'whatever the question may be, as to the policy of putting off the war, if it were in our power, surely we see enough to be sensible that it may come upon us every day'.[89]

It was easy to approach Portugal. She was not yet at war with France, her relations with Britain were reasonably close and she was not suspected of having aggrandising views of her own. Austria, Prussia and Russia were very different. On 19 December Vorontsov had approached the government on behalf of Catherine II with the suggestion that Britain join an anti-French coalition. Grenville saw this as a very important development which, if utilised, might have favourable consequences,[90] but he did not reply until after receiving Chauvelin's note. On 28–29 December Grenville replied, with messages to Vorontsov and to the British envoys at Berlin, Madrid, The Hague, St Petersburg and Vienna; and he followed these up with one to Sir James Murray, who was instructed to inform Frederick William II, then at Frankfurt, of British moves and to negotiate with him.[91] The Dutch were urged to ensure that their preparations for war were complete, while Francis Jackson, now Minister Plenipotentiary in Madrid, was instructed to renew proposals for co-operation made in accordance with orders of 5 December. Whitworth was informed that the government was acting,

[88] Grenville to Ostervald, 29 Dec. 1792, PRO FO 63/15.
[89] Cabinet Minute, 27 Dec., Grenville to Auckland, 29 Dec. 1792, 1 Jan. 1793, BL Add. 58857 fol. 75, 58921 fols. 34, 36–7.
[90] Marcum, 'Vorontsov', p. 258; Grenville to Auckland, 29 Dec. 1792, BL Add. 58921 fol. 34.
[91] Grenville to Straton, 29 Dec. 1792, Ipswich HA 239/2/308; Grenville to George III and reply, both 2 Jan. 1793, BL Add. 58857 fols. 76–8; Grenville to Murray, 4 Jan. 1793, PRO FO 29/1.

in order to put a stop to the farther progress of the French arms, and French principles, and to oblige that nation to renounce its views of aggrandizement, and to desist from that regular, and settled plan which they appear to be pursuing, and which they have lately avowed by a public decree, of encouraging, and assisting all attempts which may be made against any established governments.

Whitworth was to tell the Russian government first that Britain was already arming and intended to fulfil obligations, and was pleased that Catherine shared these views, and secondly that Russian envoys should be given powers to negotiate in pursuit of agreement on necessary measures. Grenville continued, 'the most adviseable step to be taken, would be, that sufficient explanation should be had, with the powers at war with France'.[92] They, rather than France, were seen as the key to a satisfactory peace, for Britain could only bring sufficient diplomatic pressure to bear on France if she was fully informed of Austrian and Prussian plans and enjoyed their confidence; while, if war with France was necessary, it could only be waged successfully in co-operation with them. France was to be asked to return to her 1789 frontiers and to pledge publicly not to stir up discontent in other states; in return, other powers were to promise both non-interference and the recognition of the Republic.

This proposal encapsulated the spirit of the Pitt ministry as clearly as their earlier attempt to oblige Russia, Austria and Prussia to accept the *status quo ante bellum* in eastern Europe. The anxiety about Austrian and Prussian plans in western Europe that had surfaced in the late summer of 1792 was reflected anew in the desire to limit the role of these powers. There was to be no war of ideology, no restoration of monarchy supported by Austrian and Prussian bayonets, although that was what the Austrians still wanted,[93] no larger version of the Dutch crisis of 1787 creating a new constitutional and international order. Grenville wanted a barrier against France, not measures to overthrow her government.[94] He hoped that if war broke out the Dutch army would be sufficiently strong to avoid the necessity of having to rely entirely on Prussia to protect the United Provinces.[95] Instead, Austria and Prussia were only to be allowed to seek territorial indemnification for their efforts against France if the latter power refused the terms that it was to be offered by the neutral powers, a group among which Britain was most prominent and now most active. Her role was acknowledged from a surprising

[92] Vorontsov to Grenville, 29 Dec., Grenville to Whitworth, 29 Dec., Grenville to Vorontsov, 28 Dec. 1792, PRO FO 63/23 fols. 256–71.
[93] Cobenzl to Stadion, 22 Dec. 1792, Ipswich HA 239/2/295.
[94] Grenville to Vorontsov, 28 Dec. 1792, PRO FO 65/23 fol. 259.
[95] Grenville to Auckland, 18 Dec. 1792, BL Add. 58921 fol. 29.

quarter. The Papal Nuncio in Lisbon sought a British declaration to France that the Papal States were under British protection, and a British fleet in the Mediterranean to give substance to the declaration.[96] Neutral states throughout western Europe were under pressure. In October Ferdinand III of Tuscany had been keen to see a small British squadron under Rear-Admiral Samuel Goodall anchor at Livorno. The squadron, HMS *Rodney* and two frigates, was, however, outnumbered in early December by the French fleet in the Gulf of La Spezia: fifteen of the line and sixteen frigates.[97] The French fleet under Latouche-Tréville sailed on to Naples, arriving there on 17 December, and the threat of attack led the government to agree both to acknowledge the French republic and to be neutral.[98] French pressure on Geneva led to the creation of a new-model francophile government in early December.

The British proposals of 29 December 1792 were abortive but they are of great interest for the light they throw on the motivation of the Pitt ministry. Its cautious approach to change was clearly indicated, as was its willingness to resort to interventionist diplomacy based on a collective security system. What was not proposed was even more striking. At this juncture, Britain was offered a tremendous opportunity to crush France. The domestic and diplomatic circumstances both seemed propitious. In Britain the opposition was divided, the ministry united and enjoying the confidence of both Crown and Parliament. The navy was ready for action, government finances were strong. The Royal Navy was in the unprecedented position of having 100 ships of the line, nearly half of which were new and the rest fully repaired.[99] The international situation was unprecedented. Britain had the opportunity to play a major role in what would be the strongest European coalition hitherto created, one that would include Austria, Prussia, Russia, the Empire, Spain and the Dutch. Only France and a desperately weak Poland were truly outside this system. The Family Compact was decisively broken, while Russia was no longer diverted by war with the Turks, and the Habsburg empire was considerably more stable than it had been in early 1790. As in 1745–8, it might be difficult to mobilise strength sufficiently fast to counteract French advances in the Low Countries, but the difficulties that the French were already encountering on the middle Rhine, where

---

[96] Ostervald to Grenville, 1 Dec. 1792, PRO FO 63/15.
[97] Hervey to Straton, 6 Oct., Anon. to [Hervey], 11 Dec. 1792, Ipswich HA 239/2/383, 389.
[98] Hamilton to Straton, 18 Dec. 1792, Ipswich HA 239/2/392; Grosjean, 'Relations', 37–8.
[99] Grenville to Auckland, 4 Dec. 1792, BL Add. 58921 fol. 9; P. Webb, 'Construction, repair and maintenance in the battle fleet of the Royal Navy, 1793–1815', in Black and Woodfine (eds.), *British Navy*, pp. 207–10.

they had been driven from Frankfurt on 2 December by a Hessian force assisted by the citizens, suggested that they would be unable to retain their recent gains. It was also widely assumed that domestic, particularly financial, problems would gravely hinder their war effort. On 27 January 1793 Richmond told Grenville that 351,000 troops were 'collecting against France' north of the Alps, and that this figure could be swelled by 50,000 Russians, 20,000 Dutch and 10,000 British troops.[100]

In short, the opportunity for action appeared excellent. The Nootka Sound crisis had suggested that France would not find it easy to mobilise her fleet, and her colonies, especially the crucial ones in the West Indies, were known to be rife with discontent. Thus, Britain could join in the conflict, and both revenge her losses during the American War of Independence and make fresh gains, in the West Indies and the Indian Ocean. The adhesion of Spain to the anti-French coalition would be crucial in giving Britain the margin of naval strength required to enable her to mount a whole series of amphibious operations. On 3 December Count Osterman, the Russian Vice-Chancellor, while making it clear that Russia would not heed the Prussian request for the dispatch of troops to fight France, nevertheless pressed Whitworth on the opportunity 'of annihilating the commerce and navy' of France.[101]

And yet such a prospect was not sketched out at the end of December 1792, no more than it had been behind government planning during the Dutch and Nootka Sound crises. As then, the Pitt ministry was motivated by defensive considerations. In the winter of 1792–3 it was the fate of the United Provinces, not of Saint-Domingue, that was the principal issue. Indeed British ministerial concern for the Indies was still largely defensive. In the instructions for what was the last British government attempt to keep the peace, the projected discussions between Auckland and Dumouriez, Grenville undertook that Britain would not commit hostilities while hopes of peace remained,

unless such measures should be adopted on the part of France in the interval, as would leave His Majesty no alternative. Among these must unquestionably be reckoned the plan said to be now in agitation in France, of sending immediately to the West Indies a squadron of ships of war, some of them of great force, together with a very considerable body of land forces. Even in time of the most profound peace, and with the utmost confidence that could be entertained in the good dispositions of France, such a measure would place His Majesty's colonies in that quarter in a situation of the greatest uneasiness. In the present moment … it is impossible that he should forego the advantage of his naval superiority in

---

[100] Richmond to Grenville, referring to meeting of previous day, 28 Jan. 1793, BL Add. 58937 fols. 166–70. For a larger figure, Duncan to Elgin, 5 Dec. 1792, PRO FO 26/19.
[101] Whitworth to Grenville, 4 Dec. 1792, PRO FO 65/23 fol. 242.

these seas, and suffer a large force to proceed on a destination eventually so injurious to the security of his own dominions, and to the property and interests of his subjects.[102]

Six weeks earlier there were no British plans to use the international crisis in order to destroy their principal maritime and colonial rival. Instead, it was the French who threatened an attack on the British Empire. Armand, Count of Kersaint, a naval officer, discussed such an attack in the Convention on 3 January and proposed to help Tipu Sultan. Nor was there any British interest in the plans for a weaker France on the Continent that Elgin attributed to Thugut: the revival of the Bavarian Exchange scheme, but with French Flanders being added, while Luxemburg, Alsace and Lorraine went to a Habsburg prince.[103] Instead, it was the *status quo* that was envisaged. Had they happened, the planned return to the frontiers of 1789 in western Europe and the recognition of the Republic would probably have led to a position of tension between Austria and France, especially as Habsburg power was reintroduced into Belgium. Although there is no sign that it played any role in British policy, such a situation would be in Britain's interest, especially as the reintroduction of Habsburg power would cover the United Provinces from France, while, more generally, the failure to recreate the Austro-French alliance would weaken France in western Europe and make her a less formidable rival to Britain.

Whatever the long-term implications of the British plan, it was the short-term practicality that was of consequence. As over Ochakov, such a plan arguably failed to address the concerns of the combatants adequately. In 1790–1 there was a naive estimate of Catherine II's willingness to yield to intimidation and to abandon her gains, at the end of 1792 a failure to appreciate the degree of Austrian, Prussian and French commitment to their views. The Executive Council and many French politicians sought peace but not at the price of returning all France's territorial gains, and in so far as this was a crucial issue, war with Britain was inevitable, the conclusion reached by Reinhard, the French Secretary of Legation, on 3 January 1793.[104] It is also arguable that there simply was not time to mount such a complex negotiation. To consult with Austria and Prussia *before* offering France terms would delay matters considerably, and, by then, the conflict might have spilled over into the United Provinces. On the other hand, it was necessary to bind Britain closer to Austria, Prussia and Russia. Without them, negotiations with France would not be meaningful, not least because British

---

[102] Grenville to Auckland, 4 Feb. 1793, BL Add. 34447 fols. 433–4.
[103] Elgin to Grenville, 2 Oct. 1792, PRO FO 26/19.
[104] *Correspondence of Miles* I, 442–3; Evans, 'Miles', 205.

ministerial experience of French volatility and distrust of France was such that no settlement with her would be regarded as acceptable unless guaranteed by other powers. Thus, distrust of France and the desire to win the co-operation of the major continental monarchies combined to ensure that the major diplomatic initiative launched by Britain at the end of 1792 was directed not at France, whose government was not formally informed of the proposals, but at her opponents. A British cypher clerk sold the French the details of the instructions to Whitworth of 29 December, possibly with government connivance,[105] but there was no attempt to use them as a basis for discussion. This can be seen as a missed opportunity, but French policy over the previous two months, both in general and in the specific case of discussions with British ministers, had done nothing to inspire confidence.

On 6 January 1793 Auckland observed, 'At present there is a period of calm; but it is like the sudden interruption of a blustering storm, I have no faith in it.' He was right to be sceptical. By this stage it was regarded as increasingly likely that the war would spread to include the British and the Dutch, and the subsequent game of might-have-beens as well as the historians' quest to ascribe responsibility seems more and more point-less.[106] Near midnight on New Year's Day, Auckland had not felt certain that war would take place, but the letter he sent Burges was striking for its cool-headed realisation that French domestic policy, or rather the savagery and pain of revolution, was affecting his response. It served as a parallel to the tide of loyalism in Britain and also prefigured the emotional response to the fate of Louis XVI, increasingly seen as man as much as monarch:

It is a detestable nation: almost all within it for whom I felt affection or respect are either killed or killing, or (like Madame de Rayneval and Madame de Montmorin) dead or dying broken hearted. I feel so completely antigallican that I am in danger of losing with regard to that nation every sentiment of candour and humanity, and even that coolness of judgement which we all wish to preserve in the political measures to which they force us.[107]

Had Auckland been able to see Lebrun's instructions to Chauvelin of that day, he would have been more pessimistic about the chances of

---

[105] Martin to Compatriote, 31 Dec. 1792, AE CP Ang. sup. 29 fols. 340–1; Murley, 'Anglo-French War', pp. 420–2.
[106] Auckland to Loughborough, 6 Jan. 1793, BL Add. 34446 fol. 471; Grenville to Auckland, 29 Dec. 1792, 1 Jan. 1793, BL Add. 58921 fols. 34, 36. For a similar thesis about the War of the Spanish Succession, W. Roosen, 'The Origins of the War of the Spanish Succession', in J. Black (ed.), *The Origins of War in Early Modern Europe* (Edinburgh, 1987), pp. 151–75.
[107] Auckland to Burges, 1 Jan. 1793, Bod. BB. 31 fol. 1.

preventing war. Uncertain of the position that the British ministry had left the Republic in, Lebrun, nevertheless, thought that it wanted France to declare war for domestic reasons, and he gave Chauvelin permission to return as soon as he thought he should.[108] In one respect the differences over Chauvelin's status were indeed a trivial quarrel over a matter of form, but also, far from preventing substantive discussions over the points at issue, the differences reflected what were now the crucial problems: a general mutual distrust and a commitment by both governments to positions from which they were not willing to recede. Far from detracting from negotiations, the dispute over recognition encapsulated the points at issue.

On the evening of 6 January 1793, George III wrote to Chatham stating that, in the light of signs that the French government intended to go to war with Britain, 'in the actual state of things it seems the most desirable conclusion of the present crisis'.[109] The following day, Chauvelin, who now saw war as inevitable, again compromised the attempt to discuss issues by insisting on recognition. He made protests against the Aliens Bill and the prohibition of grain exports to France,[110] but they were returned without answer because he had presented them 'in the character of Minister of the French Republic, although he had before been formally apprized that he could not be admitted to treat in that character'. Grenville informed the King that 'it was the opinion of all your Majesty's servants that no time should be lost in returning him his note as inadmissible, as any delay would have had the appearance of hesitation'. George III supported the step. Auckland, who was encouraged by signs of growing French unpopularity in the Austrian Netherlands, thought Chauvelin's memorandum on the Aliens Bill 'impertinent and highly absurd'.[111]

On 8 January Lebrun sent Chauvelin fresh instructions in response to Grenville's note of 31 December. Ehrman suggested that they 'refrained from closing the door', and from a French perspective they were somewhat conciliatory. The French position on the Scheldt was restated, but Lebrun disclaimed the idea that France was the universal arbiter of treaties, stated that she would respect other governments as she was treated and renounced any territorial gains: French troops would occupy conquests only for the duration of the war. Dutch neutrality would not be

[108] Lebrun to Chauvelin, 1 Jan. 1793, AE CP Ang. 586 fols. 4–8.
[109] George III to Chatham, 6 Jan. 1793, Aspinall, *George III* no. 821.
[110] Chauvelin to Lebrun, 7 Jan. 1793, AE CP Ang. 586 fol. 56.
[111] Grenville to George III, 7 Jan. 1793, Aspinall, *George III* no. 822; George to Grenville, 8 Jan. 1793, BL Add. 58857 fol. 79; Auckland to Straton [mid Jan. 1793], Ipswich HA 239/2/292.

infringed and there were no threats of any appeal to the British public. The Scheldt dispute should be settled in direct negotiations between the Maritime Powers and Belgium when the independence of the latter was fully established. Chauvelin, with whom it was expected Britain should negotiate, was sent fresh credentials.[112]

Nevertheless, these were totally unacceptable terms as far as the British were concerned. They entailed a separate but precarious neutrality, while the war continued, and gave Britain no role in the eventual peace settlement, and, correspondingly, no likelihood that any Anglo-French or Anglo-Belgian settlement would be guaranteed by the other powers. In addition, the possibility that a French military presence in Belgium would lead to the destabilisation of the United Provinces remained strong. Lebrun had little confidence that his instructions of the 8th would lead to amicable negotiations and a resolution of differences for, before he could receive a response from Chauvelin, he sent the latter fresh instructions on the 10th stating that Britain was to be left eight days to give her final resolution as to war or peace. Lebrun's response to a Neapolitan suggestion for Austro-French negotiations hardly suggested that there was any basis for serious discussions. Lebrun was interested in ascertaining Austrian intentions, but made it clear that a breach between Austria and Prussia would be a necessary preliminary to any agreement, and that Austria could then seek compensation for the loss of the Austrian Netherlands in the conquest of Silesia.[113]

Grenville sent an instruction on the 9th that gave a clue as to his thinking at this point and suggested that there was no way forward while the French insisted on recognition. As so often, an instruction in one of the generally overlooked 'minor' diplomatic series can throw light on the general principles motivating policy. Referring to a note exchanged between Lebrun and the Spanish *chargé d'affaires* at Paris, Grenville informed Ostervald at Lisbon that, if authorised, this meant that Spain was the first to recognise the Executive Council and to apply to it on behalf of Louis XVI and in favour of good relations, adding: 'The contemptuous manner in which this overture was received by the National Convention sufficiently proves how little a conduct of this nature was calculated even to answer the object of present security.' Grenville sought an Anglo-Portuguese concert to obtain an explanation from Spain and the arming of Portugal, whose neutrality, he warned, would not be respected by France, a claim that Kersaint's speech to the

---

[112] Lebrun to Chauvelin, 8 Jan. 1793, AE CP Ang. 584 fols. 77–9; Ehrman, *Pitt* II, 249; Murley, 'Anglo-French War', pp. 410–11.
[113] Lebrun to Chauvelin, 10 Jan. 1793, AE CP Ang. 584 fol. 92; Grosjean, 'Relations', 39–40.

Convention on 3 January justified. In response to the earlier Portuguese argument that they were not affected by or guarantors of the state of Scheldt, Grenville argued that

there are many circumstances independent of the desire for opening the Scheldt which are considered by His Majesty as calling for vigorous and decisive measures on his part... this act is considered by the King as affording one instance only of the general system adopted by the present rulers in France for overturning all existing governments, for carrying their principles into all the different countries of Europe, and for extending their own dominion by acquisitions of the utmost value and importance.

The recent Russian overtures and the current situation of Austria and Prussia were seen as giving grounds for 'a concert of measures' involving the three powers and Britain. In light of recent discussions in the National Convention, Grenville thought that his return of Chauvelin's note as inadmissible, because the latter assumed the character of Minister Plenipotentiary, might be followed 'by immediate hostilities on the part of France'. This, Grenville argued, should lead Portugal to take a different role than if war began only on account of the Scheldt dispute. Thus, in place of the interest in mediation expressed in the instructions of 31 December, there was now a more immediate stress on the threat of war. Grenville sought Portuguese concurrence 'in a general system... between the leading powers of Europe for their common interest and security', but it was clear from his instructions that this was to be aimed explicitly against France.[114] It was also clear that the precise steps by which Britain and France moved towards war would be of importance not only for the domestic political situation, but also because of the impact on Britain's allies.

Meanwhile, the French continued to seek discussions with the British government. Chauvelin's request on 9 January for a meeting with Grenville and his subsequent threat in reply to Grenville's negative answer on the 11th, that the Eden Treaty would be revoked if he did not obtain satisfaction within three days, were both without effect: the first was received with the statement that, although the British government was prepared to receive unofficial communications from the Republic via Chauvelin, French answers to British complaints already made were a prior condition of 'any new explanations'; the second was returned without comment on the 12th.[115] In accordance with Lebrun's instructions of the 8th, Chauvelin sought a meeting with Grenville to explain the situation, and this took place on the 13th, though on an unofficial footing,

---

[114] Grenville to Ostervald, 9 Jan. 1793, PRO FO 63/16.
[115] Chauvelin to Lebrun, 13 Jan. 1793, AE CP Ang. 584 fols. 123–4; Murley, 'Anglo-French War', pp. 427–8.

a defeat for French insistence on recognition. Chauvelin made it clear that poor communications were playing a major role in the crisis:

M. Chauvelin, as soon as he came into my room, began by stating that he was desirous of explaining, that all his steps subsequent to the date of my letter of the 31st ult had been taken in consequence of particular instructions from the Conseil Executif, given before they had received that letter. That they had seen in that letter one thing which had been satisfactory to them, notwithstanding the other things of which they might complain. This was the assurance which enabled them to reject the idea entertained by some persons in France of its being the intention of the government here to declare war at all events. Under this assurance they had authorised him to give to their answer a form which was not liable to the exceptions which had before been taken. He then gave me the dispatch from M. Lebrun.

Chauvelin also said 'that one of the difficulties of the present situation of the two countries was the want of a proper channel of communication. That he himself, from having no access to the king's ministers was frequently unable to give accounts of their real views and intentions.' Chauvelin complained of the manner in which he was treated in the British press; and asked crucially if he could see Grenville often 'sous le même forme'. He did not ask for permission to present his credentials. Grenville listened in silence, then stated that the seriousness of the issue meant that he could not answer at once, and the two men, their final meeting having drawn to an uneventful close, parted.[116]

On the same day, Miles saw Pitt. He had been sent a statement for the minister by Lebrun, as well as a letter from Maret, now Lebrun's deputy in Paris, offering to moderate French policy over the Scheldt and 19 November decrees, albeit in a vague fashion, and one at variance with the stand taken by the Executive Council. Though 'at a loss to imagine how a paper which you term an official dispatch can have been addressed to you', Pitt had 'no objection to seeing any information respecting the sentiments of persons in France', but he warned Miles that he would be unable to discuss the contents with him. Miles was optimistic about the French wish to negotiate and thought an honourable peace a prospect, but, after what, he claimed, was an initially welcoming response by Pitt, he found the minister hostile, a change Miles attributed to Burke's attendance at the Cabinet that day. According to Miles, Pitt then banned him from corresponding with the Executive Council, and thus closed a potentially crucial channel for negotiations.[117]

---

[116] Minutes of a Conference with M. Chauvelin, 13 Jan. 1793, BL Add. 34447 fols. 25–6; Chauvelin to Lebrun, 13 Jan. 1793, AE CP 584 fols. 125–6.
[117] Pitt to Miles, 13 Jan. 1793, PRO 30/8/102 fol. 190; Miles to Pitt, 13 Jan. 1793, *Correspondence of Miles* II, 40–3; Murley, 'Anglo-French War', p. 439; Evans, 'Miles', 204–5.

Grenville certainly thought the approach via Miles unsatisfactory and his expertise and scepticism may have had considerable influence on Pitt. On the 15th Keith, then in London, noted the report that the French had 'within these few days, lowered their tone considerably',[118] but that day Grenville sent Auckland a private letter in which he revealed clearly that the British government was unwilling 'to exclude all measures to be taken on the general view of affairs, and for the object of restraining the progress of French arms and French principles, even though we should not be the immediate objects of attack', and that satisfactory French assurances would not be sufficient. Britain required 'better security', which could only come from a guarantee by the major continental powers, as part of a peace settlement, on terms that it was readily apparent that the Republic would not accept. Grenville wrote:

the Republic ought to convince herself of the impossibility of our acquiescing in all that has happened, with no better security against its recurring than a tacit disavowal or even an express assurance. By the very messenger which brought Chauvelin's last humble paper, a sort of confidential dispatch was sent to be communicated to us through a private agent [Miles]. We disliked the mode of intercourse and have stopped it for the future. But it gave us then the previous knowledge of the substance and tone of Chauvelin's communication – and in this ... dispatch ... it is expressly said that if England perseveres in expecting too much from France the latter will attack her where she is vulnerable namely in Holland ... the danger to which she [United Provinces] would inevitably be exposed from smothering again, without extinguishing, the fire which had so nearly consumed all the countries in Europe, if a barrier had not been found here to its progress.

If we were to desist now without providing some effectual security for the future I would not answer for raising again here the same spirit which has enabled us to act so effectually ... my personal and sincere abhorrence of war where it can be avoided – But I am satisfied that nothing but vigorous and extensive and systematic measures can save us now.

That was the British response to the French approaches of the 13th. Grenville sought security, a security to be obtained from the collapse of France or the creation of a strong barrier against her, not one gained from negotiations with her. Peace or war with France was in some respects less important than 'effectual security for the future', and the last could not be gained from the Republic, for it was distrusted.[119] The abrupt and declamatory style of French policy in November 1792 had had a major effect: the Republic was seen as unpredictable and inexorable, and its claim to interpret treaties itself, in the light of universal principles that it alone declared and interpreted, aroused an outrage on Grenville's part

[118] Keith to Straton, 15 Jan. 1793, Ipswich HA 239/2/336.
[119] Grenville to Auckland, 15 Jan. 1793, BL Add. 34447 fols. 37–8, 58921 fols. 55–7.

comparable to that which others felt from the trial of Louis XVI. If there was peace it would have to be, as Fife pointed out, 'an armed one',[120] an expensive option that invited domestic political criticism from a number of directions, and if Britain remained neutral her government would have to watch, without being able to influence, the struggle on the Continent and the subsequent negotiations. That had been the policy of the previous summer, but French successes, combined with the Scheldt, 19 November and 15 December decrees, now made such inaction very dangerous, for it was clear that the entire map of western Europe might be redrawn.

And yet, not having declared war on France when she proclaimed the Scheldt open, there was no obvious reason for Britain to do so in mid-January. The need to win as much political support as possible, both in Britain and among her potential allies, made this factor of some consequence. Far from taking new provocative steps, the French approach via Miles had been conciliatory in intention. George Rose commented on the 15th, 'the concessions they are making are convincing proofs they *now* wish to avoid a rupture with us'; a conclusion supported by both Auckland and Keith, though neither thought that the French would be able to offer satisfactory terms.[121] The British response was negative. Anger with the fashion in which the French conducted negotiations, the tone and style of their diplomacy, the contradictory attitude of their different agents and the Republic's unpredictability, combined with the sense that discussions had been tried without success, with the strength of loyalism and government finances and the feeling that war could and increasingly should be waged, to produce a negative response to Chauvelin, while the other approaches were ignored.

In a letter dated 17 January 1793 and 'L'an 2ᵉᵐᵉ de la Republique française', Chauvelin had sought an interview with Grenville, and had asked whether George III would receive his credentials, because he feared that he would otherwise have to leave under the Alien Act.[122] The following day, Grenville clarified the situation by replying to the paper Chauvelin had left on 13 January. He pronounced it unsatisfactory, because the Republic had not renounced her offensive claims of the previous November, specifically the opening of the Scheldt. Grenville argued that offering to negotiate this once Belgium was independent was unsatisfactory, and he was similarly dissatisfied with the idea that only

---

[120] Fife to William Rose, 16 Jan. 1793, Aberdeen UL Tayler papers 2226/131/925.
[121] Rose to Auckland, 15 Jan. 1793, BL Add. 34447 fol. 64; Keith to Straton, 18 Jan., Auckland to Straton, 23 Jan. 1793, Ipswich HA 239/2/337, 289; Hatsell to Hey, 18 Jan. 1793, Exeter, Devon CRO 63/2/11/1/54.
[122] Chauvelin to Grenville, 17 Jan. 1793, BL Add. 34447 fols. 98–9.

then should French troops be withdrawn. The French threat to see British preparations as a possible cause of war was declared unacceptable and Chauvelin was informed that they would be continued in order to preserve the security, tranquillity and rights of Britain and her allies, and to create a barrier to ambitious views that threatened the rest of Europe, and that were made more dangerous by the propagation of principles that threatened the destruction of all social order.[123]

The Republic was therefore expected to renounce its November decrees, to evacuate the Austrian Netherlands, and to accept that Britain would remain armed. These were unrealistic assumptions; but in returning to his message of 31 December, and not seeking to find common ground with Chauvelin's note of 13 January and the approach via Miles, Grenville was reflecting not only the domestic British situation and British ministerial assumptions, but also the fact that discussions and moves since November had given ground for no realistic hopes about the prospect of a secure and lasting peace. The French had made efforts to find some common ground, but they were muddled, equivocal and changeable. That would have mattered less had the general situation been free from immediate threats, but Britain's principal ally was faced by Dumouriez's army, the campaigning season was nearing and the British ministry had to decide how best to negotiate with Austria, Prussia and Russia. Britain was arming fast, which Chauvelin reported proved that she sought war.[124]

On Sunday 20 January 1793 Pitt saw Loughborough, part of the process by which the ministry was seeking to recruit leading Whigs or at least ensure that they did not attack government policy, a process whose success Dundas had reported on to George III that morning.[125] The most prominent catch was the Prince of Wales. His acceptance of colonelcy of a dragoon regiment was seen as a clear statement of support for government policy.[126] Returning to Malmesbury's house on the 20th, Loughborough told him that 'war was a *decided measure*; that Pitt saw it was inevitable, and that the sooner it was begun the better'. The favourable state of public opinion, the prospect of gaining the French West Indies, the buoyancy of public revenue, the greater forwardness of British, compared to French, naval preparations, the favourable dispositions of the Dutch, Russia and Spain were all mentioned, though this

---

[123] Grenville to Chauvelin, 18 Jan. 1793, BL Add. 34447 fols. 110–12.
[124] Chauvelin to Lebrun, 15, 23 Jan. 1793, AE CP Ang. 586 fols. 147, 223.
[125] Dundas to George III, 20 Jan. 1793, Aspinall, *George III* no. 827. For the determination of one Northite MP to abandon 'those who are deeply pledged to confusion', H. G. H. Jolliffe, *The Jolliffes of Staffordshire* (1892), p. 65.
[126] Aspinall, *The Correspondence of George Prince of Wales 1770–1812*, II (1964), pp. 329–34; *Times* 28, 30 Jan. 1793.

list may have owed something to Pitt's desire to persuade Loughborough to become Lord Chancellor. Three days later, Malmesbury wrote to Pitt, promising his support for ministerial policy.[127] Unlike in 1775, 1754–6 and 1739, the Opposition was disintegrating as the government moved towards war.

At the same time there was no trust in French intentions. Burges warned Auckland on the 22nd that Dumouriez planned to have an army of 800,000 men and that there was 'every reason to believe that a serious attack will be made upon Holland'. Returning from a reconnaissance mission, Captain Kempthorne reported that day that French troops were moving forward towards Antwerp and that the Batavian Legion of Dutch Patriots were preparing to invade the United Provinces. In fact, the projected invasion had been postponed four days earlier.[128] Any attack could only be deterred either by the arrival of Austrian and Prussian armies on the Rhine, and, not least for this reason, those powers could not be excluded from British calculations; or, Grenville suggested, by 'raising difficulties' in the Austrian Netherlands. Far from being averse to the idea of encouraging insurrection, Grenville wrote privately to Auckland on the 22nd to express the hope that it would be possible 'to bring the Austrian government and the Vandernootists to a complete good understanding, and to co-operation in a plan for expelling the French', which he felt Britain should facilitate. Reports of the growing unpopularity of the French in Belgium encouraged belief in the possibility of an insurrection.[129]

The news of the sentence of death on Louis XVI being pronounced by the National Convention on 17 January reached London on the 21st. It was clear that this would lead to a crisis in relations. Chauvelin, who reported that newspaper attacks in pro-government papers, especially the 'infamous' *Sun*, amounted to incitements to his assassination, paid his bills and packed. He was sent instructions by Lebrun on the 22nd to leave Britain without delay, but, before these arrived, he had anyway been ordered to go by the British government.[130]

Louis XVI was executed in what is now the Place de la Concorde on the morning of Monday the 21st. News of it was one of the few messages that crossed the Channel swiftly that turbulent winter. It arrived in London on the 23rd. Chauvelin had already written that day that the

---

[127] *Malmesbury Corresp.*, II, 501–2; Malmesbury to Pitt, 23 Jan. 1793, PRO 30/8/155 fol. 95; Murley, 'Anglo-French War', p. 450.
[128] Burges to Auckland, 22 Jan., Kempthorne to Aust, 22 Jan. 1793, BL Add. 34447 fols. 185, 198; Murley, 'Anglo-French War', p. 457.
[129] Grenville to Auckland, 22 Jan. 1793, BL Add. 34447 fol. 186, 58921 fols. 73–4.
[130] Chauvelin to Lebrun, 19 Jan., Lebrun to Chauvelin, 22 Jan. 1793, AE CP Ang. 586 fols. 187, 208; Aust to Auckland, 22 Jan. 1793, BL Add. 34447 fol. 197.

government wanted war and would use the execution to stir up public support. Before the news arrived, George III told Pitt that, whenever it did, he would call a Privy Council to order Chauvelin's expulsion. When it came, the royal audience in the Drawing Room was cancelled, as was a planned visit by George III to the theatre, while the play at the Haymarket came to an abrupt end when the audience shouted out 'No Farce, No Farce' and left. Acts of mourning were a public criticism of the execution of Louis XVI, and thus of the most significant and symbolic step taken by the revolutionary government. A week later, Samuel Horsley, Bishop of St David's and a supporter of Pitt, gave the annual Martyrdom Day sermon in Westminster Abbey before the House of Lords. Marking thus the anniversary of the execution of Charles I, the individual elevated most closely to sainthood by the Church of England, Horsley delivered a powerful attack on political speculation and revolutionary theory. He dismissed the notion of an original compact arising from the abandonment of a state of nature, and instead stressed royal authority. According to Horsley, the existing constitution was the product and safeguard of a 'legal contract' between Crown and people, while the obedience of the latter was a religious duty. Horsley's forceful peroration linked the two executions:

This foul murder, and these barbarities, have filled the measure of the guilt and infamy of France. O my Country! Read the horror of thy own deed in this recent heightened imitation! Lament and weep, that this black French treason should have found its example, in the crime of thy unnatural sons!

The congregation rose to its feet in approval. The fate of religion and monarchy in Britain seemed clearly challenged by developments in France.[131]

The Privy Council met, with George III present, on 24 January and Chauvelin was ordered to leave by 1 February. This has been seen as amounting to a declaration of war,[132] though serious breaches in diplomatic relations had occurred over the previous century without the

---

[131] Grenville to George III, 23 Jan. 1793 11 a.m., C. R. Middleton, 'Some Additional Correspondence of King George III', *Notes and Queries*, June 1979, 221; Chauvelin to Lebrun, 23 Jan. 1793, AE CP Ang. 586 fol. 223; Grenville – George III corresp. on 24 Jan., Pitt to Grenville, 24 Jan. 1793, BL Add. 58857 fols. 80–5, 58906 fol. 149; Keith to Straton, 25 Jan. 1793, Ipswich HA 239/2/338; Hardman, *Louis XVI*, pp. 17, 121, 144, 188, 222, 226; S. Horsley, *Sermons*, edn H. Horsley (1816), III, 293–321; J. C. D. Clark, *English Society 1688–1832. Ideology, social structure and political practice during the ancien regime* (Cambridge, 1985), pp. 230–3; R. Hole, *Pulpits, Politics and Public Order in England 1760–1832* (Cambridge, 1989), pp. 164–5; F. C. Mather, *High Church Prophet. Bishop Samuel Horsley (1738–1806) and the Caroline Tradition in the Later Georgian Church* (Oxford, 1992), pp. 228–30.

[132] Grenville to Chauvelin, 24 Jan. 1793, BL Add. 34447 fol. 235; Murley, 'Anglo-French War', p. 453.

outbreak of war, for example between Britain and Russia (1719–30) and Britain and Sweden (1748–63). Nevertheless, in the context of Anglo-French relations in early 1793, with the fate of the United Provinces an immediate issue, and with French politicians vying to prove their revolutionary credentials in a bitter battle for power, such a breach was indeed akin to a declaration of war. When the expulsion was reported to the Convention on 30 January, Lebrun described the move as a declaration of war. On 24 January the British government decided to prepare more warships, while George III ordered the assembly of a force of 13,000 Hanoverians that was to serve in the Low Countries. Grenville repeated his interest in the idea of a Belgian rising, now seen as the best way to protect the Dutch.[133] Pro-government newspapers acted as if war had already been declared by and in response to the execution of Louis XVI. The *Times* announced on the 25th that the execution would 'invoke vengeance on his murderers. This is not the cause of monarchs only, it is the cause of every nation.' Rulers owed it 'to the happiness of their people to crush the savage regicides' and to combine in a 'coalition of all regular and well established governments and of every civilised people, against a system of anarchy'. The following day, the *Westminster Journal* was certain that the 'murder' of Louis XVI would 'be felt in the heart of every Englishman' and that 'the approaching war with France will unquestionably be the most popular in which this country has ever been involved. We have justice and expediency on our side, and the call of Europe to step forward and check the career of blood hounds ... The country is infinitely indebted for its present safety to Mr. Burke.' Miles, however, pressed Long with the argument 'that the massacre of Louis XVI could never be a pretext for hostilities after the repeated assurances given by Mr. Pitt that he would never interfere with the interior government of France'.

On 24 January 1793 Grenville wrote to Auckland, expressing his conviction that war would break out and drawing attention to his feeling that military preparations had a dynamic of their own:

The business is now brought to its crisis and I imagine that the next dispatch to you, or the next but one will announce the commencement of hostilities. Probably the French will commence them, but if not, after all lines of communication are interrupted, of necessity, and after all hope of satisfactory explanation is over I do not see how we can remain any longer les bras croisés with a great force ready for action; that force avowedly meant against France, and the language and conduct of that power giving every day more instead of less ground of offence to us and all the world.

---

[133]   George III to Pitt, 24 Jan. 1793, Aspinall, *George III* no. 829; Grenville to Auckland, 24 Jan. 1793, BL Add. 34447 fols. 232, 237.

This last horrible act of unnecessary cruelty and outrage on all men's feelings will have its effect.[134]

Next day, the Cabinet resolved on a reply to the Spanish proposal for establishing a close union, made on 1 January to Francis Jackson, Minister Plenipotentiary in Spain. St Helens was to be authorised to discuss 'a permanent system of alliance', but, in the meantime, a preliminary agreement should be proposed, including 'a concert to prevent the progress of French arms and principles' in which each power agreed to come to the assistance of the other if this led to war.[135] The idea was vague, it was not clear what opposing French principles entailed, but this did not matter greatly, as the British government was clearly preparing for war, a conflict in which foreign assistance would be vital and it was necessary to ensure that Spain remained opposed to France. War was widely seen as inevitable.[136]

And yet, war had been declared by neither side, and hostilities had not begun, either along the Dutch frontier or on the high seas. The British government was resolved to make no last diplomatic effort, and instead to prepare for war, but it did not declare it. The response from the continental powers to the British approaches of 13 November and 28–29 December had been discouraging. On 12 January Stadion and Jacobi, the Austrian and Prussian envoys in London, jointly declared to Grenville that they sought the reintroduction of monarchy in France and indemnification for themselves. The former would make any attempt by the neutral powers to mediate hopeless, the latter threatened to compromise the projected coalition against France with extraneous territorial interests and would make any alliance with Britain difficult to negotiate. Grenville made it clear to the envoys that the British government would not be a party to any indemnification at the expense of 'an unoffending' power,[137] which was most likely to be Poland. The Russian government informed Whitworth that they would not negotiate with the Republic and that they expected Britain to declare war.[138] Austria sought support for the Bavarian Exchange scheme, Prussia and Russia wanted a fresh partition of Poland. Russian troops had moved into Poland on the night of 18 May 1792; the Prussians followed in mid-January 1793, and on 23 January both powers signed the Second Partition treaty. Prussia received Danzig, Thorn, and 'Great Poland', the region around Poznan. Russia gained the western Ukraine and

---

[134] *Correspondence of Miles*, II, 52; Grenville to Auckland, 24 Jan. 1793, BL Add. 58921 fol. 75.   [135] Cabinet Minute, 25 Jan. 1793, BL Add. 58857 fol. 86.
[136] Keith to Straton, 1 Feb. 1793, Ipswich HA 239/2/339.
[137] Grenville minute, 12 Jan. 1793, PRO FO 64/27.
[138] Whitworth to Grenville, 11 Jan. 1793, PRO FO 65/24.

Belorussia. For the first time, Austria and Russia had a common frontier, while Poland lost hers with the Turkish Empire. Austria received nothing, bar the promise of support for the Bavarian Exchange.[139]

These developments were unwelcome to the British government for both prudential and ideological reasons. Grenville told Jacobi and Stadion 'in the most unequivocal terms' that Britain was against another partition, but it was clear that George III would not take 'any active measures' accordingly.[140] Resources devoted to subjugating Poland could not be used against France; the Bavarian Exchange would make the future security of Belgium an even greater problem; and a ministry that sought stability in international relations and believed that it was an ethical as well as a prudential goal, could not be expected to welcome the reorganisation of eastern Europe by rulers who had already shown themselves to be aggressive, unpredictable and heedless of British views. British envoys in central and eastern Europe were especially concerned about the changes. Morton Eden, who had little confidence anyway in the Prussian government, was provoked by the Second Partition to 'regret that the cause of the French is so very bad and wicked as to force us into the war'. William Gardiner, who had succeeded Hailes at Warsaw, was opposed to the partition and felt that the Scheldt issue was not being pushed sufficiently hard by the French to justify war. It was unlikely, after the Ochakov affair, that Britain would have taken any major diplomatic role in inspiring opposition to a second partition, but the prospect of her becoming involved in war with France made that even more improbable. In a similar fashion, it suited Catherine II for the two powers to go to war because she had been concerned about the possibility that the French Mediterranean fleet would join with the Turks in attacking Russia in the Black Sea. Eden was worried about the likely political impact of the partition in Britain, and, indeed, it was treated at the meeting between Pitt and Loughborough on 20 January 1793 as unjust and ill-timed. Though the issue of Fox's attitude towards 'his friend', Catherine, was raised, the partition served to embarrass government, not opposition. Benjamin Vaughan, MP for Calne, published a series of articles in the *Morning Chronicle* criticising the moves of Austria, Prussia and Russia against France and Poland and these were subsequently published as *Letters on the Subject of the Concert of Princes and the Dismemberment of Poland and France*. Vaughan, however, was scarcely an ordinary MP. A follower of Lansdowne, he fled to France in

---

[139] Straton to Grenville, 8, 20 Jan. 1793, PRO FO 7/32; Lord, *Second Partition*; Lukowski, *Liberty's Folly*, pp. 253–5; A. Zamoyski, *The Last King of Poland* (1992), pp. 389–93.

[140] Grenville to Morton Eden, 4 Feb. 1793, BL Add. 34447 fol. 480.

1794 when linked with revolutionary circles. Catherine herself had argued in 1787 that George III and the Prussians were hypocritical in claiming to defend German liberties with the *Fürstenbund*, but then suppressing 'the liberty of Holland' in 1787.[141]

Critics of British participation in the French Revolutionary War were to make much of the contrast between the government's acceptance of the Second Partition and its willingness to fight France, but in late January 1793 this was not a crucial issue. Grenville's instructions to Murray encapsulated government attitudes, and in them the ministry was expressing the views of the political nation more accurately and successfully than at the time of the Ochakov crisis. Prussian intervention in Poland was condemned, but the government would do nothing to oppose it.[142] Poland was far distant, Britain had no alliance with her, Prussian and Austrian support were crucially required for the defence of the United Provinces, and the doubts about policy voiced by Eden were not shared by ministers more directly involved in the crisis. The previous November Eden had suggested that it was 'altogether impracticable ... to reduce France'.[143] He had glanced into the abyss, there saw death, and not felt at peace. Two months later, the chance of victory and the means to obtain it seemed little clearer, but that was not the issue. War itself seemed inevitable and necessary, even if the means by which it was to bring victory, and the definition of victory itself (other than in the vague, albeit urgent, terms of security), were obscure.

The French were to make a last effort to keep the peace, though it was not fully authorised, and the Convention was not informed.[144] When Chauvelin was recalled on 22 January, he was informed that Maret would be sent to London to negotiate with Pitt. The following day Dumouriez wrote to Auckland from Paris suggesting a conference of the two of them, and possibly Van de Spiegel as well, on the Dutch frontier, that could be useful for the three powers, 'à L'Humanité', and possibly for the whole of Europe.[145] Maulde, carrying this letter, set off from Paris for The Hague on the 24th, Dumouriez left for Belgium the next day, and Maret set off for London: 'When he got to Dover [29th], he published with

[141] Eden to Auckland, 23 Nov. 1792, 22 Jan. 1793, Straton to Auckland, 22 Jan., Gardiner to Auckland, 2 Feb. 1793, BL Add. 58920 fol. 193, 34447 fols. 209, 206, 413–14; *Malmesbury*, II, 502; Hatsell to Ley, 6 Aug. 1792, Devon RO. 63/2/11/1/47; Marcum, 'Vorontsov', p. 76.
[142] Grenville to Murray, 20 Jan., 6 Feb. 1793, PRO FO 29/1; Grenville to Spencer, 27 Mar. 1792, BL Add. 34441 fol. 508.
[143] Eden to Auckland, 23 Nov. 1792, BL Add. 58920 fol. 193.
[144] Murley, 'Anglo-French War', pp. 458–63; Evans, 'Miles', 206. For the reports of the Spanish representative in Paris, J. Chaumé, *Les Relations Diplomatiques entre L'Espagne et La France de Varennes à la mort de Louis XVI* (Bordeaux, 1957), p. 180 fn. 15.
[145] Dumouriez to Auckland, 23 Jan. 1793, BL Add. 34447 fol. 230.

great industry and ostentation that he had letters of credence from the Executive Council, and authority to propose terms of pacification.'[146] Maret did not know that Chauvelin had been expelled, but when he discovered this at Dover he decided to press on to London and to await fresh instructions there.[147] Chauvelin had been instructed to tell the British government about the mission, but he had not done so. Unsure now about what he should do, Maret simply informed the Foreign Office that he was 'charged...with the care of the French archives and correspondence', the mission outlined in the more restrictive of his two letters of introduction.[148]

Maret saw Miles who had been warned by Pitt not to act as a go-between. Nevertheless, on 31 January 1793 Maret claimed that Pitt and Grenville were willing to see him. He added that the execution of Louis XVI had led to the success of the government's anti-French hate campaign, that the 'populace' sought and demanded war, that for fear of attack he could not leave the embassy, but that the City merchants and the gentry wanted peace. As so often with French envoys, Maret discerned a government divided into two parties, the party 'purely royalist', which sought a war of counter-revolution and did not think of anything else, and a group led by Pitt that feared the financial consequences. The *Times* of 19 November 1792 had indeed printed the rumour that Pitt would resign because his views on relations with France were irreconcilable with those of George III. In 1808 Miles, by then even less reliable than hitherto, was to claim that Pitt was ordered by the King to fight or to resign and that the government had for long determined on war with France at all events. Maret also argued in his report of 31 January 1793, that Pitt knew that he lacked the knowledge necessary to be a war minister, that the death of Louis XVI had hit his influence in the Council, that the current armaments were less than those of 1790 and 1791, that the government press was not hostile to his mission, that the ministry was disposed to listen to Maret and to receive Dumouriez' approach, and that he, Maret, sought either his recall or instructions.[149]

Maret was certainly misled by Miles. The government ordered him to leave Britain at once on 4 February, by which date he had not received fresh instructions. Grenville explained the expulsion by reference to the French embargo on British shipping, and to the speculations in public

[146] Burges to Auckland, 2 Feb. 1793, BL Add. 34447 fol. 402.
[147] Maret to Lebrun, 29 Jan. 1793, AE CP Ang. 586 fol. 298.
[148] Burges to Auckland, 2 Feb. 1793, BL Add. 34447 fol. 402; Evans, 'Miles', 206–7.
[149] *Correspondence of Miles* II, 52; Maret to Lebrun, 31 Jan. 1793, AE CP Ang. 586 fols. 344–7; W. A. Miles, *The Conduct of France towards Great Britain Examined* (1793), pp. 107–14, and *A Letter to His Royal Highness the Prince of Wales* (1808), pp. 84, 132; Evans, 'Miles', 210–11.

funds caused by rumours arising from Maret's presence.[150] It was not until two days later that the ministry learnt of what was, according to the less than reliable Miles, Maret's offer, namely the return of French conquests and negotiations with Dumouriez.[151] There had been no opportunity to find out exactly what he was willing to propose: no informal negotiations had taken place and, as Pitt told the Commons on 12 February, Maret had not submitted any proposals.

Meanwhile, on the evening of 27 January, Maulde had given Auckland Dumouriez' letter and had assured the envoy that the general wanted to make peace. Auckland was sceptical – 'I have too little faith in his powers, or in my own talents, to have any sanguine hope of such results, even if the conference should not be obviated by existing circumstances'[152] – but willing to negotiate. Delayed by poor weather in the North Sea, his letters did not reach London until 2 February. Burges was sceptical and certain that war would break out. He argued that Dumouriez, like Maret, had left Paris before he could know that Chauvelin had been expelled:

The knowledge of this latter circumstance must have convinced the French rulers, that the flimsy kind of negotiation they had been carrying on with us was at an end; and it is therefore reasonable to suppose, that the whole arrangement they had made with Dumouriez, for the purpose of bringing you to a conference, and by that means gaining time for the accomplishment of their design upon Holland, must have been changed.

Though his interpretation of French intentions is open to question, Burges was correct in his assumption that Chauvelin's expulsion had changed matters. He added the news that France had on 29 January declared an embargo on British, Dutch, Prussian and Russian shipping, with the exception of packet-boats, and he argued that last-minute negotiations could not serve any purpose:

All this forms, to my judgement, a mass of evidence conclusive on the question. And it in some measure consoles me for the delay, which must inevitably take place in your receiving the instructions you require on this curious request of M. Dumouriez; as I think it now evidently appears, that a conference with him could have been asked solely with a view of gaining time and of amusing us while he forwarded his preparations for an attack upon Holland.[153]

Nevertheless, it was decided to respond to Dumouriez' approach and to send Auckland instructions accordingly. It was in part a case of 'amusing'

[150] Grenville to Maret, 4 Feb. 1793, PRO FO 27/41; Grenville to Auckland, 4 Feb. 1793, BL Add. 34447 fol. 428.
[151] Miles to Pitt, 6 Feb. 1793, PRO 30/8/159; Miles Corresp., II, 55–63; Evans, 'Miles', 207–8.   [152] Auckland to Grenville, 29 Jan. 1793, BL Add. 34447 fol. 333.
[153] Burges to Auckland, 2 Feb. 1793, BL Add. 34447 fols. 402–4.

the general in order to delay an attack on the United Provinces, a measure sought by Auckland and Van de Spiegel. The Dutch were not in a position to withstand a major attack, and no other allied forces were yet able to offer much help. The British were unable to respond to Nagel's demand for the immediate dispatch of troops. However, in addition, Britain, which was not yet at war with France, was being given a chance of negotiating informally with a senior French official who was not demanding recognition of the Republic.

On 4 February 1793 Auckland was sent fresh instructions. Events elsewhere had already made them redundant, but they are more than a footnote on history, for they cast light on British government thinking at this crucial moment, offering another snapshot, like the instructions of 29 December, and thus providing valuable evidence in the controversy as to British intentions and, specifically, whether the ministry sought war. Grenville argued that it was unclear that any French government, however pacific, could answer for the future conduct of the state, and that, in all French explanations, there had 'appeared no disposition to give any real satisfaction', but, in light of the British wish to obtain her objectives without war, Auckland was instructed to meet Dumouriez. Such a meeting would avoid the problems of recognising the Republic, while the general was sufficiently important to give rise to hopes that he might be able to give effect to any engagements that he might contact, which was certainly not true of Chauvelin, Maret and the other agents who had been sent to London. Auckland was to say that no negotiation could take place until the embargo on British shipping ceased, that it was best to have just one channel for negotiations, that he was authorised to hear any suggestions Dumouriez might have and that the papers which had passed between Grenville and Chauvelin were to be the basis of the British position. The end of the war was seen as the best security against the renewal of unwelcome French moves. France must disavow her offensive decrees and settle with Austria, Prussia and Sardinia on such terms as they might reasonably expect. As long as French conduct was acceptable, Britain would not begin hostilities while negotiations lasted, but she would continue her preparations.[154]

On the next day, Grenville wrote to Morton Eden, who had been appointed to Vienna in order to seek better relations there. The Austrians were to be told of Dumouriez' approach and to be given assurances that the British government wanted it to lead to a general peace on terms Austria might expect. If France refused terms an alliance against her was to be proposed and Britain might be able to support indemnification for

[154] Grenville to Auckland, 4 Feb. 1793, BL Add. 34447 fols. 426–37.

Austria and Prussia. A similar dispatch was sent to Murray next day.[155] Thus, the programme of 28–29 December was to be revived: relations with France were to be placed in, and secured by, the context of a more general policy that centred on winning the support of the major continental powers. The isolationism that had characterised British policy in the last months of peace and in the first months of the French Revolutionary War was to give way to a new system. Yet, this system was understandably less than fully thought out. It was already clear that Austria, Prussia and Russia had interests of their own to pursue. It was also unlikely that the total victory required to bring France to the *status quo ante revolution* terms outlined by the British would be secured readily. Failing that, it was not obvious how Britain was to ensure that her putative allies served her interests.

On 5 February 1793, Grenville sent Auckland a private letter that threw considerable light on his instructions of the 4th. He was pessimistic about the possibility that Dumouriez' approach would lead to anything, but, nevertheless, felt it necessary to respond 'for the advantage which a week or two may give to Holland'. As throughout much of the first decade of the Pitt ministry, the key to British policy was to be sought in the United Provinces, as, more particularly, since mid-November 1792, the key was the immediate needs of the defence of the Dutch. Grenville suggested that the approach might have been designed to embarrass the British government domestically, a suggestion that was evidence of crisis paranoia, the knowledge of French attempts to inspire discontent and sensitivity to the domestic situation. The problems posed by revolutionary diplomacy were revealed in Grenville's comment that,

the facility of assertion which prevails among all those now employed by France gives them much advantage in all *verbal* communications, especially with our extreme delicacy in not disclosing ... things which we have engaged to keep secret ... a man ought to have Parliament quite present to his mind to feel the full force of all that might be said on this subject.[156]

The ministry's concern about parliamentary attitudes had been revealed a month earlier when an unprecedented idea had been advanced by Grenville: 'laying before a Secret Committee of the two Houses (very small in number) some particulars of the designs which have been in agitation'. Auckland was asked accordingly to provide material and told that it would 'be very useful in the view of embarking the nation heartily in the support of a war, if unavoidable'.[157]

---

[155] Grenville to Eden, 5 Feb. 1793, PRO FO 64/27, BL Add. 34447 fols. 474–80; Grenville to Murray, 6 Feb. 1793, PRO FO 29/1.
[156] Grenville to Auckland, 5 Feb. 1793, BL Add. 34447 fol. 483, 58921 fols. 87–8.
[157] Grenville to Auckland, 1 Jan. 1793, BL Add. 58921 fol. 38.

It is unlikely that the British reply to Dumouriez' approach could have led to anything, bar abortive discussions. The political atmosphere in Paris was not conducive to an abandonment of ideals, statements and conquests. Though some politicians were worried about the prospect of expanding the war, there is no sign that they were strong enough to force through the concessions demanded by Britain. Influential speakers in the Convention were convinced that Britain was weak, her government without principles in international affairs, that the people, especially in Ireland and Scotland, would support France and the British war-effort would collapse under the weight of internal divisions and strain, as much as thanks to French efforts. Moderates and moderation were at bay in Paris. Secret negotiations were meaningless without the political will and ability to win support for any agreement, and, under pressure from the Jacobins, their rivals were in no position to run the risk of being accused of making concessions, let alone actually to make any.[158]

The expelled Chauvelin was received in this atmosphere on 29 January and the response was furious, though certain ministers would have preferred to preserve peace. The Eden Treaty was annulled, an embargo was placed on British shipping and it was provisionally agreed that Dumouriez would be ordered to attack the Dutch. On the 31st the Executive Council decided that this attack would be mounted and the Patriots were told to incite risings. The Maret and Dumouriez peace initiatives were therefore superseded: all these decisions were taken before they could report to Paris. Indeed, fearing the likely response were they to become public, the French ministers took care to keep them a secret. The process culminated on 1 February when the National Convention decided unanimously to declare war on Britain and the United Provinces. George III was accused of supporting the Austro-Prussian alliance in its enmity towards France. Making new use of the convention that war was declared on sovereigns, and, thus, that aggression was not being committed against other peoples, the Convention also agreed to a motion that the British people were to be asked to rise by an address composed by, among others, Tom Paine. The following day, Lebrun recalled Maret. He claimed that Chauvelin's expulsion, planned British military preparations and British steps against French shipping had left no doubt of British intentions. Lebrun argued further that, having tried unsuccessfully all means of conciliation with Britain, it was clear that Dumouriez would not succeed, and that only French military success would lead the British government to appreciate the justice of France's cause. Miles was to argue that had the French

[158] *AP* 56, 110–17, 57, 16–25, 58, 112–23.

government wanted peace, it would have awaited the result of the Maret mission.[159] The news of the Convention's declaration of war reached London on 9 February 1793. George III found the news

highly agreeable ... as the mode adopted seems well calculated to rouze such a spirit in this country that I trust will curb the insolence of those despots and be a means of restoring some degree of order to that unprincipled country, whose aim at present is to destroy the foundations of every civilized state.[160]

Dundas had already sent instructions to the Governor of St Helena to detain any French ship that might call there, and had persuaded Nagel to send similar orders to the Governor of Cape Town.[161] The world war that had begun was to place immense strains on British society and yet leave Britain as the most powerful state in the world.

The causes of the Anglo-French conflict touched off a major controversy and the issue has subsequently attracted a reasonable measure of historical attention. The controversy of the time was so acute because the issue was politically crucial. The war came at once to dominate British politics; indeed relations with France had played a crucial role in the crisis of the Whigs that had become so marked since 1791. This was a crisis of division, loss of direction, and uncertainty, that led those who were unhappy with either Fox's determination to maintain opposition to the government during the international crisis or his reluctance to condemn the direction of the Revolution to look increasingly to Pitt. Some were willing to join the government, more were ready to support it or at least not to oppose it, but, whatever the decisions of individuals, they helped to weaken and fragment the Whigs. There were other causes of the crisis. The failure of the Fox–North ministry, defeat in two successive general elections (1784, 1790), the prevailing success of the Pitt government, and the obvious absence of royal backing, had all caused disappointment and lowered morale in Whig ranks from 1784 on, and the deflation of hopes raised by George III's illness in 1788–9 was especially serious.[162] The war with Revolutionary France completed the

---

[159] Lebrun to Maret, 2 Feb. 1793, AE CP Ang. 586 fols. 378–9; Miles, *Conduct of France*, pp. 110–11. For continued interest in peace D. Williams, 'The Missions of David Williams and James Tilly Matthew to England, 1793', *English Historical Review*, 53 (1938), 651–8.

[160] Middleton, 'Additional Correspondence', *Notes and Queries* (1979), 221; George III to Grenville, 9 Feb. 1793, BL Add. 58857 fol. 87.

[161] Grenville to Auckland, 8 Feb. 1793, BL Add. 58921 fol. 97.

[162] L. G. Mitchell, *Fox and the Disintegration of the Whig Party*; I. R. Christie, 'Anatomy of Opposition', *Parliamentary History*, 9 (1990). E. A. Smith, *Lord Grey, 1764–1845* (Oxford, 1990) and J. Derry, *Charles, Earl Grey. Aristocratic Reformer* (Oxford, 1992) enable the crisis to be considered from the perspective of a rising Whig politician.

division in Whig ranks and the conflict's place in domestic British politics helped to make it contentious. There was controversy even before the news of the French declaration reached London. On 5 February 1793 the *Morning Chronicle* claimed that war threatened national prosperity and the consequent reduction of the National Debt:

We might, by an open and cordial conduct, have dictated almost any conditions to France; – we might have made this country the emporium of the world... it required only plain sense, candour and integrity, to have obtained it. But... we have suffered ourselves to be cajoled by a set of vehement and malignant spirits, who having rank prejudices to gratify or having tasted the fruits of former wars, pursued only the gratifications of their passions, and did not disdain the jesuitical plan of obtaining their purposes through popular delirium.

The article, anonymous in the fashion of the period, did offer one interesting suggestion. A reduction of the National Debt, it claimed, would give Britain such a pre-eminence over other nations that 'hardly any stroke of adverse fortune' could have affected it, an instance of the contemporary argument for the economic dominance of international relations. Nevertheless, the general feature of this, as of most other articles, was its unspecific nature, and its failure to allow for the ambiguous nature of developments, the problems of diplomacy and the halting progress of negotiations. This was also true of the bulk of the pamphlet debate which began rapidly. The barrister John Bowles rushed out his *Real Grounds of the Present War with France* (1793), an appeal for public support for the war. French gains were seen as a threat to a balance of power necessary for peace and tranquillity. Revolutionary principles, especially the decree of 19 November 1792, were presented as a threat to all international order. France had sought negotiations only in order to lull the British government and to make war unpopular. The defence of religion was seen as a crucial theme by many pro-government writers and was central to a large number of sermons. *The Letter of ... Fox to the Electors of Westminster Anatomized* (1793) saw the Christian religion and civilization as under threat. Revolutionary France was associated with a 'rage for war', and with a desire to interfere in the domestic affairs of other states.[163]

[163] Anon., *Dialogues on the Rights of Britons, between A Farmer, A Sailor, and A Manufacturer. Dialogue the Third* (1793), pp. 20–1. Scholarly discussion of the polemical debate in this period has concentrated on the response to the Revolution, rather than on the implications for British foreign policy and the moves that led to war. The literature is vast. Valuable recent works include G. Pendleton, 'The English Pamphlet Literature of the Age of the French Revolution *Anatomized*', *Eighteenth-Century Life*, 5 (1978), 29–37; J. E. Cookson, *The Friends of Peace: Anti-War Liberalism in England 1793–1815* (Cambridge, 1982); R. Hole, 'British Counter-Revolutionary Popular Propaganda in the 1790s', in C. Jones (ed.), *Britain and Revolutionary France: Conflict, Subversion and Propaganda* (Exeter, 1983), pp. 53–69;

These arguments were difficult to counter, not least because Foxite writers did not wish to, and certainly did not wish to be seen to, praise the Revolution. Indeed criticism of the government was crippled by the limited appeal of France, republicanism and atheism, as, earlier, Jacobite propaganda had been harmed by France, autocracy and Catholicism. Rather than defend France, it was necessary to criticise government policy and this was difficult to do in a fashion that had a popular resonance. On 23 November 1792 Fox had been sure that war could be avoided with honour, though he had referred to Pitt as 'a great bungler ... in these businesses'. Fox's *Letter ... to the ... Electors of ... Westminster*, written in January 1793, criticised the government for not negotiating seriously with France and argued that this course alone would provide public justification for war, as it would then be possible to establish how far the French were willing to satisfy the British. After war had broken out, Fox and Sheridan, on 12 February 1793, criticised the government for failing to negotiate seriously, while, that day, Stanhope and Lauderdale told the Lords that the expulsion of Chauvelin and Maret had helped to ensure war.[164]

This stress on an avowed negotiation was placed in a context of public politics by Fox in his *Letter ... to the ... Electors ....*. He argued that, although the right to declare war was a royal prerogative, the right to grant or to withhold the means to pay for it was a 'privilege of the people' through their parliamentary representatives. Furthermore, the people had to support the burden of the war. Therefore, Fox claimed, it was reasonable that they should be informed of the purposes of the struggle, so that, if dissatisfied, they could petition Parliament for a change in policy. Fox also focused on the hypocrisy of the government. Poland was to provide an obvious basis for such a charge, but Fox pointed out that Britain had had an envoy at Versailles when Corsica was 'enslaved', envoys at the courts of the partitioning powers at the time of the First Partition, and diplomatic representation at the courts of Algiers and Morocco, whose standards scarcely conformed to what was generally judged acceptable. Therefore it was wrong to have withdrawn Gower. This pragmatic argument was joined by another blunter one, namely that France could not be conquered.

M. Butler, *Burke, Paine, Godwin and the Revolution Controversy* (Cambridge, 1984); T. P. Schofield, 'Conservative political thought in Britain in response to the French Revolution', *Historical Journal*, 29 (1986), 601–22; G. Claeys, 'The French Revolution and British political thought', *History of Political Thought*, 11 (1990), 59–80. I am grateful to John Cookson for discussing the subject with me.
[164] Russell (ed.), *Fox*, II, 379–80. For Fox's views in this period, F. O'Gorman, *The Whig Party and the French Revolution* (1967), p. 118, Mitchell, *Fox and the Disintegration of the Whig Party*, pp. 217–18.

The last point was also taken up by the prominent Liverpool doctor and opponent of the slave trade, James Currie. In February 1793 Currie criticised 'the war-hoop about sedition, insurrection and conspiracies' and that June published *A Letter, Commercial and Political ... to ... Pitt* under the pseudonym of Jasper Wilson. Currie traced the conflict to Pillnitz, argued that Britain should have remained neutral and prosperous, and claimed that in the winter of 1792–3 there had been an opportunity for Britain to restore peace to Europe. Currie saw this as lost because the 'alarmists', inspired by Burke, had taken the nation out of Pitt's hands, and driven by fears of French sedition, had pressed for war. He argued further that 'one part of the cabinet ... was warmly and decidedly for it from the first'.[165]

Currie's mixture of prudential and ideological arguments was taken up by other Foxite writers. The lawyer Thomas Erskine argued in his *Considerations on the French War* (1794) that Britain could not trust her allies, repeated the charges of hypocrisy over Poland, contrasted Pitt's position over Ochakov with his current lack of policy in eastern Europe, claimed that the government was fighting 'for the divine right of Kings' and, more interestingly offered an account of how the war, if successful, might lead to a situation that was more threatening for Britain. France was seen as the only power that could seriously resist the future efforts of Russia and Austria 'at almost universal empire'. If France was beaten, her victors would fall out over the terms, launching Britain into a new war that would threaten the total subversion of the balance of power. Three years later Erskine argued that it was pointless to fight so that Austria should regain Antwerp and Ostend from France, as Austria might soon be Britain's enemy, France her ally.[166]

Erskine's argument was an intelligent one. Very little thought had been given to the future European order. If Britain was in part fighting for the balance of power, it was not clear that the defeat of France would restore it. If she sought a collective security system, it was not clear how her allies were to be persuaded to avoid directing this to their own aggrandisement. Indemnifications could lead to fresh partitions. Such problems were avoided in ministerial pamphlets such as John Bowles' *Two Letters ...* (1796), with their stress on the present threat from France and their theme of Britain attacked.

Scholarly discussion since that period has focussed on the questions of

---

[165] Currie to Lansdowne, 12 Jan., 13 Feb. 1793, 17 Nov., 9 Dec. 1794, 18 Mar. 1797, Bowood 41; W. W. Currie, *Memoir of the Life, Writings and Correspondence of James Currie* (2 vols., 1831), I, 194–211.
[166] T. Erskine, *A View of the Causes and Consequences of the Present War with France* (1797), p. 124.

whether the war was inevitable, and if so, why, and of where responsibility for the conflict rested. A number of different arguments have been advanced, some claiming that 'diplomatic' causes were responsible for the war, but others seeking domestic causes. These have been found on both sides and full play has been made of conspiracy theories, a process helped by contemporary charges and counter-charges. It has been argued for example that Pitt sought war in order to split the Whigs, a groundless charge as the Whigs were weak anyway and had been divided by their response to the Revolution. Such charges, which corresponded with French conspiracy theories about Pitt's role, were rebutted in a scholarly fashion by J. T. Stoker whose thorough analysis, based on British and French diplomatic sources, centred on the notion that Pitt sincerely sought to preserve peace.[167]

The mutual antipathy of the two peoples and powers was an important factor in increasing and sustaining tension. Contemporary discussion of the causes of the conflict raised this point. John Gifford cited Fox's speeches against the Eden Treaty and argued that an 'antigallican spirit' was always seen as an honourable characteristic of a British mind. John Bowles similarly saw it as innate, and as crucial to British prosperity and security.[168] Nevertheless, antipathy alone did not cause war, and the most recent and most incisive scholarly consideration of the outbreak of war supports the 'conventional view' that it was concern for the Low Countries that led to war. The notion of it being an ideological war is dismissed, and it is suggested that governmental fear of French subversion led to hostility to France, but not war. Blanning also argues that the fate of the Low Countries was decisive for the French. In 1795 George Canning focussed on this issue when seeking to win support for the war: 'Tell me if any statesman that ever lived, on being shewn that France was mistress of the Netherlands and of Holland – no matter whether with Louis XIV – or with [the Revolutionary] Tallien... would not exclaim at once, "Then England *must be* at war with her".'[169] Blanning's argument can be questioned. It is clear that the Low Countries provided the occasion for war, and, it is always important to examine closely the actual steps by which conflict broke out. It is equally

---

[167] Henry, 3rd Lord Holland, *Memoirs of the Whig Party during My Time* (2 vols., 1852), p. 13; W. T. Laprade, *England and the French Revolution* (Baltimore, 1909), pp. 184–5; Stoker, *Pitt* pp. 1, 205–6.

[168] J. Gifford, *A Letter to the Hon. Thomas Erskine* (6th edn, 1797), pp. 158–60, 177, *A Second Letter to the Hon. Thomas Erskine* (4th edn, 1797), p. 35; J. Bowles, *French Aggression, Proved from Mr. Erskine's "View of the Causes of the War"* (2nd edn, 1797), p. 76.

[169] Blanning, *French Revolutionary Wars*, pp. 158–9 and works cited there; P. Jupp (ed.), *The Letter-Journal of George Canning, 1793–1795* (1991), p. 184.

clear that the British government had revealed a marked disinclination to become involved in the cause of counter-revolution in the spring of 1792, and this seems to lend substance to claims that it was not motivated by ideological considerations. Indeed, the chronology of confrontation points directly to that opposite conclusion.

Yet, Blanning separates British governmental fear and resentment of French support for subversion, rather than the French pursuit of 'a forward policy' too readily;[170] while his accurate stress on the effects of mutual miscalculations that led each side to overestimate its own strength and the problems of its rival is somewhat vitiated by his unwillingness to consider adequately the extent to which ideological issues were *also* responsible for the failure to negotiate a compromise. Fear, as much, if not more than miscalculation, was crucial, and this fear, on the British side, derived from a distrust that arose from the perception of the French government as being unwilling to accept limits to its ambitions and revolutionary pretensions. Even Fox, writing on 23 November 1792, noted: 'The French disclaim any intention of interference in Dutch affairs, but whether their disclaimer, even if sincere, is much to be relied upon, I doubt.'[171] Blanning's emphasis on misunderstanding, on 'the mutual miscalculation of their power relationship' is not only too schematic; it also fails to appreciate that the British ministry was well aware of the strength of its rival. Whatever its possible limitations, French power was readily apparent after Jemappes. As Bowles pointed out in 1794, 'the essence of peace is security'; none was offered by the policies and pretensions of revolutionary France. War was entered into through necessity, not as a consequence of the illusions of what Blanning termed the 'Coppelia effect'.[172]

The points in dispute, principally the Scheldt navigation and the territorial integrity of the United Provinces, were negotiable, as preliminary discussions in the winter of 1792–3 revealed. The French, who were after all in control of Belgium, appeared less rigid, at least in so far as their agents were concerned, than Catherine II had proved over Ochakov. Given the negotiability of the issues, war can then be explained by mutual miscalculation, the 'Coppelia effect', war by accident, error, misjudgement and illusion. This conclusion is supported by some of the evidence, not least the professions of French agents in London and The Hague.

---

[170] Blanning, *French Revolutionary Wars*, p. 159.   [171] Russell (ed.), *Fox*, II, 379.

[172] J. Bowles, *Farther Reflections submitted to the Consideration of the Combined Powers* (1794), p. 7; Blanning, *French Revolutionary Wars*, p. 123. The quote refers to the outbreak of war the previous year, but it encapsulates Blanning's general thesis, on which see p. 28. For a different view see Black's two chapters in Black (ed.), *Origins of War*.

This was certainly the view adopted by some of the critics of the Pitt ministry, especially when they focused on the failure to keep Gower at Paris or to replace him, and the unwillingness to recognize the Republic and to continue receiving Chauvelin as an accredited envoy. Yet, it is not a view supported by the British ministerial correspondence of the period. It was not so much that, as in 1755, passion and prejudice were greater factors in the drive to war than the formal issues in dispute, but rather that for the British ministry distrust became the central issue. That distrust can be treated either as 'rational' or as 'ideological', a somewhat false counterpointing. In fact, it was both. There was a 'rational' assessment that the overall thrust of French policy was aggressive in cause and/or consequence, whatever the willingness of French agents to offer or suggest compromises on particular points, and also an 'ideological' perception of this challenge. This had two dimensions, first a rigidity in the British response to French innovations and secondly a perception of French policy as ideological in its determination to new-model international relations. The tone of French policy was different, a point brought home vividly to British diplomats by the unconventional conduct of their French counterparts – Auckland reported in June 1792: 'M. de Maulde made a long visit yesterday to the Grand Pensionary, and uttered nothing but classical phrases, natural philosophy, and belles lettres'[173] – and by the manner and content of French public diplomacy, the 'megaphone' nature of the discussion of foreign policy in the Assembly and the Convention. In April 1792 Grenville wrote to Gower concerning a minor difference between the two powers: 'You will observe that my dispatch is drawn with a view to public discussion, as I imagine that considering the present state of things in France, *that* can hardly be avoided however desireable it would have been.'[174] Chauvelin shared the view, and complained that the public reading of dispatches compromised negotiations.[175]

The avowed agenda of French policy was a more serious problem for the British government. Treaties were to be recast to conform to the eternal verities of human nature, the peoples of Europe were to be given their voice, enfranchised in a new diplomatic order, organised by France and supported by the bayonets of her victorious troops. This threatened Britain as much, if not more, than its immediate manifestation in the opening of the Scheldt. The threat was less concrete and less apparently

---

[173] Auckland to Grenville, 8 June 1792, BL Add. 58920 fol. 105. Three days earlier, Auckland had referred to the strange clothes Maulde wore when Auckland gave a ball and supper in honour of George III's birthday, fol. 104.
[174] Grenville to Gower, 6 Apr. 1792, BL Add. 59021 fol. 16.
[175] Chauvelin to Dumouriez, 23 May 1792, AE CP Ang. 581 fols. 49–50.

immediate, but it was one that greatly concerned the British government, especially Grenville. He made it clear that it was the general thrust of French policy, as exemplified by their claim alone to judge the continued applicability of treaties, that was central. The willingness of the French to sponsor or encourage discontent and sedition was not separable from this, not a distraction from the vital question of the Low Countries, but an indication both of the essential objectives of French policy and of the means by which they sought to effect them. Domestic sedition was thus important, not only for its impact on British capability, but also as a vital sign of French intentions. In May 1791 Montmorin, noting the belief that the French wished to force 'tout l'univers' to adopt their new regime, had, instead, argued that it was up to each nation to judge what was best for itself. Eighteen months later, it was credible to argue that the French had bridged the two propositions by defining other nations in terms of revolutionary and pro-French populaces. The French government might complain of misleading and hostile images spread by émigrés,[176] but the course of the Revolution appeared to justify them. The policy of French agents in this respect was a crucial source of distrust. The interception of Maulde's dispatches revealed that his protestations of good intentions towards the Dutch government did not inhibit his encouragement of sedition. They suggested that no French envoy or approach could be trusted. If individual French agents, or indeed ministers, differed in private from aspects of the policy outlined above, that was of limited consequence because they were unwilling and unable to stop it in the electric public forum that was now so crucial to its development. Far from French intentions being secondary to the fact of power, it was these intentions that were the issue. It was not a question of suspicion, for hostile intentions were proclaimed in France without hesitation and equivocation.

Concern about the French encouragement of sedition did not begin at the close of 1792. That May Auckland had to reassure the Dutch government about radical associations in Britain, while Trevor, dining with Edward Gibbon at Lausanne, noted that his compatriot was 'more animated than usual', and added 'Even Mr. Gibbon who in general voit assez de sang froid seems to be alarmed at the temper of the times.'[177] Such fears were mirrored within Britain, although the strength of the forces arrayed against France that summer suggested that the source of revolution would soon fall victim to the bayonets of monarchy.

---

[176] *Recueil ... Venise*, p. 312; B. Auerbach (ed.), *Recueil ... Diète Germanique* (Paris, 1912), p. 380.
[177] Auckland to Grenville, 15 May 1792, BL Add. 58920 fol. 86; Trevor to Malmesbury, 28 May 1792, Winchester CRO Malmesbury 169.

This was crucial. It was not only that in late 1792 the United Provinces were threatened and British policy perforce shifted, a 'non-ideological' cause of conflict, but also that in late 1792 the Republic demonstrated its resilience, vitality, unpredictability and radicalism, thus lending force and focus to 'ideological' fears. Before this shift, the British government had been willing to negotiate with its French counterpart. In June 1792 Grenville sent a private letter to Auckland that was, like so many such letters, a crucial complement to his formal instructions:

> I have given no opinion in my dispatch ... as to the propriety of our entering into any explanations with France about the views and probable conduct of the Republic. In truth I feel that it is a point on which the Dutch government ought to decide, and therefore have left it absolutely to them; but the inclination of my own opinion is, that it would be wise to make sure of this opening in order to take away from them every ground or pretence of uncertainty as to the dispositions of the States General ... you think me too tolerant of the ignorance and absurdity of the French Mission here, and you hint at the propriety of my making application at Paris for the removal of M. de Chauvelin, and of your forbidding M. de Maulde your house. I own that my persuasion is extremely strong of the propriety of avoiding any sort of eclat on this subject. The quarrelling with France would give encouragement to the persons in both countries who wish to introduce French maxims of government amongst us, and would give to them the command and direction of that very prevailing wish for peace which I take to be the ruling sentiment both here and in Holland. And the showing pique and ill humour where it can be avoided, without meaning to go further, would certainly be undignified and hazardous.[178]

Thus, France was not seen as an unsuitable partner for negotiations in the summer of 1792. This was underlined, two and a half weeks later, when Gower sent Grenville a 'secret and private' letter, written in his own hand, that is of particular interest, not least because it is clear that it should not have survived: this raises the questions of how much and what has disappeared and of the extent to which the official diplomatic series creates a misleading impression. Gower wrote on 6 July:

> I have had a long conference this morning with Mr. Bonne-Carrere, whose name I mention having promised him to desire you to burn this letter; He told me that he was sensible that in the present distracted state of this country it was not to be supposed that the British Ministry would be inclined to enter into any negotiation with this government ... that from his situation in office ... Directeur du Bureau des Affaires Etrangeres, he was able to facilitate, whenever an opportunity should offer any negotiation ...

Having consulted Pitt, Grenville replied favourably: Gower was to investigate what could be obtained.[179] This opening was, however, to be

---

[178] Grenville to Auckland, 19 June 1792, BL Add. 58920 fols. 112–13.
[179] Gower to Grenville, 6 July, Grenville to Gower, 13 July 1792, BL Add. 59021 fols. 31–3.

swept aside in the agitation and disruption that engulfed France from late July. The unsettled state of affairs in Paris had already been a factor in British governmental calculations about diplomatic discussions.[180] From late July negotiations seemed even more problematic, until the situation altered once more with the Prussian retreat from Valmy. This suggested that, at least for a while, the French government would be more stable, a point made by Auckland in mid-November.[181] The context, however, was different from that of the early summer. Then, the French government did not appear to be excessively radical, either in domestic or in international matters. By November, the situation was very different, and this conditioned the attitude of British government to the possibility of negotiations, their content and nature. The rapid changes in France in July–September, especially the overthrow of the monarchy and the September Massacres, all preceded the Prussian check at Valmy, but they combined to make the new republic seem dangerous, sinister, violent and radical to an extent that could not be comprehended in British terms. Developments in France also affected opposition politicians and many who had been sympathetic towards the early stages of the Revolution changed their attitude. Fox was prepared to accept the events of 10 August 1792, but not the September Massacres. Press support for the Revolution waned.[182]

Valmy and subsequent French triumphs were seen in this new context. The non-'ideological' position of the spring no longer seemed relevant. Military success and the radicalisation of the Revolution made the French example appear more threatening. Grenville observed that 'the example of success in France cannot but be very encouraging to those who wish to make similar attacks both here and in Ireland'.[183] The need to resist this success and to block its future progress seemed more important than the specific points at dispute, precisely because the Republic could not be trusted. Auckland argued that the navigation of the Scheldt was not of much real importance, as the channel was not good for navigation, but that was not the point, for, as Auckland pointed out, the rights of the Dutch were clear and the French had unilaterally abrogated them.[184] The changing nature of the French government and political nation ensured that French aspirations, even if similar in their anti-Austrian focus, had altered between the spring and the autumn.

[180] Auckland to Grenville, 26 May, Grenville to Auckland, 19 June, Grenville to Gower, 13 July, Princess of Orange to Greffier, 17 July 1792, BL Add. 58920 fols. 101, 113, 59021 fol. 34, 58920 fol. 140.
[181] Auckland to Grenville, 15 Nov. 1792, BL Add. 58920 fol. 171.
[182] Morton Eden to Auckland, 24 Oct. 1792, BL Add. 34445 fol. 138.
[183] Grenville to Richmond, 11 Oct. 1792, BL Add. 58937 fol. 164.
[184] Auckland to Grenville, 28 Nov. 1792, BL Add. 58920 fol. 186.

French victory made the revolutionary threat apparent and concrete, at the same time as the Revolution itself seemed more alien, in no fashion a replica of the British and American Revolutions. British politicians were forced to determine and express their views in response to a series of statements from Paris that appeared hostile and without likely end; each individual declaration was less significant than the series; they were proclaimed without any sense that conciliation and negotiation were a necessary part of any process of change.

The question of whether there was any viable alternative to war with France has to address not only the discussions in the winter of 1792–3 and the circumstances of that period, but also the possibility that peace could have been preserved in subsequent years. The latter is implausible, unless it can be suggested that Pitt's government would have been prepared to accept French hegemony in western Europe, a hegemony more powerful, insistent and threatening than that toppled in 1787. This would have been possible only if the analysis advanced in France, of a feeble Britain threatened by domestic radicalism, had been accurate, but it was not. French talk about their desire for an alliance with Britain was of little assistance; it was clear that opinion was divided in Paris as to whose alliance in Britain should be sought. The Republic's attitude to treaties scarcely encouraged any reliance on French assurances and, as the instability of her politics affected her diplomatic personnel and policy, conspicuously so in the case of her representation in London, it was difficult to see whose assurances were to be sought. By going to war in early 1793, Britain benefited from the enmity towards France of the other leading continental powers.

There was little basis for any Anglo-French understanding, either short- or long-term, in the winter of 1792–3 and the only possible positive solution to the discussions was the avoidance of conflict for a while. The idea of bringing about a generally accepted agreement was even more implausible than it had been the previous summer.[185] Any Anglo-French understanding would be of an uncertain duration, might encourage radicalism in Britain, and would make it difficult to develop links with other powers or to influence their views. And yet, as Grenville appreciated, as French constancy, both domestic and international, could not be relied on, such links would be necessary, both for Dutch security and for the guaranteeing of any Anglo-French understanding. An Anglo-French agreement would have been viable in the long term only had it been part of a larger international settlement, which would have had to address the Belgian question. Distrust was as important in

[185] Grenville to Auckland, 19 June 1792, BL Add. 58920 fol. 113.

Anglo-French relations in 1792–3 as it had been in 1787 and 1790, but in 1792–3 it was no longer a question of seeing the French threat in traditional and quantifiable terms, such as naval preparations. The unpredictability and potency of French aspirations, and the links, both real and imagined, between British radicals and France made the situation appear far more threatening.

The challenge of revolution explains why Anglo-French distrust developed into an acute situation in the winter of 1792–3. Crucial to this shift, for both the fears of the British political nation and the anxieties of its government, was French resilience in 1792 and the dramatic impact of French strength in an area believed crucial to British interests, or at least vital to keep out of the hands of France. The likely consequences of a revival in French strength had been an important theme in British discussion of French developments from 1787 onwards. The possible nature of French schemes in the Low Countries had similarly been a significant aspect of the discussion of French diplomatic plans. Their combination in late 1792 was a potent one, that would have been judged dangerous prior to the radicalisation of the Revolution. Much about the crisis, not least the dispute over the Low Countries and their transition into an Anglo-French battlefield, was far from novel.

The need to defend an ally was also far from novel. In 1747–8 the British had been concerned about the French advance into the United Provinces; much of their diplomatic effort in 1748–55 was designed to prevent its recurrence. Yet, the nature of the challenge was different. In 1792–3 it was feared that the Orangist regime would collapse in the face of domestic subversion, a subversion that was much more radical in its nature than the pro-Orange agitation sponsored by the British in 1747 and 1787. The German powers that Britain would need to turn to in order to help in the defence of the Dutch were already involved in a war with France in which ideological considerations played a considerable role.

Part of the problem in assessing the impact of the Revolution on international politics, and, more specifically, on Anglo-French relations, is that there is a tendency to treat the Revolution as a unit. Yet the answer to the question of its role in giving relations an ideological slant depends in part on the specific conjuncture being considered. The challenge was, and appeared, very different in the summer and late autumn of 1792. In June 1792 Auckland could be pleased 'to observe how providentially the conduct of the Prussian and Austrian Cabinets has tended to separate us with credit from any participation in their troubled concerns'. Seven months later it was 'the hidden ways of Providence' that unaccountably delayed the French from receiving the 'justice' they deserved. Auckland's language is significant. By November 1792 the French were 'bloody barbarians', and it was necessary to resist the 'contagion' of 'this new species of French disease'. And yet it was Auckland who had proposed the idea of negotiations with France in mid-November, including the dispatch of an agent to Paris, a move that would have had an effect on the public debate within Britain.[186]

The nature of British policy ensured that her confrontation with France would be made to appear 'non-ideological'. It was necessary to put policy in the best light possible for both domestic and international reasons, and this could be done by being seen to come to the defence of an ally in accordance with treaty obligations. And yet Grenville's stress on the common danger, his argument that French policy and pretensions represented a general assault on the international system, had considerable weight. It might appear hypocritical that this was not brought forward in the summer of 1792, but then France appeared a problem not a threat: the question then was whether order could be recreated in France, not whether she would overrun her neighbours.[187]

To a considerable extent, the British governmental response in late 1792 to the Revolution's advance was a reawakening of the attitudes that had led to opposition to Catherine II's desire for aggrandisement in 1790–1. There was a common thread, a stress on international order and on the need for its enforcement by and in defence of alliances. It was against this background that Trevor in November 1792 could call for a 'union' of European countries.[188] This lends force to the contemporary argument that the British ministry was therefore inconsistent and hypocritical over the Second Partition of Poland. That was a charge that some ministers and diplomats privately accepted the weight of, though pro-government newspapers denied the charge, the St James's Chronicle stating on 16 June 1792, 'The friends of sedition in this country are extremely solicitous to confound the Polish with the French Revolution. Nothing can be more unjust, as they very essentially differ both in principle and effect.'

'Ideology' was not simply at stake on the British side. The declarations by the French and the debates they sprang from reflected the application of philosophical idealism to international relations with all the cant and the self-righteous response to the views of others that was to be

---

[186] Auckland to Grenville, 12 June 1792, BL Add. 58920 fol. 108; Auckland to Burges, 25 Jan. 1793, Bod. BB. 31 fol. 4; Auckland to Grenville, 26, 15, 16 Nov. 1792, BL Add. 58920 fols. 178–9, 171–2.
[187] The need to take the 'ideological context' seriously has also been stressed by P. Shofield, 'British Politicians and French Arms: The Ideological War of 1793–1795', History, 77 (1992), 183–201.
[188] Trevor to Grenville, Nov. 1792, BL Add. 59025 fols. 22–3.

anticipated. The new society that was being advocated and created in France was not essentially designed to be formed with reference to the concept of the territorial state. In so far as the new politics and ideology illuminated the policy of the French government, they did not encourage the limitation of policy aspirations nor compromise with the interests of territorial states. Lebrun's instructions revealed an unwillingness to accept the validity of other perceptions, and his wish to maintain peace with Britain was not accompanied by any consistent willingness to compromise with her to any serious extent. There was no sustained attempt to explain to the Convention the views of other powers. French domestic developments helped the move towards confrontation, by creating an institution – the National Assembly and later the Convention – and a political culture, that encouraged both the public expression of specific views on foreign policy and attempts to influence policy with these. The public debate on foreign policy in France in 1791–3 had a similar effect to that within Britain in 1739 and 1755: it encouraged those ministers and politicians who wished to fight and made others hesitant about expressing their opposition. More cautious French ministers lost the ability to push through their own ideas, and both the British and the Dutch governments were aware of this failure. Having failed to keep Prussia out of the opposing camp earlier in 1792, the French were set to repeat their failure with Britain. Here Blanning's 'Coppelia effect' played its role, but so also did the appeal of a new ideology and its impact on the negotiating positions of the French. In addition, Blanning's 'Coppelia effect', with its stress on the mutual miscalculation of strength, can be matched by another, more potent one, that emphasises the extent to which both countries, or at least their governments and political elites, seemed more distinct and 'extreme' in their ideologies. Alongside reports of radicalism in Britain, French agents stressed the hostility of George III, the bulk of his ministers and most of the elite. In turn, the British were given full details of the gory and inquisitorial nature of the new republic, culminating in the trial of Louis XVI. St Helens claimed in January 1793 that it would be 'extremely difficult... even to *name* the actual French government without giving it some appellation which would be either too honourable for its members to wear, or too coarse for His Majesty to use'.[189]

The massacres and other atrocities and violent acts served an important function in that they provided the specificity, the concrete examples that could apparently make events more comprehensible, that newspapers liked in their reports, and which form so obvious a contrast to the very

[189] Hampson, *Danton*, p. 93; Auckland to Grenville, 15 Nov. 1792, BL Add. 58920 fol. 170; St Helens to Grenville, 26 Jan. 1793, BL Add. 59022 fol. 48.

general nature of much comment. Under a local byline, the *Chelmsford Chronicle* of 21 September 1792 informed its readers 'such great advocates are the French for the levelling system, that they cannot, nor will suffer any one to appear in the nation above a common man; an English gentleman, well known in the county of Essex, being one day at Paris with his usual attendant servants, he attempted to ride in his phaeton [carriage] through the streets'. The account of how he was nearly hung as a consequence may have been more meaningful to some readers than Burke's diatribes.

Concern about French developments was not urgent while France seemed weak, and Burke then found his warnings had little impact; but the revival in her power changed the situation totally and fused traditional political concerns with an apparent volatility and a new distrust that both stemmed from ideological considerations. Fox and Whig papers, such as the *Morning Chronicle*, were not able to carry the bulk of Whig opinion with them over France, as they had done during the Ochakov crisis. This was partly because in the latter the ministry had ignored traditional assumptions about the nature of British foreign policy, but, more generally, because the latter crisis was simply a political one in which Whigs such as Portland and Fitzwilliam could oppose government policy without, as over France, worrying about repercussions in a tense social situation and about ideological consequences. Then, foreign policy had been sealed and separate, a source of and field for political debate, but one that did not relate to questions about the nature of British society. In 1792, the situation was very different, a return to the period when the external French challenge was matched by domestic concern over the intentions of the Stuarts, whether on the throne or, as from 1688, claimants to it. The conflation of the threat posed by the traditional enemy with a sense that British society and religion were under challenge was potent. The language used was accordingly rhetorical. In May 1792 Trevor urged Malmesbury to 'rally to the standard of the Constitution'. Two months later Carlisle explained to Fox his support for 'a stronger government...the want of which all moderate men, friends and supporters of the Administration are ready to admit...the adding that strength...is required of us all as a conscientious discharge of a public duty'.[190] By February 1793, Portland was in no doubt that the war was indeed 'ideological', a struggle that did not hinge on calculations of territorial advantage. On 12 February he declared his support in the Lords for 'a war, the object of which was, to resist doctrines that...went to the overthrow, not merely of all legitimate government, of the security

[190] Trevor to Harris, 12 May 1792, Winchester, Malmesbury 169; Carlisle to Fox, 23 July 1792, BL Add. 47568 fol. 277.

of nations, of peace and order, but even of religion itself, and of everything for which society was instituted'.[191] The combination of national enmity, a widely based desire for the maintenance of social stability and a strong religious conviction that deplored revolutionary irreligion, was a strong one and helped to sustain Britain through the years of defeat that lay ahead. Nobody on either side anticipated a conflict that would last, with only brief intervals, until 1815.

[191] Cobbett, 30, 413–14.

10 The domestic context of foreign policy

Any assessment of British foreign policy in the period 1783–93 faces a number of questions. It is necessary to consider the relative importance of the factors affecting foreign policy, but this question cannot be detached from the wider issues of the nature of British politics, the British state and British political culture in the late eighteenth century. That introduces the question of the differences between Britain and continental states, and the relationship between British foreign policy and several of the longer-term trends that are apparent in British history in this period: the development of British patriotism and the evolution of Britain as an imperial and commercial state. Indeed, the extent to which foreign policy played a role in British 'imperialism' of this period, if such a term does not suggest a misleading degree of coherence, is of considerable significance.[1]

The 'structural' features of the domestic context are fairly clear and have been discussed at some length recently, though not specifically for this period.[2] It is, therefore, pertinent to ask whether the situation was any different in 1783–93 than it had been earlier in the century. This is especially important, in light of the argument that Parliament and public opinion played a minor role in the foreign policy of the previous two decades.[3] The order in which the factors are discussed is in itself a possible indication of bias, but it seems most relevant to consider first those institutions and individuals who were directly and formally involved in the formulation and execution of foreign policy, and then to consider some of those whose role was, however important, not continuous or less direct. The former group includes the King, Cabinet ministers, diplomats and the officials in the Foreign Office; the second,

---

[1] J. Black, 'Britain and the Continent 1688–1815. Convergence or Divergence?', *British Journal for Eighteenth-Century Studies*, 15 (1992), 145–9; L. Colley, *Britons. Forging the Nation, 1707–1837* (New Haven, 1992).

[2] J. Black, *British Foreign Policy in the Age of Walpole* (Edinburgh, 1985) and *System of Ambition?* (Harlow, 1991), pp. 12–20, 38–115; Scott, *Foreign Policy*, pp. 10–28.

[3] Scott, *Foreign Policy*, pp. 7–8.

Parliament, commercial issues, public opinion and the press. Part of the discussion has, where appropriate, been included in the narrative chapters, most obviously consideration of the role and policies of George III[4] and the influence of particular ministers.[5]

George III's personal authority was far greater in 1784–8 than it had been earlier in the reign. The unpopularity of his early years and the failures associated with the American war, had, in large part, been compensated for by the discrediting of opposition with much of the political nation, as a result of what was seen as factious policies during the American war and during the domestic crisis of the early 1780s, and the particular unpopularity arising from the Fox–North ministry and the confrontation over the India Bill.[6] Aside from these particular problems facing the opposition, there was also the major general rallying of the independents, 'all the country gentlemen',[7] to the support of the Crown. Though the support of peers and MPs who considered themselves independent could not be relied upon, and was a particular problem at moments of crisis, their general backing for the Crown was an important element in the monarch's political weight. An independent MP, Sir John Sinclair, claimed in December 1789 that the 'majority of the present House of Commons are attached to the Crown rather than to the Minister'.[8]

George III's backing for Pitt was crucial to the establishment of his ministry and important to its continuation, but George did not see the appointment of relevant ministers as any reason why he should not take a major role in foreign policy, and he was constitutionally entitled and expected to take such a part. Diplomats were the king's representatives, and he played a role in their appointment. George saw foreign envoys in London, and his own diplomats before their departure, and on other occasions when they were in London if he wished. Dorset indeed complained that the King told Adhémar too much.[9] George read dispatches and private letters from diplomats. Like Louis XVI, George worked hard on foreign policy.[10] He was far more experienced than his

4 See pp. 56, 88–9, 97, 125–8.   5 See pp. 56–7, 124–5, 137–9, 160–1, 167.
6 L. Colley, 'The Apotheosis of George III: Loyalty, Royalty and the British Nation 1760–1820', *Past and Present*, 102 (Feb. 1984), 104–6, 128; Report of Lasowski, Duke Louis de La Rochefoucauld's bearleader on his trip to England in 1784, University of London Library, Mss. 138 fol. 182.
7 Philip Lloyd to Jenkinson, 21 Dec. 1783, BL Add. 38471 fol. 77.
8 Aspinall, *Correspondence of George Prince of Wales*, II, 53.
9 Luzerne to Montmorin, 3 June 1788, AE CP Ang. 565 fols. 233–4; Dorset to Stafford, 12 Apr. 1787, PRO 30/29/1/15 no. 58.
10 W. Fraser to Keith, 17 Aug. 1784, George III to [Carmarthen], 12 Nov. 1785, Burges to Grenville, 9 Sept. 1791, Grenville to George III, 1 June, 5 Sept., 25 Nov. 1792, BL Add. 35532 fol. 203, 27914 fol. 11, 58968 fol. 11, 58857 fols. 1, 32, 57; Thurlow to

ministers in the field of diplomacy. George had never travelled abroad, but Pitt and Carmarthen knew little of the Continent, and lacked his experience in the conduct of foreign policy. Carmarthen was also not the most distinguished of Foreign Secretaries, though the general tendency among scholars to dismiss him completely is questionable.[11] George had played a major role in foreign policy since his then favourite adviser, Bute, replaced Pitt the Elder as a Secretary of State at the end of 1761, and had been active in supporting particular initiatives, such as the secret discussions with France in 1772–3. With time, his confidence in his judgement increased, as did his personal authority. It was George's experience, as well as the formative views of his political apprenticeship, that led him to argue in January 1786 that foreign alliances were best avoided as likely to lead to commitments that might entail war.[12] As Elector of Hanover, George also controlled another diplomatic service and, more importantly, had an independent source of information and advice. In December 1784 the Under Secretary William Fraser complained that 'the letters from the Hanoverian Ministers are never communicated to us'. Burke claimed in 1791 that 'the conduct of Hannover will be the pulse thro' which the rest of Europe will judge of his real Sentiments'.[13]

George's role in the *Fürstenbund*, the supposed anti-Russian attitude of the 1780s and the Dutch crisis have been discussed earlier.[14] It is clear that, although his importance could be exaggerated, he was of consequence, both directly and because he was believed to take a major role. The last factor was also important in 1791–3, as George's hostility to France and her Revolution was an article of faith with French envoys and agents. There is, however, no evidence that the King forced the pace of the British response. He accepted and apparently supported the shift to inaction that affected British policy in 1791. Though this centred initially on eastern Europe, it also conditioned the response to the developing crisis caused by the Revolution and the Austrian response. George's personal dislike of developments in France did not prevent him from

Stafford, no date, 1 Oct. 1787, PRO 30/29/1/15 nos. 62, 66; Grenville to Elgin, 5 Sept. 1792, PRO FO 26/19; Middleton, 'Additional Correspondence of King George III', *Notes and Queries*, (June 1979); Hardman, *Louis XVI*, p. 88.

[11] E. Fitzmaurice, *Life of William Earl of Shelburne* (2nd edn, 2 vols., 1912), pp. 286, 291; J. Black, 'The Marquis of Carmarthen and Relations with France 1784–1787', *Francia*, 12 (1984), 283–303.

[12] C. Middleton, *The Administration of British Foreign Policy 1782–1846* (Durham, North Carolina, 1977), p. 71, and 'King George III on European Politics, 1789–1808', *Consortium on Revolutionary Europe ... Proceedings, 1989*, 39–40, 45; George III to Pitt, 24 Jan. 1786, Aspinall, *George III* no. 274.

[13] Fraser to Keith, 10 Dec. 1784, BL Add. 35533 fol. 71; Burke to Dorset, 11 Sept. 1791, KAO C 186.   [14] See pp. 88–9, 97, 125–8, 135, 138, 140.

supporting neutrality in 1792, and he wrote to Grenville to that end on 22 September.[15] If, that winter, he backed the move towards war with France, that was also the attitude of the bulk of the political nation. Agreement over essentials did not of course prevent differences over matters of detail, and the *Fürstenbund* raised the question of George's role as Elector in a particularly pointed fashion. The extent of royal power was masked, however, by a reluctance to push differences to extremes. George accepted Pitt's growing role from 1787, the transition from leading minister to effective head of the ministry which was cemented in foreign policy when his ally Grenville replaced Leeds. This necessarily reduced George's potential for intervention, for the monarch was most effective when he could arbitrate between competing ministers, but there is no sign that George resisted the process or tried to play Carmarthen/Leeds off against Pitt. There is little sign of any difference between King and ministers over the negotiation of the Triple Alliance, and disagreement over the Baltic crisis of late 1788 was settled by George's ill-health.

After his recovery, which seems to have been only partial,[16] the first major crisis was that over Nootka Sound, but, as with his grandfather and predecessor George II over the War of Jenkins' Ear, George III did not play a conspicuous role in that crisis. Both monarchs devoted less attention to colonial, maritime and commercial affairs than they did to those of the Continent, though this was more marked in the case of George II, both because of his military interests and his frequent and lengthy visits to Hanover. George III was not obviously interested in the commercial negotiations with foreign states, though there was no necessary reason why he should be: they were in part beneath his dignity as monarch, but it was also the case that the ministry was perfectly competent to undertake them. Indeed, having got ministers whom he supported, a support underlined by the conduct of the opposition, most obviously during the Regency and Ochakov crises and, in the case of Fox, during the confrontation with France, there was little reason for George to demonstrate, stress or test his authority. In one respect, it is therefore misleading to discuss royal power when considering the foreign policy of the Pitt ministry, because the impact of that power was displayed most clearly in the formation of that ministry, and, in a negative sense, in the uncertainty over the direction of policy displayed during the Regency Crisis. Royal authority in the field of foreign policy

---

[15] George III to Grenville, 22 Sept. 1792, BL Add. 58857 fol. 35.
[16] Ralph Payne to Malmesbury, 1, 9 Oct. 1789, Winchester, Malmesbury 162. His most recent biographer, however, refers to 'complete' recovery and subsequent 'good health', Brooke, *King George III*, pp. 343, 374.

had also been at issue in 1782, when peace negotiations had led to criticism of the notion that the Crown could cede territory without parliamentary approval,[17] but, thereafter, it was not an important issue, though the question of the Crown's right to fulfil treaty obligations by raising troops in the recess without parliamentary approval was raised in 1789.[18]

Only two ministers, Carmarthen and Grenville, were formally responsible for foreign policy during this period, though, if commercial negotiations are included, Hawkesbury had a major role. The role, however, of a number of ministers was well illustrated in 1791: Spanish proposals in July for a defensive and commercial alliance led to Cabinet debates. Pitt asked Hawkesbury to give in his thoughts in writing and they served as the basis of instructions sent by Grenville to St Helens.[19] If negotiations with native rulers in Asia are also discussed, it is necessary, in addition, to consider the power structure of the East India Company, both in India and in London. The government, however, could still play a direct role in Asia. After the proposed mission to China was thwarted by the death off Malaya on 10 June 1788 of the special envoy, the Hon. Charles Cathcart MP, the ministry considered a replacement, Grenville noting 'great part of the hopes which are entertained of the success of this mission rest on the greater degree of attention which, it is supposed, the Government of China will show to a person coming there, as authorised by the King, than if he came, only in the name of a trading company'. This was especially necessary, because the East India Company was opposed to any initiatives that might affect the monopoly of its 'factory' at Canton. It was also criticised for failing to aid the export of British manufactures to the Orient. George, Lord Macartney replaced Cathcart, but his embassy, which left England in 1792, failed to obtain the commercial advantages that had been sought.[20]

Other ministers played a role in foreign policy, formally through the

---

[17] *Edinburgh Advertiser* 27 Sept., *Morning Chronicle* 2 Nov. 1782.

[18] Anon., *Considerations on the Prussian Treaty*, pp. 3–4.

[19] Hawkesbury, memoire and note, Aug. 1791, Bod. BB. 61, p. 1.

[20] Grenville to Thurlow, 15 July 1789, BL Add. 58938 fols. 3–4. On the Cathcart embassy, Pritchard, *Anglo-Chinese Relations*, pp. 236–64; Ehrman, I, 418–21 (though he errs in calling Charles Cathcart, James, see *History of Parliament* II, 198). For criticism of the Company and interest in increasing manufactured exports, Garbett to Lansdowne, 15, 20, 25 Sept. 1787, 22 Apr. 1789, 31 Aug., 24 Sept., 31 Oct., 1 Nov. 1791, Mr. Scott to Directors of the Company, no date, Thomas Perceval to Garbett, 5 Dec. 1792, Bowood, 17–18. On the Macartney embassy, see most recently, A. Peyrefitte, *The Collision of Two Civilisations: The British expedition to China, 1792–4* (1993). Relations between chartered companies and overseas agents of government were not only an issue for the British: for the Compagnie du Sénégal in the late 1780s, L. Jore, *Les Établissements français sur la Côte Occidentale d'Afrique de 1758 à 1809* (Paris, 1965), pp. 114–17.

Cabinet,[21] and informally through the crucial processes of discussion and consultation that leave such a relatively light imprint in the sources. As has been pointed out recently, albeit in a different context, crucial political 'contacts' in this period 'were conducted in person', and 'almost always ... unrecorded', and, when sources survive 'everything depends on the tone in which' remarks were made, and this 'cannot be recaptured'.[22] It is also clear that informal dinner parties for Pitt's friends were one of his favoured means for doing business and maintaining unity.[23] Though Carmarthen complained in 1784 about a lack of Cabinet interest in foreign policy,[24] Cabinet ministers could discuss and approve instructions and see dispatches and appear to have done so to a certain extent.[25] They could correspond directly with British diplomats. This was obviously true of Pitt who corresponded on diplomatic topics with Eden, Ewart and Harris, but it was also true of Hawkesbury, whose correspondents included Dorset, and Thurlow, who also corresponded with the Duke and with Eden. Relatively little of Thurlow's correspondence survives, which is disappointing as it would be useful to know whence this perceptive minister derived his information and how far he tried to influence policy. Force of personality played a major role in the high politics of the period, and Thurlow, who was afraid of no man, certainly had it. He was able to dominate debates in the Lords, but could be indecisive in Cabinet. Vorontsov was impressed by Thurlow but not Carmarthen.[26]

[21] A. Aspinall, 'The Cabinet Council 1783–1835', *Proceedings of the British Academy*, 38 (1952), 145–252, is largely devoted to the early nineteenth century; R. Pares, *King George III and the Politicians* (Oxford, 1953), pp. 143–81, esp. 161–2; Ehrman, *Pitt*, I, 180–6, 628–35; Christie, 'The Cabinet in the Reign of George III, to 1790', in Christie (ed.), *Myth and Reality in late-eighteenth-century British politics and other papers* (1970), pp. 55–108, esp. 69–70, 103–5; C. Middleton, 'The Impact of the American and French Revolutions on the British Constitution: A Case Study of the British Cabinet', *Consortium on Revolutionary Europe Proceedings* 1986, 317–26, esp. 318–20.

[22] A. P. W. Malcomson, 'A Lost Natural Leader: John James Hamilton, First Marquess of Abercorn (1756–1818)', *Proceedings of the Royal Irish Academy*, 88 (1988), 83–4.

[23] Jupp (ed.), *Canning*, p. 10.

[24] Leeds Political Memoranda, BL Add. 27918 fol. 121.

[25] Richmond to Pitt, 30 June, 5 July 1787, 22 June 1790, W. Fraser to Pitt, 24 Dec. 1787, PRO 30/8/170, 30/8/137 fol. 31; Stafford to Pitt, 17 Sept. 1787, HL Hastings Mss 26018; Camden to Burges, 8 Aug. 1790, Bod. BB. 18; Aust to Auckland, 7 Sept., 1790, Aust to Grenville, 14, 17 Sept. 1791, 8 Sept. 1792, BL Add. 34433 fol. 73, 58968 fols. 18, 21, 59; Cabinet minute, 28 July 1791, BL Add. 59306 fol. 3.

[26] Richmond to Pitt, 15 Jan. 1786, PRO 30/8/170; *Daily Universal Register* 31 July 1786; Anon. report, 19 July 1787, AN. AM. B⁷ 453; Eden to Pitt, 23 Aug., J. N. to Fox, 29 Sept. 1787, BL Add. 34426 fol. 9, 47562 fol. 105; Thurlow to Burges, 5 Dec. 1789, Bod. BB. 18 fols. 88–90; R. Gore-Browne, *Chancellor Thurlow: The Life and Times of an Eighteenth Century Lawyer* (1953); McCahill, *Order and Equipoise*, pp. 113–14, 132–5, 137; Malcomson, 'Leader', 65; G. Ditchfield, 'Lord Thurlow', in R. Davis, *The House of Lords, 1720–1920* (1994); Marcum, 'Vorontsov', pp. 111–12.

Though they have been criticised as 'hopelessly disinterested in foreign affairs',[27] Camden, Howe, Stafford and, in particular, Richmond, revealed a degree of interest and were consulted,[28] although the influence of Howe, like that of his successor, Chatham, was limited largely to naval matters. Military interests played little role in policy. If naval considerations made gaining and retaining the support of the Dutch crucial, there is little sign that this view was pushed by a naval interest, though, after the experience of the War of American Independence, ministers would have known that naval power was a vital issue. Howe discussed the issue of naval forces in the Indian Ocean with both Carmarthen and Pitt.[29] Furthermore, Howe made it clear at the start of a paper of 1 January 1786 on the state of the Navy and the need for naval preparations, that Britain's problems stemmed in part from the nature of the alliances of the other European naval powers.[30] This could be seen as an indication of the Admiralty's view of the necessity of breaking those alliances, although no such remark was made. There is no sign that strategic questions, still less a military lobby, played any important role in the Anglo-French confrontation of 1792–3. The Low Countries might be important for strategic reasons, but the British ministry was unwilling to fight over the Austrian Netherlands, the Scheldt was seen as a diplomatic issue, and the British government felt compelled to defend the Dutch as an ally. Strategic questions did not feature at any length in the diplomatic or ministerial correspondence of the period, though clearly the rationale for the Dutch alliance was in large part naval and strategic, primarily so with regard to the Indian Ocean. Excluding those on half pay or retired, seventy-three of the MPs elected in 1790 held commissions in the regular army. Twenty-five naval officers were then elected, although there is no sign that either group acted as a concerted political interest or had any bearing on foreign policy.[31]

The interest and intervention of ministers varied. Sydney wrote at the time of the *Fürstenbund* controversy, 'I am so far behindhand in foreign politics.' Described in 1791 as 'the *primum mobile* of the commercial interests of this great nation', Hawkesbury became increasingly influ-

---

[27] A. G. Olson, *The Radical Duke – Career and Correspondence of Charles Lennox third Duke of Richmond* (Oxford, 1961), p. 78.

[28] Richmond's letters to Pitt, PRO 30/8/170; Carmarthen to Pitt, 26 Dec., Carmarthen to Richmond, 27 Dec. 1785, PRO 30/8/151 fols. 32–3; Robert Arbuthnot to Keith, 16 Nov. 1787, Richmond to Grenville, 5 Nov. 1791, BL Add. 35539 fol. 250, 58937 fol. 151.

[29] Howe to Carmarthen, 11 Apr. 1784, 15, 17 Apr. 1785, Pitt to Carmarthen, 30 Oct. 1784, BL Eg. 3498 fols. 178, 186–9, 64.

[30] Howe, Observations, 1 Jan. 1786, Aspinall, *George III* no. 271.

[31] Thorne, *Commons*, I, 310, 314; J. Brewer, *The Sinews of Power. War, money and the English state, 1688–1783* (London, 1989), p. 44.

ential.[32] Cabinet minutes were formal records[33] and accounts of Cabinet discussions are too few[34] to permit any conclusions as to the consistent importance of individuals. It is not clear how far such discussions were guided by informal preliminary meetings, though that is very likely. What seems clear is that Cabinet members discussed matters that were not within their formal competence. Thurlow did this most obviously, for example, during the Dutch crisis, but clearly the views of all were of importance during the Cabinet discussions over Ochakov. Cabinet discussions were clearly of importance in resolving differences over whether to support Belgian neutrality in late 1789,[35] though, as yet, the consistent united Cabinet control of policymaking that was to become important in the 1790s was only developing slowly. Changes in Cabinet composition, in particular the resignations of Leeds and Thurlow, were to be important to this process. The tightly knit ministerial group close to Pitt that was so influential in the 1780s became an important element in the Cabinet.[36] The Cabinet's role led Pitt to write to Grenville in October 1791 about a new move in British policy in eastern Europe, 'This of course, cannot be done without a Cabinet.'[37] Pitt himself took only a limited role in foreign policy in 1784–6, but even then he had distinct views and took steps to increase his knowledge. Thus, in 1785 he wrote to Carmarthen: 'To be able to form in any degree an opinion of the prospect of confederacy, on the Continent, it strikes me to be very material to ascertain with some accuracy, the relative strength and situation of the different German Princes. I feel myself at present much too ignorant of it.' Pitt, therefore, suggested that they discuss the matter with Fawcett. From 1787 on Pitt took a greater role, especially in 1790–1 as he developed a particular interest in eastern Europe.[38] This shift owed something to the impression made by particular British diplomats. Barthélemy reported in September 1791: 'M. Pitt a toujours été dirigé dans son systeme de politique extérieure d'abord par Mylord Malmesbury, ensuite à quelque égards par Mylord Auckland, et aujourd'huy par

[32] Sydney to Carmarthen, 6 Aug. 1785, BL Eg. 3498 fol. 210; George Mitchell to Hawkesbury, 1 Jan. 1791, BL Add. 38226 fol. 26.
[33] e.g. 27 Dec. 1792, 25 Jan. 1793, BL Add. 58857 fols. 75, 86.
[34] Christie, *Myth and Reality*, p. 96 and fn. 2; Middleton, 'British Cabinet', 318–19.
[35] Leeds to Fitzherbert, 1 Dec. 1789, BL Eg. 3500 fol. 115.
[36] A. F. Madden, 'The Imperial Machinery of the Younger Pitt', in H. R. Trevor-Roper (ed.), *Essays in British History* (1965), pp. 174–92; Porter, *Anglo-French Relations*, p. 17.
[37] Pitt to Grenville, 23 Oct. 1791, BL Add. 58906 fol. 110; memo on defensive alliance with Spain, 1791, Bod. BB. 61 p. 1.
[38] Pitt to Carmarthen, 27 Apr. 1785, BL Eg. 3498 fol. 108; W. Fraser to Pitt, 24 Dec. 1787, PRO 30/8/137 fol. 31; Barthélemy to Montmorin, 4 Nov. 1788, 4 Mar. 1791, AE CP Ang. 567 fol. 103, 576 fol. 276; Aust to Auckland, 7 Sept., Pitt to Leeds, Oct. 1790, BL Add. 34433 fol. 73, 33964 fol. 21.

M. Ewart.' Malmesbury pressed Ewart in 1789 on the need to 'have the case plainly and strongly stated to' Pitt and Leeds, neither of whom, he claimed, were timid or 'disposed to shrink from great measures because they are hazardous'. He also claimed 'I have always found the present Cabinet perfectly ready to act whenever anybody pressed them on.'[39] It was also the case that Pitt had more time for foreign policy by late 1790. The finances had been stabilised and the domestic political situation was now relatively quiescent. Pitt kept an eye on instructions, increasingly so in 1790 and early 1791.[40] His contributions to these instructions were generally intelligent.[41] In 1789 he had a friend, Dudley Ryder, appointed as an Under Secretary at the Foreign Office, much to Leeds' anger.[42] It has, however, been argued that the Ochakov debacle led Pitt thereafter to be less willing to adopt an independent line.[43]

Diplomats were also of consequence. Harris' famous remark about not receiving instructions worth reading and about the need for the man on the spot to formulate policy,[44] can be supported by reference to the complaints of other diplomats, not so much about the content of their instructions, but about their infrequency. This was not a new problem, though there were some serious complaints about Carmarthen, especially from Keith.[45] Circumstances played a role, most obviously with the failure to send Eden the instructions he sought during the Regency Crisis, and also with the failure to keep Keith informed at the period when relations with Prussia, not Austria, were crucial. In part, however, the transition in 1782 from the system of two Secretaries of State to the Foreign and Home Secretaries[46] created problems.

[39] Barthélemy to Montmorin, 2 Sept. 1791, AE CP Ang. 578 fols. 209–10; Malmesbury to Ewart, 29 Aug. 1789, Williamwood 147.

[40] Pitt to Leeds, 19 June 1790, PRO 30/8/102 fol. 172; Ewart to Jackson, 27 Mar. 1791, Williamwood 148.

[41] Pitt to Carmarthen, 24 Oct. 1786, 21 Nov. 1790, 31 Jan. 1791, BL Add. 27915 fols. 15, 20, 22.   [42] Leeds to Pitt, 27 July 1789, PRO 30/8/151 fol. 40.

[43] Porter, *Anglo-French Relations*, p. 16.

[44] Harris to Ewart, 15 Mar., 19 Apr. 1785, Winchester, Malmesbury 204, pp. 30, 35–40, *Malmesbury*, II, 112–13. He offered a different view to Elliot, 17 Jan. 1786, NLS 12999 fol. 116. On the subject, Black, *Foreign Policy in the Age of Walpole*, pp. 66–70, *System of Ambition?*, pp. 59–68; Scott, *Foreign Policy*, pp. 23–7.

[45] Keith to Carmarthen, 30 Jan., Carmarthen to Keith, 12 Feb., Keith to Carmarthen, 3 May, Carmarthen to Keith, 16 May, 11 July 1788, PRO FO 7/15 fols. 37, 53, 191, BL Add. 35540 fol. 228, PRO FO 7/16; Straton to Keith, 15 Aug. 1788, Keith to Ewart, 28 Sept. 1788, BL Add. 35541 fols. 49–50, 115; Keith to Carmarthen, 20, 22 Mar., Keith to Pitt, 20, 21, 22 Mar., Keith to Trevor, 25 Apr. 1789, NLS Acc. 9769 72/2/71–2, 74–6, 78.

[46] Middleton, *British Foreign Policy*, p. 10, and, 'The Foundation of the Foreign Office', in R. Bullen (ed.), *The Foreign Office 1782–1982* (Frederick, Maryland, 1984), which though very useful on the Foreign Office up to 1830 contributes little to an account of its foundation.

Under the former system, the absence of one Secretary from London or his ill-health did not prevent his colleague from filling his role,[47] and, although he would not necessarily be conversant with the details of a particular negotiation, he would be well aware of the general developments in British foreign policy and would sometimes be an experienced diplomat.

This was not the situation during Carmarthen's tenure of the Foreign Office. When he was busy on other duties, for example attendance at Parliament,[48] ill,[49] or otherwise absent, diplomatic business suffered, though Fraser and later his replacement Burges, Carmarthen's Under Secretary from August 1789, were regarded as doing much of his work.[50] Burges was certainly both able and intelligent and British diplomats thought staying in close touch with him worth while. An MP and frequent parliamentary speaker in 1787–90, who failed to win re-election in 1790, Burges was aware of the importance of parliamentary opinion. The Home Secretary, Sydney, was not a credible replacement for Carmarthen, no minister had served as a diplomat and no other minister had taken a regular role in foreign policy, let alone having any experience in fulfilling the functions of the Foreign Secretaryship. The position changed with the rise of Grenville. Though his missions to The Hague and Paris in 1787 were very short-term and were not followed by similar or even longer missions (Harris could be trusted to negotiate the Triple Alliance), Grenville's interest in foreign policy had been whetted, and he was a credible replacement to Leeds in 1791. During his period as Foreign Secretary he was away from London for much of the summer of 1792, as a result of his marriage on 18 July to Anne Pitt, like Grenville, a first cousin of William Pitt, and their subsequent honeymoon, but Dundas was able to consult and send instructions in his absence.[51] Pitt could also play a role, as he showed by drafting dispatches. His willingness to correspond with diplomats increased Pitt's influence, gave the envoys a valuable route to the centre of government and increased the degree to which they were free agents, able to appeal over the head of the Foreign Secretary. Pitt was not unique among First Lords of the Treasury in taking a role in foreign policy. Walpole had served as acting Secretary of State in 1723 and Newcastle, a long-serving Secretary of State, later, as First Lord, played an important role in foreign policy.

[47] M. A. Thomson, *The Secretaries of State 1681–1782* (Oxford, 1932), pp. 90–1.
[48] Carmarthen to Keith, 7 Mar. 1788, PRO FO 7/15 fol. 90.
[49] Thomas Jackson to Harris, 28 Sept. 1787, 7 Mar. 1788, Winchester, Malmesbury 158; Luzerne to Montmorin, 21 Apr. 1791, AE CP Ang. 577 fol. 176.
[50] Marcum, 'Vorontsov', p. 113; Luzerne to Montmorin, 12 Oct. 1790, AE CP Ang. 575 fol. 42.   [51] Aust to Grenville, 3 Sept. 1792, BL Add. 58986 fol. 55.

Whoever was responsible for foreign policy, the parliamentary session still, however, interrupted its conduct.[52]

Diplomatic posts were not always easy to fill,[53] as was demonstrated by the case of the Berlin embassy in 1785, and many diplomats complained about their conditions. Pay was a major grievance,[54] as was rank,[55] and a failure to keep them informed.[56] Appointments to junior posts created difficulties in relations with more senior diplomats, but, for the conduct of foreign policy, the most serious problems were created by disagreements between diplomats. This was most acutely the case when two served at the same court, as with Eden and Dorset in Paris in 1786–7.[57] This could lead to problems, with the envoys creating different, even clashing, impressions, and with each complaining about the other to London. This was especially a problem if ministers other than the Foreign Secretary were involved, as then the sometimes complex network of patronage that lay behind important appointments could play a role. Despite his social skills, Dorset was less than diligent in sending reports, and this forced a role onto both Hailes[58] and Eden, not that Eden, unlike Hailes, was reluctant to take it.

Clashes between envoys as they advanced different interpretations of the international system[59] and suggested clashing policies, were not necessarily harmful. They ensured that the government was offered various options and that policy was not therefore controlled by the diplomats. It would have been a different question if policy had been undermined by diplomats, but there is little sign of that. Auckland criticised the direction of policy in early 1791, but did not try to undermine it, though that was not how the situation appeared to critics.[60]

[52] Harris to Ewart, 4 Feb. 1785, Winchester, Malmesbury 204, p. 22; Aust to Liston, 4 July 1788, NLS 5551 fol. 122; Auckland to Morton Eden, 9 Jan., 1 Mar., Auckland to Spencer [Mar. 1792], BL Add. 34441 fols. 122, 395, 582; Grenville to Fife, 24 Feb. 1792, Aberdeen UL Tayler papers 2226/131/893; On Walpole, J. Black, 'An "Ignoramus" in European affairs?', *British Journal for Eighteenth-Century Studies*, 6 (1983), 55–65.   [53] Mountstuart to Liston, 22 July 1784, BL Add. 36804 fol. 80.

[54] Mountstuart to Liston, 21 Nov. 1783, Morton Eden to Eden, 31 Oct. 1784, BL Add. 36804 fol. 69, 34419 fol. 424; Keith to Frances Murray, 17 Apr. 1784, HL HM. 18940, p. 279.

[55] Elliot to Carmarthen, 1 Sept. 1784, PRO FO 22/6 fols. 261–3; Morton Eden to Keith, 18 Nov. 1785, BL Add. 35535 fol. 259.

[56] Ewart to Keith, 24 July 1784, BL Add. 35532 fol. 164; Dalrymple to Harris, 2 Sept. 1786, *Malmesbury*, II, 225; Hailes to Ewart, 31 May 1789, Matlock CRO 239 M/O 759.

[57] Dorset to Hawkesbury, 19 Oct. 1787, BL Add. 38222 fols. 135–6; Dorset to Stafford, 1, 22 Nov., 19 Dec., 1787, PRO 30/29/1/15 nos. 72–4.

[58] Carmarthen to Hailes, 22 Oct., 6 Nov., Hailes to Carmarthen, 28 Oct. 1784, BL Eg. 3499 fols. 46, 56, 44.

[59] The contradictory views of Keith and Ewart were no secret. Noailles to Montmorin, 12 June 1790, AE CP Aut. 359 fol. 322.

[60] Jackson to Burges, 6 May 1791, Bod. BB. 36 fol. 68.

He was presumably affected in part by the criticism he had received during the Dutch crisis, not least over the impression he had made on Montmorin.

Harris was the most able of the British diplomats, though it is difficult to see him as being able to match Eden's proficiency in commercial discussions, and, albeit as a result of unreasonable British demands, he was not successful in his colonial negotiations with the Dutch; though neither was Auckland. Harris was criticised for offering too many concessions in these negotiations. As already indicated, he could be criticised for having over-committed Britain in the Dutch crisis, advocating a degree of commitment that in the end was justified only by the unpredictable factor of a Prussian invasion.[61] Harris was successful in negotiating the Triple Alliance, but there was little real prospect of either Prussia or the Dutch going elsewhere for allies. Though there was talk of Prussia turning to France, there was little real prospect of this: France was obviously weak and, as an ally, discredited, while Montmorin himself was more interested in closer relations with Austria and Russia.

By backing the wrong side in the Regency Crisis, Malmesbury condemned himself to the political wilderness from early 1789,[62] and was therefore out of the diplomatic service during both the Ochakov crisis and the negotiations with Revolutionary France. Judged from his criticism in August 1789 of what he saw as a failure by Pitt and Leeds to support Ewart's negotiations and his support for increasing 'our consequence on the Continent',[63] he would probably have been a forceful advocate for confrontation with Russia. It is more interesting to consider what Malmesbury's attitude toward negotiations with Revolutionary France would have been. He was subsequently to be entrusted with such negotiations. It is difficult to see Malmesbury as advocating a different line to that actually followed had he been in the diplomatic service in late 1792. He would probably have both despised Auckland's willingness to negotiate and been very anxious to defend the United Provinces and thus his achievement of 1787. Malmesbury had been very clear in his emnity to France during his Hague embassy.[64]

Auckland was a very competent diplomat, who was revealed to be very perceptive over Ochakov. His 'political creed' turned 'on the expediency of avoiding wars abroad and innovations at home'.[65] In 1787, Auckland

[61] See pp. 140–1; Tarling, *Anglo-Dutch Rivalry*, pp. 33, 35.
[62] Malmesbury to Ewart, 29 Aug. 1789, Williamwood 147.
[63] Malmesbury to Ewart, 29 Aug. 1789, Williamwood 147.
[64] Harris to Keith, 15 Mar. 1785, Winchester, Malmesbury 204, p. 29; Harris to Pitt, 22 Dec. 1786, 9 Oct. 1787, BL Add. 28068 fol. 194, Winchester, Malmesbury 207.
[65] Auckland to Pitt, 23 Feb. 1790, PRO 30/8/110 fol. 158.

regarded good relations with both France and Spain as possible: 'It is only necessary for this purpose to establish cordially and completely that we are respectively content with our possessions and positions, and that we will concur in discountenancing all attempts to change and conquest in any quarter.'[66] His was the most influential voice in favour of such an alignment. Auckland was able to appreciate the views of Foreign Ministers he negotiated or discussed matters with, most obviously Montmorin, Floridablanca, and Van de Spiegel.[67] At times, he seemed too willing to accept their views, most obviously on his first diplomatic posting at Paris, and this led to criticism. Both at Paris and at Madrid, Eden revealed himself to be an urgent achiever, determined to make a major diplomatic initiative[68] and to ensure that he was responsible for a 'diplomatic revolution'. Eden's desire to achieve results can be related to his ambition, to the need to provide for his large family and to the hyper-activity that led him to write both a large number of dispatches and frequent and often lengthy letters to those who he thought would be influential.[69] In some respects, Eden, in his frenetic energy and determination to push new schemes, was very similar to Ewart,[70] a comparison that Eden would not have welcomed, and, like him, he felt it necessary and important to supplement his official correspondence with an attempt to win over Pitt, the Foreign Secretary, Carmarthen or Grenville, and Burges. The desire to produce important diplomatic combinations was not, however, restricted to Eden and Ewart. It was widespread and displayed by such different individuals as Pitt, Harris, and even Thurlow.[71]

After his return from Spain, Eden's diplomatic trajectory changed. He was disappointed already at having been moved from Paris to Madrid;[72] in 1789–90 he faced fresh blows in not gaining a post at home, such as the Speakership, and in not replacing Dorset at Paris.[73] The checks to his ambition and self-esteem may have been linked to the more cautious policy that he followed at The Hague. In place of the bold strategy of a major realignment in western Europe, to be achieved by an alliance with France or Spain, Auckland (Eden) was now urging a cautious response to Ewart's schemes, though envy of the latter's influence may also have

[66] Eden to Liston, 29 Oct. 1787, NLS MS. 5549 fol. 27.
[67] Auckland to Burges, 21 Aug. 1790, Bod. BB. 30 fol. 50.
[68] Eden to Liston, 29 Oct. 1787, NLS 5549 fol. 27.
[69] Eden to Pitt, 13 Apr. 1786, 27 Oct. 1787, PRO 30/8/110 fols. 20, 125; Aust to Liston, 13 June 1788, NLS 5551 fols. 89–90.
[70] Liston to Ewart, 22 Jan. 1790, Williamwood 148.
[71] Thurlow to Ewart, 17 Jan. 1791, Williamwood 148.
[72] Eden to Pitt, 19 May, 23 Aug. 1787, PRO 30/8/110 fol. 98, BL Add. 34426 fol. 10.
[73] Eden to Pitt, 12 Nov. 1788, 3 Oct. 1789, PRO 30/8/110 fols. 144, 149.

played a role. Although he did not end his career, for at least a while, as Malmesbury did, by any opportunistic moves during the Regency Crisis (which in part was an unexpected benefit of being in Madrid), Auckland suffered from a breakdown in his relations with Pitt, while Carmarthen continued to distrust him.[74] On the other hand, he had considerable success in winning Grenville's confidence. Grenville sought an experienced and confidential adviser in a field about which he knew relatively little. To a considerable extent Harris had fulfilled this role for Carmarthen, especially in 1786–8,[75] and, indeed, Carmarthen suffered from having no equivalent adviser after Harris lost his position and diplomatic connections following the Regency Crisis. Grenville and Auckland had only limited contact in the mid-1780s, but this situation changed considerably after Auckland went to The Hague, and even more after Grenville became Foreign Secretary. After the latter episode, the correspondence between the two men became an aspect of the correspondence between a Foreign Secretary and a leading diplomat, in which it was generally the case that the official correspondence was supplemented, expanded and qualified by a private correspondence. Auckland was assiduous in both his official and his private correspondence with Grenville.

The extent to which this connection could be used by Auckland to advance views of his own was limited by the post-Ochakov European diplomatic realignment and the related move of British foreign policy towards a more cautious stance. This was accentuated by Grenville's personal disinclination to take an active role, and by the change in Pitt's attitude to a comparable situation. Auckland was concerned by what he saw as 'the unsettled disposition of mankind in general', the danger of 'the whole fabric of sovereignty' being levelled 'in the dust' by popular action, and believed that the European powers should therefore avoid war with each other, which he saw as likely to facilitate this process. He wrote of France in January 1791: 'It is an immense and raging Vesuvius in the political region, and nobody can tell to what quarter its lava may next be driven, or ultimately reach.'[76] Auckland, who had spent a considerable time in Paris in the early autumn of 1789 on his way back from Madrid, was more aware of the potential significance of French developments than either Pitt or Grenville. The main line of British

---

[74] Leeds to Fitzherbert, 20 Nov. 1789, 2 Feb. 1790, BL Eg. 3500 fol. 108, Add. 28065 fol. 95.

[75] Barthélemy to Vergennes, 26 Sept. 1786, AE CP Ang. 557 fol. 320; Carmarthen to Harris, 20 Oct. 1786, BL Eg. 3500 fol. 24.

[76] Auckland to Ewart, 2 Feb. 1791, PRO 30/8/110 fol. 184; Auckland to Elgin, 12 July 1791, Broomhall 60/23/20; Auckland to Burges, 11 Jan. 1791, Bod. BB. 30 fol. 94.

policy having been set out at the time of Pillnitz, this did not alter essentially until November 1792. Auckland played a major role in the subsequent crisis, not least by stressing the vulnerability of the United Provinces and the need to take immediate steps to reassure the Dutch. He was also central to the attempt to ascertain whether French policy could be influenced by negotiations with Dumouriez, although Auckland alone was not responsible for this move and was indeed sceptical about the possibility of preserving peace.

Auckland and, in this period, Malmesbury only served in western Europe. Diplomatic correspondence between Paris or The Hague and London was frequent. Although such correspondence could be at crucial moments, most obviously late 1792, too slow, it was relatively quick compared to the situation with respect to British embassies further east in Europe. There, envoys such as Elliot, Ewart, Hailes and, allegedly, Ainslie, were better able to, or perforce felt themselves obliged to follow initiatives of their own, not obviously that they saw these as diverging from British interests and policy. They were certainly given some leeway in deciding how best to implement their orders, although that created problems. Hailes commented in 1790, 'I know from experience how necessary it is after a warm bout in business to go home in order to explain what may not have been thoroughly understood.'[77] Elliot was the most versatile of these diplomats, able to operate in the very different atmospheres of revolutionary France and *ancien régime* Denmark. Already an experienced diplomat, he played a role both in the Danish monarchical coup of 1784 and, more conspicuously, in the Baltic crisis of 1788. If Denmark did not become a British ally, and Elliot was obliged impotently to comment on and complain about Russian influence, or, as he saw it, control, this was a result of the dynamics of Baltic politics, rather than of Elliot's level of skill. His success in Paris, at least in so far as this can be gauged from the reports by Elliot and Gower, suggests not just Elliot's flexibility and adaptability, but also that his later absence from that city was harmful to British policy. In 1792 Britain lacked any representative in Paris who was able to distinguish, assess and make predictive suggestions about the different tendencies in French politics, let alone to explain, discuss and even negotiate over British policy.

'We take Your Resident at Berlin, Ewart, to be exceedingly well inform'd of continental politicks, which is not generally the case of the English Ministers abroad.' That was the verdict of the Hanoverian Ernst Brandes, in January 1787,[78] and Ewart's ability to establish good relations

[77] Carmarthen to Keith, 18 July, Carmarthen to Ainslie, 19 Dec. 1786, Hailes to Jackson, 24 Sept. 1790, PRO FO 7/12, 78/7 fol. 363, 353/66.
[78] H. Furber (ed.), *Correspondence of Edmund Burke*, V (Cambridge, 1965), p. 307.

with Prussian ministers seemed especially valuable because of poor Anglo-Prussian relations since 1762 and the extent to which British diplomatic failures in Russia were blamed on Prussia. This ability was not, however, matched by a skill in assessing Prussian intentions or in offering accurate predictions about international developments. Thus in September 1791 he promised Pitt 'a complete preponderancy all over the North', whenever Britain sent a large fleet to the Baltic.[79] Ewart has been seen as a prescient diplomat whose views prefigured the 'traditional British foreign policy of the nineteenth' century and ranked Palmerston and Disraeli among his 'unconscious disciples'. Ewart's determined advocacy of confrontation with Russia as essential to the maintenance of the Prussian alliance, was, however, as Auckland pointed out, based on a series of over-optimistic assumptions not only about the likely responses of other powers and the probable impact of Prussian power, but also on the very ability to find and hold fixed points in the foreign policies of other states, and thus to establish 'the general tranquillity of Europe on a more permanent footing than ever'.[80] Ewart also advanced too optimistic a view of Britain's international role, greeting the result of the Dutch crisis, as proof that 'Great Britain will again act that topping part in Europe to which her natural strength and resources so justly entitle her.'[81]

Liston was a bitter critic of Elliot and Ewart,[82] and he had an interesting alternative vision of international relations and British foreign policy that is worth noting, as it reveals the extent to which an experienced diplomat could reject the main thrust of British diplomacy in 1787–91. In June 1789, he wrote to Ewart:

that England, Prussia and Holland are sufficiently powerful, without any additional alliances, or any new acquisitions: that an extension of our system, or an increase of dominion, would alarm the other powers of Europe, and probably give rise to opposite combinations, of which it is impossible to foresee the consequences: that we are so formidable that nobody thinks of attacking us; and that nobody will think of it if we are wise enough to be civil to all the world, and to avoid an insolent and dictatorial conduct.

The following January, he returned to his theme:

My idea is – That Great Britain may be considered as a country-gentleman, of high rank, of great property, of increasing wealth and influence, who ought to employ himself principally in the management of his affairs; to cultivate a good

---

[79] Ewart to Pitt, 9 Sept. 1791, PRO 30/8/133 fols. 299–300.
[80] D. B. Horn, *Scottish Diplomatists 1689–1789* (1944), p. 17; Ewart to General Grenville, 19 May 1790, Williamwood 147.
[81] Ewart to Cornwallis, 1 Nov. 1787, PRO 30/11/138 fol. 195.
[82] Liston to Ewart, 24 June, Elliot to Ewart, 9 Aug. 1789, Williamwood 148, 151.

understanding with *all* his neighbours, and if possible to make enemies of none: that he ought therefore to be very cautious of erecting himself into a *judge* and a *ruler* among them ...

In March 1790 Liston advocated sitting:

serene, like the Jupiter of the ancients, to view the tempest from afar, and to let foolish mortals arrange their differences as they best may. But this would require so much apathy, and moderation, and wisdom that it is perhaps beyond the reach of human endeavour.

In light of that, Liston accepted that Britain would have 'alliances and quarrels', but he advocated defensive alliances only and a goal of 'respectable independence and tranquillity'. If 'conciliation' and 'forbearance' were practised, Liston predicted a century of peace, but he criticised the attempt to enlarge the system of the Triple Alliance, especially the approach to Gustavus III:

The idea of deciding the differences that arise among our fellow mortals, of raising up the weak and depressing the strong, of saying 'hitherto shalt thou come and no further,' is great, noble, divine; But it humiliates and irritates those who are forced to submit to our assumed authority; and they who usurp the functions would stand in need of the power of the Deity ... that heroic courage which disdains to weigh prudential reasons or to think of possible and distant consequences ... how cautious ought to be the self-created judge?[83]

His views were dismissed by Elliot: 'the sum total of Liston's politics seems to be *Do Nothing*'. They are, however, worth attention not least because of the abandonment in 1791 of the system Liston criticised. Indeed Grenville's views echoed those of Liston. Criticising Prussian policy towards the Austrian Netherlands in 1790, Liston wrote: 'I do not well conceive upon what ground she can intervene at all, unless indeed we assume that all Europe is to be considered as a Commonwealth, where what every member does concerns every member, and that consequently every one has a right to speak and to act for what he reckons the general and the particular interest.' A belief in just such a Commonwealth was central to Burke's call for action against Revolutionary France, but it was not the view taken by the government as it refused to act against France for most of 1792. As late as 6 November, Grenville defended non-intervention, adding 'In all this, I reason as an Englishman, and apply my first case, as naturally an Englishman must, to the maintenance of our own tranquillity.'[84]

[83] Liston to Ewart, 24 June 1789, 22 Jan., 9 Mar. 1790, Williamwood 148.
[84] Elliot to Ewart, 1 Aug. 1789, Liston to Ewart, 9 Mar. 1790, Williamwood 151, 148; Grenville to Auckland, 6 Nov. 1792, BL Add. 58920 fol. 162.

Such a chord had been struck repeatedly throughout the course of eighteenth-century foreign policy, not simply by critical backwoodsmen, but also by diplomats and ministers, not least First Lords of the Treasury. Such views pose a question mark against Scott's recent attack on 'writing about what policy should have been rather than what it actually was', and his related juxtaposing of 'whig' and 'tory' approaches to foreign policy, in order to marginalise and thus dismiss critics of alliance politics.[85] Scott neglects the extent to which there was, on many occasions in the century, sustained debate within governmental and indeed diplomatic circles about the objectives and methods of British foreign policy, that there was no unitary 'whig', still less governmental approach, and that the related issues of what policy should have been and should be were central to governmental concern and political debate. It was thanks to both of the latter that Stanhope and Carteret were such disastrous ministers: they divided Whig governments and lost parliamentary and public support, so that the Stanhope–Sunderland ministry had to turn to the opposition Whigs in 1720, while George II could not retain Carteret in office in 1744 and 1746.[86]

The failure to integrate the domestic dimension can weaken greatly any account of eighteenth-century foreign policy, especially if the extent to which policy differences were part of the public as well as the intra-governmental political debate is not appreciated. Pitt's retreat over Ochakov cannot be discussed without reference to domestic circumstances. Liston's views found little echo within the government in 1790, but the transition in policy the following spring, from the discourse of alliances and systems to preparations for an unwanted war, brought such ideas to the fore, as Cabinet ministers and parliamentarians were both obliged and given the opportunity to consider the objectives and methods of foreign policy. The verdict was for caution, a retreat from interventionist aspirations to circumspect actions, unsurprisingly so as the British had not fought on the Continent since 1758–62 (Gibraltar during the War of American Independence can be excluded as a special case) and successive ministries since had revealed scant willingness to enter into and give effect to commitments that would lead to fresh continental conflict. In early 1791, Auckland displayed more political sensitivity than Ewart, which was not surprising given their respective

[85] Scott, 'Second "Hundred Years War"', 450.
[86] J. Black, 'Parliament and the Political and Diplomatic Crisis of 1717–1718', *Parliamentary History Yearbook*, 3 (1984), 77–101, and 'British Foreign Policy and the War of the Austrian Succession, 1740–48', *Canadian Journal of History*, 21 (1986), 313–31. R. Hatton, *George I Elector and King* (1978) and U. Dann, *Hannover und England 1740–1760. Diplomatie und Selbsterhaltung* (Hildesheim, 1986) fail to explain the unpopularity of the policies of Stanhope and Carteret.

political experience: Auckland had been an MP since 1774 and was still in the Commons. Pitt learned the need to weigh 'prudential reasons' and 'think of possible and distant consequences' in both foreign policy and its domestic context. Leeds was replaced by Grenville, who was more aware of these factors. The more cautious response to revolutionary France and to the Second Partition (though the need to win allies against France was foremost in the latter case), testified in part to the lessons of Ochakov.

Ewart's diplomatic career was relatively brief, but many of the diplomats of the period 1783–93 were both long-serving and had much of their career prior to the Pitt ministry. This was true of, among others, Ainslie (Constantinople), Hamilton (Naples), Keith (Vienna) and Walpole (Lisbon). Though some long-serving envoys were at relatively minor embassies, such as Florence, Naples and Venice, the last referred to as 'the hospital for Foreign Ministers',[87] this was not true of all, and it is clear that diplomats such as Ainslie and Keith were greatly influenced by their earlier experience of their posts, and that this created the context within which they responded to new developments and to their instructions. In this respect, there is some basis for Harris' maxim, not least because, in the relative economy of experience, both Carmarthen and Grenville were at a disadvantage compared to many of their envoys. In addition, as Auckland wrote to his brother in March 1792:

You seem to think it odd that you have so few official letters since your arrival at Berlin: but this is always the case with respect to all the missions during a session of Parliament and at a period too when there is no matter of foreign discussion that materially engages the anxieties of administration. Under such circumstances it sometimes happens with respect to missions even of the first rank not to receive a syllable in six months. The case would be very different under a Secretary of State so efficient as your present principal [Grenville] if there were anything that necessarily required frequent despatches from him.[88]

There was, however, some criticism of the quality of British envoys,[89] though there was also praise, for example, for the very able Fitzherbert. In January 1787, Carmarthen singled him out, alongside Ainslie and Liston, for praise.[90]

---

[87] Horace Mann to Humphry Morice, 4 May 1784, Northumberland Record Office ZSW 554/45. On Ainslie and Hamilton, Bagis, *Ainslie* and Fothergill, *Sir William Hamilton, Envoy Extraordinary* (1969).

[88] Auckland to Eden, 1 Mar. 1792, BL Add. 34441 fol. 395.

[89] *Polit. Corresp.* 46, 337, in general and of Liston; Arbuthnot to Keith, 6 May 1787, BL Add. 35538 fol. 141 of Torrington; Brand to Wharton, 26 Apr. 1794, Durham, Wharton; Lewis (ed.), *Horace Walpole's Correspondence with Countess of Upper Ossory*, II (1965), p. 488.

[90] Ségur to Montmorin, 9 Oct. 1787, AE CP Russie 122 fol. 147; Carmarthen to Pitt, 14 Jan. 1787, BL Eg. 3498 fol. 171.

Diplomats had great influence on the execution of foreign policy, and were of considerable importance for its formulation. Parliamentarians, in contrast, played a less active and direct role, and one that was limited to the formulation of policy. The influence of Parliament, as a crucial institution and a sphere of politics, and in terms of the impact on policy at specific conjunctures, has been considered recently,[91] and the first ten years of the Pitt ministry did not mark a new departure in these categories. Diplomats continued to report on parliamentary developments; and on the press as well. Louis XVI, who read English well, followed parliamentary debates closely, and the Ochakov debates were followed closely in Berlin.[92]

Parliament had both direct and indirect influence. Responsibility in the field of finance entailed supporting the military expenditure and subsidies to foreign powers that were judged necessary for the pursuance of policies, most obviously Pitt's expensive programme of increasing and improving the strength of the navy. In addition, foreign policy was debated in both chambers of Parliament and thus posed the problem of parliamentary management. Cornwallis, briefly an MP before he went to the Lords, thought it impossible to be 'an efficient member of Administration' in Parliament, 'without possessing such powers and habits of parliamentary debate as would enable him to do justice to a good cause, and defend his measures as well as those of his colleagues'.[93]

Parliament's indirect influence is and was harder to gauge. The extent to which British policy, and the foreign response to British views that could play a large role in shaping British policy, were affected by the existence of Parliament and the consequent need for government to consider how best to win parliamentary support or reply to parliamentary criticisms, were unclear to contemporaries. Much clearly depended on the particular issue and occasion. As Parliament was the public forum in which the ministry formally presented and defended its policy and was criticised in a fashion that obliged it to reply, it was Parliament where the public debate over foreign policy can be seen as most intense and effective. There was an obligation to respond that was lacking in the world of print, and an immediate linkage between the taking of decisions and the debates, the debates themselves being occasioned by the

---

[91] Black, *Foreign Policy in the Age of Walpole*, pp. 75–82, *System of Ambition?*, pp. 43–58, 'A Parliamentary Foreign Policy? The "Glorious Revolution" and the Conduct of British Foreign Policy', *Parliaments, Estates and Representation*, 11 (1991), 69–80, 'Parliament and Foreign Policy 1739–63', *ibid.*, 12 (1992), 121–42, 'Parliament and Foreign Policy 1763–93', *ibid.*, 13 (1993), 153–71.

[92] Hardman, *Louis XVI*, p. 90; Jackson to Burges, 17 May 1791 Bod. BB 34 fol. 158; Hailes to Jackson, 18 Dec. 1790, PRO FO 353/66.

[93] Cornwallis to Pitt, 23 Jan. 1792, PRO 30/11/175 fol. 21.

discussion of these very decisions. Thus, the financial power of Parliament, the need to turn to it in order to obtain the financial backing necessary for policy, gave it a role in the field of foreign policy that it otherwise lacked in a direct constitutional sense.

The quality of the debates was reasonable but varied, though the *World* of 9 November 1791 criticised the geographical knowledge of opposition speakers. Precisely because the debates could serve to raise both general and specific points, the content of speeches was very varied. If it is assumed that all speakers should have offered a detailed account of the international situation in order to throw light on the diplomatic problems and choices facing Britain, then it is clearly possible to adopt a critical attitude. Such a uniform critical approach is, however, in-appropriate, because speakers presented situations in different lights, not least in order to make very disparate political points. Constitutionally and institutionally, there were no changes in the position of Parliament in 1783–93, though in terms of the politics of the period, the notion of a parliamentary foreign policy was less obvious, until the Ochakov crisis, than it had been earlier in the century. The need to be able to defend foreign policy was clearly at issue during the earlier period of the Pitt ministry, most obviously with reference to the *Fürstenbund*, the Eden Treaty, the Dutch crisis and that over Nootka Sound, but in none of those cases was there a sustained or serious challenge to the government. This was not, however, inevitable. In each case, the issue was serious and there were potentially major challenges to policy. The *Fürstenbund* raised the questions of royal influence and the need for better relations with Austria and Russia, the Eden Treaty that of the possibility of better Anglo-French relations, the Dutch crisis that of whether the British government had been misled by the hopes of such relations, that over Nootka Sound whether the ministry had failed to make precise and sufficient gains.

These challenges were not developed to any serious extent, not because there was no basis for such a critique, but because of the weakness of the opposition, the attraction, greater resonance, and relative importance of other issues, for example, the case of Warren Hastings,[94] and the fact that divisions within the government did not spill over into the parliamentary sphere. This is significant, because that had not been the case over a number of other issues, most obviously parliamentary reform, Richmond's fortification bill, the slave trade and the Hastings case. Furthermore, such a spilling over in the field of foreign policy had

---

[94] Aust to Liston, 15 Feb. 1788, NLS 5550 fol. 53. On the case see most recently G. Carnall and C. Nicholson (eds.), *The Impeachment of Warren Hastings* (Edinburgh, 1989).

occurred earlier in the century. That it did not do so in the 1780s suggests that foreign policy divisions, though important, were not central to the politics of the period, that ministers were prepared to restrict their differences to Cabinet and correspondence, and that the political system under the Pitt ministry prior to the Regency Crisis was less fluid than it had been in 1714–21 and 1739–51.

Aside from these 'structural' features, the ministry was also helped by the extent to which the particular crises prior to Ochakov were, in parliamentary terms, shortlived, and that, with the exception of the *Fürstenbund*, it was credible to present the government as following a successful policy. This was important because the Foxite Whigs were largely opportunistic in their treatment of foreign policy, and were, therefore, discouraged by signs of ministerial success. As a result of Vergennes' determination to create a new alignment, the terms of the Eden Treaty were favourable to Britain, and the ministry's willingness to solicit and win over most manufacturing and mercantile opinion helped to limit the possibility of a successful exploitation of the issue.[95] Ministerial sensitivity was also indicated in 1786 when Hawkesbury wrote to Fawkener concerning Anglo-Portuguese trade: 'I have no doubt that when you return to England you will bring with you such an answer ... or at least such information as will enable us to state a proper case to Parliament and fully to justify the proceeding we shall then be obliged to hold.'[96]

The following year the extent to which the Dutch crisis was 'close run', and that success was due to Prussia, the Turks and French finances, and the contrast between the events of 1787 and the analysis and prospectus offered by Pitt at the time of the debates over the Eden Treaty, though mentioned,[97] were not pressed home because of the extent and popularity of British success and the clear endorsement of an anti-French policy by opposition speakers at the time of those debates. Both limited the plausibility of any attack on ministerial policy.[98]

The same was essentially true of Nootka Sound. Spain was a recent enemy; expansion in the Pacific was seen as a clear national interest, not

[95] Pretyman to Addington, 3 Oct. 1786, Exeter, Devon CRO Addington (Sidmouth) MSS D152 M/C 1786 fol. 47; Sir Francis Baring MP to Lansdowne, 7 Oct. 1786, Bowood 9; Hawkesbury to Thomas Gibbons, 5 Jan., Hawkesbury to Eden, 19 Jan., Wycombe to Keith, 6 Feb. 1787, BL Add. 38309 fols. 134–7, 35538 fols. 11–12; Ewart to William Porter, 2 Feb. 1787, Williamwood 130; E. A. Smith, *Whig Principles and Party Politics. Earl Fitzwilliam and the Whig Party 1748–1833* (Manchester, 1975), pp. 95–6, 114; McCahill, *Order and Equipoise*, p. 123.
[96] Hawkesbury to Fawkener, 27 Nov. 1786, BL Add. 38309 fol. 128.
[97] *London Chronicle* 19 Jan. 1788.
[98] Arbuthnot to Keith, 25 Sept., 1, 15 Oct., John Boyd to Keith, 8 Nov. 1787, BL Add. 35539 fols. 160, 165, 190, 233; *Newcastle Chronicle*, 6, 17 Oct. 1787.

limited by any serious critique of the self-interest of the traders involved; interest in the possibility of better Anglo-Spanish relations, indeed knowledge of that aspect of the diplomatic world, was generally absent. As over the Falklands in 1770, the government was attacked in a 'domestic' rather than a 'diplomatic' context, not on the grounds that Britain had gone too far, that it had jeopardised diplomatic possibilities by an aggressive stance, but that it had not acted in a firm enough fashion and that this had led to a belated and unsatisfactory settlement.[99] Pitt the Elder had attacked the ministry's policy during the Falkland crisis in a similar fashion. Arthur Young complained in 1787 that 'to reason with a British Parliament, when her noisy factious orators are bawling for the honour of the British lion, for the rights of commerce, and freedom of navigation; that is, for a war – that such a war will cost an hundred millions sterling... they are deaf to you'.[100] A report in the *Newcastle Chronicle* on 17 November 1787 noted that 'there are not wanting those who still repine because we have no war. – This is the time, they say, to humble our *natural* enemies, without reflecting on the injustice of going to war without a cause'. A critique of ministerial moves on the grounds that they were not firm enough was understandable in political terms, but it was vulnerable to the government's ability to present such distant events as it thought most convenient. Furthermore, by early 1791 the developing crisis in relations with Russia offered a better opportunity for the opposition to attack the government and indeed seemed to be a more important issue. Parliamentarians knew more about the issue, and the intervention of Vorontsov ensured that this was even more the case.

The Ochakov crisis was the most abrupt demonstration of the impact of domestic and, in particular, parliamentary factors on foreign policy since the protracted crisis over foreign policy in 1739–44. As a result, it was unprecedented in the experience of the politicians of the period. Whatever the weaknesses of Britain's diplomatic and strategic position, it was the domestic situation that was responsible for the climbdown over Ochakov. It is clear that the magnitude of the parliamentary crisis seriously affected the ministry, sapping confidence and morale, and exacerbating divisions. Ministerial victories in the divisions were little substitute for the difficulties being faced in Parliament and the strain of sustained public pressure. The crisis with revolutionary France, on the other hand, was far less serious in parliamentary terms, because Fox and his allies had failed to derive any long-term benefit from the Ochakov

---

[99] E. A. Smith, *Lord Grey 1764–1845* (Oxford, 1990), pp. 31–2.

[100] A. Young, *Travels during the years 1787, 1788 and 1789* (2nd edn, 2 vols., 1794), I, 39. Mirabeau used the War of Jenkins' Ear to criticise the role of emotion in a popular assembly, *AP* 15, 622.

crisis,[101] and by late 1792 not only lacked the support of independents but also that of much of the Whig party. Indeed the crisis destroyed the value of such a term as a means of analysis. Fox pointed out that: 'To declare war, is, by the constitution, the prerogative of the King; but to grant or with-hold the means of carrying it on, is (by the same constitution) the privilege of the People, through their Representatives.'[102] In early 1793 there was little doubt that these representatives would support war with France. Cornwallis' successes against Tipu dulled the force of opposition criticisms of his policy in the Second Mysore War, criticisms which he dismissed as ignorant.[103]

If Parliament had an important, though episodic, role in foreign policy, the same was even more true of mercantile interests. In one respect, the period was very much one of commercial considerations, in which such interests played a major role, and indeed it is possible to see the pursuit of commercial advantage as a central theme of the foreign policy of the period.[104] And yet, as earlier in the century,[105] the theme that emerges most clearly is the determination of 'government' most generally, and the Foreign Office and British diplomats more specifically, to concentrate on political issues and to subordinate commercial questions to them. This was certainly Carmarthen's attitude,[106] and Samuel Garbett complained about a lack of support for industry and trade from ministers. He claimed that Pitt relied on poorly informed people and had no extensive ideas on commercial questions,[107] the latter a very questionable view but one that underlines the contentious nature of Pitt's reputation in the mid-1780s.

The subordination of commerce to political priorities was accentuated by trends in imperial policy, with the greater emphasis on direction from London. This was seen most clearly in the new arrangements for the government of India, but it can also be discerned in the more general stress on strategic, geopolitical and maritime issues in what may be

---

[101] *Public Advertiser* 1 Mar. 1792; Smith, *Grey*, p. 35.
[102] *Letter from … Fox, to the Worthy and Independent Electors of … Westminster* (1793), pp. 23–4. There is an important, recent discussion of representation in J. P. Reid, *The Concept of Representation in the Age of the American Revolution* (Chicago, 1989).
[103] Cornwallis to Lansdowne, 9 Oct. 1791, Bowood 40.
[104] Barthélemy to Vergennes, 5 Dec. 1786, Barthélemy to Montmorin, 28 Oct. 1790, AE CP Ang. 558 fol. 231, 579 fol. 91.
[105] Black, *Foreign Policy in the Age of Walpole*, pp. 93–117, *System of Ambition?*, pp. 87–101. See more generally P. J. Cain and A. G. Hopkins, 'Gentlemanly Capitalism and British Expansion Overseas I. The Old Colonial System, 1688–1850', *Economic History Review*, 2nd ser., 39 (1986), 502–15, 517–22.
[106] Carmarthen to Fitzherbert, 12 Nov. 1786, BL Eg. 3500 fols. 16–17.
[107] Garbett to Shelburne, 18 Nov. 1784, Garbett to Lansdowne, 13 Feb. 1785, 21 Sept. 1786, Bowood, 16–17; Money, *Experience and Identity*, p. 33.

termed imperial policy, if such a term does not convey a misleading sense of coherence. This stress was not necessarily incompatible with commercial expansion, especially given a mercantilist ethos, but it reflected a policy that was not set by merchants.[108]

Government certainly sought[109] and took heed of mercantile opinion in commercial and colonial negotiations, and was lobbied heavily to that end. There were numerous examples of competing mercantile interest groups, for example the whalers and the East India Company who clashed over whaling and sealing rights in the Indian Ocean and Pacific, though the government brokered compromises in 1786 and 1788.[110] There was a public dimension to lobbying, as in the winter of 1790–1 when the press reported pressure from Leeds on both Yorkshire MPs and the government concerning new Spanish duties.[111] The response to lobbying was sometimes immediate. A memorandum from the Africa Company in 1784 about the French establishing a post on the river Gambia, led at once to enquiries by the government. On 11 February 1791, the Governor of the Russia Company wrote to Leeds about the need for a lightship in the Kattegat to warn ships about a dangerous shoal. Four days later, orders were accordingly dispatched to Drake in Copenhagen.[112]

In addition, there is no doubt that trade was seen as a crucial objective of foreign policy, especially because of its financial benefits. Ainslie hoped that Britain would be able to mediate Russo-Turkish differences in 1787, as he thought it 'must greatly contribute to the success of our

[108] D. Mackay, 'Direction and Purpose in British Imperial Policy, 1783–1801', *Historical Journal*, 17 (1974), 487–501, and *In the Wake of Cook*, pp. 24, 52, 83; R. Hyam and G. Martin, *Reappraisals in British Imperial History* (1975), pp. 13–14; P. J. Marshall, 'The Eighteenth-Century Empire', in Black (ed.), *British Politics and Society*, pp. 194–200. For an emphasis on a coherent strategy of trade and empire, Madden, 'Imperial Machinery', p. 186, Frost, 'Nootka Sound and the Beginnings of Britain's Imperialism of Free Trade', Vancouver 1992 paper.

[109] Eden to Pitt, 25 May 1786, PRO 30/8/110 fol. 39. As a preparation for the Macartney mission, East India Company advice on exports to India, China and Japan was sought, Pritchard, *Anglo-Chinese Relations*, p. 269.

[110] Carmarthen to Pitt, 8 Apr., Garbett to Pitt, 11 June 1786, Edward Forster, Governor of the Russia Company, to Pitt, 30 Apr. 1790, Carmarthen to Eden, 26 May, Eden to Carmarthen, 14 June 1789, PRO 30/8/151 fol. 36, 30/8/138 fol. 39, 30/8/136 fols. 176/7, FO 72/14; memorial to Pitt about trade with West Africa from Liverpool merchants, Bowood 17; *Bristol Gazette and Public Advertiser*, 7 Dec. 1786; *Newcastle Courant*, 15 Jan. 1791; Auckland to Grenville, 25 Jan., 12 Feb. 1792, BL Add. 58920 fols. 63, 68; W. Bowden, 'The Influence of the Manufacturers on Some of the Early Policies of William Pitt', *American Historical Review*, 29 (1924), 655–74; Jackson, *Whaling*, pp. 101–2, 106–8; BL Add. 37873 fols. 102, 105, 154.

[111] *Newcastle Courant* 15 Jan. 1791, reprinting item from *Norfolk Chronicle*.

[112] Africa Company memorandum, 14 Aug., Evan Nepean to William Fraser, 18 Aug.. 1784, Forster to Leeds, 11 Feb., Leeds to Drake, 15 Feb. 1791, PRO FO 27/12 fols. 262–4, 30/8/136 fols. 182–4.

commercial pursuits, and to the advantage of our establishments in the Levant'. His French counterpart warned of vital French interests, 'millions of the French who in Provence and Languedoc benefit from Turkish dependence on our industry'.[113] As after the Seven Years War, the fiscal burdens of great power status and war led to a search for new sources of revenue and greater effectiveness in utilising those that already existed. The quest for commercial treaties and, more generally, the desire to use diplomatic means to assist British trade, can be seen in this light, but it would be mistaken, in doing so, to neglect the extent to which the government felt obliged to temper the drive for commercial advantage by other factors. It was anyway clear, from long experience, that other powers were not willing to yield their commercial pretensions to those of Britain without advantage or reason, and in this complex equation political factors played a major factor.

British commercial negotiations in this period have been well served by Ehrman's excellent study,[114] and it is not necessary to supplement his account. It is clear that Pitt played a major role, that indeed his primary interest in international relations was commercial, that Carmarthen was less interested, and that some diplomats were sceptical about the possibility of creating a new commercial order through diplomacy. It is clear that the considerable effort that was made had few consequences. The most important was the Eden Treaty with France, but the political benefits were slight in the short term, and outweighed in the long term by the adverse impact on French public opinion.[115] Political developments ensured that the commercial potential of the treaty was not realised.[116] Such a realisation depended on acceptable political relations, which is what Vergennes had really sought. The French pressure in forcing the negotiations to life ensured that diplomatic considerations were at the forefront, but the insistence of the British government on detailed terms revealed its determination not to ignore commercial issues. The fate of the Irish commercial propositions the previous year underlined the need to tackle domestic political and commercial pressures. Pitt shared Vergennes' aims to a certain extent, because he believed peace essential

---

[113] Ainslie to Carmarthen, 9 Aug. 1787, PRO FO 78/8 fol. 155; Choiseul-Gouffier to Montmorin, 10 Aug., Montmorin to Ségur, 9 Dec. 1787, AE CP Turquie 176 fol. 99, Russie 122 fol. 320.

[114] J. Ehrman, *The British Government and Commercial Negotiations with Europe 1783–1793* (Cambridge, 1962), though see critical review by A. R. Ryan, *History*, 49 (1964), 88–9.

[115] Eden to Carmarthen, 3 Oct. 1786, PRO FO 27/20 fol. 215; *AP*, 15, 538.

[116] On unrealised benefits for Sheffield and Manchester, Arbuthnot to Keith, 3 July 1787, BL Add. 35538 fols. 251–2; for a more positive evaluation, *Newcastle Courant*, 12 Jan. 1788, Torrington to Keith, 30 Jan., Eden to Sheffield, 14 Feb. 1788, BL Add. 35540 fol. 36, 61980 fol. 43, *Felix Farley's Bristol Journal*, 5 Apr. 1788, Young, *Travels*, I, 93.

for national recovery, but by the summer of 1787 his priorities had shifted.

In the negotiations of the period, as more generally, British diplomats supported British trade, but only in so far as it did not clash with political interests. As with imperial expansion, so with European trade, the attitude of government was considerably more cautious, more responsive to political and financial considerations, and more aware of the sectional and often contradictory[117] self-interest of commercial and industrial lobby groups, than might be suggested by any stress on a theme of a system of imperial or commercial advantage.[118] Garbett contrasted trade based on manufactured exports and commercial 'adventures',[119] and argued that Asia should become a market for 'boundless quantities of British manufactures', but that the East India Company lacked the necessary resources, interest and expertise.[120] Garbett also pressed for access for trade to Japan.[121]

British caution is made abundantly clear, in the case of imperial advantage, by the hesitation of the East India Company, both in London and Bengal, about getting involved in the Malay world. Francis Light's success in establishing a position at Penang was more than matched by the Company's refusal to heed his suggestions, and the requests from Malay princes, that Britain establish a presence elsewhere, and by its reluctance to help the Sultan of Kedah, with whom the Penang negotiations had been conducted, against his aggressive opponents.[122] This refusal reflected both a general reluctance to take on commitments, a reluctance that was political and financial in origin, and a more specific unwillingness to challenge the Dutch position in the region and thus harm Anglo-Dutch relations in both Europe and Asia. Similarly, when Cornwallis' 1792 approach to Nepal for the development of trade with the dominions of the East India Company was countered with a request for military aid against the Chinese, who in 1788–92 launched a series of attacks on Nepal, the cautious Cornwallis would go no further than offering mediation. He did, however, persist in his attempt to improve relations with Nepal and in 1792–3 also sought to develop them with the

---

[117] Hawkesbury to Garbett, 26 Dec. 1786, BL Add. 38309 fol. 133; Ryan review of Ehrman, *History* (1964), p. 89; Bowden, *Industrial Society*, pp. 181–91; Money, *Experience and Identity*, pp. 34–44; Brewer, *Sinews*, p. 249.

[118] For cautious support for trade after 1815, D. C. M. Platt, *Finance, Trade, and Politics in British Foreign Policy, 1815–1914* (Oxford, 1968).

[119] Garbett to Lansdowne, 15 Sept. 1791, Bowood 18.

[120] Garbett to Lansdowne, 15, 23 Sept. 1787, 22 Apr. 1789, 31 Aug., 24 Sept., 31 Oct. 1791, Bowood 17–18.   [121] Garbett to Lansdowne, 1 Nov. 1791, Bowood 18.

[122] Bassett, *Trade and Policy*, pp. 85–96, 106–7; Bonney, *Kedah*, p. 100; Tarling, *Anglo-Dutch Rivalry*, p. 13.

Rajah of Assam. In 1788 Cornwallis had refused to help Rajah Kirtibhum of Mallenbhum against Nepalese expansion.[123] Similarly, Sir John Macpherson's bold call for expansion in northern India was not heeded: there were no territorial gains there until part of Oudh was acquired in 1801. Macpherson's letter to Shelburne from Calcutta in December 1782 is indicative of a territorial imperialist mentality:

If your Lordship casts your eye upon the local situation of these provinces you will easily trace the boundaries which nature has traced for an Empire of which the annual ... revenue is about six millions sterling independent of the value of its manufactures. This Empire is as easily governed and secured, nay more so than the single province of Bengal in nearly the same degree that Britain as an united kingdom is more easy of protection than England in a separate state. From the Rohilla Mountains, along the Thibet Hills to the sea at Chittagong ... Scindia, the Maratha General with his army is not far from the station of our other Brigade at Cawnpore. That vicinity shows the necessity of our extension of territory for if you draw back your frontier to Patna, the Marathas would follow or some power equally dangerous as a neighbour.

Five years later, however, Macpherson argued that Britain should seek 'among Indian nations' a 'balance of their power', not her own territorial expansion.[124]

The reluctance of the British government was paralleled by that of France. Vergennes was opposed to the bold initiatives proposed by Castries. Similar caution was displayed elsewhere by Britain, and was a feature of British imperial policy both when the state was relatively weak, in 1784–6, and, thereafter, when it was stronger. In the case of the Malay world, it has been suggested that this was because there was concern not to jeopardise the negotiation of an Anglo-Dutch agreement that might leave Britain in a stronger position;[125] but this was not the case with the Caribbean. The British government did not adopt an aggressive attitude over the issue of the Mosquito Coast.[126] The need to preserve a good understanding with Spain was stressed. The opposition motion in the Lords censuring the government for abandoning the Coast to Spain by the Convention of 14 July 1786, was defeated on 16 March 1787 by 53 votes to 17. In 1786 George III approved Pitt's suggestion that 'all idea

[123] Ross (ed.), *Cornwallis*, II, 190–1; Harlow, *Second British Empire*, II, 588; Wickwire, *Cornwallis*, p. 46; Cornwallis to Dundas, 15 Oct. 1792, 25 Jan., 24 Mar. 1793, PRO 30/11/151 fols. 138, 148–9, 156; K. C. Chaudhuri, *Anglo-Nepalese Relations from the Earliest Times of the British Rule in India till the Gurkha War* (Calcutta, 1960), pp. 63–9.
[124] Macpherson to Shelburne, 6 Dec. 1782, Bowood 56; Grenville to Dundas, 26 July 1787, PRO 30/11/112 fol. 228.
[125] Tarling, *Anglo-Dutch Rivalry*, pp. 17–19; Bassett, *Trade and Policy*, v, pp. 93–4.
[126] Burdon, *Honduras*, I, 157.

of interfering in the discontents of the inhabitants of the Spanish settlements in South America' be rejected, adding 'As I ever thought the conduct of France in North America unjustifiable, I certainly can never copy so faithless an example.'[127]

That year, Richmond opposed the idea of exchanging Gibraltar and a Caribbean island, specifically Puerto Rico, in part by using the familiar notion of a satiated empire. He argued that there was no need for more sugar islands as they would be 'more ... than our number of people or riches can afford to cultivate ... The protection of such distant possessions is always difficult for this country which has so few troops to spare.'[128] Accused in the National Assembly in May 1790 of seeking 'la monarchie universelle', the British government, in fact, adopted a very cautious approach towards the prospect of exploiting difficulties in the French Caribbean colonies. Despite persistent reports that Britain would seek to gain the largest, most populous and most valuable French colony, Saint-Domingue (Haiti), and appeals for intervention by white colonists frightened by the slave rising of August 1791, the government refused to act. The colonists met with a cool response, and in August 1791 Grenville wrote to Gower that there was no intention of retaliating in the West Indies for French intervention in the War of American Independence, 'and that we are fully persuaded that all the islands in the West Indies are not worth to us one year of that invaluable tranquillity which we are now enjoying'. The 1789 demand that the French renounce their claim to Flat Isle near Anguilla was made in response to what was seen as an act of French aggression.[129]

Such a policy not only reflected the influence of Grenville, who assumed the central role in foreign policy at the same time as he became Foreign Secretary, but also the general tenor of British foreign policy since 1783. However much ministers and diplomats such as Leeds, Harris, Ewart and, from 1787, Pitt, might become interested in an interventionist foreign policy in Europe, it was essentially designed to maintain the stability of European international relations, and Britain's place in them. Similar attitudes underlay British government policy in the Indian Ocean, though aspects of British policy in the Pacific, especially the establishment of a colony in Australia, can be seen as

---

[127] Pitt to George III, 1 July 1786, Aspinall, *George III*, no. 309; George III to Pitt, 3 July 1786, Stanhope, *Pitt*, I, 480.

[128] Richmond to Carmarthen, 26 Mar. 1786, BL Eg. 3498 fol. 235.

[129] *AP* 15, 528; Gower to Grenville, 26 Aug., Grenville to Gower, 31 Aug. 1791, BL Add. 59021 fols. 9–10; Hisinger to Lessart, 17 Jan. 1792, AE CP Ang. 580 fol. 25; D. Geggus, 'The British Government and the Saint Domingue Slave Revolt 1791–1793', *English Historical Review*, 96 (1981), 290–1; Duffy, *Soldiers, Sugar and Seapower*, pp. 27–8; Leeds to Fitzgerald, 16 Oct. 1789, PRO FO 27/33A fols. 169–71.

representing a bolder and more ambitious viewpoint. Similarly, Dundas wrote of Penang in 1787: 'I have rather a predilection to it, unless something better calculated to obtain the commerce and navigation of the Eastern Seas could be secured to us, for surely the obtaining of these objects are very important.' He also approved of Cornwallis' willingness to defend the Nawab of Oudh, an ally with whom a commercial treaty was negotiated in 1787. Cornwallis had good relations with Oudh and did not follow an expansionist policy at her expense.[130]

A war of *revanche* with the Bourbons was not on the agenda, although as Cathcart argued in 1787, it was 'the uniform policy of our governments at home and abroad, to aim at the depression of the French influence in India'.[131] This was, however, seen in the light of being 'very much upon our watch' against French jealousy. Thus, Dundas, although not committed to territorial aggrandisement in India in the 1780s, pressed for a firm line against the French there.[132] Alongside undoubted interest in imperial and, more particularly, trans-oceanic commercial expansion, there was also a reluctance to extend territorial control. The India Act of 1784 declared that 'schemes of conquest and extension of dominion in India are measures repugnant to the wish, the honour, and policy of this nation'.[133] Three years later, Carmarthen complained that in the Lords Thurlow had 'reprobated any shadow of right to our settlements on the Mosquito Shore at any time and treated the soidisant subjects in that quarter (perhaps with justice at least) as a set of buccaneers merely subsisting by smuggling, and hitherto uninterrupted rather by connivance than authority', a harsh view of 'informal empire'.[134] A comprehensive frontier policy for British North America in the aftermath of the American Revolution was lacking.[135] In 1790 the far-from-radical Earl of Fife noted: 'I have no ambition for extended dominions but only to manage what we have.'. Two years later, after some opposition politicians had been shown a draft of the royal speech, Loughborough wrote to Pitt about the gains from Mysore:

It would be a satisfaction to many to find some distinct intimation that the value of these acquisitions was estimated rather by their importance as a safeguard to

---

[130] Dundas to Cornwallis, 29 July 1787, PRO 30/11/112 fol. 201; R. B. Barnett, *North India Between Empires. Awadh* [Oudh], *The Mughals, and the British 1720–1801* (Berkeley, 1980), pp. 229, 252.

[131] Cathcart to Cornwallis, 27 July 1787, PRO 30/11/138 fol. 170.

[132] Dundas to Cornwallis, 29 July 1787, PRO 30/11/112 fol. 179; Furber, *Dundas*, pp. 69, 66–7.

[133] B. B. Misra, *The Central Administration of the East India Company, 1773–1834* (Manchester, 1959), p. 32.

[134] Carmarthen to Liston, 9 Apr. 1787, NLS 5546 fol. 109.

[135] Wright, *American Frontier*, pp. 19, 26, 39.

our old possessions than as an extension of territory, and that security not conquest was the object of our military operations.[136]

There was a difference between policies that were likely to affect other European states directly and those where gains would be made at the expense of native rulers, though this gap was partially bridged by the links that existed between such princes and European powers. Britain made gains at the expense of native rulers or peoples – in Australia and southern India, at Penang and in Sierra Leone – but the process was very different in the case of European powers, as demonstrated by the only significant concession made by one to Britain in this period, the Nootka Sound settlement. In this dispute, the British government sought to avoid resort to force, essentially sought a compromise from the outset and was able to negotiate one fairly easily because it was dealing with a European power operating in accordance with familiar diplomatic conventions.

An unwanted war was the prerequisite for many gains that might otherwise be desirable. Thus, in 1771 Sir John Macpherson discussed the benefits of gaining Brazil, but recognised that war with Portugal would have to come first.[137] Commercial benefits were anticipated in 1790 from co-operation with Morocco in the event of any war with Spain, but the British government changed its position after reaching a settlement over Nootka Sound, and the British Consul, who had been made a temporary Ambassador, was informed that 'the measure of farming the duties, and excluding thereby the subjects of other nations from those ports, which might have been extremely beneficial to us in the event of a Spanish war, is not an object to be wished in time of peace'. A new treaty of peace with Morocco was, however, concluded with King Moulay Yazid on 8 April 1791.

In contrast, even though extra-European territorial goals in relations with non-European powers were also generally limited, the mechanisms for establishing a compromise settlement were less ready, and British policy was not in the hands of diplomats seeking a compromise. If, as in Australia or the Andaman Islands, no native state was acknowledged, then Britain could act in a bold fashion, taking advantage of established conventions relating to land seen as 'waste' or 'desert'. In India, the East India Company's officials made scant distinction between frontier wars and gang violence in nominally pacified regions.[138] Commander George

---

[136]   Fife to William Rose, 7 May 1790, Aberdeen UL 2226/131/817; Loughborough to Pitt, 9 Dec. 1792, PRO 30/8/153 fol. 71.

[137]   Macpherson to Shelburne, 16 July 1771, Bowood, Box 56; – to Consul Matra, 14 Nov. 1790, BL Add. 51705 fol. 7.

[138]   W. E. Washburn, 'The Moral and Legal Justifications for Dispossessing the Indians', in J. M. Smith (ed.), *Seventeenth Century America: Essays in Colonial History* (Chapel

Vancouver, who in 1791 had been sent with HMS *Discovery* and HMS *Chatham* to survey the Pacific Northwest coast and to receive back the territory seized at Nootka, claimed the coast line of what he called 'New Albion': from latitude 39° 20' north to Admiralty Inlet. The British government, however, disapproved of his success in persuading the King of Owhyee to cede his island to George III. The British were not alone in their attitude. The North American Indians had not been represented in the 1782–3 peace negotiations that had reapportioned their land.[139]

Both in Europe and elsewhere, the principal motivation behind British policy was defensive, specifically anti-French. Thus, in 1788, Cornwallis wrote of 'the port of Mootapilly which, whilst it is not in our possession, is always liable by some intrigue to fall into the hands of some other European power, and in that case would greatly embarrass us, and entirely cut off the communication between Madras and the Northern Circars'.[140] This defensive motivation took precedence over any interest in territorial or even commercial gains, and had indeed been a major theme throughout the course of eighteenth-century British imperial policy. Thus, the use of force at Ambriz to the north of the Portuguese settlements on the Angolan coast was considered in 1791 in order to protect British trade from a Portuguese attempt to create a commercial monopoly. The measure, however, was very much a reactive one and Thurlow stressed the need for 'firmness, which does not disappoint our end by raising unnecessary displeasure'.[141]

In July 1786 the Board of Control for India sent the Secret Committee of the Court of Directors instructions that clearly outlined the priorities of *official* policy: 'one universal principal ... either in the present condition of the native powers, or in any future revolutions amongst them ... that we are completely satisfied with the possessions we already have, and will engage in no war for the purpose of further acquisitions'. The Board added an important caveat, namely that if any native prince accepted European aid, Britain would back rival native rulers, but that also was a defensive provision. It has, however, been argued that as the government expected the French to interfere in Indian politics, in

Hill, 1959), pp. 24–32; A. Frost, 'New South Wales as *terra nullius*: the British denial of Aboriginal land rights', *Historical Studies*, 19 (1981), 513–23; P. J. Marshall, *Bengal: The British Bridgehead. Eastern India 1740–1828* (Cambridge, 1987), pp. 96–7.

[139] G. Vancouver, *A Voyage of Discovery to the North Pacific Ocean, and Round the World* (3 vols., 1798); R. Fisher, *Vancouver's Voyage: Charting the Northwest Coast* (Seattle, 1992); F. Merk, *The Oregon Question* (Cambridge, Mass., 1967), pp. 1–5; Wright, *American Frontier*, pp. 3, 38.

[140] Cornwallis to Campbell, 5 July 1788, PRO 30/11/159 fols. 141–2.

[141] Robert Walpole to Grenville, 13 July, 13 Aug., Grenville to Walpole, 28 July 1791, PRO FO 63/14; Grenville to Thurlow, 22 July, undated reply, BL Add. 58938 fols. 123–6; Cabinet minute, 28 July 1791, BL Add. 59306 fol. 3.

alliance with Mysore, such a stipulation was not as 'detached as it might appear'.[142] Cornwallis argued that there was a need to take steps to block the dangers he saw as posed by France and Mysore. He saw both as responsible for the hostile actions of other powers, and thus regarded the successful issue of the Dutch crisis as of great importance. In 1788, for example, Cornwallis argued that the Rajah of Cherika was unlikely to repeat the aggression he had displayed in 1786 as Tipu would not support him. He wrote in 1788 of the latter: 'Having always found great difficulty to bring myself to believe that Tipu would be mad enough, without the support of France or the Marathas' to attack Britain, and, indicating the danger of adopting too rigid a distinction between offensive and defensive strategies: 'However inconvenient it would be to our present arrangement, I cannot help thinking that it would ultimately prove for the good of the Company's affairs if Tipu was to oblige us to act against him.'[143] Cornwallis certainly presented his war with Tipu as defensive, and not as indicative of 'a change of system'.[144] In his relations with Hyderabad, Mysore and the Marathas, especially his attempt to isolate Mysore, Cornwallis faced diplomatic challenges similar to those confronting British ministers in Europe, although the constraints of British public opinion and traditional assumptions were less insistent in the case of India.

A more serious limitation on any defensive orientation was provided by the role of aggressive local officials, as in the Bay of Honduras in 1789,[145] and of unofficial bodies, most obviously the 'country' (private) traders in the East Indies and the northern Pacific, who were responsible both for the crucial moves over Penang and for the Nootka crisis. In 1785 the Spanish envoy Campo contrasted the pacific dispositions of the British government and of British 'adventurers' (not on the Mosquito Coast) who supplied the Indians of central America with arms and offered them protection.[146]

'Country' traders were more enterprising than the East India Company.[147] The impact of Meares' allegations revealed the difficulties posed by such activities, but it is nevertheless clear from the Malay world

[142] Kennedy, 'Anglo-French Rivalry', p. 183; Ingram, *British India*, pp. 26–7, 31.
[143] Cornwallis to Campbell, 30 June, 5, 31 July 1788, PRO 30/11/159 fols. 139, 141, 147.
[144] Cornwallis to Lansdowne, 21 May 1792, Bowood 40.
[145] Leeds to Merry, 25 Dec. 1789, PRO FO 72/15 fols. 375–86. On the difficulty of controlling local officials and agents, Atkin, *Russia and Iran*, p. 45.
[146] Campo to Carmarthen, 10 June 1785, BL Eg. 3504 fol. 71.
[147] E. Stokes, 'The First Century of British Rule in India', *Past and Present*, 58 (1973), 136–60; Nightingale, *Trade and Empire*, ix, pp. 240–2; Marshall, 'British Expansion in India in the Eighteenth Century: A Historical Revision', *History*, 60 (1975), 28–43; Barnett, *North India*, pp. 89–90.

that private initiatives could be rejected or ignored. Similarly, 'New Albion' led to nothing. In October 1793 Captain John Hayes hoisted the British flag on the north-west coast of New Guinea, and on behalf of George III took possession of what he called 'New Albion', the first European presence on New Guinea. Hayes' was a privately funded expedition in search of the valuable nutmeg, backed by two British merchants in Bengal. The local Papuan people were welcoming, but Cornwallis' successor as Governor-General, Sir John Shore and his council, sceptical about the economic prospects, refused to support the new settlement at Fort Coronation, and in 1795 it was abandoned. In 1790–1 Blankett had 'determined to attempt the passage (to China) through the Molucca Islands, by the channel of Timor, as not only the clearest passage, but as it might tend to establish the right of the King's subjects to the free navigation of those seas, conformable to the late treaty with Holland'. He reported on Dutch weakness on Timor and suggested that it 'certainly would not be difficult to introduce several articles of our own manufacture, amongst the innumerable inhabitants of these seas, such as knives, razors, saws, hatchets, iron pots, arms powder, shot etc.' Blankett claimed that the British would thus be able to obtain some of the products of the Moluccas and use them as the Dutch did to further their trade with China. The East India Company was indeed interested in 1790 in the prospect of a base on the Palau (Belau) islands (1000 kilometres north of New Guinea and unoccupied by any European power), that could serve to supply ships sailing to China, but was not seeking to overthrow the Dutch in Indonesia, and there was no question of Britain attacking her Dutch ally.[148] A similar contrast between national policymaking, and more aggressive private initiatives has been noted in the case of the United States, albeit with the additional complication of migration.[149]

A stress on the limited nature of British aspirations can also be questioned by considering the extent to which the extent and nature of British 'defensive' requirements had altered, with the expansion of empire, the experience of defeat in the War of American Independence and recent evidence of and fears concerning French imperial ambitions.[150] This heightened consciousness and extended range of defence centred on the Indian Ocean, most obviously in 1784–8, and led in a

---

[148] Kennedy, 'Anglo-French Rivalry', p. 353; A. Griffin, 'London, Bengal, the China Trade and the Unfrequented Extremities of Asia: The East India Company's settlement in New Guinea, 1793–95' *British Library Journal*, 16 (1990), 151–73, esp. 151–4, 164; Blankett to Hawkesbury, 1 Mar. 1791, BL Add. 38226 fols. 114–17.

[149] Stuart, *United States Expansionism*, p. 5.

[150] Kennedy, 'Anglo-French Rivalry', pp. 342–54.

'forward defence' policy to the search for a naval base to the east of India. Yet, as already suggested, there were limits to 'forward defence', both because there was no wish to risk war by challenging the clearly established interests of other European powers, and because the prime defence of Britain's imperial position was provided not by a policy of trans-oceanic aggrandisement, but by one of naval expansion and preparation. It was in the dockyards of Britain that the fate of India was to be secured.

'Forward defence' was to become far more important from 1793, as the resilience and ambitions of first Revolutionary and later Napoleonic France became apparent, and as the defeat or loss of independence at the hands of France of formerly anti-French imperial powers led to concern about their navies and colonies. France conquered the United Provinces in 1795, leading Britain to seize her colonial bases, Malacca, Trincomalee, Galle, Padang, and Cape Colony all being captured or occupied that year. Spain made peace with France the same year, ceding Santo Domingo to France. The French made a major effort in the West Indies in 1795. They failed to take Dominica, but, helped by native risings, recovered Guadeloupe and St Lucia, occupied the Dutch islands of St Martin and St Eustatius and landed on Grenada and St Vincent. The following year, French emissaries arrived in Teheran. In 1797 France took the Ionian islands from the destroyed state of Venice. Napoleon's invasion of Egypt in 1798 threatened not simply the *status quo* in the eastern Mediterranean, but also the route to India. Within five years, there were to be French plans for expeditions to India, the West Indies and Louisiana, the last acquired from Spain in 1801. Concern about French and Russian intentions led to greater British interest in the Near East. It is in these years of crisis that 'forward defence' can be seen clearly,[151] though it had been a factor in the previous years of peace. The principal thrust of empire was, however, war, war both as a means of gaining power and territory, and as a precipitant of fear. The Pitt government was reluctant to become involved in war, and did not do so until 1793. It was only then that 'forward defence' took on a new immediacy. This shift had,

---

[151] Duffy, *Soldiers, Sugar and Seapower*, pp. 141–56; *Cambridge History of Iran*, 7, 331, 373; C. de La Jonquière, *L'Expédition d'Egypte, 1798–1801* I (Paris, 1900); F.-P. Renaut, *La Question de la Louisiane, 1796–1806* (Paris, 1918); G. Blainey, *The Tyranny of Distance* (Melbourne, 1966), pp. 70–98; I. Murat, *Napoléon et le rêve américain* (Paris, 1976); M. E. Yapp, *Strategies of British India: Britain, Iran and Afghanistan 1798–1850* (Oxford, 1980); E. Ingram, *Commitment to Empire: Prophecies of the Great Game in Asia, 1797–1800* (Oxford, 1981); P. Mackesy, *War without Victory. The Downfall of Pitt, 1799–1802* (Oxford, 1984), esp. pp. 144–7; S. Förster, *Die mächtigen Diener der East India Company. Ursachen und Hintergründe der britischen Expansionspolitik in Südasien, 1793–1819* (Stuttgart, 1992).

however, been prefigured in India by governmental and popular willingness during the Third Mysore War (1790–2) to support what became a war of conquest.[152]

Concern with empire was in many respects an aspect of concern with trade, and both played a major role in public discussion about Britain's relations with foreign powers. Indeed, in so far as a 'public culture' of foreign policy can be discerned, it was one of trade and security for *Britain*, for concern about the Continent and such abstractions as the balance of power only played a major role in so far as they were seen as an aspect of the security of Britain, most obviously with the fate of the United Provinces in 1787 and 1792–3. Such limited interests reflected the conservatism of public opinion and the press. They represented a continuation of the situation in the decades after the Peace of Paris, and clashed in part with the notion of a European balance affecting Britain, but such a notion had most impact and resonance throughout the century when plausibly directed against France, and not when applied against other powers, most obviously Russia in the late 1710s or Austria in the late 1720s. Thus, Pitt's domestic political failure in 1791, the failure to persuade the 'political nation' that a Russian threat to Europe existed, that this threat affected Britain, and that it required action by her, had been prefigured earlier in the century: even during the period of Anglo-French alliance (1716–31), it had been difficult to shed an automatic assumption of hostility towards France. This had become even more intense after the mid-century wars (1739–63), and the defeats and humiliation of the War of American Independence. This hostility set the measure of the task Pitt faced in supporting the Eden Treaty, and, though to a lesser extent, that faced by Burke in defending the French *ancien régime*.

'Negative' drives, arising from hostility and fear, play a major role in many movements, ideologies and tendencies, and that was certainly true of British public culture in this period, more specifically of the patriotism of the age. That term can be used in an eighteenth-century context both to describe specific politicians and political groupings, such as the 'Cobham Cubs' in the late 1730s, who used a discourse of national interests and a wronged nation to criticise governments for their domestic and foreign policies, as well as, more generally, to focus on the development of a non-specifically partisan sense and discourse of national identity and interest. The patriotism of the 1780s lacked the clear political echoes of that of the 1730s-50s, but was nevertheless still

[152] P. J. Marshall, '"Cornwallis Triumphat"': War in India and the British Public in the Late Eighteenth Century', in L. Freedman, P. Hayes and R. O'Neill, *War, Strategy and International Politics* (Oxford, 1992), pp. 60–74.

important. It owed much to xenophobia, anti-Catholicism, and hostility to France.

Earlier in the century, Britain had seemed different, indeed exceptional, as a political society because of the importance of its public politics and the extent to which they centred on issues of policy, such as those posed by the patriotic discourse, rather than merely place and patronage. To a considerable extent this analysis, advanced most frequently by juxtaposing Britain and France, was misleading. Not only did some continental states, most obviously Sweden, Poland and the United Provinces, have a public politics, but there was also a politics in *ancien régime* states that lacked national political assemblies, a politics that was not devoid of issues.[153]

Nevertheless, despite the similarities, there was also a degree of difference between Britain and, certainly, France in the first half of the century. This was eroded by the process of public politicisation in France that led to and, to a greater extent, was stimulated by, first, the mid-century controversies centring on Jansenism and later by that arising from the Maupeou Revolution. Oliver Goldsmith, in his 'Citizen of the World' essay in the *Public Ledger* of 8 July 1760, referred to the French 'vindicating themselves into freedom'.[154] By the 1780s there was a considerable measure of convergence between aspects of the public politics of Britain and France. The greater freedom of the French press was an obvious instance, and French ministers discovered that, like their British counterparts, they could be embarrassed by press attacks on foreign powers or their envoys. 'Public opinion' came to the fore in French politics. During the commercial negotiations of 1786, Vergennes mentioned his concern about possible domestic complaints.[155] In France, in September 1787, Grenville was concerned about the strength of anti-British agitation, and he wrote: 'It is impossible to say, in a country where so much depends on public opinion, what effect may be produced by this sort of clamour; and whether that may not drive them [ministers], against their wishes, into measures of violence.'[156] Four years later, criticism of government expenditure led Malmesbury, then visiting Berlin, to observe, 'despotic as this Government is, yet the public will be

---

[153] J. Black, 'Britain and the Continent 1688–1815. Convergence or Divergence?', *British Journal for Eighteenth-Century Studies*, 15 (1992), 145–9, and *Convergence or Divergence? Britain and the Continent* (London, 1994), pp. 116–53.

[154] D. van Kley, *The Damiens Affair and the Unraveling of the Ancien Régime. Church, State, and Society in France, 1750–1770* (Princeton, 1984); D. Echeverria, *The Maupeou Revolution* (Baton Rouge, 1985). There are valuable comparative approaches in D. Jarrett, *The Begetters of Revolution. England's involvement with France 1759–1789* (1973) and N. Henshall, *The Myth of Absolutism* (Harlow, 1992), pp. 80–119.

[155] Eden to Carmarthen, 17 Apr. 1786, PRO FO 27/19 fol. 21.

[156] *Court and Cabinets*, I, 330.

listened to',[157] though Jenkinson wrote in 1792 of the Prussians that, as they lived 'under an arbitrary government', they were 'unacquainted with the variety of interests that must be consulted in a government constituted like ours'.[158] The process of Anglo-French convergence was to be both accentuated and then ruptured by the Revolution. The Estates General was not so much revived after a long interval, as created anew, and this forum of national politics rapidly developed into a body before which, in comparison with Britain, the government was politically and, though more gradually, institutionally crippled. The Revolution also led to the development of a patriotic discourse in France, one in which foreign policy played a major role, and could thus serve to exclude important political groups from the nation. This was also true of Poland, as earlier of the Dutch Patriots.[159] Later, counter-revolution was to lead to the development of a similarly divisive discourse throughout much of Europe, as peoples rallied around Country, Crown and Church and in opposition to France. The discourse in revolutionary France was initially anti-Austrian, a continuation and accentuation of the pre-revolutionary situation,[160] though it subsequently broadened to include publicly voiced hostility to all monarchical, indeed all *ancien-régime*, states, and thus, in practice, to the rest of Europe, or at least all major powers with whom revolutionary France was likely to have relations. It was as urgent, as crucial to the revolutionary atmosphere and the sense of crisis, as its anti-Russian counterpart in Poland.

The closest British equivalent was hostility to France, but, in the late 1780s and in 1790–1, this lacked the intensity either of French austrophobia or of Polish russophobia, or indeed of British francophobia earlier in the century. All political developments, not least revolutions, follow their own trajectories, and comparisons can be questionable,

---

[157] Aspinall, *George Prince of Wales*, II, no. 623.
[158] C. D. Yonge (ed.), *The Life and Administration of Robert Banks, Second Earl of Liverpool* (3 vols., 1868), I, 25.
[159] N. C. F. van Sas, 'The Patriot Perspective: New Perspectives', in Jacob and Mijnhardt (eds.), *The Dutch Republic in the Eighteenth Century*, pp. 98–9. On nationalism in this period B. F. Hyslop, *French Nationalism in 1789, According to the General Cahiers* (New York, 1934); H. Kohn, *The Idea of Nationalism: a study in its origin and background* (New York, 1945); *Actes du Colloque Patriotisme et nationalisme en Europe à l'époque de la Révolution française et de Napoléon* (Paris, 1973); E. Turczynski, *Konfession und Nation. Zur Frühgeschichte der serbischen und rumänischen Nationsbildung* (Düsseldorf, 1976); C. Prignitz, *Vaterlandsliebe und Freiheit: deutscher Patriotismus von 1750–1850* (Wiesbaden, 1981); 'The Enlightenment and the National Revival in Eastern Europe', *Canadian Review of Studies in Nationalism*, special issue (1983); O. Dann and J. Dinwiddy (eds.), *Nationalism in the Age of the French Revolution* (1988); *Transactions of the Seventh International Congress on the Enlightenment* (3 vols., Oxford, 1989), cont. pag. 1635–42.
[160] Hailes to Carmarthen, 28 Oct. 1784, BL Eg. 3499 fol. 45; *AP* 15, 538.

especially if they imply, as with certain theories about industrialisation, that there was one path, but, nevertheless, there is a sense in which English patriotism was given a tremendous boost and fresh definition by the 'Glorious Revolution', and that France and Poland underwent a similar process in the late 1780s and early 1790s. As in the English case, this patriotism was politically defined, partisan and divisive. In England it had been directed against Jacobites and those held likely to support the exiled Stuarts, such as Catholics, as much as against the principal patron of the Stuarts, Louis XIV. Indeed, Louis XIV established himself as the national enemy more by his backing for the Stuarts and their British supporters, especially the Irish Catholics, than by his activities on the Continent. War did not unite the country. The Nine Years War (1689–97) was divisive as the Tories and the Country Whigs disapproved, and the war was largely unsuccessful. The Tories deplored every victory of the Duke of Marlborough during the War of the Spanish Succession (1702–13).

English, still more British, patriotism was thus in the post-1688 period necessarily divisive, and derived much of its drive from this partisan character. The 'Glorious Revolution' led to the development of two competing theses of patriotism, one of which triumphed, and thus was able to define patriotism accordingly. Such a process was not new. It could indeed be seen on every occasion in which domestic divisions and foreign policy had interacted, for example during the Henrician Reformation and the English Civil War, and it thus had medieval roots, as with French intervention in English domestic politics in 1216–17: at the end of the reign of John and during Henry III's minority. The expansion of the dimension of public politics in the early 1690s, thanks to the move to annual Parliaments and an active press free of pre-publication censorship, as well as the lengthy conflict with France for most of the period 1689–1713, ensured that the particular patriotic discourse associated with the winning side in the British civil conflict of 1688–91, became well entrenched.

That there was, however, always a public debate over foreign policy, over goals as well as means, was amply demonstrated both during the wars of 1689–1713 and subsequently. The political intensity and resonance of this debate became, nevertheless, less important after the mid-century wars, as the foreign policy agenda that successive ministries had adopted during the reigns of Georges I and II, and that, furthermore, they could be accused of following in opposition to what could be termed national interests, had been discarded. The Seven Years War and the Elder Pitt focused the sense of nationhood and patriotism. There was a pronounced move away from continental interventionism in the 1760s, and an even more obvious abandonment of postures that could be criticised as pro-Hanoverian. Britain was at peace with all her European neighbours between 1763 and 1778: the longest period, if Anglo-Spanish hostilities in 1727 are treated as war, since the reign of James I; if not, the longest period since Walpole's ministry. The Falklands Crisis of 1770 and the Ochakov Crisis were to demonstrate, however, that the overt public dimension of foreign policy could still be of considerable and direct political importance. Lansdowne claimed in 1787 'that it is the Public which decides upon measures with us'. The same year Thurlow gave Pitt a warning that he would have done well to recall in early 1791. He argued that if the Dutch crisis led to war it would be necessary to prepare 'materials for explaining our conduct ... for giving it an acceptable colour here ... This country dreads a war, and nothing will be so difficult, as to persuade them, they are well served, in that situation, or by those, who shall have brought them into it.'[161]

In November 1785 Fox offered his friend Richard Fitzpatrick a somewhat pessimistic view of the public's ability to understand foreign policy:

I can not think as you do of the insignificancy of newspapers though I think that others over rate their importance. I am clear too that *paragraphs* alone will not do. Subjects of importance should be first treated gravely in letters or pamphlets or best of all perhaps in a series of letters, and afterwards the paragraphs do very well again as an accompaniment. It is not till a subject has been so much discussed as to become almost threadbare that *paragraphs* which consist principally in allusions can be generally understood. Secret influence, Indian government and now Irish propositions are all fit subjects therefore for paragraphs; but foreign politics must first be treated in some serious and plain way, and must be much explained to the public before any paragraphs alluding to them can be understood by one in a thousand.

Given the complexity of the *Fürstenbund*, then the leading issue colouring political views of British foreign policy, Fox's assessment was understandable. He was not arguing that public opinion was unimportant, simply that international relations were difficult to comprehend. This helped to ensure that it was easier to politicise aspects of foreign policy that struck a traditional resonance, especially Anglo-Bourbon relations, rather than those relating to eastern Europe, unless they were seen in the misleading perspective of Anglo-French animosity.[162]

There is no doubt that patriotism, in the sense of national identity and consciousness, was strong, albeit still confused by the questions of how to

---

[161] J. Black, 'The Crown, Hanover and the Shift in British Foreign Policy', in Black (ed.), *Knights Errant*, pp. 113–34; Lansdowne to Morellet, 7 Aug. 1787, Beinecke, Osborn Files, Lansdowne; Thurlow to Pitt, Sept. 1787, PRO 30/8/183 fol. 174.
[162] Fox to Fitzpatrick, [Nov. 1785], BL Add. 47580 fol. 129.

relate to Catholics, Scots and Irish. And yet, a teleological view of patriotism, that presents steadily growing patriotism and rising nationalism is not without problems. In many respects, the absence, in the early decades of George III's reign, of the forcing house of revolution and of a strong domestic challenge, as had earlier been the case from 1688, limited the urgency and vigour of patriotism, especially as a political force. The crushing defeat of Bonnie Prince Charlie at Culloden in 1746 ensured that Jacobitism was less of an option for Tories and so had less influence on the perception of them by both the Whigs and George II. In the late 1740s and 1750s, Tory cohesion and identity were seriously compromised as Tories played a major role in support of Whig alignments: those constructed first by Frederick, Prince of Wales and later by Pitt the Elder. George III's determination to exert his power completed the destruction of the old party system, dividing the Whigs and atomising the Tories. The role of competing personal groups, operating without the semi-imperatives of fear and loyalty created by the Jacobite challenge and the response to it, helped to produce ministerial and parliamentary insecurity in the 1760s as George III sought to create a ministry he could co-operate with and that could wield an effective majority in the Parliament. The situation was aggravated by fears of rapid constitutional change towards royal tyranny. The decade also witnessed an increase in extra-parliamentary political activity associated, in particular, with the favourable response to the maverick and charismatic John Wilkes in his challenges to the authority of George III, his ministers, and Parliament. There was, however, no comparison between the actual and potential extra-parliamentary action that George I and George II's ministries had to consider and that which was faced in the period 1760–90. Most extra-parliamentary action was really a matter of peaceful lobbying. It was not until the 1790s that a challenge similar to that posed by Jacobitism had to be confronted. The British supporters of the American rebels sought to alter the purpose of George III's government, not the identity of the ruling dynasty. Christopher Wyvill's attempt to found an alternative structure to Parliament failed. Whereas in the Thirteen Colonies revolution was both cause and consequence of the slipping away of authority from the established institutions of state, to new, *ad hoc* unofficial bodies, no such process took place in Britain. The pro-government *Leeds Intelligencer*, in its issue of 13 March 1781, claimed that: 'If the Patriots really believe the doctrines they profess, they must suppose the constitution to be dissolved, and then they ought to have recourse to arms. But their spirit does not keep pace with their professions.' The American crisis did not act as the earlier Franco-Jacobite crisis of 1689–1715 (and to a certain extent -46, -59 or -63) had done, in that ministerial conduct was unsure, as for example in the dispatch of the Carlisle Commission, and the domestic critics of governmental policy generally remained within the political system and certainly did not turn for support to Britain's enemies. These factors weakened any clear identification of national identity and the struggle with a foreign power and its domestic supporters. The same was even more clear of the Ochakov crisis. In the early 1790s, a sustained attempt to recreate this adversarial relationship was made in Britain. The response to the crisis in relations with revolutionary France and its real and apparent supporters in Britain was an attempt to reforge a sense of national identity, because the nature of the revolutionary challenge, both in Britain and from France and, crucially, their apparent co-operation, seemed to make this essential. Thus, in Britain and in France a similar process occurred in the early 1790s: the definition of a political perspective in which foreign and domestic challenges were closely linked, and in which it seemed crucial to mobilise mass support for a struggle with an insidious, but also all too apparent enemy. A language of nationalism in which paranoia played a major role therefore developed, though it was far from simply negative: the quasi-messianic values outlined by the revolutionaries in France were paralleled by the stress on the values of Crown, Church, political system and ideological inheritance in Britain.[163]

Such a stress on a measure of convergence between Britain and France, for even if the terms of discourse were opposing, the purposes were similar, opens up the more general and recently controversial issue of the extent to which it is helpful to regard eighteenth-century Britain as an *ancien régime* state and society, indeed of the very nature of the British state in this period. The former issue requires an examination of the situation on the Continent, as well as that in Britain. A redefinition of continental absolutism can be offered, one in which the functional and ideological limitations of the power and authority of central government are stressed, and the crucial nature of crown–elite consensus is emphasised. In addition, the very variety of *ancien régime* political culture can be emphasised, so that the differences if this is considered at say Moscow or Madrid, Milan or Mannheim, are emphasised. It then becomes more pertinent to discuss Britain as an instance of an *ancien régime* political system, while accepting that, as in the other cases of such societies, their

---

[163] L. Colley, 'Whose Nation? Class and national consciousness in Britain, 1750–1830', *Past and Present*, 113 (1986), 97–117, offers a valuable but somewhat different account of the political context of national consciousness. See also her *Britons. Forging the Nation, 1707–1837* (New Haven, 1992), and 'Britishness and Otherness: An Argument', *Journal of British Studies*, 31 (1992), 316–26.

common characteristics were matched by distinct individual features. Thus, the shared consequences of the Judaic–Christian moral and social inheritance, low-technology agrarian economies, inegalitarian, paternalistic and male-centred social organisations dominated by the inheritance of wealth and power, decentralised government and a political system that sought elite consensus and in which patronage played a major role, have to be set aside such specific characteristics as Anglicanism, a well developed system of common law, the relative sophistication of England's primary financial institutions, especially the Bank of England, and Britain's insular position. The last permitted Britain, as the only important independent island(s) state off the Continent of Europe, to rely for defence on a powerful navy and to seek to act as a major power without having a substantial army.

Other characteristics were shared with a number of other states. If Britain was a major colonial power, so also were Spain, France, the United Provinces and Portugal. If she was, thanks to the Hanoverian connection and the British dimension, part of a 'multiple kingdom', so also were other states, such as Denmark and Sweden. A stress on distinctive demographic and economic developments can be qualified by considering the situation on the Continent. The notion of British specificity can be further qualified if the aggregate nature of Britain is replaced by consideration of the differing experience of her constituent parts. At a regional level, economic variety and different social experiences emerge even more clearly, while a consideration of the particular nature of the Scottish and Irish experience in the century after the 'Glorious Revolution' casts doubt on any triumphalist interpretation of British specificity in the period.[164]

In terms of political culture and institutions, Britain was in some respects distinctive. Though not alone in having an important representative assembly (in Britain's case, three until 1707 and two thereafter), the Westminster Parliament had developed as an effective instrument of statehood, not least because the fears of executive control expressed in the late seventeenth and early eighteenth century had been, in large measure, justified. Indeed, in the debates in the National Assembly in May 1790 about how far that body should have powers over peace and war, the British Parliament was criticised on that basis.[165] Parliamentary taxation tapped national wealth, the central government was able, as a result, to borrow at a favourable rate of interest, certainly in comparison to France, and an agency existed for national legislation.

---

[164] J. Black, 'The European Idea and Britain 1688–1815', *History of European Ideas*, 17 (1993), 439–60.   [165] *AP* 15, 540, 623–4.

French ministers sought to create a body with these characteristics in the 1780s, though they wanted one that was apparently more responsive to governmental initiatives than the Westminster Parliament, and certainly were not interested in any counterpart to the British political crisis of 1782–4. Anthony Merry's mention of an older British model is interesting given the role of the aristocracy in pre-revolutionary pressures for change, 'the Parliament in France have prescribed terms for the arrangement of the constitution of that kingdom as nearly as possible similar to the Magna Charta'. The appeal of more recent British models in the pre-revolution and the early stages of the Revolution,[166] as of the Revolution itself to British radicals, is a reminder of the degree of flux in Anglo-French relations in their broadest sense, that characterised some attitudes in the late 1780s and early 1790s.[167] This was of particular concern to British conservatives, but it also reflected a sense in both states that the existing political system required major changes. This attitude had led to pressure for reform in Britain in the early 1780s, and, in some respects, in the 1780s, Pitt's ministry was a beneficiary of this attitude, at least in so far as winning a considerable measure of support was concerned.

In the 1780s political reform was blocked in Britain, though not in Ireland. The Yorkshire movement did not transform the political system and attempts at parliamentary reform were defeated in the House of Commons.[168] In October 1789, Capell Lofft, a Rational Dissenter, supporter of parliamentary reform and opponent of the slave trade, wrote:

I rejoice to hear that in America at least the cause of Negro emancipation prospers. In France there seems no reason to doubt of its success. I hope England will not persevere in that supineness to her own rights and those of mankind which instead of the first has marked her in this century the last of all Nations to

[166] Merry to Liston, 19 Dec. 1788, NLS 5552 fol. 103; *AP* 15, 534, 548, 559, 576, 585, 610, 615; G. Bonno, *La Constitution britannique devant l'opinion française de Montesquieu à Bonaparte* (Paris, 1931); E. H. Lemay, 'Les Modèles anglais et américain à l'Assemblée Constituante', *Transactions of the Fifth International Congress on the Enlightenment* (Oxford, 1980), II, 872–84; J. Censer, 'English Politics in the *Courrier d'Avignon*', in Censer and J. D. Popkin (eds.), *Press and Politics in Pre-Revolutionary France* (Berkeley, 1987), pp. 201–2.

[167] J. Grieder, *Anglomania in France 1740–1789. Fact, Fiction, and Political Discourse* (Geneva, 1985), pp. 141–6; J.-P. Jessenne and F. Wartelle, 'France Angleterre: Conflits d'images et influences sur l'engagement revolutionnaire en France septentrionale', in M. Vovelle (ed.), *L'Image de La Revolution Française* (4 vols., cont. pag., Oxford, 1989–90), 608–13.

[168] G. M. Ditchfield, 'The Parliamentary Struggle over the Repeal of the Test and Corporation Acts, 1787–1790', *English Historical Review*, 89 (1974), 551–77, and 'The House of Lords and Parliamentary Reform in the Seventeen-Eighties', *BIHR*, 54 (1981), 219.

give effect to any propositions of reform in which the interests of mankind and her own genuine honour and felicity are concerned.[169]

This sense, that Britain had fallen behind in the reform stakes, that her elite had no stake in reform, was to sharpen and become more important as radicalism developed in a dialectic with the French example.

Yet, reform has many aspects and an element of subjectivity is central to any assessment. Institutional reform was a feature of the 1780s, most obviously in the government of India, but also in public finance and in a general tightening of procedure and improvement of efficiency that was a feature of the peacetime Pitt ministry. The Sinking Fund of 1786 reorganised debt redemption, the Consolidated Fund created in 1787 brought order to government accounts, though there was still neither a single, comprehensive budget nor effective Treasury control of expenditure. Helped by commercial expansion, government revenues and the amount of bullion in the country grew appreciably.[170] This commercial expansion, and the government policies that were in part responsible, ensured 'the enthusiastic support of the manufacturing and commercial elites' for the ministry.[171] In France, in contrast, political, rather than institutional, reform came to the fore, despite the effort of the royal government to centre on the latter. The *Morning Chronicle* of 7 September 1791 praised the new French constitution as better than that of Britain, but the pace of political reform, the urgent desire to create a perfect new constitution and, crucially, the opposition of powerful domestic elements to the process of reform as well as divisions among the reformers, ensured that reform in France soon became better described as revolution, both by its supporters and by its opponents.

It would be foolish to deny that the differing results of the reform process in Britain and France in 1783–93 were in large part due to contingent factors, but it is appropriate to consider how far the differences reflected the varied nature of the two countries as *ancien régime* states. The inability of the British state to absorb imperial tensions had been demonstrated in relations with the Thirteen Colonies in the 1770s, but, it had proved more resilient in dealing with domestic tensions, including the challenging experience of defeat and loss of empire, in the 1780s. Close attention to the early 1780s, however,

---

[169] Lofft to ?, 15 Oct. 1789, Beinecke, Osborn uncat.

[170] Ehrman, *Pitt*, I, pp. 239–326; N. Baker, 'Changing Attitudes towards Government in Eighteenth-Century Britain', in A. Whiteman, J. S. Bromley and P. G. M. Dickson (eds.), *Statesmen, Scholars and Merchants* (Oxford, 1973), pp. 202–19; J. Torrence, 'Social Class and Bureaucratic Innovation: the Commissioners for Examining the Public Accounts, 1780–7', *Past and Present*, 78 (1978), 56–81; J. Clapham, *The Bank of England. A History* (2 vols., 1945), I, 256–7.

[171] F. O'Gorman, 'An Age of Progress and Reform?', *Historical Journal*, 35 (1992), 693.

suggests a less optimistic conclusion, and it is clear both then, and a decade later, that critics of the system were prepared to turn to novel and extra-parliamentary political means. The crisis in relations between George III and the Fox–North ministry created a serious political situation, and its resolution in the form of a Pitt ministry enjoying backing in Parliament was far from inevitable.

Yet, once crown–elite consensus had been restored, at least in so far as was measured by the ability of George III to co-operate with a ministry enjoying the support of Parliament, Britain was politically stable. Unlike during the period of the Jacobite challenge, this was not a question of ministerial stability but more general political instability, at least that is until the rise of domestic radicalism following the French Revolution altered the situation. Prior to that, there was a considerable measure of stability, and that was not disturbed either by the failure to introduce parliamentary reform or by the measures of the Pitt ministry. A stable and relatively united government enjoying a considerable measure of public support, therefore, faced the crisis of the early 1790s, an obvious contrast with the situation in France. The parliamentary system brought a considerable measure of elite consensus in Britain: if not necessarily support for government and its policies, then at least acceptance of its position. Indeed, in contrast to the position under Walpole, when the Revolution Settlement was still being defined and debated and con-stitutional and political conventions were being established, the situation was far more stable by the 1780s, though the controversies over George III's conduct in 1783–4 and over the nature of a regency government in 1788–9 were a reminder that conventions and their application were far from fixed. This consensus was to hold firm in 1792–4, as most of the elite lined up behind the ministry, many abandoning the Whig party.[172] The consensus was crucial in giving the government a considerable degree of room for diplomatic manoeuvre. The Ochakov climbdown indicated the difficulties that could arise if ministers took bold steps and neglected to consider how far they could go without arousing appreciable domestic disquiet and opposition, but, given greater caution, in terms of diplomatic objectives and means and the domestic presentation and defence of policy, the government could realistically hope to win support.

In France, there was no time to establish widely acceptable con-stitutional conventions, and the elite was fatally fractured. The rev-olutionary consequences justified Burke's concern on both counts. Thus, the constitutional and political differences between the two states proved more important in this period than the similarities between the two

---

[172] McCahill, *Order and Equipoise*, pp. 5, 12–14, 20–1, 153–8, 166–7.

societies, unsurprisingly so as crucial aspects of political arrangement and ideology were at stake.

The British state of the late eighteenth century experienced and survived severe challenges, greater than any until the world wars of the modern age. They were not, however, unprecedented, for the wars of 1689–1713 and 1739–63 were serious crises, domestic as much as international, political and fiscal as much as diplomatic and military. With the important exception of imperial affairs, the institutions and practices that had helped surmount the Seven Years War did not require total overhaul in order to cope with the crises of the 1770s and 1780s. This was not to be the case of the Revolutionary–Napoleonic crisis, but it was the war that was responsible for new institutions and practices, such as income tax and the census, rather than them leading to war. The same was essentially true of the growth of empire in the period. The parallel with France is instructive, for, to a considerable extent, it was the French Revolutionary War that radicalised the Revolution, just as it was to be war that changed states such as Prussia and Spain. British success in the struggle with France has also been seen as providing a crucial precondition 'for the market economy and night-watchman state of Victorian England, as well as the liberal world order which flourished under British hegemony'.[173] The relationship between international strength and economic growth had been prefigured during the Nootka Sound crisis, at the conclusion of which Auckland thought Britain:

confessedly at the head of all the nations of the earth in foreign influence and internal prosperity: with the advantage of having proved that our superiority depends on something more than mercantile energy, which will now show itself with redoubled vigour and with new security ... I do not believe that there ever existed a moment in which our country stood so high in the opinion of other nations.[174]

Any emphasis on the changes brought by war might seem to relegate the foreign policy of the first decade of the Pitt ministry to inconsequence, but it was largely thanks to foreign policy that wars were caused or avoided, while it was also crucial to their conduct. Without a history of its foreign policy, it is impossible to understand the British state of the age, a period in which it played a crucial role in world history.

---

[173] P. K. O'Brien, 'The Impact of the Revolutionary and Napoleonic Wars, 1793–1815, on the Long-Run Growth of the British Economy', *Review* [of the Fernand Braudel Center], 12 (1989), 348, *Power with Profit: The State and the Economy, 1688–1815* (1991), p. 33, and 'Political Preconditions for the Industrial Revolution', in O'Brien and R. Quinault (eds.), *The Industrial Revolution and British Society* (Cambridge, 1993), p. 151.

[174] Auckland to Sheffield, 13 Nov. 1790, BL Add. 45728 fol. 120.

11   The international system

An account of international political developments in the period 1783–93 throws up a number of questions. The most obvious, indeed conventional, one centres on the question of the extent to which the French Revolution changed the situation, most obviously in so far as French policy was concerned, but also with reference to the policy of other powers. This question can focus on the objectives of the powers concerned, most obviously on whether Revolutionary France sustained or altered the policies of its *ancien-régime* predecessor, but it can also be addressed to the related issues of the means by which policy was formulated and the methods of diplomacy, all of which contributed to a supposed revolutionary foreign policy, or at least to the foreign policy of a particular revolution. Before turning to this question, or rather set of questions, it is appropriate, however, to focus attention on two issues, first the nature of *ancien régime* international relations, both in general, and in the specific terms of the conduct of the powers in the decade prior to the outbreak of the French Revolutionary War, and secondly to assess the importance of European international relations both in this period and in that of the subsequent years of conflict. The first question is a crucial preliminary to the assessment of revolutionary change, for it is only if *ancien régime* international relations are properly understood, both in a descriptive and in a dynamic sense, that it is possible to address the issue of the impact of the French Revolution.

The conventional view is that pre-revolutionary relations were conservative, and this is linked to a sense that the warfare of the period was limited and indecisive, indeed that relatively little was at stake in it. Thus, John Childs has argued that 'eighteenth-century warfare was defensive because the international political outlook of western Europe was defensive. All states, large or small, were essentially concerned with the maintenance of the *status quo*.'[1] Such an analysis is questionable on

---

[1] J. Childs, *Armies and Warfare in Europe 1648–1789* (Manchester, 1982), p. 101, see also p. 21, K. J. Holsti, *Peace and War: armed conflicts and international order 1648–1989* (Cambridge, 1989), p. 102, and, with some qualification, R. F. Weigley, *The Age of*

both grounds. Many rulers were very ambitious in their policies and much was at stake. The notion of limited war has to be seriously qualified. Rulers achieved much through war and diplomacy. War was not only responsible for frontier changes: it was also through conflict that the Bourbons had gained and established themselves on the thrones of, successively, France, Spain and Naples, and the house of Hanover and the Romanovs retained those of Britain and Russia respectively. In the period 1680–1780 the Austrian Habsburgs had gained Hungary, the Austrian Netherlands and a dominant position in northern Italy, Russia had become both a Baltic and a Black Sea power, Prussia had become a major state. Rulers had shown themselves willing to consider substantial alterations in the international system, territorial changes that radically altered the ranking of the powers. The First Partition of Poland (1772) had been prefigured by similar schemes that had been considered on a number of occasions earlier in the century. A partition of the Swedish empire was planned and, with major modifications, executed during the Great Northern War (1700–21). The partition of the Spanish Habsburg inheritance was the central issue at stake in the War of the Spanish Succession (1701/2–13/14); that of the Austrian Habsburgs in the War of the Austrian Succession (1740–8). The partition of the Habsburg inheritance that was planned in 1741, and that did not seem too fanciful in light of the progress of the campaigns of that year, would have entailed a major redrawing of the map of central Europe.

In 1680–1780, possession of significant territories, such as Silesia and the western Milanese, was gained and retained through conflict. Far larger areas were fought for, and war plans, if successful, would have entailed substantial territorial changes and fundamental alterations in European international relations. The most ambitious plans related to the Balkans, where, on a number of occasions, the Austrians and Russians planned major conquests. Elsewhere in Europe, ambitious plans for territorial redistribution were advanced, as in northern Europe during the Great Northern War, or in 1784 when Gustavus III of Sweden was forced to drop his aggressive plans against Norway. During the Wars of the Spanish and Austrian Successions, the reversal of Louis XIV's gains along France's eastern frontier was a goal of his opponents, while during the latter conflict and the Seven Years War, the partition of Prussia was on the agenda. These schemes, though difficult to execute, were not obviously beyond the military capabilities of the powers of the period.[2]

Battles. The Quest for Decisive Warfare from Breitenfeld to Waterloo (Bloomington, 1991), p. 168.   [2] Black, *Rise of the European Powers.*

The wars of the period were waged for victory. That rulers and generals did not wish to lose trained troops on campaign or in conflict did not mean that operations were simply conducted in order to minimise losses. Hand-to-hand infantry fighting was less marked than in the major battles of the previous century, but this was a consequence of the demise of the pike and increased infantry firepower. Cold steel remained important in cavalry combat, and was also more important in infantry engagements than pictures of parallel firing lines might suggest, bayonet charges being employed by generals such as Marlborough and Charles XII of Sweden. The tactics of firepower did not necessarily reduce casualties, or imply any absence of a desire to win. The exchange of fire between nearby lines of closely packed troops could produce high casualty rates, especially if cannon could be brought to bear. Over 30,000 of the 108,000 combatants at Blenheim (1704) were casualties, as were a quarter of the Anglo-Dutch-German force at Malplaquet (1709) and about 13,000 out of 35,000 Prussians at Kolin (1757).

The importance of sieges in many campaigns is frequently cited as cause, example and consequence of the limited nature of operations and the extent to which conflicts were wars of position. Fortifications did not, however, prevent decisive campaigns, as Saxe demonstrated in the heavily fortified Low Countries in 1745–8, while sieges were far from necessarily being a soft option. Louis XIV and certain of his ministers and generals may have come to prefer caution, the concentration of massive forces to ensure predictable success in sieges, but their policies should not be regarded as typical. The combatants of the period, such as the Prussian soldiers in the Seven Years War, would not have appreciated being told that they lived in an age of limited war.[3]

Such a reassessment qualifies some of the claims made on behalf of the 1790s, not least the suggestion that warfare changed fundamentally. It also poses a question mark to the thesis that has hitherto been the principal qualification of the notion of a dramatic change in international relations stemming from the French Revolution. This is the idea that there was a major change in the second half of the eighteenth century, but that this originated not from revolutionary Paris, but from the adaptation of Enlightenment ideas by the rulers of the period in order to provide a rationale for expansionism. Thus, the First Partition of Poland is seen as a new departure, the application of the principle of reason to international relations.[4]

This thesis rests on a mistaken assessment of the previous century,

[3] Black, *A Military Revolution?*, pp. 52–7.
[4] D. E. Kaiser, *Politics and War, European Conflict from Philip II to Hitler* (Cambridge, Mass., 1990), pp. 203–10.

especially the period 1715–48 which has had relatively little attention recently, and also reflects the dominant model of the *ancien régime*, namely a resolution of the mid-seventeenth-century crisis in the shape of absolutist states and societies, whose subsequent stability was a crucial component of the *ancien régime*, but one that was faced in the second half of the eighteenth century by a general crisis.[5] This model can be challenged, but it is first necessary to address the thesis of a new-modelled and new-modelling international system.

The First Partition was greeted with outrage, but claims that new maxims had been adopted were inaccurate. Not only had treaties been cynically breached on many occasions, but the actual or planned despoliation of weak states by more powerful neighbours, alone or in combination, was far from novel. The remodelling of territorial control by agreement among some or all of the major powers, generally without heeding the views of their weaker counterparts, had been a characteristic of the extensive diplomacy over the Spanish Succession and was a feature of the peace settlements of the period. It is possible to present this diplomacy in a positive light by stressing the role of equivalents, considerations of balance and the desire to achieve a peaceful and 'rational' solution to disputes, especially in avoiding general war.[6] The reality was also that the pretensions of the weak were overridden and that such manipulative diplomacy was generally more fertile than successful.

Numerous plans for hostile seizures of territory can be found in the diplomatic correspondence from the decades before the First Partition, and they were not only propounded by rulers, such as those of Russia, who had few dynastic and other legal claims that they could advance. In 1704 Frederick I of Prussia demanded Nuremberg as his price for abandoning the Grand Alliance, in the early 1740s Spain advanced plans for major territorial changes in Italy, and in 1744 Frederick II, while suggesting substantial gains for Prussia and Saxony in Bohemia, argued that Charles Albert of Bavaria, the Emperor Charles VII, could be compensated for his claims there with the archbishopric of Salzburg and the bishopric of Passau. The Baltic was a region particularly fertile in schemes for new territorial dispositions, some not intended as hostile, such as the Holstein project in 1726 for the acquisition of Russia's conquests from Sweden by the Duke of Holstein-Gottorp, or the attempt in 1743 to elect the Crown Prince of Denmark as King of Sweden. Others would have required war, for example the plan of 1744 for concerted action against Prussia, leading to the gain of East Prussia by Poland, with Russia obtaining an equivalent in eastern Poland, and for the acquisition

[5] A good recent summary is offered by W. Doyle, *The Old European Order 1660–1800* (Oxford, 1978), pp. 295–6.   [6] R. M. Hatton, *War and Peace, 1680–1720* (1969).

of Bremen and Verden from Hanover by Denmark which was in turn to return Schleswig to Holstein-Gottorp.

Contemporaries had little doubt of the sweeping changes envisaged by many rulers. Amelot, the French Foreign Minister, commented on the 'vast ideas' of Charles VII in 1743, while in 1744 the French envoy to Charles, faced with the accusation that French policy would be seen as renewing the idea of a universal monarchy, complained that George II sought to dispose of eastern France 'like the things in his garden at Herrenhausen'. The same year a British diplomat claimed that French support for the Jacobites 'gives a flat lie to the boasted moderation and innocence of her views and must convince every subject of the republic [United Provinces], as well as of England, that not only the possessions of the House of Austria, and the Balance of Power, but even our own liberties and religion, are struck at by that ambitious power'.[7] Minor powers especially were victims of the desire for expansion. Those in the German part of the Empire, especially the vulnerable ecclesiastical principalities and Imperial Free Cities, were protected to a certain extent by respect for, and a disinclination to challenge, the Imperial constitution, supported as it was by the Imperial position of the Habsburgs and by many of the second-rank German powers. In northern Italy, however, the situation was less favourable, and the Austrians seized the Duchy of Mantua, with scant respect for justice. Their limited heed of legal rights was more than matched by the rulers of Savoy-Piedmont whose expansionist schemes were conducted simply with reference to diplomatic opportunity. Frederick II told a British envoy in 1748 that Genoa had been justified in joining the Bourbons because her territories had been disposed of by the Treaty of Worms (1743) 'against all the rights of man'. Paradoxically, he also revealed that he was willing to support a similarly illegal and unprovoked Hanoverian acquisition of the prince-bishoprics of Osnabrück and Hildesheim.[8] The fate of Genoese-owned but rebellious Corsica had also been a matter of discussion in the 1740s, while, the previous decade, Francis of Lorraine had complained impotently about the fate of his duchy. Possibly the First Partition created such a shock because Europe had been territorially stable since 1748, but it is more likely that the key element inspiring fear was the combination and seeming apparent invulnerability of the three partitioning powers. A sense of balance was lost and that destroyed any element of predictability. It was apparently no longer the case that

---

[7] AE CP Bavière 102 fol. 78, 110 fol. 71; PRO SP. 84/402 fol. 90; Lukowski, 'Guarantee or Annexation: a Note on Russian plans to acquire Polish territory prior to the First Partition of Poland', *Bulletin of the Institute of Historical Research*, 56 (1983), 60–5.

[8] *Politische Correspondenz*, VI, 100–1.

schemes would be opposed by states that could hope to block them. Such a 'window of opportunity' for major change was to disappear swiftly, just as that created by the French-inspired anti-Austrian coalition of 1741 had done, and for the same reason, for both alliances of partitioning powers collapsed.

Not only, therefore, is the notion of a new age of international relations problematic, but it also suffers from a more general chronological emphasis that underrates the first half of the eighteenth century and stresses forces for change in the second half. This is but part of a more general problem, the compartmentalisation of the eighteenth century and the creation of a chronology that treats its early years as the concluding period of the era of Louis XIV, and then, after a period much of which is in shadow, focuses on Maria Theresa, George III and the 'enlightened despots'. The nature of this chronology, and the extent of this period of shadow, varies by country and subject; but we know less of the Portugal of John V than of that of Joseph I and Pombal, less of the Spain of Philip V and Ferdinand VI than that of Charles III, less of the War of the Austrian Succession than of the Seven Years War. While this remains the case, it is difficult to establish what was novel about, for example, the 'enlightened despots' or the international relations of the partition period, and thus how aspirations and achievements should be assessed.[9] This emphasis is linked to an overly static notion of the *ancien régime*, an analytical problem that, it has been suggested, could be resolved by using the formulation early modern instead.[10] If too static an interpretation is adopted, then not only must major change in the late (second half of the) eighteenth century be sought, but the causes of this change must be assessed. Just as with 'absolutism', so the very linguistic connotations of the term *ancien régime* create problems, but, conversely, if the emphasis is rather on a more dynamic, fluid or plastic *ancien régime* or early modern period, then it is less necessary to focus on change or the causes of change in the late eighteenth century.

Such a shift leads, however, in two contrary directions. The first does not entail any emphasis on the French Revolution, instead seeing it as an extreme example of the variations present within early-modern international relations, but the second leads to not only a downplaying of the importance of developments in the two decades prior to the Revolution, but also to an exaggerated stress on the role of the Revolution itself.

[9] J. Black, 'Ancien Régime and Enlightenment', *European History Quarterly*, 22 (1992), 247–55.
[10] H. E. Bödeker and E. Hinrichs (eds.), *Alteuropa- Ancien Régime – Frühe Neuzeit. Probleme und Methoden der Forschung* (Stuttgart, 1991), pp. 11–50.

The novelty of revolutionary foreign policy and of the international relations of the revolutionary period, a related but different question, can be approached in a number of lights. These can be simplified to objectives and methods, though a new method of conducting foreign policy was itself one of the objectives of the revolutionaries. They were the heirs to an important, though far from uniform, tradition of thought about international relations. Though there were exceptions,[11] most thinkers accepted that the solution to international problems had to be found in creating a code of conduct for relations between states, rather than in joining them together in a federation or a unitary state. Natural law theories remained important and in 1758 Emmerich de Vattel's *Le Droit des Gens* appeared. This influential work, which was translated into English in 1759 and German in 1760, stressed the natural law basis of international law and emphasized the liberty of nations as a feature of natural law relating to sovereign states. This entailed not the liberty to oppress others but the peaceful enjoyment of rights.[12]

Vattel's legal framework was matched by the attempts of certain prominent French intellectuals to advocate an international order based on morality and reason. They were suspicious of the intentions and conduct both of international diplomacy and of French foreign policy, believing them to be manipulative, dishonest and aggressive. In common with natural law theorists, French writers had little understanding of dynamic elements in international relations, the scope of change and the attempt by certain powerful rulers to match diplomatic developments to their growing power. Montesquieu, for example, has been seen as displaying 'a fearful resistance to change'.[13] Just as many natural law theorists came from the federal states of the Empire and the United Provinces, with their stress on legal relationships and their, in most cases, only limited interest in aggression, so the French writers came from a power that had largely ceased to seek European territorial gains. The

---

[11] D. Heater, *The Idea of European Unity* (Leicester, 1992), pp. 65–90; E. V. Souleyman, *The Vision of World Peace in Seventeenth and Eighteenth-Century France* (New York, 1941).

[12] F. S. Ruddy, *International Law in the Enlightenment. The Background of Emmerich de Vattel's Le Droit des Gens* (Dobbs Ferry, New York, 1975).

[13] M. L. Perkins, 'Montesquieu on National Power and International Rivalry', *Studies on Voltaire and the Eighteenth Century* 238 (1965), 76; A. D. Hytier, 'Les Philosophes et le problème de la guerre', *Studies on Voltaire*, 127 (1974), 243–38; R. Niklaus, 'The Pursuit of Peace in the Enlightenment', *Essays on Diderot and the Enlightenment in Honour of Otis Fellows* (Geneva, 1974), pp. 231–45; H. Meyer, 'Voltaire on War and Peace', *Studies on Voltaire*, 144 (1976); H. Mason, 'Voltaire and War', *British Journal for Eighteenth-Century Studies*, 4 (1981), 125–38; round table on ideas of war and peace in the eighteenth century, Eighth International Congress on the Enlightenment, Bristol 1991.

bold and acquisitive aspirations and aggressive methods that had characterised French policy in 1741 were not matched under Vergennes. The *philosophes* argued that all people essentially sought peace, that national interests, if correctly understood, were naturally compatible, and that war arose from irrational causes, such as religion and the irresponsibility and self-indulgence of leaders,[14] and from the nature of diplomacy. They therefore pressed for open diplomacy, much as the harmful effects to trade of guild secrets, monopolies and tariff barriers were deplored. In line with most thought of the period, the *philosophes* held that each nation had its true interest.

Radical writers, such as Rousseau, Mercier de la Rivière, and Condorcet, argued that reform necessitated the transfer of control over foreign policy from essentially bellicose, irrational and selfish monarchs, to the people who would be led by reason and would love peace. Tom Paine blamed war on the *ancien régime* and claimed that 'man is not the enemy of man, but through the medium of a false system of government'. The stress on open diplomacy and on the expression of the popular will in foreign affairs,[15] was to bear fruit in the Revolution, and was an important element of Enlightenment thought that Kaiser's account underrates.

However, in practice the volatile and emotional ideas and atmosphere of revolutionary Paris had a considerable impact on the conduct of foreign policy. For all the high-minded talk, the conduct of policy was more difficult and confused than before. When Samuel Rogers went to the National Assembly he 'heard a very violent debate ... in which 3 or 4 often spoke at once and the bell which the President rings to impose silence, was as often rung in vain'. The Earl of Darnley 'could hear nothing but noise, clapping of hands as in a theatre, and the President with a great bell endeavouring to impose silence in vain'.[16] The fevered nature of the crucial debates there (some of the business was far less interesting or contentious), the declamatory style and extravagant arguments of the speakers and the frequent interventions of the spectators on the side of action and against compromise, all combined to produce a context within which it was difficult to conduct not just diplomacy as conventionally understood, but also any negotiations in which mutual understanding and concessions were to play a role.

[14] Mason, 'Voltaire', 133–4.
[15] Howe, 'Revolutionary Perspectives on Old Regime Foreign Policy', *Consortium on Revolutionary Europe. Proceedings 1987*, 265–75; T. Paine, *The Rights of Man, Part I* (1791) in B. Kuklick (ed.), *Thomas Paine. Political Writings* (Cambridge, 1989), p. 142.
[16] Rogers to his sister, 4 Feb. 1791, Beinecke, Osborn Files, Samuel Rogers; Darnley to Malmesbury, 20 Dec. 1789, Winchester, Malmesbury 149; Murley, *Anglo-French War*, pp. 375, 388–405; Blanning, *French Revolutionary Wars*, pp. 111–12.

To a certain extent, the attitudes aroused in revolutionary Paris were not without precedent. The *philosophes* had blamed religion for many wars, arguing that religious fanaticism had enslaved and aroused the people, and there is a degree to which the universalist pretensions and the alarming or invigorating energy, if not fanaticism, of revolutionary foreign policy can be seen as similar to the 'Enlightenment view' of such episodes as the Crusades or the post-Reformation wars of religion.

Though, obviously, not in the Balkans, religious animosity had ceased to be as important in international relations as it had been in the century after Westphalia,[17] a period mistakenly assumed to be one in which such divisions had played little role. The willingness of Catholic rulers to join the *Fürstenbund*, and the improvement in relations between Britain and the Papacy were interesting indications of the general trend. Though British envoys continued to intercede on behalf of co-religionists, for example the Waldensians,[18] Stormont, when Secretary of State, wrote to Keith in 1782 about a forthcoming visit by Pius VI to Vienna:

If he comes as Pope... you cannot, with any propriety, wait upon him, or show him, in your public character, as a Protestant Minister, any mark of respect. If he should come incognito and appear either as a temporal Prince, or as a Bishop, there can in that case be no objection to your showing him every mark of attention.

Four years later, Hawkesbury was pleased to observe from Pius' reported 'expressions in favour of the King, that prejudices arising from different sentiments of religion are almost wholly extinguished even in the Court of Rome'; and in 1791 Cardinal Antonelli, the Prefect of the Congregation for the Propagation of the Faith, who had authority over the Irish Catholic Church, instructed the four archbishops there on the religious duty of obedience to the government of George III. The following year, the Papacy sought British assistance in deterring the threat of French attack. Once atheistic France had been identified with AntiChrist, Catholics could appear as allies.[19]

Religious issues and tension had ceased to play a major role in international relations between Christian powers, but some of the central aspects of confessional international relations also characterised the

---

[17] J. Burkhardt, *Abschied vom Religionskrieg: Der siebenjährige Krieg und die päpstliche Diplomatie* (Tübingen, 1985).

[18] Trevor to Fox, 27 Dec. 1783, PRO FO 62/3 pp. 306–7.

[19] Stormont to Keith, 22 Mar. 1782, PRO FO 7/4; Hawkesbury to Louis Dutens, 24 Nov. 1786, BL Add. 38309 fol. 127; M. Buschkühl, *Great Britain and the Holy See 1746–1870* (Blackrock, 1982), p. 25; Ostervald to Grenville, 1 Dec. 1792, PRO FO 63/15; *Daily Universal Register* 17 Jan. 1785; Black, *The British Abroad. The Grand Tour in the Eighteenth Century* (Stroud, 1992), p. 245; A. Robinson, 'Identifying the Beast: Samuel Horsley and the Problem of Papal AntiChrist', *Journal of Ecclesiastical History*, 43 (1992), 607.

revolutionary phase. This was true of universalist, utopian and sometimes millenarian aims, of a paranoid style, of fanaticism, of a degree of
popular participation and mobilisation; and of a rejection of limited
means and goals, of a traditional legal and institutional framework for the
formulation, conduct and discussion of international relations, and of a
diplomacy of compromise, exigency and expediency. There is also an
interesting parallel between the interaction, tension and clash of the
universalist message of individual creeds or of revolutionary pro-
grammes, widely seen as subversive of all order, and the specific,
generally more local and localised, requirements and policies of particular
groups in both contexts. The tendency to see modern revolutions in
secular terms, which is the view of revolutionary theorists and of most
revolutionaries, has led to an underrating of their shared structural
characteristics with confessional violence, not least such violence aimed
at overthrowing established structures, and attacking either the established faith, or the faith of an important section of the community.
Thus, the radical ideas and institutions of the Catholic League prefigured
those of the Revolution and Counter-Revolution. In addition, the
Revolutionary-Napoleonic crisis led to the intensification of religious
identity and the exacerbation of confessional violence, both within and
outside France.[20]

The extent to which early-modern confessional activity prefigured
subsequent revolutionary movements is less true of foreign than of
domestic policy, because the success of such groups in gaining control of
the central institutions of the state was limited, though the foreign policy
of the Parliaments of Interregnum England represented an obvious
example. Their policy, like that of Cromwell, can be seen in 'secular'
terms, primarily mercantilist at the expense of the Dutch and strategic at

[20] H. G. Koenigsberger, 'The Organisation of Revolutionary Parties in France and the
Netherlands during the Sixteenth Century', *Journal of Modern History*, 27 (1955),
335–51; O. De Lamar Jensen, *Diplomacy and Dogmatism: Bernardino de Mendoza and
the French Catholic League* (Cambridge, Mass., 1964); J. H. M. Salmon, 'The Paris
Sixteen, 1584–94: the Social Analysis of a Revolutionary Movement', *Journal of Modern
History*, 44 (1972), 540–76; E. Barnavi, *Le Parti de Dieu: Etude sociale et politique des
chefs de la Ligue parisienne, 1585–1594* (Brussels, 1980); P. Benedict, *Rouen during the
Wars of Religion* (Cambridge, 1981), pp. 182–9; R. Harding, 'Revolution and Reform in
the Holy League: Angers, Rennes, Nantes', *Journal of Modern History*, 53 (1981),
379–416; R. Descimon, *Qui étaient les Seize? Mythes et réalités de Ligue parisienne,
1585–1594* (Paris, 1983); M. Greengrass, 'The *Sainte Union* in the Provinces: The case
of Toulouse', *Sixteenth Century Journal*, 14 (1983), 469–96; Greengrass, 'The Sixteen;
Radical Politics in Paris during the League', *History*, 69 (1984), 432–9; R. A. Schneider,
Public Life in Toulouse, 1463–1789 (Ithaca, 1989), pp. 120–31; B. B. Diefendorf,
Beneath the Cross: Catholics and Huguenots in Sixteenth-Century Paris (New York,
1991); J. N. Hood, 'Protestant-Catholic Relations and the Roots of the First Popular
Counterrevolutionary Movement in France', *Journal of Modern History*, 43 (1971),
245–75.

that of Spain, but there is an alternative view that would rather stress ideological factors, and this new analysis has been carried forward to the discussion of the Second Anglo-Dutch War.[21]

The revolutionary crisis of the late eighteenth century as a second general crisis akin in some respects to the Reformation might appear fanciful, but it is less so if the continuities between the 'Middle Ages' and the 'Early-Modern period' or the *ancien régime* are considered, and also if the religious dimensions of the Age of Revolutions are appreciated. They are readily apparent in the American Revolution, and in the hostile response evoked by the French Revolution in much of Europe. Though operating from a different basis, Burke also highlighted similarities between the Reformation and the Revolution in his *Thoughts on French Affairs* (1791), as did Novalis, the German Romantic poet and writer Friedrich Leopold, Freiherr von Hardenberg, in his essay *Die Christheit oder Europa* written in 1799, when he discussed what he termed 'a second Reformation', and Fichte. Miles compared the zeal of the revolutionary troops to that of early Islamic warriors and wrote of 'this new species of Mahometanism'.[22]

Britain played a major role in the rallying to Church and Crown that proved such an obvious feature of the 1790s across much of Europe, and, indeed, in Britain closer relations between the government and the Catholic Church were an aspect of this rallying around authority and the cause of religion. A critical James Currie argued in February 1793 that

[21] C. Wilson, *Profit and Power. A Study of England and the Dutch Wars* (1957), pp. 48–61; J. R. Jones, *Britain and Europe in the Seventeenth Century* (1966), pp. 46–9. Jones, *Britain and the World 1649–1815* (1980), p. 53 emphasises the determination of a 'small and tight-knit republican faction' to survive 'in a hostile world'. H.-C. Junge, *Flottenpolitik und Revolution. Die Entstehung der englischen Seemacht während der Herrschaft Cromwells* (Stuttgart, 1980); R. Brenner, *Merchants and Revolution. Commercial Change, Political Conflict and London Overseas Traders, 1550–1653* (Princeton, 1993); R. Crabtree, 'The Idea of a Protestant Foreign Policy', in I. Roots (ed.), *Cromwell. A profile* (1973), pp. 160–89; J. N. Bowman, *The Protestant Interest in Cromwell's Foreign Relations* (Heidelberg, 1990); S. C. A. Pincus, *Protestantism and Patriotism: Ideology and the Making of English Foreign Policy, 1650–1665* (Ph.D. thesis, Harvard, 1990) and 'Popery, Trade and Universal Monarchy: The Ideological Context of the Outbreak of the Second Anglo-Dutch War', *English Historical Review*, 107 (1992), 1–29. I have benefitted from reading unpublished material by Dr. Pincus.

[22] N. O. Hatch, *The Sacred Cause of Liberty: Republican Thought and the Millenium in Revolutionary New England* (New Haven, 1977); R. M. Bloch, *Visionary Republic: Millenial Themes in American Thought, 1756–1800* (Cambridge, 1985); J. C. D. Clark, 'The American Revolution: A War of Religion?', *History Today*, 39 (Dec. 1989); 'Revolution in the English Atlantic Empire', in E. E. Rice (ed.), *Revolution and Counter-Revolution* (Oxford, 1990), pp. 60–73; Burke, Everyman edition of the *Reflections* (1910), pp. 288–90; E. Burke, *Thoughts on French Affairs* in D. E. Ritchie (ed.), *Edmund Burke. Further Reflections on the Revolution in France* (Indianapolis, 1992), pp. 208–9; Novalis, *Hymns to the Night and Other Selected Writings* edn C. E. Passage (Indianapolis, 1960), p. 55; *Correspondence of Miles* I, 345.

the English were motivated by Anglican zeal, and 'John Bull such a priest-ridden animal. Everything bold and liberal appears to his eye with a sectarian hue, and the idle disputes about the trinity have been one powerful cause of the war with France.'[23] In the Austrian Netherlands, Naples, the Tyrol, Portugal, Russia and Spain opposition to the French was to take on the aspect of a religious crusade, as indeed was also the case with domestic opponents of the Revolution. The revolutionaries themselves were, however, also inspired by a quasi-religious zeal, not so much for the new religion that they invented, but for the utopian possibilities that they appeared to be creating for mankind. This zeal made diplomatic compromise not practical politics in the winters of 1791–2 and 1792–3, but, as already suggested, it can be seen not so much as a new force in international relations, but as a revival, in a new form, of the politics, policies and paranoia of zeal last seen so urgently in the maelstrom of Reformation confessional violence. Parallels between the sixteenth and early seventeenth centuries and the 1790s are very striking in terms of rhetoric and mentalities. The Wars of Religion did not preclude alliances that were fundamentally explicable only in terms of mutual political interest, such as those of Henry II of France and the German Protestants or Richelieu's France and the Swedes, though these had their pendant in the eventual accommodation of Revolutionary France with some *ancien régime* states, for example the South German princes.

Though the Revolution released, energised and directed French resources,[24] so that the country was able and willing to play a more forceful role in international relations, much about the Revolution was unsurprisingly traditional; albeit in a more violent form, it was, like all human life, in tension between the past and the future. The technological and organisational changes summarised by the phrase Industrial Revolution were still restricted in their impact. The major transformations in theoretical and applied science and technology in most fields, whether warfare, transportation, the generation and distribution of power, medicine, contraception or agricultural yields, were yet to come, as was the possibility of mass politicisation presented by mass education, widespread literacy and the creation of a more intense political world thanks to the rapid and frequent communication of ideas. The national

---

[23] Papers of Sir John Cox Hippisley, Ipswich, East Suffolk CRO; M. Buschkühl, *Great Britain and the Holy See 1746–1870* (Blackrock, Co. Dublin, 1982), pp. 25–39; G. Scott, *Gothic Rage Undone. English Monks in the Age of Enlightenment* (Downside, 1992), pp. 217–18; Currie to Lansdowne, 13 Feb. 1793, Bowood 41.

[24] An important recent work that casts valuable light on an aspect of this process is J.-L. Rosenthal, *The Fruits of Revolution. Property Rights, Litigation and French Agriculture, 1700–1860* (Cambridge, 1992). See, more generally, Kennedy, 'Anglo-French Rivalry', p. 350.

politics that these changes, as well as the ideology of nationalism and widespread migration to the towns, were to permit, was rather a creation of the nineteenth century than of the revolutionary period.

Nevertheless, even if the 1780s and 1790s can be seen in large part in terms of continuity, of the tensions of the so-called early modern period, even if parallels can be found in the Reformation, the Revolution still represented a break from *ancien régime* diplomacy. The revolutionaries thought of themselves as acting in a new fashion, an important aspect of novelty in response to a culture that was primarily reverential of and referential to the past. Avignon became French and the position in Alsace altered not in response to international treaty, but as a result of what were held to be popular will and natural rights. The argument that treaties entered into by rulers could not bind people was subversive. The subordination of foreign policy and the Foreign Minister to control by a committee of a popular assembly was new: control passed from the executive to the legislature. John Trevor cited revolutionary sentiment in Italy and Flanders, when arguing 'that the present war and all that is connected with it, differs from every other'.[25]

Particular episodes over the previous century prefigured some of the experience of the revolutionary period. This is true of the xenophobic popular pressure in Britain in 1738–9 for war with Spain that played a role in limiting the options of the Walpole ministry, and thus helped to cause the War of Jenkins' Ear, or of the outburst of popular action that drove occupying Austrian forces from Genoa in 1746 and then sustained the city against Austrian attack, even if that was largely a response to Austrian financial and other demands. The Revolution was still different because it affected France, the most populous state in western Europe, the paradigm of European monarchy and the most important western European participant in continental international relations, because the radicalisation of the Revolution was unprecedented for any large polity, and because the French Revolutionary Wars involved and affected all of Europe.

The last point might seem to answer the question of the importance of European international relations in this period, but it does so only to a certain extent. The essential geopolitical position in 1788 was unchanged in 1815: Britain was the leading European maritime power, Russia its land counterpart, and Europe was divided among a number of rival sovereign powers, unable and unwilling to create any permanent system of effective co-operation. The defeat of Napoleon led to a reversal of the trend which had culminated in 1810–12 with much of Europe, including

[25] Rothaus, 'War and Peace', 120–38; Trevor to Grenville, 1 Dec. 1792, PRO FO 67/10.

the Low Countries, Hamburg, Lübeck, Genoa, Tuscany, Savoy-Piedmont, the Papal States, Trieste, Dalmatia and Catalonia being part of France, while client states, such as the new kingdoms of Bavaria, Italy and Westphalia, were similarly engorged. Europe returned to the situation that distinguished it from so many of the other heavily populated regions of the world, multiple kingship.

A stress on geopolitical continuity does not imply neglect of important changes. The Prussian acquisition of the Rhineland at the Congress of Vienna led to a fundamental re-orientation of Prussian policy westwards. This had a substantial influence on the geopolitical situation as she, rather than the Old Alliance or, more particularly, the Habsburg Emperor, now represented the barrier to French eastern expansion. Prussia was thus cast in the role of champion of German national integrity against France. Aside from this shift, which had been prefigured by Prussia's role in the Dutch crisis in 1787, the Revolutionary-Napoleonic period also led to crucial internal changes in the states that were occupied or influenced by France. French hegemony produced reform and secularisation.

British maritime and Russian land power were both enhanced by the sustained conflicts of the Revolutionary-Napoleonic period. Of the islands lying off the European mainland, only Britain was both independent and a major power. This allowed, indeed required, her to concentrate on her naval forces, unlike her continental counterparts who, even if also maritime powers, as most obviously with France and Spain, devoted major resources to their armies. This concentration had been crucial to Britain's success in defeating the Bourbons in the struggle for oceanic mastery in 1739–63 and surviving the attempt to reverse the verdict during the War of American Independence. By the late 1780s Britain had emerged clearly again as the strongest naval power in the world, the European state best placed to project her power across the globe. The foundation of a colony in Australia in 1788 and the challenge to Spain's position on the Pacific seaboard of the new world in the Nootka Sound crisis were but consequences of this inherent strength. The distinctive feature of the post-medieval European maritime empires was their desire and ability to project their power across the globe: by the late eighteenth century, Britain was clearly most successful in doing so.

The Revolutionary-Napoleonic period dramatically accentuated this relative strength, giving Britain clear maritime and trans-oceanic commercial superiority. In territorial terms, Britain made extensive gains. Some of these were achieved at the expense of other European powers. They were mostly the islands that European maritime powers had been best placed to seize: the Seychelles, Mauritius, Trinidad,

Tobago, coastal Ceylon and the 'land-islands' of Cape Colony, Essequibo and Demerara (Guiana). Others, such as much of southern India and large areas elsewhere in the sub-continent, were gains at the expense of indigenous rulers. At the same time, the other European empires were being swept away or suffering major losses. This was true, and even more so by 1830, of the French, Spanish, Dutch and Portuguese empires. Aside from losses to Britain, these were dramatically affected by the successful independence movements in Central and South America, while the gain of West and East Florida from Spain by the United States was an early indication of American aggressive strength. Even before the outbreak of the Revolutionary Wars, the French empire and French overseas interests were seriously affected by the Revolution. The process of revolution in the French colonies shattered their unity, the slaves of the West Indian colonies revolted, and everywhere France suffered a loss of prestige. Thus, for example, Jezzar Ahmed Pasha, the governor of Palestine, felt able to expel the French merchants who enjoyed a monopoly of Palestine's external sea trade at the end of 1790, only inviting them back in 1791 on his own terms.[26] During the Revolutionary and Napoleonic Wars, British naval strength emasculated the French, Dutch and Spanish empires as military and strategic threats and commercial rivals. British naval power had helped to make the French control of Louisiana redundant, and Napoleon's sale of it in 1803 was an apt symbol of the Eurocentricism that was such a characteristic feature of his policies, after the failure of the Egyptian expedition; although it was also an attempt to bring the United States into conflict with Britain.

It was largely thanks to the British navy that in 1815 so much of the trans-oceanic European world outside the New Hemisphere could be coloured red on the map; largely due to successful rebellions in South and Central American that by 1830 the vast majority of European possessions abroad were British. Some of the others, most obviously the Dutch East Indies[27] and, later, the Portuguese colonies in Africa, were, in part, dependent territories. The Anglo-American position in the Oregon Country ensured that Russian-ruled Alaska was not going to serve as the basis for expansion further south. This situation was not to last; indeed 1830 was the date of the French occupation of Algiers, the basis of their subsequent North African empire. Nevertheless, the unique imperial oceanic position that Britain occupied in the Rev-

---

[26] A. Cohen, *Palestine in the Eighteenth Century* (Jerusalem, 1973), p. 21.

[27] J. A. de Moor, '"A Very Unpleasant Relationship". Trade and Strategy in the Eastern Seas: Anglo-Dutch relations in the nineteenth century from a colonial perspective', in G. J. A. Raven and N. A. M. Rodger (eds.), *Navies and Armies. The Anglo-Dutch Relationship in War and Peace 1688–1988* (Edinburgh, 1990), pp. 49–69.

olutionary, Napoleonic and post-Napoleonic period was to be of crucial importance to the economic and cultural development of the state in the nineteenth century. France was to become a great imperial power again; Portugal and the Dutch were to make gains, Germany, Italy, Belgium (and the United States) to become imperial powers, but for none of these was empire as important, as central a feature of public culture (or elite careers), as it was for Britain.

Any parallel with Russia might appear surprising. Although Catherine II revived the thrust of Russian naval power developed under Peter the Great, and was thus able to make Russia a force on which hopes were built or to be feared in the Mediterranean, a position that was sustained under her successor, and although Russian activity in the Pacific was not inconsiderable,[28] Russia was essentially a land power. Indeed she possessed the largest army in Europe.[29] The Russian domination of eastern Europe was strengthened during the Revolutionary-Napoleonic period and in the subsequent peace settlement, strengthened with the support, or at least consent, of Britain.[30] Finland was acquired from Sweden (1809), Bessarabia from the Turks (1812) and much of central Poland, now known as the Kingdom of Poland, from Austria and Prussia (1815). In addition, Russia made major gains in the Caucasus, with the acquisition of Georgia and Baku. And yet Russia was similar to Britain in strategic terms in one important respect, the two powers prefiguring the position of the United States and the Soviet Union for the 1917–90 period. Both in a way were outside Europe, able to protect their home base or centres of power from other European states, yet also able to play a major role in European politics. The isolation should not be overstated. With reason, British government feared invasion on a number of occasions from 1690 to 1809. Russia was invaded, by Sweden in 1708–9

[28] Bode, *Flottenpolitik Katharinas II*; P. Venturi, *End of the Old Regime in Europe 1768–1776. The First Crisis*, pp. 3–153; N. Saul, *Russia and the Mediterranean, 1797–1807* (Chicago, 1970); R. V. Makarova, *Russians on the Pacific, 1743–1799* (Kingston, Ontario, 1975) and G. Barratt, *Russia and the South Pacific 1696–1840* (3 vols., Vancouver, 1988–90), though see J. R. Gibson, 'A Notable Absence: the Lateness and Lameness of Russian Discovery and Exploration in the North Pacific, 1639–1803', paper given at the Vancouver conference on Exploration and Discovery, 1992.
[29] W. H. Pintner, *Russia as a Great Power, 1709–1856* (Washington, 1976), 'Russia's Military Style, Russian Society and Russian Power in the Eighteenth Century', in A. G. Cross (ed.), *Russia and the West in the Eighteenth Century* (Newtonville, Mass., 1983), pp. 262–70, 'The Burden of Defense in Imperial Russia, 1725–1914', *Russian Review*, 43 (1984), 231–59.
[30] C. J. Fedorak, 'In Search of a Necessary Ally: Addington, Hawkesbury, and Russia, 1801–1804', *International History Review*, 13 (1991), 245. A recent study of co-operation between the two powers is provided by W. H. Flayhart, *Counterpoint to Trafalgar. The Anglo-Russian Invasion of Naples, 1805–1806* (Columbia, South Carolina, 1992).

and by Napoleon in 1812, attacked, as by Sweden in 1741 and 1788, or threatened, for example by Prussia in 1791. Nevertheless, the strategic position of Britain and Russia was different to that of other European states; and, just as they had avoided the ravages of the Thirty Years War, so they were to see off Napoleon and thus thwart the last attempt before the age of nationalism to new-model the European political space.[31] The Treaty of Vienna (1815) was explicitly designed to, and provided for, not a balance of power, but a balance of satisfaction. Russia was dominant in eastern Europe, Britain on the oceans, and there was no balance of power in either sphere.

If attention is focused on the positions of Britain and Russia, then it can be argued that the outbreak of the French Revolutionary Wars did not bring much material change. The conflict between France and her neighbours was one in which Russia and, still more, Britain, was heavily involved, but it, nevertheless, also enabled, indeed in some respects obliged, them to pursue a policy of territorial gains that simultaneously ended real or apparent threats and established hegemony.[32] Heavily committed to her continental position, France was unable to stop Britain, while a French-organised coalition was unsuccessful in preventing Russia from consolidating her position in eastern Europe. Rather, however, than seeking causes in the form of the debilitating strains between France and her continental neighbours, it is appropriate to note that the situation was essentially a continuation of the pre-revolutionary position. Russia had dominated eastern Europe for several decades. The Prussians had no wish to repeat the punishing experience of Russian invasion during the Seven Years War; the Austrians were concerned about Russia's advance against the Turks. Though the Turks did not collapse as readily as had been anticipated, and Russian gains in peace settlements (1700, 1739, 1774,[33] 1792) were less than had been expected, it was, nevertheless, the case that Russian expansionism was a dynamic force and that Russia was a more powerfully unpredictable neighbour for Austria than Poland had been.

The outbreak of the Revolutionary War gave Russia an opportunity to launch the Second Partition of Poland (1793), and this was to lead to the Third Partition (1795), steps that were unwelcome to Austria. The expansion of Russia has been seen as the expression of a territorial

[31] R. Glover, *Britain at bay: defence against Bonaparte, 1803–14* (1973); V. R. Ham, 'Strategies of Coalition and Isolation: British War Policy and North-West Europe, 1803–1810' (unpublished D.Phil., Oxford, 1977), p. 292; S. Woolf, *Napoleon's Integration of Europe* (1991).

[32] M. Atkin, *Russia and Iran, 1780–1828* (Minneapolis, 1980).

[33] R. Davison, '"Russian Skill and Turkish Imbecility": The Treaty of Kuchuk Kainardji Reconsidered', *Slavic Review*, 35 (1976), 463–83.

'revolution' in eastern Europe.[34] Russian hegemony in eastern Europe was, however, not a product of the outbreak of this war, but rather of the respective strength of the powers. This had been demonstrated in 1788–90 by her ability to fight Sweden and Turkey simultaneously and in 1790–1 by Catherine II's conviction that she could resist Anglo-Prussian pressure over the terms on which she should settle with the Turks.

British naval hegemony was, similarly, not dependent on the outbreak of the French Revolution, though that was to weaken the French navy. British successes during the Revolutionary-Napoleonic wars, the defeats suffered by the French, Dutch, Danes and Spaniards, and the disruption of Dutch and Spanish forces caused by French occupation, were all important, but, as with Russian victories, they reflected relative strength and the situation prior to the Revolution. Britain had beaten the Bourbons in the mid-eighteenth century struggle for naval mastery and had survived the major challenge to her maritime and imperial position mounted during the War of American Independence. The conflict ended with a strong British navy and a weakened French counterpart. Post-war construction left the British navy even stronger at the onset of the next Anglo-French conflict,[35] but her success in the Dutch crisis (1787) had already dramatically weakened France's potential challenge to Britain's imperial position. British strength was further demonstrated and accentuated by the resolution of the Nootka Sound crisis (1790): a conspicuously successful British naval armament, obvious weakness in the French navy, disarray in the Franco-Spanish alliance.

Thus, just as the Ochakov Crisis bore testimony to fears of Russian intentions and strength, but showed that active diplomacy supported by the mobilisation of the military forces of Britain and Prussia and the prospect of Polish assistance, could be no more successful in preventing Turkish losses than the diplomatic pressure directed at preventing the Russian acquisition of the Crimea in 1783–4, so British strength was already apparent before the French Revolutionary Wars. The need, in light of the contemporary and future importance of British and Russian power, to avoid a Franco-centric approach, explains why it is necessary

[34] F. Salomon, 'The Foreign Policy of William Pitt in the First Decade of his Ministry in its European significance', *Transactions of the Royal Historical Society*, new series, 10 (1896), 112.

[35] D. Baugh, 'Why did Britain lose command of the sea', in Black and Woodfine (eds.), *British Navy*, pp. 149–69; J. Dull, *The French Navy and American Independence* (Princeton, 1975), pp. 316–17; P. Webb, 'Rebuilding and repair of the fleet', *BIHR*, 50 (1977), 194–209; R. J. B. Knight, 'The Building and Maintenance of the British Fleet during the Anglo-French wars 1688–1815', in M. Acerra, J. Merino and J. Meyer (eds.), *Les Marines de Guerre Européennes XVII-XVIII⁰ siècles* (Paris, 1985), p. 42.

to devote attention to the Dutch, Nootka Sound and Ochakov crises, but the outbreak of the French Revolutionary Wars was also of consequence. They reflected and helped to emphasise a crucial development of the 1790s, the revival of the 'Western Question'.

The 'Western Question' can be seen in a number of ways, principally as three related issues: the question of whether any power was to dominate western Europe and, if so, which; the response to France of her neighbours; and the particular issue of France's expansion east into the Empire, south-east into Italy and north-east into the Low Countries. As a result of the economic, political and military problems that affected Spain in 1640–1714 and the accession of a branch of the Bourbons to the throne of Spain, this 'Question' had ceased to be an issue of Spanish power. Instead, the revival of French strength under Louis XIV, the ambition and energy of the King, and the size of his armed forces ensured that it had become one of French power. This had led to western European international relations being articulated around the axes of support for or hostility to France. Hostility had led to the 'Old Alliance' or the 'Old System', the fusion of Anglo-Dutch and Habsburg energies in a common struggle against France, and this had conditioned the attitudes and aspirations of a large number of politicians, including many British ministers and diplomats, although there had always been individuals who had challenged the basic suppositions of policy or the degree to which Britain was committed to her allies.[36]

The defeat of Louis XIV in the War of Spanish Succession, the relative passivity of the Orléans Regency (1715–23) and the French ministries of the 1720s and the rise of Austrian and Russian power, had led to a different diplomatic agenda in the late 1710s and 1720s, one in which French intentions and power were not major issues. They became more prominent again in 1733–48, in years of French victories and diplomatic successes, but were, in turn, relegated by defeat during the Seven Years War, France's relative post-war quiescence, and the strength, resilience and independence that Austria, Russia and Prussia demonstrated in the war and in subsequent post-war diplomacy. France was not only relatively weaker, but she also acted as a 'satisfied' power. These changes made the 'Old System' redundant and also undercut the strategic thesis that France could be weakened as a maritime enemy by the efforts of Britain's continental allies. They also made it possible for

[36] J. A. Downie, 'Polemical Strategy and Swift's *The Conduct of the Allies*', *Prose Studies*, 4 (1981), 134–45; J. Black, 'The Tory view of Eighteenth-Century British Foreign Policy', *Historical Journal*, 31 (1988), 469–77; H. J. Müllenbrock, 'Alexander Pope's *Windsor Forest* (1713): Genre and Political Propaganda', *Studi Settecenteschi*, 11–12 (1988–9), 9–15; J. Black, 'Swift and Foreign Policy Revisited', in H. Real and R. Rodino (eds.), *Reading Swift* (Munich, 1993), pp. 61–70.

French ministers to discuss the advantages of co-operating with Britain in continental diplomacy.[37]

The Revolution did not revive the 'Western Question' for several years, for France was obviously weak in 1789–90, though British anxiety in late 1789 about French intentions towards the Austrian Netherlands was an augury for the future. If the debates of the National Assembly during the Nootka Sound crisis demonstrated French unpredictability, the French response also indicated the weakness of her government, the willingness of some of the most prominent 'popular' leaders to negotiate with a foreign power, and the problems facing any French naval mobilisation. If French policy in 1791–2 played a major role in causing war with Austria, it was not the threat posed by French power that was foremost in the minds of the rulers and ministers of Prussia, Austria and, indeed, Britain, although France's weaker neighbours, such as Trier, and indeed Spain, were more worried about the situation. France was invaded with at least as much confidence as Britain and Prussia had shown in planning war with Russia in 1791, if not with far more. She appeared obviously weaker than Russia, and was certainly more divided, accessible and vulnerable to invasion.

France's unexpected successes in September–November 1792 altered the situation dramatically and forced the European powers to appreciate the strength, energy and unpredictability of French power. They led directly to the entry into the war of Britain and the United Provinces. Alongside a stress on the new challenge posed by Revolutionary France, there was also a sense of continuity in terms of territorial expansion, expressed best by Portland when he wrote on 16 November 1792: 'the same spirit of lust for Power actuates the conduct of the French in their Republican as in their Monarchical form of Government, and ... they are not less intent upon governing Europe than they were in Lewis the 14th's time'.[38] There were to be other dramatic French advances in the 1790s. The frontiers of Italy, the Rhineland and the Low Countries had been stable for the half-century after 1748; now Europe was to be remoulded, new political spaces created, frontiers redrawn. The auxiliary republics of the 1790s became the ancillary kingdoms of the 1800s. France became an empire; the Holy Roman Empire came to an end. As the Second and Third Partitions, as well as much else of the diplomacy of 1793–1815,

---

[37] D. Baugh, 'Great Britain's "Blue-Water" Policy, 1689–1815', *International History Review*, 10 (1988), 50; J. Black, 'On the "Old System" and the "Diplomatic Revolution" of the Eighteenth Century', *International History Review*, 12 (1990), 321; Stormont to 4th Earl of Rochford, Secretary of State for the Southern Department, 1 June 1774, PRO SP. 78/292 fol. 104; Vergennes to Noailles, then Ambassador in London, 8 Mar. 1777, AE CP Ang. 522 fol. 50.

[38] Turberville, *Welbeck*, II, 225–6.

were to demonstrate, the French challenge did not lead to the shelving of all other interests and ambitions, while, indeed, the revolutionary forces were to suffer serious defeats, as at Neerwinden (1793), Amberg (1796), Stockach (1799) and Ostrach (1799) at the hands of the very impressive Austrian army, and in 1799 at the hands of the Russians. And yet, French successes in the 1790s, culminating in the military failure and political collapse of the Second Coalition, were to be followed the following decade by triumphs that gave Napoleonic France a military reach in Europe hitherto surpassed only by the Roman Empire.[39]

Though oppressive, widely unpopular[40] and eventually defeated, Revolutionary and Napoleonic rule was of great importance, not least for its energising of nationalism and for its role in provoking governmental change in a number of states, most obviously Prussia, an echo of the impact of mid-eighteenth-century defeats on the Austrian state. The Revolutionary Wars did indeed change France and Europe more than the Revolution itself, and they also had a decisive impact on the course of the latter. It is therefore important to consider how far the wars were the product of the Revolution and what was distinctive about revolutionary foreign policy. While Foreign Minister in 1792, Dumouriez introduced some changes in the organisation of the ministry and of the diplomats, though, as is generally the case in revolutionary episodes, changes in personnel were more important.[41] Even more so was the changed nature of the politicisation of foreign policy.

Ancien régime foreign policy was heavily politicised, in that the autonomy of the small-scale 'foreign offices' responsible for the bureaucratic aspects of policy was very limited; policy was decided at the highest levels, usually by the monarch and his intimate advisors, and often in a Court context, rather than in a more bureaucratic institutional framework; and the decisions reflected, in part, the issues and personalities at stake in Court politics. Thus the direction of foreign policy was often the outcome of unrelated domestic struggles. This situation was not of course uniform. Just as the nature of the *ancien régime* was far from

[39] G. E. Rothenberg, *Napoleon's Great Adversaries: The Archduke Charles and the Austrian Army 1792–1814* (Bloomington, 1982); A. B. Rodger, *The War of the Second Coalition* (Oxford, 1964); P. Mackesy, *Statesmen at War: The Strategy of Overthrow* (1974), *War without Victory. The Downfall of Pitt, 1799–1802* (Oxford, 1984); P. W. Schroeder, 'The Collapse of the Second Coalition', *Journal of Modern History*, 59 (1987), 244–90.

[40] T. C. W. Blanning, *The French Revolution in Germany: Occupation and Resistance in the Rhineland 1792–1802* (Oxford, 1983); D. M. G. Sutherland, *France 1789–1815. Revolution and Counterrevolution* (1985), pp. 14, 107–14, 439.

[41] F. Masson, *Le Département des Affaires Étrangères pendant la Révolution, 1789–1804* (Paris, 1877), pp. 161–8; *Les Affaires Étrangères et le Corps Diplomatique Français*, I, 285–6, 312–13; P. Howe, 'Belgian Influence on French Policy, 1789–1793', *Consortium on Revolutionary Europe 1986*, 218–19.

uniform, the political culture and constitutional arrangements of Poland and the United Provinces being obviously different to those of France and Spain, so also were there variations in the conduct of foreign policy.

The Revolution led to a major change in the French situation, in that the politicisation of foreign policy was more public, thanks to the role given to the National Assembly, and the situation was less stable as a result of the unpredictability of and rapid changes in French domestic politics. Equally important, in 1792, was the uncertain constitutional position, which centred on the power and eventually life of the King. War seemed necessary to many critics of Louis XVI in order to undermine the royal position and then to conserve in power those who sought such a goal. There were also, however, supporters of the Crown who saw war as the best chance of reviving royal power, either through French victory (Narbonne) or defeat (Marie Antoinette). French foreign policy was affected by the, at best, uneasy and, more often, competing nature of the policies of the King, the ministry and the Assembly, and these, in turn, were far from united, there being competing views in both the royal Court and the successive ministries. The outbreak of war added fresh complexity as certain generals started to negotiate on their own authority and in pursuit of their own objectives.

Thus, above any other specific characteristic of a revolutionary foreign policy, the most apparent one in 1792 was confusion, a lack of certainty as to the likely policy that would be followed and as to who was making the crucial decisions and how best they could be influenced. If the British discovered this during Elliot's secret negotiations in Paris in 1790, it was obviously also the case in 1792–3 when British ministers had to consider what weight to attach to French agents in London, and subsequently to the prospect of negotiations with Dumouriez.

Confusion was not the monopoly of revolutionary governments. Prussian policy under Frederick William II was seen as unstable, conflicting aims being pursued by ministers and favourites with little real cohesion provided by the self-indulgent monarch. British ministers and diplomats could also convey clashing impressions, as Eden and Harris did in 1787 and Auckland and Ewart in early 1791. The French situation was worse, however, because, as in Britain in 1754–6,[42] domestic uncertainty, indeed, a lack of strong government, made it difficult for the National Assembly to accept the need for compromise even though individual ministers and politicians realised that it was necessary. The added problems posed by the universal message of the Revolution, its rejection of the past in favour of a new order, as for example in the

---

[42] T. R. Clayton, 'The Duke of Newcastle, the Earl of Halifax, and the American Origins of the Seven Years War', *Historical Journal*, 24 (1981), 571–603.

Scheldt decree, ensured that there was scant willingness to accept the discipline of negotiations.

It was not, therefore, surprising, that the pro-British sentiments that were voiced in 1789-early 1792 were unrealistic, based in large part on a misreading of British policy, if not the British political system,[43] and not offering any sensible basis for co-operation. Their lack of realism was matched by the subsequent failure, as Anglo-French tension rose in 1792, to understand what was going on in Britain, and by the conviction that any hostile governmental response would be overcome by the will of the British public.

A conviction of the value of open diplomacy and a pursuit of a public foreign policy was not necessarily incompatible with the maintenance of former alliances and enmities, nor did it need to arouse a hostile response from former allies. In November 1792 Thomas Walpole, Envoy Extraordinary in Munich, reported that Karl Theodor was near death and that his heir had 'received and given audience to a new French minister, and I am sure that many of his counsellors and perhaps those most in confidence are strongly attached to a French alliance – be the government of France what it may – monarchical or republican'.[44] The willingness of powers to negotiate with a regicide regime was striking. The Treaties of Basle between France and Prussia, the United Provinces and Spain (1795) were followed by the Franco-Sardinian Armistice of Cherasco (1796), the Franco-Austrian treaties of Campo Formio (1797) and Lunéville (1801) and the Anglo-French Treaty of Amiens (1802). Yet Cherasco, Campo Formio and Lunéville were very much the products of military exhaustion, failure or defeat. More apparent in 1791–2, was the unwillingness of governments to fight France or, once war had begun, to join in against her. Personalities played a major role. Leopold II was unwilling to fight; Francis II more enthusiastic for war. Traditional interests and objectives can also be stressed, as obviously with the shift in British policy following the dramatic change in French fortunes and apparent objectives in the Low Countries. Such an argument would emphasise continuity, with the pursuit of power as the consistent theme, and minimise the role of ideological considerations, both on the French side and on that of her rivals. Continuity can also be stressed if an effort is made to distinguish clearly between on the one hand revolutionary ideologies and ideals, and on the other actual policies,

---

[43] C. Mazauric, 'Sur le patriotisme Jacobin. L'Angleterre vue de Rouen', *Sur la Révolution française* (Paris, 1970), pp. 163–79; E. H. Lemay, 'Les Modèles anglais et américain à l'Assemblée Constituante', *Transactions of the Fifth International Congress on the Enlightenment* (Oxford, 1980), II, 872–84; Jarrett, *Revolution*, pp. 263–76.

[44] Walpole to Burges, 22 Nov. 1792, BB 44 fol. 133.

what ministries in Paris did or tried to do. However radical the speeches made by revolutionary orators, many of the presuppositions underlying government policy were usually to a large extent traditional. Ideas about France's traditional allies, notably the Ottoman Empire and the Poles, were largely as they had been under the *ancien régime*. The hostility of the revolutionaries to the Austrian alliance had deep pre-revolutionary roots; and the tendency to look to Prussia as a possible or likely ally went back to the 1740s. The idea of closer relations with the German states, other than Austria and Prussia, was also revived.[45] It can, therefore, be argued that though revolutionary emotion altered much of the tone of French policy it had much less effect on its substance and thus the situation after 1792–3 was one of the pursuit by greatly expanded means of aims which were not in themselves essentially new.

Against this must be set the new element of distrust in relations that the Revolution introduced, a distrust that was paranoid, that linked alleged domestic and foreign threats and that echoed the fevered anxieties of Reformation relations. This distrust, which characterised the Revolutionaries, and their opponents, as well as neutral powers, affected the content and character of policy and relations. Louis XIV had aroused considerable distrust, but posed less of a domestic threat than the Reformation and Revolutionary counterparts. Despite the similarities that have been found between *ancien régime* and revolutionary policy, both in terms of French goals (Sorel) and of the application of reason (Kaiser), revolutionary ideals and the logic of domestic politics pushed France towards war in a fashion that was totally different from the impact of domestic pressures elsewhere. It had proved possible to avoid war over the Scheldt and the *Fürstenbund* in 1784–5, and to negotiate peace settlements in eastern Europe in 1790–2. Such a process of compromise was not possible in the case of France.

It is clear that at the end of 1792, British policy was crucially affected by a conviction that revolutionary France would not accept any limits or heed any deterrents. This conclusion was not without basis in 1792–3. Speakers in the National Assembly returned frequently to the theme of the link between domestic and foreign enemies. The actions of the *émigrés*, the real and rumoured Austrian connections of the royal Court, and the obvious sentiments of most foreign monarchs, lent substance to such accusations, as did a strong sense that French interests had been betrayed since 1756 by her Austrian alliance, an alliance for which the fault lay with the Bourbon monarchy. Thus, the Girondin Pierre Vergniaud declared in January 1792, in a speech in which the threat to

[45] *Recueil ... Diète Germanique*, pp. 376–7.

the Revolution was stressed and the call 'aux armes' reiterated, 'que la rupture de ce traité est une révolution aussi nécessaire dans l'ordre politique, soit pour l'Europe, soit pour la France, que la destruction de la Bastille l'a été pour notre régénération intérieure'. After wild applause from Assembly and spectators, Vergniaud continued by claiming that hostile Austrian actions had broken the treaty, and that he knew no other policy 'pour un peuple libre, que la justice'. He later drew attention to Demosthenes stirring up the Athenians against the threat from Philip of Macedonia and to Frederick II launching a pre-emptive attack against a hostile league in 1756.[46]

Vergniaud's mention of Frederick is interesting, for, at the same time as revolutionary speakers asserted universal principles of conduct in international relations and called for a new order of allied national popular wills, they also displayed an eclecticism that led them to search the past for heroic models who could be emulated. Frederick II was frequently cited, for example by the Girondin Armand Gensonné on 14 January 1792,[47] but so also was Henry IV, an apparently suitable counterpoint of regal energy and anti-Habsburg activity to the enervated and suspect current holder of the throne. It was in foreign policy that the traditional themes displayed by some revolutionaries was apparent, for, alongside the appeal to the new order, there was a determined rejection of the Austrian alliance, an attempt to argue that, as a result of the alliance, all had gone wrong with French foreign policy. This could unite both traditional critics of an alignment that had not lacked enemies under the *ancien régime* and enthusiasts for a new order, not least those who were suspicious of the royal Court. Foreign policy played a major role in the Revolutionaries' critique of the royal government.

These different themes can be seen in December 1791 and January 1792 when Brissot and his allies led, persuaded and cajoled the National Assembly towards a heightening of the confrontation with Austria that was designed to lead to war. One critic of this policy, Gérardin, who sought an adjournment, pointed out that 'il est toujours dangereux d'engager une assemblée delibérante dans un mouvement d'enthousiasme',[48] but such arguments were not heeded. Instead, the Assembly had just loudly applauded Guadet who had laid out yet another aspect of the new diplomacy, 'On parle de congrès! Les députés des nations réunies pour assurer la liberté du monde, voilà le seul congrès possible aujourd'hui en Europe, voilà le seul probable!'[49]

Possibly with time and careful negotiation and under the pressure of domestic difficulties, some sort of *modus vivendi* could have emerged,

---

[46] *AP* 37, 491–3.   [47] *AP* 37, 412.   [48] *AP* 37, 415; Hampson, *Danton*, p. 93.
[49] *AP* 37, 413.

such as that suggested by Grenville's talk of historical parallels and eventual recognition. Time, however, was lacking; while the thesis of the interrelationship of domestic and foreign threats, a theme reiterated frequently in both France and her neighbours from the outset of the Revolution, and one that became more potent from 1791, made the sort of compromise sought by the British government unacceptable to many rulers and politicians. The idea that domestic change within France could be accepted so long as she renounced proselytism was not one that enough French politicians were willing to accept and fight for in 1792–3 to make it credible. Equally, it was not a notion that was welcome to most European rulers, although it might have been enough to discourage some from intervening in the Revolutionary Wars. It was only French success in late 1792 that made the issue of French proselytism in its most potent and durable form, territorial expansion, one of immediate concern throughout western Europe. At that point, only the British government offered a real solution, one of compromise based essentially on revolution in one country. It was flawed, not because of the British reluctance to negotiate publicly and formally, and, thus, in granting recognition, surrender part of her negotiating hand and limit Britain's chances of developing a common front with France's enemies, but rather because compromise over the Scheldt or the decree of 19 November was no more on the table in Paris with those who were setting the pace of French politics, than was compromise over Louis XVI's head. To compromise was to betray the Revolution. That self-serving, shallow and harsh thesis was to cause far more blood to flow outside France than it cost to the people of that great country.

Ideology can thus be stressed, but a question remains as to how best to conceptualise the international relations of the period, for, whatever the changes in France, most powers in the early 1790s were governed by the same ruling groups, if not rulers and ministers, as in the pre-revolutionary period. There are obvious contrasts between the language of system and clear national interests beloved by contemporaries and by most historians, and the confused and confusing manner in which developments occurred, the often kaleidoscopic nature of alliances, the short-term character of so many alignments and speculations. For the modern scholar, the starkest problem is not only the conventional challenge of how best to describe in a relatively small number of words the complexity of the past, but also how to make sense of, and at the same time move away from, the detailed level of short-term changes, without destroying the character of thought and action in this period by subsuming it into a level of schematic abstraction centring on a systemic approach. There is the related problem of lacunae in the sources, and the difficulties in establishing and assessing both sources and methodology created by a wider conception of foreign policy than the largely diplomatic one.[50]

It is difficult to see much of value in a systemic approach to the pre-revolutionary period. A purpose of the narrative chapters has been to indicate that contingent factors played a major role. This is clearly true of the crises, the Dutch and Balkan ones of 1787, Nootka Sound and Ochakov, but it is also so of the alliances and alignments of the period. These could be and were rationalised in systemic terms, most obviously through the discussion of national interests and the balance of power, but both had a somewhat spurious precision. Albeit discussing the following century, two political scientists felt able to conclude that 'to grace the conceptual and empirical chaos of the balance of power literature with the label "theory" is much too generous', and there is much truth in this observation if 'theory' is to be regarded as precise and scientific. In practice, contemporary conceptualisation offered in the related notions of natural interests and the balance of power, both a precise and mechanistic language and a flexible thesis that could be applied widely, and frequently in a contradictory fashion.[51]

The fictional Sir Roderick Horsefield remarked in 1966 'I tell you, Poirot, nothing's more difficult nowadays than the question of allies. They can change overnight.'[52] The same was even more true of the early 1790s, and it is clear that the role of change, chance and opportunism must be central to any conceptualisation of international relations in this period. In their search for advantage and security, rulers were willing to change policies and allies frequently and unilaterally, while simultaneous contradictory negotiations were commonplace. This emerges clearly from a narrative account of the period, as does the strong contemporary sense of uncertainty over present and future developments. The common eighteenth-century sense of history with its stress on the role of individuals and the play of circumstances, is in large part vindicated as far as the international relations of the period are concerned, and they were the most important aspects of governmental activity.

[50] O. Feldbaek, *Denmark and the Armed Neutrality. Small Power Policy in a World War* (Copenhagen, 1980), pp. 219–21; J. P. Aguet 'Un "Combat pour L'Histoire"': Lucien Febvre et L'Histoire Diplomatique', and S. Friedländer and M. Molnar, 'Histoire nouvelle et histoire des relations internationales', in Friedländer et al. (eds.), *L'Historien et les relations internationales* (Geneva, 1981), pp. 14, 82; Black, *A System of Ambition?*, pp. 7–11.
[51] J. D. Singer and M. Small, 'Alliance Aggregation and the Onset of War, 1815–1945', in Singer (ed.), *Quantitative International Politics: Insights and Evidence* (New York, 1968), p. 285; J. Black, 'The Theory of the Balance of Power in the First Half of the Eighteenth Century: a note on sources', *Review of International Studies*, 9 (1983), 55–61.
[52] A. Christie, *Third Girl* (1st published 1966, Fontana edn 1968), p. 103.

Index

Index

Basle, 379
Basra, 48
Batavia, 148, 415
Batavian Legion,
Battles: Amberg, 539; Babadag, 322;
  Blenheim, 521; Cape Kaliakra, 322;
  Fokshani, 214; Hogland, 182;
  Jemappes, 408; Kolin, 521; Machin,
  322; Malplaquet, 521; Martineshti,
  214; Mehadia, 214; Narva, 289;
  Neerwinden, 539; Ostrach, 539;
  Poltava, 289; Saints, 12; Stockach,
  539; Slatina, 188; Turnhout, 210;
  Valmy, 404, 405, 406;
  Yorktown, 11
Bavaria, 5, 64–5, 83, 113, 149, 178, 185
Bavarian Exchange, 63, 82–5, 91, 128,
  132, 135, 159, 171, 394, 436, 448–9
Bayreuth, 65, 394
Beauchamp, Francis, Viscount, 187
Beckwith, George, 240
Béhaine, Pigneau de, 44
Belgrade, 149, 188, 214, 288
Belgrave, Robert, Viscount, 312–13
Belize, 32–3
Bender, 214, 216, 274, 287
Bengal, 44, 146, 505
Benkulen, 37
Berne, 378
Bernstorff, Count Andreas Peter von, 72,
  74, 183–4, 197, 309
Bessarabia, 216, 274, 282, 323, 534
Bezborodko, Alexander, Prince, 126
Bintinaye, Chevalier de La, 371
Birkenstock, Johann Melchior, 217
Birmingham, 327
Bischoffwerder, Johann Rudolf von, 175,
  185, 297, 318, 320
Black Sea, 46, 50–1, 113–14, 187, 272,
  275, 282–3, 289, 298–9, 311–13, 318,
  322, 365, 449
Blair, Lieutenant Archibald, 34
Blankett, Captain John, 45–6, 505
Blanning, T. C. W., 3, 5, 127, 268, 379,
  460–1, 469
Bligh, Captain William, 253
Bo-daw-hpaya, 44
Board of Control for India, 35, 40, 51–2,
  503
Boddam, Governor, 34, 38
Bogle, George, 312
Bohemia, 5, 62, 280
Bois-le-Duc, 209
Bombay, 48, 147
Bonaparte, Napoleon, 50, 323, 506, 531,
  535

Bonnecarrère, Guillaume de, 395–6, 464
Borneo, 37
Bosnia, 188
Botany Bay, 44
Bouillé, Marquis de, 368
Bourgoing, 229
Bowles, John, 457, 459, 461
Braam, J. P. van, 37
Brabant, 143, 204–5, 209–10, 212, 217,
  265
Brand, Thomas, 107, 153
Brandes, Ernst, 486
Brazil, 502
Breda, 205, 209, 425
Breisgau, 378
Brest, 103, 154, 250, 252, 385, 418, 432
Breteuil, Louis, Baron de, 155, 207, 338,
  410
Brienne, Etienne Charles, Loménie de,
  131, 135, 141, 153–4, 166
Brissot de Warville, Jacques Pierre, 373,
  380, 381, 543
Britain,
  action against radicals, 390–1, 411, 422
  and Austria, 58–9, 61, 79–82, 119,
    168–9, 200–1, 216–22, 257–65, 293–5,
    361, 383, 388, 415
  and Austrian Netherlands, 59, 203–15,
    265–7
  and France, 68–72, 101–12, 116–17,
    147–55, 160–7, 238–42, 329, 330–3,
    338, 346, 348, 349, 350, 351, 353,
    354, 355, 357, 362, 363, 365, 385,
    387, 389, 390, 430, 454, 456, 506,
    507–8, 509, 515
  and Ireland, 413, 416, 422
  and Prussia, 85, 93–5, 119–22, 145,
    167–8, 173–82, 195–7, 201, 204–6,
    216–23, 257–65, 284, 297–9, 329, 332,
    342, 361, 383, 415, 450, 487, 538
  and Russia, 61, 89–92, 168, 187, 197,
    273–5, 283, 285–325, 359, 363, 366,
    383, 447, 487, 494, 538
  and Spain, 9, 225–56, 330, 346, 349,
    493–4, 511, 531
  and the United Provinces, 98, 118,
    147–55, 179, 206, 243, 329, 333, 341,
    384
  Francophobia, 460, 474, 509, 511
  social unrest, 517
Broglie, Duke de, 64
Brunswick, Duchy of, 113, 144, 176, 208
Brunswick, Karl Wilhelm Ferdinand,
  Duke of, 118, 134, 145, 147, 151,
  397, 401, 403, 407, 409
Brussels, 210, 408, 410

547

Index

Index

Index